OPERETTA

A Theatrical History

OPERETTA

A Theatrical History

RICHARD TRAUBNER

OXFORD UNIVERSITY PRESS

New York   Oxford

To Andrea,
WITH LOVE

Oxford University Press

Oxford   New York   Toronto
Delhi   Bombay   Calcutta   Madras   Karachi
Petaling Jaya   Singapore   Hong Kong   Tokyo
Nairobi   Dar es Salaam   Cape Town
Melbourne   Auckland

and associated companies in
Berlin   Ibadan

Library of Congress Cataloging in Publication Data

Traubner, Richard.
Operetta: a theatrical history.

Includes bibliography and index.
1. Operetta—History and criticism.   I. Title.
ML1900.T7   782.81'09   77-27684
ISBN 0-385-13232-8   AACR2
ISBN 0-19-520778-5 (PBK.)

2 4 6 8 10 9 7 5 3 1

Printed in the United States of America

FRONTISPIECE: The glamorous Lily Elsie and her rather wistful-looking American co-star, Joseph Coyne, as the widow and Danilo in the London production of *The Merry Widow* (Daly's, 1907).

CONTENTS

ACKNOWLEDGMENTS

The following individuals and institutions were of invaluable assistance in the preparation of this book. My heartfelt thanks to them all, alphabetically:

Alan Abrams, Reginald Allen, Antonio de Almeida, the Austrian Institute, New York, Kathy Bayer, Ian Bevan, the Bibliothèque Nationale, Paris, the entire staff of the Billy Rose Theatre and Music Collections, Lincoln Center, New York, Edith Böheim, Gerald Bordman, Russell Brown, John Cannon, Carlos Clarens, Mervyn E. Clay, Danièlle Cornille, John Coveney, Ken Dixon, Gail D'Luhy, Frederick and Phyllis Doppelt, Bridget D'Oyly Carte, D.B.E., Ingrid Eckardt, Chris Ellis, William K. Everson, Harry Forbes, George Forrest and Robert Wright, Charles Forsythe, Beverley Vawter Gallegos, Kurt Gänzl, Louise Gault, John Gillett, Sam Goldsman, Paul Gover, Henry Anatole Grunwald, Paul Gumhalter, Howard Hart, Hans Heinsheimer, Michael Hofmann, Erzsi Horváth, Arthur Jacobs, Richard Jarman, Charles, Vera, and Yvonne Kálmán, Larry Kardish, Peter Kemp, Courtney and Caroline Kenny, Hilary Knight, Richard Kutner, Andrew Lamb, Robert Lantz, Tom Mack, Adrienne Mancia, Kenneth Mandelbaum, Dennis C. Miller, Norman Miller, Allan and Bob Morris and families, William Mount-Burke, Richard C. Norton, Patrick O'Connor, the Österreichische Nationalbibliothek, Vienna, Sheila Porter, Robert Pourvoyeur, Colin Prestige, Terence Rees, Johannes Reuther, Glenn Rounds, Brian Salesky, Helen Salomon, Ingrid Scheib-Rothbart, Alexander Schouvaloff, Eugene and Lillian Schuster, Beverly Sills, Alfred E. Simon, Dinah Spinetti, Ruth, Käthe, and Walter Strasser, Michael G. Thomas, Richard Toeman, Romano Tozzi, Milton Traubner, Muriel Traubner, Albert Truelove, Douglas Tunstell, the staff of the Volksoper, Vienna, Hugh Wheeler, Susan Woelzl, John Wolfson, Peter Wood, Hope and Jay Yampol, and Pablo Zinger.

INTRODUCTION

O PERETTA! Flowing champagne, ceaseless waltzing, risqué *couplets,* Graustarkian uniforms and glittering ballgowns, romancing and dancing! Gaiety and lightheartedness, sentiment and *Schmalz*. From Offenbach's *opéras-bouffes* in the 1850s and '60s, to Gilbert and Sullivan's comic operas in the 1870s and '80s, from the Golden Age of Suppé and Strauss II to the Silver Era of Lehár and Kálmán, through the Broadway operettas of the 1920s up to the romantic American musicals of the '40s and '50s, operettas have kept audiences enthralled for more than a century. Though the Second World War changed the course of operetta, its mutations continue, and recent productions on stage, film, and television continue to attract new generations to the older masterpieces.

Operetta attracted its audiences principally by means of its contagious melodies, though many other factors contributed to its popularity: clever libretti, satirical jibes, romantic intrigue, mesmerizing stars, lovely chorus girls, and scenic splendor. But the songs were always the most important element in this popular genre.

This is a theatrical history of a genre that is remembered today principally for its music. Many can hum items ranging from the Letter Song from *La Périchole* to "Wanting You," but it is becoming increasingly difficult to recall the works these tunes are from, operettas which were once hugely, internationally popular but which are now less frequently performed. Even the names of operetta composers are forgotten by the general public. With the exception of some of the lyrics from the Gilbert and Sullivan operettas in English-speaking countries (almost always exceptions to general operetta rules), the words to operetta songs are seldom remembered, and not much energy has been expended glorifying the operetta libretto as literature.

For the sake of convenience and order, this book examines the major operettas, within the confines of their eras, by composer.

The history of operetta is a theatrical one. From their very inception in mid-nineteenth-century Paris, operettas were intended as entertainments not for opera houses (where some did wind up eventually) but for boulevard theatres, for popular consumption. In this sense, they were analogous to the popular Broadway musical comedies of the past sixty years. Operetta similarly appealed to all classes of theatregoers, from those in the orchestra (stalls) to the upper galleries. From almost the beginning of operetta's existence, these works were expected to show profits by running fairly substantial numbers of consecutive, or nearly consecutive, performances. The subsidized patronage of royalty and the wealthy at the opera houses or court theatres of Europe did not create them; operettas from the start had to cater to the public's taste. Profit motivation had as much to do with the conception of operetta as the artistic desires of its composers.

By the end of the nineteenth century, operettas were among the most popular of theatrical attractions, with companies and theatres devoted principally to their presentation all over Europe and the New World. Before the 1914–18 destruction of the social conditions that had seen this golden age of operetta flourish, brilliant (and lesser) composers, librettists, stars, and impresarios collaborated to produce these satiric, romantic, extremely melodic, and glamorous works. By the end of the nineteenth century, Paris, Vienna, and London were the capitals of operetta, with hundreds of operetta troupes playing other cities throughout the world. After World War I, Berlin, Budapest, and New York increased their exports to such an extent that they joined the list of principal operetta cities.

The death of operetta was thought to have occurred during the 1930s, brought about by a variety of conditions including the ascendancy of the more spectacular singing screen, with its cheaper tickets, the jazzy musicals and revues on Broadway in the 1920s, radio, and the suppression in Germany of Jewish talent. There were also socioeconomic and political factors which had increased audience awareness and sophistication, so that the plots which had served operetta librettists for more than fifty years were found wanting: tales of disguised royalty in the Hungarian countryside or Cinderella plots involving the crossing of class barriers would no longer titillate audiences in the mid-twentieth century.

After the War, the Broadway "musical"—stressing romance and often escapism—naturally extended the major characteristics of European and American operettas of the 1920s and '30s, while musical comedy and revue, which had seen triumphs in the '20s and '30s, perpetuated in many ways the gaiety and charm of operettas that had heretofore contained farcical or satirical elements. Because of the preeminence today of the American terms *musical* and *musical comedy,* the word operetta is now used solely to denote works that were written before the 1940s.

In the United States, operetta primarily conjures up the basically romantic works of Victor Herbert, Sigmund Romberg, and Rudolf Friml, written in a period that spanned about thirty years. Operettas produced prior to 1900 were often called comic operas, as they were in England. In France the term *opérette* also connotes twentieth-century works (often produced with spectacular effects), while *opéra-bouffe* is the term used for the works of Offenbach, and *opéra-*

comique (officially, but often grandiosely) the definition used by the authors themselves to describe the works of Offenbach's rivals and successors, as these often played up romantic elements. Britain's greatest works, the Savoy series of Gilbert and Sullivan, were comic operas, while their descendants at the turn of the century were called musical comedies, originally so-called to distinguish them from continental works. Today, the British will even use the term musical comedy to describe a thoroughly romantic European operetta. It would be considered box-office poison today to call the commercial presentation of an operetta just that; musical is the preferred term in Britain and the United States.

There exist certain definite traits that distinguish operetta from neighboring genres. The first has to do with the "-etta" in operetta and the "light" in light opera, a term that I resist, as it may imply a lack of musical thought or preparation, while assuming it is in some way a variant of grand opera. Operetta means a little opera (originally because it was in one act) and light opera means, or *should* mean, an opera that literally takes itself lightly. It is not heavy or grand, in a worldly or tragic sense, and, most importantly, should not be pretentious. This does not mean that a happy end of the plot is the necessary result (though it usually is) or that every song need be happy and frivolous—far from it. It is the basically entertaining nature of operetta to promote good feeling and even joy, leaving the darker, weightier aspects of theatrical presentation to dramas, melodramas, and grand operas. Sentiment and romance have traditionally played important roles in operetta, but rarely despair.

This unpretentiousness applies to the operetta score, which, besides being ideally ravishing and dramatically apt, is designed to be played by a theatre orchestra (rather than an operatic-symphonic one) and to be popular enough to be played night after night. Should the audience whistle its tunes on leaving the theatre, and should the sales of sheet music and recordings of the score prosper, supporting further performances, the composer has succeeded. There have been instances of operettas written for private performances, of course, but most were written for commercial ventures as income-producing entities. By unpretentious, I mean accessible, to a large segment of the population.

This commercial unpretentiousness has always given operetta a bad name in the highest circles of musical art, where profits are not ordinarily placed before artistic creation. It is for this reason that some classical composers, players, devotees, and primarily critics have looked down on operetta as a bastard art form, unworthy of serious recognition. And continue to do so. It is not an elitist art form, conceived for the highly educated and wealthy and in some respects kept alive by it.

Alfred Grünwald wrote the libretti to such memorable operettas as Leo Fall's *Die Rose von Stambul* (1916), Oscar Straus's *Der letzte Walzer* (1921), Emmerich Kálmán's *Die Bajadere* (1921), *Gräfin Mariza* (1924), and *Die Zirkusprinzessin* (1926), and Paul Ábrahám's *Viktoria und ihr Husar* (1930) and *Die Blume von Hawaii* (1931), among many others, all but the Ábrahám works in collaboration with Julius Brammer. After Grünwald's arrival in the United States in 1938, he began writing *A History of Operetta*, which was unfinished at his death. His comments on operetta remain just as valid today as they were in the 1940s, and it is a pleasure to make them public for the first time.[1]

> Serious writers on music, the "superior" critics, all those music esthetes who prowl about the sacred halls of music with dead-earnest faces as self-appointed guardians of the sacred Forms and Traditions, look upon operetta as something highly distasteful. They never gave it much attention, whenever possible they have tried to stifle it by a conspiracy of silence, and if they do speak of it they are always careful to express their great disdain . . .
>
> That is why one can find hardly a word about operetta in even the thickest tomes about music old or new. It is just as if it had never existed. Now and again, but very rarely, musical historians do condescend to mention Offenbach, and when it is absolutely necessary even Johann Strauss, but there it ends . . .
>
> What we must recognize is that operetta is a distinct art form, and a very important one, in view of its unquestioned universal popularity. It was born, it grew up, developed, reached heights now already regarded as classical, passed through an occasional period of decline, was reborn again: that is, it has a history, just as drama and opera have . . .

Operettas were written and played at the same time as operas, *opéras-comiques,* and other symphonic pieces of music, and in many instances were enjoyed by the same people who supported these forms. Operettas were recognized as theatrical as much as musical offerings, and in many cases the principal operetta singers were known first, and primarily, as comedians or café singers, rather than as operatic singers. There were considerable strides in the late nineteenth century in turning stilted, convention-riddled *opéra-comique* construction and staging into a new, dynamic, and frequently hilarious theatrical form, with much more attention paid to dramatic and musical characterization, wit, and frivolity, and a more intelligent use of the chorus. The work of Offenbach, Sullivan, Messager, and their librettists will be noted in this respect.

What happened to operetta around the turn of the century parallels in many ways what happened to French *opéra-comique* around the turn of the previous century: comedy and satire (if any) were relegated to subplots while the principals indulged in increasingly formula romantic entanglements, usually in a fairly exotic setting that provided a degree of spectacle to mask the libretto's conventionalism. Sadly, the public today equates the terms operetta and *opéra-comique* with the more romantic, sentimental pieces rather than the sprightlier, more exuberant comic works which started both forms. It is one purpose of this book to resurrect appreciation for the delightful and today forgotten masterpieces of the least pretentious operettas, in which will often be found the loveliest music and most charming libretti. Some may indeed be moored to their historical periods, requiring considerable expertise in having them presented anew to the public. My task is first to make these works known.

---

[1]Excerpts quoted from *A History of Operetta* by Alfred Grünwald. Translated from the German by Julian Leigh. Quoted by permission of the author's son, Henry Anatole Grunwald.

The public, after all is said and done, is generally a good arbiter of taste. Those operettas that ran for hundreds of performances may or may not have had the most musicianly of scores, or the most intelligent libretti. They may have owed much of their success to a certain star, or to a celebrated company. But, in so many instances, they worked, and, by virtue of revivals, continue to work their charms on succeeding audiences. *La Belle Hélène, Les Cloches de Corneville, The Mikado, Die Fledermaus, Die lustige Witwe, Gräfin Mariza, Im weissen Rössl,* and *My Fair Lady* continue to hold the stage in their respective countries. As we will see when we come to them, they were also international successes at the time of their original productions. These and many other works remain operetta masterpieces.

In the next category are works which may have been colossal hits in their day but were never or seldom seen again. Time and changing values have worked against *L'Oeil crevé, Madame Favart, The Geisha, Chu Chin Chow, Robin Hood, Nanon,* and *Die Dollarprinzessin,* preventing their continued reappearance. And then there are operettas which may have failed originally but which remain the connoisseur's delight, and thus have a slightly better chance of revival because these connoisseurs will attempt to have them staged. Chabrier's *L'Étoile* is a perfect example.

Masses of operettas were written in the period from 1855 to 1930. Most of these are forgotten, for whatever reason. Just as a grand opera specialist has to turn to obscure listings for information on obscure works, the operetta specialist must look elsewhere for obscure operettas and their composers. I apologize if I have left out any reader's favorite work. Also, one could go on for years listing operetta antecedents: Italian *opera buffa,* German *Singspiel,* and British ballad opera. I list only a few examples that I think are significant. For others, the specialist will have to go elsewhere, with the author's good wishes.

I *do* list most of the significant works of every major operetta composer, though not necessarily all, as that would again be too picayune for my and your tastes. On the other hand, I will stress relatively unknown works (especially those unknown in the United States) which should be heard. The public originally rejected, quite rationally, a great deal that remains worthless. I pray for the day when companies will record obscure Offenbach or Johann Strauss works, but the chance of their being performed is not only slim but silly. There are many weak works here, which frankly do not merit stage revival, with all of today's expenses and risks.

As to the libretto question, there are, of course, several important librettists and teams, and most will be mentioned, but I see no reason to mention every one in every case. I am not the first to admit that many libretti are spurious, or, conversely, that the good ones have helped the famous masterpieces live. The leading Viennese librettist Alfred Grünwald stated similar ideas forty years ago:

> In operetta, as in opera, the libretto plays a decisive part. One might think that a self-evident fact, yet it is constantly overlooked . . . Beaumarchais, who wrote *The*

Marriage of Figaro once said, "That which is too stupid to be spoken is sung." I hereby make a present of the quotation to critics who are not acquainted with it or have forgotten it. Can it be that the author had a presentiment of all the operetta librettos to which his words could properly apply?

Many excellently composed operettas suffer because the music is only a drape for the frame supplied by a poor book. On the other hand, there is scarcely one really successful operetta in which the libretto does not play an important part . . .[2]

Patrick J. Smith, in his definitive study of opera librettos, states:

. . . the [opera] libretto is a sufficiently minor art form to permit a greater degree of generalization than, say, the novel. "If you've read one, you've read them all" may be an exaggeration, but, with the exception of the major librettists and some isolated librettos, it is not a gross exaggeration.[3]

This would not be an exaggeration in the operetta genre, either, in which only a few major librettists did not simply follow formulas. Henri Meilhac and Ludovic Halévy and W. S. Gilbert were the undisputed masters, indeed, the creators. There were others who were either prolific or witty, but most, admittedly, are not remembered as librettists, in the way we remember Lorenzo da Ponte or Arrigo Boito.

Operetta librettists frequently worked in teams, or even trios, as did many *vaudevillistes* in nineteenth-century France. If nothing else, several authors writing together would assuredly get the text written more quickly, in time for the composer to set it and for the manager to present it. In the highly competitive pre-radio and television era, speed was desirable. This may have accounted for a lack of consistency of tone in most operetta librettos. Most of the teams, admittedly, are even less well known today than the names of operetta composers: Zell and Genée, Chivot and Duru, Nuitter and Tréfeu, Willner and Bodanzky, Bernauer and Schanzer . . . a succession of writing partnerships that sounds like a list of law firms. Like lawyers, they provided a service—to keep the plot going, to provide a framework for certain operetta conventions (like the baritone entrance song or the middle finale), and to provide ideally memorable lyrics.

The conventions of the French operetta libretto became as standardized as those for French opera and *opéra-comique,* once they had been set. Foremost was the use of dialogue. As Patrick J. Smith notes, in reference to the dialogue in *opéra-comique:*

The alternation of stretches of spoken dialogue with ensembles or arias was vital to the structure of the libretto and of the opera . . . [the dialogue] not only fleshed out the stick figures of the arias but also provided a measure of Gallic irony in the give-and-take of the conversation, which undercut the moorings of the verse.[4]

[2]Ibid.
[3]Smith, Patrick J., *The Tenth Muse*, p. viii.
[4]Ibid., p. 290.

As Smith points out, prose dialogue required singing actors rather than acting singers; no more so than in the first comic operettas, for which popular boulevard comedians were sought. The leading female parts in the Offenbach *opéras-bouffes* may have required good singing, but the stars engaged for these parts were just as likely to have been trained in the *café-concert* as in the Conservatoire.

The writers picked for the first French operettas were generally *vaudevillistes*, playwrights who wrote boulevard farces, usually with lyrics for a number of songs. These writers often parodied contemporary society by burlesquing a well-known myth, classical story, or fairy tale (as in the case of Meilhac and Halévy's libretti for *La Belle Hélène* and *Barbe-Bleue*) but they also dealt with modern-dress farcical situations. The first Viennese librettists, trained in the Viennese farce-*vaudeville* school, merely adapted or translated French libretti; many famous Viennese operettas are based on French originals. British librettists all fell in the shadow of W. S. Gilbert, as did a great many American writers. The powerfully romantic operettas of the Edwardian age and the 1920s, in Europe and in the United States, had libretti that more often than not were cast from the same molds. Few of these were textually interesting, neither the lyrics nor the dialogue being remarkable. Operetta conventions by this time were harrowingly conventional.

This book is not a collection of plot synopses. There have been several, and these are especially useful for works seen or heard in foreign languages. Operettas, popular entertainments that they are, have traditionally been performed in the vernacular. Should older translations of operettas be unplayable, it is time for new ones.

Just as the recording industry has promoted opera appreciation in this century more decisively than any other single force (except perhaps radio), records should assist the public's knowledge of operetta in years to come. Although British, American, German, and French companies consistently re-record or reissue the same famous works, because these always make money, their exploration into the hidden, neglected operetta repertory should be encouraged. Records often lead to performances.

Perhaps because the genre is considered a "light" one, there has been little documentation of it in English, save for dozens of books on Gilbert and Sullivan and some on the American musical, the excellent ones by Gerald Bordman being quite worthwhile. It is for this reason that the American sections of this history are not given quite the same weight as the European ones, which have not had adequate American or British documentation. Another reason for this is that American operettas (as opposed to more recent musicals) have never had the international acceptance that French or Austrian works have traditionally enjoyed. American works of the 1890–1920 period enjoyed only a brief local vogue, and only the operettas of Victor Herbert seem to have really survived that period. Although only a comparatively small number of European works from this period are still done with any regularity, there are some other interesting examples whose quality—alive today on recordings and on radio broadcasts—seems very high, and deserving of reappraisal. Some information on these, and their composers, is included.

In Britain, the same period produced a great many frothy musical comedies and more romantic operettas, the tunes and even stars of which are still recalled today by older members of the public. Many of these continental and British works were produced in America with considerable success, though the reverse was not true. This should help explain the definite European slant of this history; the American works have happily received much attention elsewhere.

Again, it would be quite impossible and ultimately foolish to list every operetta composed internationally. Similarly, the foreign-performance listings are by no means complete, but merely an indication of the worldwide popularity of so many works. The principal operetta cities have always been Paris, Vienna, London, Berlin, Budapest, and New York, as these are the places where operetta activity was greatest, and where operettas with international circulation were created and where they are still performed. Cities like Moscow, Warsaw, Prague, and Munich, among others, still have active operetta houses, but none of them has given the world a lasting operetta hit.

This book is also directed at opera snobs who constantly say, "Ugh! Operetta!" Let me stand up and say that the best operettas are in many ways more intelligent, entertaining, and musically stimulating than some of the operas currently on the stage today, not to mention those bores lurking in the wings, like those dredged up by *bel canto* aficionados. The opera snob has little sense of proportion. If it is an opera—preferably a serious one by a known composer that has been neglected—it is worth his attention, whereas any operetta will be ignored. Stage music should hardly be valued simply because of the composer's name or the emotional terrain of the libretto in question. Classical purists who dislike musical theatre and opera generally can be forgiven, but for an opera fan to resist operetta on a charge of triviality can only be chalked up to that fan's ignorance of operetta (and an ignorance of widespread libretto triviality in opera) or to a taste for vocal and orchestral pyrotechnics which in many instances have little to do with the plot in question. There are still thousands of people who consider Shakespeare's comedies less important than his tragedies and correspondingly prefer "serious" works to comedies.

Critics have conversely resisted operettas that attempt to be serious, or thoroughgoingly romantic, rather than trivial. Composers (and librettists) are chastised for going beyond their terrain. The public has often embraced such works with open arms, while the critics carped. Indeed, during the "Silver" Viennese era (after 1905, and especially in the 1920s) audiences admired unsatiric, romantic works which often had moments of operatic grandeur. Yet the musical establishment, after spending years damning or ignoring what they considered trivial operetta music, now turned around and accused operetta writers of being too serious. This type of operetta-scorn manifested itself as early as the 1880s, as librettist Alfred Grünwald recalled:

. . . long before this the critics were incensed by any attempt on the part of the operetta to be like the opera. The well-known Viennese critic Hanslick, who had made himself forever immortally ridiculous with his judgement of the work of Richard Wagner, wrote about Johann Strauss's *Gypsy Baron* that the Waltz King, in a trumped-up second finale, had unfortunately struck some suddenly tragic, operatic notes which he might much better have left to those who were more qualified for that kind of thing. However, the willful public disagreed with the critic. It flocked to a hundred performances of *The Gypsy Baron* . . .[5]

There are good, or effective operas, and bad, or ineffective ones, good operettas and bad ones. And those in between: those that need work, those with one good song, and those with silly books. I do know that *Die Fledermaus* is as great a masterpiece in its genre as *Die Meistersinger von Nürnberg* is in its. Why must we constantly pit one against the other and try to decide which is more culturally important. Let's enjoy both!

A Note on Theatres, Premières, Show and Song Titles: Theatres and opening nights are generally listed in parentheses, as, for example: (Shaftesbury, 9 October 1910). The city should be apparent from the surrounding sentences or paragraphs. Occasionally, the English translation of a foreign title and the show's run are also given within the parentheses. English translations of foreign show titles are generally given in Roman letters; what these shows were actually called in English-language productions are usually indicated by *italicized* titles. For example, *Der Vogelhändler* (The Birdseller), but, in performance, *The Tyrolean*.

Where a translation of a song title or a first line is listed with only the first letter capitalized, as in (When you go to the fair), this is my ideally literal translation of the title. When it is given with the principal words capitalized, as in (When You Go to the Fair), this means that the song was translated and published that way in its English version, and that the English or American librettist may have given the title or first line a freer translation. Foreign capitalization generally follows foreign usage.

The five years since the first appearance of this book have seen several interesting operetta developments. In America, producing organizations and record companies have been reexamining vintage musical comedies and romantic operettas, treating them as classical works. Spurred on by the popularity of opera-star recordings (by no means a new development, as there have been studio recordings of shows since the beginning of the century) these "crossover" discs of *Show Boat, My Fair Lady, Of Thee I Sing, Carousel, South Pacific*, and others are answering the public's demand for melody, romance, and wit in a heavy-metal, acid-rock world.

In some cases, recordings have resulted in full-fledged revivals, particularly in London, to compete with such wildly successful pop operas as *The Phantom of the Opera* (1986) and

---

[5]Grünwald, ibid.

Les Misérables (1985). These two shows were playing at the end of 1988 in Vienna, which welcomed *Cats* at the Theater an der Wien for an unprecedented run in 1983. Spectacularly mounted British productions are for the moment in vogue, and there have been local attempts to create the same sort of show. In Barcelona in 1988, for example, one could see *Mar i cel*, a new musical historical melodrama.

Europeans remain basically conservative, producing and recording the same tried and true operettas, occasionally in bizarre productions. The quantitative tally of staged operetta performances has probably not risen since 1983. Some companies will only present *Die Fledermaus* or *Die lustige Witwe*, while others have decided to forego the genre altogether—influential Dramaturgs and their public would rather see a company challenged with *Die Walküre* than have it present another production of *Der Bettelstudent*.

And yet, opera stars like Plácido Domingo are responsible to some extent for making other operettas popular once again today. Spanish opera stars continue to concertize and record excerpts from their beloved zarzuelas, and occasionally appear in them: Alfredo Kraus starred in 1988 in a full production at Barcelona's Liceo of the Vives masterwork, *Doña Francisquita*. Zarzuelas were virtually unknown outside of Spain and Latin America in the early 1980s. Happily, this is hardly the case today, since the spectacular revue from Madrid, the *Antología de la Zarzuela*, has been acclaimed internationally.

In Germany and Austria there have been a few courageous repertoire choices. Straus's *Der tapfere Soldat (The Chocolate Soldier)* and his Wagner burlesque, *Die lustigen Nibelungen*, have been seen for the first time in years. The East Berlin Komische Oper presented Gilbert and Sullivan's *Iolanthe* to enthusiastic audiences who had never heard of it, while a Gilbert and Sullivan revue was seen at the Vienna Volksoper. But Viennese operetta abroad has been winning new fans, particularly in Japan, where audiences have been revelling in Volksoper tours, and in America and Australia, where Kálmán works not seen for fifty years are suddenly popular again.

In Britain, the rebirth of the D'Oyly Carte Opera Company occurred in between runs of the English National Opera's de-Japanned *Mikado* and the New Sadler's Wells Opera productions of *Bitter-Sweet* and *The Gondoliers*, while tours of *Perchance to Dream* and *King's Rhapsody* roamed the provinces. Gilbert and Sullivan succeeds while a revival of Herbert and Ellis *(Bless the Bride)* does not. In France, there are even some new operettas, beside the yearly Lopez creations. Distinguished revivals of Chabrier and Messager works have been seen and recorded in Lyon. But Paris does not support, as London does, a company regularly doing operetta classics—and the loss of the Opéra Comique as a second opera house only aggravates this problem. With *Cats* finally opening in Paris in 1989, one wonders what future Parisian tastes will be.

It is once again my hope that this book will prompt impresarios to look retrospectively and mount new productions of the many delightful operettas that are awaiting their kiss of life.

For this edition, factual errors, misspellings, and typos have been corrected. I thank my earnest readers for pointing some of these out, and hope any others I may have missed are brought to my attention.

November, 1988   R. T.

OVERTURE

ACCORDING to most French dictionaries of the mid-nineteenth century, the word *opérette* was taken from the German *Operette,* itself derived from the Italian term *operetta.* The *-ette* or *-etta* designated something diminutive, a "little" opera or a "little" *opéra-comique.* There was substantial agreement that operettas were performed in "little theatres or salons," and several dictionaries, particularly the musical ones, named Mozart as the originator of the term.

The Dictionnaire de l'Académie française (1878, 1935) called operetta a "dramatic composition of which the action is gay or comic and the music light." The 1957 Larousse de la Musique called operetta a "genre derived from *opera buffa* which was born and developed in the course of the nineteenth century." The more recent Webster's Third New International Dictionary (1976) termed it "a light musical-dramatic production having usually a romantic plot and containing spoken dialogue and dancing scenes." And the 1979 Concise Oxford Dictionary of Opera calls it "a term used for a play with an overture, songs, interludes, and dances." These definitions are admittedly vague.

Part of the difficulty rests not only with the half-truths in many definitions but also with changes in meaning over centuries and from country to country of terms that scholars have used (or should use) in defining the genre. Thus, the original Italian word *operetta* meant something different in Mozart's day from what it does now, while it still means something quite different in France and in England. *Opéra-comique,* which deserves and has received comprehensive studies on its own, was something else entirely in eighteenth-century France than the form it became in the nineteenth century, and it could not and still cannot be translated with accuracy into the English term comic opera, which

---

Boston's Bijou Theatre was a leading regional operetta theatre in the United States. This programme cover illustrates the second act of Gilbert and Sullivan's *Iolanthe,* and was used regularly in the 1880s.

1

itself meant something (specifically) different in the 1880s than its present (general) meaning.

To make matters even more delightfully confusing, as in an operetta plot, the Italian term *opera buffa* could definitely not be translated into the French *opéra-bouffe* after the 1850s. Furthermore, there are other important French terms which had meanings different from their British or American usage, then and now: *vaudeville, pantomime,* and *burlesque* being the most vital for our discussion.

Surprisingly, an Italian term is used to describe a specific genre to which the Italians themselves have not contributed one work that has been universally popular. *Opera buffa* undoubtedly had an influence on operetta, but so did several other theatrical forms. The French *opéra-comique* has more of a claim, though not an exclusive one, to operetta's parentage. When Camille Saint-Saëns, at the 1921 opening of the American Conservatory in Fontainebleau, claimed that operetta was the "daughter of *opéra-comique* who went astray . . . not that daughters who go astray are always without charm," he neglected to inform us who the real father was. And it would be impossible to pinpoint him accurately, because *opéra-comique* had many lovers.

Operetta is of French extraction, and most non-French operettas heard today are based on French models dating from no earlier than the 1850s. Nevertheless, there were specific Italian influences. *Intermezzi,* short musical entertainments sandwiched between the acts of a play, were given in Florence as early as 1539. As these developed, the interlude was eventually placed within the context of the *opera seria,* offering comic relief. Pergolesi's *La Serva Padrona* (The Maid-Mistress, 1733) was the most celebrated *intermezzo,* paving the way for the popular Italian *opera buffa* of the eighteenth and nineteenth centuries. It would indeed be easy to say that Italian *opera buffa* gave the French the idea of operetta, but this would be misleading, as the French had their own antecedents long before. Operetta was perhaps more a comic French reaction to both serious Italian (and French) grand operas and needlessly serious French *opéras-comiques,* based on models that were both French and Italian.

This Franco-Italian correspondence goes back to 1283, when Adam de la Halle had offered *Le Jeu de Robin et de Marion* (The Play of Robin and Marion) to the French court at Naples, a comic play into which he had inserted popular songs of the day to fit the dramatic-comic action, a practice which was to continue well into the nineteenth century. Robin and Marion were the ancestors of the types of musical entertainments popular at the Parisian fairgrounds in the late seventeenth and early eighteenth centuries. The Foire Saint-Germain, held from February to April near the present church of Saint-Germain-des-Prés, and the Foire Saint-Laurent, given during August and September where the Gare de l'Est now stands, were the popular haunts of those seeking vulgar thrills, from acrobatics to coarse satirical songs, along with all manner of circus-like sideshow attractions. Appealing to certain members of the nobility, the bourgeoisie, and the rabble, the fairs were, at least, democratic.

At the same time, serious Italian opera was claiming the attention of the upper classes and the court, and the French *comédie ballet,* often with music by Italians like Jean-Baptiste Lully (1632–1687), was delighting Molière's audiences with its skillful mixture of spectacle, comedy, and singing. The most famous and popular of these remains Molière and Lully's *Le Bourgeois Gentilhomme.* First seen at the château of Chambord (14 October 1670), it was for the *divertissement* of the King, as the first edition stated. Louis XIV was suitably diverted, telling its author after the second performance: "Really, Molière, you haven't yet done anything that has diverted me more, and your play is excellent." In the original cast Molière himself was the first Monsieur Jourdain and a man the first Madame Jourdain. Lully's score was originally much longer than the version we hear today, with the ballet sections far more built-up than present-day tastes would warrant. But such brilliantly funny moments as the dancing lesson, the interrupted musicale, and the whole false-Turkish ceremony at the end of the play, in which Jourdain is created a *"Grand Mamamouchi,"* were musical sequences that continue to enchant us three hundred years later with their sprightly blend of comedy and music. *Le Bourgeois Gentilhomme* was also a commercial French success, in spite of its royal-command genesis. It was produced for the general public at the Palais-Royal (23 November 1670) and made some 1,397 *livres* on its first night. The play was repeated some forty-two times in the next two years—a substantial "run" for that period. Molière's influence on all future French comedy is of course obvious, but he also wrote what were in effect the first significant French musical comedies, which were thus important stepping-stones on the road to French operetta.

Lully was also responsible for attractions at the Académie Royale de Musique (the Opéra), which, in the interests of crimping any outside competition from musical entertainments, had licensing restrictions enacted to prevent the number of actor-singers and musicians appearing elsewhere. At one time, these permitted one actor plus four violins and an oboe. These rules were roughly equivalent to British regulations at the same time involving the "patent theatres," patented to prevent other theatres from establishing claims on audiences.

The Parisian fairs found the serious operas, with their elaborate machines, stock mythological characters, and stilted mannerisms fair game for parody. Satirical songs were already common: the original meaning of *vaudeville* was a song with a familiar melody to which new satiric, scabrous, or risqué words were applied. There was also the *comédie à ariettes* (comedy with little airs), which originally burlesqued arias from Italian operas, with French lyrics. Possibly because the parodies and the *vaudevilles* were getting too popular and too searing, the three official patent theatres, the Opéra, the Comédie-Française, and the Comédie-Italienne successfully had the fair plays with songs banned at various times during the 1707–15 period. To circumvent this, the wily fair actors had the *audience* sing instead of the actors, by having them follow the words on *écriteaux,* placards or banners suspended from the tops of their platforms, while the actors pranced and mimed about the stage.

The Opéra eventually relented, permitting singing at the fairs, and plays consisting entirely of *vaudevilles* became popular. By 1715 came the first usage of the term *opéra-comique* to describe a form similar to what had been called *pièces en vaudevilles,* while at the same time dialogue began creeping back into these entertainments to separate the songs. In 1718, the Comédie-Française, already a graying institution not yet forty years old, had the Duc d'Orléans stop their performance because the dialogue stretches were assuming uncomfortably long periods.

The new genre continued to purvey the old recipe for popularity: satire (both social and musico-dramatic), characters drawn generally from the *commedia dell'arte,* songs that were immediately hummable (whether familiar or new), and varying amounts of ribald indecency. One of the most famous *opéras-comiques* of the first half of the eighteenth century was Charles-Simon Favart's (1710–1792) *La Chercheuse d'Esprit* (1741), a licentious and graceful work remembered because it is used in Offenbach's *Madame Favart* (1878), an operetta that recreates this very period. The present Opéra-Comique theatre in Paris, the Salle Favart, is named after Favart, who provided some hundred and fifty libretti for the most celebrated *opéra-comique* composers of later years, Grétry, Philidor, and Gluck.

A revival of Pergolesi's intermezzo *La Serva Padrona* in Paris in 1752 started a clamor for Italian or Italian-style works without parody and satire, with domestic situations treated in a natural, healthily comic style. *Opera buffa* had begun its world conquest. French composers began to compose sophisticated scores, with more elaborate part-writing and enlarged orchestration, for sentimental or comic libretti. Philidor's *Tom Jones* (1765), Monsigny's *Le Déserteur* (1769), and Grétry's *Richard Coeur de Lion* (1784) were sentimental, even pathetic *opéras-comiques,* and the last was well on the way to the historical-romantic grand opera so beloved in the nineteenth century. By the time of the Revolution of 1789, the prominent *opéras-comiques* had ceased being *comique.*

The Romantic movement contributed to this trend, with exotic and novel-like plots being popular, making the music of the *opéra-comique* more and more like *opéra.* François Adrien Boïeldieu managed to be comic and romantic with his *Ma Tante Aurore* (1803), while the much later *La Dame Blanche* (1825) was nearly entirely romantic, after Walter Scott. It was *La Dame Blanche* (Opéra-Comique, 10 December 1825) that decisively changed *opéra-comique,* requiring virtuoso operatic voices singing against complicated, heavily charged orchestrations.

In 1817, Gioacchino Rossini's *L'Italiana in Algeri* (1813), his first great *opera buffa,* was presented in Paris. This started an affair between Paris audiences and the comic and dramatic works of the Italian composer that was legalized, as it were, with Rossini's move to Paris several years later. *Le Comte Ory* (1828) was

---

Auber's *Le Cheval de Bronze,* libretto by Scribe, was first presented at the Opéra-Comique in 1835. The exoticism and spectacle of its oriental setting and the accessibility of its tunes were two qualities that continued into the *opéra-bouffe* period. (What was originally comparatively light in 1835 was transformed into a grand opera in Auber's 1857 amplification.)

witty and scintillating as few French works then were, explaining the taste for *opera buffa*. But there was some native comic relief. While Parisians fell for Meyerbeer in the 1830s, several delightful *opéras-comiques* were produced that are still heard because of their lighthearted, gay music and charming, unpretentious plots: Daniel François Esprit Auber's *Fra Diavolo* (1830), Louis Joseph Ferdinand Hérold's *Le Pré aux Clercs* (1832), and Adolphe Adam's *Le Postillon de Longjumeau* (1836). Eugène Scribe, besides fathering the "well-made play," was one of the most prominent librettists of his time, writing not only the words for *Fra Diavolo* but also those for *Le Comte Ory, La Dame Blanche,* Adam's sweet *Le Chalet* (1834), Auber's *chinoiserie, Le Cheval de Bronze* (1835), and two other captivating works by Auber: *Le Domino Noir* (1837) and *Les Diamants de la Couronne* (1841). (Scribe's complete *oeuvre* runs to seventy-six volumes.) Auber's infectious scores had a verve obtained by exploiting dance rhythms, like the then-popular galop and polka, which unmistakably influenced operetta. It was also safe to say that much of their jaunty appeal as well as the construction of their elaborate finales came from the good influence of Rossini, whose works remain the best of *opera buffa*.

Adolphe Adam (1803–1856) helped bring back some of the jollity of the fairgrounds to the *opéra-comique*, their own descendant. Although Adam studied with Boïeldieu at the Conservatoire, he worked in a *café-concert,* and wrote the music for some two dozen *vaudevilles.*

He wrote for the Opéra-Comique from 1829; in 1834 his one-act *Le Chalet* brought him to prominence. He too was influenced by Rossini, and his style was comic and reasonably unpretentious. *Le Chalet* (Opéra-Comique, 25 September 1834) had a libretto by Scribe and Melesville set in Switzerland, with "the mountains of Appenzel" seen through the doors of the titular abode. Derived from a story by Goethe, the slight plot told of timid Daniel and his loved one, Bettly, whose chalet is besieged by a company of Swiss soldiers fighting for Austria, led by the swaggering Max. *"Vivent le vin, l'amour et le tabac / Voilà le refrain du bivouac!"* sing Max and his mercenaries as they pilfer poor Bettly's supplies. Rousing military songs like this kept *Le Chalet* popular for years, one of Adam's most enduring works. In 1840, it was superseded by Donizetti's *La Fille du Régiment* at the same Opéra-Comique, a more ambitious work that also had fun with martial rhythms and characters.

Without Rossini, operetta may very well have developed very differently in Paris, where the maestro chose to live. The Rossinian influence happily continued in Adam's future works, along with the refinement that Boïeldieu had encouraged. In the 1850s, concurrent with Hervé but still before the advent of the Offenbach successes, Adam was writing one-act *opéras-comiques* which were virtual operettas. *La Poupée de Nuremberg* (1852) is the only one remembered today. Adam even managed to write one for Offenbach's Bouffes-Parisiens in 1856, *Les Pantins de Violette,* set in a *commedia dell'arte* environment, and produced a few days before Adam's death. The original pierrot was soon to be Offenbach's greatest star, Hortense Schneider.

The comedy of the Italian *intermezzi* had long since developed into *opera buffa,* whose history is less complicated than that of its French cousin. One need only mention the major composers and their high points in this distinguished cavalcade of brilliant and enduring works: Pergolesi's *La Serva Padrona* (1733), which caused such an éclat in Paris twenty years later, works by Paisiello (including his own *Barbiere di Siviglia* in 1782), Cimarosa, and Salieri, and naturally the triumphs of the Austrian, Mozart. Were it not for the *opera buffa* convention of the *recitativo secco, Le Nozze di Figaro* (1786) would be one ot the greatest *opéras-comiques.* In fact, it was performed with dialogue replacing the *recitativo* when it was first done at the Paris Opéra in 1793, and many times since at the Opéra-Comique. Of course, it had the advantage of a superb source, the 1784 comedy by Beaumarchais. One can understand the French devotion to the spoken word that would lead them to speak rather than sing the dialogue, which is certainly better than the spoken dialogue in *Die Zauberflöte.* The characters in *Le Nozze di Figaro* are musically alive with a comic verisimilitude previously rare on the musical stage, its songs and ensembles have everything to do with carrying the story forward, and the finale to Act II is the peerless mold into which all others of its type are poured. It also retains the elegance of its original play, and the elegance of Mozart's music was a quality for which many future operetta composers, including Offenbach, Sullivan, and Messager, would strive. In this sense, Mozart's influence on operetta has been profound.

It is also important to stress again that, although works like *Le Nozze di Figaro* were written by royal command (because of the very different financing of theatrical works in the eighteenth century), they were often great successes with the general public. The first night of *Le Nozze di Figaro* in Prague in 1787 was an amazing triumph: virtually all of its thirty-odd numbers had to be repeated, and several songs became such great hits that Mozart could expect a laugh when he quoted *"Non più andrai"* in the last act of *Don Giovanni* in its Prague première in 1787. Were the entire structure of royalties, copyrights, and publishing different in the late 1700s, Mozart's career would no doubt have been vastly different and his fortune considerably improved.

Mozart wrote several other works in Italian and German which were forerunners of operetta. *Die Zauberflöte* (1791) is a principal one because it is a *Singspiel*, or song-play, and because it has folk, fairy-play, or pantomime elements which would similarly influence later operetta creators. *The Magic Flute* is, of course, more than that, but its commingling of romantic, serious, and farcical elements, in typical *Singspiel* fashion, was a tradition that would be continued in Viennese operetta. It was in the one-act form, however, that Mozart influenced Offenbach, and he even called some of his short trifles operettas—little operas that could be written after lunch in one afternoon. One of the best of these was undoubtedly *Der Schauspieldirektor* (The Impresario, 1786), written the same year as *Figaro* for a fête at Schönbrunn Palace. Offenbach thought so highly of it that he had it produced in his second season at the Bouffes-Parisiens, with a new libretto by Léon Battu and Ludovic Halévy that considerably changed the original story.

Both the short and the lengthened form of the Italian *opera buffa* were carried over into the new century by two remarkably prolific composers: Rossini (1792–1868) and Donizetti (1797–1848). Gioacchino Rossini's earliest one-act successes, like *La Scala di Seta* (1812) and *Il Signor Bruschino* (1813), were based on Italian or French comedies that offered little of the social or political criticism of Beaumarchais, being rather typical farces of the Molière or Goldoni types. *L'Italiana in Algeri* (1813), in two acts, was an even greater triumph, in Venice, and later in Paris (1817). Its infectious gaiety almost assuredly had its effect later on Adam and Auber. *Il Barbiere di Siviglia* (1816) and *La Cenerentola* (1817) had even greater appeal. The score to *L'Italiana in Algeri* was written in three weeks, that of *Il Barbiere di Siviglia* in less than two, and who knows how long *Cenerentola* took. All three are totally delicious, bubbling, sparkling works, as alive today as they ever were.

Gaetano Donizetti had a similarly prolific career, starting it as a frank Rossini imitator. Donizetti was perhaps more successful with sentimental subjects (as far as current critical opinion is concerned), though three of his *opere buffe* have persisted quite happily to the present day. *L'Elisir d'Amore* (1832) was actually a setting of an Italian reworking of Scribe's libretto *Le Philtre,* written originally in 1831 for Auber. Even more French were *La Fille du Régiment* (1840) and *Don Pasquale* (1843), both first produced in Paris.

Rossini and, to a lesser extent, Donizetti, with their infectious styles, gave the ailing *opéra-comique* a shot in the arm, but the serious-sentimental Rossini and Donizetti had as much of an effect, leading to overblown *opéras-comiques* as well as grand *opéras,* and it was this wing that again triumphed after 1830. *Le Comte Ory* (1828) was Rossini's last great comic work, based this time on a *vaudeville* by Scribe and Delestre-Poirson that had first been performed in 1816. Without *Ory,* it is unlikely Auber and Adam would have composed such works as *Fra Diavolo* (1830) or *Le Postillon de Longjumeau* (1836), which brought a measure of jollity and good humor back to *opéra-comique.*

The influence of the better *opere buffe* on French and English operetta is obvious, even in specific instances. When Offenbach paid homage to Rossini and Mozart in his second season at the Bouffes-Parisiens by mounting *Il Signor Bruschino* and *Der Schauspieldirektor,* he admitted his influences. Gilbert and Sullivan's *The Sorcerer* (1877) could not very likely have been written had not both authors known Donizetti's *L'Elisir d'Amore.* Both Offenbach and Sullivan knew their Italian operas thoroughly; and Rossini rather graciously called Offenbach *"le Mozart des Champs-Élysées."* The *"Rossini* of the Champs-Élysées" might have been just as apt.

There were several other French composers who provided scores for cheerful *opéras-comiques* while also writing heavier works. Most of these are merely memories today. Jacques Fromental Halévy, whose nephew Ludovic would become France's greatest operetta co-librettist, saw "lightning" strike twice in 1835 when the Opéra produced his grand *La Juive* and the Opéra-Comique mounted his charming *L'Éclair* (Lightning), both big successes. Amboise Thomas's *Le Caïd* (1849) gave the Opéra-Comique a so-called *opéra-bouffe* before the term had its Offenbach associations; it was more after the Rossini style of *opera buffa.* Charles Gounod's *Le Médecin malgré lui* (1858) set Molière virtually word-for-word, with only middling results. Victor Massé's *Galathée* (1852) and *Les Noces de Jeannette* (1853) were very much in and of the transitional period between *opéra-comique* and *opérette. Jeannette* is still impressive for its cheery, folksy good spirits, and a good deal of this was due to the libretto by Jules Barbier and Michel Carré (who wrote the book for Gounod's *Faust* in 1859). It is a lovely one-acter, surely deserving of revival, and not far removed from some of the later *paysanneries* of Offenbach, via Mozart. Even more neglected is the same composer's two-act *Galathée* (by the same librettists), one of innumerable musical versions of the Pygmalion-Galatea story that have been written, leading notably to Suppé's *Die schöne Galathee* (1865) and Loewe's *My Fair Lady* (1956). *Galathée* very significantly treated a classical myth humorously, something Offenbach and his librettists could not have failed to notice. The lofty Grecian statues of mythology were humanized and made funny—especially by the piece's non-Racinian dialogue.

There were, of course, many *opéras-comiques* written after the advent of Offenbach and Hervé, but the distinction between *opéra* and *opéra-comique* was progressively becoming whether or not the work had dialogue. Both *Faust* and *Carmen* were *opéras-comiques*. Gaiety and fun had by then moved over entirely to operetta, although many composers and librettists, especially after 1870, still rather grandly called their operettas *opéras-comiques* when they were in fact merely more sentimental than the *opéras-bouffes* of the 1860s. The same sentiment that helped reduce *opéra-comique* to a teary, tedious genre returned after the Franco-Prussian War to modify the bite and silliness that so delightfully distinguished the original operettas.

The development of the *opéra-comique* as an individual (though changeable) genre from its origins as the fairground *comédie en vaudevilles* did not exclude a development of the latter form. Becoming what would later be called simply a *vaudeville,* comedies or farces with songs retained their great appeal to Parisians right through the nineteenth century. Scribe himself was, again, among the most famous of *comédie-vaudeville* dramatists during the 1820s and '30s. His extremely complicated plots were infamous—playful, witty, and strewn with songs. One, *La Chatte métamorphosée en femme* (1827), provided the basis for a one-act Offenbach operetta thirty years later. The music in Scribe's play was all borrowed: from other *vaudevilles,* from popular street songs, even two airs by Beethoven! By the 1850s, the leading *farceur* and *vaudevilliste* was another Eugène, Labiche, whose *Le Chapeau de paille d'Italie* (The Italian Straw Hat, 1851, written with Marc Michel) remains his most famous work. Satire, directed against middle-class foibles and bourgeois morality, was ever-present in the nineteenth-century *vaudeville.*

So were puns, *doubles entendres,* gags, topical asides to the audience, and all the other comic pleasantries that had been forced out of the more formalized, more sentimental *opéra-comique* during the eighteenth century. Another medium for topical satire was the *revue,* which developed the fairground spoof—similarly left out of *opéra-comique*—and reached a high plateau by the 1840s, with the productions of the *frères* Cogniard at the Théâtre de la Porte-Saint-Martin. Like the *vaudeville,* the *revue* continued its ascent through the operetta period, well into this century. Parodies and burlesques of the latest operas, operettas, and plays were only to be expected in the latest *revue.*

The development of the popular, nontheatrical, French song deserves (like the history of the *opéra-comique*) a tome to itself. By the end of the eighteenth century, the then-suburban cabarets in the fashionable public gardens were a popular setting for their performance. Visitors were regaled with comic, satirical, or sentimental songs, done in the *chansonnier* style that has persisted to this day. Audiences were naturally expected to join in the *refrains.* The first well-known song author was Béranger, a true descendant of the troubadours of old. His songs were heard throughout the nineteenth and well into the twentieth centuries—even Yvette Guilbert sang them. The music-hall style would eventually lead to the revue songs of Maurice Chevalier, Mistinguett, Charles Trenet, and Edith Piaf, in some instances written by operetta composers.

In 1851, S.A.C.E.M., the French Society of Authors, Composers and Publishers of Music, was created to give profits to songwriters from the public performance of their songs. By the advent of the Second Empire (the Offenbach era in the theatre), the popularity of the *cafés-concerts* (or *cafés-chantants,* early music halls) was so intense that the previously frequented popular theatres on the Boulevard du Temple were emptied. The lower and lower-middle classes wanted "pop" music, rather than pantomimes, or tumbling acts, or cheap farces. Les Ambassadeurs, le Café de France, le Café Anglais were all the rage, as were the public *bals* which satisfied dancing urges. Both the music halls and the *bals* had a direct influence on the infant operetta, requiring songs (for the most part) to be accessible to untrained ears. They had to be catchy and, if possible, eminently danceable. This democratization accounted for many mediocre operettas throughout the nineteenth and early twentieth centuries, the direct opposite of the witty, musically and lyrically inspired creations of Offenbach and Meilhac and Halévy. But Offenbach and his librettists were hardly unaware of the *café-concert:* many of their stars, like Hortense Schneider, were groomed there, and the valuable training in diction, comic values, and "putting across" songs were unmistakable facets of the very first and greatest operettas.

Operetta had elements of the music hall and the *vaudeville* in it from the start, particularly in many of its comic *couplets,* or humorous verse songs. Neither Hervé nor Offenbach resisted writing catchy songs that would appeal to audiences at first hearing; their music was for everyone. The musical burlesques that would only be appreciated by those classes of theatregoers who knew their music were effectively balanced by songs that were destined to become popular hits. Furthermore, their authors knew the publicity value of hit songs, which were permitted to be sung (out of costume) in the cafés.

The other popular form of entertainment, the public ball, similarly had an influence on operetta as well as being an advertising medium for it. It is very apparent that popular dance music had a huge impetus in the creation of operetta everywhere, nowhere more obviously than in Vienna, where the waltz and the polka and the march were among the principal means of musical expression in operetta. In France, Offenbach used these and other dance structures (the boléro, the galop) in his works, eliciting as much foot-tapping from his audiences as humming-along. And nothing helped sell operetta in the pre-Gramophone era as much as the millions of copies sold of sheet music based on these works and arranged for the dancing of waltzes, polkas, quadrilles, and lancers.

All these genres, popular entertainments stemming ultimately from the late seventeenth- and early eighteenth-century Parisian fairs, were responsible for the birth of operetta after 1850. The works mentioned may well be counted as the ancestors of operetta, but none should really be called an operetta, because operetta as we know it was specifically a Paris original created after 1850. *Fra*

Diavolo, or *Le Comte Ory,* or *Le Postillon de Longjumeau,* delightful as they are, are not operettas because they represent the development of *opéra-comique,* and the original operettas of the 1850s were frankly closer to the *vaudeville* and the *revue* in spirit.

The gestation of operetta in England might seem to have followed a surprisingly similar path as it did in France, but, in fact, the British operetta was based more on French models of the post-1850 period than on popular native works. It is curious that London also had fairground entertainments in the seventeenth and eighteenth centuries (and legal troubles with the patent theatres), that it had elaborate spectacles with music and dancing—masques and otherwise—from Elizabethan times, and that it developed its own ballad opera in the eighteenth century, which was roughly equivalent to the *comédie en vaudevilles* and the original *opéra-comique,* using preexisting music with new words.

One of the first and greatest of all ballad operas was the 1728 triumph, *The Beggar's Opera* (Lincoln's Inn Fields, 29 January), produced by John Rich and written by John Gay ("it made Rich gay and Gay rich"), with music adapted from popular ballads and even Handel. By the time of the première of *The Beggar's Opera,* Italian opera had reached an intense level of British popularity, particularly after the establishment of the Queen's Theatre in 1705 as a home for Italian opera, where it seemed Handel could turn out a new opera every fortnight. These were invariably stagnant mythological or classical affairs that merely existed for vocal *tours-de-force.* By 1726, Handel had become a British subject, and two years later John Gay pricked the bubble that was an inflated convention by producing something new and British.

The chief song-source was a six-volume songbook published a decade before that included a vast number of ballads and other songs. Surprisingly, *The Beggar's Opera* was originally intended to be performed without an orchestra; the actors were meant to sing the songs without accompaniment. Indeed, Gay's play was good enough to be played *a cappella,* but Rich wanted an orchestra. Accordingly, the German Dr. Johann Christian Pepusch was called in to do the orchestrations, although it is by no means clear that he helped Gay choose the songs.

In 1728, the political jibes at the Robert Walpole government were considered merciless; today, these jests have lost a great deal of meaning, and in an age when anything can be (and has been) musicalized, the Swiftian irony of this tale of highwaymen and thieves, in which the coarsest citizens were made the heroes of an opera patched together out of popular ballads and street songs, has nowhere near the sensational effect it had in 1728. Pretty as these ballads are, they are not recognizable to modern ears, and thus *cannot* have the same effect today as they originally had with their new words. However, the work remains funny, and its attack on corruption is still vital, even if we are ignorant of the fact that Song No. XXI, "If the heart of a man is deprest with cares," is sung to the tune of "Would you have a young virgin of fifteen years."

The Beggar's Opera's original cast was led by Lavinia Fenton, whose Polly was so winning that she won herself the hand of the Duke of Bolton in marriage. The original run of what Jonathan Swift called the "Newgate Pastoral" was a (then) phenomenal 63 nights. The work naturally saw dozens of spin-offs, including *The Quaker's Wedding, The Beggar's Wedding,* and *Polly,* Gay's own sequel. This was banned by the Lord Chancellor in 1729 but has been presented as a novelty several times since. *The Beggar's Opera* was produced constantly in the eighteenth century, in America, too, and was later revived in London in 1820, 1836 (Covent Garden), and 1878 (Avenue). But none of these had runs to equal Nigel Playfair's legendary production at the Lyric, Hammersmith, in 1920, which was seen for 1,463 performances. This version's success was due to not only the tasteful new arrangements of Frederic Austin, but also the lovely, intimate theatre, a perfect cast, and the magical décor and costumes of Claude Lovat-Fraser. *The Beggar's Opera* was given a needlessly heavy operatization in 1948 by Benjamin Britten. And it served as the backbone of the Brecht-Weill *Die Dreigroschenoper* (1928), two centuries after the original first night.

Ballad opera was, as in France, pruned of much of its original satire and raucousness by the middle of the eighteenth century by composers like Thomas Arne and his librettist Isaac Bickerstaffe. *Thomas and Sally* (1760) was undoubtedly their most famous opera, but the works of his contemporaries are today largely in limbo—they certainly failed to obtain the international popularity of French works of the same period. And the same thing can be said of early nineteenth-century works, whether comic or not, until the advent of the "British Bellini," Michael William Balfe. His frankly Italian operas have nothing to do with operetta, but his best moments, in *The Bohemian Girl* (1843), have either an Italian flashiness or a sweet Irish simplicity which could not have failed to impress Sullivan, who edited a vocal score of *The Bohemian Girl* for the publisher Boosey during his pre-operetta days. This was assuredly a worldwide hit, and remains one of the few British musical theatre pieces written between *The Beggar's Opera* and *Trial by Jury* that is still performed (and not very often, at that).

The *café-concert* idea was not exclusively French. The British also liked the idea of a song or two with their public drinking. Again, the lower-middle and working classes were the chief patrons of what became the music hall, beginning its real career around 1850. There had been tavern supper-rooms, and various saloons with songs, but it was not until the mid-nineteenth century that music halls began to proliferate. Charles Morton, who ran the Canterbury and Oxford halls, was later a famous operetta manager. He turned the Philharmonic Music Hall in Islington into a theatre, presenting Offenbach's *Geneviève de Brabant* and Lecocq's *La Fille de Madame Angot* in notable productions. He later rescued D'Oyly Carte's foundering English Opera House by turning it into a variety theatre, the Palace. Variety was the natural extension of music hall, in a theatrical rather than a tavern setting.

The greatest stars of British music hall and variety specialized—as in France—in easily memorized songs with catchy refrains, generally comic but often sentimental. Their influence on Arthur Sullivan was not remarkable, though one cannot disassociate a song like "A Policeman's Lot Is Not a Happy One," from *The Pirates of Penzance* (1879), from the music hall. Later on, however, the dividing line between some of the numbers in English musical comedy and those in variety would be quite dim, as on the Continent.

More important to the genesis of the Gilbert and Sullivan style were the extravaganzas of James Robinson Planché, perhaps in some ways the English equivalents of the Viennese *Zauberspiele* of Ferdinand Raimund and Johann Nestroy, dramatic fairy tales with allegorical figures and music. These were, in both countries, in some ways variations on *vaudeville;* in England they led to burlesque—a travesty on some famous opera, play, or story, with interpolated songs—and to pantomime (as it was known in the latter 1800s and into this century). Gilbert's earliest stage works were in burlesque, and he also had his own well-known *Bab Ballads* to draw upon when it came to writing operettas, the first of which were written for Mr. and Mrs. (Thomas) German Reed.[1]

[1]For full accounts see plays collected and edited by Isaac Goldberg, *New and Original Extravaganzas*, and Jane Stedman, *Gilbert Before Sullivan*.

"How happy could I be with either, were t'other dear charmer away." Macheath (Frederick Ranalow) loves both Lucy (Violet Marquesita, left) and Polly (Sylvia Nelis) in *The Beggar's Opera*. Nigel Playfair's revival of Gay's 1728 ballad opera at the Lyric, Hammersmith, opened in 1920 and was seen for 1,463 performances.

Their "entertainments," as they were called, were specifically meant to cater to those of the middle and upper classes who in the Victorian era would never be seen in a theatre and certainly not in a music hall.

The Viennese operetta is today perhaps the strongest surviving national school (always excluding Gilbert and Sullivan). More of its works, particularly from the latter, or "Silver" period, are performed today than comparable works from other lands during the same period, and the years from *The Merry Widow* (1905) to the First World War saw an international Viennese dominance. For many, the glamor of operetta remains a peculiarly Viennese quality. Just as the Viennese were able to contribute to the development of Italian opera, they appropriated French operetta and eventually made it their own when Viennese managers refused to pay high sums to import Parisian models.

The waltz was the Austrian ingredient that transformed Viennese operetta. (Not that the French hadn't used it: a famous example from Offenbach is the great waltz first heard during the overture of *La Belle Hélène,* taken from the finale to Act II.) A waltz in the second-act finale of a comic opera, *Una Cosa rara,* by Vicente Martín y Soler, caused a furor in Vienna in 1786. So exciting was this event that Mozart used a waltz in *Don Giovanni* (and quotes a passage from *Una Cosa rara* as well). In the early nineteenth century, the waltz still had trappings of the *Ländler* when Franz Schubert wrote his measured dances, but the waltz was gaining tremendous popularity at public dances. In 1819, Carl Maria von Weber's *Invitation to the Dance* gave classical stature to the piano waltz, leading to the concert waltzes of Lanner and the Strauss dynasty.

The *Singspiel* was popular in Austria, as it was in Germany, and the Viennese variety was inclined to be influenced by the popular *Zauberspiel* (magic play) and *Posse* (farce), both with songs. All had the element of Viennese wit and sly humor that to some degree was carried over to the new operetta.

There were many practitioners of *Singspiel,* including several composers celebrated for other musical endeavors. Franz Schubert composed five *Singspiele*—most in one act—and even more full-length operas which are almost never staged. One reason given for this is that their libretti are poor, another is that Schubert's music for the stage is insufficiently dramatic. A further excuse is that they are simply not great Schubert. A combination of all three reasons is probably the truth. Schubert also wrote songs for farces and incidental music for dramas. Recent recordings of several of the one-act *Singspiele* have revealed a number of nice items, but rarely a full score that opera-house managers would want to mount. The most "popular" are *Die Verschworenen* and *Die Zwillingsbrüder,* the latter apparently the only one performed during Schubert's lifetime, in 1820. Felix Mendelssohn-Bartholdy left a one-act work, *Die Heimkehr aus der Fremde* (The Return from Abroad, 1829), which has a vitality that makes one regret he did not live longer to compose more for the musical stage, especially since Mendelssohnian elegance has been so admired in the operettas of Sullivan and other composers. Composed privately for his parents' silver wedding anniversary, the work was seen publicly only after the composer's death, in Leipzig in 1851. It was presented the same year at the Haymarket, London, under the title *Son and Stranger,* and the patter song *"Ich bin ein vielgereister Mann,"* known in English as "I Am a Roamer," is still sometimes heard.

Two German composers still played today bridge the gap between Mozart and Suppé: Albert Lortzing (1801–1851) and Otto Nicolai (1810–1849). Lortzing's *Zar und Zimmermann* (1837) and Nicolai's *Die lustigen Weiber von Windsor* (1849) even get occasional airings outside German-speaking borders. Both are nearly operettas, even if one was, properly, a *Singspiel* and the other a *komische Oper.* As critics have pointed out, these works and their fellows were the German equivalents of the French *opéras-comiques* of Adam and his contemporaries, but they had perhaps an even more distinct influence on classical post-1850 operetta, especially Viennese, than some of the more routine French works. They were distinctly German (particularly Lortzing's works), which is why they have not traveled too well: scenes from German peasant life have not had quite the same appeal abroad as do those of Ruritanian royalty. It is a testament to their durability that Lortzing and Nicolai are still performed today—one cannot say the same of Boïeldieu or Adam or any of the principal French *opéra-comique* composers.

One hears the influence of Mozart in Lortzing, and also Weber. Lortzing, in turn, influenced Wagner, as well as Johann Strauss II. *Hans Sachs* (1840) was a forerunner of *Die Meistersinger.* Marie's first song in the first act of *Zar und Zimmermann* is directly en route to the first scene between Adele and Rosalinde in *Die Fledermaus.* Lortzing, besides being a composer and his own librettist, was an actor, born into a theatrical family. His theatrical sense was thus very sure, perhaps more impressive in some instances than his musical originality. His comic scenes were extremely effective, and not always heavy-handed in the usual Prussian fashion.

After sojourns in Cologne and Detmold, during which he wrote several *vaudevilles,* Lortzing and his family moved to Leipzig, where his best works were written and produced: *Zar und Zimmermann* (Tsar and Carpenter, 1837) and *Der Wildschütz* (The Poacher, 1842). *Zar und Zimmermann* was not the first musical version of a play by three French authors, *Le Bourgmestre de Saradam;* there had been others, by composers Grétry, Mercadante, and Donizetti. The plot was based on a historical anecdote, that Tsar Peter the Great worked incognito in Holland as a carpenter in a shipyard. The townspeople were supposed to have been Dutch, complete with a wooden-shoes dance in the last act, but they sounded German, and the leading character, the Burgomaster Van Bett, was a precursor of Wagner's Beckmesser, the all-knowing, fatuous official. "Oh, I am clever and wise," he sings in his famous entrance song (and several times thereafter), and he is of course anything but that. This big bass *Auftrittslied* (entrance song) was patterned after the Rossini-Donizetti type, and it would later resurface in such famous songs as the "Kiss on the Shoulder" entrance of Colonel Ollendorf in Millöcker's *Der Bettelstudent,* while the song's patter of infinitive verbs would appear again in Dr. Blind's part in the Act I trio of *Die Fledermaus*.

Particularly impressive was the chorus-lesson scene that opens Act III, in which Van Bett instructs the townsfolk to learn a chorus of praise for the Tsar, gentle mock-Handel long before Sullivan attempted the same thing. The sentimental songs beloved all over Europe in the nineteenth century (and not just in *opéra-comique*) are present in *Zar und Zimmermann*. One, the song of the French ambassador, *"Lebe wohl, mein flandrisch Mädchen,"* is quite lovely, and another is the Tsar's scepter song in the last act. Lortzing's duets have an attractive folksiness, and the celebrated sextet in Act II begins very imposingly *a cappella* and ends with a rapid-fire *cabaletta*. Lortzing's style was quite influential on the young Viennese operetta.

Zar und Zimmerman was in Berlin in 1839, in Vienna in 1842, in New York in 1857, and in London in 1871 in English, as *Peter the Shipwright*. *Der Wildschütz* has been done abroad, fitfully, but rarely *Undine* (1845, a romantic opera), *Der Waffenschmied* (The Armorer, 1845), or even the excellent *Die Opernprobe* (The Opera Rehearsal, 1851). Several one-act works have been lost or forgotten, among them the interestingly titled *Szenen aus Mozarts Leben* (1830) and *Eine Berliner Grisette*. One wonders what these lighter pieces were like. Very likely they were among the first German operettas.

Otto Nicolai is remembered solely for his *Die Lustigen Weiber von Windsor,* and it is of heavier cast than Lortzing's works. Nicolai was also a conductor and, like so many operetta composers, an organist. *Die Lustigen Weiber von Windsor,* with libretto by Hermann Mosenthal, was from Shakespeare, who was later to inspire Verdi and Vaughan Williams with the same play. It is brilliantly scored—the overture is rightly famous on its own—and in many sections it suggests parts of future operettas. This "comic-fantastic" opera is accurately, again, *opéra-comique,* requiring in this case more elaborate singing than we expect in operetta.

Josef Lanner (1801–1843) and the elder Johann Strauss (1804–1849) supplied the ball-mad Viennese with two formidable dance orchestras, catering to those of whatever class whose nightly desire was to whirl and twirl in three-quarter time. Dance music in other time-signatures was also required: polkas, marches, quadrilles, and galops. In pre-operetta days, popular operas and *opéras-comiques* would sometimes supply the melodies for these Lanner- and Strauss-arranged compositions. During the heyday of Viennese operetta, the latest Strauss II show would as a matter of course be good for six or more dance arrangements for the ballroom or the home spinet.

Leading with their violins (which so influenced the style of their waltzes), Johann Strauss II (1825–1899) and his brothers Josef and Eduard carried on their father's traditions and brought the concert waltz to its highest plateau. The activity that had originally started in the *Heurigen,* the suburban inns, was now, for the most part, in the center of a greatly expanding city, where sumptuous balls were a glittering facet of Viennese life in the twilight of the Habsburg era.

Strauss II's greatest and most popular waltzes were written from 1867, with the performance of *An der schönen blauen Donau* (The Blue Danube) at the Dianasaal; works like *Künstlerleben* (Artist's Life), *Geschichten aus dem Wienerwald* (Tales from the Vienna Woods), and *Wein, Weib und Gesang* (Wine, Women and Song) were written before he turned his attention to the stage.

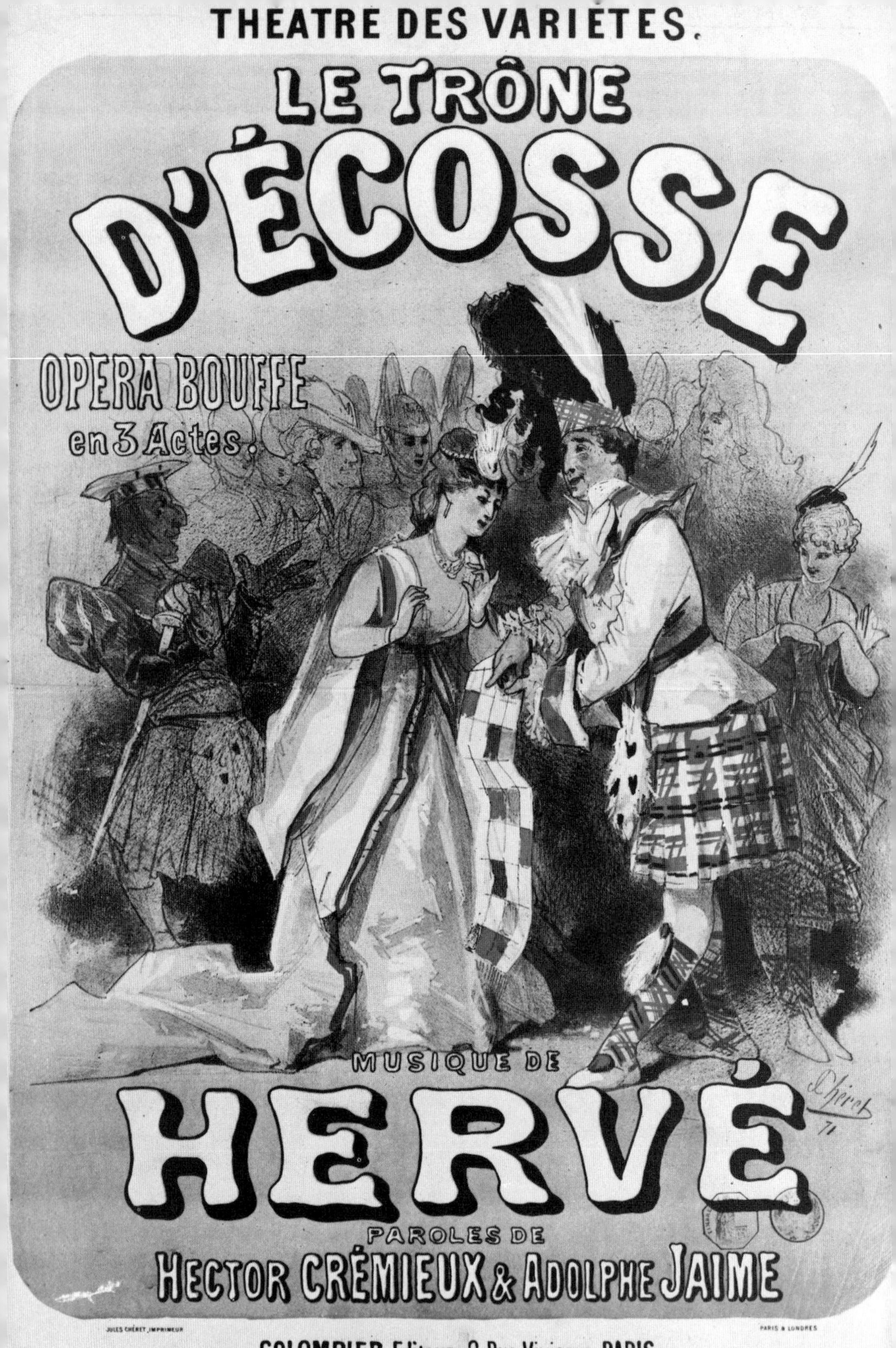
THEATRE DES VARIETES.
LE TRÔNE D'ÉCOSSE
OPERA BOUFFE
en 3 Actes.
MUSIQUE DE
HERVÉ
PAROLES DE
HECTOR CRÉMIEUX & ADOLPHE JAIME
JULES CHÉRET, IMPRIMEUR
PARIS & LONDRES
COLOMBIER, Editeur, 6, Rue Vivienne, PARIS.

BEGINNERS, PLEASE!

T HOUGH there were antecedents of operetta in countries other than France, it took the French to refine the form—first in the short, one-act works which were as much an extension of the *vaudeville* as a corruption of the *opéra-comique* and later in the full-length, usually three-act *opéras-bouffes*. These were invariably more ambitious musically than their shorter relatives.

The term *opérette* had been used before 1850, and there were composers who were writing short comic scenes or sketches before the advent of Hervé, but none of these was of more than passing interest, and their composers' names are generally forgotten. Offenbach is considered the father of French operetta—but so is Hervé. Both should be given credit. One can oversimplify the truth by saying that Hervé sired the short French operetta (though none of Hervé's short works are heard today), while the short operetta, brought to a high level by Offenbach (whose one-act works are still done today), was developed by Offenbach into the longer operetta.

Hervé's later, full-length operettas, resting on the scaffolding created by Offenbach and his librettists, became immensely popular when Offenbach's career was just about to begin its decline in the late 1860s. For many years, the two composers were rivals, often bitter ones. And, late in Hervé's career, years after Offenbach's death, Hervé wrote his one operetta still performed regularly today, *Mam'zelle Nitouche* (1883).

If there is no disputing the musical superiority of Offenbach over Hervé, one can still give Hervé the palm for his zany libretti and the spirit of inanity so much a part of the first operettas.

A poster by Jules Chéret for Hervé's *Le Trône d'Écosse* (Variétés, 1871). Chéret (1836–1932) was France's greatest theatre-poster artist, and his intensely theatrical designs for the operettas of Offenbach, Hervé, and other composers were instrumental in publicizing the gaiety and color awaiting customers at their theatres. *Le Trône d'Écosse* obviously took place in a very *opéra-bouffe* Scotland. Collection of Lucy Broido.

It is appropriate that the life story of Florimond Ronger, popularly known by one of his pseudonyms, **Hervé,** (1825–1892) is as fanciful as the genre he helped create. Born in 1825 to a brigadier of the gendarmerie and a Spanish lady, Hervé was an outstanding choirboy at the Saint-Roch church in Paris, and was encouraged from an early age to pursue a musical career. He was enrolled as a Conservatoire student, studied with Auber, and at the age of fifteen was playing the organ at the chapel of the church of Bicêtre. His playing so impressed a *curé* named Paradis that he was hired to provide music and some instruction for the inmates of an adjacent insane asylum. His poor, widowed mother was also hired to do the laundry. Besides playing and teaching, Hervé managed to organize some of the insane to present his own setting of a *vaudeville* by Scribe and Saintine, *L'Ours et le Pacha* (The Bear and the Pasha, 1842). This event so impressed the medical community at the time that there appeared a paper or two on the *"musicothérapie"* at Bicêtre.

But Hervé was not content being exclusively an organist or musical therapist. He longed for the stage. So he contrived to spend his days at the chapel and his evenings at suburban theatres, acting in minor and then bigger roles, and occasionally singing in his fine tenor voice. In 1845 he won a competition to become the organist at Saint-Eustache, one of the most prestigious parishes in Paris; he stayed at this post for eight years, leading a double life. It was during his tenure at Saint-Eustache that he took his final *nom de théâtre* from one of his students, the Marquis d'Hervé. This entire schizophrenic experience served as the basis of the story of his most famous operetta, *Mam'zelle Nitouche.*

In 1848, he composed a one-act "grotesque scene" entitled *Don Quichotte et Sancho Pança* for the composer Adolphe Adam's ill-fated "Théâtre National." This burlesque of literature, written for the comedian Désiré, was a precursor of the *opéra-bouffe,* and was seen at other theatres with success, in spite of the Revolution of 1848. The composer Reynaldo Hahn described what he considered the birth of operetta:

> In 1847, an overweight and short actor named Désiré, the spoiled child of the Théâtre Montmartre, went to see one of his friends, who was tall, and thin, and the organist at Saint-Eustache. He said to him: "I want to give a benefit performance for myself, and it's imperative that I play in something new. You, who are so droll when you act, and who has such funny ideas, you who compose so prettily and so easily: write me a little something for two people that you can play with me."
>
> The organist at Saint-Eustache thought about what the fat little man was saying to him. "Agreed," he answered, "and I've already found the title: it will be called *Don Quichotte et Sancho Pança.*"
>
> This incoherent fantasy, but with an irresistible buffoonery, was played by the thin author and his fat friend with an extraordinary success, and was striking in its novelty. It had as a subtitle: *"Tableau grotesque."* It was really not an *opéra-comique.*
>
> What was it, then?
>
> It was a thing for which no name had previously existed: it was an operetta; it was simply the first French operetta.

As the term itself had been used before, Hahn's statement was not entirely accurate, but in essence Hervé's work was among the first in the operetta style.

In 1851 Hervé secured another post, as musical director at the Théâtre du Palais-Royal; he managed to have four works presented there, one in five acts (*Les Folies dramatiques*, 1853), the others in one. *Les Folies dramatiques*, written with two other librettists, parodied all the types of entertainments then popular on Parisian stages: comedies, *vaudevilles*, dramas, tragedies, ballets, operas—and particularly Italian opera singers, who were mercilessly deflated.

In 1854, Hervé became the director of the Folies-Concertantes, a small theatre in the Boulevard du Temple. At first, he gave pantomimes, then things he called "lyric eccentricities" or perhaps "an asphyxiation in one act." The Folies-Concertantes was kept from presenting anything other than *"spectacles-concerts"* (concert shows) in one act, and with only two characters. (These same licensing restrictions, dating back to 1807, hampered Offenbach, as we will observe, and were the major reason preventing the birth of the full-scale operetta before the 1860s, when these laws were lifted.)

Hervé did not confine his activities to theatre direction. In his long and prosperous career, he wrote more than one hundred and twenty operettas, at least half of which were in two or more acts, plus the libretti, in many cases. He additionally staged, starred in, or conducted most of them, often at the same time, according to contemporary reports. He did not monopolize the composition entirely—he gave both Delibes and Offenbach their early chances at the Folies-Nouvelles, the new name for the renovated Folies-Concertantes, dating from 1854–55. In the same season Offenbach was to start his triumphant career at the Bouffes-Parisiens. Within a few short years Hervé and Offenbach would become notoriously jealous of each other. Neither would permit his work to appear in the other's theatre, nor were they evidently on speaking terms. (A reconciliation was achieved by 1878, when Hervé played the part of Aristée/Pluton in a revival of *Orphée aux Enfers*.)

It would be difficult to discuss individually the dozens of forgotten short works Hervé provided for his various theatres, except to mention that they were reportedly amusing, satirical, fanciful, and perhaps not quite as musically interesting as the works Offenbach was churning out at the same time. Hervé's musical parody was heavy-handed, his songs were more rhythmic than melodic, and the skits found in his libretti were so tied to then-current events that their future life was severely questionable—indeed, they were seldom revived. In his two years at the Folies-Concertantes, Hervé's succession of blithe one-act operettas must have convinced Offenbach that he could write along the same lines. Had Hervé been a more gifted composer he would be remembered today as the Father of Operetta. Perhaps he was too busy directing, acting, and singing to channel all his talents into composing. It was not until the 1860s, well after Offenbach's first full-length hits, that Hervé hit his stride, composing his best works after the middle of the decade. By this time, the *opéra-bouffe* characteristics were well established: its infectious gaiety, its burlesque and satire—of whatever institution, its zany characters and situations, its fast pacing and rapid rhythms, and its complete unpretentiousness.

Les Chevaliers de la Table Ronde (The Knights of the Round Table, Bouffes-Parisiens, 17 November 1866) was the first three-act *opéra-bouffe* in the Offenbach style for Hervé, and it fared fairly well, but nothing like the next three-act *bouffe*, *L'Oeil crevé* (a French idiom meaning, literally, the burst eye, but also implying something hitting you right in the eye). *L'Oeil crevé* (Folies-Dramatiques, 12 October 1867) was one of the most spectacular hits of the 1860s, achieving an initial run of more than 10 months. And the critics were virtually unanimous in their praise. "Hervé's music is distinguished, spiritual, joyous, really crazy, really Parisian . . . and wise! The orchestration is full of delicious details," said the critic from *Le Figaro*.

There were parodies of both Rossini's *Guillaume Tell* and Weber's *Der Freischütz* in Hervé's libretto, which was, however, no more coherent than his usual inanities. Obviously, the topical references and interpolated gags were popular, but the general zaniness and non-sequiturs were also admired. The lyrics were good, though without the sheen and metrical finesse of Meilhac-Halévy creations. Looking back on his libretti, we find that their genial unstructuredness and very fast, zippy *dialogues* would, possibly, bear reexamination.

Foreign managers were looking for French works other than Offenbach's to fill the demand for *opéra-bouffe*. *L'Oeil crevé* was the first big Hervé work in Vienna, where it was called *Der Pfeil im Auge* (An Arrow in the Eye, Theater an der Wien, 29 February 1868). In London, it appeared, in H. B. Farnie's English version, as *L'Oeil Crevé!, or, The Merry Toxophilites* (Opera Comique, 1872).

Henry Brougham Farnie was almost singlehandedly responsible for the initial success of French *opéra-bouffe* in England. A literary hack without any noticeable talent for witty dialogue and even less for rhyming ability, he worked fast and managed to retain just enough French raciness to get his English versions by the Lord Chamberlain (the censor) and still titillate London audiences. He scoured Paris for properties and often had the English libretto of a particular work finished before his return to London. The first Farnie adaptation to create a stir was of the Offenbach-Meilhac-Halévy *Geneviève de Brabant* in 1871.

But greater triumphs awaited Hervé. Just as *L'Oeil crevé* had appeared—startlingly—right after *La Grande-Duchesse de Gérolstein*, *Chilpéric* (Folies-Dramatiques, 24 October 1868) opened a few weeks after the premiere of *La Périchole*, and was, similarly, an international success. *Chilpéric*, a travesty of sixth-century French history, was just as anachronistic as its predecessor, and the situations were healthily and delightfully vulgar. Hervé, far more than Offenbach himself, was responsible for giving *opéra-bouffe* a low reputation. His jokes were often risqué, the choruses were often dominated by females, and their outfitting was as scanty as possible by 1860s standards. Hervé himself starred in the title role of Chilpéric, supported by the magnificent and underdressed Blanche d'Antigny as his wife (and later murderer), Frédégonde. The big hits were the *air du Jambon*, the Ham Song, which had to be repeated—often—and the Song of the Blue Butterfly. Musical and dramatic barbs were aimed at such works as *Die Zauberflöte*, *Les Huguenots*, and even *Lohengrin* in *Chilpéric*.

König Chilperich played at the Carltheater, Vienna, in 1869, and the following year at the Lyceum, London. Julia Mathews and Hervé himself starred in the British adaptation by H. B. Farnie, along with a well-chosen bevy of beauteous chorus girls, who at one point stuck out their bare legs from the wings, twelve ladies on each side of the stage. Another memorable moment occurred when the entire cast opened up multicolored umbrellas during a finale *galop*.

Hervé made a tremendous impression in London, particularly on the ladies. Emily Soldene, the celebrated English *opéra-bouffe* prima donna who succeeded Hervé as Chilpéric at the Lyceum, and whose reminiscences furnish a marvelous picture of this era,[1] remembered the creator-star as

> . . . an elegant, charming artist; such gaiety, such grace, such distinction, such perfection of style, such expressive hands, they were, if possible, more expressive than his face; not much voice, but what wonders he did with it! And then his delightfully broken English, not too broken, just broken enough . . . no wonder the women went down in regiments before this redoubtable foreign fascinator; at least, that's what they used to say. It was even whispered that the principal cleaner, age 67, was not entirely unaffected by his magnetic influence.

Soldene went on to relate the story of an "insolent" and "arrogant" actress with a "triple-expansive bust" who impertinently replied to Hervé's stage direction at a rehearsal. The "maestro" said, in a gentle, beseeching tone:

> "Come here, *ma fille.*"
> "*Ma fille!*" marched up, posing like an angry pouter pigeon. "Ah!" said he, touching the bust delicately and inquiringly with the tip of his delicate finger, "One can buy that, *mais, ma foi*, one cannot buy this," tapping his forehead violently, "buy this; *comprenez, ma fille?*—understand?"[2]

It should be added that it was well known at that time that chorus girls stuffed their garments with newspapers at strategic points to correct any insufficiencies.

The Prince of Wales (later Edward VII) was a regular supporter of French *opéra-bouffe*, both in Paris and in London. After the first act of a performance of *Chilpéric* in London, he asked Hervé if he might give an encore of the Ham Song, which was sung in the first act on horseback. As if to add to the merry zaniness of the story, Hervé obliged by riding into the Act II bedroom set on a horse, singing the royal command encore.

A revival of *Chilpéric* at the Théâtre des Variétés in 1895 inspired Toulouse-Lautrec's painting of Marcelle Lender dancing the role of Galswinthe. The artist visited the Variétés more than twenty times to study her.

Le petit Faust (28 April 1869) was another smash—more than two hundred performances at the Folies-Dramatiques. Hervé was Faust, Blanche d'Antigny, Marguerite. Hector Crémieux and Adolphe Jaime did the book and lyrics this time, leaving Hervé more time to work on his music and to rehearse himself as Faust. The libretto was as rambling and silly as ever, but the lyrics were quite

[1]Soldene, Emily. *My Theatrical and Musical Recollections*, pp. 65–66.
[2]Ibid.

polished (even pithy, as in Méphisto's first *rondeau*) and the gaiety and vulgarity quite unbridled. Hervé's tunes were both lovely and catchy, and the faster they were, the more insistently memorable they became. Written a decade after the première of Gounod's opera (1859) but produced only two months after the version we know today was presented at the Opéra, *Le petit Faust* was partially a musical burlesque of the opera, but also a twisting of its dramatic incidents, done in pure *opéra-bouffe* style. Thus, the libretto has the old Faust in Act I teaching an unruly co-ed class the elements of anatomy. Siébel is one of the students. (In the Gounod and the Hervé, Siébel is a trousers role. In the Hervé, so is Méphisto.) Faust asks "Monsieur Siébel" if he is a man—"Prove it!" he shouts. Stage directions were not needed; it was a piquant, saucy libretto. Valentin leads a glorious military chorus, but his sentiments are far from those in *"Gloire immortelle."* Rather, "When a soldier goes to war / He embraces his father / (Chorus) And if he has no father? / (Valentin) He embraces his mother," and so on, all rhymes ending with *-ère*. Very silly, and great fun.

Delightful as the first act was (preceded by a stunning overture), with its jumping opening chorus, Marguerite's entrance song *("Fleur de candeur")*, and her *"Viv' l'amour, l'jeunesse"* at the finale, the second act was even more invigorating. The brilliant triple chorus of students, cocottes, and old men opened this Kermesse scene, followed soon by Méphisto's song of the Persian prince and the flea, *"le satrape et la puce,"* which played with the words *satrape* and *s'attrape* (to get bitten). Better yet was the waltz-ensemble in which Marguerites from many lands were introduced for Faust's delectation. Méphisto then stopped the show with the simple, very touching Four Seasons waltz, *"Par l'ombre d'un rêve"* (In the shadow of a dream), after which a direct burlesque of the Gounod garden scene broke down into yodeling *à la tyrolienne,* the common comic opera way of dealing with anything German. It is a wonderful score that deserves to be heard again, but the production would have to include a horse-drawn cab, among other effects. A spectacular remounting and enlargement (including a ballet of the Seven Deadly Sins) in 1882 at the Porte Saint-Martin Theatre, with Hervé's corrections and additions, was followed by other revivals into this century.

Little Faust followed *Chilpéric* at the Lyceum, London, in 1870, with Emily Soldene as Marguerite, and Mlle. Debreux as Méphisto, and that same year Richard Genée adapted the libretto for the Vienna première at the Theater an der Wien, as *Doctor Faust junior. Les Turcs* (Folies-Dramatiques, 23 December 1869), a burlesque of Racine's *Bajazet* by Hector Crémieux and Adolphe Jaime, was very well thought of by the critics, and was very well advertised by a magnificent poster by Jules Chéret.

Hervé wrote a new "operatic extravaganza," *Aladdin the 2nd,* for London's Gaiety Theatre in a period of exile from France during the Franco-Prussian War (26 December 1870). It was the Christmas attraction at this well-known theatre, whose stars were the ever-popular J. L. Toole and Nellie (Ellen) Farren. *Aladdin the 2nd* was one of the first Japanese spectacles ever put upon the London stage, and its librettist, Alfred Thompson, was also responsible for the beautiful costumes. It was very likely that both W. S. Gilbert and Arthur Sullivan saw *Aladdin the 2nd;* it was a Japanese operetta, and Toole played a character named Kokoliko. The next year's Christmas attraction at the Gaiety was the first Gilbert and Sullivan work, *Thespis,* also starring Toole.

Le Nouvel Aladin was not terribly popular at the Folies-Nouvelles at the end of 1871; it had been preceded by *Le Trône d'Écosse* (The Throne of Scotland) at the Variétés. There is a conspiracy against Queen Jane of Scotland, and the Scots want in her place a descendant of Robert Bruce. A traveling wine salesman, Robert Mouton, is thought to look like Bruce and is proclaimed king. Dozens of popular songs and anything recognizably Scottish (or English) were burlesqued by Hervé and his librettists, Hector Crémieux and Adolphe Jaime. The chief conspirator's name was MacRazor. In the excellent opening cast were the Variétés regulars, José Dupuis and Céline Chaumont. Again, a waltz in the overture was admired, as was Hervé's orchestration.

A series of three-acters followed in the 1870s, none of them achieving anywhere near the popularity of his '60s output. He then tried something else. He embarked on a new pathway at the Théâtre des Variétés, with *La Femme à Papa* (1879), a *vaudeville-opérette* in which clowning predominated over singing, and Anna Judic became its reigning star. Born Anna Damiens, she made her debut at the *café-chantant* Eldorado in 1867, where her big song hit was *"Ne me chatouillez pas!"* (Don't tickle me!). She sang for Offenbach *(Le Roi Carotte)* before making her debut at the Variétés in a revival of *La Belle Hélène* in 1876.

With the great success of *La Femme à Papa,* Hervé more or less dropped the *opéra-bouffe* form and concentrated on the *vaudeville-opérette.* His last two successes were quite potent: *Lili* (Variétés, 10 January 1882) and *Mam'zelle Nitouche* (Variétés, 26 January 1883, 212 performances), which were written by Albert Millaud and Ernest Blum, with the venerable Henri Meilhac adding his touch of genius to *Nitouche.* Meilhac's touch must have been considerable—*Mam'zelle Nitouche* remains the only Hervé work performed today.

Both works were designed expressly for Judic, and she triumphed in both. Everyone waited for her big songs: in *Lili* there was a *chanson provençale,* in *Mam'zelle Nitouche* it was *"Babet et Cadet."* *Nitouche* had the story that had semi-autobiographical elements. It was about a young organist who composed for the stage, and the demure convent-girl (Judic) who joins him in leading a double life. By the third act, they are required to get back to the convent disguised as dragoons. The *"compositeur toqué,"* the crazy composer, was modeled on Hervé himself. The Variétés comedian Baron was the Hervé character:

> *Pour le théâtre, Floridor,*
> *Et pour le couvent, Célestin;*
> *Aimable et gai, c'est Floridor,*
> *Grave et dévot, c'est Célestin!*

(For the theatre, Floridor, and for the convent, Célestin; amiable and gay, it's

Floridor, grave and devout, it's Célestin!) The music was certainly fresh, and irresistibly tuneful, but the whole was still not up to Hervé's *opéra-bouffe* standard of the 1860s. This was no more than a *vaudeville à couplets,* and the couplets and ensembles that stood out were the regulation military-accented songs that were popular near the end of the century, not only in the theatre but also in the cafés, such as the song of the bass drum ("Along the rue Lafayette").

Mam'zelle Nitouche was popular all over Europe, particularly Eastern and Northern Europe. The Viennese première took place in 1890 (Theater an der Wien, 19 April). In Budapest, both *Lili* and *Nitouche* (called *Nebáncsvirág* at one point) were enthusiastically welcomed by Magyar audiences, and to this day *Nitouche* can be found in the repertoires of many Hungarian and other Soviet-bloc countries. An English version of *Nitouche* appeared in London with May Yohe. It has been revived countless times in Paris and all over France. There have been several film versions. One, made in 1931, starred Raimu as the organist-composer.

There were further works in the span of this amazing fifty-year career, but little of note. *Le Vertigo* (Renaissance, 1883) was an old-style *opéra-bouffe*—not wanted—and a Variétés production of 1884, *La Cosaque,* was similarly a failure, even with Meilhac on hand to co-write the libretto. After the embarrassing failure of *Fla-Fla* (Menus-Plaisirs, 1886), which lasted only five nights, Hervé went back to London, where in the same year he composed two now-forgotten operettas, *Babil et Bijou* and *Frivoli* (with Marie Tempest and Emily Soldene at Drury Lane) and a series of grand ballets for the Empire Theatre. In 1892, his name returned to the Parisian kiosks: *Bacchanale* was presented at the Menus-Plaisirs, but only a few times. A cruel review in *Le Figaro* so aggravated Hervé's asthma that he died a few days later, 3 November 1892, at the age of sixty-seven.

Hervé remains virtually unknown in the United States. Apart from tours of companies performing *L'Oeil crevé* and *Chilpéric,* there was only one other notable English version of his works given on Broadway: *Papa's Wife* (Manhattan, 13 November 1899), presented by Florenz Ziegfeld for and with his wife, Anna Held. This amalgamated elements of *La Femme à Papa* and *Mam'zelle Nitouche,* adding new music by Reginald De Koven. This was reputedly the first show in which Ziegfeld displayed what would become his trademark—the Ziegfeld girls.

For all its popularity, *Mam'zelle Nitouche* should not be taken as the definitive Hervé operetta. In an age of Monty Python and other examples of truly bizarre, far-out humor, not to mention a very liberal attitude toward sex, the libretti to Hervé's three principal *opéra-bouffes, L'Oeil crevé, Chilpéric,* and *Le petit Faust,* ought to be looked at for possible stage revivals.

Jakob (Jacques) Offenbach (1819–1880), the second son of Issac Juda Eberst, a wandering cantor, was born June 20, 1819, in the Glockenstrasse, Cologne. His father had been a resident of Offenbach, outside Frankfurt, and he adopted the town's name as his own. But life as a cantor was not well-paying, and to supplement his income Herr Offenbach often played the violin in local taverns. All the Offenbach children were musical, and by the age of eight Jakob was composing little songs, moving on to the cello the next year. The elder Offenbach was vastly proud of Jakob, and often had him, with his brother and a sister, perform in various taverns around Cologne.

The father was sufficiently impressed with his son's cello-playing to take him and his brother Julius to the Paris Conservatoire in November 1833. Cherubini, its famous director, was then a crotchety seventy-three, and disinclined to admit very young students (Offenbach was fourteen), especially foreigners. (Cherubini, born Italian, had turned away the twelve-year-old Liszt for that reason.) But after some pressure from his father, and several impressive auditions, young Jakob was accepted. The two brothers found lodgings in a very humble house near the rue des Martyrs, and for pocket money Jakob, now Jacques, often sang in the local synagogue choir. Young Offenbach was frankly too good for the cello lessons he was receiving from his master, Vaslin; his mind was on the stage. He went to the Opéra, the Opéra-Comique, and all the popular theatres at that time situated in and around the Boulevard du Temple. He admired all the popular *opéras-comiques* of the reigning composers—Adam, Auber, Hérold—and eventually played them when he was engaged as cellist by the orchestra of the Opéra-Comique.

The 1830s, besides being notable for the great popularity of *opéra-comique,* Italian comic opera, and the grand operas of Meyerbeer and his contemporaries, was also an age of public *bals* and their flashy conductors, like "the mystical Jullien" (as W. S. Gilbert called him) who attracted thousands to his Jardin Turc in the Boulevard du Temple to hear dance music. Quadrilles, polkas, and waltzes based on themes from the latest operatic hits were intensely popular, as were the latest waltzes imported from Vienna (sometimes by Strauss or Lanner). Offenbach's earliest published compositions were symphonic waltzes in this mode; some were played by Jullien. The first was entitled *Fleurs d'hiver,* the next, using synagogue motifs, was *Rebecca.*

The other source of popular music was the salon, where, apart from more classical compositions, sentimental tunes were all the rage—drawing room or parlor ballads, we might call them. Offenbach composed several works in this vein, but more importantly made the right connections while playing his virtuoso cello at many a salon. He gave his first public concert at Pape's Musical Instrument Store in the beginning of 1839 and was asked to compose a few numbers for a *vaudeville* at the Théâtre du Palais-Royal the same year, *Pascal et Chambord* (2 March 1839). With a plot set in the Napoleonic wars, the piece failed.

Further salon recitals led to his meeting John Mitchell, an English concert and theatre manager with a lovely stepdaughter, Herminie d'Alcain. Young Offenbach was much taken with her and dedicated his first popular-song success to her, the appropriately titled *À toi* (To you). Mitchell arranged a very successful cello tour of England for Offenbach (he played before the young Queen Victoria) and was probably delighted when Jacques proposed marriage to Herminie. There was one major condition, that Offenbach have himself baptized a Catholic, which the young musician did, in 1844. The pair were married that summer.

Two years later, Offenbach presented a burlesque of Félicien David's pseudo-oriental symphonic ode *Le Désert* at the Comtesse Bertin de Vaux's salon, and furnished the score to another military *vaudeville, L'Alcôve,* produced at the author's expense at the Salle la Tour d'Auvergne (24 April 1847). Adolphe Adam managed to see it (it did not run long) and promised to commission Offenbach to write a new comic opera for the new Théâtre-Lyrique, but the revolutionary disturbances of 1848 intervened. Offenbach, not yet a Frenchman, thought it wise to leave France, and he moved with his wife and daughter to Cologne. Life in Germany was far from prosperous, though songs like "The German Fatherland" and the "Song of the German Boys" enjoyed some circulation. *L'Alcôve* was produced in a German version in Cologne in January 1849, again with little success.

A short while after his return to Paris, in 1850, Arsène Houssaye, director of the Comédie-Française, appointed Offenbach *chef d'orchestre,* a post he held for six years. It was a fortunate appointment, as he constantly had his own compositions aired, in addition to the usual opera suites and other incidental music he conducted. But the actors resented his having the orchestra enlarged, as the removal of the *fauteuils d'orchestre* (front stalls) deprived them of some of their shared profits. Offenbach also composed incidental numbers for some plays, including Beaumarchais's *Le Barbier de Séville* and *Le Mariage de Figaro;* one song, the *Chanson de Fortunio,* was written for Alfred de Musset's *Le Chandelier.* Though it was sung by an actor with a poor bass voice, the insistent melody of Fortunio's song haunted all who heard it and subsequently became the hit tune in Offenbach's one-act *opéra-bouffe* written eleven years later.

On 12 May 1853, two years after the restoration of Imperial rule in Paris, a concert at the Salle Hertz featured a one-act Offenbach pastorale called *Le Trésor à Mathurin,* performed by singers from the Opéra-Comique. They were prepared to sing it for their director but, no, the Salle Favart would not consider such trifles. Four years later this work became the very successful *Le Mariage aux lanternes.* The next Offenbach work was *Pépito,* produced at the Variétés with no success (28 October 1853), though the influential critic Jules Janin (of whom we shall hear more presently) liked it. *Oyayaye ou la Reine des Îles* (Queen of the Isles), accepted by Hervé's Théâtre des Folies-Nouvelles in June 1855, was more successful. It was about a Parisian double-bass player shipwrecked on an island with a cannibal queen. Hervé was the star. Offenbach by this time had already applied to the ministries and police officials to open his own theatre to present his own works.

Jacques Offenbach around 1861, about the time of *M. Choufleuri restera chez lui le . . .*

Eighteen fifty-five was the year of the Second Empire's first Exposition, designed by Napoléon III to turn people's attention to the glories of France and the world and away from its problems. In the Carré Marigny in the Champs-Élysées (now the site of the Théâtre Marigny) stood the Théâtre Lacaze, a tiny wooden structure dedicated to magic shows. As this foundering establishment was right near the grounds of the Exposition, due to open in May, Offenbach obtained a license, formed a company of wealthy investors, made himself managing director, and leased the theatre. *Le Figaro* announced at the end of May:

> Our friend Jacques Offenbach, the cellist, conductor of the Théâtre-Français, has just leased a new theatre that he will manage, opposite the Olympic Circus, enticingly named "Bouffes-Parisiens." The title says everything about the repertoire. It is a theatre more than anything consecrated to openhearted laughter, to fantasy, to light and smart melody, to bold refrains.

The Bouffes-Parisiens was very rickety, very steep, and not entirely insulated. A cartoon at the time was captioned "Stratagem of young Offenbach, who made his theatre with a ladder." But it was very intimate and perfectly suited to musical comedy on summer evenings.

Offenbach had twenty days to arrange the opening programme, billed for 5 July 1855. When other writers withdrew, he asked his friend Ludovic Halévy, a young government worker to write a prologue. Halévy was the nephew of Offenbach's former composition teacher at the Conservatoire, the composer Fromental Halévy *(La Juive)*. Another friend, Jules Moinaux, supplied a libretto in one act, and a pantomime was devised. A company of actors was hired, including the popular pierrot Legrand and the equally popular harlequin De-grudder, and Offenbach composed and arranged the music. Rehearsals did not proceed smoothly, as Halévy and several others thought *Les Deux Aveugles* (The Two Blind Beggars), the last item on the bill, tasteless and vulgar. But Berthe-lier, who starred in the piece (after having created 1855's *café-concert* song hit, "*Vive la France!*"), insisted on playing it.

July 5 arrived. The prologue, *Entrez, Messieurs, Mesdames!*, by Méry and Ser-vières (Halévy's pseudonym because of his government job), was followed by *Une Nuit blanche*, a sentimental one-act pastoral comic opera, *Arlequin Barbier*, a pantomime in four scenes, and *Les Deux Aveugles*, "*bouffonnerie musicale*," or farce, in one act. All had music by Offenbach save for the pantomime, for which Offenbach arranged Rossini melodies. *Les Deux Aveugles* was the sensation; the musical satire of two sham blind beggars was found irresistibly funny, and all went home that night humming the bolero. Berthelier, as Giraffier, and Pradeau, as Patachon, became even more popular, and the house was full every evening, the little house everyone called "*la bonbonnière*," the candy box.

Other one-act operettas followed, *Le Rêve d'une Nuit d'Été* (A Summer Night's Dream, 30 July), *Le Violoneux* (The Fiddler, 31 August), and *Madame Papillon* (Mrs. Butterfly, 3 October). The first concerned two English visitors to Paris, the second was based on an old Breton legend, and the third was about an old lady (played *en travesti* by Pradeau) who comes to Paris to seek romance. All were popular, tuneful, charming, but the public clamored for *Les Deux Aveu-gles*, which eventually was given a command performance for the Emperor in the Tuileries to celebrate the end of the Crimean War. Performances of *Les Deux Aveugles* were given abroad, in London in 1856, in New York in 1858, and the following year in English as *Going Blind*, and in Vienna in 1863, but they did not by any means create an international rage for Offenbach.

Parisians were disinclined to sit in a drafty theatre in November (the Expo-sition had closed), so new winter headquarters for the Bouffes-Parisiens had to be found. This time it was the Théâtre des Jeunes-Élèves in the Passage Cho-iseul (where, rebuilt in 1863, it still stands). The Bouffes-Parisiens, in its *Salle d'Hiver*, opened memorably on 29 December 1855 with *Ba-ta-clan*, Halévy and Offenbach's still-popular "*chinoiserie musicale*," cleverly burlesquing Italian op-era, Chinese language, dress, and manners, and, very pointedly, Meyerbeer. An ensemble in *Les Huguenots* was mercilessly pitted against the title march—a "Chinese" anthem (mostly pidgin Italian) set to a supposedly oriental but very catchy martial tune vocally imitating the braying of trumpets. Anything that smacked of pompousness—especially Meyerbeer—was fair game for Offenbach and his librettists. Though many of their little one-acters were simply sentimental farces or bucolic romances, the opportunity to burlesque a musical or theatrical trend often presented itself. In *Ba-ta-clan*, moreover, the "Chinese" characters all turn out to be Parisians; there was a lovely waltz celebrating the city's *bals*. As *Ching Chow Hi*, Offenbach's "extravaganza" played in English at the St. George's Opera House, London, in 1867; Vienna had already seen it as *Tschin-Tschin* at the Carltheater in 1860.

Ba-ta-clan was faced with the same arbitrary licensing restrictions (dating from a Napoleonic edict of 1807) that Offenbach had encountered at the summer Bouffes—four characters only on the stage (three, originally). But the opening-night audience adored the antics of the four actors: Messrs. Pradeau, Berthelier, and Guyot and Mlle. Dalmont. "People laughed, clapped, shouted as at a miracle," raved the critic Jules Janin, and they left the theatre dancing. Several weeks later, a *café-concert* called the Ba-ta-clan opened (one still exists in Paris).

But the winterized Bouffes-Parisiens, which cost 80,000 francs to revamp, had to have a supply of operettas; Offenbach could not write them all. In an antiquarian search for other works, Offenbach was responsible for revivals of Rossini's *Il Signor Bruschino* and Mozart's *Der Schauspieldirektor*. He also commissioned Adolphe Adam's last stage work, *Les Pantins de Violette* (Violette's Puppets, 29 April 1856). In the summer of 1856, after the company had moved back into its summer home, Offenbach announced a competition for the composition of a one-act operetta to a libretto by Halévy and Battu, *Le Docteur Miracle*. (The operetta's plot has nothing to do with the E. T. A. Hoffmann story chosen for one of the acts of Offenbach's final work, *Les Contes d'Hoffmann*.) Only French composers were eligible, and they could not have had works produced previously by the Opéra or Opéra-Comique. The prize was twelve hundred francs, a gold medal, and performance of the finished work by the Bouffes. There were two winners the next year: Charles Lecocq and Georges Bizet.

In the meantime, Offenbach had produced his *Elodie ou la Forfait nocturne, Le Postillon en gage*, and, most impressively, *Tromb-al-ca-zar, ou Les Criminels dramatiques* (3 April 1856), with a cast that included Pradeau, Léonce (a famous clown), and Mlle. Hortense Schneider, a newcomer from Bordeaux, who had made her debut in a *café-concert* before appearing in *Le Violoneux*. One of the zanier ensembles in *Tromb-al-ca-zar*, a situation comedy about an *hôtelier* mistaken for a ferocious robber, sang of Bayonne ham. A great success, *Tromb-al-ca-zar* was followed (12 June 1856) by *La Rose de Saint-Flour*, again with Pradeau and Schneider, and again a success. Other productions in 1856 included *Les Dragées de Baptême* (Baptismal Wafers), written no doubt to honor the recent birth of the Prince Imperial, and *Le "66"!*, about a peasant who mistakes the

number 99 for the winning 66 in a lottery. Both *Tromb-al-ca-zar* and *Le "66"!* were later done in London (1870, 1876) in English.

The year 1857 opened with a *féerie, Les Trois Baisers du diable* (The Three Kisses of the Devil), and then *Croquefer, ou Le Dernier des Paladins* (12 February 1857), which dared to add a fifth character, antagonizing the censors. This turned out to be a mute warrior, who produced only barks and grunts during a contraband quintet! *Croquefer* was produced in London as *The Last of the Paladins* in 1868, in Vienna as *Ritter Eisenfrass* in 1864, and in New York as recently as the 1970s.

New Offenbach compositions followed merrily in 1857: *Dragonnette* (30 April), *Une Demoiselle en loterie* (A Lottery Girl, 27 July), *Le Mariage aux lanternes* (Marriage by Lanternlight, the revision of *Le Trésor à Mathurin*, 10 October), *Les Deux Pêcheurs* (The Two Fishermen, 16 November). *Dragonnette* had a stirring patriotic finale, *"Vive la France!"*, while *Une Demoiselle en loterie* introduced Lise Tautin, Offenbach's first Eurydice a year later, in another lottery tale. These were all either *opérette*, *opéra-bouffe*, or even *opérette-bouffe;* they were mildly successful, whether in Paris or on tour in London, Vienna, or Lyon, where the Bouffes-Parisiens troupe went on their first national tour in the summer of 1857. The London season at the St. James's Theatre (commencing 20 May 1857) originally featured half the Bouffes company; during the British première of *Croque-fer* (a benefit for the composer) Offenbach appeared on the stage to perform a cello solo. Queen Victoria put her royal seal of approval on the season by attending a performance.

The tours of the Bouffes-Parisiens company had a momentous impact on operetta history, prompting Viennese and London composers and librettists to come up with national equivalents of the short operetta form. The most important of these were Suppé's *Das Pensionat* (1860) and Sullivan's *Cox and Box* (1867). These two landmark works led to the development of their respective operetta schools in Austria-Hungary and Great Britain

The year 1858 saw the licensing restrictions lifted, finally allowing Offenbach for the first time an unlimited number of characters and a chorus. But other one-acters, including two particularly fine ones, followed: *Mesdames de la Halle* (The Ladies of Les Halles, 3 March) and the delightful *La Chatte métamorphosée en femme* (The Cat Turned into a Woman, 19 April), based on a Scribe and Melesville *vaudeville*. *Mesdames de la Halle* was set in the Paris produce market and featured in its amplified cast two coarse vegetable-sellers played by men. This was revived, to great hilarity, at the Opéra-Comique in 1979, as part of an Offenbach triple bill. The feline operetta has recently been seen again in East Berlin and New York. The summer tour of 1858 took the company to Berlin and Bad Ems, at that time one of the leading German spas, and one particularly popular with Parisians. The Bouffes-Parisiens, whether in Paris or on tour abroad, was an institution. The Emperor's stepbrother, the Duc de Morny, was a regular visitor, as were the leading composers, journalists and writers. But tours and new productions, especially like the one given *Mesdames de la Halle,* were expensive, prices were going up, and the Bouffes-Parisiens company was deep in debt.

By the summer of 1858 Offenbach was being hounded by bailiffs, forced at least once to check into a Paris hotel incognito or to flee to Germany. His talents

---

Henri Meilhac (left) and Ludovic Halévy, the foremost French operetta librettists. Offenbach may be seen whizzing by on a bicycle.

had never been in business organization and he was over-lavish in his decorations for the theatre and its productions. But he was astute enough to realize he needed a big hit to keep the theatre full nightly for months and months.

A libretto sketch on the Orpheus legend had been prepared months before by Ludovic Halévy but had been put aside because of the four-character, one-act restriction. Offenbach had Halévy and Hector Crémieux work on it, though at this time Halévy had just been appointed General Secretary to the Ministry for Algeria and did not want to sign his name to the libretto. The work is nevertheless dedicated to him, and he apparently helped write it.

Orphée aux Enfers (Orpheus in the Underworld), as it was called, was Offenbach's first two-act work, though in its original Bouffes-Parisiens version it was not a full evening's length; other pieces supported the bill. The original cast was as follows:

Aristée/Pluton	MM.	Léonce
Jupiter		Désiré
Orphée		Tayau
John Styx		Bache
Mercure		J. Paul
Bacchus		Antognini
Mars		Fioquet
Eurydice	MMes.	Tautin
Diane		Chabert
L'Opinion Publique		Mace
Vénus		Garnier
Cupidon		Geoffrey
Junon		Enjalbert
Minerve		Cico

The opening night (21 October 1858) hardly seemed historic at the time. There was no hitch throughout the evening, but no one seemed terribly excited, except perhaps by the galop in the bacchanale at the end of the operetta.

The critics were on the whole lukewarm. Only a few recognized how good *Orphée* was or how popular it would become. Among them was Jules Noriac, on the *Figaro-Programme*. His telegraphic rhyming review began as follows:

Inouï,	Incredible,
Splendide,	Splendid,
Ébouriffant,	Astounding,
Gracieux,	Graceful,
Charmant,	Charming,
Spirituel,	Witty,
Amusant,	Amusing,
Réussi,	Successful,
Parfait,	Perfect,
Mélodieux,	Melodious,

l'opéra	the opera
d'Orphée	of Orpheus
(c'est un	(it's an
opéra)	opera)
sera	will be
incontesta-	incontesta-
blement (ce	bly (this
mot n'en finit	word will never
pas)	finish)
le	the
plus	most
grand	enormous
succès	success
de	of
l'hiver.	the winter.

Offenbach was not entirely satisfied, so the morning after the première saw him making some of his *"bedides goupures"* (little cuts). If *Orphée* failed, with its expensive sets and costumes designed by Gustave Doré, the Bouffes would fail with it. Business did get better until about a month and a half later. Early in 1859, there was further surgery on *Orphée,* and at that point fate, in the person of Jules Janin, intervened. In a notice for the *Journal des Débats,* he denounced the revised *Orphée* as a "profanation of holy and glorious antiquity." Offenbach and Crémieux had in fact used a bit of Janin's purple prose for a speech of Pluton's, and when the source of this flowery extract was revealed in a letter by Offenbach to *Le Figaro,* Paris was thoroughly titillated. All this lurid publicity aided the box office, and the COMPLET (SOLD OUT) sign appeared continually. This increased the public's mania to see the operetta, as did the band arrangements, the quadrilles and other dance medleys, and the barrel organs throughout Paris that played nothing but *Orphée aux Enfers* during 1859. The cast was totally exhausted by the 228th performance, and the piece was reluctantly retired, but only for a few weeks. In April 1860, the Emperor had a command performance at the Théâtre-Italien, with the extra forces of their orchestra and chorus. The programme also consisted of *Le Violoneux,* the ballet star Emma Livry in a scene from *La Sylphide,* and Offenbach's Wagner travesty, *Le Musicien de l'Avenir* (The Composer of the Future). *Orphée,* naturally, made the greatest impression, with its fabulous hit songs, its revealing Doré costumes, and its burlesque of antiquity.

Not that such burlesques were at all a new thing—hardly so. Offenbach may very well have seen a revue at the Vaudeville in 1846 by Clairville, *Les Dieux d'Olympe à Paris* (The Olympian Gods in Paris). Instead of going to the Underworld, the gods appear in Paris. Victor Massé's *Galathée* (1852) had similarly contemporized an antique myth. But the *Enfers* of *Orphée* was made to seem quite Parisian, maybe one of the glamorous private parties—with hints perhaps of an orgy—which made headlines in 1858. When Janin objected to the desecration of antiquity, he might instead have been blasting the less classical easy virtue of Second Empire morality, here thinly disguised by Grecian draperies. Jupiter may very well have represented the Emperor (a well-known womanizer) and Orphée, a bored middle-class married man. L'Opinion Publique (Public Opinion, the character representing the Greek chorus, in this case played by a statuesque mezzo-soprano) has to force an unwilling Orphée to go after his abducted wife. The entire company gives in to libidinous pleasure, exemplified by Eurydice's hymn to Bacchus ("*Évohé!*") and the *galop infernal, or cancan,* presented as a raucous alternative to the minuet. And the operetta ends happily as Jupiter hurls a thunderbolt at Orphée *forcing* him to look back and thus have his wife remain in Hades—to her delight—while Orphée is again free, to the consternation of L'Opinion Publique. When the gods get restless—indeed, revolutionary—near the end of Act I, Jupiter's solution is to distract the gods by taking them down to the Underworld—a panacea similar to Napoléon's Exposition three years before.

Critics and historians can go on about the social satire in *Orphée aux Enfers,* though it is hardly likely Crémieux, Halévy, or Offenbach meant their satire to incite a revolt against the régime of Napoléon III or the prosperous citizens who supported the Bouffes-Parisiens. As many critics have said, Offenbach's position was very much one of a court jester. His and his librettists' aim was to make people laugh, perhaps even warn of impending events, but certainly not to preach or correct. He was certainly a political opportunist, using government contacts to ultimately benefit himself financially, running away from France when things got nasty, and returning only when the situation looked calm.

What is more important is that *Orphée aux Enfers* was the first great operetta, and the model for future operettas, whether French, English, or Austrian. It contains the scaffolding for all the other great full-length Offenbach works. Orphée is the first major tenor hero, Eurydice, the first full-length soprano heroine (low soprano, even mezzo later on), Cupidon, the first soubrette of importance, and so on. The stock company of operetta, though it had existed from the earliest days of the Bouffes, was now enlarged, thanks to the dropping of the licensing restrictions. More importantly, the chorus, for the first time, became an impressive unit of the operetta, an essential part of the action rather than an echo. Whereas in grand opera and *opéra-comique* the chorus often only wandered in when necessary to support the principals, usually in time for the finale, the Offenbach operetta chorus was essential to the action, and it danced and looked attractive, to boot.

A brilliant score also helped. In a genre where the richness of orchestration declines as the years sweep by, *Orphée aux Enfers* weds a fittingly classical sound to its irresistible melodies. With what was a small theatre band (compared to the mammoth at the Opéra) Offenbach managed to produce an effervescent sheen that many composers have failed to produce with a symphony orchestra.

Members of the first-run cast of the first classical full-length operetta, Offenbach's *Orphée aux Enfers* (Bouffes-Parisiens, 1858), as depicted in the original vocal score.

ORPHÉE
Mr MARCHAND

JUPITER
Mr DÉSIRÉ

JOHN STYX
Mr BACHE

BERGER d'ARCADIE
Mr LÉONCE

Orphée is the earliest full-length work in the current operetta repertoire, and it sounds it. For all its musical satire, melodic snoring, playing around with the sacred Gluck, and the rush of its bacchanale, some sections sound as if written by Auber or Adam or even eighteenth-century composers in their finer moments. Frankly operatic, too—as in the first duet between Orphée and Eurydice—compared to some of Offenbach's earlier *couplets.* Some musical satire is lost today. The violin passage with which Orphée annoys his long-suffering wife, which was perhaps meant to sound hideously, irritatingly sentimental, now seems charming. Aristée's entrance song *is* a sentimental pastoral song, but with mock-sentimental words. The quotation from Gluck's *Orphée* is not nearly as well known today as it was in 1858. Other numbers are just blazingly memorable: Diane's "hunting" *couplets* describing her meeting with Actéon by the fountain, *"Quand j'étais Roi de Béotie,"* the mournful recounting of a royal past sung by Pluton's servant, John Styx (first played by Bache, a frightfully thin recruit with a high voice from the Comédie-Française) and the unforgettable *cancan,* easily Offenbach's most famous creation.

More vital to operetta are such choice morsels as the *rondeau des Métamorphoses,* during which Diane, Vénus, Cupidon, Minerve, and Pluton remind Jupiter of his amorous exploits on earth in various disguises:

> *Ah! ah! ah! Ah! ah! ah,*
> *Ne prends plus l'air patelin,*
> *On connaît tes farces, Jupin!*

"Don't take a patronizing air with us, Jupie, we all know your escapades!" The tune to this clever refrain is cheeky and catchy, paving the way for similar ensembles in later *offenbachiades;* the entrance of the Kings of Greece in *La Belle Hélène* is a prime example. More important is the Act I finale, first of a series of superb middle-act finales which are the crowning glories of the great operettas of the nineteenth century. Long, convoluted, chock-full of many melodies, and usually finishing with some extremely rapid patter or play on words, they would become more and more elaborate and brilliant in later years, often adding a waltz as a climax.

Orphée's Act I finale begins in a whisper *("Il s'approche! Il s'avance!")* and ends *presto,* playing with *"Partons, marchons, la, la, la"* (which is echoed later in the even sillier *"Pars pour la Crète, pars, pars, pars"* in the Act I finale of *La Belle Hélène*). The act would always end in a galop, with the entire company going off somewhere, an endearing feature of French operetta. Gluck's *Orphée* and the revolutionary *Marseillaise* are sacrilegiously quoted along the way, the former held as sacrosanct, the latter then considered subversive.

The Act II bacchanale is certainly a show-stopping sequence, with its hymn to Bacchus, sung by an Eurydice crowned in grapevines, and its *galop infernal,* is preceded, for comic effect, by a minuet, a charming eighteenth-century pastiche Offenbach was so good at. For many, the gayest, sauciest number remains the insouciant *duo de la Mouche* (Fly duet) in Act II, during which Eurydice is ravished by a fly—Jupiter in disguise. This is operetta at its operatic best, using the mode of grand opera, both in vocal line and instrumentation, for comic effect. A situation right out of a boulevard *vaudeville* is set by Offenbach in the style of the Académie Nationale de la Musique, to which is added the buzzing *"zi"* of the fly. The effect, with fat Jupiter dressed in a pantomime insect cos-

---

Jupiter (M. Guy) disguised as a fly in the 1903 revival of Offenbach's *Orphée aux Enfers* (Variétés).

tume (and supposed to be tiny) courting Eurydice, is the early apogee of French operetta.

Orphée was such a financial triumph in Paris and on tour (the 1859 receipts at the Bouffes-Parisiens exceeded 419,581 francs) that Offenbach was able to build a house at Étretat, which he appropriately christened the Villa d'Orphée. *Orphée aux Enfers* has been revived many times in Paris. The first and most important remounting was a greatly aggrandized version for the Théâtre de la Gaîté in 1874. The Gaîté revived that production through the '70s and '80s, but by 1903 the work was in the hands of the Variétés: in 1903, a lovely production with the boulevard comedian Max Dearly as Mercure, in 1912, and in 1931, when Dearly took the role of Jupiter. The Opéra-Comique had *Orphée* in its repertoire in the early 1970s.

In London, the work first appeared in English in December 1865, as *Orpheus in the Haymarket,* in J. R. Planché's version at the Theatre Royal, Haymarket. The Sadler's Wells Opera (now the English National Opera) revived the work with enormous success in the 1950s. In New York, it was first heard in German at the Stadt Theater in 1861. Germany and Austria-Hungary were long the champion *Orpheus in der Unterwelt* promoters—the work is still a regular staple in the repertoires of central European opera houses. The German most closely associated with *Orphée* was Max Reinhardt, who staged the operetta in the first decade of this century and for many seasons subsequently in various cities. In Austria, a German version by and with the celebrated actor-playwright Johann Nestroy was given at the Carltheater (17 March 1860).

Offenbach created two short operettas for the Bouffes, *Un Mari à la porte* (22 June 1859) and *Les Vivandières de la Grande Armée* (6 July 1859) before the next eagerly-awaited, full-length work, *Geneviève de Brabant* (Bouffes-Parisiens, 19 November 1859). Lise Tautin, who had danced so provocatively as the frenzied Eurydice, was cast as Drogan, the gay and scintillating pastry cook of old Flanders. A splendid house watched the new "profanation" of old, but the operetta failed to win many admirers, probably because of its weak libretto by Étienne Tréfeu and Crémieux, larded with too many poor jokes and puns. A revised version, incorporating a riotous gendarmes duet, was more of a success at the Théâtre des Menus-Plaisirs eight years later. The gendarmes became United States Marines when the tune was appropriated for "From the Halls of Montezuma." In the 1867 revival, the gendarmes were medieval soldiers rather than policemen.

The year 1860 saw one short work at the Bouffes: *Daphnis et Chloé* (10 February), plus a revue, and a ballet for the Opéra, *Le Papillon,* choreographed by

---

Offenbach's *Geneviève de Brabant:* a music cover depicting the original London performances in 1871, based on Offenbach's revised version of 1867. British sheet-music illustrations at this time were invariably based on sketches made by artists at first nights, so that the costumes and settings shown were quite accurate indications of the original productions in London.

the legendary Marie Taglioni for Emma Livry. Mlle. Livry met a sad end shortly afterward when her skirt caught fire on going too near the footlights. The hit *"valse des rayons"* is still heard these days as the sadistic *apache* dance (named for the Parisian thugs). *Le Papillon* appeared several times on the bill with the first Paris production of *Tannhäuser*. It is fair to report that by this time Wagner was not fond of Offenbach, though he later thought him Mozart-like. Perhaps smarting from Offenbach's ridicule in the *Musicien de l'Avenir,* Wagner referred to the warmth of Offenbach's music as having come from the "dung heap." *Le Papillon* has recently been revived in England and the United States, more or less as a comic novelty, in a reorchestrated version.

Barkouf managed the hitherto impossible for Offenbach: it was accepted and presented by the Opéra-Comique on Christmas Eve, 1861. This was the composer's first work officially in this vein (and the first in three acts), with a libretto by Scribe and Boisseau. The star of *Barkouf* was a fearsome Pakistani canine—the critics called the opera a *"chiennerie"* (which one can translate with the implications of the female gender). The total failure of *Barkouf* did not daunt Offenbach; soon afterward the Bouffes was performing *La Chanson de Fortunio* (5 January 1861), a Crémieux-Halévy "sequel" to the story told by Alfred de Musset in his play *Le Chandelier* (1850), for which Offenbach had written the original Song of Fortunio.

By 1861, Offenbach had been made a French citizen and had been given the medal and ribbon of the Légion d'Honneur, no doubt proposed by his friend the Duc de Morny, stepbrother of Napoléon III and the Bouffes' greatest fan. Morny had written a libretto of his own, eventually titled *M. Choufleuri restera chez lui le . . .* (M. Cauliflower will be at home the . . .). During rehearsals for *M. Choufleuri* the libretto was amended by at least three other authors, including Halévy and Crémieux, though "Saint-Rémy" (whom everyone knew to be Morny) was exceptionally proud of his work, spending more time at the Bouffes than at his office.

The rehearsals took place in between performances of the latest two-act operetta, *Le Pont des Soupirs* (The Bridge of Sighs, Bouffes-Parisiens, 23 March 1861), a burlesque of melodrama set, as the title indicates, in Venice. Its première, starring Désiré and Lise Tautin, was heartily cheered, and there was praise for the delicacy of Offenbach's score—especially the elaborate choral writing. But the Crémieux-Halévy book was too trivial to survive a four-act expansion produced at the Variétés seven years later. *The Bridge of Sighs,* English by Henry S. Leigh, was seen at the St. James's, London, in 1872, and a German version was at the Carltheater, Vienna, a year later.

After a preview in the Palais-Bourbon in the presence of the Emperor, the Morny-Offenbach *opéra-bouffe* opened the 1861–62 season at the Bouffes-Parisiens on the fourteenth of September. By this time the theatre was under the direction of Alphonse Varney. *M. Choufleuri* lasted little more than a month, a *succès d'estime,* perhaps, but still performed today with regularity, because its ruthless burlesque of Italian opera singers appeals to current opera singers. Among the *offenbachiades* appearing that same season at the Bouffes-Parisiens were two (now-forgotten) three-act *opéras-bouffes: Le Roman comique* (10 December 1861) and *Le Voyage de MM. Dunanan, père et fils* (23 March 1862).

The summer of 1862, as usual, was spent at Bad Ems, where Offenbach went for his gout. Most of the Bouffes company were in Brussels, where *Orphée aux Enfers* was a tremendous hit. A smaller group was in Vienna, performing Offenbach to further acclaim. Offenbach generally managed to have two or three short works produced at the Kursaal at Ems. In 1862 *Les Bavards* (The Gossips) had its first performance there. Charles Nuitter's libretto was based on a Cervantes comedy, *Los Habladores* (1624). The work was altered for the Bouffes in February 1863, alternating with the ever-popular *Orphée*. Saint-Säens called *Les Bavards* "a little masterpiece," and it was instantly popular abroad. It was seen in Russia in 1867, in Rio de Janeiro in 1871, and in Madrid in 1872. In 1924, it entered the repertoire of the Opéra-Comique.

The one-act pace had slowed down, revivals kept the Bouffes full, and at the end of the 1862–63 season the theatre was rebuilt. In 1863 the Théâtre du Palais-Royal's production of a one-act *vaudeville* by a new team—Henri Meilhac and Ludovic Halévy—was a considerable hit. Called *Le Brésilien*, it starred Hortense Schneider, late of the Bouffes-Parisiens, and featured an Offenbach song, *"Voulez-vous accepter mon bras?"* (Will you take my arm?), which became the raging hit. Back in Bad Ems in the summer of '63, Offenbach was challenged at a party to write an operetta in one week. He said "assuredly," provided he got a libretto within twenty-four hours. It just happened that one Paul Boisselot had a libretto in his valise, a *"conversation alsacienne"* in one act entitled *Lieschen et Fritzchen* (Lizzy and Fritzy). One of the back-and-forth duets (so charmingly used later in *La Vie Parisienne*) began *"Je suis alsacienne,"* with the reply *"Je suis alsacien,"* and was introduced by a charming young singer with whom Offenbach soon had a long-lasting affair, Mlle. Zulma Bouffar. Produced the following Saturday, *Lieschen et Fritzchen* was an immediate hit and was seen later at the Bouffes with la Bouffar, in January 1864. Another Offenbach success at Ems and Paris that season was *Il Signor Fagotto,* which Rossini admired.

Offenbach had gone to Vienna several times to supervise the authentic production of some of his works in the early 1860s, to try to counteract the pirated versions. In 1864, Offenbach was again in the Austrian capital to see the Court Opera's (forerunner of the Vienna State Opera) spectacular production of his three-act romantic opera *Die Rheinnixen* (The Rhine Nymphs, 1864). It lasted only eight performances, but is remembered for its Goblins' Song, which became the immortal barcarolle in *Les Contes d'Hoffmann*. Consecutive failures in larger forms, *opéra-comique* and now a large-scale opera, made Offenbach yearn for a grand success in his primary field, operetta.

In the spring of 1864, the Bouffes-Parisiens had a new three-act *opéra-bouffe, Les Géorgiennes* (16 March), libretto by Jules Moineaux. This spectacular had a *Lysistrata*-ish plot, complete with a voluptuous chorus line of women, led by Ugalde and Bouffar, performing the *"Marseillaise des femmes."* This had a Women's Liberation refrain, *"À bas les hommes!"* (Down with men). The lineup of comely young amazons was not the only memorable item in the opera, which also featured the imposing entrance of Léonce aboard an elephant. *Les Géorgiennes* had a profitable run of over a hundred performances, followed by a provincial tour featuring the Bouffes in *Orphée, Fortunio,* and *Mesdames de la Halle.* A London version of *Les Géorgiennes* was seen in 1875 with Richard Temple, later Gilbert and Sullivan's principal bass-baritone, in the role originally played by Pradeau.

The 1864 summer at Ems saw three new operettas. Let this extract from one of Offenbach's letters to his wife illustrate a typical day:

> At 6:30, I got up and bathed.
> At 9, Désiré and Paul came to practice *Jeanne* [*qui pleure et Jean qui rit*].
> At 10, I attended the dress rehearsal of *Fortunio.*
> At 11, lunch.
> At 12, rehearsal of *Le Soldat* [*magicien*].
> At 2:30, visit of M. Talleyrand, Minister of France to Berlin, who asked to come to present me to his wife.
> At 4, my bath.
> It's 5 o'clock, I'm writing to you.
> At 6, I dine.
> Tonight, at 7:30, the ensemble from *Jeanne* and *Le Soldat* chez moi.

(Most people went to spas for relaxation!) *Jeanne qui pleure et Jean qui rit* (Crying Jean and Laughing John) was heard at the Bouffes-Parisiens that November. *Le Soldat magicien* became the subtitle of *Le Fifre enchanté* (The Enchanted Fife).

Offenbach, however, had been having trouble with the new management over business matters at the Bouffes; there had been litigation several months before. Although the court decided in the composer's favor, bad feelings remained. And at this very time Hortense Schneider was embroiled in a dispute over salary with M. Plunkett, the director of the Palais-Royal, who was hankering for an Offenbach operetta for his theatre. Meilhac and Halévy had been preparing another mythological work, hoping to repeat the success of *Orphée,* this time based on the saga of Helen of Troy. The original draft was called *La Prise de Troie* (The Taking of Troy), though the final libretto ended with the abduction of Helen by Paris. The collaborators realized they had to have Hortense Schneider as Hélène. Hearing she was leaving Paris to stay with her mother in Bordeaux, Offenbach rushed to her apartment and tried to coax her with Hélène's music. She no doubt thought it lovely, but nothing would make her act on the boards of the Palais-Royal under Plunkett, where the work was slated to première. She left Paris.

Two famous interpreters of *La Belle Hélène:* the Paris original, Hortense Schneider (left), and the first Viennese queen, Marie Geistinger. They reigned for years as the most beloved of all operetta stars in their respective cities, and Offenbach revered both.

A telegram arrived the next day in Bordeaux: "Plans canceled at Palais-Royal, possible at the Variétés. Answer." Mlle. Schneider responded with the then-unheard-of terms: "I want 2,000 francs a month." "Conditions accepted, come quickly," came the reply. *"Parfait!* I only ask for a week's rest," wired back Schneider. But two days later she was back in Paris to learn the part.

Henri Meilhac (1831–1897) and **Ludovic Halévy** (1834–1908) had been at the same *lycée* together but were not friends, as Meilhac was some years older than Halévy. After their start with *Le Brésilien,* they went on to write not only the principal operetta libretti for Offenbach and other composers, but also many internationally popular *vaudevilles* and other plays.

La Belle Hélène was constructed in what would become their typical fashion, with Meilhac sketching out the plot and the principal scenes. Some of the dialogue was Halévy's, as were most of the lyrics, though some were joint efforts. Meilhac was once described as *"notre cher paresseux Meilhac,"* our dear, lazy Meilhac. Halévy was more industrious, but still no match for the fanatical Offenbach, who did most of his orchestration at home while talking to his family or friends, his children screaming in the background, his right hand scratching away.

When presented with the text, the censors took a wary view of Calchas, the *Belle Hélène* soothsayer who seemed to be debasing the clergy, and several lines had to be eliminated. Rehearsals proceeded furiously at the Variétés—some were held during the intermissions of the then-current revue—and the composer, wracked with gout, was far from enchanted with his orchestra of twenty-six, conducted by Lindheim. There was also considerable friction between *la Schneider* and Mlle. Léa Silly, who was cast as Oreste, Hélène's nephew; any attempt by Silly to show her talents was fiercely resented by Schneider. The Saturday night dress rehearsal (14 December 1864) was filled with friends and admirers who did not seem to admire some portions of the play. The tenor, José Dupuis, was met with stony silence when he first sang Paris's entrance song, *"Au Mont Ida."* After a sleepless night, during which he had decided to leave the company, Dupuis went to see Offenbach. Before Dupuis could say a word, Offenbach led him to the piano and played three new settings for the song which had failed. "Choose one!" cried Offenbach, and both agreed the first new version was the best.

The first night (17 December 1864) was more successful, but there were still critics who, amazingly, carped about their classics being travestied. After the second week, however, the receipts rose to the capacity level and stayed there for months. Auber was entranced with Schneider's voice, and the dramatist Victorien Sardou wrote Offenbach a warm note:

> . . . This is a great success for you, my dear friend, and a delicious evening for us . . . this morning, when I awoke, I cried out seeking to remind myself of the delicious air of Dupuis in the first act and the two romances of Schneider, and the finale to the first act, and the finale of the second, and the whole rest of the play . . . Your actors have served you very well: Dupuis and Grenier are very amusing, Mlle. Schneider played as only she knows how, and also sang with an art I had thought forgotten.
>
> I see nothing, happy man, to detract from your triumph and I have only one regret: that is, not to have been part of it.

La Belle Hélène is more than an elaborate copy of *Orphée aux Enfers*. It transcends the former to even higher Olympian heights in the operetta canon. Its finales are funnier, more elaborate, and involve an even greater use of the chorus; the orchestrations are richer, the tunes more plentiful, and there is a waltz of great grace and beauty in Act II.

The subject matter, in this case Greek legend in addition to purely supernatural mythology, is not exactly cheerful, but Meilhac and Halévy manage to keep the proceedings lighthearted all the way. The dénouement, however, has not pleased many producers—the Trojan War is not to be burlesqued, say they— so modern productions often substitute a revised third act of more serious implications (and often with interpolated songs that have nothing to do with *La Belle Hélène*). This is misguided; the original third act is the best, and producers should realize that the spirit of jest and burlesque must be maintained right through the very end of the piece. *La Belle Hélène* is not a mopey *opéra-comique*, it is a mocking *opéra-bouffe*.

The usual *vaudeville* characters are more sharply etched in music than ever before, depicting the more obvious boulevard types everyone knew. Calchas is the bribe-hungry public official, foreshadowing Gilbert's Pooh-Bah a decade later. The Kings of Greece are all petty, inept, unroyal monarchs, and Ménélas is, of course, operetta's most delightful cuckold. Oreste, played by Mlle. Silly in a racy trousers costume plus monocle, is the adolescent dandy so prominent on the boulevards. To have this part played by a man (as it is sometimes today) is to miss all the sexual fun. If we keep Cherubino, Octavian, and Oscar women, we should keep Oreste a woman as well. Paris is an experienced lover, knowing just how to handle not only the ladies but even the goddesses, as he explains in his entrance song. The love affair between Paris and Hélène is quite graphically handled in the operetta, a refreshingly modern change from the usual thin romantic goings-on. Their dialogue in the second act is the close, intimate banter of two prospective lovers, and their love duet is at the same time genuinely beautiful and slightly mocking, not to mention erotic. So erotic that, for a revival of the operetta at London's Alhambra in 1873, the published libretto noted that the duet was "cut short by an order from the Lord Chamberlain's office, the whole duet having been previously excised when the original opera in French was performed at the St. James's, with Madame Schneider."

The book for *La Belle Hélène* is filled with jokes and one-liners, and we can only imagine the personal styles and sight gags of the original cast, which included the popular performers of the Variétés company. Most were known as comedians rather than singers, and it was for this company that Meilhac, Halévy, and Offenbach specifically tailored their finished script. The elaborate *charade* in Act I, a riddle that Paris solves with the word "locomotive" (three thousand years too early), the "goose game" in Act II, and the beach party scene in Act III all look rather thin on paper. They depend on expert comic acting, and, in each case, on a vast *assemblage* of crazy types in any particular scene. By British-American (post–Gilbert and Sullivan) standards, this usually undisciplined collection of zanies seems totally anarchic. Precisely so, and it was always an essential feature of Offenbach/Meilhac-Halévy comedy.

Hélène played London's St. James's Theatre in 1867–68 in the original version, with Schneider in tow. (The St. James's was often called "The French Theatre" because it constantly housed tours of the Bouffes-Parisiens, the Comédie-Française, and other Parisian theatres.) It is easy to see Gilbert admiring Hélène's "*Un mari sage*" (a prudent husband) in the Act II finale. Hélène's topsy-turvy explanation for her husband's discovery of her and her lover Paris in bed is that Ménélas has been imprudent—he should not have returned without warning after his departure for Crete. The idea of the entire chorus echoing this very private dispute *à trois*, in its tripping four-syllable way, is a brilliant comic touch, and one that is essentially of operetta. And there are other marvelous moments—the "*homme à la pomme*" (man with the apple) fugue, which works in few other languages; the repetitions in the *couplets* of the Kings of Greece (*Le*

roi barbu qui s'avance, -bu qui s'avance, -bu qui s'avance; or, The bearded king who comes forward); and, of course, the exquisite waltz ending of the Act II finale. And one may not omit the *"trio patriotique,"* the irresistible bolero in the seaside scene of Act III.

La Belle Hélène enjoyed a very long run, made Schneider the uncontested queen of the Paris musical stage, and made Offenbach very wealthy, from sheet-music royalties and performing rights. In Vienna, *Die schöne Helena* played the Theater an der Wien (17 March 1865). *Helen, or Taken from the Greek* (pun intended) appeared at London's Adelphi in 1866 with a female Paris, and an English version was seen in Chicago the following year. There have been many revivals in Paris, notable ones being at the Variétés in 1899 and at the Mogador in 1960. *La Belle Hélène* was another of Max Reinhardt's favorite Offenbach works. His many stagings appeared all over Europe, including a 1930 mounting in Berlin with Jarmila Novotna (Helena) and Max Hansen (Menelaus) and the memorable C. B. Cochran production—again at the (new) Adelphi—in 1932, with Evelyn Laye, George Robey (Menelaus), and W. H. Berry (Calchas). These had their scores rearranged by Erich Wolfgang Korngold, with a new third act in London that dealt directly with the Trojan War. Oliver Messel supplied the sumptuous sets and costumes, which included an all-white boudoir in Act II which set London a-tizzy. *Helen Goes to Troy* was the name given to the New York version with Novotna planned by Reinhardt before his death in 1943.

Meanwhile, back at the Bouffes, a new piece was needed, so *Les Bergers* (The Shepherds), a decorative three-act *opéra-comique* was furnished. The first act was set in antiquity, the second was a Watteau pastorale ("*J'ai nagé en plein Watteau*"—loosely, "I've been wallowing in Watteau"—Offenbach was reported to have said), and the third a Courbet landscape. Audiences on 11 December 1865 did not take kindly to it, in spite of a lavish production and Offenbach's delight in eighteenth-century pastiche. After *Les Bergers,* no Offenbach work would be produced at the Bouffes until 1868 (30 September) when *L'Île de Tulipatan* opened.

The long run of *La Belle Hélène* was followed at the Variétés by *Barbe-Bleue* (Bluebeard, 5 February 1866). If *Hélène*'s subject matter was not exactly comic, *Barbe-Bleue*'s was really horrific. Several expressed doubts as to the propriety of using the gruesome story for a comic operetta, but the Bluebeard legend had been very popular throughout Europe in comic versions, particularly in British pantomime.

Barbe-Bleue returned its creators to the farcical Middle Ages of *Geneviève de Brabant*. In the Meilhac and Halévy treatment, as opposed to the more macabre Charles Perrault tale, Bluebeard has not actually killed his wives. His alchemist Popolani has given them sleeping potions and placed them in a cave. This made everything more palatable, and would naturally have seemed very amusing to French audiences, which may have looked upon bigamy as an attractive custom.

Barbe-Bleue's score is one of Offenbach's greatest, as major revivals in recent years in Berlin, Paris, and London have proved. There are many delectable moments. There is a synagogue introduction to the delightful "title" song, "*Ma première femme est morte*" (My first wife is dead), with its wide-eyed lyrics and its final declaration that no widower is as gay as Bluebeard. Several numbers sung by Boulotte, the feisty, unlettered heroine first portrayed by Hortense Schneider, have an earthy swagger, and there is a sensational South American dance to end Act I. *Barbe-Bleue*'s other main satirical thrust was at fawning courtiers, and supporting José Dupuis as King Bluebeard was a court of Variétés comedians, most of whom had starred in *La Belle Hélène:* Grenier, Kopp, Couder, and Hittemans. Certainly, the fairy-tale atmosphere was (and still is) enticing to the scenic designers and costumers and a fortune was spent on the original production. This faith in the piece was rewarded; the profits returned were substantial.

Helen of Troy's all-white bedroom, designed by Oliver Messel, for the C. B. Cochran–Max Reinhardt production of *Helen!,* Adelphi, London, 1932. The absence of color on such a vast scale was then considered revolutionary in scenic design—certainly for an Offenbach operetta.

By the fall of 1866 *Barbe-Bleue* had been presented outside France. *Bluebeard Repaired* (in H. Bellingham's one-act English traduction) appeared at London's Olympic Theatre (2 June 1866) and *Blaubart* was seen at the Theater an der Wien (21 September 1866), while New Yorkers had to wait another two years to see it, in French (Niblo's Gardens, 13 July 1868). Schneider and Dupuis performed it at the St. James's, London, in 1869. *Kékszakáll* delighted Budapestians in 1870. There were three major Parisian revivals: 1888, Variétés, with Jeanne Granier as Boulotte; 1904, Variétés, with Anna Tariol-Baugé; and 1971, Théâtre de Paris, with spectacular sets and costumes by Carzou. London's English National Opera mounted a version in the 1960s, but Walter Felsenstein's East Berlin Komische Oper production of *Ritter Blaubart*, originating in 1963, is easily the most popular staging of the century.

La Belle Hélène and *Barbe-Bleue* had been so successful at the Variétés that the rival manager Plunkett of the Palais-Royal commissioned the three creators to write something similar for the forthcoming Exposition of 1867, something equally elaborate, with fantastic décor and costumes and a hopefully disrespectful treatment of either a myth or a fairy tale. Instead, Offenbach was setting *La Vie Parisienne*, a boulevard *vaudeville* based loosely on a one-act Meilhac and Halévy effort, *Le Photographe*, which had been produced at the Palais-Royal in 1864. Offenbach was delighted with the Palais-Royal players: "How charming! How exquisite! They don't need to know how to sing. We're not at the Opéra-Comique! If they are funny it's enough for me." However, the composer had his enchanting protégée Zulma Bouffar in mind for the part of Gabrielle, the glove-seller, and Plunkett was obliged to engage this outsider.

The rehearsals were depressing. Brasseur (who originated the triple roles of the Brazilian, Frick, and Prosper) and Hyacinthe (the first Baron von Gondremarck) were voiceless every day. Herminie (Métella) didn't care for her role at all, and Mlle. Paurelle (Pauline) didn't bother to have her costume properly fitted as she didn't think the show would last more than three nights. Plunkett was worried about morale and, even worse, the two librettists were just about ready to give up. The dénouement was criticized; in fact, the whole company hated the final two acts. Only Offenbach believed in the operetta's success. He sat in his usual place up against the footlights and remarked, when happy, *"C'est très pien"* (Very good), or else *"Ça n'est pas ça de tout"* (That's not it at all) when he wanted something done again. He never lost his Frankfurt accent.

The collaborators and Plunkett invited everyone they could think of to the first night and encouraged everyone to applaud heartily. Offenbach wrote to Hortense Schneider, who would never have appeared for Plunkett, ". . . you must be at our première. A première of mine without my dear daughters, Hé-

---

Ingrid Czerny as Fleurette and Hans Nocker as Bluebeard in the celebrated Walter Felsenstein production of Offenbach's *Barbe-Bleue* at the Komische Oper, East Berlin. Komische Oper/Arvid Lagenpusch.

lène and Boulotte, would be an impossible thing. Till tomorrow then. I hope you will go through more than one pair of gloves applauding the adorable things that I have done in our *Vie Parisienne*. Your respectful father, Jacques Offenbach."

But any anxiousness was unnecessary, as *La Vie Parisienne* was a sensation from the first act. Even the severest critics were intoxicated: Jules Claretie said that the play's effect on the audience was as if "the whole house had been taking hashish." The opening night at the Palais-Royal was 31 October 1866; the Emperor and Eugénie attended the fifty-eighth performance and the piece had a very long run. Offenbach would later have three hits simultaneously on the boards at three theatres: *La Vie Parisienne*, *La Grande-Duchesse de Gérolstein*, and a revival of *Orphée aux Enfers*.

La Vie Parisienne was an obvious crowd-pleaser for visitors to the Paris Exposition as the plot revolves around the adventures of tourists visiting the city. A Swedish baron and baroness and a super-rich Brazilian fall into the clutches of two hard-up and amorous boulevardiers in a first act set in a Paris railway station. The rest of the operetta is complicated by a host of servants and working-class people, including a glove-seller (Bouffar) and a bootmaker (Brasseur, who also played the Brazilian and a waiter).

La Vie Parisienne was really Offenbach's first major full-length operetta success in modern dress, dealing with topical subjects and characters and leading the way to musical comedy, via many delightful and saucy Victorian and Edwardian operettas. La Vie Parisienne is partly responsible for (and very similar in plot and construction to) Die Fledermaus (1874), the Johann Strauss cornerstone of Viennese operetta. Not surprisingly, as Die Fledermaus is based on a Meilhac and Halévy play, Le Réveillon. One notices immediately the similarity of the party acts. One thinks of Paris when one thinks of Offenbach, and none of his works is more Parisian than La Vie Parisienne. The score is impudent, bright, and only sentimental for Métella's bittersweet Parisian rondeaux. A high point of musical foolery is "Votre habit a craqué dans le dos" (Your coat is split down the back), which leads into a third-act finale of increasingly drunken revelry—ending with another cancan. La Vie Parisienne is hardly serious; it is rather a joyous paean to Paris—a Paris which, in spite of loose morality and politically borrowed time, was still an enchanting city in 1866.

There have been several notable Paris revivals. The first, under the direction of the composer, was at the Variétés in 1873. By this time, the original five scenes had been reduced to four. For the Exposition of 1889, Paris saw the operetta again, and also in 1892 and 1904. The glittering revival of 1911 (again at the Variétés) featured sumptuous décors and costumes. Max Dearly as the boulevardier Bobinet, and the great Mistinguett (well before her Casino de Paris days) in a small part. Dearly repeated his role at the Mogador in 1931. Another famous revival was the Jean-Louis Barrault Théâtre de France version of 1958, which played at the New York City Center briefly in the early 1960s. Here again, a company of actors, including Barrault and Madeleine Renaud, took on an *opéra-bouffe,* with brilliant results.

La Vie Parisienne has had a checkered career in English. First heard in that language in London in 1872 (Royal Holborn Theatre), a totally rearranged version by H. B. Farnie entitled simply *La Vie* played at the Avenue Theatre eleven years later, with Lionel Brough as the Baron. Neither engagement proved a happy one. Two subsequent productions were better received: in 1929, a new rearrangement by A. P. Herbert for the Lyric, Hammersmith, and the more faithful 1961 version for the Sadler's Wells Company by Geoffrey Dunn. In New York, Farnie's anglicization of *La Vie Parisienne* played at the Bijou in 1883, and another version was heard in 1945 during the New Opera Company season at the City Center. A new translation by the present author was heard in 1975, performed by the New York Lyric Opera.

Yves Robert rehearses Michel Roux (Baron von Gondremarck) and the ladies in a Paris revival of *La Vie Parisienne.* This sumptuous 1980 production reopened the Châtelet, the eternal home of *l'opérette à grand spectacle.* It included a three-story boulevard mansion and an actual train to bring in the Brazilian and his fellow travelers in Act I. Théâtre Musical de Paris/Enguerand.

GRAND DUCHESS of Gerolstein

VALSE

The

MUSGRAVE.

THE EMPEROR OF OPERETTA

E IGHTEEN sixty-seven was the year of the Universal Exposition in Paris. The visitors who came that spring to see the pavilions erected in the Champs de Mars also saw a new, Haussmann–ized city of wide boulevards, proud, pleasure-loving Parisians, and masses of fireworks and fêtes. Everyone crowded the boulevard theatres, the Opéra, with its new façade, and the waltz concerts conducted by a handsome Viennese visitor, Johann Strauss II. As the Palais-Royal readied its production of *La Vie Parisienne* for an October 1866 opening, Hippolyte Cogniard, the manager of the Variétés, demanded a new piece from Offenbach and Meilhac and Halévy to open in time for the Exposition. The librettists commenced work on *La Chambre rouge,* but by mid–October Halévy would refer to the new work, with satisfaction, as *La Grande-Duchesse.* Gérolstein was added later, after the censors insisted there be no misunderstanding with Luxembourg. Gérolstein was a fictitious place created by the novelist Eugène Sue.

Having graciously invited Hortense Schneider to the première of *La Vie Parisienne,* Offenbach coaxed her into accepting a contract for the new operetta at the Variétés which would pay her 4,500 francs a month to play the Grand Duchess. However popular it may have been, her Boulotte in *Barbe-Bleue* would be nothing compared to the international fame she would receive as the fictitious monarch in the next Variétés operetta. Yet her well-known temperament disrupted rehearsals continuously, her personal version of the libretto being at odds with the librettists'. Dupuis, playing her paramour, Fritz, claimed at one point that he could sing his role only three times weekly, as it was too strenuous. Even Offenbach fussed: he wanted *"touze"* drums onstage for one military moment, but instead of twelve he had to settle for three.

The presentation of the saber in the first-act finale of Offenbach's *La Grande-Duchesse de Gérolstein* (Variétés, 1867), topped with portraits of General Boum, the Grand Duchess, and Fritz. A splendid British music cover issued at the time of the Covent Garden production of 1867.

These were minor troubles compared to censorship questions. The libretto was seen as parodying such things as the petty, pre-Bismarck German courts, the romance of Catherine the Great and Potemkin, the dictatorial rule of Spain's Bourbon Queen Isabel II and her court, and, most obviously, the activities of Napoléon III and his court. To make the latter less obvious, the time was set back to the early eighteenth century. During an exchange of dialogue, Fritz mentions a campaign he had successfully ended in eighteen days—but as the Austrians and the Prussians had just fought for that length of time at Sadowa (ominously for the French), the line was altered to read "four days." The censors also forbade Schneider to wear an elaborate military cross with ribbon; the star was later to have her revenge by being photographed for publicity purposes with the outlawed decoration.

The first night, 12 April 1867, saw both the *beau-* and *demi-monde* well represented. The terribly fashionable Princess Pauline von Metternich was there, dressed in the newest shade—"Bismarck brown"—and without a crinoline; Rothschild, Hanslick (the Viennese music critic), and many other notables packed the Variétés. Schneider almost refused to go on, what with her nerves and the embargo on her military cross. At the height of her tears, Offenbach could do nothing but run into the pit and begin the overture. As soon as Hortense heard the stirring opening notes of *"Voici le sabre de mon père,"* she dried her tears and smiled "like a circus horse hearing a polka," as she later recalled.

The first act went magnificently and the audience danced into the foyer for the interval humming the same Saber Song. But the remainder of the evening seemed anticlimactic after the show-stopping *"Dites-lui"* (Tell Him . . .) sung by Schneider early in Act II, and the première went on well past midnight. The authors and composer began cutting and revising immediately after the première. These changes, including a revised Act II finale, were completed by the third night, and the result was a complete triumph, confirmed by Sarcey in the *Journal Illustré,* who called it as good or better than *La Belle Hélène* and *Barbe-Bleue.* And everyone, Parisians or visitors to the Exposition, simply had to see it.

The Emperor visited the Variétés alone, on April 24, but brought Eugénie to a later performance. The Prince of Wales, Europe's leading *bon vivant* at twenty-six, had to appeal personally to Mlle. Schneider for a box for the performance on May 15, and the star managed to secure one only after having made a round of Paris's ticket brokers. Though ostensibly coming to see the Exposition, Tsar Alexander II wired ahead from Cologne to obtain a box for June 1, the date of his arrival. And, after paying his respects at the local Russian Orthodox church (no doubt for his safe arrival after assassination attempts), he rushed to the theatre with the Duke Vladimir. Prosper Mérimée attended the theatre that night and remarked that "Mlle. Schneider's legs seem to have produced a great effect on Vladimir."

Bismarck came also that June, and remarked to his secretary that the operetta was *"tout à fait ça,"* referring to the satiric picture of the fragmented German landscape given in the piece. Bismarck would, of course, have the last laugh three years later. Other visitors to Mlle. Schneider's *loge* included the Grand

Duke Constantin and the kings of Bavaria, Portugal, and Sweden. The Sultan of Turkey came on June 30, dressed "like an English clergyman," according to Mérimée. Ismail Pasha, the Viceroy of Egypt, went nightly to revel in Mlle. Schneider's performance and dressing room. This provoked a former admirer of the actress, Xavier Feuillant, to appear one evening in the opposite stage box *also* wearing a fez. The Emperor Franz Josef made the *faux pas* of missing the show, and the *Nain Jaune,* a humorous journal, slyly included an article suggesting that the Grand Duchy of Gérolstein declare war on Austria.

One afternoon at the Exposition, Mlle. Schneider's carriage was stopped at the entrance reserved for royalty. She was permitted to pass when she explained that she was the Grande-Duchesse of Gérolstein. She was indeed "the Empress of Operetta," as one critic called her, also saying "her caressing and feminine smile is the most audacious of passports." It was a royal climax to a career built as much on sensuous charm as on beauty (which she had) or vocal ability (which we can never be sure of—even the severest critics were reputed to have lost their faculties in her presence). *"La Snèder,"* as some Parisians called her, remains certainly the most legendary diva of operetta, French or otherwise, helped by the fact that she was too early for recordings. We can look at photographs, but her voice remains a mystery.

The rest of the Variétés' original cast included Dupuis as the simple-minded but handsome private, Couder as the hilariously swaggering General Boum (who preferred gunpowder to snuff), and Élise Garait as the peasant girl Wanda. Their antics helped make *La Grande-Duchesse* one of the greatest hits in French theatrical history, and the Variétés' most memorable production, a fact confirmed today by the presence of a full-length portrait of Schneider as the Grand Duchess above the Circle bar.

Theatre managers in Europe and the United States who had heard of the fabulous success of Schneider in *La Grande-Duchesse* became even more interested when reports of the record-breaking box-office receipts were received. *La Belle Hélène, Barbe-Bleue,* and the first few days of *La Grande-Duchesse* had grossed something like the equivalent of $600,000 (in 1867 dollars). An entire *opéra-bouffe* company was imported from Paris to appear at the French Theatre, New York, on 24 September 1867. It opened with Lucille Tostée in *La Grande-Duchesse.* (The Théâtre Français was at the corner of Fourteenth Street and Sixth Avenue; the top price was two dollars for a box seat.) So great and immediate was the success of the operetta that the tunes were "hummed, whistled, played until the ear was worn to shreds," according to George Odell, in his *Annals of the New York Stage. La Grande-Duchesse* (still in French) started a raging fever for French *opéra-bouffe* which went unchecked until a British operetta, Gilbert and Sullivan's *H.M.S. Pinafore,* began another craze eleven years later.

England first saw the Duchess at Covent Garden in an English version by Charles Kenney (18 November 1867). The star was the Australian Julia Mathews, and the operetta was revived at the Olympic in May 1868, running alongside a successful summer repertory season by the Offenbach company at the St. James's. Schneider played Eurydice, Hélène, Boulotte, and the Grand Duchess, getting most of her acclaim in the latter role (possibly from the snobs who could say they had seen it in Paris during the Exposition).

Mrs. Howard Paul (who in 1877 created the role of Lady Sangazure in *The Sorcerer* for Gilbert and Sullivan) was one of the first English Duchesses. Another was Emily Soldene, who at one point wore Julia Mathews's costume, complete with a huge grease stain in the middle of the lap. The dresser explained to Miss Soldene: "Lor', miss, that's where Miss Mathews used to put 'er fried fish!" If Mathews was considered "clever, but rather coarse," she could take consolation in the fact that some of Schneider's "suggestive" gestures were considered quite improper for respectable London theatregoers. The English craze for *opéra-bouffe,* started primarily by the success of *The Grand Duchess,* ran concurrently with the American mania and was similarly supplanted by Gilbert and Sullivan.

Vienna had already succumbed to Offenbach, but the success of *Die Grossherzogin von Gerolstein* at the Theater an der Wien (13 May 1867) was phenomenal. Marie Geistinger, who later managed the theatre herself, was the Viennese favorite in the title part. Berlin fell the following year, with Lina Mayr playing the Duchess at the Friedrich-Wilhelmstädtisches Theater. *Gerolsteini nagyhercegnö* followed in Budapest. The other principal cities of the old and new worlds capitulated in time.

In 1878, the French War Minister voiced his opposition to a Paris revival of *La Grande-Duchesse,* on the grounds that it burlesqued the army (!), but further Parisian revivals occurred in 1887 (Variétés, with Anna Judic) and in 1890 (Variétés, with Jeanne Granier). Perhaps because of its burlesque of German militarism, *La Grande-Duchesse* would hardly have seemed in good taste during either of the two World Wars, but it was in fact a tremendous success for Fritzi Massary at Berlin's Metropoltheater in 1916. It was more than likely banned during the Nazi era because of Offenbach's (and Halévy's) Jewish background. It was revived at the Gaîté-Lyrique in 1948 (with Germaine Roger) and in the early 1960s at the Marigny (with Suzanne Lafaye). In 1981, Régine Crespin appeared as the Grand Duchess at the newly reopened Châtelet.

The most celebrated New York revivals and American tours starred Lillian Russell. When the beautiful songstress appeared at the Casino in 1890, she made her first-act entrance on a sleigh, wrapped in ermine, amid a blinding paper snowstorm. (Seasonal considerations in the synopsis of scenes—hitherto unknown—allowed effects such as these as well as a prodigious number of elaborate costumes for Miss Russell, all looking rather more like the 1890s than the specified 1720s.) The critic for the New York *Dramatic Mirror* felt that the French singers who had played the Duchess "surpassed Miss Russell in the naughtiness and chic that the role really requires, but not one of the Frenchwomen ever sang as well or looked as handsome as our own Lillian." *Town Topics* was more poetic: "In the *Grand Duchess* she fills the eye like a splurge of roses and amazes the ear with an abundance of melody equal to a virgin wood at summer sunrise."

Miss Russell also had the distinction of making the first overtly publicized long-distance telephone call. An elaborate apparatus was set up in her dressing room, where, during the intermission, she sang the Saber Song into a metal funnel. In Washington, President Grover Cleveland listened appreciatively at the other end. The Santa Fe, Baltimore, and New York City operas have produced the operetta more recently.

The most notable British revival was at the Savoy, produced by Richard D'Oyly Carte. W. S. Gilbert, whose last collaboration with Sullivan, *The Grand Duke*, had just proved more or less a fiasco, was in the audience on the first night, 4 December 1897. The then-standard Kenney translation was dropped in favor of a new book by Charles Brookfield which entirely bowdlerized the last act, plus new lyrics by Adrian Ross. The orchestrations were "strengthened" by Ernest Ford. In the cast were no less than three of George Grossmith's Savoy successors in the Gilbert and Sullivan patter roles: Walter Passmore (as Boum), Henry Lytton (as Paul), and C. H. Workman (as a peasant).

La Grande-Duchesse de Gérolstein was incontestably Offenbach's greatest hit in terms of worldwide popularity. In France, it was as much a social as a musical attraction. In spite of a few well-placed, admittedly exciting numbers, much of the score is not Offenbach or Meilhac and Halévy at their most felicitous or winning. It has neither the brilliant clarity nor the high-voltage gaiety of either *La Belle Hélène* or *La Vie Parisienne;* there are *longueurs* that seem to last entire scenes, due to a story which peters out from the middle of Act II, as the first-nighters were quick to observe. The militaristic rum-te-tums often appear without any dexterous orchestration to ennoble them. On the other hand, there are certain moments which prove so exciting in performance that they manage to make the audience forget the weaker sections of the operetta: the Grand Duchess's review of the troops, *"Ah, que j'aime les militaires!"* (Oh, how I love the military), her duet with Fritz, *"C'est un fameux régiment,"* and the rattling Saber Song which closes Act I. There is little else after Act I save for the plaintive *"Dites-lui";* the catchy comic conspiracy trio in Act II is a long, long rehash of the patriotic trio in *La Belle Hélène,* without as much brio. Yet for all its shortcomings, the Grand Duchess continues to draw crowds whenever she appears. Offenbach knew as well as anyone the powers of a German band.

Since the failure of *Barkouf* at the Opéra-Comique on Christmas Eve, 1861, Offenbach dreamed of a triumphant return to the Salle Favart. *Robinson Crusoé* (20 November 1867) was no triumph, but it came off considerably better than his canine work six years before. Defoe's original had to be twisted by librettists Cormon and Crémieux into something Gallicly different to accommodate the large Opéra-Comique company. Their Crusoé, after discovering his *girl* Friday (played by Célestine Galli-Marié, later the original Carmen), was met by his wife Edwige (Mlle. Cico), her servant, Suzanne, and a band of dancing savages. M. Sainte-Foy stopped the show with his song of the *"pot au feu"* (stew pot), with its cannibalistic references. With its English basis, this *opéra-comique* has recently found favor with British audiences. Opera Rara, at the 1973 Camden Festival, London, produced the work successfully. Its more elaborate vocal lines (which sound rather overwritten at times) would appeal to an opera company not wishing to stoop down to the level of operetta.

More typically Offenbach was *Le Château à Toto,* which the Palais-Royal produced on 6 May 1868. Too typical, it seemed—the music was found smacking of the past without providing anything new and the Meilhac-Halévy satire on decadent nobility was considered unamusing. On the other hand, the shorter (one-act) *L'Île de Tulipatan,* originally composed at Bad Ems and reproduced at the opening of the Bouffes-Parisiens season in September, was genuinely funny and charming. Henri Chivot and Alfred Duru's book concerned a boy raised as a girl and a girl raised as a boy, and attendant family problems. This was apparently enough for one act; a charming Paris revival in 1982 confirmed the work's agreeable silliness. On the same opening programme was *Le Fifre enchanté* (The Magic Fife), originally *Le Soldat magicien* at Ems in 1864, harmless and unmemorable.

A week later came the première of *La Périchole* at the Variétés (6 October 1868). Conceived as a vehicle for Schneider, the title part she played was based on a historical character, a Micaëla Villegas. A well-known actress in eighteenth-century Peru, she was at one time the mistress of its Viceroy. During a tiff, she apparently so displeased her master that he called her a *"perra chola"* (native bitch) and drove her out of his palace. Prosper Mérimée dramatized his own story as the one-act *Le Carrosse du Saint-Sacrement* (The Coach of the Holy Sacrament), and it was produced (without success) at the Comédie-Française in 1850. (It was only popular later, after a successful revival at the Vieux Colombier in 1920 which led to a new production at the Comédie. Jean Renoir's *Le Carrosse d'Or* [The Golden Coach], an Italian-French film co-production of 1952 with Anna Magnani, treats the same story.)

Meilhac and Halévy borrowed only the setting, not the plot, from Mérimée, and they did him greater justice later with their superb libretto for Bizet's *Carmen* (1875). "Meil" and "Hal" (as the composer affectionately called his librettists) had given Offenbach a two-act book set in a fanciful eighteenth-century Lima, with a triangle love-story of the Viceroy, a street singer, and her poor fellow artist Piquillo. The satire which so permeated *La Belle Hélène* and Offenbach's earlier works was no longer much in vogue—the *offenbachiades* were veering closer to *opéra-comique,* and operatic burlesques within operetta were somewhat wasted on an increasingly more democratic audience. Offenbach's main contribution in this vein in *La Périchole* was a takeoff, *"Quel marché de bassesse!",* on a scene from Donizetti's *La Favorite* (1840). There were a few jokes at the expense of court life *chez* Napoléon III, but little else of import in the libretto: some

---

The sale of dance arrangements of themes from operettas was one of the principal means of popularizing these works. This appeared with the first English production of *La Périchole* at the Royalty Theatre in 1875. The part of the Viceroy (far left) was taken by Fred Sullivan, whose brother Arthur supplied the music for an afterpiece later added to the bill: *Trial by Jury.*

LA Périchole WALTZ,

FROM

Offenbach's Opera

Charles Coote

silly comics (one name taken from a cigar label—Panatellas), a drunken wedding, and an idiotic dinner scene just before the presentation at the court.

But it did have a touching love scene in the first act, climaxed by La Périchole's Letter Song, the words of which Halévy adapted from the letter Manon Lescaut sends to Des Grieux in the Abbé Prévost's novel, beginning: *"Je te jure, mon cher chevalier, que tu es l'idole de mon coeur . . ."* (I swear to you, my dear knight, that you are the idol of my heart . . .). This new note of pathos was not sustained in the weaker second act. In the original cast, Schneider was La Périchole, Dupuis, her street-singing partner, Piquillo, and Grenier, Don Andrès, the Viceroy—all favorite stars perfectly cast.

The first night seemed to confirm the feeling of success which had pervaded the rehearsals, the audience particularly enjoying the finales. The critics noted the easy superiority of the scintillating score over the meager book. Francisque Sarcey disliked the court satire, and claimed that the public was tired of operetta. This was not quite true; Parisians were interested in other recent works, among them successes by the experienced Hervé *(Chilpéric)* and a new composer, Lecocq *(Fleur-de-Thé),* and they were becoming keen on more romantic subjects—the hallmark of post-1870 French operetta—which in fact *La Périchole* did anticipate.

The critic Edmond Tarbé rebutted the charge that Offenbach was played out: "The maestro's muse is clothed in a *moiré* dress of changing shades—it's always the same dress, but not always the same reflection." The authors and composer made some cuts and changes on the morning immediately following the première. The new operetta *was* a success—by the fiftieth performance it had grossed 206,590 francs—and it was popular enough to be burlesqued at the Alcazar, in tandem with Hervé's aforementioned hit, as *Chilpérichole*. The Letter Song swept France, though curiously enough on the first night only the upper *galeries* appreciated it; the wealthy *tout Paris* below was possibly startled by this pathetic note in an Offenbach *opéra-bouffe*.

Following a spectacularly enlarged revival of *Orphée aux Enfers* in 1874, Offenbach, Meilhac, and Halévy decided to produce *La Périchole* and to pad out their admittedly flimsy second act. The *séguidille* which originally appeared just before the Act II finale was transferred (perhaps inadvisedly) to Act I, and a new Act III, in two scenes, was created—the first scene in the Viceroy's dungeon for recalcitrant husbands. This certainly improved matters dramatically and has been performed more than once as a subtle burlesque of *Fidelio*. It served as a good setting for Périchole's declaration, *"Tu n'es pas beau, tu n'es pas riche"* (You aren't handsome, you aren't rich), with its enchanting refrain, *"Je t'adore, brigand . . ."* (I love you, brigand). The *br* in *brigand,* according to one of Offenbach's grandsons, was inimitably gurgled by Schneider.

In spite of these enlargements and improvements, this production did not run long, but there were further repeats at the Variétés (1876—with Anna Judic; 1878—the year of an Exposition; 1895—with Jeanne Granier). The most popular reprise by far was produced in honor of Offenbach's 150th birthday at the Théâtre de Paris in 1969 with Jane Rhodes as La Périchole in a gorgeous, if slightly overbearing décor by the painter Carzou.

New York witnessed the first principal foreign production (Pike's Opera House, 4 January 1869) in French. Five days later, *Périchole, die Strassensängerin* opened at the Theater an der Wien, Vienna. The first British presentation, in French, with Hortense Schneider, occurred during the 1870 summer season at the Princess's Theatre (now the site of an Oxford Street Woolworth's). By the end of that year the operetta had been seen in such cities as Berlin, St. Petersburg, and, closer to its setting, Buenos Aires and Rio de Janeiro. The first London production in English (Royalty, 30 January 1875) was managed by Richard D'Oyly Carte, who later arranged for a new supporting piece: the second joint opus and first great success of Gilbert and Sullivan, *Trial by Jury* (25 March). It goes without saying that the genesis of British operetta was in many ways modeled directly on the Offenbach-Meilhac-Halévy collaborations. Gilbert not only borrowed his basic operetta framework and construction from the *offenbachiades* of Meilhac and Halévy, but also in at least one or two instances used lines or business from *La Périchole* itself: Piquillo's attempted suicide has a descendant in Nanki-Poo's similar scene in *The Mikado* (1885). Gilbert adapted several works by Meilhac and Halévy for the English stage, including the next Offenbach-Variétés hit, *Les Brigands* (1869). Gilbert, coincidentally, financed the building of the Garrick Theatre, where *La Périchole* was seen again in the West End (1897) with Florence St. John, *"prima donna assoluta"* of comic opera, as one

---

Joan Sutherland as La Périchole in a 1973 television series designed to get people interested in opera. The soprano, like many other great opera stars of past and present, loves operetta and has recorded many selections. Courtesy of Kroll Productions, Inc.

English critic called her. Two years previously, her American counterpart, Lillian Russell, appeared in the part at the Knickerbocker, New York.

Another New York performance of singular interest was the Moscow Art Theatre Musical Studio version, translated and staged by Nemirovich-Danchenko (Jolson's, 21 December 1925). Olga Baclanova starred in what the *World*'s Samuel Chotzinoff called "a very nice and simple musical comedy . . . almost turned into an Ibsen problem play . . . Everybody acts as if he were doing the 'Lower Depths' of Gorky." More recent but no more like the original was the Metropolitan Opera version of 1956, a "spectacular" staged by Cyril Ritchard (with himself as Don Andrès, plus Patrice Munsel), translated by Maurice Valency, with interpolated ballets and songs from *Fantasio* and *La Grande-Duchesse de Gérolstein*.

The Opéra-Comique played another Offenbach work on 10 March 1869, *Vert-Vert*, the musical story of a parrot. Meilhac and Nuitter collaborated on the libretto, set in a boarding school for young ladies, complete with visiting dragoon guards, dancing lessons, and a pleasant Offenbach score. It met with success, though some criticized his elevating a *vaudeville* into a comic opera. And why not? *La Vie Parisienne* was a perfect precedent. Less successful that season was the Meilhac/Halévy/Offenbach homage to Hortense Schneider, *La Diva* (Bouffes-Parisiens, 22 March 1869), a thinly veiled musical autobiography of the actress with new songs.

La Princesse de Trébizonde, a three-act *opéra-bouffe* by Nuitter and Tréfeu, appeared at the Bouffes-Parisiens on 7 December 1869. Making her debut in operetta was Céline Chaumont, as a girl-juggler who poses as a wax figure of the title princess, falling in love, of course, with a real prince. Her vivacious spirits were admired, as was her impeccable diction. A short run of four months gave Parisians a chance to see Mlle. Chaumont; they were tired of exaggerated situations and the old *bouffe* style, which included a burlesque of a number from Rossini's *William Tell*.

Operatic voices, again, were hardly required at the Bouffes; star quality was everything. The critic for London's *Daily Telegraph,* reporting on Chaumont, stated:

> Above all, little Mlle. Chaumont puzzles everybody who hears her. With no more voice than that of a cat when you squeeze her tail, she contrives, by her artful singing, to put more expression into the music than could be imagined by less clever persons. All who would know how to sing without a voice should give heed to Mlle. Chaumont.

La Princesse de Trébizonde was the first full-length Offenbach at London's Gaiety Theatre (16 April 1870), with a cast including J. L. Toole and Nellie Farren. It was in New York the following year (Wallack's, 11 September 1871) and in Vienna in 1873 (Carltheater, 1 February).

But Parisians preferred *Les Brigands* (Variétés, 10 December 1869) which continued the romantic streak exemplified in *La Périchole,* and with Spanish characters, to boot. Indeed, the boots *("les bottes, les bottes, les bottes")* of the royal carabiniers tramped the *opéra-bouffe* to immense success. In a double-chorus situation (which Gilbert and Sullivan were to echo most uncannily in the second act of *The Pirates of Penzance* a decade later) a band of robbers and the police meet at the end of Act I. The rest of the score is a bit top-heavy. Most of the best songs (and there were many) are in Act I—the entrance song of Falsacappa, the bandit chief (played by Dupuis), another for Fiorella, his daughter (Aimée triumphed in this part), and the lovely numbers for Fragoletto, the peasant lad (originally intended for Schneider, but refused by her, and played by Zulma Bouffar).

Les *Brigands* was an affectionate return to the *Fra Diavolo* type of *opéra-comique,* and it retained sufficient romance and wildness of setting to appeal to admirers of the sentimental. The Meilhac-Halévy satire was there for those who wanted it: "One must steal according to the position one occupies in society," claims the Duke of Mantua; the carabiniers are never there when they're wanted ("we're always late," they chant). The military aspect of *Les Brigands,* the easy-to-remember martial rhythms, the comic swagger of the officers, and the carabinier uniforms themselves helped ensure the operetta's popularity, just as they helped bring *La Grande-Duchesse* to worldwide fame. Offenbach realized that "the public is tired of little tunes, and so am I." In fact, though he may indeed have tried to set situations to music, the "little tunes" of *Les Brigands* proved irresistible.

Echoes of *Les Brigands* in *The Pirates of Penzance* were more than a chance occurrence. Gilbert translated the operetta, thus providing history with a rare delight, an operetta with words by Gilbert and music by Offenbach. In 1871, the Boosey firm commissioned Gilbert to prepare an English version of *Les Brigands.* However, the Globe Theatre at more or less the same time had asked Henry S. Leigh to prepare *his* version for a production in April. Leigh's got produced, Gilbert's did not, though Boosey did publish his libretto for copyright reasons. Leigh's version was called *Fal-sac-ap-pa* (Globe, 22 April 1871); the *Illustrated London News* could not "recommend it as a musical or dramatic performance." Gilbert's version was finally produced in the same year as *The Gondoliers* (Avenue, 16 September 1889). It was not a great success. Gilbert insisted he had never polished his work for the stage; slight textual revisions were made in the vocal score published around the turn of the century by Boosey—but not by Gilbert. The Gilbert-Offenbach *Brigands* was very pleasantly revived as a fringe event in the 1982 Edinburgh Festival.

Les Brigands has nevertheless been quite popular in France (there was a television film in the 1970s) and throughout Europe—particularly in Berlin, where the actor-manager Gustaf Gründgens staged it in the early '30s. There was a revival directed by Peter Ustinov at the Deutsche Oper (West Berlin) in 1979.

La Romance de la Rose, a one-acter woven around "The Last Rose of Summer," was Offenbach's last creation of the 1860s (Bouffes-Parisiens, 11 December 1869).

As the sóldiers tramped on the boards of the Variétés, German boots were ready to march on Paris. On 2 September 1870, the Emperor capitulated at the Battle of Sedan. The theatres closed, and Offenbach, a naturalized Frenchman, was still ashamed of his German origins. He left Paris for his villa at Étretat, thence on to Italy, Spain, and finally Vienna, where he conducted the Viennese production of *Les Brigands* (Theater an der Wien, 12 March 1870). The Second Empire was over. However much Offenbach may have mocked its shortcomings, by 1870 he was considered to have represented it musically. Would the public stand for the old genre after the Commune? Charles Lecocq, who had himself had several successful works in the late '60s, predicted that operetta would be killed by Prussian shells. (This seems a bit unfair; Berlin was very fond of French operetta.) Happily for himself—and us—Lecocq was proved wrong.

Offenbach launched right back into operetta on returning to Paris in the fall of 1871. *Les Brigands* was revived at the Variétés and *Boule de Neige* (Snowball) flopped at the Théâtre de la Gaîté (14 December), a theatre once famous for its melodramas and now to be celebrated for its elaborate *féeries,* pantomimes or extravaganzas. *Boule de Neige* was actually *Barkouf* trussed up as an elaborate *opéra-bouffe;* no matter, the snowball was still a dog.

The next piece at the Gaîté was a hit: *Le Roi Carotte* (King Carrot), to a libretto by Victorien Sardou. Highly satiric, it managed to aim its darts at Bonapartists, monarchists, and republicans, and by placing part of the action in Germany, it noted how inefficient the French were when compared to the German might. This was considered too offensive in view of the French war losses, and the action was shifted to a very fictitious Hungary. Simply explained, the allegorical story had a king dethroned by an evil fairy who turns vegetables into people, with King Carrot as their monarch. The new régime is even worse than the former, and the old king is restored to power. What was fascinating was that Sardou's libretto had been written *before* the war, in 1869.

The première was enthusiastically received, for the most part, on 15 January 1872, and the operetta ran 149 performances. There was a lot to admire—four acts and seventeen scenes of unparalleled extravagance in sets and costumes, a grand scene at Pompeii, a long, tuneful score, a ballet of insects, an ant chorus, Zulma Bouffar, and a newcomer Offenbach had seen singing at the Eldorado *café-concert* and at the Folies-Bergères, Anna Judic. She was to become one of the most famous operetta stars of the century. The production cost six thousand francs a night to run, but made a daily profit of three thousand francs. The London version was at the Alhambra (3 June 1872), the Viennese at the Theater an der Wien (23 December 1876).

If *Le Roi Carotte* was heading in the direction of spectacular revue, *Fantasio,* which opened a scant three days later at the Opéra-Comique (18 January 1872), was pushing *opéra-bouffe* again to loftier plateaux. This comic opera had a libretto adapted from Alfred de Musset's play and starred Galli-Marié. *Fantasio* had a lovely first act but not much else and was withdrawn after about two weeks, though the Viennese version the next month was better-liked. By now it seems apparent at this late stage of the composer's career—taking into account his usual working habits, starting with the first act and working to the end—that Offenbach poured all his more ebullient and diverting composition into the beginning of each of his later works and may have been so tired out working under such great pressure that the last acts of these works often seem uninspired. Perhaps he began to lose interest after Act I; in spite of some charming numbers in their final acts, the scores of *La Grande-Duchesse*, *La Périchole*, *Les Brigands*, *Fantasio*, and others up to 1880 are top-heavy, lovely up front but thin and repetitious afterward.

In Vienna, *Der schwarze Korsar* (The Black Pirate) opened at the Theater an der Wien in the autumn of 1872 (21 September), starring the theatre's directress, Marie Geistinger. Vienna was Offenbach-mad, but this work flopped. The German text was by Offenbach himself, with help from Richard Genée, the theatre conductor, and it was basically to blame for the work's swift sinking. Genée later provided the libretti for many important Viennese operettas.

The Variétés, no doubt wishing to have as great a hit on its hands as the revival of *Les Brigands*, put on *Les Braconniers* (The Poachers) on 29 January 1873. Unfortunately, it was too similar to *Les Brigands* for comfort, and in spite of a stellar cast (Bouffar, Dupuis, Berthelier, Léonce) it failed to achieve more than a two-month run.

With the staggering Paris success of Lecocq's *La Fille de Madame Angot* (21 February 1873) staring Offenbach in the face, the elder composer had the choice of following his own trend, wisely taken up by Lecocq, of romanticizing and sweetening the old *opéra-bouffe* as he had done in *La Périchole* and *Les Brigands*, or instead writing more spectacular extravaganzas like *Le Roi Carotte*. The fact that he decided to do both was risky enough, but he additionally (and most unwisely, as it turned out) took over the management of the Théâtre de la Gaîté. Never a very good businessman, the complicated realities of running a theatre profitably were glossed over by Offenbach's wildly extravagant spending. He luxuriously refurbished the house and hired a huge company of costly singers, dancers, comedians, and extra orchestra members. Elaborate scenic and costumic staffs and equipment were engaged. It was Offenbach's notion to alternate his standard hits, in the new dressed-up and enlarged versions, with dramatic spectacles, produced in a similarly lavish fashion.

In the meantime, some new short works *(La Leçon de Chant, La Permission de 10 heures)* appeared at assorted theatres followed by *La Jolie Parfumeuse*, a three-act operetta for the Renaissance (29 November 1873), libretto by Crémieux and Blum. Louise Théo, another Offenbach find from the Eldorado, drew Parisians for 200 performances as Rose Michon, a young married woman seduced by a rich financier, whose mistress manages to have her sent back to house and husband. The music was refined and witty rather than outstandingly tuneful, a common later-Offenbach characteristic. Kate Santley was London's Rose at the Alhambra (18 May 1874).

For tunes, spectacle, and an aggrandized version of the early Offenbach, Paris turned to the inflated version of *Orphée aux Enfers* which opened at the Gaîté on 7 February 1874. No expense was spared for this ultra-lavish production. Grévin designed costumes for a greatly enlarged list of principal parts, a chorus of one hundred and twenty, and a massive sixty-girl *corps de ballet*. He had to design not four scenes (as in the original version) but twelve, complete with an omnibus to carry the gods to the gates of the Underworld at the end of Act I. It was marked *LIGNE P. Y.–CHAMPS-ÉLYSÉES–BARRIÈRE D'ENFER,* the first stop being a play on the words "country of Greece," or *"pays grec."* Note that the route went via the Champs-Élysées, doubtless to allow the gods a few hours in Paris's playground.

This was an *opéra-féerie,* to be sure, and it was so successful financially that the takings by the hundredth performance amounted to some 1,800,000 francs. In 1874, the one-act *Bagatelle* premièred at the Bouffes-Parisiens (21 May), while the latest piece for the Renaissance, starring Judic was the three-act *bouffe, Madame l'Archiduc* (libretto by Millaud and Halévy, with contributions by Meilhac in the first act (31 October). Their story concerned an Italian prince and a waitress. Emily Soldene played the part in London (Opera Comique, 13 January 1876) and, earlier, Marie Geistinger in Vienna (Theater an der Wien, 16 January 1875). London's Alhambra Theatre commissioned Offenbach to write *Dick Whittington and His Cat* for its 1874–75 Christmas pantomime. The contract would pay the librettists and composer 60,000 francs.

The tremendous success of *Orphée aux Enfers,* which by now had racked up more than eight hundred performances, again proved hard to equal. Its successor at the Gaîté, an elaborate production of Sardou's play, *La Haine* (Hate), could hardly approach it in popularity, and the dozens of expensive suits of period armor, ordered but never used, were rather cunningly employed in a revamped and gussied-up revival of *Geneviève de Brabant.* The Variétés, pining for a new three-act Meilhac/Halévy/Offenbach creation, got one on 19 October 1875. *La Boulangère a des écus* (roughly: This bakeress has plenty of dough) was promised for Schneider, but when she once walked out of a rehearsal her part went the next day to Aimée. Schneider sued the Variétés, which had managed to lure Schneider back from a Russian engagement for this part, and won her case. *La Boulangère* enjoyed some success, helped by an infectious *tyrolienne* and the title song, and by a strong cast that also included Dupuis, Léonce, and Paola Marié. But it was a weak effort by the three collaborators and it was to be their last together. The plot concerned a financial scandal during the eighteenth century.

Geneviève de Brabant and its huge sets and ballets collapsed at the Gaîté. Offenbach, heedless of the vast sums lost in producing two failures at the Gaîté, embarked on yet another expensive project, a Sardou version of *Don Quixote.* But impending financial ruin intervened. Rather than go through the painful

---

The first scene in the spectacular version of Offenbach's *Le Voyage dans la Lune* directed by Jérôme Savary for the East Berlin Komische Oper, 1978. Setting by Reinhart Zimmermann, costumes by Eleonore Kleiber. Komische Oper/Arvid Lagenpusch.

and humiliating process of bankruptcy, Offenbach bravely took the initiative, sold his interests in the Gaîté, gave up or leased his property, and mortgaged three years of his forthcoming royalties. He promised to pay everyone back, down to the last *rat* of the ballet, and such was his prestige and generosity in the theatre world that everyone backed him up. A large amount of money was promised if he would tour the United States in 1876 playing his own compositions; overcoming his fear of ocean travel and the anxiety of being away from his beloved family for so long, he accepted. The American tour was a great success, and he even managed to write a book about it, *Notes d'un Musicien en Voyage* (1877).

Vizentini, Offenbach's musical assistant at the Gaîté, had taken over the reins of the theatre, and he produced his former boss's *Le Voyage dans la Lune* (A Trip to the Moon) on 26 November 1875. Zulma Bouffar, who had again taken Paris by storm in Johann Strauss's *La Reine Indigo*, returned to Gaîté for this *opéra-féerie*, merely suggested by Jules Verne's story and inspired by the great success of *Le Tour du Monde en 80 Jours* at the Porte Saint-Martin the year before. The spectacular effects far overshadowed the music, however, with a huge cannon in which the voyagers were shot to the moon dominating the stage. The lunar landscape in the second act was a scenic triumph as well, but not perhaps as startling as the massive volcano eruption in the fourth act. There were some twenty other scenes of equal extravagance and, for once, a funny and satiric book by Albert Vanloo, Eugène Leterrier, and Arnold Mortier. It also did well at the Theater an der Wien in 1876.

East Berlin's Komische Oper, long the home of the celebrated Walter Felsen-

stein production of *Ritter Blaubart (Barbe-Bleue)*, unveiled in 1979 a truly spectacular version of *Le Voyage dans la Lune*. A French director, Jérôme Savary, and the brilliant house designers, Reinhart Zimmermann and Eleonore Kleiber, wisely decided to base their work on the original Paris production, with added suggestions of the famous Méliès trick film of 1902. By moving the huge company and the immense sets with speed and gusto, but allowing enough of the raffishness of the libretto to shine through in the broad comic acting, Savary and his designers pulled off a spectacular true to the original.

La Créole (3 November 1875) was a full-length work for the Bouffes-Parisiens, with a libretto by Meilhac and Millaud, set in the period of Louis XVI and concerning the love of a musketeer for a native of Guadeloupe. It did better, with a better cast, in an 1886 London revival *(The Commodore)* than it had at the Bouffes a decade before with Anna Judic. Long after it had been forgotten, *La Créole* was revived for Josephine Baker at the Marigny (17 December 1934). La Baker did not have to blacken herself with licorice juice, as did la Judic! The libretto had been thoroughly overhauled by Albert Willemetz.

Two more forgettable works were put on at the Bouffes in 1876: the one-act *Pierrette et Jacquot* and the four-act *La Boîte au lait*. And then came another science-fiction operetta, with a libretto by Mortier and Gille "based" on Jules Verne, *Le Docteur Ox* (Variétés, 26 January 1876). In this, the Docteur Ox and his assistant Ygène (Ox . . . ygène) . . . the story hardly mattered in this sumptuous production, and José Dupuis and Anna Judic stopped the show nightly with their "Flemish" couplets.

By 1877, some critics claimed that the composer had played himself out, that his fountain of melody had dried up. (Lecocq scored another ravishing triumph that year, the intoxicating *Le petit Duc.*) *La Foire Saint-Laurent* (10 February 1877), the first of three Offenbach operettas contracted for the Folies-Dramatiques, was no better, though it allowed the composer to pay homage to the Parisian fair that nurtured operetta.

More of an opportunity for pastiche came with the second Folies-Dramatiques operetta, the slightly more successful *Madame Favart* (libretto by Chivot and Duru, 28 December 1878). It was a raging hit in London, produced and with a libretto by H. B. Farnie that held the British spellbound for 502 performances and many more on tour (Strand, 12 April 1879). London's fascination was principally for its operetta queen, Florence St. John, in the part created by Juliette Simon-Girard. This was one of Offenbach's best late scores. The *ronde des vignes* ("*Ma mère aux vignes m'envoyait,*" My mother sent me to the vines) is the most famous song, and the rest of the numbers have considerable charm, though without the insistent tunefulness of Lecocq at this period. *Maître Péronilla* and *La Marocaine*, both from 1878–79, failed.

Just when all hope had vanished for another Offenbach triumph, the old mas-

---

Alfred Concanen's rendering of a scene from Offenbach's *Madame Favart*, first presented in London in 1879 and an enormous success there at the Strand Theatre.

ter surprised everyone with *La Fille du Tambour-Major*. The Théâtre des Folies-Dramatiques witnessed cheering and bravos at the première, 13 December 1879, almost fifteen years to the day after the brilliant première of *La Belle Hélène*. Few could believe that the gout-ridden composer who had not had a hit in so long could have written so exciting, so thrilling a score, set to an amusing libretto by Chivot and Duru, Lecocq's writers. Instead of Marie from *La Fille du Régiment,* there is Stella de Monthabor, and, as in the Donizetti work, the military songs carry the day. The *chanson du départ* at the close of the operetta was a tremendous thrill, especially for Offenbach, who even at that late stage was still honoring older composers—Méhul in this case, almost totally forgotten by that time, one must add. Simon-Girard made a totally favorable impression as Stella; her partner was M. Simon-Max. At the *souper de la centième* (the supper commemorating the one-hundredth performance) these two regaled the old composer with a medley of his greatest successes. Offenbach could not even remember where some had come from! As he listened to the affectionate tribute that evening at the Hôtel Continental, the thought must have occurred to him that some of his recent music was, if not pedestrian, lacking in any real character. Like most operetta composers, he placed at least part of the blame on the flimsy nature of the libretti he had to set. The fact remains, however, that Offenbach took on too many assignments late in his career, goaded by basic business necessities. Meilhac and Halévy, who wrote his greatest successes, had sought the greener pastures of straight plays, grander operas like Bizet's *Carmen,* and, in Halévy's case, prose. They also had provided the adorable libretto for Lecocq's *Le petit Duc;* Offenbach must have smarted from that. They did not work with him anymore.

In spite of rapidly declining health, Offenbach accepted a commission from the Renaissance, Lecocq's house, no doubt to prove he could still write one success after another, much as Lecocq had been doing in the 1870s. (*Belle Lurette* was produced posthumously, 30 October 1880.) Offenbach's powers and interest were involved with another project, one he held in the very highest esteem: *Les Contes d'Hoffmann* (The Tales of Hoffmann). A drama by Barbier and Carré (authors of *Faust*'s libretto for Gounod) based on several tales by E. T. A. Hoffmann and produced at the Odéon in 1851 apparently made an impression on the young Offenbach, who conducted the orchestra. Beginning in 1878, Offenbach worked furiously on *Hoffmann.* "I have . . . a terrible, invincible vice, that is always to work," he claimed, and spent more time revising numbers from *Hoffmann* than he had given to the entire composition and orchestration of many of his three-act operettas.

Offenbach held an "audition" of his new *opéra-comique* for various impresarios and friends at one of his famous Friday evening musicales. Perhaps as much out of respect to a dying titan as out of genuine admiration for the new piece, the directors of the Opéra-Comique and the Ringtheater (Vienna) took options on it. Offenbach never quite finished the piano version, but he did leave notes for much of the orchestration at the time of his death, 3 October 1880. Offenbach's gout had racked his entire body; his lungs, then his heart gave way. There is an affectionate anecdote told of how Léonce, the original Pluton in *Orphée aux Enfers,* came to call on the composer the following morning, only to be told that Offenbach had passed away in his sleep. "How surprised he will be when he wakes up" was the actor's reply.

Les Contes d'Hoffmann was produced at the Opéra-Comique on 10 February 1881 in a version that differed greatly from the composer's wishes, with orchestrations by Ernest Guiraud. A Viennese production followed in December, but on the second night the Ringtheater caught fire in one of the nineteenth century's tragic theatre disasters. The reception in Paris was initially favorable, although it took some time for the work to gain its present worldwide popularity. *Les Contes d'Hoffmann* is generally produced nowadays as a straightforward grand opera, the spoken dialogue of the original *opéra-comique* version having been musicalized into recitative form. In spite of the heavier story and its correspondingly weightier treatment, several songs might have come out of Offenbach's operettas. Most of the items in the Olympia finale, including the celebrated doll-song, *"Les oiseaux dans la charmille,"* and the waltz-plus-galop end, the drinking song from the Venetian scene, and the *couplets ("Jour et nuit je me mets en quatre")* from the Antonia episode are a few examples. However, their treatment in *Hoffmann* is admittedly more operatic, both vocally and orchestrally, and the extended scenes of dramatic singing are like little that previously came from Offenbach's pen. Forecasts of this weightier style were, however, indicated in previous *opéra-comique* works like *Robinson Crusoé.*

This is not to say that Offenbach's sole career goal was to write a grand opera. Although he labored long on the score during the last years of his life, during a painful period of severe gout, he quickly put aside *Hoffmann* for another operetta, *Belle Lurette,* when that commission was received. In recent years, the reconstructed Fritz Oeser edition of *Hoffmann* supposedly restores something of the composer and authors' original intentions for their opera, before managements and singers in Paris, Vienna, and elsewhere made the changes that people today have come to expect in performances and recordings. The Oeser edition would have been impossible without the research of musicologist-conductor Antonio de Almeida, who has been a champion of the "original" version. However, in spite of critically acclaimed presentations in Miami and elsewhere, this *Hoffmann* has not yet supplanted the familiar grand-opera edition, probably because leading international opera stars are reluctant to relearn their parts. Thus, performances at the Salzburg Festival in 1981 used a hodgepodge of the old and new editions, while the 1982 Metropolitan Opera production stuck to the standard version, even though it committed itself to the expense of treating New Yorkers to new sets and costumes.

French music critics, usually in a deprecating way, have used the term *"musiquette"* when discussing operetta, often applying it to Offenbach. If one translates this to mean "miniature music" or "little music," one might take it quite literally (in a symphonic sense) and apply it to the small theatre orchestras Offenbach usually employed, as compared to the enormous symphonies used to play the "serious" music of the late nineteenth century. As an orchestrator, quite apart from any innate melodic gifts, Offenbach was a master miniaturist, knowing exactly how to use every instrument to its best advantage. Rather in the way one associates the big bands of the 1930s and '40s with their bandleaders, the Offenbach sound is unmistakably personal and sparkling. For buoyancy, high spirits, and pure *joie de vivre,* Offenbach has few equals. He had the happy faculty of making even the most banal of tunes quite riveting. Fortunately, he was also a remarkably fertile melodist. Naturally, in a great field of over one hundred stage works, there are bound to be some arid, repetitious patches, but, taken separately, many of the hundreds of tunes he wrote will always sound fresh and endearing.

Offenbach was also capable of big effects, in spite of his pit orchestra. The operatic travesties of the 1850s (particularly sections of *Orphée aux Enfers*) sound tremendously grand and glorious, and the later *opéras-comiques* (culminating in *Les Contes d'Hoffmann*) have a heavier weight than the *bouffes.* But these very *bouffes* are the greatest examples of the art of Offenbach, showing how music can be funny in itself, besides being entrancingly melodic and cleverly orchestrated. Most of his works still performed today have libretti by Meilhac and Halévy, and to them must go half the credit for keeping Offenbach in the repertoire. They were fundamentally responsible for the idea that operetta could be satirical, that it could be funny and intelligent at the same time, or even *silly* and intelligent. Offenbach's and Meilhac's and Halévy's operettas were not cheapened or watered-down *opéras-comiques,* catering to the masses. Nor were they purely extravagant burlesques. They were instead *opéras-bouffes,* with witty lyrics and dialogue, unusual plots, and an *esprit* which resulted from the artful combination of high-spirited words and music. The "Mozart of the Champs-Élysées" was divine, glorious, inspired, but never stuffy, high-minded, or pedantic. That he was beloved by the theatregoing public of his day is a testament to his "popular" and rarely condescending nature. His place was not in the Conservatoire, it was in the boulevard theatre, and he was so essentially devoid of "seriousness" that one cannot help but find his work amusing and likable. That he was also a composer of genius has only tightened his hold on a gratefully smiling posterity.

POST-1870 PARIS

T HE FRANCO-Prussian War (1870) did not immediately change the taste of Parisians for certain kinds of operetta, but it was a decisive blow against *opéra-bouffe*. Before the war, Second Empire frivolity sanctioned entertainments that were lighthearted, silly, boisterous, licentious (certainly by British standards), and satirical, with the accent clearly on gaiety. The pettiness of the court and government of Napoléon III and the specter of Bismarck had already been alluded to in two *offenbachiades: La Périchole* and *La Grande-Duchesse de Gérolstein,* and by the late 1860s there were critics already condemning the satire in the libretti, possibly because these situations were simply becoming too serious to satirize.

The war and the Commune confirmed how serious they were, and quite abruptly ended not only the reign of Napoléon (who fled to England) but also the frivolity connected with his reign, at least for several months. By the autumn of 1871, theatrical activity began to flourish again. At first, Parisians wanted the same fare they had had during the Empire: folly, gaiety, the lightest operettas. *Les Brigands,* even though it had forecast the sound of military boots approaching, was enthusiastically reprised at the Variétés; the Bouffes-Parisiens remounted *Les Bavards* and *La Princesse de Trébizonde,* also by Offenbach. *Le Roi Carotte* was a spectacular hit for Offenbach at the Gaîté in January 1872. Hervé's *Le Trône d'Écosse* next appeared at the Variétés. But all of the 1871–72 operettas were swept aside by the triumph of Charles Lecocq's *La Fille de Madame Angot* at the end of 1872, in Brussels. When it arrived in Paris in 1873, Lecocq effectively replaced Offenbach as the emperor of operetta.

The operettas of the Third Republic became more differentiated than the ever-popular *opéras-bouffes* of the previous decades. With composers like Planquette, romance, preferably of the sentimental, costumed kind, became entirely more popular than the satire that had previously reigned in Offenbach's heyday. Comedy was not—needless to say—banished, so that by the 1880s the *vaude-*

ville-opérette had achieved a position of strength as a vehicle for established stars and exceptionally lightweight scores. And the exotic spectacle of the first operettas was aggrandized in the 1870s into the bloated *féeries* that became forerunners of the *opérettes à grand spectacle,* works which seem to please modern French audiences more than the classic operettas of the last century—a sad predicament. Since the 1870s, wit and satire have had a difficult time with increasingly bourgeois and petit-bourgeois audiences that prefer sighing over a good love story, preferably decked out in lavish costumes, to laughing at the vices of the current government. The riotous, rapid-fire buffoonery was softened into a less raucous, more refined gaiety. Lecocq, Planquette, their librettists and their followers tailored their operettas to the tastes of this new era.

Alexandre-**Charles Lecocq** (1832–1918) was born in Paris to unprosperous parents whose financial condition barred an operation for their crippled son. Always on crutches, the boy possibly compensated emotionally for his visible affliction by studying theory and composition assiduously, without making too many close friendships at school or later in his professional life. While he was at the Conservatoire under Auber in 1849, with fellow students Georges Bizet and Camille Saint-Saëns (the latter one of his few friends), his work was disliked by his composition teacher Fromental Halévy. Needing funds, he gave piano lessons from the age of sixteen; he also played piano at several of the public *bals.*

In 1856, Lecocq shared with Bizet the grand prize in Offenbach's operetta competition at the Bouffes-Parisiens. Each of the entering composers were given a libretto by Ludovic Halévy and Léon Battu entitled *Le Docteur Miracle.* The jury was composed of, among others, Thomas, Auber, Halévy, Gounod, Massé, and Scribe, and their two choices reflected the judges' background in *opéra-comique,* as well as their admiration for the comic works of Rossini.

Bizet's work was probably more Rossinian. Lecocq, although he admitted to having written in the *"genre italien,"* did call his work an *opéra-bouffe,* and it probably seemed a more modern score. The joint prize pleased no one, least of all the composers themselves. Bizet's operetta was to have been given the first hearing, but Lecocq objected so violently that lots had to be drawn. Lecocq won on this round, and his version was heard 8 April 1857. Bizet's came the next evening—hardly an ideal arrangement. In the end, Lecocq's work is forgotten while Bizet's continues to be broadcast and recorded, and occasionally performed, as at the Spoleto Festival, Charleston, South Carolina, in 1980. Lecocq had his score printed while Bizet's remained unpublished until the present century.

Equally forgotten are roughly a dozen short works such as *Huis Clos* (No Exit, 1859), *Liline et Valentin* (1864), and *Le Myosotis* (1866), easily the most charming and the most assured of these early efforts. It had the comedian Brasseur as Schnitzberg, a cellist who "played" his main solo on a mouth organ concealed in the instrument. The two-act *L'Amour et son carquois* (Cupid's Quiver,

1868) was longer, but not any better received. Lecocq's first true success was the three-act *Fleur-de-Thé* (Tea Flower, Athénée, 11 April 1868). The choristers walked out after the dress rehearsal because they hadn't been paid, but the Athénée's manager William Busnach managed to scrape some money together to get them back. A heat wave didn't stop the crowds coming to see the new three-act *chinoiserie* by Henri Chivot and Alfred Duru. Lecocq was not fond of being compared to Offenbach; he and Offenbach had not been friendly since *Docteur Miracle* and he carefully tried to avoid the familiar rhythms and *alsaciens* which had characterized Offenbach's one-acters. The two clowns Désiré and Léonce were applauded nightly as the Tien-Tien and Kaolin, and their echo duet, *"Je vois tout—Il voit tout!"* was a sensation. The bald-headed Désiré also entertained with *"Je suis clairvoyant comme un sphinx."*

The plot of *Fleur-de-Thé* concerned a cook, sailing on a French boat, forced by Chinese law to marry a mandarin's daughter, and later rescued by his French wife who staves off the Chinese troops by making them drunk on champagne. As *The Pearl of Pekin, Fleur-de-Thé* was seen in New York in 1871 and in 1888, the latter version with additional songs by Gustave Kerker. Richard D'Oyly Carte also produced *Fleur-de-Thé* at the Criterion Theatre in London with Emily Soldene (1876).

Other one-acters followed at the better theatres until the 1870 war, when operetta production in Paris ceased for several weeks. The manager of the Brussels Fantaisies-Parisiennes, Humbert, who had successfully put on *Fleur-de-Thé*, commissioned a new full-length work with a libretto by Lecocq's by-now regular librettists Chivot and Duru, plus Jules Clairville, a well-known *vaudeville* writer. The plot merrily concerned a group of one hundred Englishmen who requisition the Admiralty to send a hundred virgins to aid in populating a tropical island. But the boat gets lost . . . the delightful complications of *Les Cent Vierges* would take up too much room here. The songs were what mattered, particularly a *valse chantée* in the second act which would set a precedent for Lecocq. There was also an "omelette" quartet (there had been an omelette song in *Le Docteur Miracle*) and several engaging choruses and *couplets*. The Brussels première (16 March 1872) was followed by a hit production at the Variétés two months later with some of the original cast.

Marie Aimée, who had given New York its first taste of Lecocq with *Fleur-de-Thé*, was seen in 1871 in *Les Cent Vierges,* one of several Lecocq operettas with the star to follow (in French) in New York well into the 1880s. An English adaptation of *Les Cent Vierges* was given at the Gaiety, London (14 September 1874) as *The Island of Bachelors*—the original title was too scandalous for Anglo-Saxon ears. Nevertheless, it was presented as a burlesque in the true, slightly off-color, Gaiety tradition and it served as a good vehicle for the beloved Nellie Farren.

Brussels and Paris were ready for the next Lecocq, which turned out to be his masterpiece: *La Fille de Madame Angot*. The librettists this time were Clairville, Siraudin, and Koning. The original Brussels idea was to do an *opéra-bouffe* of

Romeo and Juliet, but this was abandoned along with several other plans in favor of an operetta to take place during the time of the Directoire (1795–99). There had been many plays set in this colorful period (a costumier's dream) but no operettas. The authors then hit on the idea of making the central character the daughter of Madame Angot, making their play a "sequel" to the many plays since the eighteenth century which had dealt with this popular folklore character.

Madame Angot was the fishwife who suddenly acquired a fortune but not the manners to go with it. Her coarse ways, earthy language, and fists-on-the-hips stance, depicted amid upper-class surroundings, were always good for a laugh. The librettists made her daughter, Clairette, a much sweeter girl, but still one who knew (by the third act) she had to be a forceful character: *"De la mère Angot, j'suis la fille, j'suis la fille!"* (I am the daughter of Mother Angot!) she sings exultantly.

But Angot's daughter was not enough. Other actual Directoire figures were woven into Clairette's adventures: Ange Pitou, a *chansonnier* of dissident royalist songs, and Mlle. Lange, a glamorous star of the Comédie-Française who found herself in prison as often as Pitou, but who was released and sustained by several wealthy lovers, including the Directoire minister Barras. Thus, when Clairette sings at the close of Act I: *"Barras est roi, et Lange est sa reine. . . ."* (Barras is king, and Lange his queen), this tuneful act of sedition gets her arrested—which is just what she wants, to save herself from having to marry the weak hairdresser, Pomponnet.

The librettists cleverly mixed up these characters and added a women's chorus of *merveilleuses* and a men's of conspirators and hussars of Augereau—each group with its distinctive dress and pose. It is doubtful anyone in the 1874 audience could remember the 1798 period, but the costumes caused much the same *coup de théâtre* as the 1912 costumes did with *My Fair Lady* audiences nearly a century later. It was a gorgeous, elegant show, and easily the most spectacularly tuneful and beautiful score since the heyday of Offenbach. The political nature of the first two acts evaporates in the third, when Clairette enigmatically returns to Pomponnet. We are left wondering whether this conventional operetta-finale marriage would last for the daughter of the unconventional Madame Angot.

The overture is one of the best ever written for a French operetta. There follows a succession of tremendously effective numbers: the opening ensemble in Les Halles, Pomponnet's excited *couplets* anticipating his forthcoming marriage, the fabulous legend of Madame Angot *("Marchande de marée"),* Pitou's *"Certainement, j'aimais Clairette"* (Certainly I've loved Clairette), one of the most attractive French baritone entrances, sensuous, ironic, and forceful all at once,

---

Two vignettes from the second act of Lecocq's *La Fille de Madame Angot* (Brussels, Fantaisies-Parisiennes, 1872), from an edition of the libretto illustrated by P. Hadol. At right, the cavorting conspirators; at left, the actress Mlle. Lange and Clairette (still in her wedding dress) reminisce laughingly of their childhood together.

the *"chanson politique,"* written by Pitou but sung by Clairette, as instantly memorable as such a song would have been in 1798 to catch on.

The second act is highlighted (as in *Les Cent Vierges*) by a sung waltz, *"Tournez, tournez."* Mlle. Lange is forced to disguise a royalist conspirators' meeting in her house as a wedding ball for Clairette so that a battalion of hussars will not arrest them all. The hussars are heard offstage, and as they approach the waltzing is already in progress. Various secret confidences are exchanged as the couples waltz around the room; the dancing stops as each person sings. It is one of the most exultant of all operetta finales. The waltz is, however, only a climax to an impressive array of Act II solos, duets, and ensembles. Mlle. Lange and the *merveilleuses* sing of the conquests of the manly *soldats d'Augereau* and naughtily stress the word *"hommes"*; they know that *les femmes* have the ultimate conquests in their boudoirs. Pomponnet defends Clairette's "real innocence" in a sweet romance; Clairette and Lange laughingly reminisce of happy childhood days together, complete with a radiant laughing refrain. And Lange and Pitou have a "political" duet which, again, has more to do with sexual attraction than anything else. Most startling of all is the conspirators' chorus at the beginning of the finale:

> *Quand on conspire,*
> *Quand, sans frayeur,*
> *On peut se dire*
> *Conspirateur.*

(When one conspires, without fear, one can call oneself a conspirator.) They tiptoe in with their distinctive high black collars, blond wigs, and crooked sticks—

the royalist plotters, the *incroyables*—to a halting, whispering chorus that caused an immediate sensation.

The third act is a typically weaker third sister to the other two, but one can't complain when the first two have been so entrancing.

Lecocq was a first-class melodist. It is no wonder that sheet-music sales of dance arrangements from this and his other operettas enjoyed such a huge vogue. The essential dance-ability of his tunes (based, obviously enough, on dance rhythms) was no deterrent to their being sung, and they had a rhythmic vigor lacking in so many dreary tunes then being churned out.

The Brussels opening night (4 December 1872, Fantaisies-Parisiennes) was a "heroic" success, as one critic reported—each succeeding song was more popular than the last. The glittering costumes by Grévin created a *"tableau vivant du Directoire,"* as historian Louis Schneider aptly stated. The Folies-Dramatiques, Paris, which had at first rejected the piece, embraced it enthusiastically when its success in Brussels was assured, and imported Mlle. Desclauzas to recreate her Brussels Lange (21 February 1873). Paola Marié was the acclaimed Paris Clairette. The gallantry of the Augereau hussars averted a serious disaster in the second act when they quickly put out a little conflagration—the drapes in Mlle. Lange's ballroom were too close to some candles. The public didn't even notice—they were enraptured by that waltz. Every number had to be repeated at the première, and the performance was in fact repeated 411 times in Paris, a record run.

Librettist Koning shrewdly bought the provincial rights the next morning, beating the Folies-Dramatiques manager Cantin and causing that gentleman no end of ill feelings. Cantin gave increasingly meager suppers for the 100th, 200th, and 300th performance celebrations, but was thoughtful enough to give his star, Paola Marié, two Corot canvases at the first of those suppers. (Generous only in retrospect; the pictures were worth far less then.)

Koning, meanwhile, was making a fortune. Within a year *La Fille de Madame Angot* had played in over a hundred French cities. Lecocq's masterpiece was gay, gorgeous, sentimental, full of hummable tunes, masterfully orchestrated. Yet it was called an *opéra-comique,* and that was precisely what its pretensions were, to avoid the silliness, satire, and buffoonery that had marked the *bouffes* of Offenbach and Hervé. Comic characters there were, to be sure, but the focus was as much on the love story as on the foolery, and the dramatic tension was not caused by a series of crazy characters. It was more in the *Périchole* than in the *Grande-Duchesse* mold; the public wanted costumed escape, but it preferred real romance to mocking satire.

The royalist vs. republican issue may indeed have had a satirical thrust in 1873 France, so soon after the fall of the Second Empire. Yet in spite of its exceedingly French theme, *Angot* was popular in many European monarchies. *Angot, die Tochter der Halle* ravished Vienna (Carltheater, 3 January 1874) and Berlin saw it the same year. It was performed in London, in French, at the St. James's in the May following the February Paris première, and by the fall in English (Philharmonic, Islington, 4 October 1873).

Italy admired it tremendously; it even sent a children's company to London (Criterion, 1878). A major Paris revival in 1888 at the Eden Theatre teamed up operetta superstars Anna Judic as Lange and Jeanne Granier as Clairette. In 1918, as a Victory operetta, it entered the répertoire of the Opéra-Comique; a not-too-surprising distinction as the authors had originally called it an *opéra-comique*. It has been given in New York since its première there in 1873 (Broadway, 25 August) but not lately. At the New Theatre, the Metropolitan Opera Company performed *Angot* with Frances Alda as Clairette (1909), and in 1925 the Nemi-rovich-Danchenko company gave it in Russian at Jolson's Theatre. A centenary revival in Brussels (1974) failed to give off any sparks.

By January 1873, the Brussels Fantaisies-Parisiennes had already commissioned another Lecocq, this time with a libretto by Leterrier and Vanloo that concerned female twins mistaken for each other on their wedding morning in a Spanish Africa complete with Arab and pirate bands. Realizing he had to do something novel to avoid comparisons with *Angot,* Lecocq tried to make the new operetta, *Giroflé-Girofla* (Fantaisies-Parisiennes, 21 March 1874) more like Italian *opera buffa.* Looking back in 1890, Lecocq remembered writing the score with "great pleasure and great ease," and his satisfaction and happiness shone out in every page. For this was a frank, sudden return to pure nonsense. And it worked admirably well, with a combination of zaniness and tenderness that proved attractive to Parisians. Lecocq's fertile invention, particularly in the ensembles (a sextet in Act I, a quintet in Act II), was formidable.

W. S. Gilbert may very well have been attracted to *Giroflé-Girofla:* a pair of twins mistaken for each other, an ironic pirates' chorus, and the character Don Boléro d'Alcarazas may very well have influenced his future libretti.

The Brussels success was repeated in Paris (Renaissance, 12 November 1874) and a new star was born—Jeanne Granier. Not entirely unknown—she had replaced Louise Théo in *La jolie Parfumeuse* for Offenbach—she created a larger sensation this time as she had *two* roles instead of one. She would become to Lecocq what Schneider had been to Offenbach, what Judic would be to Hervé, *créatrice* and star. *Giroflé-Girofla* enjoyed engagements in most of the world's capitals: London (Philharmonic, Islington, 3 October 1874) and New York (Lyceum, 4 February 1875) and even its "native" Spain, in 1875. A major Paris revival occurred in 1903 (Gaîté) but since then *Giroflé-Girofla* has enjoyed more pronounced success in Germany and in Russia. A vaguely constructivist production, with designs by Grigori Yakoulov, was presented by the Moscow Art Theatre's musical wing in 1922.

Two nights after the Paris première of *Giroflé-Girofla* came *Les Prés Saint-Gervais* at the Variétés. This had a libretto by Victorien Sardou (with Philippe Gille) based on a play he had written years before. The libretto was a bit too serious for the Variétés, where it did not fare well (49 performances); a bit livened up for London it did a little better (Criterion, 28 November 1874). Lecocq's own score annotations (1916) complained that the third act was "impossible," and that it needed a greater comédienne to play the travesty role of

LA GIROFLE GIROFLA

VALSE,

ON LECOCQ'S POPULAR OPERA BOUFFE,

BY

CHARLES COOTE.

Alfred Concanen lith.

A. Concanen del et lith.

Ent. Sta. Hall.

LONDON,
ENOCH & SONS, 19, HOLLES St. CAVENDISH SQre W.
Stannard & Son, Lith.

SOLO ... 4/
DUET. ... 4/
FULL ORCHESTRA 1/4 NET
SEPTETT. ... 1/ NET

the Prince de Conti than it had originally (Mme. Peschard). *Le Pompon* (Folies-Dramatiques, 10 November 1875) lasted a mere fourteen performances, but Lecocq had presold his score to his publisher for a tidy fee.

Lecocq had become as prolific as Offenbach in his heyday: a month after *Le Pompon* came *La petite Mariée* (The Little Bride; Renaissance, 21 December 1875) with Jeanne Granier in a sort of Italian remodeling of *Giroflé-Girofla*. This, too, was successfully presented in London and New York. A decade before Gilbert and Sullivan's *The Mikado* came *Kosiki* (Renaissance, 18 October 1876), a Japanese operetta by Busnach and Liorat, with Zulma Bouffar in the travesty title role of the son of the Mikado—a pre-Nanki-Poo of sorts! *Kosiki,* in spite of its fantastic locale, was more of an *opéra-comique* musically, with less comic embroidery than usual for Lecocq. Perhaps a little more comedy would have elongated its month-and-a-half run.

La Marjolaine (Renaissance, 3 February 1877) was more of a success, with Bouffar in a Flemish plot. But not nearly so much as the next Lecocq work, *Le petit Duc* (Renaissance, 25 January 1878), which is, by general consensus, the composer's second greatest effort. The little Duke of Parthenay (played *en travesti* by Jeanne Granier) is discovered at the court of Louis XIV at Versailles at the beginning of the eighteenth century, where he has just married his little duchess (he is eighteen, she is younger). However, by order of the king, the duke must be trained and the duchess sequestered in a convent for some time before they can consummate their union. This permitted Granier, as the duke, to disguise her-himself as a young maid in order to enter the convent. A flimsy plot, yes, but abounding in strong scenes and charming lyrics, written by the twin *doyens* of the operetta libretto: Meilhac and Halévy. Their first effort for Lecocq was a triumph, and left no doubt that the composer had succeeded Offenbach, as Lecocq now had Offenbach's writers in his camp. *Le petit Duc* also had the fortune of coinciding with the Paris Exposition of 1878; it was *the* show to see just as *La Grande-Duchesse de Gérolstein* had been a decade before.

Le petit Duc clearly foreshadows Messager—a slight story depending as much or more on charm than on satire or humor. Both composers were fond of little strokes of pastiche; Lecocq had just prepared and published the first piano-vocal score of Rameau's *Castor et Pollux*. There are gavottes and other eighteenth-century touches, including several almost Mozartian accompaniments, and a *solfège,* or singing-lesson song, in Act II which has always been popular in France. But the best numbers are the most exultant: the sincerely beautiful female duet, *"C'est pourtant bien doux,"* which starts formally with *"je vous aime"* (I love you) and ends gloriously with the familiar *"je t'aime."* Modern performances ruin the effect by making the duke a man; it loses a theatrical and harmonic piquancy. Other applauded numbers were the pages' chorus, *"Il a l'oreille basse,"* the march-rondo, *Pas de femmes!,* and, very happily, the marvelous extended finales to Acts I and II.

Lecocq's *Giroflé-Girofla:* an impression of the London production (Philharmonic, Islington, 1874) by the outstanding English music-cover artist, Alfred Concanen.

Focusing on the *travesti* swagger of the little duke, and brimming with the combination of military and convent that was later to characterize two other hits, *Les Mousquetaires au Couvent* (1880) and *Mam'zelle Nitouche* (1883), *Le petit Duc* was hard-put to fail, especially considering its cast. Granier was an irresistible duke, the part of the duchess was played by Mily-Meyer, and others in the superb original cast included Desclauzas as the Mother Superior and the comedians Berthelier, Urbain, and Vauthier. Curiously, *The Little Duke* was not quite as popular in London or New York as it had been in Paris. Perhaps the score was too French—too elegant, too mannered for Anglo-Saxon tastes. *Der kleine Herzog* appeared at the Vienna Carltheater in 1878, and rapidly everywhere else. The rage for Parisian operetta was still feverish before the ascendancy of the Viennese and Londonian varieties.

At the luncheon for the hundredth performance given for the cast at the Pavillon Henri IV at Saint-Germain, a young dragoon approached Granier with a gorgeous bouquet "from the colonel and regiment officers of dragoons of the garrison at Saint-Germain, to the Colonel Duke of Parthenay." Granier, delighted by the surprise, kissed the young officer on both cheeks.

After 301 performances of *Le petit Duc,* the Renaissance had a new Lecocq: *La Camargo* (20 November 1878). Based on the exploits of a famous eighteenth-century dancer (La Camargo) and the celebrated thief Mandrin, the new operetta had lovely parts for Zulma Bouffar as the dancer and the rest of the Renaissance company, beautifully costumed and set by the director Koning.

Le grand Casimir (Variétés, 11 January 1879), *La petite Mademoiselle* (Renaissance, 12 April 1879), *La jolie Persane* (Renaissance, 28 October 1879), and *Janot* (Renaissance, 21 January 1881) were not big hits, even though the second and last had Meilhac and Halévy libretti. *Le Jour et la Nuit* (Day and Night, Nouveautés, 5 November 1881) marked the first important role for a new operetta star, Marguerite Ugalde, as Manola. Opposite her was the old comic favorite, Berthelier. Returning to the silliness of *Giroflé-Girofla* and *La petite Mariée,* librettists Leterrier and Vanloo provided Lecocq with another Mediterranean-set hit. Written and rehearsed in two months, *Le Jour et la Nuit* so taxed Lecocq's health that he was unable to conduct the first night, but the operetta enjoyed a great success; by the hundredth performance it had earned more than 432,000 francs. As *Manola,* it played in the United States; in Vienna, it was *Tag und Nacht.* As the Paris production ran almost two hundred times at the Nouveautés, a follow-up was ordered: *Le Coeur et la Main* (Heart and Hand, Nouveautés, 19 October 1882)—again set in Iberia, this time with a libretto by Nuitter and Beaumont. It seemed like a copy of *Le Jour et la Nuit,* and it shared similar defects: a weak third act, a tendency to bawdiness that had not disfigured *La Fille de Madame Angot* or *Le petit Duc,* and not quite the melodic sparkle of his earlier works. Perhaps the sameness of the libretti failed to offer sufficient challenge. *Le Coeur et la Main* appeared in England as *Incognita.*

Jeanne Granier strikes a victorious pose in one of her greatest triumphs, the *travesti* title role in Lecocq's *Le petit Duc* (Renaissance, 1878).

The presentation of *La Princesse des Canaries* (Folies-Dramatiques, 9 February 1883) began a downhill slide, as far as survival was concerned. Two works were done at the Opéra-Comique, *Plutus* (1886) and *Le Cygne* (a ballet, 1899), the rest at the popular operetta theatres. Lecocq died in 1918, leaving some unproduced works, and he just missed hearing Reynaldo Hahn conduct the Armistice revival of *La Fille de Madame Angot,* his undisputed masterwork, at the Opéra-Comique.

Lecocq's three big international hits, *La Fille de Madame Angot, Giroflé-Girofla,* and *Le petit Duc* still hold the stage, or deserve to. New versions in foreign languages may be needed, but the music is unwaveringly potent. Many critics maintain that Lecocq was a better harmonist than Offenbach and a more refined orchestrator, although the startling immediacy of Offenbach's tunes was something Lecocq did not always achieve. In each of Lecocq's other pieces are at least a few numbers deserving of appraisal. In English-speaking countries, Lecocq is solely remembered as the source of the ballet *Mam'zelle Angot,* first presented by the (American) Ballet Theatre in 1943 and produced by the Sadler's Wells Ballet in 1947 and the Australian Ballet in 1971. Should producers want to look beyond Offenbach in the next few years, they need only take one step to discover his heir apparent.

Robert Planquette (1848–1903) will always be remembered for one work—
Les Cloches de Corneville—which in aggregate number of performances worldwide may well be the most popular French operetta ever written. There was
usually a new Planquette operetta performed every season from 1878 to 1897,
and some were substantial hits. Only *Les Cloches de Corneville* and *Rip* survived
the turn of the century. Planquette had a distinct gift for rhythmic variety and
the pulsations which keep songs alive but was less well equipped in the department of melody and admittedly deficient in the instrumental/harmony area (some
sections of his scores were "sent out" for orchestration). However, to some,
the composer of *"J'ai fait trois fois le tour du monde"* and *"Va, petit mousse"* (both
from *Les Cloches*) could not and still cannot be faulted. Contemporary popularity and sheer endurance speak well for at least this principal work.

A Parisian, born into a family of Norman origins in 1848, Planquette attended the Conservatoire, where he excelled at the piano but was not particu-

larly proficient in harmonic studies. He was reputed to have had a beautiful tenor voice, used to good effect when performing his own songs. One of these, the 1867 march of the "Sambre et Meuse" regiment, was picked up by the young Lucien Fugère at the Ba-ta-clan, who turned it into a spectacular national success. (Jeanette MacDonald sings it to the Emperor Napoléon III in the 1937 film *Maytime*.) Planquette excelled at marches throughout his career—several can be found in his operettas. A few short works made their appearance in the 1870s, with intriguing titles like *Méfie-toi de Pharaon* (Beware of Pharaoh). In 1876, he presented his credentials to the Folies-Dramatiques, which gave him a libretto first refused by Hervé because there were not enough puns in it.

The opening of *Les Cloches de Corneville* (The Bells of Corneville, known in English as *The Chimes of Normandy*, Folies-Dramatiques, 19 April 1877) was well-applauded by the public, though there were also detractors who thought the libretto by Clairville (of *La Fille de Madame Angot* fame) and Charles Gabet too reminiscent of *Martha* and *La Dame Blanche*. Whether or not this is true, the plot has proved itself popular over the years with producing groups and audiences. Yet this throwback to the past was dangerous, for it was this type of cliché-ridden, sentimental *opéra-comique* that Offenbach and Hervé had tried to kill off by inventing the modern operetta. Planquette and his librettists had decisively tipped the scales in favor of sentiment and romance. Perhaps tired of the over-elaborate Offenbach spectacles at other theatres, the 1877 public readily warmed to a romantic story about a set of Norman bells that would ring when the Marquis Henri de Corneville, the rightful owner of a château, returned to his home.

Planquette's score is rarely lacking in spirit, the songs have considerable movement to them, and each character has his or her opening song to establish themselves. Serpolette, the country wench, has several ditties which set a rollicking tone, Germaine has sedate, sweet (and rather trite) little arias, and the Marquis a fashionable *valse-rondeau*, the celebrated *"J'ai fait trois fois le tour du monde"* (I've been around the world three times). Several numbers are undeniably irresistible, no matter how musically boring, thanks to their virulently catchy refrains: the *"digue, digue, digue"* of the "title" song, the so-called "legend of the bells," sung by Germaine, and most of the first-act finale, with a weak, obvious counterpoint chorus of servants—one *knows* the counterpoint is coming because the separate parts are so hollow by themselves. Plus Serpolette's overworked *"Voyez ceci, voyez cela"* and *"Vive le cidre de Normandie"* in Act III, a crowd-pleasing drinking song. But these are happily offset by a fair amount of genuinely interesting musical moments: the truly charming barcarolle of Grenicheux, *"Va, petit mousse"* (literally, Go, little cabin boy), the delightful, Bizet-esque quartet in Act II, *"Fermons les yeux,"* an almost Meyerbeerian "ancestors" cho-

---

Planquette's *Les Cloches de Corneville*, always popular in France, was similarly successful in England and America as *The Chimes of Normandy*. In the London presentation (Folly, 1878—sheet-music cover by Alfred Concanen) Shiel Barry played the part of the villain, Gaspard.

rus, and the ensemble in the same act devoted to putting the timid Grenicheux into a suit of armor.

Les Cloches de Corneville's charm, wholly different from the more vital Lecocq and Offenbach pieces then popular, harked back to both the seventeenth century in setting and the early nineteenth in musical and dramatic conventions, yet 1877 audiences adored it, giving it a fabulously lengthy original run of over five hundred performances. And in 1878 it was parodied at the Bouffes du Nord as *"Les Cornes de Clochenville."*

Wherever *Les Cloches* rang, success followed. It astonished Vienna in September 1878 (Theater an der Wien); it dazzled Berlin and was a perennial success in New York. But its greatest triumph was in London. The entrepreneur-librettist H. B. Farnie convinced Alexander Henderson to go into partnership with him to produce Farnie's English edition at the Folly Theatre. Violet Cameron was engaged to play Germaine, and Shiel Barry, an actor who specialized in Irish parts, the miser Gaspard. But before long the producers and the cast lost confidence in the work, especially by the opening night (28 February 1878), when Barry, suffering from a shocking cold, was forced to gasp and crackle his lines. Business the first two weeks, although not bad, did not seem to indicate a long run, but word-of-mouth succeeded in filling the theatre almost every night thereafter for its momentous 705-performance run (including a transfer to the Globe). And Barry was partly to thank; he retained his gasping, raspy voice at each performance. *Les Cloches de Corneville* appealed to all, and its touring career, particularly in France, England, and the United States, was long and profitable, and filled with many stars and stars-to-be.

Quite naturally, various managers sought another Planquette hit of *Cloches* dimensions to fill their theatres and purses. A diverting cast including Mlle. Silly and Brasseur gave *La Cantinière* (The Canteen Girl, Théâtre des Nouveautés, 26 October 1880) a short run. Another military operetta the same year, *Les Voltigeurs de la 32ᵉ* (The Light Infantrymen of the 32nd Regiment), at the Renaissance, was even less successful in Paris, in spite of a fine cast (Jeanne Granier, Mily-Meyer, and Marie Desclauzas), but did tolerably well in London as *The Old Guard* (Avenue, 1887), another Farnie adaptation starring the popular comedian Arthur Roberts. Both of Planquette's 1880 works showed the unmistakable influence (in libretto and in score) of Offenbach's recent *La Fille du Tambour-Major*.

Farnie himself contracted Planquette to provide his next score, for the English stage. This was *Rip van Winkle*, based on Washington Irving, but even more on the Dion Boucicault–Joseph Jefferson stage version which had proven so vastly popular. According to one anecdote, Farnie met the actor Fred Leslie (who did not know the librettist) at a seaside resort on holiday, and, flattering him and managing to excite Leslie with Irving's story of the man who slept for twenty

---

Fred Leslie in the title role of the London production of Planquette's *Rip Van Winkle* (Comedy, 1882), which predated the Paris version.

years (Leslie had apparently never seen the play), roped him into a contract on the spot for £25 a week. The operetta was rehearsed for some eight weeks by Boucicault himself when the general rehearsal time at this period was more like a week. It opened at the Comedy Theatre, 14 October 1882, with Leslie scoring an immense triumph as Rip, outstripping Jefferson's popularity, at least in England. And the supporting cast was equally glittering: Lionel Brough, W. S. Penley (later to triumph in the straight comedy *The Private Secretary*), and Violet Cameron. Leslie, however, thought the £25 salary a dirty trick, and demanded more, which the management refused to provide. The show closed at the height of its furor, and Farnie and Henderson were forced to renegotiate a new contract with Leslie. After a successfully resumed London engagement, Leslie toured to even greater acclaim in the provinces.

Rip, the French version by Meilhac and Gille, appeared two years later at the Folies-Dramatiques (11 November 1884), scoring a bull's-eye, but in a theatre a bit too small for this type of thing—a true operetta *à grand spectacle.* Nevertheless, the streak of *américano-anglomanie* present in late nineteenth-century Paris ensured a healthy first run of over 120 performances. Meilhac and Gille, no doubt familiar with another Irving creation, added the character of "Ischabod" to the plot.

Rip has had several important Paris revivals, all at larger theatres much more suited to it, like the Gaîté, Mogador, and Porte Saint–Martin (1933, with suave André Baugé in a perfect role for his talents). No one, however, has mounted it recently, and the score is primarily to blame. It is sentimental rather than exciting, which is what this score *should* be, given its plot. Yet it is typically Planquette: the overture is pleasant but uninspiring, the opening chorus might well serve for any other operetta (it is not remotely "American" or "English colonial"), and the comic numbers are merely commonplace. One of the great hits of the first act, Rip's first solo, with its refrain *"C'est un rien . . . un souf-fle . . . un rien!"*, does not appear in the original British version. On the other hand, the *"légende des Catskills"* must have been more effective in the London production, calling for a ghostly chorus; in the French, it is only a duet between Rip and Nelly, curiously looking ahead to a 1920s Romberg-type romantic song.

The first-act finale has very little tension. As for the second act, the expectations of a great ghost ensemble are never satisfied: the simpler *choeur des ancêtres* in *Les Cloches de Corneville* has a far more robust and exciting character. Only Sullivan, in the later *Ruddigore* (1887), met the challenge of setting a supernatural scene in operetta with a jaunty, full-blooded vigor. The fabled *chanson de l'écho* is bewitching, with its shepherd's-pipe refrains, but again, sentimental rather than spellbinding. Of course, the ending of the story *is* sentimental, but one has the right to expect an eerier operetta than this. In the original cast were the Odéon tragedien Brémont as Rip, Mily-Meyer as Kate, and Simon-Max as Ischabod. *"Rip-Rip"* played the Theater an der Wien in 1883, and was operatized for the Volksoper in 1909.

Another British operetta to première a Planquette score was *Nell Gwynne* (Avenue, 7 February 1884) with words by Farnie; this was transformed for Paris into *La Princesse Colombine* (Nouveautés, 7 December 1886). The London production fared marginally better, and *Surcouf* (Folies-Dramatiques, 6 October 1887) did better still. *Surcouf* became *Paul Jones* in London. Apart from *Le Talisman* (1893), set in Louis XV's Versailles, and *Mam'zelle Quat'sous* (1897), a military work, none of the composer's other works achieved anywhere near the acclaim or box-office receipts of *Les Cloches* and *Rip,* both revived many times. Among the more notable revivals of *Les Cloches* was the 1940 Châtelet production with André Baugé and the producer-director Henri Varna himself as old Gaspard.

Unlike most of his contemporaries, who were survived by only one great hit, **Edmond Audran** left several, and not only in Paris. Yet, today, his works are seldom performed, in spite of their appealing good spirits and quite professional sheen. The son of an Opéra-Comique tenor, Edmond (1842–1901) attended Paris's École Niedermeyer; Messager was later one of its more famed graduates. The Niedermeyer school was celebrated for its organists, who were graduated to the principal church organs of France. (It was also accused of fostering, in composition, an organish style without any harmonic variety, all the instruments playing more or less the same thing.) In due course, Audran was the organist at a church in Marseille, and, like Hervé before him, he found time to compose little operettas for local stages.

Marseille was the site of his first substantial full-length operetta, *Le grand Mogol* (Gymnase, 24 February 1877). This netted sixty performances and considerable acclaim for both Audran and his leading lady, the lovely Jeanne-Alfrédine Tréfouret, who later took the more manageable appellation of Jane Hading. (Is it possible, in searching for a then very fashionable English stage name, she accidently left out an "r"?) *Le grand Mogol*, an Indian affair set in eighteenth-century Delhi concerning a prince who had to remain pure in order to become the Grand Mogul, was most notable for the "Kiribiribi" song in the first act. Paris did not see the operetta until 1884 (Gaîté, 19 September), the same year London saw an English version, at the Comedy Theatre, with Florence St. John, Fred Leslie, and Arthur Roberts.

Miss Hading went directly into the company of the Palais-Royal; Audran was courted by the Bouffes-Parisiens. Its manager Cantin was sufficiently impressed with *Le grand Mogol* to put on the next Audran-Chivot work, this time written with Chivot's usual collaborator, Duru. It was *Les Noces d'Olivette* (Olivette's Wedding, Bouffes-Parisiens, 13 November 1879). This had a fair run but might be forgotten today were it not for H. B. Farnie's English version, which followed the lengthy engagement of Offenbach's *Madame Favart* at London's (old) Strand Theatre (18 September 1880). *Olivette*, as it was more simply called, ran some 466 performances (in those days a phenomenal engagement), due in part to the stars Violet Cameron and Florence St. John. It was very popular on tour, and in the United States (Bijou, New York, 25 December 1880), well into the present century.

Cantin had the good sense to continue his association with Audran and his librettists. Their next production, *La Mascotte*, was one of the greatest of Bouffes-Parisiens hits (29 December 1880). This had 460 basically consecutive performances through the end of 1882, and by 1885 it had reached its thousandth. The story? In sixteenth-century Italy, a farm girl is supposed to bring good luck to whomever is fortunate enough to possess her, although she must remain a virgin or her powers are lost. When Bettina, the luck-bringing turkey-girl, finally succumbs to her beloved shepherd, Pippo, her gifts are miraculously retained, and all ends well. The characters are so irresistibly bright and the situations so endearingly silly that the piece seldom bores. This lighthearted plot, largely devoid of satire, was furnished with a complementarily *soufflé*-ish score. Audran managed to be as forthrightly rhythmic as he was obviously, ingeniously, melodic—his great virtue. The result was a pure crowd-pleaser, demanding neither intense concentration on the audience's part nor elaborate orchestration on Audran's. The band was reduced and no one seemed to mind.

Similarly, the finales were somewhat shortened, a trait that would become increasingly prevalent during the 1880s. Yet we don't mind if *La Mascotte*'s Act I finale is short and snappy when it ends with a galop worthy of Offenbach: *"En poste! Houp-là!"* The songs in *La Mascotte* provide more of a sense of dramatic aptness than usual, being fully integrated in the plot. Audran's basically Mediterranean sunniness, as opposed to the more intellectual gaiety of Offenbach, shines through his work.

Not that one can't excise some of the songs and perform them singly—many are positive gems. The legend of the *mascotte* (with its soaring waltz refrain) was admired by many baritones, and the song of the orangutan (which admittedly has nothing at all to do with the plot) was a familiar parlor favorite for years. The latter is only slightly less risqué than the first-act *"le . . . je ne sais quoi"* of Fritellini—referring, innocently enough, to that "extra" quality he has that appeals to the ladies. This must have appeared especially saucy to London as well as Paris audiences. Songs and suggestions such as these no doubt gave French operetta that "extra" quality so abhorrent to W. S. Gilbert, to name one puritan out of a vast audience of admirers. Some of *La Mascotte*'s finest moments include the lightweight but fascinating superstition *couplets* of the comic, Prince Lorenzo, with their choral patter repeats, Bettina's entrance song ("Let Me Go!"), and the famous animal duet, complete with yodeled farmyard noises in praise of turkeys and sheep:

> *J'aim' b'en mes dindons!*
> *J'aim' b'en mes moutons!*

The score was instantly admired at the première: many numbers had to be repeated. Morlet, the Opéra-Comique baritone so admired as Brissac in the earlier production of Varney's *Les Mousquetaires au Couvent,* was Pippo, Mlle. Montbazon was an attractive Bettina, and Hittemans was the outrageously superstitious prince. The luck of the mascot herself rubbed off on what has subsequently proved itself Audran's masterwork. The London production, translated by Farnie and Reece, which opened the Comedy Theatre on 15 October 1881, achieved the considerable run of 199 performances—half the success *Olivette* was, but making up for it later as a decided provincial favorite. Violet Cameron again appeared as an Audran heroine, and the comic Lionel Brough was first noticed by Londoners in a major role. The first English-language U.S. performance was in Boston (Gaiety, 11 April 1881) and *The Mascot* was as popular on tour as it was in the metropolitan centers. (It was again seen in New York in 1909 at the Manhattan Opera House and at Jolson's Theatre in 1926.)

Gillette de Narbonne (Bouffes-Parisiens, 11 November 1882), an infectious Mediterranean confection with a cast of Bouffes-Parisiens regulars, couldn't help but succeed, and indeed proved a substantial triumph. Based on a Boccaccio tale and set in the Middle Ages, it was just the sort of regionalism Audran did best. The Provençal song with its refrain *"Digué li qué vengué mon bon"* was particularly applauded. *Les Pommes d'or* and *La Dormeuse éveillée* were not received as well, but the first Paris production of *Le grand Mogol,* amplified for the occasion (Gaîté, 19 September 1884), was on the boards 248 times. *The Grand Mogul,*

An American poster advertising Audran's *La Mascotte* (c. 1881). Library of Congress.

THE MASCOT

A.S.SEER'S PRINT. N.Y. (COPYRIGHTED)

also known as *The Snake Charmer,* had already been seen in New York in 1881, with Britain's Selina Dolaro.

In 1886 followed *La Cigale et la Fourmi* (The Grasshopper and the Ant, Gaîté, 30 October), Chivot and Duru's operetta retelling of La Fontaine's fable. Jeanne Granier, one of operetta's true queens, was cast as the grasshopper. *"Ma mère, j'entends le violon"* was the smash song hit, equally popular in London as "Mother Dear, I Hear the Violin." *La Cigale* (Lyric, 9 October 1890) had an English book by the librettist of *Cox and Box,* F. C. Burnand, with additional lyrics by Gilbert à Beckett and some new music by Ivan Caryll. Geraldine Ulmar, who

had triumphed as Elsie in Gilbert and Sullivan's *The Yeomen of the Guard*, and who was Gianetta in their *Gondoliers*, went right into *La Cigale* when it began its 423-performance engagement at the Lyric. Audran's works in London fairly consistently outran their Parisian counterparts in their original runs. Nor was Audran unknown in Central Europe: *Der Glücksengel (La Mascotte)* was a substantial hit at the Theater an der Wien, as it was in Berlin and Budapest. A Hungarian company played it—*Az üdvöske*—in Vienna. The Carltheater and the Theater an der Wien shared between them *Olivette, Der Grossmogul,* and *Gillette de Narbonne* as well.

The golden days of Audran's career had passed, but he kept up a furious activity right up to his death, composing on the average two scores per season. In 1890 he achieved what was probably his greatest financial success, *Miss Helyett* (Miss Eliot, Bouffes-Parisiens, 12 November). This had a staggering total of 816 Bouffes performances. One regretfully has to credit Maxime Boucheron's naughty book, a romance concerning an American girl, who, having fallen off a cliff in the Pyrénées, is thankfully saved by a branch which catches her dress, turning her upside down and revealing what is underneath. An itinerant artist sketches the sight before rescuing her. On this scanty premise an entire plot was woven, embroidered with a score which Parisians found quite gay and scintillating, and they madly applauded Bianca Duhamel in the title role. Retitled *Miss Decima* (was this really more pronounceable than *Miss Eliot?*) and starring absolutely no one (Criterion, 23 July 1891), F. C. Burnand's English version had some popularity. In New York, a Broadway version (Star, 3 November 1891), with the original title, starred Mrs. Leslie Carter under the direction of David Belasco.

One has to wade through several mediocre works before reaching, six years later, Audran's final opus of any lasting worth: *La Poupée* (The Doll, Gaîté, 21 October 1896). The story of an automaton—popular since works like Adam's one-act *opéra-comique*, *La Poupée de Nuremberg* (1852), the Delibes ballet *Coppélia* (1870), and the Olympia act of Offenbach's *Les Contes d'Hoffmann* (1880)—was given the elaborate production one would expect at the Gaîté. But scenes laid in the time of Louis XV in a monastery, a doll store, and a château could not really overcome an insipid story, or a score that most critics called tasteful but lacking in dynamism. While Paris supported it for 121 showings, London backed a surprising 576 performances (Prince of Wales's, 24 February 1897) with Courtice Pounds (the Savoy favorite) and Willie Edouin, and this during a period when French operetta had been overshadowed by the increasingly popular early musical comedies and such native works as *The Geisha*.

The year 1896 also saw *Monsieur Lohengrin* (Bouffes-Parisiens, 30 November), which had an interesting libretto and a little of the parody-Wagner one might have expected. However, parody and musical burlesque were Offenbachian traits, not Audranian ones. The composer died in 1901, certainly not outmoded in style—his later works were usually right up to date in their boulevard mannerisms. The earlier *Olivette*, *La Mascotte*, and *Gillette de Narbonne* are however the works one would like to see and hear again today.

Louis Varney (1844–1908) could claim some forty or so works to his credit, of which only *Les Mousquetaires au Couvent* (The Musketeers in the Convent) has survived—and this was his very first full-length attempt. His career did not go downhill by any means: he could always be counted upon to provide at least one or two works a season, but none of his other works seized France with quite the fervor of his first try. He was the son of Alphonse Varney, Offenbach's conductor at the Bouffes-Parisiens and later (1862) its director. After the Franco-Prussian War the younger Varney was conducting the orchestra at various Paris theatres, as well as providing short works and songs.

In 1879, Cantin, then director of the Bouffes-Parisiens, asked the younger

---

The notorious scene in Act II of Varney's *Les Mousquetaires au Couvent* (Bouffes-Parisiens, 1880) in which the drunk false-monk Brissac scandalizes a convent with a "sermon" on profane love. There is a somewhat similar scene in Gilbert and Sullivan's *Princess Ida* (1884).

Varney to set music to a libretto by Paul Ferrier and Jules Prével. Based on an 1835 *vaudeville* by Saint-Hilaire and Duport, *L'Habit ne fait pas le moine* (The Habit Does Not Make the Monk), the book bore some resemblance to that of Rossini's *Comte Ory,* but was chiefly distinguished by its Louis XIII–Cardinal Richelieu-era setting, an unusual one for operetta up to that time. Having absolutely nothing to do with Alexandre Dumas (yet), the story told of two musketeers who disguise themselves as Capuchin monks in order to enter a convent and abduct some *pensionnaires.* In the end they are forgiven, as the sleeping monks from whom they borrowed habits are in fact two conspirators who would have assassinated Richelieu.

This hoary plot had proved itself popular already. Ferrier and Prével enlivened it with attractive, newly drawn characters, some amusing dialogue and bright lyrics. Varney apparently gave the work his greatest effort, but he did not quite have time to finish it. The première being imminent, he farmed out several items (including the chattering chorus of *pensionnaires* in Act II and the ebullient Act III "ladder" quintet) to his colleague, the conductor/composer Achille Mansour, to compose.

Cantin cast the work extremely well, with the famed actor Frédéric Achard as Brissac, the more swaggering of the Musketeers, and the tenor Marcelin as his more romantic friend. The comic Hittemans was the Abbé Bridaine and the women were equally well portrayed. Varney's first work was enthusiastically received from the very start (Bouffes-Parisiens, 16 March 1880) and when, after a few weeks, the original Brissac had to appear elsewhere, Varney composed two new songs for his replacement, the Opéra-Comique baritone Morlet: *"Pour faire un brave mousquetaire"* (To make a good musketeer) in Act I, and the second-act drunken *ariette,* *"Ah, quel déjeuner j'ai fait!"* (What a lunch I've had!). These proved even more sensational than anything yet heard in the score. *Les Mousquetaires* was easily the biggest operetta hit in France since *Les Cloches de Corneville,* and Varney was besieged for new works.

Thanks to Planquette and his librettists, satire and topicality were now out of favor, and in their place was the provincial folktale or semihistorical anecdote, replete with legend songs, country dances, and the sentimental love songs which would tip the scales as the 1890s neared, whether in Paris or London, New York or Vienna. High spirits would remain, and in *Les Mousquetaires au Couvent* Varney supplied them abundantly. His melodies and rhythms were infectious, particularly in the entrance songs of Bridaine, Brissac, and Marie, and in the charming (if slightly underdeveloped) ensembles, like the ebullient male trio *("Une femme, une femme!")* in the first act and the Latin-flecked chorale during the finale involving the false monks. Also pleasant are Simonne's robust *"Zon, zon, zon"* and her rapid-fire anthem in praise of the wine of Vouvray, both in the first act. *Les Mousquetaires* remains one of the most popular of the *petit-bourgeois* operettas, until recently a staple in the provinces and occasionally the subject of a Parisian revival.

Les Mousquetaires opened at the old Globe Theatre, London (31 October 1880)— "the music's by Varney, the words are by Farnie"—to mixed notices. *Punch* thought the book not only dull, but vulgar, with a "commonplace and ineffective" series of songs. Thanks to thin walls, the *Musketeers* company could no doubt hear the original *Pirates of Penzance* cast playing the adjacent Opera Comique to considerably more acclaim. After the *Pinafore* mania began, anything English was bound to be more appreciated, especially in the United States. In spite of Farnie's English libretto, it did not achieve anywhere near the success of his *Les Cloches de Corneville* in English.

The Bouffes-Parisiens had the pleasure of producing Varney's second major work, *Coquelicot* (2 March 1882), again based on an old *vaudeville,* but what had triumphed before failed this time. The Folies-Dramatiques got the next opus, *Fanfan la Tulipe* (21 October 1882), which fared better—a military spectacle complete with the battle of Fontenoy. It also had some engaging mock-popular songs in the correct period style. (The 1952 French film with Gérard Philipe dealt with the same character.) An expected operetta appeared in 1885: a musical version of the popular dramatization of Dumas's *The Three Musketeers* (which the author had written with Auguste Macquet in 1845). This was *Les petits Mousquetaires* (5 March, Folies-Dramatiques), libretto by Ferrier and Prével, and there was nothing little about its success—149 performances, attributable not only to the familiar exploits of Athos, Porthos, and Aramis and to Varney's carefree tunes, but also to a gorgeous cast, including Marguerite Ugalde, *en travesti* as D'Artagnan, Mlle. Desclauzas, and Simon-Max. It was the first of several popular operettas based on this durable classic, and one, by virtue of its story, that might stand a modern producer's inspection.

Varney's subsequent works may have been set in interesting locales—*Dix Jours aux Pyrénées* (Ten Days in the Pyrénées, 1888)—or may have had interesting characters—*Le Chien du Régiment* (The Dog of the Regiment, 1902)—but none were as successful as his first great hit. By the turn of the century he was correctly describing his works as *vaudevilles-opérettes* to account for the lack of formal Offenbach-Lecocq conventions. There was a distinct leaning toward the military in much of his work, and also a weak-willed tendency to write revue or *café-concert*-like *couplets* to stick into the bland libretti he had to set. But then, the plots and lyrics got no more than they deserved. Varney may not have had a distinguished career, but he wrote right up to his last years and did manage to be at least diverting, if not original.

Among other French composers *not* remembered today for their operettas are Delibes, Bizet, Gounod, Massenet, and Chabrier. **Léo Delibes** (1836–1891) will always be associated with his ballets, *Coppélia* and *Sylvia,* and his *opéra-comique, Lakmé* (1883), but his first stage work was produced by and with Hervé at the Folies-Nouvelles: *Deux Sous de Charbon,* a *"saynète* [sketch] *musicale"* (9 February 1856). The title's two pennies' worth of coal was meant to effect the suicide of a pair of lovers, but the news of the death of the hero's rich uncle saves the day. Subsequent short operettas appeared that year at the Bouffes-Parisiens under the aegis of Delibes's friend Offenbach: *Les Deux vieilles gardes* (8 August 1856) was the first success, with a greatly admired "punch" duet and a polka danced by the two old guardians—Mmes. Potichon and Vertuchoux. This was performed in London as *The Patient*. *Six Demoiselles à marier* (Six Girls to Marry Off, 12 November 1856) was similarly lively, but *L'Omelette à la Follembûche* (8 June 1859) was more lively still, with a libretto by the authors of the 1852 *comédie-vaudeville* hit *Le Chapeau de paille d'Italie* (The Italian Straw Hat), Eugène Labiche and Marc Michel.

Among the craziest of these dozen or so one-acters was *L'Écossais de Chatou* (The Scotsman from Chatou, Bouffes-Parisiens, 16 January 1869) with a libretto by Adolphe Jaime and Philippe Gille—librettists for Offenbach *(Le Docteur Ox)* and, later, for Delibes *(Lakmé)*. This was about a *bourgeois,* who, having heard the song from Boïeldieu's *La Dame Blanche* about free hospitality in the mountains of Scotland, decides to open a rent-free chalet for foreigners at Chatou. In this exceptionally zany plot, complications too numerous to detail ensue, but everything ends with a *schottisch* danced by the company. Félix Clément and Pierre Larousse described it in their Dictionnaire des Opéras (1905):

> As for the final scene, it resembles those of all the operettas represented in France, since *Orphée aux Enfers,* where the actors succeed, in a *sarabande* as ugly to see as it is crazy, in depriving the lyric art of all its dignity, grace, and its decency.

Most of Delibes's operettas were short until 1869 (Variétés, 24 April), when *La Cour du Roi Pétaud* was presented—a three-act *opéra-bouffe* with a libretto by Jaime and Gille. Zulma Bouffar and Marie Aimée starred in this satirical piece that attacked the monarchy of King Pétaud III but also managed to have its lyrical moments—particularly a lovely third-act love duet. In the twilight years of the Second Empire, it had become increasingly popular for *opéra-bouffe* to ridicule royalty and rulers—hence *La Périchole,* the year before. Zulma Bouffar played the travesty role of Prince Léo (perhaps named after the composer), and his/her song before the statue of Love was quite popular. *Le Roi l'a dit* (The King Said So) was another royal affair, but this was an *opéra-comique,* and first performed at that theatre (1873). We can be thankful it is still performed, albeit very rarely, giving us an indication of the Delibes style in musical comedy. In 1880, Delibes honored his friend by finishing and orchestrating Offenbach's last operetta, *Belle Lurette.*

Georges Bizet (1838–1875), the composer of the world's most popular French opera, *Carmen* (1875, written as an *opéra-comique*), was also responsible for several operettas. The first was the probably unperformed *La Maison du docteur* (The Doctor's House, 1854), but the second was *Le Docteur Miracle,* which alternated with Lecocq's operetta written to the same Léon Battu and Ludovic Halévy libretto in April 1857. Bizet's version, played second, was and has remained the public's favorite. Bizet had already won two Prix de Rome competitions for serious works; now he triumphed in an Offenbach-initiated operetta competition. He was nineteen; two years before, he had written his miraculous Symphony in C. Not yet quite sure which path suited him best, he wrote a full-length *opera buffa* to an Italian libretto in 1858, *Don Procopio,* which was perhaps more a throwback to the Rossini-Donizetti age than a contemporary Parisian *opéra-bouffe*. *Don Procopio* was not performed in the composer's lifetime, receiving a Monte Carlo première in 1906. Had Bizet started a little later, after the Offenbach successes of the late 1850s and 1860s, he might have been content to stick with operetta, but by 1863 he had chosen a more romantic route with *Les Pêcheurs de Perles* (The Pearl Fishers). In fact, he dallied with the operetta form only twice more in his tragically brief life. In December 1867, *Malbrough s'en va-t-en guerre,* a compendium operetta with music also by Delibes, Émile Jonas, and Isidore Legouix, was produced. Bizet sketched the first act for this Théâtre de l'Athénée production, but it was Delibes who orchestrated it for him. Bizet was too busy with *La Jolie Fille de Perth. Malbrough* lasted a month, under the direction of the theatre director, William Busnach, who also wrote the libretto for an unpublished and unplayed Bizet operetta, *Sol-si-ré-pif-pan* (1872). *Carmen* had its first night two months before Bizet's death in 1875. Parts of that masterwork, such as the quintet in Act II and the ebullient choruses, make one wish Bizet had expended more of an effort in the domain of operetta, but he apparently lacked the *un*-seriousness of purpose that a good operetta composer must have. Bizet had Meilhac and Halévy for *Carmen;* how nice it would have been had they given him an *opéra-bouffe* to set.

Charles Gounod (1818–1893) was another opera composer who lacked the truly humorous, lighthearted touch necessary for *opéra-bouffe,* though he lived right through its golden years. *Le Médecin malgré lui* (1858), based on Molière's short comedy of 1666, was the play more or less set to music. Gounod's three-act *Philémon et Baucis* (1860) began as a single act for Baden, later enlarged to two for revivals at the Opéra-Comique, where it tallied up a respectable number of performances over the years. Gounod was too sentimental for true operetta, even though many of the (comparatively) light moments in *Faust* or *Roméo et Juliette* would seem to have indicated a certain proximity to the form. *Faust* (1859) was burlesqued most famously by Hervé ten years later, and also in Terrasse's *Faust en ménage* (1924). And the Jewel Song received a brilliant operetta send-up in "Glitter and Be Gay," from Leonard Bernstein's *Candide* (1957).

The public's and the recording industry's current fascination with the operas of Jules Massenet (1842–1912) has yet to reveal any true or lasting operettas. *La Grand' Tante* (1867) was more an *opéra-comique,* as was *Don César de Bazan* (1872), but *L'Adorable Bel-Boul* (1874) was a one-act operetta, privately performed with the young Jeanne Granier in the cast. By the end of the century Massenet was celebrated for works quite outside our scope. Even *Cendrillon* (1879), the Cinderella story that might have been a charming operetta, was turned into something entirely too formidable. Again, as so many "serious" composers were to discover, operetta was not something that one could easily write by shifting into a lower gear.

L'Étoile has been one of the most neglected of great French operettas, although this masterwork by **Emmanuel Chabrier** (1841–1894) has suddenly been revived in Brussels and in several other cities. *L'Étoile* is one of several operettas (not always publicly performed) by the composer of the popular *España* and the seldom-produced *opéra-comique, Le Roi malgré lui* (1887). *L'Étoile* is totally irresistible, containing one of the most delightful of French stage scores, and a libretto so bizarre or silly that it seems more charming and surreal today than many modern works. Trained as a lawyer, Chabrier held a post in the Interior Ministry. Two salon operettas composed in 1863–64 had libretti by the poet Paul Verlaine (with Lucien Viotti): *Vaucochard et Fils 1er* and *Fisch-ton-kan.* Excerpts from both were performed at the Paris Conservatoire in 1941, with the participation of Francis Poulenc.

L'Étoile (The Star, Bouffes-Parisiens, 28 November 1877) had a book by Letterier and Vanloo, who had two years before given Lecocq a huge hit in *Giroflé-Girofla. L'Étoile* also had a vaguely Eastern-Moorish flavor, with lavish costumes by Grévin. The story concerns King Ouf the First, who customarily celebrates his birthday with a ritual impalement. A young peddler, Lazuli, is picked as the victim, until an astrologer informs the King that the royal life will expire whenever Lazuli's ends, as they share the same star. And so forth.

There was nothing seriously wrong with (and certainly nothing serious about) the book. The music, however, caused logistical problems, especially as Chabrier had scored the entire work without providing a piano score for the rehearsals. The Bouffes-Parisiens orchestra then protested it was too difficult to play. It was indeed an extraordinarily fine score, brimming with terse orchestration and unusually subtle harmonies for operetta, unlike some of the scores the Bouffes had been used to at that time. It is bubbly, but it is the very finest champagne. If an overture is any indication of things to come, one would have the highest expectations after hearing *L'Étoile*'s. It reminds one of the best, comparable to Lecocq's or Sullivan's preambles. The Peddler's Song, the *chanson du colporteur,* sung by Paola Marié on the first night to acclaim,

> Oui, je suis Lazuli,
> Le colporteur joli,
> Le fournisseur des dames,

(Yes, I am Lazuli, the handsome peddler, provider to the ladies) is only exceeded in charm by the very next number, the title *romance de l'étoile.* How much more touching and beautiful this is than the average romantic operetta song. The music associated with King Ouf and his court is properly "oriental," but always in a humorous way, and the fun reaches a hilarious climax in the Act I finale with King Ouf's *couplets du pal* (Impalement Song).

Verlaine contributed the words to this section, as well as the lyrics for the duet of the Green Chartreuse in Act II, which effectively parodies Italian opera. In Act II, song follows song with suavity and grace. Particularly ingratiating are Lazuli's *couplets,* ending with *"un mari ne gêne guère, un mari ne gêne pas!"* (A husband is hardly a bother, not a bother at all!), a kissing quartet, and, again, a superior finale, beginning with a gunshot (*The Yeomen of the Guard* would later have a great ensemble beginning with a shot).

Delightful as *L'Étoile* sounds today in comparison with so many other works of the period, and however well it was received by the critics and première audience, it was perhaps both too silly and too subtle for the general public. The original production closed after its forty-eighth performance, ostensibly because of the illness of one of the actors. The real motivation, as Rollo Myers points out in his Chabrier biography, may have been the contract which had Chabrier, Leterrier, and Vanloo receiving a big fee after the *cinquantième* from the Bouffes director.

Brussels saw the first revival in 1909 (there was another, undistinguished one at the Brussels Monnaie in 1977 for the operetta's centenary), but the most famous Paris reprise occurred during the Nazi Occupation at the Opéra-Comique (10 April 1941). Fanély Revoil won all hearts as Lazuli, and selections were finally recorded to give a broader public an idea of Chabrier's charms. Debussy adored playing through the score of *L'Étoile* and Vincent d'Indy called it "as brilliant as *Le Barbier* [*de Séville*] and more comic and musical than all the preceding operettas."

Marie Jansen did the trousers part of Lazuli in the first New York production, *The Merry Monarch* (Broadway, 18 August 1890), for Francis Wilson's company. This had a considerably altered libretto by J. Cheever Goodwin and a virtually new score—sadly cutting out huge chunks of Chabrier—by Woolson Morse. The London version was called, more accurately, *The Lucky Star* (Savoy, 7 January 1899). This enjoyed the longest consecutive run of all—149 performances—though Chabrier was given no credit as composer: Ivan Caryll took that honor, while stealing a bit of the Frenchman's Act I finale and several of the Goodwin-Morse songs as well. Walter Passmore was the King, succeeding the Parisian Daubray and the New York Wilson, and Emmie Owen was in the travesty role, with the lovely Ruth Vincent as the Princess. When *L'Étoile* was given by the Mannes School of Music in New York in January 1969 (as *The Horoscope*), the *Times* critic Harold Schonberg remarked that the young lady playing Lazuli "could go places." She was Frederica von Stade.

The limited original success of *L'Étoile* may have disillusioned Chabrier, but he sprang back in May 1879 with another operetta, the one-act *Une Éducation manquée* (An Incomplete Education), again with a libretto by Leterrier and Vanloo. This was the story of a young man (again a breeches part—played by Jane Hading) who has been tutored in everything except what to do on his wedding night . . . a delightful little French sketch with appropriately frolicsome music. It is still revived today. Diaghilev had recitatives added by Darius Milhaud for his 1934 production, designed by Juan Gris.

After the success of *Une Éducation manquée* Chabrier left his government job and devoted his career to music, but unfortunately not to any further *opéras-bouffes*. A pity, as his succeeding operas, written in a grander style, are seldom looked at or heard today. As far as operetta is concerned, judging from the finesse and spirit of *L'Étoile* and *Une Éducation manquée*, Chabrier's was *une carrière manquée*.

VIENNA GOLD

T
HERE is a parallel between the inception of Viennese operetta and
the beginning of the Parisian variety. Franz von Suppé's position in
Vienna was quite similar to Hervé's in Paris. One could say that both
were the first major operetta composers—even creators—in their respective cities, but both were superseded by other musicians within a few years:
Jacques Offenbach, and Johann Strauss II. And later, after periods of eclipse,
both sprang back with three-act works in the Offenbach or Strauss style which
were more deliriously popular than anything they had written previously.

Both Suppé and Strauss were specifically influenced by Offenbach. Suppé's
early short works frankly imitated Offenbach's, and Strauss was said to have
been personally coaxed by the French master to compose for the stage. But if
the structure was unmistakably Parisian (as much derived from Meilhac and
Halévy as from Offenbach), the music would become unmistakably, unforget-
tably, Viennese in the space of a very short time.

La Belle Hélène was a tremendous hit in Vienna in 1865 (Theater an der Wien),
confirming a rage for French operetta that persisted for at least another decade.
At the same time, when Strauss was composing some of his greatest concert
waltzes, many of the popular French operettas contained similarly popular waltzes.
In January 1874, the Viennese saw Lecocq's *La Fille de Madame Angot*, which,
like *La Belle Hélène*, had a sweeping Act II finale waltz. It was inevitable that
the waltz would grow in prominence within the confines of the new Viennese
operetta. By April of that year, Strauss gave Vienna and the world the greatest
of all Viennese operettas, *Die Fledermaus*, the golden standard by which other
Viennese operettas are measured today. No one wrote waltzes like Strauss, and
no one would write waltz-operettas like Strauss, though legions tried. Since *Die
Fledermaus*, no self-respecting Viennese operetta could get away from the fact

---

Johann Strauss II caricatured around the time of *Der Zigeunerbaron* (1885).

that the waltz was the *Wiener Blut* (Viennese Blood) running through its veins, its life-force. As librettists Alfred Grünwald and Julius Brammer stated in the refrain of the principal waltz from *Die Rose von Stambul*, music by Leo Fall (1916): *"Ein Walzer muss es sein"*—it *must* be a waltz.

Another major influence on the new Viennese operetta was the *Posse mit Gesang*, the Vienna musical farce equivalent of the Parisian *vaudeville*. Although these were frequently just as boisterous as their French counterparts, they were often more sentimental and *gemütlich* (cosy), Viennese characteristics that could be naturally exploited in music by the use of the waltz. The nostalgia for *Alt-Wien*, the Vienna that old-timers remembered with affection, was also something that went back as far as the early days of operetta.

Franz von Suppé (1819–1895) was in many ways the father of Viennese operetta, yet today he is principally known for his overtures. If only people would ask: "Overtures to *what?*" Overtures to many delightful operettas which, for the most part, go unperformed today. Of a field of some forty operettas and nearly two hundred assorted *vaudevilles*, burlesques, farces, and parodies, only two are still popular: the three-act *Boccaccio* (1879) and the one-act *Die schöne Galathee* (1865). Yet at one time Suppé's *Fatinitza* (1876), for one, enjoyed a huge vogue around the globe, particularly in the United States.

Suppé's early *Singspiele,* burlesques, and farces, dating from the 1840s and written before the influence of Offenbach was felt in Vienna, were partially the progenitors of the classical Viennese operetta, steeped in the tradition of the popular *bourgeois* comedies of the Biedermieier period and yet showing the unmistakable influence of the waltzes of Johann Strauss I and Joseph Lanner. When Offenbach finally arrived in Vienna with his Bouffes-Parisiens company in 1858, Suppé seems to have been the composer to have been most influenced by the French *bouffonnerie,* turning out a succession of one-act works which Parisianized the rough edges of his earlier farces and at the same time retained enough sentiment to keep them Viennese.

Francesco Ezechiele Ermenegildo Cavaliere de Suppe-Demelli was born somewhere in Spalato, Dalmatia (now Split, Yugoslavia), perhaps on a boat, on 18 April 1819. His father was of Belgian extraction, his mother of Czech/Polish origin, and the boy was raised as an Italian. The father of Viennese operetta was never able to speak German perfectly. Suppé showed a certain virtuosity on the flute at the age of eleven, but his father wanted him to be a lawyer, so he was sent to Padua to study. With his father's death in 1835, the boy's family went to Vienna, where Franz studied music at the Polytechnic Institute under Ignaz von Seyfried, a former pupil of Mozart. He played the flute in various orchestras, taught Italian, and in 1837 and 1841 wrote two operas, neither of which were performed but both of which may have been influenced by Gaetano Donizetti.

By 1841 he was a volunteer assistant conductor at the Theater in der Josefstadt, when a *Posse* (farce), *Jung lustig, im Alter traurig* (Jolly When Young, Sad

When Old), was performed with his overture and incidental music and songs—the first of many of these plays-with-music Suppé would write. In 1845, when he was twenty-five, Suppé was engaged with Albert Lortzing by the Theater an der Wien's director Franz Pokorny to conduct and to compose *Singspiele* and other plays and sketches.

One overture, which had been used twice before without any notice, was refurbished to serve as a prelude to the comedy *Dichter und Bauer* (Poet and Peasant). This became a universal triumph, but Suppé's compensation was only eight *Thaler*. His first three-act work, an opera, appeared in 1847: *Das Mädchen vom Lande* (The Country Girl, Theater an der Wien, 7 August 1847), really a *Singspiel* that mirrored the works of Lortzing, Cornelius, and Nicolai. The *Singspiel* was an overworked and possibly played-out type of musical theatre by the late '40s. By the 1850s, with the first performances of the Offenbach one-acters at Vienna's Carltheater, the capital preferred the new, definitely French, theatrical form.

In 1848, Pokorny transferred his activities to the Kärntnertor theatre and asked Suppé for further comic compositions. Through the 1850s, the composer supplied music for various properties, including a "dramatic poem," *Tannenhäuser* (1852, a parody), and a "life-portrait," *Mozart* (1854). The one-act comic opera *Paragraph Drei* (Paragraph Three, 1858), based on a French source, was a failure, but Suppé persisted. He was especially encouraged not only by the Viennese reception of Offenbach's company, but also by the success in Vienna of unauthorized performances of such works as *Die Hochzeit bei Lanternenschein* (*Le Mariage aux Lanternes,* 1857) and Nestroy's 1860 version of *Orphée aux Enfers* at the Carltheater (17 March).

24 November 1860 is considered by many the birthdate of the true Viennese operetta, with the production of Suppé's *Das Pensionat* (The Boarding School) at the Theater an der Wien, by then under the direction of the late Pokorny's son, Alois. Pokorny, Jr. did not have enough cash to obtain the rights for the first Viennese productions of Offenbach—that privilege went for several years to the Carltheater—but he was responsible for a cheaper alternative, the new Viennese variety. *Das Pensionat,* with its Spanish setting, proved to be the first Viennese operetta to travel. In 1861, it was heard (in German) at the Stadt Theater, New York (18 November).

After Pokorny went bankrupt in 1862, Suppé transferred most of his activities to the Kai-Theater, where he conducted several new one-acters, including *Die Kartenschlägerin* and *Zehn Mädchen und kein Mann* (both 1862). The former did not appeal to the public originally, and was revised in 1865 as *Pique Dame. Zehn Mädchen und kein Mann,* very likely influenced by Delibes's *Six Demoiselles à marier* (1856), was a much more accomplished work and the public liked it. *Ten Girls and No Man,* increased by fifteen females, appeared at the Vienna Opera in 1873 as *Fünfundzwanzig Mädchen und kein Mann!* It even appeared at Drury Lane, London, the following year, as *Ten of 'Em.* A British version performed by the Guildhall School of Music in 1981 at London's Sadler's Wells Theatre revealed the work to be a pure delight, very much in the *Bouffes-Parisiens* style, but with an even more ambitious series of musical parodies than was usually attempted by Offenbach in a short operetta, and a Viennese predilection for martial swagger that was to become a Suppé characteristic.

In 1863, *Flotte Bursche* (The Jolly Students, Kai-Theater, 18 April) was more popular still, its pre-*Student Prince* antics and genial melodies delighting the Viennese. But in 1863, the Kai-Theater burned, so Suppé joined with Karl Treumann, the popular actor-manager at the Carltheater, where he composed many more *Possen,* sketches, and further incidental music, in addition to *Franz Schubert* (1864), a precursor of *Das Dreimäderlhaus,* using motifs from the *Erlkönig,* the *Wanderer,* and other Schubert "hits." It was successful enough to have been revived in 1886.

In 1865 came his most enduring one-act success, *Die schöne Galathee* (The Beautiful Galatea), obviously modeled, in both title and style, on Offenbach's *La Belle Hélène,* which had seized Vienna earlier that year with Marie Geistinger in the title role. In fact, *Die schöne Galathee* had its première in Berlin (Meysel's Theater, 30 June 1865). The libretto, by "Poly Henrion" (pseudonym of Karl Leopold Kohl von Kohlenegg, certainly a much more operetta-ish name!), was a treatment of the Pygmalion myth used countless times before and since, (and in 1852 by Massé and librettists Barbier and Carré for their *opéra-comique*). The *"komisch-mythologische"* operetta was seen in Vienna the following autumn (Carltheater, 9 September 1865), but did not prompt critical bravos. The libretto was not really satirical, in the sense of *Orphée aux Enfers* or *La Belle Hélène,* but more a situation comedy played in togas. Yet the music was excellent, and the overture nothing short of sensational. Starting buoyantly, then becoming almost Wagneresque, it ended with a waltz so potent, so Viennese, that Frederick Loewe must have unconsciously paid homage to it when he composed the Embassy Waltz for *My Fair Lady* (1956). Suppé excelled at more than overtures. He was adept at languorous waltzes, blithe *couplets* in the French style, and elaborate Italianate ensembles, such as the spectacular trio, *"Seht den Schmuck, den ich für Euch gebracht,"* and the subsequent drinking quintet—almost a march—*"Hell im Glas."* These reflect the past—Rossini, perhaps—but they also have an unmistakable Viennese flavor, as does the penultimate kiss-duet, which gives a piquant foreshadowing of the *Duidu* ensemble in *Die Fledermaus.*

There have been numerous revivals in Vienna and the rest of the German-speaking world. *Die schöne Galathee* remains a repertory staple. London first heard *Ganymede and Galatea* in 1872. New York, after German performances in 1867 at the Stadt Theater, saw *The Beautiful Galatea* at Tony Pastor's in 1882, on a double bill with *Trial by Jury.*

The one-act *"Operette militär,"* *Leichte Kavallerie* (Light Cavalry), again, famous today only for its overture, followed on 24 March 1866 at the Carltheater.

A vignette from the first production of Suppé's *Die schöne Galathee* (Berlin, Meysel's, 1865), showing the statue coming to life. Suppé's melodious one-act "comic-mythological" operetta is one of the few one-act Viennese works still performed.

(The German film version of 1935, which brought Marika Rökk to Nazi-era fame, has virtually nothing to do with the work.) *Freigeister* (Free Spirits, 23 October 1866) was another Carltheater hit, as was the three-act *Banditenstreiche* (27 April 1867), the latter still occasionally performed in Germany. The "Bandits' Tricks" was in the line of *Fra Diavolo*-like pieces, with the noble eighteenth-century Neapolitan bandit Malandrino outfitting a peasant girl with a thousand stolen ducats in order to marry her.

One of the reasons for the lack of a substantial full-length Suppé operetta in the Parisian manner from 1867 to 1876 was the appearance of Johann Strauss II's operettas on the Viennese stage—supposedly spurred on by Offenbach himself. Apart from *Banditenstreiche*, Suppé had failed to come up with any work as popular as Strauss's *Die Fledermaus* (1874), though one cannot say he didn't have the chance, as well as the goading of the theatre managers, who from 1864 had been looking for something as beautiful as *Die schöne Helena*. Suppé had responded with his *Galathee*, but however *schöne* it was, it was not quite the full-length blockbuster the Carltheater or the Theater an der Wien wanted. Though Suppé had assuredly pointed the way toward the development of the Viennese operetta, and by virtue of his timing may be said to have fathered it, Strauss, in the 1870s, actually got it going with *Indigo, Der Karneval in Rom, Die Fledermaus, Cagliostro in Wien,* and *Prinz Methusalem* at either the Theater an der Wien or the Carltheater.

It was time for Suppé to prove he could write a three-act comic opera of equal weight, and, rightly sensing that a good libretto might help, he turned to

Strauss's librettists, F. Zell and Richard Genée *(Die Fledermaus, Cagliostro in Wien)*, who came up with *Fatinitza* (Carltheater, 5 January 1876). This was based on Scribe and Auber's *opéra-comique, La Circassienne* (1861), but the writers made an important change in having the role of the young Russian officer Vladimir played by a woman, allowing for him (the actress) to masquerade as a Turkish woman (Fatinitza) in the course of the regimental story. Antonie Link, who had charmed Vienna as its first Mam'zelle Angot and its original Prinz Methusalem, was Vladimir.

Fatinitza was both a huge critical and public triumph and a reassurance to both Suppé and Carltheater manager Franz Jauner, besides being a moneymaking property of unparalleled worth. The celebrated march-trio *"Vorwärts mit frischem Mut"* (Forward with good cheer), kept rather short but effectively repeated in the operetta and drummed into Viennese ears, assured a huge sheet-music sale by the summer of 1877, not to mention separate sales of the other songs and dance arrangements. Suppé received about 36,000 *Gulden* for the first 100 performances, reached 30 January 1878; and Jauner, who owned the rights, was also well enriched.

Performances popped up everywhere: in London (Alhambra, 20 June 1878), Paris (Nouveautés, 15 March 1879), and New York (Fifth Avenue, 22 April 1879). The London production ran some 100 nights, but the New York version had the misfortune of appearing at the time of the first New York productions of *H.M.S. Pinafore*.

A production in 1880 at Booth's Theatre, with Adelaide Phillips as Vladimir, was beautifully mounted and more heartily welcomed, after Suppé's *Boccaccio* had clicked. *Fatinitza* toured extensively under several managements for decades, and had a notable Broadway revival at the Broadway Theatre in 1904 with Fritzi Scheff, for which Harry B. Smith wrote a new English version.

In early 1878, Zell and Genée presented Suppé with the book for what would become one of the most popular of all Viennese operettas, *Boccaccio,* or *Der Prinz von Palermo.* Out of the receipts from *Fatinitza,* Suppé, nearly sixty, had bought an estate in Gars, Lower Austria (later a Suppé museum), where he might very well have retired, cultivating the asparagus he so admired and writing cookbooks. He did not work at all that summer, and was forced to cram his composing into the space of four weeks in autumn, clothing himself supposedly in six vests, a very heavy dressing gown, several pairs of stockings and felt-lined slippers, and a fur cap—plus a foot warmer and, no doubt, a roaring fire in the stove, to protect himself from the Vienna chill. This warmth overflowed into the operetta, one of those happy ones set in Italy, allowing for all sorts of native dances.

The tumultuous première (Carltheater, 1 February 1879) surpassed the reception accorded *Fatinitza,* and it must have seemed to Vienna that Suppé had consolidated a comeback that would well-nigh drive Strauss off the map: the Waltz King's *Blindekuh* had been a debacle a few weeks before. The role of Boccaccio was taken by Antonie Link (women would traditionally play the part until the 1930s) and Rosa Streitmann was his beloved Fiametta in a clever libretto which placed the actual poet Boccaccio in his own Florence in a barely biographical story. Boccaccio's name alone must have intrigued a good many theatregoers to visit the many theatres all over the world in which Suppé's *Meisterwerk* played, but it has little to do with *The Decameron*. It appeared at the Folies-Dramatiques, Paris (29 March 1882), and was the second attraction at the new Comedy Theatre, London (22 April 1882), with Violet Cameron as Boccaccio. It was first heard in New York (Thalia, 23 April 1880) in German, and three weeks later in English. It was fittingly popular in Italy, where it was last given a major revival in Rome (Opera, 1970). The McCaull Company toured it in 1888, with De Wolf Hopper in a comedy part, and Fritzi Scheff played it at the Broadway in 1905. Many, many performers appeared in numerous companies in the United States: Frank Moulan, Raymond Hitchcock, William Danforth, Bertram Peacock, Herbert Waterous.

The most prestigious revival took place at the Metropolitan Opera, New York (2 January 1931). Conductor Artur Bodanzky had the dialogue replaced with recitative and added music from other Suppé pieces *(Donna Juanita* and *Pique Dame* among them) in order to bolster up the title role as a flashy vehicle for Maria Jeritza. It was grandly designed by Joseph Urban. An effort on Gatti-Casazza's part to leaven the fare at the Met, it succeeded, and plans were soon set to revive *Donna Juanita* the following season. The Bodanzky version of *Boccaccio* was given at the Vienna Staatsoper in 1932.

But there were several who carped, not so much at the Met's decision to stage a comic opera, but at its aggrandizement of the Suppé original, and the irksome idea of doing it entirely in German for an American audience. Lawrence Gilman, of the *Herald Tribune,* didn't care for the original:

> . . . so far as its form and style are concerned, it is light opera, but in effect—especially as it was done last night—it is heavy as lead: heavy with the weight of laborious levity and a vacuous mind. The work itself, musically and dramatically, is weak and indigent stuff . . . the score is for the most part a trite and feeble thing—full of tepid tunes and rhythms . . .

The choruses, finales, and orchestration might today seem overwritten and heavy-handed, especially when compared to other operettas of its era. Take, for example, the entire opening scene in front of the church of Santa Maria Novella. Despite several Italianate passages, it is a thoroughly German-operatic beginning, ponderous and full of dull repeats. The "lively" students are more heavy Heidelbergian than frolicsome Florentine, and the announcement of new stories by Boccaccio provokes a convoluted scene of no particular lyric merit.

Compare this opening to those in two other "Italian" operettas: in Strauss II's *Eine Nacht in Venedig,* the ebullient piazza chorus *"Wenn vom Lido sacht,"* the vendors' cries, and the lilting entrance of Pappacoda (his *"Makkaroni"* song), or the astounding opera-within-an-operetta which is the first twenty minutes of Sullivan's *The Gondoliers* (1889). Both have sections in Italian—the Sullivan, most memorably—and both have the Italianate sunniness necessary to operetta and lacking in Suppé's beginning. But the situation quickly improves.

The operetta's first interesting number is Boccaccio's swaggering *"Ich sehe einen jungen Mann dort stehn,"* with its surging refrain. From there on, *Boccaccio* remains musically exciting, reaching high spots in the first act with two graceful duets between Fiametta and Boccaccio, the student song *(". . . Immer in undici, dodici, tredici"),* the similarly folkish cooper's song *(". . . Bumti-rapata . . . bumti, bumti, bumti, rapata!"),* an entrancing Viennese waltz-trio for Fiametta, Isabella, and Peronella in the second act, and, in the third act, a famous love duet *("Florenz hat schöne Frauen,"* or *"Ma bella fiorentina,"* if you prefer), and the march, *"Der Witz, die Laune,"* repeated to end the operetta. *Boccaccio's* third act may be as short as the usual operetta third act but, luckily, Suppé's final-act inspiration did not run out.

Boccaccio must have been more fun with a female in the lead—to say that this has gone out of fashion is nonsense. Oreste, in *La Belle Hélène,* le petit Duc, and Boccaccio have no more right to be played by men than Cherubino does in Mozart's *Figaro.* Certainly, many would rather have seen Maria Jeritza than Allan Jones (New Yorker Theatre) as Boccaccio in 1931–32, if only for the enchantment of transvestism, which has never really been as acceptable or amusing in America as it has been in Europe.

Donna Juanita (Carltheater, 21 February 1880) continued the Zell-Genée-Suppé fortunes, and proved a great international success as well. It is still a favorite in Russia. Set in late eighteenth-century Spain, it is basically a rehash of the plot of *Fatinitza,* with a young French cadet (again played by a woman) disguising himself as the seductive Donna Juanita in order to penetrate the Spanish lines. Like its two famous predecessors, it has a wonderful overture, but the score itself was thought too much like those of *Boccaccio* and *Fatinitza* for it to hold much interest. The first production in English was given at the Fifth Avenue Theatre, New York (16 May 1881), and this too was Bodanzky-ized for Jeritza in 1932. Olin Downes remarked on her Metropolitan romp in the *Times:* "Douglas Fairbanks could not have outdone her in athletics."

Nothing after *Donna Juanita* has endured, though several were very popular in their time: *Der Gascogner* (Theater an der Wien, 22 March 1881), based on a Eugène Sue novel, was an outright flop, but *Die Afrikareise* (A Trip to Africa, Theater an der Wien, 17 March 1883), a vehicle for Alexander Girardi, was a popular attraction in the United States, appearing first in English at the Standard, New York, later the same year. Both operettas had books by Richard Genée and Moritz West. *Die Afrikareise* took place in Egypt in and around the "Pharaone" Hotel, Cairo. It had a bit of *Aïda* about it, set as it was on the banks of the Nile, with an Abyssinian slave girl; the other characters were primarily Italians. Lillian Russell appeared in it at the Standard, New York, during 1887.

Of Suppé's final works, only *Die Jagd nach dem Glück* (The Hunt for Happiness, Carltheater, 27 October 1888), a failure in Vienna, was popular abroad. It had a substantial run in New York as *Clover* (Palmer's, 9 May 1889), produced by Colonel McCaull with De Wolf Hopper, Jefferson De Angelis, Mathilde Cottrelly, and Eugene Oudin. There was a more ambitious opera, *Des Matrosens*

Heimkehr (1885), another comic opera, *Bellmann* (1887)—neither caught the public's fancy—and a couple of *pasticcios* constructed after Suppé's death: *Das Modell* (1895) and *Die Pariserin* (1898) being two.

The composer-conductor who had so delighted Vienna with his fundamentally cheerful music and podium antics (he very elaborately and publicly self-administered snuff before each of his famous overtures, so that each was preceded by a big sneeze) was toward the end of his life affected by the death he obviously saw approaching. He devoted much of his time to religious music and at the same time had his house rigged up with deathly items like coffins, used on occasion for sleeping.

Perhaps such *bizarreries* are understandable—Suppé died horribly of stomach cancer, literally starving to death. The end came 21 May 1895, six days after the death of his collaborator Richard Genée, who in turn had died only a few weeks after *his* partner, Zell. The actor Alexander Girardi remarked on the librettists, with sincere affection, "They even did this together!" Suppé received an impressive funeral, with all his theatrical and musical colleagues present save one, his rival Johann Strauss. Strauss was, if anything, even more preoccupied with death than Suppé and would not attend. But he did send a wreath to the grave "in sincere reverence."

One might honestly claim that with **Johann Strauss II** (1825–1899) the Viennese operetta of the "Golden Age" reached its finest hour (or even eight or nine hours). Certainly, *Die Fledermaus* is one of those inexhaustible creations that at once define an entire genre while at the same time provide its best moments. *Der Zigeunerbaron*, among its virtues, not altogether unconciously serves as a musical monument to the Austro-Hungarian Empire, and *Eine Nacht in Venedig* remains a *ca' d'oro* of irresistible melody (in search of a libretto). Yet these three works alone, plus the lamentably popular posthumous *pasticcio*, *Wiener Blut*, are all that have remained in the repertoire, supplanted in this century by such variations on a biographical theme as *Walzer aus Wien*, *The Great Waltz*, and *Valses de Vienne*, all dealing musically with the lives of the Strausses, *père et fils*.

Setting aside the unparalleled popularity of the Gilbert and Sullivan output, Strauss's operetta survival rate is by no means a lowly figure. Three or four works are twice or three times as many as we remember today of his contemporaries: Millöcker's (*Der Bettelstudent*, *Gasparone*), Zeller's (*Der Vogelhändler*), or Suppé's (*Boccaccio*, *Die schöne Galathee*). Not forgetting that Strauss is far better known as the world's greatest waltz composer. Yet it is undeniable that his other operettas, originally popular on both continents, seem today unplayable.

Why? The charge that a stupid libretto has prevented eternal success is a false one—we have shown and will continue to point out exceptions to this belief. The claim that Strauss himself was underinspired by spurious libretti is equally unsound, as is the oft-repeated definition of Strauss as an "undramatic" composer without a true theatre sense, which even he confessed. *Eine Nacht in Ve-*

nedig, for one, refutes all these charges—it was and has remained popular in spite of its silly book and dumb lyrics (which have wisely been repaired over the years). Its music is quite inspired and even dramatic, though Strauss himself confessed not to have known a thing about the plot when he was setting the lyrics. The finales to Acts I and II of both *Die Fledermaus* and *Der Zigeunerbaron* (and the first-act end of *Eine Nacht in Venedig*) remain unsurpassed in German-language operetta for comic or dramatic theatricality, perhaps a reason why both are played all over the world at opera houses as well as regular theatres.

Critics who then pointed out that only the waltzes were notable in the lesser Strauss operettas ultimately provide the key to fully appreciating these works: they *are* waltz-operettas, yes, but more accurately *dance* operettas, with many other dance rhythms represented. When the critic Eduard Hanslick stated that "the waltz stops the action" in a Strauss operetta, was he being entirely uncomplimentary? Was he expecting music-drama in a popular musical comedy? There is more "drama" in a Strauss operetta waltz than in the vast majority of French or Viennese *couplets.*

Listening today, as one can, to radio broadcasts or recordings of such comparative novelties as *Cagliostro in Wien, Der Karneval in Rom,* or *Der lustige Krieg,* one is forced to agree with the 1870s critics: the waltzes are outstandingly better than the other numbers. However, the plot of *Der lustige Krieg* is attractively silly; wrapped around *"Nur für Natur"* it might make a very pleasant evening—certainly a more ebullient one than any number of other works from the later "Silver Age." Not for nothing was Johann Strauss II the *Walzerkönig;* though others would approach him, none would capture his sensuousness. The *Schatz* (treasure) waltz in *Zigeunerbaron* or *"Brüderlein und Schwesterlein"* from *Fledermaus* are two different examples of what made Strauss as sexually attractive in his musical day and way as Elvis Presley or the Beatles were in later years. It is impossible to sit still during a Strauss operetta; one finds oneself swaying to the music. More than that, the contagious *bonhomie,* the impulse to relate one's good feelings to the other members of the audience, is omnipresent. This is a special quality in music, and one on which operetta, and particularly Johann Strauss II, capitalized.

One could hardly accuse Strauss of carelessness—his best works, waltzes as well as operettas, are models of craftsmanship and thought. We *do* know that his personal history and eccentricities (which we emphatically will *not* dwell upon here—they have been meticulously and/or fancifully set down in many books, musical plays, and films) might at times have made him less conscientious about certain operettas. But he cared so actively about their reception that one must assume he cared about their writing and execution. Strauss was an extremely self-conscious man, with "the most musical brain in Europe," according to Richard Wagner. A reexamination of the other Strauss operettas is overdue, especially in his native Austria. The Vienna Volksoper, subsidized to the hilt and able to afford a risk from time to time, should begin looking at these neglected works. By all means, rewrite the books if necessary and extract numbers from the weaker scores for interpolation into the new libretti. The staff and artists might be pleasantly surprised with the results, if not the basically conservative Volksoper audience.

The first meeting between Offenbach and Strauss may have taken place at the 1864 Vienna Concordia-Ball, for which both composers had been invited to write waltzes. Offenbach's *Abendblätter* (Evening Papers) had to be repeated five times; Strauss's *Morgenblätter* was surprisingly unpopular. Popular legend, probably perpetrated by a Berlin journalist in the 1880s, had it that the composers were *zum goldenen Lamm* (at the Golden Lamb Inn) when Offenbach said to Strauss, "Why haven't you written any operettas?" However fanciful the story, it is not impossible to imagine Strauss having been piqued by Offenbach's huge operetta successes in Vienna during the 1860s.

Die lustigen Weiber von Wien (The Merry Wives of Vienna) would have been Strauss's first stage work. His first wife, Jetty Treffz, had taken some of his musical sketches to Maximilian Steiner, director of the Theater an der Wien. Steiner had these set to lyrics and sung to a delighted Strauss, who by October 1869 was at work on his first operetta. The libretto, by Josef Braun, one of Suppé's regular textwriters, took place in contemporary Vienna at midnight on New Year's Eve. Braun wanted the popular Viennese star Josefine Gallmeyer, but "Pepi" had quit the Theater an der Wien four years before after a disagreement with Director Steiner. As they could not lure her away from the Carltheater, where she had just created a sensation as Gabrielle in *La Vie Parisienne, Die lustigen Weiber von Wien* was withdrawn from Steiner and canceled.

Steiner, though fazed, persisted. On 10 February 1871, a new work, *Indigo und die vierzig Räuber* (Indigo and the Forty Thieves) received its première at the Theater an der Wien with the composer conducting. The program announced: "Text from an old subject arranged and staged by the Director, M. Steiner." No librettist or librettists were listed, until wags referred to the operetta as *Indigo und die vierzig Textdichter*—the "forty librettists" having plundered various sources for the new text. However poor the libretto, the first night was a sensation. All Vienna was there (some had to pay exorbitant prices to attend) and the critic Wimmer recorded the enthusiasm following the waltz song *"Ja, so singt man, ja, so singt man in der Stadt, wo ich geboren . . ."* (Yes, that's how they sing in the town of my birth):

The entire audience broke out in a cry . . . everyone believed that Strauss would take the violin from the first violinist, and play as he had once done at Sperl's, at Zeisig's, at Dommayer's, at Unger and Schwender's, for dancing.

Hanslick thought the piece was too long, but liked the orchestrations. The long evening started at seven o'clock and ended at eleven; the three acts and four scenes contained several ballets for the *bayadères,* moors, and mulattos in the large cast, which included Jani Szika as Ali Baba, the donkey driver, and Marie Geistinger, Pepi Gallmeyer's arch-rival and the original Viennese *belle Hélène,* as Fantasca.

Indigo's opening night was the most memorable Vienna had seen since the première one year before of *Die Meistersinger* at the Court Opera. Such was its reception that Strauss was forced to conduct the second night as well. It received seventy performances in all. The piece was internationally circulated; what theatre manager could refuse a Johann Strauss score, especially with a big waltz hit? By 1874 it had reached Budapest, and the next year it received a glittering, much amplified, production as *La Reine Indigo* at the Théâtre de la Renaissance, Paris (27 April 1875). The Offenbach star Zulma Bouffar was Fantasca, but some of the other names were changed; Ali Baba was now Babazouck, and the harem girls Zaire and Florinda were now called Banana and Piastrella. Paris saw an obviously racier show: Romadour in Vienna was merely a high priest, in Paris he was Chief of the White Eunuchs. "The Blue Danube," that irresistible waltz, was dropped into the middle of the last act (sung in the wings by a chorus of sailors), to go along with Bouffar's big waltz song, *"Ô flamme enivrante, ô philtre vermeil!"* London saw it at the Alhambra in September 1877, in an F. C. Burnand translation, New York in August 1891, at the Casino. *Indigo*

enjoyed a new life as *1001 Nacht,* in two acts with prologue and epilogue, with a new libretto by Leo Stein and Carl Lindau and rearranged melodies by Ernst Reiterer (Volksoper, 27 October 1907). The big hit song was now *"Nun lachst du mir wieder, du flüchtiges Glück!"*

The insecure Strauss had not been certain of success. It was reported that on the day of the première of *Indigo* he was driving with a friend in a *Fiaker* which passed by a kiosk on which there was a poster advertising the operetta. Strauss reportedly fainted on seeing it. Yet he was not altogether without hope for the future: during the *Indigo* rehearsals with Geistinger he supposedly composed her next big song, *"Die Glocken, sie hallen"* (The Bells are ringing), for *Der Karneval in Rom* (Roman Carnival), which opened a little more than a year later (Theater an der Wien, 1 March 1873). Many librettists, alone and in teams, had offered their wares to Strauss, who in the end had gone back to Josef Braun and his reworking of Victorien Sardou's well-known *Piccolino* (1865). This was operatized at least once before, in 1869, and once again in 1876, the latter with a score by Ernest Guiraud (the man who "filled in" Bizet's *Carmen* and finished *Les Contes d'Hoffmann* for Offenbach). Strauss's reputation as a stage composer, after only a *succès d'estime,* was high enough for the director Herbeck to want *Karneval in Rom* for his Hofoper, but the court authorities at that time would not permit a comic operetta in its sacred precincts. At the Theater an der Wien, the opening went superbly, most of the raves going to Geistinger as Marie, an Alpine maiden entangled with the painter Arthur Bryk (Albin Swoboda). Bryk was loosely but obviously based on the popular Viennese artist and party-giver Hans Makart. *Das Fremdenblatt,* the Viennese paper, noted Strauss's two styles: the light one for the humorous scenes, and the darker, more operatic one for the romantic passages. The Italian setting also permitted Strauss the native rhythms that he adored using.

Der Karneval in Rom was well timed to play during the Vienna Exhibition, which opened 1 May 1873; all performances at this time were sold out. But a week later came Black Friday, the famous Börse (Vienna Stock Market) crash, with its nasty financial repercussions throughout Europe. This had a deleterious effect on all theatrical activity. *Der Karneval in Rom* ran a very respectable 81 performances, but was seldom heard again until 1912, when a revised version, *Der blaue Held* (The Blue Hero) was heard, again at the Theater an der Wien.

In Paris, *Le Réveillon,* a three-act comedy by Meilhac and Halévy (Palais Royal, 10 September 1872), was produced at the home of *La Vie Parisienne,* one of the authors' great Offenbach hits. A *réveillon* is a Christmas Eve or New Year's Eve supper. One can be sure Strauss saw *Pariser Leben* in its popular production at the Carltheater in 1867, and it is equally likely that librettists Richard Genée and Karl Haffner would have seen it as well. *Le Réveillon* was the basis of the libretto for the next Strauss work, *Die Fledermaus,* which corresponds to the French

---

Karl Adolf Friese as the High Priest Romadour in the original production of Johann Strauss's *Indigo* (Theater an der Wien, 1871). Österreichische Nationalbibliothek.

original in many respects. The major changes involve the names and the locale. Thus, Gaillardin became Eisenstein; Fanny, Rosalinde; the Prince Yermontoff, Prince Orlofsky; Pernette, Adele. Alfred retained his name, but was now an opera singer rather than a fiddle-brandishing orchestra leader. There was a great deal of dancing in *Le Réveillon,* even a bit of Rossini, plus the now-celebrated drunken jailer scene in Act III. Before awarding the laurels to MM. Meilhac and Halévy, one must note that *they* owed much to a farce by Roderich Benedix, *Das Gefängnis* (The Prison), produced in Berlin in the 1840s before a Viennese production in 1851.

The French play went through various Viennese hands. Franz Jauner, director of the Carltheater, had his house-writer Karl Haffner translate and adapt *Le Réveillon* to Viennese tastes. But it wasn't right, and the play wound up at the Theater an der Wien on Steiner's desk. At this point, the publisher-agent Gustav Lewy suggested that the play would make a good libretto for Strauss. Richard Genée was called in to prepare a new version from the French original, at a hundred *Gulden* per act. (This type of contract may explain why Viennese operettas were invariably in three rather than two acts.) Thus, much of the text, and all the lyrics, are Genée's. Genée himself credited only the characters' names to Haffner, with whom he generously shared his billing on the playbill.

The stock market collapse was on many minds when Strauss began composing the new operetta in seclusion at his villa at Hietzing. We are asked to believe the work was composed in the space of six weeks. Is this really unbelievable? Strauss was pleased not only with the truly brilliant libretto, but also with the opportunity it presented to write a good deal of non-sung dance music, and these virtues must have fired him to write so magnificently and concentratedly. Besides the glorious overture, surely one of the three or four greatest written for an operetta, Strauss wrote a series of national dances *(spanisch, schottisch, russisch, polka, ungarisch)* for the second act which are seldom performed today and generally replaced with a more popular Strauss waltz—as well as the long *mélodrame* during the mimed scene in which Frank, the prison governor, drunkenly returns to his office at the beginning of Act III. During the dress rehearsal Marie Geistinger, the theatre's co-director and star (Rosalinde), complained that the scene was too long: "It's so boring when no one says a word for so long." Strauss was willing to cut it immediately, but Genée insisted on its retention, even though not one word of his was spoken during the scene.

The locale had been switched from Meilhac and Halévy's Paris not to Vienna itself but "a spa near a big city," presumably a place like Bad Ischl, and there were new sets designed to depict the Eisensteins' parlor, Orlofsky's ballroom—not the jail. (Theatres at that time constantly reused scenery.) The cast was large, augmented by the dancers for the second act, and it was very likely thought by the management that "The Bat" would succeed in spite of its nasty title.

The programme for the first night of the greatest of all Viennese operettas, *Die Fledermaus,* on Easter Sunday, 1874. There were new settings for acts one and two (by Alfred Moser) but none, presumably, for the third-act jail scene. Wiener Stadtbibliothek.

K. k. priv. Theater an der Wien.

Unter der Direktion Geiſtinger & Steiner.

Sonntag den 5. April 1874.

Zum erſtenmale:

Die Fledermaus.

Komiſche Operette in 3 Alten nach Meilhac und Halevy's „Reveillon", bearbeitet von
C. Haffner und Richard Genée. **Musik von Johann Strauss.**
Tänze arrangirt von der Balletmeiſterin Frau Thereſe v. Kilony.
Die neuen Dekorationen des erſten und zweiten Aktes von Herrn Alfred Moſer. — Die
neuen Koſtüme angefertigt vom Obergadrobier Herrn Schulze
Möbel von Aug. Kitſchelt's Erben (Rudolf Kitſchelt), k. k. Hoflieferant.

Gabriel von Eiſenſtein, Rentier	. . . .	Hr. Szika.
Roſalinde, ſeine Frau	. . . .	Marie Geiſtinger.
Frank, Gefängniß-Direktor	. . . .	Hr. Frieſe.
Prinz Orlofski	. . . .	Frl. Rittinger.
Alfred, ſein Gesanglehrer	. . . .	Hr. Rüdinger.
Dr. Falke, Notar	. . . .	Hr. Lebrecht.
Dr. Blind, Advolat	. . . .	Hr. Rott.
Adele, Stubenmädchen Roſalindens	. . . .	Fr. Charles-Hirſch a. G.
Ali-Bey, ein Egypter	. . . .	Hr. Romani.
Ramuſin, Gesandſchafts-Attaché	. . . .	Hr. Jäger.
Murray, Amerikaner	. . . .	Hr. Liebold.
Carikoni, ein Marquis	. . . .	Hr. Thalboth.
Lord Middleton	. . . .	Hr. Fink.
Baron Oskar	. . . .	Hr. Mellin.
Froſch, Gerichtsdiener	. . . .	Hr. Schreiber.
Yvan, Kammerdiener des Prinzen	. . . .	Hr. Gärtner.
Ida,	. . . .	Frl. Jules.
Melanie,	. . . .	Frl. Kopf.
Felicita,	. . . .	Frl. Schindler.
Sidi,	. . . .	Frl. Treuge.
Minni, Gäſte des	. . . .	Frl. R. Grünfeld.
Fauſtine, Prinzen	. . . .	Frl. A. Grünfeld.
Silvia, Orlofski	. . . .	Frl. Künzler.
Sabine,	. . . .	Frl. Stubel.
Bertha,	. . . .	Frl. Steinburg.
Lori,	. . . .	Frl. Donner.
Paula,	. . . .	Fr. Romani.
Erſter) Diener des Prinzen	. . . .	Hr. Buchner.
Zweiter)	. . . .	Hr. Kuſchle.
Ein Amtsdiener	. . . .	Hr. Schweßlak.

Herren und Damen. Masken. Bediente.
Die Handlung ſpielt in einem Badeorte, in der Nähe einer großen Stadt.

Vorkommende Tänze:

1. **Spanisch,** ausgeführt von Frl. Grillich und 8 Damen vom Ballet.
2. **Schottisch,** Frl. Geraldini, Fechtner, Wollſchack, Meier und Wieſt.
3. **Russisch,** Frl. Angelina Boneſi, Frl. Stubenvoll, Nagelſchmidt, Gwerkofsky, Guhr, Schmidt und Großeli.
4. **Polka,** Frl. Walter, Frl. Raab und Anna Thorn.
5. **Ungarisch,** ausgeführt von Frl. Benda und Herrn Couqui.

Anfang 7 Uhr.

K. k. Hoftheater-Druckerei. (B. N. St. G.)

The reviewers felt otherwise, after the première at the Theater an der Wien on Easter Sunday, 5 April 1874. The critic Eduard Hanslick called it "a potpourri of waltz and polka motives," and another complained that the champagne song in the second act was flat. Though by no means a failure, the original series of *Fledermaus* performances during 1874 totaled 68.

In Berlin, *Die Fledermaus* was received more cordially in June 1874, and celebrations for its 200th performance in 1876 were held when the Vienna production reached only half that number. In November 1874, there were performances in New York (Thalia, 21 November) in German, but these were hardly noticed. Geistinger recreated her part of Rosalinde in New York in 1881.

One thing that set *Die Fledermaus* apart from many other Viennese and French operettas of the day was that it was in modern dress, which presumably made audiences expecting costumed frivolity a bit discomfited, though the party in Act II no doubt purposely compensated for this omission. Today, naturally, the period elements make the operetta more attractive, but we thereby lose a certain contemporaneousness.

The initial British *Die Fledermaus* performances (Alhambra, 18 December 1876) were not terribly admired, while the first Parisian production was legally constrained from approximating *Le Réveillon* by Meilhac and Halévy. The management of the Théâtre de la Renaissance was even more concerned that a modern-dress operetta would not attract; consequently, the story and period were altered, and bits of *Cagliostro in Wien* (which had appeared in Vienna in 1875) were added. This bastardization, concocted by Wilder and Delacour, was entitled *La Tzigane* (The Gypsy Girl), and despite the charms of Zulma Bouffar and a marvelous poster by Jules Chéret, it achieved only a fair run of 86 performances in 1877.

Subsequent productions changed the fortunes of *Die Fledermaus*, making it a worldwide repertory favorite and money-maker, and, critically, *the* Viennese Golden Age operetta *in excelsis*. During the 1800s it competed with other works (even some by Strauss) and usually lost, in terms of audience response. The Casino Theatre in New York gave it in 1885 with De Wolf Hopper (as Frank) and Mathilde Cottrelly (as Adele) but it never achieved the great success in New York or on tour of *The Queen's Lace Handkerchief*. The British spurned it until *Night Birds* revived interest in 1911 (Lyric, 30 December), a version that was put on the following season in New York as *The Merry Countess*, with José Collins and the "Dolly Twins" (Sisters). The first production of *La Chauve-Souris*, the literal translation of *The Bat*, with a new book by Paul Ferrier (using some of the characters' names from *Le Réveillon*), was given in Paris (22 April 1904) at the Variétés—the first chance for the French to hear the original score—

Nightbirds, the 1911 London adaptation of *Die Fledermaus* at the Lyric Theatre. In this scene from Act II, Countess Rosalinda Cliquot (Constance Drever) is not recognized by her husband "Max" (or Eisenstein, played by the ex-Savoyard C. H. Workman), here talking to "Dr. Berncastler" (or Falke, Claude Flemming). The operetta was presented in (what was then) modern dress, as were many older works at the turn of the century.

but this caused no great éclat. There was no major Parisian revival in French until 1933. *La Chauve-Souris* enjoyed an extremely lush revival in 1969 at the Opéra-Comique, in a beautiful production designed by André Levasseur.

In London, *Die Fledermaus* entered the repertoire of the Royal Opera, Covent Garden, in German, in 1930. It was first done there in English in 1937. A major revival took place at Covent Garden in 1977, with an international cast performing in several tongues. Though a mishmash, the Julia Trevelyan Oman sets and costumes proved attractive to an international audience watching the proceedings on television by satellite.

The most acclaimed revival of all was Max Reinhardt's, for the Deutsches Theater, Berlin, in 1928 (8 June). Produced as a summer money-maker, the production was so admired by press and public that it was chosen as the twenty-fifth jubilee production at that theatre two years later. The Erich Wolfgang Korngold musical adaptation made Reinhardt receptive to *Fledermaus;* the score was thoroughly altered but (from all accounts) brilliantly, in spite of interpolations from other Strauss works. Hermann Thimig was a *parlando* Eisenstein, and Oskar Karlweis was a male Prince Orlofsky.

Reinhardt opened the show with the overture played against a *Heurige* scene. Dr. Falke, seated alone amid spring foliage, smoked a cigarette in a holder. Near the end of the scene he rose, paid his bill, and danced to the final waltz strains, his cape becoming the wings of a bat. The motif for the work was established early and memorably. The Act II party *chez* Orlofsky employed a revolving stage, the guests arriving one by one in a vestibule and then being admitted into a grand Biedermeier ballroom that spun into view.

It was probably the most memorable staging *Fledermaus* ever received and it was repeated in several cities. The Ernst Stern turntable was subsequently used for a Shubert production on Broadway two years later, unimaginatively called *A Wonderful Night* (Majestic, 31 October). Archie Leach appeared as "Max Grunewald" (read Eisenstein). The actor later dropped his singing to become Hollywood's Cary Grant. Strauss's widow, Adele, joined with Reinhardt to sue the Shuberts for the unauthorized use of their property. But Frau Strauss died the next year.

In 1933 (Pigalle, 28 December), Parisians saw *La Chauve-Souris* for the first time in thirty-one years, with Jarmila Novotna, Lotte Schöne, and the great actor Jules Berry in principal roles. Its success was not repeated in Milan, however; Reinhardt had predicted that *Il Pipistrello* (among its other titles) would not be welcomed in other countries as it had been in Germany and Austria. But in New York, in 1942, as *Rosalinda* ("entire production under the supervision of Max Reinhardt"), the operetta was a triumph, running 502 performances at the 44th Street Theatre.

In 1950, Rudolf Bing produced a popular version at the Metropolitan Opera, New York, with a libretto by Howard Dietz and staging by Garson Kanin. Broadway comedian Jack Gilford caused a sensation as Frosch, the role Danny Kaye had passed up, and the piece was so successful that a transcontinental tour was planned for thirty-eight weeks. There have been at least three ballet versions of the operetta, and it remains the most recorded Viennese operetta of the Golden Age.

Why? George P. Upton will explain:

> It would be impossible to name the conspicuous numbers in this animated and sprightly work without making a catalogue of them all. The opera is a grand potpourri of waltz and polka motives and fresh, bright melodies. The composer does not linger long with the dialogue, but goes from one waltz melody to another in a most bewildering manner, interspersing them with romanzas, drinking-songs, czardas, an almost endless variety of dance rhythms and choruses of a brilliant sort. It is a charming mixture of Viennese gayety and French drollery, and, like his "Roman Carnival" and "Queen Indigo," is the very essence of the dance.[1]

During the original Viennese run of *Die Fledermaus,* the creator of the part of Dr. Falke died tragically onstage, and the role was assumed by the increasingly popular Alexander Girardi, an ex-locksmith from Graz who had scored a great hit in 1871 in a Millöcker *Posse, Drei Paar Schuhe* (Three Pairs of Shoes), along with Marie Geistinger. In 1874, Girardi and Josefine Gallmeyer appeared as Claudius and Ophelia in an operetta-parody by J. Hopp, *Hammlet.* He was becoming a top star at the Strampfertheater when the Theater an der Wien lured him away with the promise of a Johann Strauss part for him to create—Blasoni, the knavish assistant to the Count in *Cagliostro in Wien* (Theater an der Wien, 27 February 1875).

Zell and Genée's libretto was set in 1783–84, the centenary of the Viennese victory over the Turks, when Cagliostro was supposedly visiting the city (he

---

[1]George P. Upton, *The Standard Light Operas,* pp. 175–76.

The Act II finale of *Die Fledermaus* at Reinhardt's Deutsches Theater, Berlin, 1928. Once again, a famous acting company took on a classic operetta, with fabulous results. Particularly stunning was the ingenious revolving setting, here depicting Prince Orlofsky's ballroom. The comedian Oskar Karlweis, flaunting tradition, was a male prince (seen in the white tunic). Österreichische Nationalbibliothek.

was actually then in Strasbourg). Scribe and Adam's *Cagliostro,* an *opéra-comique* (1844), had a quite different plot set in Versailles in 1780. Like *Karneval in Rom* and several forthcoming works, *Cagliostro* wedded Austrian and Italian motifs, and even had a popular czardas, but the Viennese were awaiting one thing: *the waltz.* And Girardi sang it (*"Könnt' ich mit Ihnen fliegen durch Leben"*—If only I could fly with you through life). Geistinger appeared as Lorenza, and Friese sang the title role, but the evening was Girardi's, thanks to the waltz which had to be encored several times nightly for 56 performances. A notable revival of a new edition occurred in Danzig in 1941.

Prinz Methusalem, for which Karl Treumann provided the text, was the only Carltheater Strauss operetta (3 January 1877). The book was written originally in French by the team of Wilder and Delacour, who had translated *Indigo* and *Fledermaus* for the Paris stage. This was an Offenbachian story of two rival countries at war, Trocadero and Rikarak. Nonsensical characters—Carbonazzi, Vulcanio, Sophistika, Trombonius—filled the complementarily silly story, which the critics claimed could not possibly have prompted so charming and well-formed a score from Strauss. They may have been right, as it was rumored that Strauss did not even wait for the German text before composing the music. The Carltheater cast included Antonie Link in the breeches title role, with Josef Matras as the Prince of Trocadero, whose comic song with the refrain about "the dotlet on the i" was best-liked.

The Folies Dramatiques Theatre, London (originally the Novelty and later the Kingsway), produced *Prince Methusalem* (19 May 1883) during its short career as an operetta house to critical and public mockery, and it was given at the Casino, New York, a month later, with Francis Wilson as Trocadero and Mathilde Cottrelly "not vocally equal" to the part of Methusalem, according to the *Telegram.* This ran a respectable 102 performances, chiefly notable for Wilson's "Dotlet on the I."

Francis Wilson had appeared as Sir Joseph Porter in a San Francisco *Pinafore,* after which he became a leading comedian in the McCaull Opera Company, which first presented *The Queen's Lace Handkerchief* (the 1880 Strauss work) for a very long run at Rudolph Aronson's Casino Theatre, New York. Wilson took over the part of Don Sancho in New York, and became a sort of U.S. equivalent of Alexander Girardi, enjoying an even longer career which included, among other Girardi originals, Zsupán in *Der Zigeunerbaron* and Marsillac in Genée's *Nanon.* His greatest part was as Cadeaux in Jakobowski's *Erminie* (1885).

The less said about *Blindekuh* (Blindman's Buff), the better. It was a complicated comedy by Rudolf Kneisel, with one of Strauss's weakest scores (Theater an der Wien, 18 December 1878), composed right after the death of his first wife. Seven weeks would pass before Strauss remarried, to a woman nearly twenty-five years younger than he, not odd when one realizes that Jetty Treffz had been considerably older than her husband. *Das Spitzentuch der Königin* (The Queen's Lace Handkerchief, Theater an der Wien, 1 October 1880) fared much better, and was the biggest Strauss operetta success in America in the nineteenth century. The book by Heinrich Bohrmann-Riegen (lyrics by Richard Genée) had been written for but turned down by Suppé, who was busy writing *Donna Juanita*. This had a story mixing Cervantes up with the Queen of Portugal, who had written a compromising note on her handkerchief: "The Queen loves you, though you are no King." Set in far-off 1580 and with an attractively Iberian atmosphere for Strauss to work with, this was the biggest Strauss operetta success in years.

Girardi made the greatest impression as Don Sancho, though Cervantes had the best songs. One was *"Wo die wilde Rose erblüht"* (Where the wild rose blooms), which became part of the famous *Rosen aus dem Süden* (Roses from the South) waltz, which also included other music from the operetta, including a section of the king's *Trüffel-couplet*. *The Queen's Lace Handkerchief* opened the brand-new Casino Theatre, New York (21 October 1882), for manager Rudolph Aronson. But if New Yorkers were ready for the latest Strauss hit, the theatre wasn't—the heating system had not been completely installed by the première, and performances were curtailed after a few very cold evenings. The operetta was sent on tour, returning to New York that December to a warmer reception. It ran 130 performances and could have gone on were it not for a previously contracted season with Maurice Grau's French Opera Company. In spite of a cold start, the beautiful Moorish-styled theatre with its large pit holding thirty musicians—then a large number for comic opera—would be one of the late nineteenth century's leading operetta theatres.

Zell rejoined Genée to provide Strauss his next success, *Der lustige Krieg* (The Merry War, Theater an der Wien, 25 November 1881). Again, a rococo Italian setting, a plot concerning two rival states, and clever lyrics inspired some enchanting music. There was nothing unique about the libretto, a typical affair with disguised dukes, but it was somewhat cleverer than the librettists' much-maligned successor, *A Night in Venice*. There were two principal comedians: Girardi, as the Marchese Filippo Sebastiani, and Felix Schweighofer, as Balthasar Groot, a Dutch tulip-grower. Schweighofer, who was earlier seen as Count Villalobos in *Das Spitzentuch der Königin,* later created several important parts, including Pappacoda in *Eine Nacht in Venedig* and Colonel Ollendorf in Millöcker's *Der Bettelstudent*. He began his career as an accountant, in Brünn (Brno), after which he worked for a furrier, a lawyer, and finally the Federal Railroads, before becoming an actor. Girardi, whose part was rather small (and who was doubtless jealous of Schweighofer), wanted it beefed up and made more sympathetic and human. After actually quitting the company when the authors said no, Girardi returned with the promise of a new song. Among Strauss's sketches was one melody that would do, and, with words by a folksinger named Franz Wagner (Genée was too busy with another work), the song became an immediate and later an international hit:

> *Nur für Natur*
> *hegte sie Sympathie . . .*

(She had sympathy only for nature . . .)

By this time Girardi, or "Xandi," was as much of an attraction in himself as a Strauss score. *Die Neue Freie Presse* noted, "Today the operetta recipe of the Viennese theatre is very simple: You take a Girardi, pour in a *couplet* around him, and the success is ready." The poet and dramatist Hermann Bahr noted, somewhat later, the effect Girardi had on Austro-Hungarian romance:

> The fact is that for twenty years now every actor, even in the remotest provinces, has to imitate the vulgar and yet mysterious, shakingly excited voice of Girardi, and has to take over his gestures . . . But that fact is not the worst of it; obviously the worst is that there's really nobody among the younger people who will be able to court a girl without unconsciously and spontaneously trying to imitate Girardi.

The Merry War played London's Alhambra (15 October 1882) during one of the theatre's non-music-hall periods, and was also seen in New York that year, in English and in German. A new translation was heard at the Casino following Millöcker's *The Beggar Student* in 1884 (69 performances, with the great English comedian Fred Leslie as Groot). The original Viennese engagement was dampened (as were attractions at all theatres) by the tragic Ringtheater fire, during the second performance of Offenbach's *Tales of Hoffmann*. In the panic, over three hundred people died. Fortunately, Strauss had attended the *first* night

Der lustige Krieg showed that Strauss was not unaware of the element which made Suppé's *Fatinitza* and *Boccaccio* so successful: the march. As would befit a "military" work dealing with war, there are plenty of marches in *The Merry War*, the leading one first occurring in the long (but not unpleasant) potpourri overture.

Following the mild success of Millöcker's *Gräfin Dubarry* and *Apajune* and the more popular Suppé works, Zell and Genée were firmly established as *the* popular purveyors of operetta libretti for the three leading composers. According to popular legend, at the beginning of 1882, Zell and Genée had two new libretti ready: one based on Polish history *(Der Bettelstudent)* and another *(Venezianische Nächte)* loosely based on a fairly successful Parisian *opéra-comique*, *Le Château Trompette* (1860) by Gevaert—book by Cormon and Carré. As the latter was definitely the weaker piece, they reasoned that the more established composer, Strauss, would ensure its success with a more expansive score. Capitalizing on Strauss's insecurity, they left both libretti with him, and when Strauss wisely told them he wanted to set the better *Bettelstudent,* the librettists informed him how delighted they were, as Millöcker wanted the other work badly. This was all Strauss had to hear: he insisted on having the Venetian work. (One wonders what wonders Strauss would have made of *Bettelstudent* and Millöcker of the other!) This story has possibly been disproved by chronology *(Der Bettelstudent* has its première almost a year before *Eine Nacht in Venedig*) and by the fact that Strauss had been talking to Zell and Genée about an operetta set in Venice for several years before they actually wrote it.

Eine Nacht in Venedig started badly in Berlin and has not yet shaken off (in reputation, anyway) the ill luck associated with the première (Friedrich-Wilhelmstädtisches Theater, 3 October 1883). The more sophisticated Berlin audience burst out laughing, not at the comedy, unfortunately, but at the inanities of the plot and the preposterous lyrics. The celebrated *Lagunen-Walzer* originally began:

> At night the cats are gray
> And tenderly sing meow.

This was too much for the audience, which drowned out the rest of the performance with catcalls and howls. The lyrics were subsequently changed to the more memorable and slightly more intelligent

> *Ach wie so herrlich zu schau'n*
> *Sind all' die lieblichen Frau'n . . .*

(Ah, how splendid to see all the lovely ladies.)

In a letter to his friend Paul Lindau after the Berlin fiasco, Strauss eagerly put the blame on the book and the fact that he had not seen the dialogue:

> The nature of the book is such that with the best will in the world I could find no inspiration in it. Its coloring is neither poetic nor humorous. It is a scatterbrained, bombastic affair without a trace of action. Nor does it require any music . . . I never saw the libretto dialogue, only the words of the songs. So I put too much nobility into some parts of it and that was unsuitable to the whole . . . At the last rehearsals, where I discovered the whole story, I was simply horrified. No genuine feeling, no truth, no sense, nothing but tomfoolery.[2]

Zell, Genée, and Strauss did indeed work separately on their operettas, for a time. After the location, characters, plot, and sequence of scenes had originally been decided upon, Zell concentrated on the dialogue, Genée on the lyrics, and Strauss on the score—to fit the situations—Genée often setting words to Strauss's music. In the spring of 1883, the press reported that Zell had read the libretto and Strauss had gone through some of the score at a Viennese gathering. In the summer, Strauss was at his country house in Schönau, Lower Austria, keeping in close contact with Genée. (Genée, also a composer, helped Strauss at times with the manuscript: his handwriting is there, and he often made musical suggestions to Strauss.)

The Berlin cast included Ottilie Collin as Annina, the fishergirl (whom Strauss, very impressed, imported to Vienna to create a leading role in his next work), and Jani Szika (the original Vienna Eisenstein in *Fledermaus*) as Caramello. But however impressed Strauss was with his cast, with the able director Fritzsche, and with the luxurious new interior of the theatre, he had very real doubts about the qualities of the text. In spite of last-minute alterations—Strauss wanted the copyists to go more slowly so he could touch things up—the reaction at the première was worse than anticipated and further revisions by all three collaborators were hastily initiated.

The upcoming first night at the Theater an der Wien spurred the workers on; the Viennese press had actively chronicled the Berlin débâcle and a repetition in Vienna was to be avoided at all costs. The Viennese première was a miraculous

---

[2]H. E. Jacob, *Johann Strauss, Father and Son*, p. 293.

vindication of the revisions—every number was sung at least twice, and the antics of Girardi (Caramello) and Schweighofer (Pappacoda) were praised to the skies. One paper noted: "On the 9th/10th October 1883, *A Night in Venice* was played for the first, second, and third time, as the public wanted to hear almost every number sung again . . . endless handclapping . . . the gentlemen rose to their feet . . . the ladies looked out of their boxes . . . the gallery cried till its throat was sore . . ." Girardi, vastly excited by his new part when Strauss originally played it for him, wanted to run out to take singing lessons. The composer threatened to throw the score in the Wien—the Danube tributary which then ran outside the door of the Theater an der Wien. (Hence, its name; it is now straddled by the Viktualienmarkt, specializing in some of Vienna's most luscious *Delikatessen*). It was also a good idea to transfer from the Duke to Girardi/Caramello the revised lagoon waltz, slowed down and sensuously played up.

The revisions were also incorporated into the Berlin production, so that by 15 October Strauss was able to thank Fritzsche happily for the "fine reception which *A Night in Venice* is now having every evening in Berlin." Yet, in spite of its huge success in Vienna, and the popularity of his dance arrangements of the show's tunes (waltz, galop, quadrille, and three polkas), Strauss was never very happy with this Venetian night.

The Viennese critics hadn't liked the book any more than the Berlin press, and the basic problem was an old one: the dangling third act. The amorous intrigue was and is no more objectionable than that found in a great many other Viennese or Parisian libretti. Perhaps if Zell and Genée had examined the Gilbertian libretti they reworked so well for the Viennese stage, they might have discovered how dramatically sound and economical *two* acts were instead of three. The end of the second act of *A Night in Venice,* then as now, is really the end of the operetta, dramatically and musically. Some admire the "Pigeons of San Marco" ensemble, but the third act is otherwise unnecessary, even with revisions. The most famous of these altered versions first appeared in Vienna in October 1923, with the music "enriched" by Erich Wolfgang Korngold. Richard Tauber triumphed as the Duke of Urbino. A Korngoldization was later heard at the Vienna Staatsoper (23 June 1929).

Korngold reduced some of the numbers, including the overture, to speed up the action, and replaced some of the cut material with music from other operettas. In the first-act duet between Pappacoda and Ciboletta, he cut the original refrain and added a theme from a drinking song and chorus in Act I of *Prinz Methusalem*. The now-celebrated *"Sei mir gegrüsst, du holdes Venezia"* was a song

Die Librettisten Zell und Genée

FRANZÖSISCHE BÜHNEN-LITERATUR.

bei der Arbeit.

from the later *Simplizius*. *"Treu sein, das liegt mir nicht"* was originally sung by Annina, but now by the Duke.

A Night in Venice was first heard in English in New York (Daly's, 19 April 1884) under the auspices of J. C. Duff's Comic Opera, and it was revived four years later by the Castle Square Opera Company at the American Theatre. There were very few revivals otherwise, the most splendid and spectacular ever being the 1952–53 Michael Todd production at the newly rebuilt Jones Beach Marine Theater, New York, with actual gondolas plying Zach's Bay and a cast of hundreds cavorting in a huge revolving décor by Raoul Pène du Bois. There was no French version until the Opéra at Monte Carlo gave it in 1930, and Britain had to wait until World War II for it—though the English National Opera recently (1976) added it to its repertoire in a glossy new English version

that failed at the box office. It remains especially popular in Eastern Europe: *Egy éj Velencében* first appeared in Budapest in 1887. It has been successfully produced on water at Bregenz, and it remains a decided favorite at the Volks-oper, Vienna, where a new production was mounted for the 150th Strauss Birthday Celebrations in 1975. Granting the existence of its well-chosen and rightfully popular interpolations, *Eine Nacht in Venedig* is assuredly number three or four in the Strauss operetta hit parade and is today more popular outside German-speaking areas than either *Wiener Blut* or even *Der Zigeunerbaron,* making it number two in these countries. So much for a bad libretto!

By the time of *Der Zigeunerbaron* (The Gypsy Baron, Theater an der Wien, 24 October 1885), Strauss was more than a national hero. He was an institution, one as cherished as the venerable Emperor himself, and one idolized throughout the Empire. In Hungary in 1883, to conduct the first night in Budapest of *Der lustige Krieg,* Strauss was introduced to the famous Magyar author Maurus Jo-kai, whose novel *Saffi* had been acclaimed. Jokai convinced Strauss that it would make an excellent comic opera, and Ignatz Schnitzer, a Hungarian journalist living in Vienna, was proposed as a librettist. That Schnitzer is remembered for nothing else is not surprising: his libretto for *Zigeunerbaron* is a model of bad construction and little wit. Yet, as a libretto for a musical version of a popular romantic story, for a composer with grand-operatic yearnings (like Sullivan and Offenbach), *Der Zigeunerbaron* was extremely effective in performance, was cheered to the skies at its première, and is still reproduced regularly in virtually its original form.

Theater an der Wien manager Franz Jauner allowed Strauss and Schnitzer ample time to do it right. (Because Jauner had been the Ringtheater director at the time of its fire, he had kept out of the public eye for some time. It was during this period that Girardi was named artistic director of the Theater an der Wien, while in fact Jauner ran the show.) The writing and composition took approximately two years, and Strauss, still smarting over the ineptitudes of the libretto for *Eine Nacht in Venedig,* for the first time paid careful attention to the book and lyrics in advance, basing his music on the exact moods of the story requirements. He and Schnitzer went over the lyrics again and again until Strauss was satisfied. The three-act plot hampered Schnitzer, but it allowed Strauss two glorious finales. *The Gypsy Baron* did have its colorful characters, none more memorable than Zsupán, the pigbreeder just returned from the Spanish wars, juicily played by Girardi. The audience enjoyed the moment when Girardi revealed his waistcoat, from which dangled stolen knives and watches.

Strauss and Jauner knew that an operetta extolling the Dual Monarchy would be politically admired (it was) and that it would make a fortune in Hungary as well as in Austria (it did). The Vienna production was therefore frankly conceived as a patriotic spectacular. Jauner's gypsy village was intensely realistic, with real horses, straw, even actual gypsy clothes. In fact, Strauss had written to Schnitzer saying he wanted "eighty to a hundred soldiers on foot and on horseback, *vivandières* in Spanish, Hungarian, and Viennese costumes . . ."

The dress rehearsal went badly—traditionally a good sign—and the première was a total triumph, with the audience screaming for repeats of nearly every number. There were countless curtain calls after each act. There were 84 consecutive performances at first; by 1935 the Theater an der Wien had seen 477 in all. Supporting Girardi in the original cast were Karl Streitmann as Barinkay and Ottilie Collin as Saffi, the two lovers. If certain critics felt, as Hanslick remarked, that "Strauss has strayed close to the dangerous borderline of grand opera," this was not necessarily meant negatively, and Strauss was happy to hear it. *Der Zigeunerbaron,* the most grandly operatic of his works played today, has been in the repertories of the Vienna and the Budapest Operas since the turn of the century, and is heard at many others as well. The first Budapest production, however, was at the Nepszínház, with Strauss conducting in the spring of 1886. The audiences went wild, flattered by the Hungarian setting and Strauss's Magyar colorings. The effect of the Budapest première can be compared to the opening performance of *Gone with the Wind* (the 1939 film) in Atlanta: a lavish period piece romantically dealing with two opposing but eventually united lands.

The score of *The Gypsy Baron* is generally rated Strauss's number two work, directly after *Die Fledermaus.* It has a magnificent, often concertized, overture, dominated by the *Schatzwalzer* (Treasure Waltz) of Act II, and there is a charming orchestral picture of the *puzsta* just before the chorus begins its doleful opening song. The operetta abounds in brilliant entrance songs. Hungarian flavoring is

---

An advertising card for the initial U.S. tour of Johann Strauss's *Der Zigeunerbaron,* presented by (Heinrich) Conried's Opera Company all over the country in 1886.

pushed aside for Barinkay's *"Als flotter Geist"* and its sensual Viennese waltz-refrain, *"Ja! das alles auf Ehr' "* (Yes, I swear it's all true!). The entrance of the soubrette, Arsena (Zuspán's daughter), is a radiant scene, followed by an even lovelier duet and ensemble with Barinkay, *"Sieh' da, ein herrlich Frauenbild"* (How fine a figure of a woman). Saffi, the gypsy maiden, has a stirring csárdás, and the pigbreeder Zsupán his hilariously illiterate *"Ja, das Schreiben und das Lesen"* (Yeah, writing and reading), which was a Girardi sensation at the première. The two big finales are among the most excitingly operatic Strauss ever wrote, the first dominated by a stirring reprise of Saffi's gypsy song and capped by the exultant coronation of Barinkay as the gypsy baron:

> *Das ist mein Thron,*
> *Weil ich Baron*
> *Der Zigeuner bin!*

The second finale features the military swagger of Count Peter Homonay, who has previously regaled all with another csárdás, the gripping Recruiting Song. Another magnificent number in Act II is the duet with chorus, *"Wer uns getraut?"* (Who married us?), a romantic description of a wedding ceremony performed by forest creatures. Act III is relieved by Zsupán's amusing account of his army adventures.

Felix Weingartner admitted *Der Zigeunerbaron* into the Vienna Opera as a Christmas attraction (26 December 1910). An attractive new production was given there as late as 1976. The operetta remains a staple at the Vienna Volks-oper. In America, *The Gypsy Baron* was unmemorably revived by the Metro-politan Opera in 1957, hoping to repeat the success of its earlier *Fledermaus* and *La Périchole,* but the lavish production, with Walter Slezak as Zsupán, failed to charm either the press or the house's subscribers and was the Metropolitan's last operetta to this date. *Le Baron Tzigane* attained a two-month run in Paris in 1895 (Folies-Dramatiques, 20 December); in London, it was not seen until 1935, in an amateur production. London's Sadler's Wells Opera subsequently pro-duced the operetta and recorded selections from it in English.

Strauss was never to write another work as good or as acclaimed as *Der Zigeunerbaron*. Ignatz Schnitzer suggested an adaptation of the play *Der Schelm von Bergen* (The Rogue from Bergen), the story of an executioner with a distaste for his trade, but this theme had already been popularized through the extraor-dinary Viennese success of *The Mikado*. Instead, the young librettist Victor Léon adapted the familiar German story "Simplicius Simplicissimus" into *Simplizius* (Theater an der Wien, 17 December 1887). In spite of Girardi playing the title role, the story, set in the Thirty Years War, was too serious for operetta tastes, and it lasted only thirty performances after a harshly criticized première.

Five years later, Strauss's fondly cherished dream of an opera for the Hofoper was realized on the first day of January 1892, when *Ritter Pásmán* (Knight Pás-mán) was presented—libretto by Ludwig Doczi. It was entirely through-com-posed, and concerned a Hungarian king in love with his vassal's wife. The story was, again, too serious for Strauss's audiences, though they liked the "national dances" in the third act, which Hanslick termed "the crown jewel" of the score. In treating another Hungarian story, it was hoped for another triumph of the *Zigeunerbaron* order, but in spite of several productions in other European cities, Strauss's knight has seldom reappeared. The Opera performed it only nine times, and it was said to have died of "acute text-failure."

Fürstin Ninetta (Theater an der Wien, 10 January 1893), with a libretto by Hugo Wittmann and Julius Bauer, had its première graced by the presence of the Emperor Franz-Josef. Its first night seemed to augur well for the future, and the Princess Ninetta was seen some seventy-six times, but she was quickly forgotten, save for a Pizzicato Polka that still enchants. More than a year and a half later came *Jabuka* (Theater an der Wien, 12 October 1894), which had the good fortune to coincide with the celebrations in honor of the fiftieth anniversary of Strauss's debut at Dommayer's. Girardi's impersonation of an Egyptian Finance Minister, Kassim Pasha, was the highlight of *Fürstin Ninetta;* in *Jabuka*, which had a Croatian setting, he was Joschko—his interpolated verse in honor of Strauss in the third act of the operetta's première had the composer and the audience in jubilation. But *Jabuka* was no second *Zigeunerbaron*, despite the intent of its authors, Gustav Davis and Max Kalbeck. Nor was *Waldmeister* (Theater an der Wien, 4 December 1895), for which Davis supplied an even creakier book, set in a small town in Saxony. The overture has been its principal virtue, still receiving concert performances. Girardi now played a provincial professor, Erasmus Friedrich Müller, with a broad Saxonian accent. The audience, as expected, adored him in any role, and even the critics (Hanslick among them) liked the continual stream of melody issuing from the seventy-year-old Strauss. There was a radio broadcast of it from Berlin in the Weimar era.

The final Strauss operetta was *Die Göttin der Vernunft* (The Goddess of Reason, Theater an der Wien, 13 March 1897). The librettists, A. M. Willner and Bernhard Buchbinder, had prepared a scenario which Strauss liked. Unfortunately, the finished libretto was not as entertaining, and Strauss wisely asked to be released from his contract. But the librettists insisted he compose the score, as they had fulfilled *their* part of the contract. Strauss could not escape, as the publishing and performance rights had already been sold, thanks to Adele, his third wife. These acrimonious beginnings did not bode well for the score, which was soon completely forgotten. Felix Salten (later popular as the author of *Bambi*) was called in to tinker with a new libretto for a 1909 version called *Reiche Mädchen* (Rich Girls), produced the same year Willner revised his plot for the much more successful *Der Graf von Luxemburg,* music by Lehár.

Obviously, one cannot blame the failure of all these operettas solely on bad libretti, nor on Strauss's presumed ignorance of stage practicalities. *A Night in Venice* has endured with a mediocre book, and the *Zigeunerbaron* text is hardly a model of wit or perception. Many melodies from the other operettas gained tremendous currency, most notably the tunes that went into "Roses from the South." Attempts to take melodies like these and fashion them into new operettas have resulted in at least two famous *pasticcios: Wiener Blut* (1899) and *Walzer aus Wien* (1931).

Franz von Suppé   Richard Genée   C. Millöcker

THE SCHOOL OF
STRAUSS II

T
HE THEATER an der Wien and the Carltheater had become the temples of Viennese operetta. Had today's long-run syndrome (and attendant advertising) existed in the 1870s, the works of Strauss and Suppé alone would have filled these theatres for months and months, but managers then had to have a supply of many works by other authors and composers to fill up their theatrical calendars. French works were still popular, but other Viennese composers, eager for the success of Strauss and Suppé, were writing operettas, and managers like Steiner and Jauner encouraged them. Millöcker, Zeller, Genée, and other composers and their librettists thus had their chances. Curiously, the libretti to almost all the great Viennese operettas of this period were by Genée and his partner, Zell.

The Viennese works of the 1870s and '80s were similar to the Parisian operettas in their dependence not only on popular composers but also on big stars, like Alexander Girardi or Marie Geistinger. On the whole, their plots were apt to be as sentimental as some of their French counterparts, and there were few in modern dress. The spectacular *féeries* were typically Parisian, however; Viennese managers were less inclined to spend such sums for works which were not expected to have long, consecutive runs. The lavishness and taste for which Paris was celebrated were rarely associated with Viennese operettas, which up to the 1920s were nearly always dowdily mounted, often with secondhand sets and costumes. The waltz, again, was of greater importance. Girardi himself was not known to have had a great voice, but voices were similarly subservient to the Viennese way with a waltz.

Comparatively few of these golden works are played today: the public has not clamored for their revival. Attempts to rekindle an interest in the less well-

---

Three composers of the Golden Era of Viennese operetta: Franz von Suppé, Richard Genée, and Karl Millöcker. Genée was also the leading librettist (with F. Zell).

133

known efforts of composers like Millöcker or Zeller, or even Strauss and Suppé, have usually failed. By and large, the Viennese audience is a conservative one, and it sadly seems to prefer the Silver Age operetta to the more musically interesting older variety.

Karl Millöcker (1842–1899) was the son of a Viennese goldsmith. His musical bent led him to the Vienna Conservatory, and in 1858 he became flautist in the orchestra of the Theater in der Josefstadt, then led by Franz von Suppé. Within six years he had become a theatre conductor himself, at the Thalia Theater in Graz. His first operettas appeared there in 1865, one-acters entitled *Der tote Gast* (The Dead Guest) and *Die lustigen Binder* (The Merry Binders). He married the theatre's star, and returned to Vienna, where he conducted at the Theater an der Wien and at the Harmonie-Theater. In 1867, at the age of twenty-five, his third one-act work, *Diana,* appeared at the Harmonie, and it was followed by a string of *Possen,* plays and ballets with Millöcker incidental music.

After a spell in Budapest, during which the three-act *Die Fraueninsel* (The Isle of Women, 1867) was presented, Millöcker again returned to Vienna, this time as principal conductor at the Theater an der Wien, under the joint direction of Marie Geistinger and Maximilian Steiner. In 1871, with Alexander Girardi leading the cast, *Drei Paar Schuhe* (Three Pairs of Shoes, 5 January 1871) proved a success—though it was, strictly speaking, a *Lebensbild* (life-picture), a farce with songs. Two of the songs became enormously popular: *"I' und mein Bua"* (I and my boy) and *"Bei Tag bin I' hektisch, bei Nacht elektrisch!"* (By day I am hectic, by night electric). The story was about a Viennese shoemaker and his wife, common folk pursuing ordinary lives. Following the popularity of *Drei Paar Schuhe* there were less exciting works, such as the *Singspiel, Der nagende Wurm* (The Burrowing Worm, 1872), the *"lokal"* operetta *Abenteuer in Wien* (Adventure in Vienna, 1873), and *Die Musik des Teufels* (The Devil's Music, 1875), described as a "fantastical musical play," all at the Theater an der Wien. During this period, Millöcker was inevitably receiving more attention as the conductor of the first runs of works like *Die Fledermaus* (1874), and there is no doubt that these had a profound influence on the more suave and less *lokal* Millöcker style that was to appear in the next decade.

Meanwhile, there was another fortuitous Girardi-Millöcker combination at the Theater an der Wien: *Das verwunschene Schloss* (The Haunted Castle, 23 March 1878). Alois Berla's plot about a haunted castle was somewhat similar to the Planquette operetta *Les Cloches de Corneville,* which had appeared a scant year earlier in Paris; the Viennese première, however, took place after Millöcker's work. Instead of a Normandy landscape, there was the equally quaint Austrian Tyrol, with its catchy dialect songs; the most popular air was *"O, du himmelblauer See!"* (O, heavenly blue lake). But there was no evil miser nor a secreted treasure in this story, rather a cowherd, Andredl (Girardi), discovering a reveling count throwing nightly parties up in the castle. Accurately called a *Volksoperette,* the Viennese at first thought it too *volks*-y, but after years of quite lucrative provincial productions it returned in triumph to the Theater an der Wien in 1893 and received a total of 63 performances up to 1909. The *Himmelblauer See* waltz was probably the first Millöcker song to gain fame outside of Austria.

Gräfin Dubarry (Countess Dubarry, Theater an der Wien, 31 October 1879) had a libretto by Strauss's and Suppé's front-rank librettists, Zell and Genée, "adapted freely from the French." The critics liked it and, as usual, liked Girardi, but the piece failed . . . until 1931, when, as *Die Dubarry*, it had its book altered by Knepler and Welleminsky and its score revamped by Theo Mackeben, at that time best known as the original conductor of the Brecht-Weill *Die Dreigroschenoper* (1928). The Berlin production premièred at the Admiralspalast Theater: *Die Dubarry* was a smash, and several of the Mackeben-Millöcker melodies became so popular that foreign productions of the new work were arranged. The biggest hit song was *"Ich schenk' mein Herz"* (I Give My Heart), adapted from the original song *"Charmant, charmant,"* and at least two others were very popular: the "title" song, *"Ja, so ist sie, die Dubarry,"* and the charming waltz-duet, *"Es lockt die Nacht"* (The Night entices). Starring as Dubarry was the Hungarian soprano Gitta Alpar, whom Berliners had earlier applauded in *La Traviata*. Reviewing the British version (His Majesty's, 14 April 1932), James Agate's first-night notice contained an elaborate plot summary that closely followed the historical facts—The Dubarry did not—ending with a guillotine finish: "I make a present of it to the screen, with the title 'Versailles Dances.' " (*Congress Dances* had recently been released in Britain; the vogue for operetta with royal backgrounds was at a new height with the opening of the Reinhardt *Helen!*) The 1931–32 *Dubarry*, according to Agate, had a "mannerless hoyden for a du Barry, a Louis Quinze lacking the rudiments of characterization, and not enough story to engross a child of twelve . . ." Agate winced at such rhymes (by Desmond Carter) as "I will win applause / From the spec-ta-tors," and found the star, Anny Ahlers, "at her first entrance [presenting] the complete Amazon, militant Valkyrie, and Germanic Fury, all three at maximum pressure."

Some time after the London first night, Fräulein Ahlers jumped out of a window to her death, so comparatively few Britons had the opportunity of seeing her. Nevertheless, the production tallied 397 performances, as compared to the Broadway edition's 87, starring Grace Moore. *Dubarry* was popular in Paris (Porte Saint-Martin, 21 October 1933) with Fanély Revoil, as well as in Vienna (Theater an der Wien, 30 August 1935) and in Budapest. *Die Dubarry* was filmed in Germany in 1951, under the supervision of Mackeben himself, but there had already been a British version called *I Give My Heart* in 1935, with Gitta Alpar and Owen Nares—a quite entertaining and tastefully mounted film which retained a few of the principal airs.

Apajune der Wassermann (Apajune the Water Sprite) was the next three-act work to appear at the Theater an der Wien (18 December 1880), again with Girardi cavorting as a folksy Austrian in a Zell and Genée libretto. It accrued over fifty performances, but was not seen again in Vienna until a much more popular mounting at the Carltheater in 1904 with Mizzi Günther and Louis Treumann (who the next year would be the original *Merry Widow* stars). *Apa-*

june was performed in New York at the Bijou Theatre (25 February 1882), and there was a more spectacular mounting at the Casino in 1885, with Francis Wilson and Mathilde Cottrelly. *Die Jungfrau von Belleville* (The Maiden from Belleville, Theater an der Wien, 29 October 1881) was similarly Zell + Genée + Girardi, but this time reverting to the French setting that figured in *Gräfin Dubarry*. The new work was not widely acclaimed. Parisians saw the operetta in 1888 at the Folies-Dramatiques, the same theatre in which the original *comédie-vaudeville* upon which the musical version was based had been performed in 1835: *Agnès de Belleville*. New Yorkers resisted the operetta in 1885.

Finally, in 1882, Millöcker had an international triumph: *Der Bettelstudent* (The Beggar Student, Theater an der Wien, 6 December 1882). Zell and Genée's libretto was again based on a French play, Victorien Sardou's *Fernande* (Gymnase, 1870), which in turn used materials that went into Bulwer-Lytton's melodrama, *The Lady of Lyons*. The legend that had Johann Strauss choosing the libretto to *Eine Nacht in Venedig* over *Der Bettelstudent*'s has already been related. *Der Bettelstudent* is about a powerful colonel who is spurned by an aristocratic lady with whom he is in love. To taunt the girl, he has a poor student disguise himself as a prince to win the girl's love—he's really noble—and the student eventually marries her. *Der Bettelstudent* made one ingenious change from its French original. The story was reset in 1704 Poland, then occupied by Saxon forces. This gave the operetta a rare revolutionary fervor, an excitement ordinarily lacking in this type of work. The byplay of the blustery Saxons (epitomized by the swaggering, burly Colonel Ollendorf) and the colorfully garbed Poles was calculated to enchant Viennese auditors, who no doubt felt superior to both parties. Nor did it bother Prussian audiences, in Berlin. Girardi was given a less comic, more romantic part than usual, as the beggar student's friend (and, later, secretary), and Schweighofer, fresh from his triumph as the tulip-grower in *Der lustige Krieg,* was Colonel Ollendorf. Given new costumes, lavish settings, and a large cast, *Der Bettelstudent* was a hit from its first night in Vienna.

The score is by far Millöcker's finest, and deservedly one of the most popular of Viennese operettas in terms of performance statistics. Its far-reaching appeal was assured very early in the first act with *"Ach, ich hab' sie ja nur auf die Schulter geküsst"* (Oh, I only kissed her on the shoulder, known as the "Kiss on the Shoulder" waltz). Colonel Ollendorf had kissed the Countess Nowalska's daughter on the shoulder and had received a slap in the face from her fan. As in *Die Fledermaus,* the plot hinged on an embarrassment that had occurred before the play began.

The other delightful number in the Act I jail scene is the entrance–duet of the two arrested students Jan Janicki (blond) and Symon Rymanowicz (brunette, as indicated in the script). The scene moves to a market fair, in which we are introduced to the impoverished Countess and her two daughters, followed by the brilliant ensemble welcoming the appearance of the disguised Jan and Symon, whom Ollendorf shows off in their borrowed finery:

> *Das ist der Fürst Wybicki*
> *Mit seinem Sekretär!*

(This is the Prince Wybicki, with his secretary.) Ten times over a millionaire, as the rhyme goes. *"Ich knüpfte manche zarte Bande,"* Symon's song in praise of the Polish woman, is justifiably celebrated. He compares her features to all the ladies he has met in every part of the world, discovering that the ideal (Polish) woman actually has a "Slavic, Bohemian" upper lip, "Parisian" little feet, and a "British" figure. The first-act finale is dominated by a stirring march.

Act II's riches are led by two entrancing love duets. The first, beginning quietly and ending passionately, is Jan and Bronislawa's *"Durch diesen Kuss"* (By this kiss), ending with its soaring command, "Love me! Love me!" The second, soon after, is Symon and Laura's more playful *"Ich setz' den Fall"* (Let us pretend . . . that I wasn't a nobleman, and so forth), a hypothetical duet that nevertheless ends with emphatic declarations of love. In addition, there are Ollendorf's *"Schwamm drüber"* (Forget it), *couplets* that can be used as a vehicle for

---

The greatest star of the Golden Age of Viennese operetta, Alexander Girardi, as Symon in Millöcker's *Der Bettelstudent* (Theater an der Wien, 1882).

topical encores, and a scintillating finale, including a robust drinking song and the dramatic exposure of Ollendorf's revengeful trick to the lady on whose shoulder he planted a kiss.

Act III, as usual the weak link, nevertheless has the attractive *couplets* for Symon, *"Ich hab' kein Geld"* (I have no money), which Girardi made his own, and a nice, long finale.

Der Bettelstudent made Millöcker wealthy, with sheet-music sales and revenues garnered from strategically timed benefit performances for the composer. For two years after its première, the Theater an der Wien played *Der Bettelstudent* at least one performance in every four, and it remains to this day a very popular work in Germany, though the number of its play-dates in Austria have curiously declined during the last few years.

Der Bettelstudent was a huge hit in Berlin (Friedrich-Wilhelmstädisches Theater, 24 January 1883) and was soon seen all over Germany. In New York, it received both German and English productions in the same month, October 1883. McCaull's company at the Casino racked up 107 performances, with W. T. Carleton and Bertha Ricci as the first romantic pair. De Wolf Hopper at one point played Colonel Ollendorf for the McCaull Company, scoring one of his earliest successes. A different translation was heard in London at the Alhambra on 12 April 1884, with Marion Hood, London's first Mabel in *The Pirates of Penzance,* as a *travesti* Symon, and the Paris première had to wait until 1889 (Menus-Plaisirs, 18 January). Both were hardly notable for their receipts.

Der Bettelstudent has since been revived all over the world, but remains a favorite in Northern and Eastern rather than Western Europe. It has been filmed at least five times in Germany (1922, 1927, 1931, 1936, and 1956), the most distinctive version being the Nazi-era production directed by Georg Jacoby, with Marika Rökk, Ida Wüst, plus Fritz Kampers and Johannes Heesters—the ideal Ollendorf and Symon, respectively. Though heavily Saxonian at times, it remains the most exciting and glittering of all 1930s Viennese-operetta film adaptations, very much a German-language equivalent of the MacDonald-Eddy films Hollywood was then making of such native operettas as *Naughty Marietta* (1935). The theme of Millöcker's operetta—Polish resistance to Germany—was hardly a theme to appeal to the Propaganda Ministry after the Polish Blitzkrieg.

Next in chronology as well as popularity among Millöcker's operettas is *Gasparone* (Theater an der Wien, 26 January 1884), a latter-day *Fra Diavolo* Italian bandit story. One of its waltzes seized the public from the first night: *"Er soll dein Herr sein, wie stolz das klingt"* (He shall be your man), which was sung by Girardi in its typical third-act position. The original lyrics would be replaced—in the streets—with "Mother, the man with the cakes is here!" The big Girardi-waltz was something the Viennese patiently waited for. The rest of the score was prime Millöcker, straddling a silly Zell and Genée book that has generally been revised for modern revivals, though the 1820 Sicilian setting and the profusion of colorful Italian dances continue to enchant.

Gasparone had 36 consecutive performances in Vienna from its première, followed by 24 more in 1884. By September it was pleasing Berliners, and early in 1885 it had a dual première in New York—in German at the Thalia and in English at the Standard (21 February), the latter given by the McCaull Company after a revival of *Apajune*. As Millöcker was a certified Aryan, *Gasparone* and other works could be performed during the Third Reich. Notable revivals occurred in the 1930s, the same decade during which an UFA production was released with the two stars of *Der Bettelstudent,* Heesters and Rökk (1937). The cinematic musical adaptation, was, however, considerably freer than the more faithful one by arranger Alois Melichar for *Der Bettelstudent*. After a picturesque prologue, a band of robbers discovered in the woods turn out to be 1938 dancing girls, led by Miss Rökk singing *"Ja, die Frauen sind gefährlich"* (Yes, women are dangerous) in a nightclub setting. *Gasparone* has recently enjoyed an upsurge of interest in Germany, probably because people were beginning to tire of *Der Bettelstudent*. A lovely new production at the Vienna Volksoper in 1980 did not, however, reveal a score as fully exciting as that for *Der Bettelstudent*.

None of Millöcker's subsequent works have retained any real hold on the stage, though several were quite popular—surprisingly—in the United States in the 1880s and '90s. *Der Feldprediger* (The Army Chaplain, Theater an der Wien, 31 October 1884) probably enjoyed greater acclaim in America than in Austria. Sydney Rosenfeld's New York version of the Wittmann-Wohlmuth libretto was entitled *The Black Hussar* (Wallack's, 4 May 1885), and with De Wolf Hopper and Digby Bell as the principal comedians it ran over a hundred performances in its initial run. Its big waltz was *"Nur ein Traum"* (Only a dream). *Der Feldprediger* was an army operetta set at the time of Napoléon's Russian campaign in 1812–13; its successor, *Der Viceadmiral* (Theater an der Wien, 9 October 1886) was a naval operetta, its first act taking place in Cadiz during the Armada era on board the Spanish ship *Guadeloupe*. *Der Viceadmiral* took some time to sail to the United States, arriving at the Casino, New York, in 1892 (18 June) for a profitable stay. *Der Viceadmiral* was revived comparatively recently by the Vienna Volksoper (1957) with Lotte Rysanek in the cast and with Zell and Genée thoroughly revised for modern ears

Die sieben Schwaben (The Seven Swabians, 1887), a folk-operetta, was notable for its Girardi part, and so was *Der arme Jonathan* (Poor Jonathan, Theater an der Wien, 4 January 1890), a huge hit for its theatre and composer. This had three acts by Wittmann and Bauer set in contemporary Boston, Monaco, and New York, with "Mister Vandergold," a rich American, changing places with a pauper, Jonathan Tripp (Girardi), and learning about work and life. There were over a hundred consecutive performances in Vienna—possibly on account of the fascination for seeing Billy, a black servant, but more likely because of its modern story. The operetta was the subject of a Walter Felsenstein revival in East Berlin in 1959. The New York version (Casino, 6 October 1890) was a triumph with Jefferson De Angelis in the Girardi part, the glamorous Lillian Russell, and a third act reset in West Point. One of the reasons for the change was to allow the Casino's manager Rudolf Aronson to incorporate his new march, "The National Guard," into the action. *Poor Jonathan*'s run was anything but poor, running most of the 1890–91 season.

At the age of forty-eight, Millöcker's health began to fail, and his works appeared with less frequency. *Das Sonntagskind* (Sunday's Child, Theater an der Wien, 16 January 1892), set in Scotland, included a charming duet between Edgar and Sylvia, *"Auf unsers Hochlands Bergen"* (In our Highland mountains). A New York critic, on viewing the Broadway version at the Casino (18 April 1892), mentioned that "there are here and there reminiscences of the lakes, kirks, kilts, and ale of the historic land," but the score was more *wienerisch* than *schottisch.* The American title was *The Child of Fortune. Der Probekuss* (The Trial Kiss, Theater an der Wien, 22 December 1894) with Girardi as Pfeifli, with his big waltz, *"Überall hör' ich nur Vreneli,"* and *Das Nordlicht* (Northern Light, Theater an der Wien, 22 December 1896) were the last two works. The first took place in the Black Forest, the second in Russia, but neither was up to the old standard. Millöcker died a wealthy man in the closing minutes of the eighteen-nineties, late on New Year's Eve, 1899.

Various *pasticcios* were concocted from Millöcker music well into the new century, among them *Jung Heidelberg* (1904), *Cousin Bobby* (1906), and *Eine Entzückende Frau* (1939). Few of the Millöcker-Zell and Genée works are heard today in their original state. The *Gasparone* performing edition generally used today dates from the 1932 revision by the composer Ernst Steffan, and *Der Bettelstudent's* book has similarly been revised. *Der Bettelstudent* remains a triumph of the Golden Age, and a new look at the other Millöcker operettas might be a very good idea.

Franz Friedrich **Richard Genée** (1823–1895) is remembered today as the Viennese Golden Era's greatest librettist; with **F. Zell** (real name Camillo Walzel, 1829–1895), he wrote the libretti for dozens of German versions of French and, later, English operettas. They became the Viennese equivalents of Meilhac and Halévy during a period of ten years, from *Cagliostro in Wien* (1875) to *Gasparone* (1884), with books and lyrics for such works as *Boccaccio* (1879), *Der lustige Krieg* (1881), *Der Bettelstudent* (1882), and *Eine Nacht in Venedig* (1883) in between. They were the principal librettists for Strauss II, Millöcker, and Suppé, and thus cornered the market. Had copyrights been as developed then as they are today, their heirs would be very, very wealthy, as the major Golden Era works still performed have their words. Zell, it has been reported, was the "Meilhac" of the partnership—he outlined the plots and suggested much of the dialogue—while Genée was the "Halévy," doing the lyrics and tightening up the script.

Genée, born in Danzig (then in Prussia), began studying medicine in Berlin but switched to music, becoming, like his future collaborators Millöcker and Suppé, a theatre conductor, in Danzig, Cologne, and Düsseldorf. His opera *Der Geiger aus Tirol* (The Violinist from the Tyrol) was produced in Danzig in 1857,

---

Gasparone was filmed by UFA in 1937, with Marika Rökk (top) and Johannes Heesters (center) in a modernized version of the original libretto. As this music cover honestly points out, the music was by Peter Kreuder and Friedrich Schröder, based on themes by Karl Millöcker. The Nazi film office, headed by Goebbels, actively promoted the filming of escapist operettas.

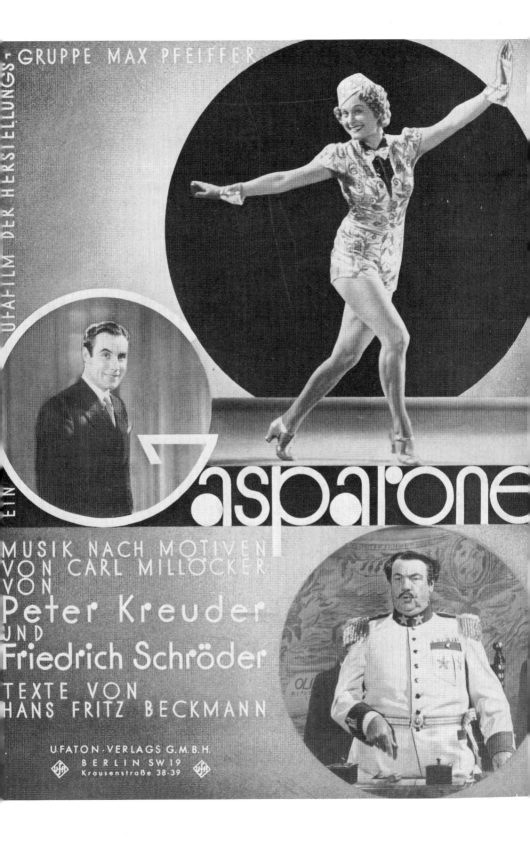

GRUPPE MAX PFEIFFER

EIN UFAFILM DER HERSTELLUNGS-

Gasparone

MUSIK NACH MOTIVEN
VON CARL MILLOCKER
VON

Peter Kreuder
UND
Friedrich Schröder

TEXTE VON
HANS FRITZ BECKMANN

UFATON-VERLAGS G.M.B.H.
BERLIN SW 19
Krausenstraße 38-39

and several works followed, including one written with Friedrich von Flotow. In 1868 he was a conductor at the Theater an der Wien, just at the time the popular French operettas were entering their triumphal period; Genée was there to rework the libretti. On the basis of his revisions of Josef Braun's text for Strauss's *Karneval in Rom* (1873), Genée was the man called in to rewrite (and ultimately discard) the Carl Haffner translation of Meilhac and Halévy's *Le Réveillon*. The result was *Die Fledermaus*.

"F. Zell" was born in Magdeburg in 1829. His family moved to Austria-Hungary, and young Zell, after a spell as a Danube steamboat captain, looked destined for a long career in the Austrian War Ministry. Instead, he retired in 1873 to set up his partnership with Genée. In 1876 came the first of Genée's two most popular self-composed operettas, with libretti by him and his collaborator: *Der Seekadett* (Theater an der Wien, 24 October). Based on a popular French *vaudeville,* the sea cadet reappeared in its musical reincarnation in London and New York in 1880. In the former production at the Globe, additions were supplied by the conductor, Edward Solomon. *The Naval Cadets,* as it was called, starred Selina Dolaro and Violet Cameron, but with weak reviews it did not last. Ada Rehan (better remembered for her Shakespeare parts) appeared in the Augustin Daly production in New York, known as *The Royal Middy.*

Nanon, die Wirtin vom Goldenen Lamm (Nanon, the Mistress of "The Golden Lamb") was also based on a French comedy, set in the Paris of Louis XIV. Written two years before Millöcker's *Gräfin Dubarry,* it was one of the first of several popular works mixing real French history and pure operetta fancy. Characters included the real Ninon de l'Enclos and the Marquise de Maintenon as well as the Sun King himself. The date of the action was listed as 1685, but in that same year both de Maintenon and Ninon de l'Enclos were beyond fifty, so the facts were already modified before the story of the innkeeper-turned-*marquise* developed. The première in Vienna was hardly notable, but in Berlin, at the Wallner Theater, there was a series of 300 performances, and when the piece returned to Vienna in 1885, it was much more of a hit.

During that period, when German stages everywhere performed it, the work was produced in New York (Casino, 29 June 1885), where it ran nearly a half year. There was a revival with Marie Tempest at the same theatre in 1892.

On the revival of *Nanon* at the Theater an der Wien in 1885, the *Neues Wiener Tageblatt* critic noted that Genée, "as a master in the art of orchestration, as an excellent musician, who understands the theatre deeply . . . ," exhibited unique talents, especially when coupled with his remarkable literary prowess.

Genée's other operettas remain history-book titles: *Im Wunderlande der Pyramiden* (1877), *Die letzten Mohikaner* (Theater an der Wien, 4 January 1879, after James Fenimore Cooper), *Nisida* (1880), up to *Freund Felix* (1893). This writer, for one, would like to see and hear what he did with the American story.

Carl Zeller (1842–1898) was born in the Lower Austrian village of St. Peter in der Au. He mastered several instruments as a child and was a boy soprano in the Vienna *Sängerknaben*, the Imperial Boys Choir. He later studied both law and music but went into the civil service, composing church music, men's choruses, marches, dances, and songs in his spare time. He rose rapidly in his government bureau (Arts and Education) and in 1876 gained some attention with a comic opera set in Scotland, *Joconde* (Theater an der Wien, 18 March 1876).

Der Vagabund (Carltheater, 30 October 1886), an operetta set in Russia, did not increase his public. *Der Vogelhändler* (The Birdseller, Theater an der Wien, 10 January 1891) did. The libretto was by two Germans living in Vienna, Moritz West and Ludwig Held. West had written Zeller's earliest libretti. Held was the cultural editor of the *Neues Wiener Tageblatt*, a friend of Alexander Girardi's, and a well-practiced translator of French comedies. One of these was *Ce que deviennent les roses*, a *vaudeville* by Varin and De Biéville (1857) which became the basis for the operetta. The libretto was suggested by and apparently written during a holiday in the Tyrol, and shows it: the speech and the setting were carefully modeled on Tyrolean folk and on an actual Papageno type who dealt in birds in that area. But because of censorship problems (either real or anticipated), the operetta's setting was changed to the Rhine Palatinate, near Mannheim, in Germany. This has made *Der Vogelhändler* as popular in Germany as in Austria. The *roses* of the French original remained, becoming roses of the Tyrol variety. As the operetta's most famous song, from the first-act finale, informs:

> *Schenkt man sich Rosen in Tirol*
> *Weisst du, was das bedeuten soll?*
> *Man schenkt die Rosen nicht allein,*
> *Man gibt sich selber mit auch d'rein!*

(When one gives roses in the Tyrol, do you know what that means? One doesn't give simply roses, one gives oneself along with them!) The original singer of the above was Girardi, who created the role of the birdseller, Adam. He caused a Viennese sensation with his second-act song as well, the heavily dialected *"Wie mei Ahn'l zwanzig Joahr' "* (When my grandpa was twenty), with its "nightingale" refrain:

> *Noh amal, noh amal, noh amal,*
> *Sing' nur, sing' Nochtigoll*

(Once more, once more, once more, sing, just sing, nightingale.)

The West and Held libretto is an extremely complicated amalgam of rustic characters and disguised *noblesse*, but its folksy diction and peasant ways have made it a true *Volksoperette*—a comparatively rare souvenir from this stage of the Golden Era. Consequently, it has not been quite as popular outside of German-speaking areas as have other, more cosmopolitan works. Musically, it has much charm, not only in the famous solos, like the sprightly *"Ich bin die Christel von der Post,"* the entrance song of the post-office girl, but also in the expansive ensembles, which show Zeller's affection for choral writing—the sequence in

the Act I finale including the march, *"Ja, den Strauss im Pavillon / Seine Durchlaucht hat ihn schon"* (His Highness has already got the bouquet in the pavilion) is very attractive, as is the earlier entrance waltz of the Electress, *"Fröhliche Pfalz, Gott erhalt's"* (May God preserve our happy Palatinate).

Der Vogelhändler had a consecutive run of 50 performances in its first series at the Theater an der Wien with a cast that included, besides Girardi as the birdseller, Ilka Palmay as the post-office girl and Ottilie Collin as the Princess. German-language performances followed everywhere. However, Zeller's superior in the Ministry of Arts and Education disapproved of his theatrical work, even if foreign governments were overjoyed with *Der Vogelhändler*. Zeller received decorations from at least five European countries—not bad for an amateur composer.

Der Vogelhändler had the distinction of sharing the bill with the first New York engagement of Mascagni's *Cavalleria Rusticana* (Casino, 5 October 1891). Called *The Tyrolean*, Zeller's operetta starred Britain's great star Marie Tempest *en travesti* as Adam. This ran a hundred performances, but America has not seen any major revival since. *Der Vogelhändler* has been filmed no less than four times, the most fondly remembered version being the 1940 Geza von Bolvary production with Johannes Heesters, Leo Slezak, and Theo Lingen.

Der Obersteiger (The Mine Foreman, Theater an der Wien, 6 January 1894) had a libretto by Held and West which tried too carefully to repeat the successful elements of its predecessor. Once again, the setting was in Germany, and the title Girardi part was once more a country worker, involved with a disguised countess, but finally marrying a local lacemaker. The music was lively and varied, and the public liked it even if the critics argued, rightfully, that it was too similar to *Der Vogelhändler*. Zeller's final operetta, *Der Kellermeister* (The Cellar Master, Raimundtheater, 21 December 1901) was billed as a *Singspiel,* the genre to which Zeller's works refer so particularly. Girardi again starred, and had a hit with *"Lass dir Zeit"* (Take your time), but little else was remembered. As both Zeller and Held had since died, West alone did another one of his provincially set libretti, and the music was enriched by Johann Brandl, but in vain. The rustic *Singspiel* elements that made *Der Vogelhändler* so attractive were not so easily recaptured.

Zeller met a sad, sordid end. In 1893, at the age of fifty-one, he fell on some ice, injuring his spine. He sued, but in the course of the trial he was convicted of perjury and sentenced to a year in prison. He suffered a stroke and died in Baden-bei-Wien, before the humiliating sentence began. To call Zeller a one-operetta composer would not be wholly fair. He was, after all, an amateur of sorts, and *Der Obersteiger* was quite popular—it is still done occasionally—and its waltz, *"Sei nicht bös' "* (Don't be cross), is often recorded. If *Der Vogelhändler* alone is known today internationally, it remains one of the best operettas of the 1890s, thoughtfully composed in the old golden style, and not at all the cheapened musical comedy that began polluting the form at this time.

More prolific than Zeller, but not as everlastingly popular, was **Karl Michael Ziehrer** (1843–1922). The son of a prosperous hatmaker, Ziehrer was also sent to the Vienna Conservatory. In 1863, he conducted his own orchestra (financed by his father) and was soon on his way as the last of the celebrated Habsburg conductor-composers of dance music. In 1866, his first operetta appeared, a one-act work entitled *Mahomeds Paradies* (1866). This caused no stir; nor did his second, *Das Orakel zu Delphi* (in Linz, 1872), or his later tries, like *Wiener Kinder* (1881). In 1870 he became a top military bandmaster, much in demand for all kinds of affairs. He continued to compose his waltzes, marches, and polkas, many for his new outfit, the "Hoch und Deutschmeister" Regiment. In 1888, he finally enjoyed a slight stage success with *Ein Deutschmeister* (Carltheater, 28 November), which had a military setting. Not as popular was *Der bleiche Zauberer* (The White Magician, 1890), based on an American Indian story by James Fenimore Cooper; Richard Genée had done *Die letzten Mohikaner* in 1878.

In 1899, Ziehrer hit the jackpot with a summer operetta, an entertainment designed for the "Venedig in Wien" theatre in the Prater. With a libretto by Leopold Krenn and Carl Lindau, *Die Landstreicher* (The Tramps, 29 July 1899)

The elaborate unit set for Zeller's *Der Vogelhändler* at the Vienna Volksoper. One of the Volksoper's most successful recent productions, *Vogelhändler* has a special folksy appeal to all Austrians—even the sophisticated Viennese Volksoper/Elisabeth Hausmann.

concerned a husband and wife involved in various fracases after discovering a 1,000-*Mark* note and a diamond necklace. If it was merely a colorful mix of turn-of-the-century farce and country (South German) folk antics, it was opulently mounted. The result pleased everyone, especially the waltz, *"Sei gepriesen, du lauschige Nacht"* (Glory to this cosy night), and the march, *"Der Zauber der Montur"* (The magic of a uniform). There was a tremendously long run of over 1,500 performances during several summer seasons, surely a record, but it is seldom revived today. Francis Wilson appeared in a Broadway version in 1901, entitled *The Strollers,* with the Ziehrer music replaced by a score by Ludwig Englander.

Die drei Wünsche (The Three Wishes, Carltheater, 9 March 1901) was well received, but the next work, *Der Fremdenführer* (The Tour Guide, Theater an der Wien, 11 October 1902), in spite of an initial run of even fewer performances (45) was the subject of two elaborate revivals. The first was at the Raimundtheater during World War II. In 1943, the romance of the good old days of Vienna was inevitably appealing. It reappeared at the Vienna Volksoper in 1978, enriched with four other Ziehrer compositions, including a romance from an operetta written a century previously for the Ringtheater, *König Jerome.* The original book was found both "unlogical and theatrically ineffective" and was altered. Willi Thaler and Alexander Girardi were in the 1902 production; Erich Kuchar and Alois Aichorn took their roles seventy-six years later.

After *Der Fremdenführer,* Ziehrer turned out one or two works a year until the 1914–18 war, many for Alexander Girardi at the Theater an der Wien; Edmund Eysler supplied similarly ephemeral works for the star. At the same time, separate waltzes and other compositions based on Ziehrer's stage melodies enjoyed a late-Habsburg vogue. These operettas included *Der Schatzmeister* (The Treasurer, 1904), *Fesche Geister* (Free Spirits, 1905), and *Ein tolles Mädel* (A Crazy Girl, 1907), the last receiving over 200 performances in an era that had suddenly become silvered thanks to Lehár and his fellow composers. *Ein tolles Mädel* was Broadwayized as *Mlle. Mischief* the following year. *Liebeswalzer* (1908), even more successful, became *The Kiss Waltz* in New York, with Jerome Kern songs added. The Emperor Franz-Josef appointed Ziehrer the royal *Hofballmusikdirektor* in 1908, succeeding to the dynasty previously controlled by the Strauss family. Unbeknown to anyone at the time, Ziehrer had the distinction of being the last in this line, and he conducted the final court ball in February 1914.

Richard Heuberger (1850–1914) was born in Graz, the son of a bandage manufacturer. He was trained as an engineer but music proved a stronger attraction, and by the late 1870s he was in charge of various singing academies and choirs. In the 1880s and '90s he was a prominent music critic for newspapers in Vienna and in Munich, and he later wrote books on musical subjects. His first stage work, *Das Abenteuer einer Neujahrsnacht* (New Year's Adventure), came in 1886 in Leipzig, and there were a few more, none achieving any great fame, save one: *Der Opernball* (The Opera Ball, Theater an der Wien, 5 January 1898).

Victor Léon and Heinrich von Waldberg wrote the libretto. When Heuberger suggested to the latter at a café that the farce *Les Dominos roses* (1876) by Alfred Delacour and Alfred Hennequin would make an excellent operetta, von Waldberg told him he had already been thinking about the same play. The plot was a sort of modernized *Fledermaus,* with similar characters going to a masked ball, only this time the action was kept in Paris. The critic Max Kalbeck wrote after the première that *Der Opernball,* "With its piquant polka, mazurka-march and waltz rhythms that sparkle and prickle . . . is no ordinary sparkling wine, rather a fiery, bubbly champagne." It had an excellent overture, and, anticipating the Silver Age, *Der Opernball* used its principal waltz for a descriptively dramatic, sensual scene. That waltz was the luscious *"Gehen wir ins Chambre séparée."* This lilting enticement to a private dining room has outstripped the operetta itself in immortality and remains the principal reason for the operetta's revival. However, the first act is delightful, and there are numerous other waltzes, especially one in the Act II finale, which command respect.

Der Opernball has had a happy career in Central Europe, and it remains a staple at the Vienna Volksoper. A production opened on Broadway (Liberty, 12 February 1912) with Marie Cahill, and the New York *Times* called the score "really insinuating and soothing." The adaptation was by Sydney Rosenfeld and Clare Kummer. In 1931, it entered the Vienna Staatsoper. Two German film versions appeared, one in 1939, a delightfully Viennese-Parisian bit of *frou-frou* but lacking most of the score, and the other in 1956.

As conventional as the libretto to *Der Opernball* was, it was better than any of the subsequent libretti Heuberger set. Those productions were failures. *Ihre Excellenz* (Theater an der Wien, 28 January 1899), not to be confused with Gilbert's *His Excellency,* was probably the best of them, and one of the last was a *Don Quichotte* (1910), given at the *"Hölle"* of the Theater an der Wien, which would lead one to believe it was a modest, tuneful affair that perhaps looked back to the Golden Era; the era that, in fact, Heuberger ended with *Der Opernball.* That he was the last of his age was proved by the fact that Heuberger was to have been the composer of *Die lustige Witwe* (The Merry Widow, 1905), the first of the Silver Age operettas. Commissioned to set the Léon-Stein libretto, he was unable to come up with any music to satisfy the Theater an der Wien, and so Lehár was given his historic chance.

J. E. JACKSON

THE SAVOY TRADITION

T HE RAGE for Offenbach in London can be traced back to the season of his one-act operettas at the St. James's Theatre in 1857, presented by the Bouffes-Parisiens company under the aegis of the composer. A few English-language Offenbach adaptations followed in the early 1860s. In 1865 *Orphée aux Enfers* played with some success as the endearingly titled *Orpheus in the Haymarket*. *Bluebeard Repaired (Barbe-Bleue)* appeared at the Olympic in June 1866 and that same month saw *Helen, or Taken from the Greek* at the Adelphi Theatre. *La Grande-Duchesse de Gérolstein* came over, in English, to the Theatre Royal, Covent Garden, in November 1867.

Hortense Schneider, who decamped to the St. James's, London, for three summer seasons in a row (1868–70), recreated her famous Paris parts (adding Eurydice) and especially delighted the fashionable audiences who could say they had already seen her as the Grand Duchess during the Paris Exhibition of 1867. Yet many critics and playgoers complained of Mlle. Schneider's suggestive gestures and the extremely risqué situations in these French importations. Some librettists attempted cleaning up some of the double entendres when these words were anglicized, but breeches parts and scanty attire lured other patrons to certain London theatres which were becoming well known for operetta by the 1870s.

In the programme for the British production of Offenbach's *La jolie Parfumeuse,* called *The Pretty Perfumeress* at the Alhambra in 1874, translator Henry J. Byron was forced to publish this statement:

The English version of *La jolie Parfumeuse* is not put forward as an exact translation or even close adaptation of the French libretto. The words of the songs, concerted pieces, choruses, etc., are simply freely rendered in English, but in the treatment of

An 1879 American poster for *H.M.S. Pinafore* stressing the romantic conflict of the heroine, Josephine. *Pinafore*'s success in the United States was unprecedented, as was its impact on the American musical stage. Library of Congress.

the dialogue and general construction of the piece, I trust I may not be considered presumptuous in claiming the performance of a different task.

The original libretto is remarkably clever, but is altogether inadmissable in an English theatre. I have had, therefore, to retain simply the "backbone" of the opera, providing dialogue which should still give a fair notion of the original, whilst avoiding anything that could give the slightest offence. I have, in fact, had to almost pull the old house to pieces and build another with the same materials.

A notable London operetta theatre was the Gaiety, managed by John Hollingshead and famous specifically for burlesque, but later for continental comic opera. Burlesque in the British sense meant a travesty of some popular or familiar work, often a grand opera, a play, or a fairy tale and usually with songs interpolated from *other* operas or operettas. Certain elements of the extravaganza and the pantomime were utilized: the "principal boy" played by a girl, the low comedian, and the shower of puns. Hollingshead opened his new theatre with the then-customary triple bill on 21 December 1868 that included *Robert the Devil, or The Nun, the Dun and the Son of a Gun,* a burlesque of Meyerbeer's *Robert le Diable.* It had new words set to Meyerbeer melodies, but it also had tunes by Hérold, Bellini, Hervé, and Offenbach. The author had already travestied Donizetti's *L'Elisir d'Amore* and *La Fille du Régiment;* he later was to take on Balfe's *Bohemian Girl* and Bellini's *Norma.* His name: **William Schwenck Gilbert** (1836–1911).

The Gaiety had no real rival for burlesque, but other theatres became famous for their operetta performances: the Olympic, the Philharmonic, Islington, the Alhambra, and others. All this activity and the irresistible Offenbach and other melodies readied the London public for the Gilbert and Sullivan revolution of the late 1870s.

A sizable segment of the mid-Victorian population, however, would not set foot inside a theatre. Plays—and players—were considered so immoral that it became necessary to disguise them as other forms, not of entertainment, but of education. Plays were "illustrations," acts were "parts," and the actors' roles were "assumptions." The musical world, steeped in the gloomy, didactic churchiness of this period, supplied oratorios and cantatas by the dozens, based on religious or similarly pious subjects to satisfy the public's real craving for opera and other musical-stage works. **Arthur Seymour Sullivan** (1842–1900) became very famous as a result of his compositions in this mode. A great segment of the middle class preferred to see anything in any way instructive: dioramas, panoramas, scientific lectures with magic-lantern slides. Minstrel shows were also considered innocent and proper. The music hall, which saw its real beginnings at this time, was not yet considered the middle-class popular entertainment it became by the 1890s; in the 1860s it had a distinctly lower-class patronage.

Richard D'Oyly Carte (name misspelled on the pillar) exhibiting his fabulous performing midgets, W. S. Gilbert (left) and Arthur Sullivan (in dress), at the time of the première of *Iolanthe* (Savoy, 1882). A cartoon from *Punch.*

An Advertising Carte.

The German Reed Gallery of Illustration "entertainments" were part of the foundation of Gilbert and Sullivan and the national school of British operetta. These "illustrations" were held in a hall resembling a drawing room more than a theatre, with a piano, a harmonium, and sometimes a harp as the orchestra. Librettist F. C. Burnand described the proceedings as if "you were attending a meeting . . . and that the attendants were somehow not very distantly related to pew-openers, or might even have been pew-openers themselves only slightly disguised." Besides various piano entertainments and solo and other comedy sketches (a sort of Victorian equivalent of nightclub acts), one-act comic operettas and farces were offered. The operettas were clearly modeled on the one-act *opéras-bouffes* of Offenbach, but without any Parisian vulgarities, in order to appeal to their middle-class audience. Domestic comedies, exotic vignettes, and typical farce plots involving mistaken identities provided the stories. The music was simple and tuneful, and obviously not intended for a full orchestra. In 1867,

German Reed leased the larger St. George's Hall, engaged a large chorus and orchestra, and undertook a season of "English" opera: *The Beggar's Opera, Ching Chow Hi* (Offenbach's *Ba-ta-clan*), Sullivan and Burnand's *The Contrabandista,* and an adaptation of Scribe and Auber's *L'Ambassadrice.* Though not a financial success, this season was a courageous milestone in the history of English operetta.

Of the various librettists and composers working for the Reeds, W. S. Gilbert and Arthur Sullivan, separately, were the most famous. It was through a German Reed piece, *Ages Ago,* that its librettist, Gilbert, first met Sullivan in 1869, through the agency of its composer, Frederic Clay. The year 1869 had started out auspiciously with the long-running German Reed production of Sullivan's first operetta, *Cox and Box.* It had first been produced at a private party at Moray Lodge in London on 26 May 1866. Burnand had the intriguing idea of musicalizing Morton's 1847 farce, *Box and Cox,* and asked Sullivan to write the score. Sullivan, the white hope of serious British music, and a popular parlour balladist as well, seized the chance to enter the theatre world. Many actors saw another amateur performance a year later at Burnand's home. Such was the fun of that midnight matinée that there were clamors to have it reproduced, and charity performances followed in Manchester and London. German Reed then acquired it for his Gallery.

Cox and Box was an intimate three-character work in both the Reed and Bouffes-Parisiens traditions. Although Burnand was hardly as great a librettist as Gilbert would become, he had a clever plot to work with and a piece that was never intended to be more than a *bouffonnerie.* Because the amateur company that first presented it was all-male, the part of Mrs. Bouncer in the farce was masculated into Sgt. Bouncer, complete with an obligatory Franco-Italian *rataplan,* the military number popular in comic and even grand opera at the time. The situations so dear to farce are admirably wedded to other operatic motifs: Mr. Cox and Mr. Box, one of whom works during the day and the other at night, meet accidentally in the room rented to both, unbeknown to each other, by the unscrupulous landlord Bouncer. The scene starts ("Who are you, sir") in melodramatic operatic fashion and ends with Bouncer's cheery solution to any problem—his *rataplan.* Box sings a lullaby to his rasher of bacon, a charming *berceuse.* And near the end he has an extended romance concerning his attempted suicide, complete with a very descriptive passage about a lonely, rocky cliff. (The surging orchestration was added for later performances by Sullivan, who wrote the score originally for piano alone.)

Cox and Box obviously proved Sullivan's knack for operetta, and the collaborators set to work on *The Contrabandista, or The Law of the Ladrones,* but this two-act work met with little success in its St. George's Hall performances in 1867.

Gilbert, meanwhile, was writing humorous verses (with captivating woodblock illustrations) for the magazine *Fun,* one of many humorous magazines then flooding the newsstands. Forty-four were collected and published as the now-immortal *Bab Ballads* in 1869, the same year Gilbert wrote a piece for the Gallery of Illustration, *No Cards* (which ironically played with Sullivan's *Cox and Box* for some time). *Ages Ago* followed that year, complete with ghosts stepping out of portraits (as in the later *Ruddigore*). Gilbert started the 1870s with a slew of successful comedies, including *The Palace of Truth* and *Pygmalion and Galatea;* Sullivan gloriously entered the decade with his oratorio, *The Prodigal Son,* and the acclaimed incidental music for a Manchester production of *The Merchant of Venice.*[1]

John Hollingshead, having convinced the duo to work together, produced the first Gilbert and Sullivan collaboration on Boxing Day (26 December), 1871 at his Gaiety Theatre, with the Gaiety favorites Nellie (Ellen) Farren and J. L. Toole in the leading roles. Expected at the same time to adhere to the burlesque traditions of the theatre and the pantomime-extravanganza *de rigueur* at Christmas, *Thespis, or The Gods Grown Old* was hardly the unmitigated failure it is thought to have been. It ran well into the following year, surpassing many other seasonal divertissements, and although it was found underrehearsed by the critics, they admired much of the music and the libretto of this "grotesque opera," and even saw a future for the collaborators together.

Thespis owes a great deal to *Orphée aux Enfers* in its mixture of gods and mortals, the latter group having climbed the summit of Mount Olympus for a picnic. Being actors, they change places with the weary gods, who are as bored with their jobs as the *Orphée* deities. The libretto has survived to this day, but Sullivan destroyed or conveniently lost the score and orchestra parts, so, aside from two numbers (one published and the other transferred to *The Pirates of Penzance*), we have no music left from *Thespis*. There always exists the Savoyard theory that the other *Thespis* tunes are present, *incognito,* in the other scores.

That golden future would not have been realized were it not for Richard D'Oyly Carte, in 1875 a thirty-one-year-old concert and lecture agent who was then managing the Royalty Theatre. Offenbach's *La Périchole* was the attraction, as usual supported by various one-act pieces for which Carte was always on the lookout. Gilbert had recently adapted a one-page "operetta" from *Fun* into a libretto for the Carl Rosa Opera Company when Mme. Rosa died. Meeting Gilbert and informing him of his need for a short operetta, preferably British, Carte was told about *Trial by Jury*. Carte immediately suggested Sullivan as the composer. Gilbert went to Sullivan's flat a few days later and read the manuscript to him,

> . . . in a gradual crescendo of indignation, in the manner of a man considerably disappointed with what he had written. As soon as he came to the last word, he closed up the manuscript violently, apparently unconscious of the fact that he had achieved his purpose as far as I was concerned, inasmuch as I was screaming with laughter the whole time . . .

---

[1]For fuller descriptions of the lives and careers of Gilbert and Sullivan separately or together, the reader is referred to any of the many standard biographies and histories: Allen, Baily, Cellier and Bridgeman, Pearson, Young, etc. (See Bibliography.)

as Sullivan recalled. Sullivan set about composing the score, and within weeks it was rehearsed and ready. The tremendously enthusiastic first night took place 25 March 1875. The reviews were ecstatic. *Punch* complained it was too short! *The Times:* "It seems, as in the great Wagnerian operas, as though poem and music had proceeded simultaneously from one and the same brain."

Many critics consider *Trial by Jury* one of the best Gilbert and Sullivan works, and in some ways it is unsurpassed—a delectable *hors-d'oeuvre* filled with everything they would do in the later works, but fresh and original here. Although it is technically a real *opera buffa,* with recitatives, arias, ensembles, and no dialogue (Gilbert called it a "dramatic cantata"), its musical model and the satiric drollery of the libretto are pure operetta. Gilbert's book and lyrics extravagantly travesty a breach-of-promise court case, and the realism of the court setting lends *Trial by Jury* an "artistic verisimilitude" previously unusual for operetta. Humor in most operettas came from exaggerated settings and costumes, transvestism, and extensive mugging, none of which was to be part of the Gilbertian plan.

Commenting on the usual operetta productions of the early 1870s, Gilbert described this proposed revolution in a 1906 speech:

When Sullivan and I began to collaborate, English comic opera had practically ceased to exist. Such musical entertainments as held the stage were adaptations of the crapulous plots of the operas of Offenbach, Audran and Lecocq. The plots had generally been bowdlerized out of intelligibility, and when they had not been subjected to this treatment they were frankly improper; whereas the ladies' dresses suggested that the management had gone on the principle of doing a little and doing it well. We set out with the determination to prove that these elements were not essential to the success of humorous opera. We resolved that our plots, however ridiculous, should be coherent, that our dialogue should be void of offence; on artistic principles, no man should play a woman's part and no woman a man's. Finally, we agreed that no lady of the company should be required to wear a dress that she could not wear with absolute propriety at a private fancy ball; and I believe I may say that we proved our case.

The first numbers in *Trial by Jury* are unmistakably of the Offenbach-Lecocq school (particularly in the orchestration of the tink-a-tank "guitar" refrain and the end of the Defendant's song), but the music suddenly assumes a mock-Handelian tone for the Judge's entrance. The Learned Judge, originally played by Sullivan's brother, Fred, sang the first of a series of songs in Gilbert and Sullivan describing how a person of low position has risen to the top of his profession, "When I, Good Friends, Was Called to the Bar." The felicity of Gilbert's lyrics is matched by the tact of Sullivan's setting, which lets every word be heard. The music is sprightly and the beloved choral repetitions enchant; however, after many such settings and more furious patter in the later operettas, Sullivan tired of taking second place.

Other elements distinguish *Trial:* the bizarre realism on Gilbert's part to have the bride and her bridal party attend the trial in their wedding wardrobe, the *bel canto* burlesque *à la* Bellini ("A Nice Dilemma We Have Here") which is rather out of place in a British court, but straight out of *La Sonnambula ("D'un pensier")*. And quite silly with English words such as *wit* (in "That calls for all our wit") with the consonant *t* foiling what would in Italian be a free vowel. This bit of grand opera is unexpected, and Sullivan had his singers give it the full Italian ham treatment. The original stage directions for the ending called for two plaster Cupids in barristers' wigs to descend from the flies and "red fire," but modern productions do without this effect.

Trial by Jury was easily the best British operetta up to that date, and it was entirely British; what could be more British than a British courtroom? D'Oyly Carte kept it running successfully for 200 performances, but, strangely enough, its success did not lead immediately to another Gilbert and Sullivan work. In 1876 the death of Sullivan's brother spawned *The Lost Chord,* Sullivan's (very popular) tribute. Gilbert was busy with several plays, including the hit *Broken Hearts,* and both Gilbert and Sullivan collaborated on operettas with other writers: *The Zoo* (Sullivan and B. C. Stephenson) and *Princess Toto* (Gilbert and Frederic Clay), in 1875–76. Carte was occupied in 1876 with the formation of the Comedy Opera Company, the purpose of which was to commission and

---

An artist's impression of the first night of *Trial by Jury,* Gilbert and Sullivan's one-act "dramatic cantata," at the Royalty Theatre, London, 25 March 1875. The role of the Judge (top) was played by Sullivan's brother, Fred, who also played the role of the Viceroy in *La Périchole* on the same bill. Bridget D'Oyly Carte, D.B.E.

perform British light opera. Burnand, Alfred Cellier, and Frederic Clay were among those approached, but in the end it was Gilbert and Sullivan who finally agreed to furnish the first full-length work for Carte's new company. The original terms of the June 1877 agreement were two hundred guineas for delivery of the manuscript words and music, and six guineas per performance in royalties to the pair, less the two hundred. Carte then leased "a distinctly second-rate theatre" in the Strand, the Opera Comique.

The Sorcerer was based on a story of Gilbert's, *The Elixir of Love,* which had appeared in the Christmas 1876 number of *The Graphic.* Gilbert had already burlesqued the Donizetti opera in his very first play, *Dulcamara;* his love of philters, potions, and pills would never die, and the "lozenge" plot was one that would later annoy Sullivan when it was reintroduced. Gilbert's story concerned an entire village succumbing to the effects of an aphrodisiac supplied by an old-established magician's firm in St. Martin's Lane. For the role of the magician, John Wellington Wells, the authors chose a provincial concert entertainer, George Grossmith, but the directors of the Comedy Opera Company were against the choice, as was Grossmith's family. Grossmith himself was unsure and said to Gilbert he thought the part would require a fine voice. "That is exactly what we don't want," replied Gilbert. Rutland Barrington was engaged for the part of Dr. Daly, at £6 a week, though the actor had some misgivings about playing a burlesque vicar. Barrington was not asked to audition for Sullivan; Gilbert wanted actors who could sing rather than singers who might be able to act. Mrs. Howard Paul was originally hired to play Lady Sangazure *and* Ahrimanes, a spirit in the second act, but the latter role was deleted, leaving Mrs. Paul with only the first "old lady" contralto part of the Savoy series.

Gilbert was laying the foundation for the future operas with the cast of *The Sorcerer.* Grossmith played the comedy-baritone parts right up to Jack Point in *The Yeomen of the Guard,* Barrington continued up to *The Grand Duke* (Ludwig) and beyond (into the new century), and Richard Temple (Marmaduke) stayed on through *Yeomen*'s Sergeant Meryll. The contralto parts were taken over by others (most notably Rosina Brandram) and the tenor, soprano, and soubrette parts were firmly established in *The Sorcerer.* Each succeeding opera would have parts for Carte's virtual repertory company.

Once in D'Oyly Carte's Gilbert and Sullivan troupes in London or on tour, actors tended to be associated with Gilbert and Sullivan parts, and many had long careers with the company. Perhaps most celebrated among George Grossmith's successors in this century were Henry Lytton, who was knighted late in his career, and Martyn Green, both of whom appeared not nearly as notably in musical comedy. In the contralto parts, Lytton's partner Bertha Lewis had a brilliant career cut short after a car accident. A later contralto, Gillian Knight, has moved on to grand opera, as has Valerie Masterson, presently one of Britain's leading sopranos. A D'Oyly Carte tenor equally famed for his work outside Gilbert and Sullivan was Derek Oldham, who appeared prominently in London productions of American and European operettas in the 1920s.

With an established troupe of actors and his dramaturgical skills, Gilbert had created the ideal scaffolding for the British operetta, a format neither he nor succeeding librettists saw fit to alter. Gilbert's skill as a stage director was also startlingly apparent. He allowed no digressions from the script, he made his players act with the utmost seriousness, and he stressed the clarity of enunciation which became a trademark of the Gilbert and Sullivan artist. Sullivan also had his way, demanding full-blown Italian opera parody for the first-act finale. "I want you to think you are at Covent Garden Opera and not at the Opera Comique," he said at a rehearsal of *The Sorcerer*.

The Opera Comique had opened in 1870 in what was then a seedy area (now the Aldwych) and was called "Theatre Royal Tunnels" because its underground auditorium was reached by several long, drafty passageways. Nevertheless, the prospect of a full-length work by the author and composer of *Trial by Jury* ensured a fashionable house on 17 November 1877. The *Times* led the parade of praise for the libretto ("an extravaganza of the best, set forth in Mr. Gilbert's raciest manner, full of genial humour and such droll fancies as come to him readily"), the score ("above all, the music is spontaneous, appearing invariably to spring out of dramatic situations"), and the production ("a more careful first performance of a new work of its kind has rarely been witnessed"). *The Sorcerer* was a success, but it was more than that. It was "another nail in the coffin of *opéra-bouffe* from the French," as Sullivan noted, proving that English comic opera had indeed arrived. It is a simple country tale, charming if not vintage Gilbert and Sullivan. Its music is sometimes dainty, sometimes vigorous, and always tuneful, but, perhaps because of the garden-party gentility of the story, it has not achieved great popular success.

When *The Sorcerer* was scarcely a month and a half old, Sullivan received a letter from Gilbert containing the sketch plot of his new "Entirely Original Nautical Comic Opera." The directors of the Opera Comique, threatening to take off *The Sorcerer* every time the receipts went down, were anxious for a new piece. Though utterly original, some elements of *H.M.S. Pinafore* can be traced back to several Gilbert *Bab Ballads,* such as "Captain Reece," "Joe Golightly," and "The Bumboat Woman's Story," among others written for *Fun*.

Gilbert's libretto was written with some of the stars from the *Sorcerer* company in mind. George Grossmith would be Sir Joseph Porter, First Lord of the Admiralty, Captain Corcoran would be played by Rutland Barrington. Hebe was originally written for the contralto from *The Sorcerer,* Mrs. Howard Paul, but after some disagreements with the management she left the cast, and the part of Hebe was taken over by her much more attractive understudy, Jessie Bond.

For the historical authenticity Gilbert insisted upon, he and Sullivan visited the Portsmouth harbor in April 1878, to inspect the deck of H.M.S. *Victory*. The librettist made copious drawings of the ship and the riggings, which he reproduced on a model stage. And he meticulously sketched out the uniforms for the play, which were made by a naval supplier at Portsmouth to ensure their accuracy. Gilbert staged the play on his model stage using colored blocks of wood to represent the principals and chorus. Thus, when rehearsals began, Gilbert had a firm notion of every movement he wanted. He never allowed digressions from his staging or dialogue; no gags or interpolations. And he made his actors perform with the utmost seriousness, so that the often ridiculous dialogue and lyrics seemed all the more amusing. It is this combination of absurdity and sincerity that is the hallmark of the Gilbert and Sullivan operettas.

The first night, 25 May 1878, gave every indication that *H.M.S. Pinafore* would be the popular operetta it was to become. The house had been sold out days before the *première*. Five numbers were encored during the performance. The reviews the next day were mostly favorable, but one notice called the play "a frothy production destined soon to subside into nothingness," and within a few days it looked as if this prediction would be an accurate one. London was suffering from an intense heat wave, and the theatre was so cramped and stuffy that audiences perspired and gasped during the not-too-well-attended performances. With receipts dropping to less that £40 a night, the directors of the Comedy Opera Company posted closing notices on several occasions (Carte had to run in and remove them) and the salaries of the company were cut by one third around the beginning of August.

Near the end of the month, Sullivan decided to include a medley of the tunes from *Pinafore* in a Promenade Concert he was conducting at Covent Garden. The arrangement was by Hamilton Clarke, who assisted Sullivan on the composition of some of the future overtures. The audience loved it, and soon everyone had to see *H.M.S. Pinafore*. The advance bookings increased, and within a few weeks the music was so popular that 10,000 copies of the vocal score were sold in a single day. The directors of the Comedy Opera Company were now drawing £500 a week. (They wanted even more, however, and they split from Carte to set up their own *Pinafore* company at the nearby Olympic Theatre. This led to a lawsuit, and the rival company quickly closed.) The original version ran some 700 performances, which was by far the longest consecutive run London had ever seen for any musical play. There was even a children's company with juvenile actors playing matinée performances.

While the London production ran, *Pinafore*-mania struck in America. On 25 November 1878, six months after the London first night, the first American production of *H.M.S. Pinafore* opened at the Boston Museum. In December, San Francisco saw the operetta for the first time. By March 1879, New York had eight different companies playing *Pinafore,* and Philadelphia had six, including the first German version. Because of the lack of a reciprocal copyright law between Britain and the United States, Gilbert, Sullivan, and D'Oyly Carte received nothing for these pirated American performances of *Pinafore,* which by the spring of 1879 had become the most popular theatrical attraction the country had ever seen.

The songs and dialogue were so familiar by this time that it was difficult for an American to escape a reference to *Pinafore*—especially in the press—in the course of a single day. Scenes from the operetta appeared on thousands of brightly colored advertising cards and in children's books. The songs were sung, whistled, and hummed universally, and the temptation to break into snatches from *Pinafore* was very great. A clergyman at a funeral closed his eulogy with the following phrase: "We shall miss him very much." And a mourner quickly added: "and so will his sisters, and his cousins, and his aunts!"

Performances in America hardly conformed to the original London version. In one New York production, the part of Ralph Rackstraw was taken by a woman, which Gilbert would never have tolerated. (What, never? . . . No, never!) A black company played in New York and Philadelphia, and one New York version had several interpolated numbers, including Handel's Hallelujah Chorus.

In June of 1879, Carte sailed for New York. He felt sure that America would welcome the original British version, and he made arrangements with a New York manager to present his own *Pinafore,* to be followed by a new Gilbert and Sullivan opera at the end of 1879. This New York première was arranged to prevent American pirates from stealing a London production and legally presenting it in the United States without paying royalties to the British authors. Gilbert had said, "I will not have another libretto of mine produced if the Americans are going to steal it. It's not that I need the money so much, but it upsets my digestion." Appropriately enough, the new opera was called *The Pirates of Penzance.*

Gilbert and Sullivan arrived in New York that November and were given a great reception as they arrived in the harbor. For the next few weeks they were lionized by Society. The New York cast and orchestra were a mixture of Americans and Britons and included the original Hebe from London, Jessie Bond. But the most important cast member on the New York first night, 1 December 1879, was W. S. Gilbert himself, who put on a false beard and appeared *incognito* to the audience as a sailor. The New York press and public alike adored the original *H.M.S. Pinafore,* and it is from this date that one can call the success of the Gilbert and Sullivan operettas *officially* international.

It is not difficult to see what made *H.M.S. Pinafore* the great triumph it became. The very idea of having a comic opera set on board a ship of Her Majesty's Navy was a brilliant idea of Gilbert's. Aside from the sheer theatrical novelty, the patriotic associations of a British man-of-war must have been very gratifying to the audiences of Victoria's reign. A chorus of sisters, cousins, and aunts was charming and pretty, and a chorus of sailors was as bracing as the sea air. Gilbert's passion for realistic settings and costumes probably made audiences feel they were visiting Portsmouth harbor on a sunny afternoon—what could be more exciting *and* patriotic?

Sir Joseph Porter, the leading comic character, was actually based on Gilbert's contemporary, W. H. Smith, who was appointed First Lord of the Admiralty by Disraeli. Smith's beginnings were similar to Porter's, as neither had ever been to sea; Smith headed the newspaper and book-selling establishments that still bear his name. Gilbert explained the situation in a story version written for children in 1908:

. . . You would naturally think that the person who commanded the entire Navy would be the most accomplished sailor who could be found, but that is not the way in which such things are managed in England. Sir Joseph Porter, who had risen from a very humble position to be a lawyer and then a Member of Parliament, was, I believe, the only man in England who knew nothing whatever about ships.

Sir Joseph's haughty attitude toward Captain Corcoran and his daughter, whom he nevertheless desires to marry, struck the original audiences as being quaint and amusing: Sir Joseph was really of "the lower middle class," while the Captain and Josephine were socially superior, being in the Royal Navy. But this situation is shattered when it is discovered that the Captain and Ralph were exchanged in childhood (a favorite device of Gilbert's which he used again in *The Gondoliers* eleven years later). Apart from the social satire, the witty and memorable dialogue enabled *Pinafore* to sail to the United States and the rest of the world. Gilbert's lyrics, while clear and amusing, gave only a hint of the more brilliant efforts which were to follow.

It was Sullivan's score, however, that was the great popularizer. From the breezy, vibrant opening chorus, to Little Buttercup's charming street-song-ish aria, to the rousing entrance of the Captain, the music was a continuous stream of "hit" songs, all easily memorable. Sir Joseph's "When I Was a Lad" was the precursor of even more celebrated patter songs, like the Major-General's song in *The Pirates of Penzance,* or "I've Got a Little List" in *The Mikado.* Then there were the patriotic choruses "A British Tar Is a Soaring Soul" and "He Is an Englishman," complete with Handelian *fioritura.* Josephine has a full-blown operatic *scena* in the second act. But the greatest success in actual performance was usually the trio in the second act, "Never Mind the Why and Wherefore," which sometimes received as many as seven encores. Various bits of business were devised by many of the famous comedians playing Sir Joseph, including Henry Lytton and Martyn Green. Today, *H.M.S. Pinafore* remains as popular as ever in the English-speaking world—even more popular in the United States than in Britain, a topsy-turvy fact that Gilbert would enjoy.

When Gilbert and Sullivan had moved into rooms at 45 East Twentieth Street, it was discovered that the composer had left his sketches for Act I of the new operetta back in London. This aggravated the composition of *The Pirates,* which had to be seriously rushed when receipts for *Pinafore* at the Fifth Avenue Theatre began to fall from the middle of December. Although the première of *Pinafore* had been critically startling, enabling the American public to see how this sort of thing ought to be staged and sung, the *Pinafore* craze was on the wane by the end of 1879. Rehearsals began for the new piece very soon after the

The wildly popular New York Shakespeare Festival production of *The Pirates of Penzance,* as produced in Central Park's Delacorte Theatre in 1980, a century after the New York premiere. Kneeling, center, are Rex Smith (Frederic) and Kevin Kline (Pirate King) in the show-stopping "With Cat-like Tread" in Act II. Martha Swope.

Pinafore first night under a cloak of intense secrecy—no American pirates would be able to get hold of *The Pirates* when the orchestra parts were locked in a safe after every rehearsal. The orchestra apparently thought a great deal of the score; it considered the music grand opera rather than comic and requested higher salaries for its extra effort. Gilbert assisted Sullivan with the music as best he could—it was he who suggested interpolating "Climbing Over Rocky Mountain" from *Thespis* to the Cornish coast of *Pirates* to serve as the entrance song of General Stanley's daughters, and it was Gilbert, with Alfred Cellier and Frederic Clay, who actually helped write out the orchestra parts for the hastily composed overture the night before the première.

In his careful efforts to secure the American copyright for *The Pirates of Penzance,* D'Oyly Carte had not overlooked the British rights. A hastily assembled libretto-and-score was sent to England several days before the New Year's Eve New York première, to Carte's "second" *Pinafore* touring company. The then-unknown Richard Mansfield was playing Sir Joseph Porter, leading a company which in mid-December had reached Devon. During the engagement at Torquay, the company trotted down to nearby Paignton to give a matinée of *Pirates* on 30 December 1879, strictly for copyright. The Royal Bijou Theatre was hardly packed that afternoon, and Mansfield remembered that they all read from scripts in hand, wearing their *Pinafore* costumes—the pirates tied handkerchiefs around their heads to distinguish them from British seamen. All these arrangements were skillfully handled by Carte's secretary, Helen Lenoir, later to become Mrs. D'Oyly Carte.

The New York première was certainly more glittering, with a large section of Society represented in the better sections of the Fifth Avenue Theatre. In spite of an impressive reception, *Pirates* lasted only a few weeks in New York, though Carte arranged for three additional companies to tour *Pirates* in the United States. The London première, 3 April 1880, was cheered by the Opera Comique public, which especially liked Barrington as the Sergeant of Police, and by most of the critics. The *Times* dissented—it considered *The Sorcerer* "in our opinion the masterpiece of its joint authors."

Some consider *The Pirates* a sort of dry-land *Pinafore*—some even go so far as to call it dry-docked. Musically, however, *Pirates* is a great deal more ambitious, taking grand-opera conceits prevalent in *Pinafore* and *Sorcerer* and elaborating them further. Again, Italo-French music is placed into the most English setting, and the incongruity that arises is even more pronounced than it was in the prior works. Frederic and Ruth, in Act I, have a duet right out of Verdi; Mabel's coloratura entrance song is a pastiche Gounod waltz, rendered all the more amusing by the bloodless rendition is has usually received from legions of British coloratura sopranos. In the second act, the heroics of "When the Foeman Bares His Steel" never fail to impress, with the weight and grandeur of its double chorus. Yet the simpler songs remain the most eternally popular: "When a felon's not engaged in his employment" ("A Policeman's Lot Is Not a Happy One") which might very well have been sung in a contemporary music hall, and the Major-General's "model" of a patter song, one of Gilbert's greatest efforts in this sphere. Often overlooked are the engaging "Paradox" trio in Act II, and the fiery "Away, Away!" which follows. The scene between the two male choruses (pirates and police), featuring the very loud "With Catlike Tread," is directly borrowed from a similar situation in Offenbach's *Les Brigands,* which Gilbert translated in 1871. Sullivan must have remembered it as well, for one section of his music sounds remarkably similar to the Offenbach: perhaps this was an *hommage* of sorts.

Gilbert's supreme credo, that of treating a ridiculous notion with the utmost seriousness, comes into full play in *Pirates,* though cloaked with a surface burlesque of the blood-and-thunder melodrama then still popular in the provinces and the poorer sections of London. "The Slave of Duty" was the subtitle on the opening night (altered from the onetime "Love and Duty") and this refers specifically to Frederic, who must obey his Sense of Duty though he is pressured to act otherwise. A few laughs are still extracted from this situation, but the main charm for *Pirates*-viewers today remains the affectionate send-up of the pirates themselves, who take care never to molest orphans ("We are orphans ourselves, and know what it is") and are commandeered by the swaggering Pirate King (who had the name Richard in the original New York production). Though originally dressed like toy-theatre villains, these pirates are for the most part well mannered; the Major-General's daughters are ready to marry them within minutes after they have been captured. These "daughters" (more accurately wards in chancery) are an equally delightful bunch—with their marvelous chattering chorus, "How Beautifully Blue the Sky," in Act I—as are the Police, mindlessly blowing their truncheons like trumpets. On a purely romantic level, *Pirates* is considerably more exotic than its predecessors. Did Gilbert's topsy-turvyness make him populate this wild, rocky Cornish beach with fairly ordinary, serious, duty-minded Britons—or did he (perhaps at the same time) populate a rather ordinary, middle-class British seaside resort with some wild types?

The Pirates of Penzance has remained a steadily popular Gilbert and Sullivan work for over a century, but it received a tremendous new lease on life with the New York Shakespeare Festival presentation at the *al fresco* Delacorte Theatre, Central Park, in the summer of 1980. The original idea to present Gilbert and Sullivan was Joseph Papp's, which led to discussions with director Wilford Leach and the pop singer Linda Ronstadt. Once the engagement of Miss Ronstadt was confirmed, there was an attempt to freshly rethink the operetta, at once remaining faithful to Gilbert's libretto while releasing it from the accepted D'Oyly Carte-inspired tradition. Sullivan's music was reorchestrated by William Elliott to meet the exigencies of an outdoor presentation (and to keep the orchestra small for budgetary reasons): the resulting sound was certainly different from the original, although the buoyant spirit of Sullivan's style was retained and the new sound rarely lapsed into the rock sound purists feared.

Surrounding Miss Ronstadt was an unusual cast of Britons (George Rose and Patricia Routledge) and Americans (Kevin Kline and Rex Smith), all of whom received as many critical bravos as did Miss Ronstadt. She was nevertheless a potent draw, bringing in people who knew nothing about Gilbert and Sullivan and in at least one instance thought "The Pirates" was a back-up group for her rock concert. Mr. Leach's staging was the principal success of the venture in the end, and the show's cohesiveness and panache caused nearly every critic to shout with joy. The mere mention of "*new* musical hit" must have warmed every Savoyard's heart (and every operettamane's as well). The production was predictably transferred to Broadway (Uris, 8 January 1981) where it continued to run and earn more money weekly than any previous Gilbert and Sullivan operetta ever had. It was awarded a Tony as "best musical revival," and brought Kevin Kline overnight stardom as a most untraditionally young, virile, and loony Pirate King. Touring companies, a London company, and a film have followed, but as of this writing there have been no other attempts to rethink Gilbert and Sullivan for Broadway, save for a Stratford, Canada, *Mikado* (1987).

After a successful run at the Opera Comique, *Pirates* was followed by *Patience, or, Bunthorne's Bride* (23 April 1881). This was based originally on a Gilbert *Bab Ballad*, "The Rival Curates," but the two protagonists were changed to Aesthetic poets in light of the reigning literary-artistic movement, and because Gilbert did not think a piece about two clerics would be fondly received. There had already been a successful comedy burlesquing the excesses of the

movement—F. C. Burnand's *The Colonel*, and George du Maurier's cartoons in *Punch* had the same balloon-bursting effect. In *Patience*, Reginald Bunthorne, a fleshly poet, and Archibald Grosvenor, an idyllic poet, could be seen as caricatures of, possibly, Oscar Wilde and Algernon Swinburne, with James McNeill Whistler thrown in, as indicated in Bunthorne's makeup. Gilbert had no severe hatred for the Aesthetics, but he disliked their idolatrous followers, as personified in the operetta by the twenty love-sick maidens. As the satire is leveled at blinded souls enraptured by a fad, the operetta remains remarkably pertinent, enhanced pictorially by the now-historical 1880s atmosphere.

The book is consistently amusing—one of Gilbert's most hilarious—but the subtle score is not one of Sullivan's most popular ones today. Various critics have accused it of being somewhat "churchy," though in its stained-glass, moody, Pre-Raphaelite way, it is perfectly in character with the libretto. There are many moments of verve and jubilance to make up for the "aesthetic" musical sections—the brilliant entrance of the "Soldiers of Our Queen," with their scarlet tunics, gold braid, white gloves, and shiny helmets; the blithe and brilliant fable of "The Magnet and the Churn," almost a *Bab Ballad* set to music; and the exceptionally comic duet, "So Go to Him and Say to Him," which always stops the show with its wild gestures and dancing. If the character of Patience is a bit too ingenuous for some tastes, she serves as a perfect "straight woman" for the more outrageous characters.

The long run of *Patience* was not entirely at the Opera Comique. On 10 October 1881, *Patience* skipped across the Strand to inaugurate the brand-new Savoy Theatre. Enlarged and brightened settings were required for the larger stage and *the* electricity, used for the first time to illuminate a London theatre. Actually, the stage itself was not electrified on opening night—the power of the generator was sufficient only for the auditorium lighting. However, first-nighters for the next operetta, *Iolanthe,* saw a fully electric show, complete with battery-powered stars in the fairies' hair.

The Savoy was built for the express purpose of presenting the Gilbert and Sullivan operettas; it is appropriate that *Iolanthe* (Savoy, 25 November 1882) was the first original Savoy work, for it is in many ways one of the very best of the series. The simple idea of intertwining a band of fairies with the House of Lords is a Gilbertian stroke of whimsical genius, the author carrying out the plot in his most logical, concise way, punctuating it with what are probably the cleverest and most refined lyrics in English. Sullivan, inspired by the fantastic goings-on in Arcadia and Westminster, by Gilbert's "excruciatingly witty" dialogue, and by the unearthly sheen of his lyrics, has provided a score which at once brings to mind Mendelssohn, Mozart, the English countryside, and Britannia the Mighty. *Iolanthe* is Sullivan's most Sullivanian score, reflecting his German training, his operetta knack—rhythmic and melodic, with a genuine respect for the gentle simplicity of the English folk song as well as the simpleminded, tuneful Victorian popular song—not to mention a new-found weight and coloration in his ingenious orchestration for the relatively small theatre band. His overture, hardly the slapdash potpourri he usually turned out the night before the première (or entrusted to an arranger), is symphonically one of his two greatest, the other being the one for *The Yeomen of the Guard.* Amazingly, he scored this overture in seven hours, a scant forty-eight before the curtain!

Using the test of a great operetta—looking at its middle finale (either in the first or second act)—one can see that *Iolanthe* ranks with the very greatest examples: *La Belle Hélène, Die Fledermaus, La Fille de Madame Angot,* a few others. The deft sequence of more than fourteen songs, one giving way to another in quick succession, Sullivan's rhythmic variations, the *hauteur* and intelligent fun of Gilbert's words, and the dramatically exciting, though patently ridiculous conflict between the peers and the fairies all unite to create an intellectual-musical tension that is relieved only by the march ("Young Strephon Is the Kind of Lout") at the very end. It is one thing to write a ridiculous scene; it is quite another to make it rivetingly dramatic. In Gilbert's scheme, the confrontation

---

Tom McDonnell as Grosvenor in the 1975 English National Opera production of *Patience.* Standing behind him in this tense moment during the Act I finale are Sandra Dugdale (Patience) and Derek Hammond Stroud (Bunthorne). The settings by John Stoddart helped make this one of the ENO's outstanding operetta productions. English National Opera.

between fairies and peers is a natural occurrence, not the usual ha-ha silliness in a British pantomime or burlesque of the period. And it is made dramatic through the agency of Sullivan's music.

The chemistry of these two collaborators, so often explained by various critics and authors, remains elusive. Did Sullivan support or enliven Gilbert's verses, giving them immortality? Yes, but Gilbert's words conferred immortality on Sullivan's music, very often. And Sullivan's work elsewhere, with other librettists, remains surprisingly pedestrian. By the same token, we have yet to see a truly successful revival of a straight Gilbert play, or of one of *his* other operettas with different composers.

There is relatively little mystery about their working habits together: we know that Gilbert wrote the libretto first, then sent it on to Sullivan to compose. We know, contrary to popular belief, that they did meet to discuss their work in progress. We know (obviously enough) that they attended rehearsals together and made changes. We know that they both conferred after the first nights and made often extensive alterations.

On the other hand, we also know that the drafts Gilbert sent Sullivan were very much a crystallization of many months of constant rewriting, down to a point where Gilbert knew he had achieved his desired ends. We know that he arrived at blocking rehearsals with the movements thoroughly worked out in advance, and that he seldom altered his staging after it was copiously written out in his prompt books. We know that Sullivan preferred working at the last minute, to meet the ultimate deadline of the actual rehearsals and the first night; that his brilliant scoring must have been equally spontaneous. Such were the separate talents of these two men, not forgetting their very long periods of practice in the theatre and in music. That these talents meshed so magnificently is not altogether mysterious, and we should simply be grateful they got together. "A Sullivan is of no use without a Gilbert," Sullivan remarked after several unsuccessful works with other librettists. And *vice versa,* we might add.

The first night of *Iolanthe* summoned forth a particularly brilliant house: the Prince of Wales, the Prime Minister, Lords, Ladies, Gentlemen—and the devoted gallery-ites who adored the Gilbert and Sullivan works as much as the gentry. Gilbert may have gotten complicated, but his audience could rarely accuse him of being obtuse, or pretentious. Similarly, though musicologists were in the house, reveling in orchestral ornamentation, most of the audience cared more for memorable tunes based primarily on dance rhythms. If there were several foreign terms not readily understood by all, this was a lyrical indulgence to be relished. Most of the jokes were easily comprehended and even topical in nature. "He's a Parliamentary Pickford, he carries everything!" cries one of the fairies, referring to the half-fairy Strephon's ability to get bills passed. Everyone then knew of the moving firm of Pickford's and its slogan, "We Carry Every-

---

A programme from the original run of *Iolanthe* at the Savoy (1882). Rosina Brandram, who subsequently played the "heavy" female parts, appeared in the curtain-raiser.

At **8**, the Original Vaudeville,

By FRANK DESPREZ,

Music by EATON FANING,

called

"MOCK TURTLES"

Mr. Wranglebury	.. .. ..	Mr. ERIC LEWIS
Mrs. Wranglebury	.. .. ..	Miss MINNA LOUIS
Mrs. Bowcher	.. ..	Miss BRANDRAM
Jane	.. ..	Miss SYBIL GREY

"IOLANTHE"

The Peer and the Peri,

FAIRY OPERA.

Words by
W. S. GILBERT.

Music by
ARTHUR SULLIVAN.

At 8.40

Dramatis Personæ.

The Lord Chancellor	.. ...	Mr. GEORGE GROSSMITH
The Earl of Mountararat,		Mr. RUTLAND BARRINGTON
The Earl Tolloller..	.. .. ..	Mr. DURWARD LELY
Private Willis { *of the Grenadier Guards* }		Mr. CHAS. MANNERS
Strephon *(an Arcadian Shepherd)*	..	Mr. R. TEMPLE
Queen of the Fairies	.. .. ..	Miss ALICE BARNETT
Iolanthe *(a Fairy—Strephon's Mother)*		Miss JESSIE BOND
Leila	*Fairies*	Miss JULIA GWYNNE
Celia		Miss FORTESCUE
Fleta		Miss SYBIL GREY
Phyllis *(an Arcadian Shepherdess and Ward in Chancery)*		Miss LEONORA BRAHAM

Chorus of Dukes, Marquises, Earls, Viscounts, Barons and Fairies.

thing." When the Fairy Queen appealed to Captain Shaw to "quench [her] great love," with "cold cascade" on opening night, she extended her arms toward the stalls where Captain Eyre Massey Shaw was seated. Everyone recognized the popular Chief of the London Fire Brigade. But topical references did not figure all that frequently in the astounding Nightmare Song, to this day quite unmatched in its brilliance as *the* most respected patter song in Gilbert and Sullivan, if not in all operetta.

Strangely enough, several critics thought *Iolanthe* not up to the level of the previous *Patience*. One noted "the same set of puppets that Mr. Gilbert has dressed over and over before." In fact, *Iolanthe* did not have as long a run as *Patience;* perhaps if Gilbert had left the title *Perola,* which he changed at the last minute to thwart would-be pirates, his superstitious liking for the letter "P" would have been justified (*Pinafore, Pirates of Penzance, Patience,* even *Iolanthe*'s subtitle, *The Peer and the Peri*). Not that the same letter had any effect on the next Savoy piece *Princess Ida,* which had one of the shortest Gilbert and Sullivan runs (5 January 1884, 246 performances). This was based on Gilbert's "respectful *perversion*" of Alfred Tennyson's long poem, *The Princess,* which had been produced without any great success at the Olympic Theatre in 1870. One reason for its unenthusiastic reception might have been the tedious blank-verse dialogue, unfortunately retained in the operetta libretto fourteen years later. It sounded uncomfortably stodgy then, and still does today. Possibly smarting from the "redressed puppets" accusation, Gilbert wrote his new libretto in three acts (actually two plus a prologue), with new dramatic weight given to the formerly less significant ingénue-soprano, Princess Ida, and much less than before to the Grossmith and Barrington parts (Kings Gama and Hildebrand, respectively). This was unfortunate; George Grossmith and Rutland Barrington were two stars everyone came to see, and Grossmith didn't appear at all in the second (and best) act.

Musically, the opening night critics were virtually unanimous—this was Sullivan's best score to date, a contention easily accepted by many today. Certainly, the second act *is* superb, probably by itself one of the best things the partners ever did, with its string of intoxicating and hauntingly melodious numbers: the women's-university students' lovely paean to Princess Ida, followed by her entrance plea to Minerva, "O, Goddess Wise"; the hilarious extended scene during which Prince Hilarion and his two cronies climb over the walls, illegally entering the off-limits-to-men confines of the university; the trio *en travesti* ("I Am a Maiden, Cold and Stately"); the appealingly somber quartet, "The World Is But a Broken Toy"; the sprightly tale of the Ape and the Lady; the glorious dancing quintet, "The Woman of the Wisest Wit"; the dainty pastiche duet between Melissa and Lady Blanche, "Now Wouldn't You Like to Rule the Roast," calling to mind, in its sarcasm, *"Via resti servita, madama brillante"* from *Le Nozze di Figaro;* the luncheon bell chorus, followed by the vivacious kissing song, also in a "medieval" mode; and the very stirring finale, one of Sullivan's most grand-operatic, with the Princess soaring over a massive chorus with her high B-flat.

The original production, painted by Hawes Craven (Act II) and Henry Emden (Acts I and III), was "amongst the most beautiful pictures ever exhibited on any stage" (a reference in particular to the sumptuous opening tableau), according to the *Theatre*'s critic, Beatty-Kingston. Though this elaborate production was a boon to the original version, subsequent producers have been loathe to spend much money on *Princess Ida,* as it has never been good box-office. Coupled with scenic exigencies is the need for a superb dramatic soprano and no less than two good tenors; it is hard enough to find one. Indeed, when the D'Oyly Carte Opera Company revived *Princess Ida* memorably in 1922, it was obliged to find an outside soprano, Winifred Lawson, to sing the title role. It was acclaimed then as a resurrected Savoy treasure, but audiences still asked for it rarely. When its scenery and costumes later became victims of the Blitz, the management felt no need to replace them until fifteen years had elapsed. Nevertheless, possibly by virtue of its scarcity, *Princess Ida* remains the connoisseur's Gilbert and Sullivan, the centerpiece of their collaboration, between *Iolanthe* and *The Mikado.* It is a storehouse of the best of Sullivan, if not of Gilbert—though his jabs at the excesses of women's rights couldn't be more pointed today.

Gilbert's next libretto, however, was his greatest, in terms of worldwide popularity: *The Mikado.* The British vogue for things Japanese was partly caused by the Aesthetic movement pilloried in *Patience;* certainly, by 1885, it had manifested itself in every middle-class household—fans, screens, lacquer boxes, china, advertising cards, calendars, stationery. Gilbert, as legend has it, had a Japanese sword on his study wall, which supposedly crashed to the floor one day, inspiring the Master to write his new operetta. Whether or not this fanciful tale is true, we know he had visited the then-very-popular Japanese Village in Knightsbridge, possibly looking for new ideas (or household souvenirs) when Sullivan had rejected a new "lozenge" plot.

D'Oyly Carte spared no expense producing *The Mikado;* he had Liberty make many of the costumes, had others imported from Paris—authentic embroidered silk Japanese creations. Gilbert had a Japanese woman from the Knightsbridge Village visit the Savoy to teach the company authentic Japanese mannerisms and to supervise the makeup, dressing, and fan manipulations. The designs were sumptuously painted by Hawes Craven. All this was good publicity, especially needed after the comparatively short run of *Princess Ida.* But rehearsals got more and more frantic as the first night approached, with many Sullivan numbers still undelivered. Sullivan's colleague Hamilton Clarke was pressed into service to score the overture from the composer's notes. At the dress rehearsal, Gilbert

---

OVERLEAF: A recreation of the original opening night of *Iolanthe* at the Savoy, with the authors joining the cast for the curtain calls, for the 1953 film *The Story of Gilbert and Sullivan.* In the center are Maurice Evans (Sullivan), Robert Morley (Gilbert), and Martyn Green (George Grossmith, as the Lord Chancellor). In the original run, the fairies had electric lights in their headpieces, powered by batteries strapped under their costumes.

wanted to cut the Mikado's "My Object All Sublime," but the chorus success-fully bade him keep it in. First-night nervousness was severe on 14 March 1885. George Grossmith, as Ko-Ko, the Lord High Executioner, had such stage fright that his knees shook, adding so greatly to the evening's amusement that he was obliged to retain a bit of it in subsequent performances. Rutland Barrington remembered the excitement in his memoirs:

> Never during the whole of my experience have I assisted at such an enthusiastic first night as greeted this delightful work. From the moment the curtain rose on the Court swells in Japanese plate attitudes to its final fall it was one long succession of uproarious laughter and overwhelming applause for the music.

The critical reaction was, for the most part, very enthusiastic as well. Savoy expert Reginald Allen has claimed that *The Mikado* was the world's most valu-able stage property for more than seventy years after the première; it has cer-tainly been the world's most popular Gilbert and Sullivan operetta, translated into more languages and performed in more countries than any other. The rea-sons for this refute the traditional view that *The Mikado* is England more or less thoroughly "Japanned," that the operetta merely masks an attack on English institutions. *The Mikado*'s initial success and its popularity abroad were due in no small measure to its Japanese trappings. *The Mikado* is very much a fantastic comedy about death, in which no death ever occurs. There is nothing exclu-sively English about the characters: the bribe-hungry Pooh-Bah exists in every country, as do the "cheap" timid tailor, the giggling schoolgirls, and Katisha, one of the most waspish and most pathetic of Gilbert's elderly ladies.

Apart from the attraction of the *japonaiserie,* Gilbert's plot happens to be one of his most clearly motivated and single-minded. We are never bored for an instant with the extraneous embellishments which sabotage some of the later works. The story concerns the coincidence of two circumstances: the Lord High Executioner's search for someone to behead, and the Crown Prince's escape from the Imperial Court to avoid marrying Katisha. Critic Beatty-Kingston *(The Theatre)* on Gilbert's libretto: "The text of *The Mikado* sparkles with countless gems of wit . . . and its author's rhyming and rhythmic gifts have never been more splendidly displayed; as for the dialogue, it is positively so full of points and hits as to keep the wits of the audience constantly on the strain." The dialogue Gilbert provided for *Pinafore,* for *Patience,* for *Iolanthe* was very funny, very lucid, very often quite crystalline in its pre-Wildean and pre-Shavian bril-liance. *The Mikado* is Gilbert's *Hamlet,* as far as quotable and memorable lines and lyrics go.

A best-selling quadrille "on airs from Gilbert and Sullivan's Opera" by Bucalossi. At center is George Grossmith as Ko-Ko. *The Mikado* only intensified an already strong Victorian love of *japonaiserie* in decoration, as shown in this magnificent sheet-music cover.

The Mikado is certainly Sullivan's best-known and most popular score. If that is a measure of its greatness (as critic Thomas Dunhill argued), then The Mikado is his greatest work. His music is, for the most part, quite un-Japanese, but there are occasional touches of Orientalia. The opening chorus begins pentatonically, and the "Miya Sama" march that begins the overture and later introduces the Emperor is actually an old Japanese war march. Other numbers are pure English Sullivan, so defiantly melodious that one happily hums them again after listening to them a thousand times. And the less-often-hummed songs always prove pleasant surprises in performance. Nanki-Poo's "A Wandering Minstrel I" is "a catalogue . . . through every passion ranging," which includes a sample sentimental ballad, a patriotic march, a sea chantey, and a bit of a lullaby. It is somewhat akin to Adele's audition song in Die Fledermaus, Act III. The entrance of the schoolgirls has the same startling effect as the entrance of the Dragoons or the Peers, the chorus of the opposite sex making its first appearance after several minutes of just men (or women). The glittering trio of "Three Little Maids" owes as much in performance to gesture and movement as the men's opening chorus, "If You Want to Know Who We Are." The Act I finale, again one of the best, builds to a thoroughly Verdian climax with Katisha sounding a bit like Amneris in Aïda, Act IV, Scene I. If it doesn't have the power of Patience's Rigoletto-Act II-like first-act finale coda, or the majesty of Princess Ida's second-act end, it does have the incomparably cheeky "For He's Going to Marry Yum-Yum," which Verdi could never imitate. It is so dramatically exciting that one spends the interval wondering what Katisha has up her sleeve (besides her right elbow, "which has a fascination few can resist!").

Act II, if well played, is perhaps the funniest of the Savoy canon, owing a great deal to dancing and slapstick—again, thoroughly international commodities, insuring The Mikado's success abroad. Musically, it opens with a female chorus ("Braid the Raven Hair") similar to the toilette opening Act II of La Belle Hélène, though the central solo portion is staccatoed to lend a more "eastern" flavor. Then follows Yum-Yum's lovely solo, "The Sun, Whose Rays Are All Ablaze," which had been transferred from its original place in the middle of Act I after the first night. Musicologists have pointed out that the madrigal "Brightly Dawns Our Wedding Day" is actually a glee, but this news does not detract from our enjoyment of this tearfully joyous ensemble. "Here's a How-de-do" is among the most-encored numbers in Gilbert and Sullivan today—audiences expect different funny business for each repetition. The arrival of the Mikado, eagerly awaited by all, finally occurs halfway into the second act; it is rare nowadays that we see anything resembling the grotesquely "senile grin and wad-

---

A scene from the second act of The Mikado, as seen in Victor Schertzinger's 1939 film version with (left to right) Sydney Granville as Pooh-Bah, Elizabeth Paynter as Pitti-Sing, Gregory Stroud as Pish-Tush, Martyn Green as Ko-Ko, Constance Willis as Katisha, and John Barclay as the Mikado. Although the film was magnificent to look at, the public was by and large unimpressed, and further plans to film the Savoy operettas were dropped.

dling walk" of the originator of the part, Richard Temple, or the ferocity of some of his illustrious successors, like Darrell Fancourt. Too often he is simply unimposing, giving little bite to his justifiably famous (and blessedly retained) "My Object All Sublime."

The other comic ensembles ("The Criminal Cried," "See How the Fates Their Gifts Allot"—which *is* labeled a glee—"The Flowers That Bloom in the Spring," "There Is Beauty in the Bellow of the Blast") are balanced by two touching, most affecting numbers: "Alone, and Yet Alive . . . Hearts Do Not Break," sung by Katisha on realizing her adored Nanki-Poo is dead (he really isn't), and "Titwillow," sung by Ko-Ko to win over Katisha's affections (which he does). However touching "Titwillow" may sound today, it is important to remember that up to Martyn Green's tenure in the Grossmith roles the song was embellished with falsetto refrains and other comic business. *The Mikado* will always be *the* vehicle for such additions, for added bits of pantomime, for elaborate sight-gags, for extraneous dancing, for topical references—in some instances sanctioned by Gilbert. Though notoriously against gagging since his early days in the theatre, Gilbert apparently was willing to allow a bit of it so long as he had seen and approved it first. Woe betide the performer who chose to insert his own business—D'Oyly Carte would fine him (or her). It was his tight control over stage direction and stage behavior which earned Gilbert later accolades as the first modern director, certainly the first in the British musical theatre.

The Mikado has been memorably made hot, black, swinging, and red, and has been seen many times on television, on the ballet stage, and even on ice. Its movie versions go back to 1907, when sequences were filmed to accompany the first "complete" set of records that were done of a Gilbert and Sullivan work; there were two subsequent films, in 1939 and 1967.

The success of *The Mikado* was truly worldwide, and it has proved a quite durable favorite. In 1886, D'Oyly Carte sent a company that had just been in New York to tour Germany and Austria-Hungary with *The Mikado* and *H.M.S. Pinafore;* further D'Oyly Carte troupes appeared the following year in the same countries, plus Holland, with *Patience* also in the repertoire. German-language versions then began to proliferate, with a notable première in Vienna of *The Mikado* (Theater an der Wien, 2 March 1888). The translation was by Zell and Genée, and the cast included Sebastian Steltzer as Ko-Ko, Hans Pokorny as Pooh-Bah, and Ottilie Collin as Yum-Yum. The ladies of the chorus were individually identified—something Gilbert had never done—with such names as Ami-tzing, Bet-ti-bo, and Tish-fu.

By the late 1880s and '90s, *The Mikado* was all over Europe, including Spain and Russia (a memorable production by Constantin Stanislavsky in 1887), and was subsequently produced virtually everywhere, including Japan itself. A memorable German production of the operetta was the lavish revue version staged by Erik Charell at the Grosses Schauspielhaus, Berlin, in 1927, featuring Max Pallenberg's celebrated Ko-Ko. Although *The Mikado* has been seen in Brussels, the French never welcomed Gilbert and Sullivan. Apart from a broadcast in the 1960s, the only *Mikado* ever seen by Parisians was the unsuccessful French version of the London *Black Mikado* of 1975.

Budapest saw *The Mikado* first in 1886 (Népszínház, 10 December). Ilka Palmay, one of the original Three Little Maids, later went into D'Oyly Carte's production of *The Grand Duke* in London. There were several other Hungarian Gilbert and Sullivans—mostly *Mikados*—and Hungarian Radio even broadcast *A házasságszédelgö,* or *Trial by Jury,* fairly recently.

With *The Mikado* so potent an attraction, other Continental managers tried some of the other Gilbert and Sullivan operettas, but never with the same success. *Patience,* or *Dragoner und Dichter,* appeared in Vienna (Carltheater, 28 May 1887), as did, later, *Trial by Jury, The Pirates of Penzance, The Yeomen of the Guard,* and *The Gondoliers.* Even Gilbert's *His Excellency* was seen at the Carltheater. More recently, there have been several new translations performed in Denmark.

Ruddigore (Savoy, 22 January 1887), like *Princess Ida,* was not revived by the D'Oyly Carte until the 1920s, but since that time it has been growing more and more popular. Coming as it did right after the phenomenally successful 672-performance run of *The Mikado,* this (or any) operetta would have had a hard time living up to its illustrious predecessor, and *Ruddygore* (as it was originally spelled) did not please audiences expecting the exoticism and gaiety of *The Mikado*. Where *The Mikado* treats a gloomy subject farcically, *Ruddigore*'s second act *is* gloomy (the ghostly picture gallery), and the ending is somewhat unsavory, with Sir Roderic explaining that all the long-dead ghosts are "practically alive." But the elements that burlesque the gothic thriller are today among the most attractive qualities of *Ruddigore*, a vindication of Gilbert's original satirical intentions.

The first act is contrastingly charming and airy, harking back to the fresh seacoasts of *Pinafore* and *Pirates;* here the picturesque Cornish fishing village of Rederring. We are first introduced to one of the most bizarre choruses Gilbert had yet devised, a group of "professional" bridesmaids who are naturally interested in seeing everyone wed. (They are rewarded at the operetta's close with husbands for themselves—the resurrected ghosts lately sprung from their picture frames!) After their opening chorus, Gilbert's succession of amusing characters follow one by one with a distinctive entrance-song, to our and the first-night audience's delight. Particularly admired was Richard Dauntless's "I Shipped, D'ye See, in a Revenue Sloop," and the hornpipe that follows. But the second act (the opening of which was delayed due to the complicated scenery) fared badly, and the final scene and elongated finale were met with hisses and boos from a small section of the house. The *Times* explained: "We have no hesitation in attributing the hissing and booing to the feebleness of the second act and the downright stupidity of its dénouement." Gilbert was forced to make several changes in the days following the première; the title spelling was changed to avoid connotations with the word "bloody" and the second act was somewhat tightened. Though *Ruddigore* has many fans today, and these rightly point to the ghost scene including "When the Night Wind Howls" as one of Sullivan's best pieces of descriptive music, the second act as a whole is one of Gilbert's weakest. Even the glittering patter trio, "My Eyes Are Fully Open to My Awful Situation," and the preceding staid duet, "I Once Was a Very Abandoned Person," fail to save it. Gilbert, in a later interview, admitted that he was surprised Sullivan hadn't treated the ghost scenes "more humorously."

There are other things that make *Ruddigore* unconvincing. The picture gallery transformation scene rarely comes across effectively—even on the opening night it was criticized. Robin Oakapple, the young protagonist, is usually played by someone nearer sixty than thirty-five; the present Act II finale (a reprise of "Oh, Happy the Lily When Kissed By the Bee") is boring compared to the original, which happily brought in the salty breezes of Act I to clear the murky air of the haunted castle. Though plagued by ill luck from the start of its run—George Grossmith, as Robin, had to be replaced due to illness after the first week by the unknown Henry Lytton—and always branded a failure, *Ruddigore* ran nine months and made each of its partners around £10,000. "I could do with a few more such failures," Gilbert told Rutland Barrington.

The Yeomen of the Guard (Savoy, 3 October 1888) was, if anything, even more solemn than *Ruddigore*. The third in a sort of trilogy of Gilbert and Sullivan black comedies, *Yeomen* is all gloomy dignity, occasionally leavened by some quaint humor and a fair amount of genuine excitement. *The Mikado* was a "Japanese" comic opera, *Ruddigore* was "supernatural," but *Yeomen* was simply an "opera," and its heavy dramatic qualities evoke the serious Sullivan of grand opera, the composer of *Ivanhoe,* which followed four years later. Because *Yeomen* is probably the most realistic of the stories, and possibly the most sentimental, those expecting the usual Gilbert wit, cynicism, and paradox will not find them readily. Sullivan, on the other hand, was delighted with this "story of human interest and probability," a welcome change for a musician who persistently thought anything comic was doomed to oblivion, as far as posterity was concerned. Gilbert, interestingly enough, felt the same way, and although he once said, "Posterity will know as little of me as I will know of Posterity," he did feel his sentimental dramas would endure longer than his operettas. Taking into account the fact that both shared this sentimental streak, it is little wonder that *Yeomen* was their mutual favorite, but another reason may be that they worked so amicably during this period, thanks to Sullivan's enthusiasm for the book.

Set as it is in the most prestigious British place of execution, the Tower of London, *Yeomen*'s score matches its grim libretto in solemnity and often rises to moments of grandeur. *Yeomen* is an atmospheric operetta, a mood piece, and the separate numbers lack the extractability those in the more comic pieces possess. But the atypical qualities of this Savoy work, the same that attracted Sullivan originally ("Pretty story, no topsy-turvydom, very human and funny also") are the features which pleased the original audiences and impress today's audiences no less.

Nothing sets the mood of *Yeomen* better than its enthrallingly exciting overture, probably Sullivan's best (with *Iolanthe*'s), which he composed in the course of twelve hours. His mastery of the economical and creative use of a small theatre pit band makes it seem rather like a huge symphony. *Yeomen*'s first act opens unlike all the others; instead of a chorus, Phoebe Meryll, a lone mezzo-soprano, sings a song while at her spinning wheel ("tearful in character," as Gilbert called it). Jessie Bond, the original Phoebe, remembered her nerves on the first night, finally having to scream at the equally worried Gilbert to leave her alone. The entrancing "I Have a Song to Sing, O!" introduces us to Jack Point and Elsie Maynard, strolling players. The irony is that Point is a professional jester, the one Grossmith part that by rights should be the funniest, but is in fact the most tragic. This was to be Grossmith's Gilbert and Sullivan swan song—he was to leave the Savoy and resume his career as a piano-entertainer at concert tours (rather akin to today's Victor Borge, though Grossmith was more involved with comic songs than comic pianism). The reason was simple: Grossmith realized he would earn far more solo than in the Savoy harness. Jack Point is quite as difficult a part to play as Robin Oakapple, taxing the best of the comedy baritones, though in this case advanced age is no barrier to an effective characterization, as Point "should die at the end," according to the author, referring to his work as a tragedy. The original stage directions state: "Point falls insensible at their feet."

The same medievalism found somewhat stultifying in sections of *Princess Ida* reappears in *Yeomen*'s dialogue, but it is less objectionable in the context of the rather more sentimental story. The plot, incidentally, is quite similar to that of *Maritana,* Wallace's very popular 1845 opera, based, in turn, on the French *vaudeville, Don César de Bazan,* which had served as the vehicle for many plays and operas. The Don is married to a gypsy dancer while in prison awaiting execution—later escaping it and reappearing disguised as a monk, whereupon the officially married couple fall in love with each other. The same thing, more or less, occurs in *Yeomen.* Whatever excuses Gilbert may have offered, it seems certain he knew *Maritana;* however borrowed Gilbert's plot may be, *Yeomen* is continually performed today while *Maritana* is totally forgotten. Gilbert, like Shakespeare, lives on, with original or purloined plots.

The second act of *The Yeomen of the Guard,* like the first, has its ups and downs, its moments of operatic thrills and its pedestrian sections, but even the lesser moments have a certain antique charm due to either words (Colonel Fairfax's "Free from His Fetters Grim") or music (the trio, "A Man Who Would Woo a Fair Maid"). The end of the act has a mournful, autumnal, bittersweet atmosphere, as if anticipating the near end of the glory of Gilbert and Sullivan. But the grand finale is superbly operatic and emotionally affecting. The audience smiles as poor, despairing Elsie gives herself up to her supposedly dead husband, only to find out it is the same man she had fallen in love with in Act II. But tears begin to well as "I Have a Song to Sing, O!" is gently reprised, reaching a swelling climax as Point dies of a broken heart. So effective is the finale that any prior deficiencies are forgotten.

In one of its boldest attempts to break the traditional scenic mold of Gilbert and Sullivan, the D'Oyly Carte had Peter Goffin discard the old, familiarly realistic Tower Green setting in 1939, replacing it with a more symbolized representation. This was a mistake, as *Yeomen* is very much an operetta dependent on the realistic, picture-book Shakespearianism championed by Henry Irving and later by Herbert Beerbohm Tree.

After these somewhat morbid subjects, *The Gondoliers* (Savoy, 7 December 1889) returns to the fantastic, social-satirical Gilbert of old and the ebullient and experienced Sullivan, ever fresh. *The Gondoliers* is quite accurately a sunny vacation in Venice after some rainy months in England. Gilbert's winning libretto plus the Italian setting inspired Sullivan to provide what many consider his most joyous, most mature score, beguilingly tuneful from beginning to end. Although it is complicated, Gilbert's plot cleverly exposes the folly of an excessively republican government, where "everyone is some*bo*dee and no one's any*body*," as the Grand Inquisitor Don Alhambra del Bolero recounts in his famed second-act song. Because *The Gondoliers* satirizes democratic equality, at that time a quaint notion in Britain but one always taken seriously in America, it has never been exceedingly popular in the United States. The first American production, at the Park Theatre, New York (7 January 1890), was a disaster—locals called it the "Gone-dollars" after its premature demise.

In the first part of Act I, Gilbert allowed Sullivan some twenty minutes without dialogue, a mini–*opera buffa* with a section actually in Italian. This is one of their most infectiously happy conceits, a return to the true dialogueless comic opera of *Trial by Jury* fifteen years before. Thomas Dunhill, one of Sullivan's best and most perceptive critics, called *The Gondoliers* "easily the most contin- uously sunny and untroubled" of the Gilbert and Sullivan works. Also, by vir- tue of its eighteenth-century setting, it is, with *Iolanthe,* the most elegant and royal of the operettas, complete with its "Regular Royal Queen," the song which so captivated Queen Victoria at a command performance at Windsor during its original London run.

The *Gondoliers* was a smash hit from the first night, and the reviews were unanimously the very best Gilbert and Sullivan had ever received—the *Illustrated London News* highlighting the reason for *The Gondoliers'* tremendous *joie de vivre:* "Mr. W. S. Gilbert has returned to the Gilbert of the past, and everyone is delighted. He is himself again . . . the Gilbert who on Saturday night was cheered till the audience was weary of cheering any more." Gilbert had left the melodrama of *Ruddigore* and *Yeomen* and had thankfully returned to his true métier, the topsy-turvy tale. Sullivan had his hand in the success as well, of course. In an interview he granted the *Home News* a week before the première, the composer revealed one of the more entrancing features of his score—its speed: ". . . nearly all the numbers are rapid. You will hear very little slow music in it."

The *Gondoliers* is the summit of Gilbert and Sullivan, the author and com- poser in their best form; most critics recalled *The Mikado* and *Pinafore* when discussing it. The twelfth work was in many ways the best of the first dozen and, of these, ten or eleven are consistently revived throughout the English- speaking world today. In fact, revivals of several of the more popular works were interspersed between the original runs of the Savoy operettas. The sunny cordiality surrounding *The Gondoliers* was shattered in 1890 by the notorious "carpet" quarrel, a disagreement which no doubt affected the future of Gilbert and Sullivan, but which has been blown rather out of proportion, giving the mistaken impression that the partners were *always* at odds.[2] During the period of the disagreement, Sullivan had an opportunity to write his cherished grand opera, *Ivanhoe,* which opened D'Oyly Carte's Royal English Opera (now the Palace Theatre) in 1891. *Ivanhoe* is outside the scope of the present book, though it could be argued that Sullivan's better moments were the ones which bore the closest resemblance to the scores of his comic operettas. He also turned out a comic opera without Gilbert during this break, *Haddon Hall* (1892). Gilbert had preceded him that year with the slightly more successful *The Mountebanks* (Lyric,

[2]For a detailed description of the quarrel, see Leslie Baily's *Gilbert & Sullivan Book.*

Martyn Green and Evelyn Gardiner as the Duke and Duchess of Plaza-Toro in Gilbert and Sullivan's *The Gondoliers*. This 1929 production, with its elegant eighteenth-century sets and costumes by Charles Ricketts, reopened the Savoy Theatre after it had been made thoroughly art déco inside and out.

4 January 1892). It must have chagrined Sullivan to know that the magic-potion libretto he had rejected wound up in the hands of Alfred Cellier, who had recently composed the operetta *Dorothy* (1886), which outran even *The Mikado*. With 229 performances, *The Mountebanks* did not prove nearly as popular as *Dorothy*. Gilbert's mélange of monks, magic, automatons, and madness—and suggestions of Meilhac and Halévy's *Les Brigands*, which Gilbert had translated, and which had just appeared at the Avenue Theatre—were not as attractive to audiences as the flimsier book to *Dorothy*. The Italian names were sillier than those for Gilbert's *Gondoliers* characters: Risotto and Minestra were two of the principal females. The London cast included J. Robertson and Geraldine Ulmar; in New York (Garden, 11 January 1892), Hayden Coffin and Lillian Russell

were the stars. There have been very few amateur revivals, chiefly noted for the automatons' duet, "Put a Penny in the Slot."

The dispute between Gilbert and Sullivan and D'Oyly Carte having been settled to the satisfaction of the parties concerned, the writing and production of the next Savoy operetta was initiated. This was *Utopia, Limited, or, The Flowers of Progress,* which had a quite successful première 7 October 1894 at the Savoy.

With nothing terribly memorable produced since *The Gondoliers,* press and public both turned to Gilbert and Sullivan to give the British musical stage another masterwork. *Utopia* was thus originally overpraised. The public, however, came to realize that the latest Savoy piece was not up to par. Though Gilbert's libretto was admired for its satirical barbs strung out on an interesting premise (the conversion of a South Sea isle into a Company, Limited, with British customs), pointed jokes here and there were no substitute for a clear and interesting plot, which in this case was hardly utopian and very limited. The characters are basically to blame, being for the most part indistinguishable from each other; Gilbert's policy of having no stars (which he inaugurated in *The Gondoliers* because of some hoity-toity Savoy players) had gone overboard here, leaving a book with too many characters and too few to admire. Sullivan's rhythmical and orchestral élan was admired, particularly by G. B. Shaw (then writing musical criticism), but his melodic invention had reached the point where tunes echoed not only older popular Sullivan numbers, but also songs already sung in the same operetta. A trio in Act II sounds alarmingly similar to a trio sung by the same people in Act I. One of the brightest spots in the first act is the brief quotation from the Captain's song in *Pinafore;* this brought the house down originally *and* in the first D'Oyly Carte revival in March 1975.

There are several lovely moments—the princesses' duet in Act I ("Although of Native Maids the Cream"), the last section of the first-act finale, and, most winningly, the Christy Minstrel takeoff, complete with tambourines and vigorous dancing. Gilbert had not forgotten that his first true "production numbers" (in the modern musical comedy sense), the hornpipe in *Ruddigore* and the cachucha in *The Gondoliers,* had made a tremendously favorable impression. He therefore had two in *Utopia,* the minstrel scene and the drawing-room court procession, both in Act II. But these are high points of a middling-to-weak score. Its slight original popularity, coupled with D'Oyly Carte's most expensive production to date, prevented its reentry into the D'Oyly Carte repertoire until the revival of 1975, in honor of the Gilbert and Sullivan Centenary at the Savoy Theatre. This revival did not—once again—prove itself a durable favorite.

The Grand Duke, the last Gilbert and Sullivan operetta, was the last breath from a dying colossus, but in some ways it is more attractive today than its predecessor. Though grossly overburdened with dialogue (page after page of boring exchanges without any musical relief) and a complex story concerning nothing of any particular interest or whimsy, it is musically more interesting than *Utopia,* showing a more continentalized Sullivan with a suave waltz or two. Rather than bore the reader with distressing examples, let it be stated that it took Gilbert a paragraph in *The Grand Duke* to say what he had said in *Iolanthe*, for example, in a sentence. Nevertheless, his lyrics show their distinctive flair time and again, and there was even a song with a refrain mostly in French, made up ingeniously out of gambling expressions. To the very end, Gilbert had no lyrical peer, and he still has yet to meet his match in operetta. And Sullivan at his weakest was still head and shoulders above any of his contempories in England (and most of his operetta descendants) in terms of the sophistication and gaiety of his scores. *The Grand Duke* received a concert rendition by the D'Oyly Carte Opera Company the night following the *Utopia* revival in 1975.

The *fait accompli* of the Gilbert and Sullivan partnership and the works it produced is truly remarkable. With the exception of Offenbach and Meilhac/Halévy, there has been no operetta collaboration to match it with regard to the number of masterpieces spawned. But more incredible still is the persistent popularity enjoyed by the majority of these fourteen operettas, not to mention the tremendous amounts of money generated thereby. Savoyards can be found everywhere in the English-speaking world, supporting countless thousands of amateur productions.

The Gilbert and Sullivan operettas were among the first British productions of any kind to achieve the kind of consecutive long runs we are used to today. Prior to the last quarter of the nineteenth century, plays were rarely produced successively one evening after another. (In fact, *The Beggar's Opera,* which ran sixty-two consecutive times in 1728, held the long-run record for nearly a hundred years.) The Gilbert and Sullivan operettas enjoyed a series of amazingly long runs beginning in 1878 with the presentation of *H.M.S. Pinafore* (700 performances), with *The Mikado* (672), *Patience* (578), and *The Gondoliers* (554) thereafter, in order of duration. But these were easily beaten by the British productions of *Les Cloches de Corneville* in 1878 (705) and the amazing run of Alfred Cellier's *Dorothy* (931), while other French works like *La Poupée* (576) and *Madame Favart* (502) also had lengthy runs that easily outran their original Parisian counterparts. By the turn of the century, *A Chinese Honeymoon* would pass the thousand-performance mark, and during the First World War, *Chu Chin Chow* more than doubled that record.

Not that the golden future of Gilbert and Sullivan was always assured. After a few revivals of the more popular works in the 1890s, and two repertory seasons at the Savoy in the 1900s, it was generally thought that the Gilbert and Sullivan operas would not be seen again in the West End. The D'Oyly Carte Company toured the provinces and appeared quietly in suburban London theatres; Gilbert and Sullivan was considered old-hat and provincial right through World War I. It was a courageous move on Rupert D'Oyly Carte's part to book the company for a season at the Princes Theatre (now the Shaftesbury) in 1919—the public had voiced a decided preference during the War for the opulent spectacle-operetta *(Chu Chin Chow)* and the snazzy revue *(Hullo, Tango!)*. But the Princes season caught on like wildfire. The public queued up for miles right up to the Second World War, and the critics glowingly reappraised their national treasures. A new generation witnessed the D'Oyly Carte's "golden age," comparing the merits of its top stars of the 1920s and '30s (Henry Lytton, Derek Oldham, Leslie Rands, Bertha Lewis, Marjorie Eyre, Winifred Lawson, and, perhaps most of all, Darrell Fancourt) with those remembered by their parents and the original Savoy artists still perhaps recalled by their grandparents. It is this family fondness for Gilbert and Sullivan—its attraction to every age group—which has always augured well for its future.

Rupert D'Oyly Carte's other wise decision was to resume the extensive North American engagements that his father had commenced with the original New York premières of the operettas in the 1880s and '90s. These, often timed for copyright reasons to coincide with the London first nights, were followed by D'Oyly Carte-licensed productions and tours which developed the considerable American appetite for the Savoy operettas. In 1927, Canadian cities were visited with such acclaim that a more extensive tour was organized two years later to also include some United States venues. The Depression apparently affected further plans, until 3 September 1934, when the D'Oyly Carte began a siege at the Martin Beck Theatre that lasted fifteen weeks. This triumphant engagement had critics, Savoyards, the general public, and, significantly, musical comedy writers, in a considerable state of excitement. With a hiatus for World War II, and intervals of a few years during which time the company switched to different American managements, the visits of the D'Oyly Carte Opera Company were eagerly awaited by many Americans and Canadians.

In 1948, on the death of Rupert D'Oyly Carte, his daughter Bridget took over the management of what became her company. In 1961, at the time of the expiry of Gilbert's copyright, Bridget D'Oyly Carte formed The D'Oyly Carte Opera Trust Ltd. and Bridget D'Oyly Carte Ltd. in order to smoothly continue the operations of the company. Although the release of the Gilbert and Sullivan works into public domain had little effect on D'Oyly Carte audiences, the financial situation of the company was not perhaps as assured in the 1960s and '70s as it had been in years past, due to the changing conditions in touring the British Isles, the changing tastes of the public, and increased costs everywhere. Though there were still American tours in the 1970s, and a very emotional Centenary Season at the Savoy Theatre in 1975 (during which every operetta was played, in order), the D'Oyly Carte was not in the best of health.

In the 1980–81 season, the Arts Council of Great Britain refused to give the D'Oyly Carte funds to assist the company's running, stating in a report that its productions and personnel were too "old" and unimaginative to deserve state aid. The report was rightly attacked by some, who maintained that if D'Oyly Carte *had* been receiving government funds all along, like the English National Opera, its productions would undoubtedly have been fresher. Though the company had been assisted by underwriting from Barclays Bank, profits continued to dwindle, and deficits rose so drastically that the D'Oyly Carte was forced to announce that the closing performance of the London season at the Adelphi Theatre on 27 February 1982 would be the last for the present company. The demise of the D'Oyly Carte has been a tragic loss for Savoyards everywhere.

The British critic Gervase Hughes commented on Sullivan's superiority:

. . . that many of us would rank *Pinafore*, *Iolanthe*, *The Mikado*, and *The Gondoliers* just above *La Belle Hélène*, *Véronique*, *Die Fledermaus*, and *The Merry Widow* is not due in the very least to patriotic sentiment or insular prejudice. (In matters musical our people have rarely been guilty of either.) At the risk of being accused of "British boastfulness" I put forward in all seriousness the proposition that thanks to Arthur Sullivan we have developed greater artistic sensibility, so far as operetta is concerned, than our friends on the continent who know him not.[3]

I would venture to comment that the reason "our friends on the continent" know him not is W. S. Gilbert. Just as there have been few English translations to do justice to the better European operetta libretti, there have been few good continental versions of Gilbert's libretti, the *best* operetta books of them all, unequivocally. Gilbert created a very British world of comic characters and types, much as Dickens had—all the operettas save four or five are set in Great Britain—but Dickens has been popular internationally. It must therefore be the lyrics which have kept Gilbert and Sullivan for the most part in England, the Commonwealth, and the United States. Their dexterity and retainability remain perplexingly undextrous and unmemorable in various translations. Sullivan's music may rarely attain the frenzied gaiety and fury of Offenbach's, or the creamy sensuousness and élan of Strauss's, but on the whole his orchestrations and his melodies certainly bear comparison with the best operetta has to offer.

Their efforts had an inestimable effect on the British and American musical theatre—musical comedy would have been impossible without them. Do not forget, on the other hand, that Gilbert and Sullivan could not have existed without Offenbach and his librettists. Offenbach's melody, variety, satire, and orchestration influenced Sullivan, of course, but Gilbert's libretti would not have been possible without Meilhac and Halévy paving the way with their satirical, fanciful plots, their bizarre characters, and their witty, polished, ingenious lyrics.

It is interesting to recall the broad popular appeal of Gilbert and Sullivan, who truly entertained high, low, and middlebrow in the late nineteenth century, and who were so popular as to drive French operetta almost completely off the English-speaking stage. Not only because their scores were tuneful, or because the libretti were amusing, or because of that remarkable oil-vinegar suspension that kept the two forces together so magnificently. Much of their great popularity was due to the *intelligence* of the operettas, musically and literarily. They were "funny without being vulgar," a perfection that was attributable to a great extent to Gilbert. In terms of advertising, Sullivan's melodies probably have more to do with the operettas remaining so popular after all these years. A great deal of the intelligence of the operettas was originally due to stagecraft—the superb productions directed by Gilbert and so tastefully mounted by D'Oyly Carte. They were simply the best musical productions of the Victorian age.

---

[3]Gervase Hughes, *Composers of Operetta*, p. 199.

THE EDWARDESIAN ERA

I F THE Opera Comique and the Savoy dominated London musical-theatre activity in the 1870s and '80s, their position was later weakened with the ascendancy of Daly's and the Gaiety in the "naughty nineties." The "sacred lamp of burlesque" had been kept aglow at the Gaiety by John Hollingshead; Daly's had been built by the American Augustin Daly as a showcase for the Shakespearian actress Ada Rehan. Both theatres would eventually come under the control of impresario George Edwardes, one for the new "musical comedy," the other for more romantic operettas. King Edward VII was still the dashing Prince of Wales in the last two decades of Victoria's century, but the types of musical shows favored during his forthcoming reign were already being created during the Edwardesian era.

After *The Gondoliers* and, more urgently, after *The Grand Duke,* it was realized that the Savoy stream of perfection may have run dry. Thus, the 1890s and the Edwardian age, as far as British operetta was concerned, were spent trying to live up to Gilbert and Sullivan. The critics and the public were more lenient toward the succeeding composers, often overpraising them, while nearly everyone waited in vain for the new Gilbert, who did not really materialize until Noël Coward, in the 1920s. Proficient lyricists, like Adrian Ross, and capable book-writers, like Frederick Lonsdale, wrote excellent material. But there were no creators, in the sense that Gilbert created his own world, peopled with memorable characters, interesting stories, witty dialogue, and his thoroughly matchless lyrics.

Several composers were touted at the time as being the successors to Sullivan. One was **Edward Solomon** (1853–1895), born in London, the son of a music-hall pianist. A versatile and proficient pianist himself, he was also an accomplished orchestrator, and his work was respected by Arthur Sullivan. He wrote

---

A costume design by C. Wilhelm (William Charles Pitcher) for the original production of Monckton and Talbot's *The Arcadians* (Shaftesbury, 1909)—arguably the greatest Edwardian operetta.

several short works for the German Reed entertainments, followed by some dozen full-length works, including—probably the most popular—*Billee Taylor* (Imperial, 30 October 1880), and then *Claude Duval* (1881), *Polly, or the Pet of the Regiment* (1884), *Pepita, or the Girl with Glass Eyes* (1888), and *The Red Hussar* (1889). In the last-named operetta, Marie Tempest made a sensational debut in New York (Palmer's, 5 August 1890), but Solomon's favorite star was America's operetta queen, Lillian Russell, who starred as *Polly* and *Pepita* and who became the second Mrs. Solomon.

Solomon's chief fault seemed to have been a lack of a Gilbert—an affliction shared by most of his composer colleagues. Textually uninspired, and without—so it seems—any melodies to linger into this century, his operettas are today forgotten, though his name remains remembered as having been Lillian Russell's husband, thanks to Don Ameche's impersonation in the 1940 film *Lillian Russell*.

At the Savoy, Richard D'Oyly Carte was faced in 1891 with the ultimate fact that the Gilbert-Sullivan partnership would not go on forever. His impulse then was astute: if not Gilbert and Sullivan, then the same type of comic opera; the Savoy audience would demand it. He commissioned Solomon to provide *The Nautch Girl* (Savoy, 30 June 1891). Most of the critics found the music the best thing in it, cleverly written, tuneful, and showing off the Savoy regulars to best advantage. There was even a reminiscence of the Hallelujah Chorus in the first-act quartet, which Sullivan himself admired at the last rehearsal. The Indian setting gave the Percy Anderson costumes a chance to shine, as did audience favorites Jessie Bond (Chinna Loofa) and Rutland Barrington (Punka, Rajah of Chutneypore). (Bond and Barrington had also toured outside the Savoy in a duologue act with music by Solomon, emulating the provincial successes of George Grossmith's "Piano and I.") The story was the typical British topsy-turvy-in-a-foreign-country Savoy type, as in *The Mikado,* grafted onto the mystery-of-the-idol's-jeweled-eye kind of plot that had served thrillers for years. It ran a not-unrespectable 200 performances and was followed by a revival of another Solomon work, *The Vicar of Bray* (1882), which was revised with a new libretto by Sydney Grundy.

Grundy furnished the libretto for Sullivan's first operetta in years without Gilbert, *Haddon Hall* (Savoy, 24 September 1892). It was based on the old comedy *Dorothy Vernon of Haddon Hall,* wherein Miss Vernon elopes with a Catholic boy in Royalist-Roundhead-Puritan days. "The clock of Time has been put forward a century," stated the programme, no doubt to allow for the attractive costumes designed by Percy Anderson. But Grundy's book was romantic, and not exceptionally funny, so that its anachronisms became jarring rather than amusing. There was much that was familiar from Gilbert and Sullivan: an En-

---

Marie Tempest's three outfits in Solomon's *The Red Hussar* (Lyric, 1889). Before her defection to light comedy in 1900, Miss Tempest played such roles as Fiametta in *Boccaccio,* the title roles of *Dorothy* and *Erminie,* and even Adam in *Der Vogelhändler.*

glish country dance, a madrigal, a touching song for the contralto (Gilbert and Sullivan's star Rosina Brandram), and various choral effects, all done with Sullivan's usual sprightly and sentimental verve. But Grundy's basically padded-out, unhumorous book and banal, often insipid lyrics have not helped it endure.

Jane Annie, or, The Good Conduct Prize (Savoy, 3 May 1893) had the distinction of a libretto by James M. Barrie *and* Arthur Conan Doyle. An unlikely combination, true, and in spite of a Sullivanesque score by the Savoy's assistant musical director, Ernest Ford, the operetta garnered only a scant 50 performances. (Sullivan himself had declined to set the libretto.) Rutland Barrington, who played a university proctor, remembered in his memoirs that Ford's score contained "some very excellent music," but also stated that he had never ". . . been able to discover with certitude what it was all about . . . The second act was full of allusions to golf, and the scene was actually laid on a golf green, and the whole thing seemed to puzzle our audiences very much . . . . I myself played a Proctor, and, for some reason which I have forgotten, hid myself in a clock."[1] This had a first act set in a ladies' seminary—Jane Annie (Dorothy Vane) being a "good girl," and Bab (Decima Moore) a "bad" one. Needless to say, Bab ran away with the best numbers and the critics' hearts, while at least one reviewer noted that the Bab associated with Gilbert had influenced the book. A chorus of lancers, complete with a lusty military song encored by Scott Fishe, and Rosina Brandram as an elderly schoolmistress were in the true Savoy comic opera tradition, but London audiences had their hearts set on the

---

[1]*Rutland Barrington by Himself,* p. 95.

real article that D'Oyly Carte had already announced—the new work by Gilbert and Sullivan themselves that was to be *Utopia, Limited.*

The comparative failure (245 performances) of *Utopia* forced D'Oyly Carte to try something new—a new English operetta with a French score. This was Messager's *Mirette* (3 July 1894). This gypsy tale failed, despite an excellent cast, and the fact that "in the dresses and scenery, all previous efforts at this theatre have been eclipsed," according to the *Illustrated London News.* Messager's failure in London did not daunt him; several years later he headed Covent Garden, and in 1919 he provided a lovely score for the British operetta *Monsieur Beaucaire.*

The Chieftain (Savoy, 12 December 1894) was an enlargement of Sullivan and Burnand's *The Contrabandista* (1868), with most of the new material occurring in Act II. "Some idea of the dramatic style, which, in the later sixties, Mr. Gilbert attempted to reform, may be gained by listening to the first act," remarked a gentleman of the London press, who also scorned Sullivan's "dainty drawing-room ballads being interspersed with concerted pieces which might have been written by Vincent Wallace." Audiences apparently did not want *Maritana* throwbacks, but several of the numbers have a comic flair and musical freshness that recall the first Sullivan-Burnand collaboration, *Cox and Box,* including a saucily rhymed bolero and a duet in Act II with hilarious school-French verses. The part of Mr. Grigg was taken in London by Walter Passmore, already acclaimed "the best vocalist of comic opera comedians," and in New York (Abbey's, 9 September 1895) by Francis Wilson, in the unusually restrained part (for him) of a Clapham tourist in the Spanish mountains.

D'Oyly Carte, not wishing to take any chances, remounted *The Mikado* in 1895 and saw it run without a hitch until the latest, and last, of the Gilbert and Sullivan works was ready. *The Grand Duke,* however, was not as popular a monarch as *The Mikado.* The only thing to do was to bring the Japanese operetta back once again. The aggregate number of *Mikado* performances for the sixteen-month stretch between 1895 and 1897 was 353, or about fifty out of seventy weeks. The conviction that Gilbert and Sullivan would never provide another work together to equal the success of *The Mikado* and its colleagues must have been strong enough after the failure of *The Grand Duke* to have prevented them from ever collaborating again.

It would have been easy for Richard D'Oyly Carte to have spent the rest of the 1890s reviving the Gilbert and Sullivan operettas, one after another. In fact, he did, but the outrageous success of his ex-stage-manager George Edwardes's productions at the Gaiety and at Daly's no doubt filled him with jealousy, and there was a fruitless succession of failures at the Savoy that could not compete with *The Geisha* (760 performances), *San Toy* (768), *A Runaway Girl* (593), or *The Shop Girl* (544). To make matters worse, critics and public attending the Savoy were ever comparing these new shows to the Gilbert and Sullivan revivals which invariably preceded them. *His Majesty* (Savoy, 20 February 1897) had a score by Alexander MacKenzie, which, to the *Illustrated London News,* "relied almost entirely upon the manners and customs of his chosen ideal," while Burnand's treatment was "so clearly Gilbertian that he unfailingly provokes comparison." George Grossmith played 6 performances, the operetta lasted only 56 more, and the most enduring memento from the production was Dudley Hardy's poster depicting the title character, Ferdinand the Fifth of Vingolia, in the guise of a playing card.

In the late '90s, interspersed between popular revivals of the Gilbert and Sullivan favorites, often conducted by the composer on opening nights, were unsuccessful new versions of Offenbach's *The Grand Duchess of Gérolstein* (4 December 1897), Chabrier's *L'Étoile* (7 January 1899)—the latter twice-removed from its French original—and Arthur Sullivan's last three operettas, all written to non-Gilbert books.

The Beauty Stone (Savoy, 28 May 1898) was a "romantic musical drama" set in the fifteenth century in the imaginary city of Mirlemont, somewhere in Flanders. Though in some ways more pathetic than *The Yeomen of the Guard,* concerning a crippled girl, Arthur Wing Pinero's book hinged on an element Gilbert would have admired—a talisman. If not a lozenge, the beauty stone was sufficiently and improbably magical for Sullivan to have shied away from it, but he nevertheless tackled Comyns Carr's lyrics. For some reason. Gilbert was not sent first-night tickets for his former partner's new opus. This further chilled a relationship that was already cool, and deprived Gilbert of the chance to hear the especially admired weaving duet, "Click, Clack, For Ever the Shuttle Flies," and the Devil's description of the beauty stone. Walter Passmore was the Devil, and Ruth Vincent, Henry Lytton, and Rosina Brandram filled out the cast. The production was typical Savoy-lavish: nine scenes under the supervision of W. Telbin, and lovely costumes as well. Too serious for London tastes, *The Beauty Stone* lasted a mere fifty performances.

The Rose of Persia was a happier affair (Savoy, 29 November 1899, 213 performances), with Basil Hood's more carefree book and some captivating lyrics, but there were those who would only accept Gilbert with Sullivan, among them the critic for the New York *Times,* writing about the production in New York at Daly's in September 1900: "Mr. Basil Hood has in one feature of the construction of the libretto equalled Mr. Gilbert. He has written it in two acts." The same reviewer found Sullivan's orchestration "an unceasing joy to hear," even if this critic's astute ear recognized scraps of *Il Trovatore, Der fliegende Holländer,* and *Cavalleria Rusticana.* When the piece was revived in 1935 at the Princes, London, the London *Times* called it a cross between *The Mikado* and the Arabian Nights with "threats of beheadings and hopes of weddings," a good description, and one that might also be applied to Chabrier's *L'Étoile,* which in its modified version had preceded *The Rose of Persia* by less than a year at the Savoy in its English version. With characters like Rose-in-Bloom, Heart's Desire, Hassan, and the Sultana Zubeydeh, *The Rose of Persia* was a precursor of the fabulously successful *Chu Chin Chow* fifteen years later. Every performance of *The Rose of Persia* was stopped by Robert Evett singing the drinking song, "I Care Not If the Cup I Hold," and it remains the best-known number.

Judging from inadequate amateur performances and recordings, there is a lot that is likable in *The Rose of Persia,* but it might seem a bit too precious to be revived today.

The claim that **Edward German** (1862–1936) "inherited" the mantle of Arthur Sullivan on the latter's death in 1901 is not without some truth, even if the Savoy management itself and the press did trumpet this proclamation. For, in retrospect, German's achievements in British operetta within the Edwardian confines of 1900–11 were considerable, as far as musicianly inspiration and orchestral dexterity were concerned. It was possibly a matter of managerial taste: the Savoy (under the D'Oyly Cartes) would never admit any music-hall trappings into the temple of operetta (well, hardly ever . . .) whereas Edwardes, despite all his Savoy training, would, and did, prosperously pandering to the turn of the century's less particular tastes.

In this sense, German was already an anachronism by as early as 1902, the year of his best-regarded work, *Merrie England.* The Gaiety and other theatres had developed the public's liking for the triteness of the new musical comedy, and the comedy, while often topical, had generally little to do with the plot. Satire of the Gilbertian type had for the most part disappeared and German's *Merrie England* took off more or less where *The Yeomen of the Guard* left off, but increased the pageantry to include not only processions of yeomen but also actual historical figures like Sir Walter Raleigh. *A Princess of Kensington,* with a book by Basil Hood, had elements of *Iolanthe* (fairies) and *Pinafore* (sailors), and *Fallen Fairies* had fairies by Gilbert himself. *Tom Jones,* in spite of several redundant songs and a grossly bowdlerized libretto, is one of German's most fortuitous creations. If German had a European counterpart, it was perhaps Messager. Both had "national" characteristics, unerring good taste, and considerable charm. But Messager moved with the times, besides being a far more prolific and gifted composer, while German steadfastly stayed behind.

Edward German Jones studied at the Royal Academy of Music and in 1888 became musical director of the Globe Theatre. For more than a decade, he composed incidental music for several Shakespeare plays; his music from *Henry VIII* is still performed.

German was chosen to finish Sullivan's *The Emerald Isle,* uncompleted at his death (22 November 1900). D'Oyly Carte, who had made the choice, died within a few months of Sullivan, so that when the audience assembled at the Savoy for the première of the new operetta (27 April 1901), it became virtually a memorial service for two thirds of the great triumvirate. The *Times* called it "an audience whose sympathetic admiration was a foregone conclusion." A cast of Savoy stalwarts (Lytton, Passmore, Brandram) and handsome costumes (Percy Anderson) and sets (W. Harford) set in rural Ireland, c. 1801, also aided the audience's admiration for a score that was only partially Sullivan's and a Basil Hood book of many jokes but little wit. The press reported that the opening chorus and a rollicking song for Terence, "I'm Descended from Brian Boru," were the only things actually written *and* scored by Sullivan, though he was reported to have left an outline of most of Act I, as well as sketches for some numbers in the second act. German was thus responsible for virtually all the orchestrations and a good portion of the tunes. *The Emerald Isle, or the Caves of Carric-Cleena* had a not bad (but not Gilbert-and-Sullivan-length) run of 205 performances and has been revived. The New York performances (Herald Square, 1 September 1902) by the Jefferson de Angelis Company fared less well. One review opined that "in this Sullivan-German score there is much to enjoy but little to bring away. Unctuously Irish, with rhythms that make the listener vibrate responsively . . . The whole score, without plagiarizing, is included in the body of musical literature of, say, the last fifteen years. It wants the personal stamp of originality."

Merrie England was not much more original, but it happily harked back to the pageantry and color of German's Shakespeare scores, set as it was in Elizabethan days. Shakespeare did not actually appear, but nearly everyone else did: Elizabeth herself, Raleigh, and the Earl of Essex. And it had a lovely succession of graceful melodies and stirring patriotic numbers, interspersed with comic numbers which were seldom very sparkling, and a ponderous romantic plot which in the end defeated its audiences. The 120-time Savoy run was not at all spectacular, but then, neither were the notices. Appearing as it did (2 April 1902) after the first revival of the superlative *Iolanthe*—with Rosina Brandram recreating her Fairy Queen nearly twenty years later, critics and audiences alike could not really help but look at Hood and German in terms of their predecessors.

Yet there was a great deal that was admirable in *Merrie England,* and this enabled it to enjoy a long and immense popularity with amateur operatic societies throughout the Empire. In the first place, it was a "historical" pageant, besides being a tuneful operetta, and in the second, it did not pose as many vocal or comico-dramatic obstacles to an untrained company as did some of Sullivan's works, though it *is* an expensive show, if mounted properly.

The tunes were, admittedly, very memorable: "The Yeomen of England," a patriotic anthem with little Sullivanian vigor but much appeal to a strong baritone (Henry Lytton, originally); the majestic entrance of the Queen; her "O, Peaceful England"; Raleigh's syrupy "English Rose," a tenor love song with a built-in patriotic punch; and, best of all, two songs for Bessie Throckmorton, the waltz-song, "Who Shall Say that Love is Cruel?", and the simple, lovely, lute-accompanied "She Had a Letter from Her Love." The choruses, invariably mentioning "the merry month of May," are all fairly similar to one another, but the dance music has a British feeling Vaughan Williams or even Sullivan would have admired.

This simple, folksy quality, unfortunately, applies to Hood's undistinguished, simple-minded lyrics, in this case antiqued with haths, doths, troths, derrydowns, and hey nonny nos. The Act I finale, one of the last decent British operetta finales, was not in the Sullivan-Offenbach mold, but was instead a more soaring, romantic concoction, spoiled at the end by the appearance of a

troupe of Morris dancers who wreck one of the operetta's most dramatic moments. The second-act finale—"Robin Hood's Wedding"—is also pleasant.

The book has been altered for subsequent revivals, including one at the Princes during World War II (revision by Edward Knoblock, with Heddle Nash and Dennis Noble) and the Sadler's Wells remounting of 1960 (improvements by Dennis Arundell, with June Bronhill and Peter Glossop). *Merrie England* was also the opening attraction at the open-air Scarborough Theatre in 1932 with its sets on an island, the entrance of Elizabeth staged on barges.

A Princess of Kensington (Savoy, 22 January 1903) ran just about as long (115 performances), though there was a more conscious effort this time to be more Gilbertian, at least in whimsy, with fairies again invading London, as in *Iolanthe*. The book was by Basil Hood. It failed in New York the same year.

Tom Jones (Apollo, 17 April 1907) is easily the best of German's scores, song for song. This was a success for its romantic leads, Hayden Coffin and Ruth Vincent, and for its principal comedian, Dan Rolyat, but not for its management—the run was only 110 performances. The opening chorus, "Don't You Find the Weather Charming," has a Messagerian grace, albeit anglicized with tally-hos, and the contrapuntal section—so early in the course of an operetta—promises much. Squire Western's dialectical "On a January Morning in Zumerzetsheer" gives a nice treatment to the usual entrance *couplets,* as does Tom

Jones's "West Country Lad." Both have a robust country swagger quite unusual in British operetta, and German uses the chorus in both numbers with some cleverness.

The soprano songs are charmingly operatic: "Today My Spinet," in Act I, and the entrancing coloratura "For To-night," a Gounodian waltz which Joan Sutherland, for one, has included in her repertoire. The ensembles are quite polished. The trio "Wisdom says 'Festina Lente' " and the madrigal-quartet "Here's a Paradox for Lovers," both in Act I, have a dramatic and musical sheen, if not bounce, worthy of (again) Messager but without the Sullivan shine. But there were dubious hangovers from *Merrie England*—all treated better, to be sure, but still irksome: "dream-o'-day Jill" instead of "Jill-all-alone," a Morris dance, and dozens of heigh-hos, derry-downs, and such. (One gets the impression that German *asked* for this type of song.) The "English Rose" blossoms here into the more dramatic and now baritonal "If Love's Content," for the title character—a cut above the typical heroic love declarations of the time. German did attempt a bit of eighteenth-century pastiche. The orchestral introduction to Sophia's "Love Maketh the Heart a Garden Fair" (Act II) is a fetching example. The opening of Act III, in Ranelagh Gardens, a lively Morris dance, is followed by a snobbish gavotte, anticipating the Ascot chorus in *My Fair Lady*. All in all, *Tom Jones* (1907), along with Messager's *Monsieur Beaucaire* (1919) and Fall's *Madame Pompadour* (1921), are among the most graceful twentieth-century operettas to be set in the 1700s.

Perhaps the British musical comedies of the turn of the century seem sillier to us than contemporary continental works because they *are* in English. While some very proficient lyricists were around then, like Adrian Ross, the prevailing fondness was for quaint, flowery lyrics. Others had to be easily remembered without necessarily having to buy a libretto. Arm-in-arm with this music-hall memory-trick repetition went a similar need for simple-minded tunes.

The British variety of musical comedy popular in the '90s and into the new century had its origins not only in earlier British and foreign operettas but also in the Gaiety burlesques. The pre-1885 Gaiety Theatre was the chief purveyor of light musical entertainment in London. Its manager John Hollingshead had, in his prestigious career, presented many worthwhile foreign operettas, had started or developed the careers of several British authors and composers, including Gilbert and Sullivan, and had given London some of its most cherished musical stars: Nellie Farren, J. L. Toole, and many others. More fundamentally, he kept

---

Edward German's *Tom Jones* (Apollo, 1907) carried on the Sullivan tradition in certain ways, among them the use of the madrigal. German's scores exult in choral and ensemble writing, and his librettists accordingly provided hundreds of fa-la-las, derry-down-derrys, and other such effects. This operetta was much tamer than Fielding's novel and the later film, but the score is undoubtedly pretty. Ruth Vincent (Sophia) and Hayden Coffin (Tom) are the lovers on the right—two of the best-voiced and most personable operetta stars of their age.

alive through the Victorian age the traditions of the extravaganza and other British forms which might have died from an attack of prudery. By making playgoing comfortable and respectable, he bridged the gap between the extravaganza and Savoy opera, and provided 1868–85 audiences with happy entertainment.

But by 1885, with the triumphant success of *The Mikado* at the Savoy in March of that year, John Hollingshead and George Edwardes, like other West End musical managers, saw that the frank imitation of the Gilbert and Sullivan operettas was no easy affair, and that their huge runs seemed just as impossible to imitate. There had been attempts in many theatres, but it was found more expedient to present anglicized French works. The craze for Offenbach and Lecocq, though waning, had by no means died out in the late 1870s and early '80s. The Gaiety, for example, was attempting to rival the huge success of *Pinafore, Pirates,* and *Patience* with revivals of Lecocq's *Le petit Duc, La petite Mariée,* and the first British performances of Offenbach's *Belle Lurette* in 1881, while at the same time presenting native works which had some popularity, but which were *not* enormous successes. Most of these were composed by Edward Solomon with libretti by H. P. Stephens: a revival of *Billee Taylor* (1880), *Lord Bateman* (1882), even a musical version of *Through the Looking Glass,* after Lewis Carroll (1882). Alternating with these was the typical Gaiety fare of burlesque, pantomime, comedy, farce, and visits from the Comédie-Française.

In 1880, the first amplified burlesque in three acts was presented at the Gaiety at Christmas: *The Forty Thieves,* by Robert Reece. This was to be the prototype of the entertainment which, when given modern stories rather than old ones, when rid of some of the saucier trappings of old burlesque, and when infused with some of the dignity and romance of the Savoy operetta and the popular appeal of the music hall, would become within fifteen years the Gaiety species of musical comedy. F. C. Burnand, the librettist still remembered today for *Cox and Box,* wrote some burlesques in the '80s, *Whittington and His Cat* (1881), *Bluebeard* (1883), *Mazeppa* (1885), until another burlesque, *Little Jack Sheppard* (1885), by H. P. Stephens and W. Yardley, really caught on, running 155 nights, considered a record for a burlesque. This was, in more ways than one, a variation on *The Beggar's Opera,* with its highwaymen, interpolated songs, and a fairly coherent, continuous plot.

For *Little Jack Sheppard,* George Edwardes joined John Hollingshead as a partner. This was the last burlesque produced by the latter, who retired from his beloved theatre in the summer of 1886. To Edwardes was entrusted the "sacred lamp of burlesque," and Edwardes spent the next decade producing them at the Gaiety. The great popularity of these burlettas (as some called them) seems to have been caused by the talents of Nellie Farren and Fred Leslie. Farren was a small woman who, terribly sensitive about growing any larger, was reputed to have eaten nothing but bread and butter. She had been in the Gilbert-Sullivan *Thespis* in 1871. Leslie, who died young in 1892 of typhoid, was considered by those who saw him to have been the finest, funniest, and most inventive comedian ever to have appeared on the British musical stage. The pair were often starred in some of the "up-to-date" burlesques that included: *Monte Cristo Junr.*, *Miss Esmeralda* (from Hugo's *Notre-Dame de Paris*), another "melodramatic burlesque," *Frankenstein* (Leslie as the Monster), *Faust-Up-To-Date* (with Florence St. John as Marguerite), *Ruy Blas, or, The Blasé Roué, Carmen-Up-To-Data, Joan of Arc, Cinder-Ellen Up-Too-Late,* and *Don Juan*. These had music composed by Meyer Lutz, the Gaiety conductor, or by his successor, the Belgian-born Félix Tilkins, whose *nom de théâtre* was Ivan Caryll. Very little of musical worth has survived, and the literary standards were correspondingly low. But the topicality and verve of the comic numbers and the freewheeling gaiety of the whole would remain the trademarks of the theatre of that name.

George Edwardes's tastes were higher, as were his sights. He toured his Gaiety burlesques—with extremely profitable visits also to America and Australia—to pay for more ambitious works leaning more toward comic opera. The first of these, early in his Gaiety management, was *Dorothy* (25 September 1886), with music by the Gilbert and Sullivan conductor **Alfred Cellier** (1844–1891) and a book by B. C. Stephenson. Based on a popular comedy set in the eighteenth century, *Dorothy* was a comic opera with a derivative, though tuneful score that not unsuccessfully smacked of both the Savoy and the "period" works that Edward German would later compose. However, it lacked any truly memorable songs. Three weeks after the première, Hayden Coffin, the very handsome romantic lead, was given the new song, "Queen of My Heart," which was serenaded to the heroine by the light of a fireplace in Act II. A double encore was generally required, but there were insufficient Gaiety-goers by then and the piece was taken off.

The Gaiety's accountant, J. H. Leslie, thought he could succeed where Edwardes had failed. He bought the entire show—the rights, the sets, and the costumes—from Edwardes for £1,000 and remounted it at the Prince of Wales's Theatre. The one significant change he made was to replace the original Dorothy, Marion Hood, with Marie Tempest, who thereupon commenced her meteoric career. *Dorothy* ran and ran, and made Leslie a fortune, out of which he built the Lyric Theatre in Shaftesbury Avenue, dedicating it to lyric works of the *Dorothy* type.

Alfred Cellier also composed *Doris* (1889), a close cousin of *Dorothy*'s, and *The Mountebanks* (1892), a posthumous operetta with Gilbert's libretto. One would like to be able to hear his much earlier works, *The Sultan of Mocha* (1874) and *The Tower of London* (1875), produced in Manchester prior to the Gilbert and Sullivan heyday. (To ease any possible confusion, Alfred's brother, François Cellier, 1849–1914, was the original conductor of the *later* Gilbert and Sullivan works at the Savoy. His original 1891 operetta, *Captain Billy*, has recently received an amateur performance and recording.)

Edwardes's sale of *Dorothy* was the first of two big mistakes in an otherwise hugely successful career. The second was to turn down the rights to Oscar Straus's *Der tapfere Soldat*, which would become *The Chocolate Soldier* in 1910.

Edwardes was bruised by the failure of *Dorothy* at the Gaiety, caused as much by the theatre's reputation as by any managerial error. In future, he would confine his more ambitious pieces to Daly's. At the Gaiety, and at other theatres, he sought a new type of entertainment. After the final revival of the first of the successful three-act Gaiety burlesques, *Little Jack Sheppard,* in August 1893, with Seymour Hicks and Ellaline Terriss (later one of the most popular musical comedy teams), Edwardes mounted *A Gaiety Girl* at the Prince of Wales's. This had a score by Sidney Jones, and was, for all practical purposes, the first Gaiety musical comedy, as the title indicates, although it did not appear at that theatre. *A Gaiety Girl* had been preceded by *In Town* (a "musical farce," 1892) and *Morocco Bound* (1893, "a farcical musical comedy"), but Edwardes managed to take hold of the infant and shape it to his own needs.

Shortly after *Morocco Bound* came Edwardes's first musical comedy at the Gaiety itself—*The Shop Girl* (24 November 1894) by Adrian Ross, who was to be the chief Edwardian lyricist, and composer Ivan Caryll, with extra melodies by Lionel Monckton. Considered by several theatre historians the first true British musical comedy, *The Shop Girl* was certainly a prototype for the gay, tuneful, brainless, but very luxurious shows that Edwardes and his rivals would send out of their factories to play the West End and tour endlessly.

Edwardes had effected a change that hit much of Europe in the 1890s, when the public clamored more for modern-dress stories than for satiric or burlesque plots. Musical comedy drew on burlesque, on comic opera, and even on the social drawing-room dramas of the '90s. Importantly, the principal comedian, who in Gilbert and Sullivan had been dignified by the rank of Lord Chancellor, Major-General, and even Duke, now reverted to low-comedy Cockney types, complete with gags and music-hall funny songs, the very stuff Gilbert had banished from the Savoy. Put in for comedy, sticking out in burlesque fashion, and no longer strictly part of a totally conceived comic plot, this new type of principal comedian signaled the breakdown of the libretto, and ultimately the score.

One might accuse "Gaiety George" Edwardes of having watered down British operetta, but this would not be fair. He produced, at Daly's and at other theatres, several excellent operettas and "musical plays," and in 1907 he revitalized the English form by injecting the Viennese *Merry Widow* into its thinned-out bloodstream. Certainly, no one can deny the great popularity of the Edwardes species of operetta and musical comedy. There were 260 theatres in the British Isles in 1901, plus smaller playing venues (like corn exchanges) that were visited by touring companies. Musical plays were the most popular attractions, and Edwardes made fortunes in the provinces, which helped pay for the more ambitious West End productions of the types of comic opera he professed to admire more than anything else, and which often lost money in London because of the expensive productions he lavished on them. If his musical comedies had music-hall features, this may have been a deliberate way to actually compete with the newly built, hugely popular, enormously profitable music halls that were springing up everywhere in Britain.

In her book on her father, *Freddy Lonsdale,* Frances Donaldson gives a generalized but accurate critique of the Edwardian musical comedy type for which Lonsdale later wrote some libretti (pp. 69–71):

. . . these productions seem to have reached almost the lowest point of art of any theatrical tradition . . . Much attention was paid to the scenery and dresses, enormous choruses of beautiful girls were engaged, the leading ladies had to be young and attractive, and always there was at least one big part for a comedian . . . Nothing very strenuous was required of anyone but the comedians. The stars and the chorus were not expected either to dance, except in an inconsequent and graceful manner, or to be able to sing. Some of the music was charming, but little was of real merit.

Commenting on the comedians, Ms. Donaldson added:

. . . one or two, such as George Robey and . . . W. H. Berry, possessed the real comic spirit, but all too often they only worked extremely hard. They derived from the English music-hall, but they were expected to be less broad, more sophisticated and to manage without the more outrageous jokes permitted to artistes in that sphere. In order to make up for these disadvantages, they relied to a great extent on exaggerated clothes and make-up, and for the rest on spontaneous inspiration (such was their position in the theatre that they often wrote their own lines, altered their performance nightly, and took liberties with the script and the rest of the cast that were permitted to no one else). When their inspiration flagged, they relied on holding the line that had failed of effect, while making distressed and india-rubber faces until the audience laughed from sheer embarrassment.

Perhaps more important than the comedians were the ladies, the *girls* of the titles: *A Gaiety Girl* (1893), *My Girl* and *The Circus Girl* (1896), *A Runaway Girl* (1898), *The Casino Girl* (1900), *A Country Girl* and *The Girl from Kay's* (1902), *The School Girl, The Earl and the Girl,* and *The Cherry Girl* (all 1903), and others, not to mention various maids, from *The French Maid* (1897) through *The Medal and the Maid* (1903) and the triumphant *Maid of the Mountains* (1917) to *A Southern Maid* (1920). The other titles referred for the most part to the principal female character: *The Gay Parisienne* (1896), *The Geisha* (1896), *Kitty Grey* (1901), *My Lady Molly* and *The Duchess of Dantzic* (1903), and *The Beauty of Bath* (1906), to give some examples.

By this time, the Gaiety Girls were known for their extravagant, up-to-date dress, not for the *undress* of yesteryear. And the casts were turning into a stock company like the one that resided at the Savoy. People went to the Gaiety for all their favorite artists there, and to Daly's or The Prince of Wales's for others.

The plot formats were also fairly regularized, but they were in some measure borrowed from French operetta. In the first act would appear a middle-class setting: a department store was a favorite venue. In the second act, the company would *go* somewhere, a place like the Riviera, or a fancy bazaar in Kensington, or the Franco-British Exhibition in White City. If there was a third act, it might take place in a ballroom, or else a hotel suite. This formula persevered: *No! No! Nanette* had a similar synopsis of scenes in 1925. The idea of the whole company taking off somewhere must ultimately stem from *Orphée aux Enfers,* when the gods descend *en masse* to hell. There is no need to go into any of the Edwardian plots even slightly. Few of them would stand up unrevised today; the jokes are so exceedingly witless that one has to pore through page after page of the script to find anything remotely amusing in even the best of them. Similarly, Edwardian audiences didn't have the same curiosity for the text that Savoy audiences had. Though cleverly done in certain instances, there was no libretto to compare with those for *Patience* or *Iolanthe,* and few lyrics like those delightedly scanned in the new electric light by Savoy patrons.

From the very start, Edwardes cared little about the integrity of a score by *one* composer. If the second act needed a new comic turn, or a love song, he turned to a number of specialists for material; later on, Jerome Kern would begin his career as one of these interpolating composers. Edwardes would just as well have had his audiences go out describing the dresses as repeating the jokes or humming the tunes. Indeed, *The Play Pictorial,* London's leading theatre magazine, had a regular column meticulously outlining each frock in each musical comedy.

After a while, all the musicals, like the dresses, would begin looking exactly alike. Even the hit songs were of the same, simple music-hall variety, distinguished principally by the personalities who sang or, rather, delivered them. Yet there were several composers and lyricists, even authors, who managed to rise above the assembly line with something worthwhile, even occasionally coming up with a complete operetta of some value. These composers were Sidney Jones, Lionel Monckton, and, to a lesser extent, Ivan Caryll, Leslie Stuart, Paul Rubens, and Howard Talbot.

Sidney Jones (1869–1946) was another of those successful musical theatre composers who were sons of bandmasters. Like Lehár, he became a bandmaster before becoming a theatre conductor. When George Edwardes received the book of a "musical comedy" entitled *A Gaiety Girl,* written by the drama critic of the *Sporting Times,* and found he liked it, he commissioned Jones to write the score and Percy Greenbank to do the lyrics. The critic's name was Jimmy Davis, but he was so often in debt that he devised the pen name Owen Hall. The *Times* admired Jones's "lively and catching" music, and acknowledged that "the piece was received with a degree of favour on Saturday night which augurs its success with people of the class to whom it appeals."

Large numbers of that class of people were evidently amused enough to support a long run at both the Prince of Wales's (14 October 1893) and a transfer to Daly's, to sit through a joke-filled but slight story of the rivalry between a Gaiety artiste (Decima Moore) and an upper-class lady (Marie Studholme) for a well-connected young officer (Hayden Coffin). Coffin stopped the show with a patriotic interpolation, "Tommy Atkins," which had only the slightest bearing on the plot. The clothes were what made the piece, with the female members of the cast constantly changing them at a moment's notice and regaling the audience with a fashion parade in every scene. These caused as much of a sensation in New York (Daly's, 18 September 1894) as in London, and set the style for native musical comedies based on the Britannic mode, with a similar vogue for English millinery and drapery.

Edwardes's production of Jones's *An Artist's Model* (Daly's, 2 February, 1895) was in a style similar to *A Gaiety Girl* and *The Shop Girl*. "Vaudeville is the word to describe *An Artist's Model*. If we haven't the word in our dictionaries, it is only because the thing does not exist in this country; and we are obliged to Mr. Hall for bringing it in fashion," wrote one London reviewer. The big song hit was Letty Lind's "Tom-tit," which was "obviously modelled" on Gilbert's "The Magnet and the Churn," from *Patience*. Another big success was, of all things, Zeller's *"Sei nicht bös',"* well known then as "The *Obersteiger* Waltz," sung as a duet. It was one thing for Edwardes to interpolate native material, but the Viennese copyright owners refused further airings of the Zeller waltz, and a substitute was found.

In *An Artist's Model*, Marie Tempest made a triumphant return to the West End after five years in the States. Hayden Coffin and Maurice Farkoa (a Turk who invariably played romantic Frenchmen) repeated their roles in New York (Broadway, 30 December 1895), where the British postcard-favorite Marie Studholme regaled all with "Tom-tit." Alison Skipworth, later a Hollywood attraction, received early notice in the Broadway company. The London production ran for 405 performances, first of an astonishing series at Daly's, which would gradually replace the Savoy in popularity as London's premier operetta theatre.

The success of the second revival of *The Mikado* at the Savoy (6 November 1895) was responsible in part for a profusion of Asian—Japanese, Chinese, Indian—operettas right through the turn of the century. First, and most prominent, was Sidney Jones's *The Geisha*, generally regarded as his best operetta. It had as much right to a Japanese locale as any work: *Madama Butterfly* (1904) has also done well with a similar setting, and the stimulus for both bittersweet plots was probably Pierre Loti's novel *Madame Chrysanthème* (1887), which had already been turned into a *comédie-lyrique* by André Messager in 1893. This had a French Lieutenant, Pierre, romancing in Japan; for Jones, it was the English Lieutenant Reg. Fairfax; for Puccini (via Belasco), the American Lieutenant B. F. Pinkerton.

The Geisha's first night was an unqualified triumph (Daly's, 25 April 1896). With lovely sets by W. Telbin and costumes by Percy Anderson, it was ensured an authentic Japanese look by Edwardes's engagement of Arthur Diósy, of the Japanese Legation, to train the cast in proper deportment. Diósy, incidentally, was supposed to have supplied Arthur Sullivan with the actual war march that appears in *The Mikado*, "Miya Sama." *The Geisha*, too, had a Japanese march in the second act: *"Koi-wa-se-ni-sumu."* Rutland Barrington appeared as the Marquis Imari—he hardly sang, as the part had been created by another actor—and Hayden Coffin was reunited with his Dorothy of ten years before, Marie

Tempest. "Queen Marie" of Daly's never used the stage door. Her carriage was waiting for her every night at the royal entrance.

During the long London run, the world at large saw in *The Geisha* a successor to *The Mikado* and a continuation of the sprightly Gilbert and Sullivan works London used to supply. A Broadway production opened at Daly's (New York, 9 September 1896) with a mixed British-American cast. Its 160 performances were 600 short of the British run, though tours aggregated the number, and there were New York revivals. Isadora Duncan was a member of the company for a brief spell. In Paris, *La Geisha* was received poorly at the Athénée-Comique in 1898, but Vienna and Berlin rapturously welcomed the play as if it were the new *Mikado*. The Carltheater production in 1897 was followed by an even more popular Theater an der Wien mounting four years later, while Budapest had already welcomed *A gésák* in 1897. Other cities were thoroughly captivated—particularly in Italy; a juvenile company was seen in Rome in the 1890s.

Owen Hall's book and the lyrics of Harry Greenbank would serve as a model of the period: increased romantic interest, generally of some potentially tragic or hopeless character, plus an increased reliance on the catch-phrase comic song, generally (painfully) of the most insipid type. Satire was thrown into the back of the carriage, and the whimsical framework of Gilbert's inspired plots was replaced in *The Geisha* and similar works by stories where comedy derived from the strangeness of the locale and its effect on the British characters discovered therein. The characters seldom changed, from 1892 to 1907, and even after. No British librettist created anything like the panorama of great beings Gilbert immortalized: Pooh-Bah, the Duchess of Plaza-Toro, Jack Point, and so many more.

Gilbert had also avoided the now-offensive phraseology that figures in *The Geisha* and its successors. These were usually sung by the comic "Chinese" character. In the Japanese *Geisha* he appears as Wun-Hi, surely enough, a laundryman. His song, "Chin Chin Chinaman," is a catalogue of Chinatown English. The melody is, however, irresistible, and so are those for such numbers as the kissing duet (another *Mikado* borrowing), O Mimosa San's waltz-refrained "A Geisha's Life," one of several rousing nautical choruses, "Jack's the Boy," and "Chon Kina."

The *Times* admired the score's attempt to rise above music–hall triviality, particularly "the 'madrigalian' movement in the first finale," and it found the scoring "generally very refined and skillful." Yet the biggest hits were Letty Lind's singing of Lionel Monckton's "The Toy Monkey," his catchy "Jack's the Boy," and the "Jewel of Asia," which had music by James Philp. If this was Jones's finest score, not all of its high points were his.

Daly's Theatre, at the north end of Leicester Square, was London's premier theatre for operetta in its day, although it was built by the American manager Augustin Daly as a showcase for his dramatic productions. After its takeover by impresario George Edwardes, Daly's housed musical plays almost exclusively, of which Jones's *A Greek Slave* was one in 1898.

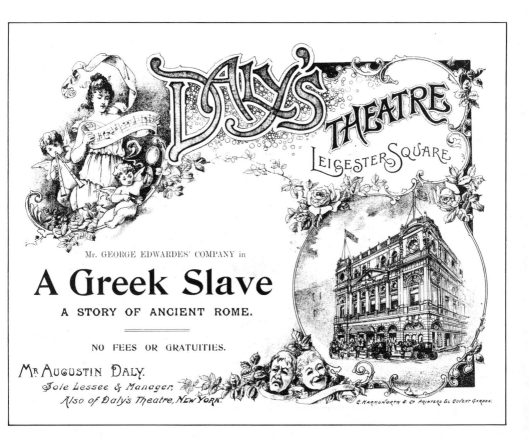

The much less successful Edwardes-Jones *A Greek Slave* (8 June 1898), set in Rome, A.D. 90, had followed *The Geisha* at Daly's. Apparently, audiences preferred to see *The Geisha*'s stars—Tempest, Lind, Coffin, Barrington—in kimonos rather than togas. Jones and Greenbank, with Edward Morton and Lionel Monckton in tow, provided Daly's with an even more successful Eastern show three years later, *San Toy,* which ran 778 performances (21 October 1899). *San Toy* substituted the Chinese town of Pynka Pong for rural Japan, but everything else was quite the same: Marie Tempest as a Mandarin's daughter, Rutland Barrington as the Mandarin, Huntley Wright and Gracie Leigh as the interracial comedy couple, and a British lieutenant, this time played by Lionel Mackinder.

Daly's audiences adored it all: the glittering cast, the overwhelming production, and the quaintly oriental milieu (in which songs were heard that, in certain cases, would not have survived the average music-hall). Rutland Barrington was given a memorably inane entrance song in *San Toy,* about his six wives. Purebred-Savoy Barrington was worried about playing a polygamist. Edwardes reassured him by saying, "They don't mind what you do, Rutty, as long as they just see you."

Marie Tempest by this time had had quite enough of Edwardes's strict regimen at Daly's (things were apparently easier at the Gaiety) and sought an es-

SAN TOY

A CHINESE MUSICAL COMEDY.

W. George

MUSIC by

Sidney Jones.

VOCAL SCORE
6/- net.

KEITH PROWSE & Co
LONDON, E.C.

H.G. BANKS, Litho.

cape. A pair of long trousers was ordered for San Toy; "No doubt correct, but I hated them," recalled Miss Tempest later. She cut them into shorts and went on the stage. Edwardes told her to either wear the costume as designed or leave Daly's. She walked off the stage, and never appeared again in operetta. Marie Tempest went on to become one of the most accomplished comediennes in Britain—in some of the worst vehicles (often written by her husband)—and remained popular well into the 1930s. From the glowing accounts of her operetta performances in the United Kingdom and the United States in the 1880s and from the few recordings we have of her special voice, it is futile but fascinating to imagine what her operetta triumphs would have been in this century.

Further "oriental" operettas included *A Chinese Honeymoon* (Strand, 5 October 1901) with a score by Howard Talbot (1865–1928) and a book by George Dance, which, after a pre–West End tour, established the reputation of impresario Frank Curzon and became the first London production to run over 1,000 performances. The run in New York (Casino, 2 June 1902), produced by the Shuberts, was half as long, but admirable all the same. Legions of East-Enders were attracted to the old Strand for this amiable, if perhaps low-brow, spin-off of *The Geisha,* with its catchy songs. Louie Freear was the much-acclaimed star. Talbot had two other works with Eastern locales open within three days of each other in 1905: *The Blue Moon* (Lyric, 28 August) and *The White Chrysanthemum* (Criterion, 31 August). These had superb casts, with many Savoy graduates— Walter Passmore and Courtice Pounds in the former and Rutland Barrington, Isabel Jay, and Henry Lytton in the latter. Both were somewhat more operetta-ish than *A Chinese Honeymoon,* as befitted their excellent casts, and both harked back to *The Geisha.* Paul Rubens helped with *The Blue Moon,* which was produced by Robert Courtneidge, a Scottish actor who had made a name for himself in Manchester. Spotted by George Edwardes, he became one of the best musical comedy producers, also producing the noted musical-comedy comedienne, his daughter Cicely. *The Blue Moon* ran only 182 performances, possibly because Indian romances in the musical theatre were said to have been unlucky, but those who saw it liked comic Willie Edouin, Passmore singing Rubens's "Oh, Be Careful of the Crocodile," the truly beautiful Florence Smithson, and those fresh young ladies, Carrie Moore and Billie Burke. James T. Powers and Ethel Jackson headed the Casino cast in New York (3 November 1906).

The White Chrysanthemum, which took one back to Japan, was another Curzon production, again with a lieutenant falling in love with a native. The twist was that she was actually Sybil, a British girl escaping a marriage not to her liking. The libretto came up with names that hardly differed from *The Geisha's.* The lieutenant was Reginald and the girl O San. If Sin Chong was not quite Wun Hi, his material was startlingly similar, with roads of vellees.

Marie Tempest as *San Toy* in Jones's oriental operetta (Daly's, 1899). Her face appeared in this piece of china on the vocal score cover.

The Girl Behind the Counter (Wyndham's, 21 April 1906) and *The Belle of Brittany* (Queen's, 24 October 1908) were slightly more impressive and more popular, but it is for his contributions to *The Arcadians* that Talbot will be recalled. We can also thank Talbot for orchestrating Lionel Monckton's melodies; Monckton did not do his own. He ended his career with those Pinero-based musical comedies, *The Boy* and *Who's Hooper?*

Lionel Monckton (plus Talbot and Rubens) had two Eastern shows: *The Cingalee* (Daly's, 5 March 1904) set in Ceylon, and *The Mousmé* (Shaftesbury, 9 September 1911), which was as thoroughly Japanese as *The Mikado,* without any occidental characters. The Queen and Princess Alexandra attended the first night of *The Cingalee,* which lasted four hours, thanks to the numerous encores. Most admired in Edwardes's production were the sets, by Hawes Craven, including "Boobhamba's Palace, by the Lake at Kandy" and the spectacular scene of the revels on the Buddhist New Year's Eve. Monckton's sextet, "The Island of Gay Ceylon," was praised; so was Rubens's "White and Brown Girl." But the piece flopped. *The Mousmé* fared even less well, though Florence Smithson's song to/with her samisen, by Talbot and Greenbank, continues to haunt, and there was a spectacular earthquake sequence in the final act.

Sidney Jones was by no means through with the East after *San Toy* in 1899. The new century brought yet another Chinese operetta, *See-See* (20 June 1906, Prince of Wales's), with an Adrian Ross–Charles Brookfield libretto. The spectacular Peking settings and robes were filled with the likes of Denise Orme and Maurice Farkoa, who refused to shave off his French-looking moustache, wearing it with a braided pigtail.

In 1903, Jones had his *My Lady Molly* and *The Medal and the Maid* open within two months of one another, at Terry's (14 March) and the Lyric (25 April), respectively. The former was the more interesting and more accomplished work, the story of a girl masquerading as an army captain in a semi-military Georgian uniform in the eighteenth century. Sybil Arundale shone as "Captain Romney," and Decima Moore, the Savoy's first Casilda in *The Gondoliers,* soubretted. Almost every other number was encored on the opening night, but "Our Captious Critic," in *The Illustrated Sporting and Dramatic News,* carped about "the indispensable comic opera innkeeper [who] always has a song about five minutes past eight."

The King of Cadonia (Prince of Wales's, 3 September 1908), music by Sidney Jones, book by Frederick Lonsdale, and lyrics by Adrian Ross, had a riotous first night and a long run of 330 performances, though the *Times* commented, "There is no wit." It was so frankly Graustarkian that one critic, when asked if he admired the operetta, remarked, "I liked it very much. But then I always have. I liked it when it was *The Prisoner of Zenda.*" Jones's score proved that the care and effort that distinguished the late nineteenth century were still alive in at least one British composer, but the main attraction of this operetta was Bertram Wallis, the exceedingly tall and handsome singer who from this point reigned as one of the Edwardian age's most glamorous matinée idols and one of its biggest male postcard-sellers. He was teamed with Isabel Jay, who had started at the Savoy and was now Mrs. Frank Curzon, wife of the theatre manager.

The King of Cadonia brought Frederick Lonsdale to the front rank of dramatists, though his peak period was to fall in the 1920s, with such straight comedies as *The Last of Mrs. Cheyney* (1925) and *On Approval* (1927). The libretto conceded to the sudden British fashion for Middle European uniforms and national dresses, but it had an added Anthony Hope-ish vibrancy, complete with attempted assassinations and disguised monarchs. Ivor Novello later paid tribute to Lonsdale and Jones by naming one of the characters in *Glamorous Night* Militza, after Malitza, played by Gracie Leigh in *The King of Cadonia,* and by having a plot brimming with anarchist assassins somewhere in Ruritania. During the run of *King's Rhapsody* (1950), Novello confessed all to Lonsdale by saying "You know what this play is based on? When I was quite young I was taken to see *The King of Cadonia,* and I thought then: This is how a musical comedy should be written. One day I shall write one like that myself."

The final Sidney Jones works, *The Girl from Utah* (Adelphi, 18 October 1913) and *The Happy Day* (Daly's, 13 May 1916), were written with Rubens, with interpolations by Jerome Kern that tended to overshadow the Jones songs. The most famous of these was "They Didn't Believe Me," from *The Girl from Utah.*

Tunewise, **Lionel Monckton** (1861–1924) was king of the Edwardesian era. Though virtually unknown outside of Britain today, his best songs—and there were quite a few—live on. Thanks to the piecemeal construction of these musical comedies, and Edwardes's sure sense of giving the right material to his stars (even if the principal composer couldn't come up with all of it), Monckton could not call an entire score his own. Yet the major percentage of *A Country Girl* (1902), *The Cingalee* (1904), *Our Miss Gibbs* (1909), *The Arcadians* (1909), and *The Quaker Girl* (1910) were his, and songs like "Moonstruck," "Arcady Is Ever Young," and "Come to the Ball" remain among the most appealing examples of British musical comedy hits. Fortunately, some of Monckton's scores are on such an outstandingly high level of accomplishment that one can easily see how much Noël Coward, Ivor Novello, and Vivian Ellis both admired and owed Lionel Monckton. The refinement, the "Englishness," and the haunting quality Monckton so often achieved with the simplest melodies and most facile harmonies must have also appealed to Jerome Kern, who was in London during this period.

Lionel Monckton was destined for the bar, but up at Oxford he became involved with university theatricals. After a while as a barrister, and after a spell as music critic for the *Daily Telegraph,* his song contributions went from amateur to Gaiety productions in the mid-1890s. His "Soldiers in the Park" enjoyed great acclaim in *A Runaway Girl* (Gaiety, 21 May 1898). He contributed numbers to *The Geisha* and *San Toy* at Daly's. *A Country Girl,* book by James T. Tanner and lyrics by Adrian Ross and Percy Greenbank, refreshed Daly's audiences weary of the Orient (18 January 1902) and freed Hayden Coffin, Huntley Wright, and the rest of the company from kimonos, yellow faces, and Chinee accents. Only Rutland Barrington was still an Eastern potentate, the Rajah of Bhong, complete with the by-now-expected topical song, "Peace!", for which Barrington often wrote his own verses (and was occasionally reprimanded by the Lord Chamberlain's Office for political reasons). As Barrington diplomatically put it, "Owing to the elasticity of George Edwardes's contracts with his authors and composers he was able to introduce songs by other people . . ." Paul Rubens's "Coo," sung by Lilian Eldee, and "Mrs. Brown," sung by Huntley Wright *en travesti,* were especially popular in 1902 but audiences today remember Monckton's plaintive "Under the Deodar," the nautical "Yo Ho, Little Girls, Yo Ho," and "Try again, Johnnie," the latter an Evie Greene favorite. Many comedy numbers and interpolated songs smacked of the music hall, but this outré raffishness was always popular and had its antecedents in the risqué *couplets* of French operetta. It remained difficult to keep the *café-concert* out of *opérette.*

A *Country Girl* had a long run of 729 performances, and was admired by many of the New York critics on its Broadway première (Daly's, 22 September 1902), though one claimed that Monckton had "tuned up his fiddle smoothly, inventing new tunes, adapting old ones, chiefly from *The Mikado.*" The New York version included several numbers cut from the London production, and, of course, had to supply new topical verses for the Rajah of Bhong's song. Paris audiences enjoyed A *Country Girl* in 1904 at the Olympia with a strong cast including Mariette Sully, Max Dearly, and Alice Bonheur, and Central Europe got a taste of Monckton—*Az utahi lány,* in Budapest, after the big success of Jones's A *gésák* and San *Toy.*

One beyond-the-ordinary Gaiety work was *The Girls of Gottenberg* (15 May 1907), the book by Grossmith and L. E. Berman, the lyrics by Adrian Ross and Basil Hood. This was a musicalization of the celebrated Prussian incident which later became Carl Zuckmayer's play and later still two films, the adventures of the "Captain" of Köpenick. Working with the familiar Edwardes company, the collaborators at least provided an interesting idea, based on truth, and one New York critic reviewing the Broadway version was delighted by the fact that it was "an out-and-out comical play set to music," without the need for "vaudeville comedians" or "improper costumes." The London production offered May de Sousa's singing, "with its pianissimo high notes . . . very welcome in these days when singing on the light opera stage is so rare," as one critic reported. But best of all Gertie Millar and Teddy Payne singing Monckton's "Two Little Sausages," and, with George Grossmith, the trio *"Sprechen-Sie Deutsch, mein Herr?".* Plus a most amusing song about the *Rheingold.*

Another co-composition by Monckton and Caryll was Our *Miss Gibbs,* judged by most historians as one of the two or three best Gaiety triumphs (23 January 1909). The *Daily Express* called it "almost the ideal musical comedy." It ran two years (636 times), and in the first-night cast were Gertie Millar, George Grossmith, Edmund Payne, Denise Orme, Maisie Gay, and Gladys Cooper.

The plot devised by "Cryptos" (James Tanner) was of the typical department-store-salesgirl-meets-disguised-rich-earl-spurns-and-finally-accepts-him variety. But the settings were right up to date—Garrods (read Harrods) Kensington store and the White City amusement/exhibition park—and an element of the plot dealt with the theft of the Ascot Gold Cup. It was Messager (or his librettists) made English, and such was the appeal of Gertie Millar doing her "Moonstruck" number in a dark blue pierrot costume ("I'm such a silly when the moon comes out") that all London had to see it. Grossmith had two very popular interpolated numbers: "Bertie the Bounder" and "Yip-i-addy-i-ay." In the face of the sudden fascination for Viennese operetta, *Our Miss Gibbs* reinforced Basically British Values. But *Our Miss Gibbs* was too British to travel—it lasted a mere two months at the Knickerbocker, New York, in 1910 (29 August) with Pauline Chase in the title role. In New York, the second act took place in the Japanese garden of the "Jap-Anglo Exhibition." "Of course, an audience let loose in a dress-making establishment doesn't care much about plot, so it is not surprising that the gowns surpass the narrative in prominence," wrote one New York critic.

On 28 April 1909 at the Shaftesbury Theatre, the curtain rose on what was indisputably the greatest operetta (or musical comedy, if you will) of the Edwardian age. Beautifully produced by Robert Courtneidge, and with a large cast including Phyllis Dare, Florence Smithson, Ada Blanche, Dan Rolyat, Alfred Lester, Nelson Keys, and, later into the run, Cicely Courtneidge, *The Arcadians* happily superimposed a fantastical Arcadia on contemporary London, much in the way *Iolanthe* had a quarter century before. Not that Mark Ambient and A. M. Thompson's dialogue was quite as clever as Gilbert's, nor were Arthur Wimperis's lyrics on as high a level, but in 1909 the plot seemed significantly more intelligent than the average musical-comedy story. This prompted B. W. Findon, a well-known Gilbert and Sullivan admirer, to remark that "a more exquisite or amusing entertainment than 'The Arcadians' has not been seen since the days when genuine comic opera was the vogue . . . the central motive is Gilbertian in its whimsicality and the adroitness with which it is developed."

The plot told of an aging aviator, grounded in Arcadia. Immersed in the "Well of Truth," he comes up a youth, and takes a number of Arcadians to London to "set up the truth in England for ever more, and banish the lie." After adventures at the Askwood race course and at the Arcadian Restaurant, the hero returns to his elderly self, to the astonishment of his earthly wife. The dialogue and the jokes, especially in the racing act, are so of their period as to be virtually incomprehensible today, but the score is so strong that, with the right revisions, *The Arcadians* could stand a full revival in Britain. (The score has had two excellent studio recordings which have helped keep it fresh.)

From the opening chorus ("Arcadians Are We") to the final reprise of the intoxicating "All Down Piccadilly," Monckton and Talbot have no dull moments, and many that would have dignified a late nineteenth-century operetta: "The Pipes of Pan" and "The Girl with the Brogue" (Monckton), "I Like London" and "Half-past Two" (Talbot). The cast was singularly unconfident of success. Musicals set in Ceylon and India were traditionally bad luck, but fantasies were thought even less appealing, and it was not until the dress rehearsal that even Courtneidge guessed he would have a hit. He had given the play a first-class production, with lovely costumes by Wilhelm (who had designed some of the Gilbert and Sullivan works) and colorful sets. The racing scene was easily one of the most magnificent *tableaux* ever seen on the London stage. Apart from the fact that a horse came on stage—always a spectacular effect—the elegantly dressed assemblage followed the event facing the audience, the race taking place imaginarily somewhere in the stalls. It is hard to believe Cecil Beaton had not seen the black-and-white photographs of the original West End or Broadway productions when preparing the Ascot scene in *My Fair Lady* a half century later, though it *is* possible he did not.

Robert Courtneidge had every right to be proud of *The Arcadians;* appearing near the end of the popular era of British musical comedy, it was the best example of its genre. If it had music-hall moments, like "I've Gotter Motter," they were *excellent* music hall, fitting into the libretto and befitting the characterizations. The melodies were enchanting, rather than merely pretty, and were aided by expert orchestrations by Talbot. The original cast, though admittedly strewn with Courtneidge regulars, was less of a stock company in the Edwardes sense, and the libretto was sufficiently novel to give the actors a chance to seem part of an ensemble rather than "sticking out" like Teddy Payne or George Grossmith, Jr. did at the Gaiety. Courtneidge celebrated his *Arcadian* anniversaries with magnificent souvenir programmes, reflecting an understandable and thoroughly deserved pride.

Henry Savage had the first option on the American rights for *The Arcadians,* but curiously turned them down after seeing the exciting dress rehearsal. Charles Frohman picked them up and produced the operetta at the Liberty on 17 January 1910. Frank Moulan and Julia Sanderson played the parts originated by Rolyat and Dare, and the show clocked 193 performances—not as long as London's run but still quite respectable.

The Quaker Girl (Adelphi, 5 November 1910), written and produced by the same team that provided *Our Miss Gibbs* (less Caryll), was less intrinsically British than its predecessor and even more tuneful. The story had Prudence, the Quaker maid (Gertie Millar, disarming all), wooed by an American diplomat (Joseph Coyne, London's Danilo), and ending up a fashion model in gay Paris, where she actually drinks champagne! The combination of Quaker morality and speech and Parisian high-life and fashion proved irresistible to both London and New York (Park, 23 October 1911), where Ina Claire played the Millar part; in the West End, 536 performances, in New York, 246. A totally charming

---

The "Askwood" racing scene in Act II of *The Arcadians,* almost a half century before the Ascot of *My Fair Lady*.

Photo Foulsham & Banfield

"The Deuce Wins"

Monckton score accounted for this popularity: the "title" song of the operetta, reflecting the quaint Tanner dialogue, strewn with thees and thous, "Tony from America," "When a bad, bad boy like me, meets a good, good girl like you," and a grand slow waltz, sung by Georges Carvey as Prince Carlo, "Come to the Ball," were standouts.

After *The Mousmé* (1911) came *The Dancing Mistress* (19 October 1912), which was the next Monckton show at the Adelphi after the short run of Kálmán's *Autumn Manoeuvres* (1912). Gertie Millar singing her husband's songs would seem to have warranted a success as big as that of *The Quaker Girl*, but this was not the case. *The Dancing Mistress* danced only 242 times, after which Ina Claire, fresh from her New York triumph in the Millar part in *The Quaker Girl*, played the Adelphi in the Caryll-Kern *The Girl from Utah*. Revue claimed Monckton's and Millar's attentions during most of the 1914–18 war, until *The Boy* (Adelphi, 14 September 1917) reunited Monckton with Talbot. This was more modern musical comedy than *The Arcadians*—and a huge hit (801 performances). A healthy sign was that it was a funny British musical based on a great British farce, Arthur Wing Pinero's *The Magistrate* (1885). It gave W. H. Berry a chance to shine and, taking a cue from *The Boy,* the Adelphi management next produced

Who's Hooper? (13 September 1919), again with Berry and again based on Pinero (*In Chancery,* 1884), with a score by Talbot and Ivor Novello. Although *Who's Hooper?* did well, the fashion for musicalizing the sprightlier English comedies of the past was sadly not to persist.

The immortality of **Leslie Stuart** (1864–1928) rests today on one or two songs, principally the double sextette from *Florodora* (Lyric, 11 November 1899), which begins: "Tell me, pretty maiden, / Are there any more at home like you?" The "quaint, irregular rhythm" (as one London critic put it) captivated all ears, though there will be few to hear it in future years, as it is hardly the type of song one would hear on today's radio. *Florodora,* one of the last shows of the 1890s, was Stuart's first theatrical assignment. His work was not unknown, however; his songs "Lily of Laguna" and "Soldiers of the Queen" had been extremely popular in the music halls and with military bands. Stuart was born in Southport, Lancashire, in 1866 and had early experience as an organist. On the strength of some of his songs in early musical comedies, Stuart did most of the score of *Florodora.*

Florodora was a perfume manufactured in the South Seas, and poor Dolores, the manufacturer-heroine, has been robbed of the secret formula, in Owen Hall's libretto. Evie Greene was Dolores, Willie Edouin was a busy-fingered phrenologist, and Ada Reeve was an *aristocrate* with another Stuart hit to sing, "Tact." *Florodora* ran a year and a half in London, and, after a slow start, even longer on Broadway (Casino, 10 November 1900, 552 performances).

But could Mr. Stuart repeat his success? Several managers gave him the chance. *The Silver Slipper* (Lyric, 1 June 1901), *The School Girl* (Prince of Wales's, 9 May 1903), *The Belle of Mayfair* (Vaudeville, 11 April 1906), *Havana* (Gaiety, 25 April 1908), and *Peggy* (Gaiety, 4 March 1911) were *Florodora*'s followers, in some cases turning in sizable runs and profits, but without adding any memorable scores or libretti to the operetta Olympus.

The *Florodora* girls were so celebrated in the United States that they became an American equivalent of the Gaiety Girls, marrying well, and even achieving celluloid immortality in a 1930 film, *The Florodora Girl.* The sextette, in fact, became a popular vaudeville staple and it is for this reason, along with its long original Broadway run, that the show has often been assumed to have been of U.S. origin. American or British companies looking at the score today might also find the tenor solo, "The Shade of the Palm," to have a certain palm-court fragrance. An Off-Off-Broadway New York revival (1981) revealed that Owen Hall's book was a somewhat more entertaining relic than the Stuart score.

Paul Rubens (1876–1917) deserves some distinction for having, at times, written his own book and lyrics, and for having written a number of engaging tunes. Up at Oxford—like Monckton—he began writing ditties while studying law, and had several songs successfully interpolated into Edwardes musical comedies of the late 1890s. He wrote three songs for *Florodora,* several for *The Toreador* (1901) and *A Country Girl* (1902), and was then signed to do a complete work for Edwardes, *Three Little Maids* (Apollo, 10 May 1902). Rubens became the house composer for Frank Curzon's Prince of Wales's after *Three Little Maids* transferred. *Lady Madcap* (17 December 1904) and *Miss Hook of Holland* (31 January 1907) came next—the latter one of his better efforts. In this "Dutch Musical Incident" Isabel Jay and Walter Hyde were the sweethearts on the Zuyder Zee. "Little Miss Wooden Shoes" and "Soldiers of the Netherlands" were hummed about London during the work's 462-performance run. *Dear Little Denmark* (1 September 1909) was a bit too similar, and *The Balkan Princess* (19 February 1910) was not much better, save for its sprightly Frederick Lonsdale book, imitating the intervening Stuart work, *The King of Cadonia,* a bit too closely as well. Isabel Jay did create a stir with what became known as the *"Balkan Princess* Toque," a blue chiffon headdress which she wore in Act II. Since *The Merry Widow,* it was not a bad idea to have a hat associated with a show. *The Sunshine Girl* (Gaiety, 24 February 1912), *Tonight's the Night* (Gaiety, 18 April 1915), *Betty* (Daly's, 24 April 1915), a Cinderella adaptation, and *Tina* (Adelphi, 2 November 1915) were the last batch of Rubens operettas; *After the Girl* (1914) was a "revuesical comedy." The violin song from *Tina,* sung by Phyllis Dare to a duke disguised as a violinist (Godfrey Tearle), continues to enchant. W. H. Berry was up to his old tricks as Van Dam, the Cocoa King, and the three acts took place in such fashionable purlieus as Venice, "Beauville-sur-Mer," and Paris. Most of Rubens's last works effortlessly achieved runs of about a year, as the public was easy to please during the war, and he continued to contribute to other productions. When Seymour Hicks took over Daly's for *The Happy Day,* the score was shared between Sidney Jones and Paul Rubens. After having achieved a considerable American success, dark-haired José Collins, illegitimate daughter of Lottie "Ta-Ra-Ra-Boom-De-Ay" Collins, burst forth on the London stage with Rubens's still-fetching "Oh, For a Night in Bohemia." It would be a foretaste of her next, legendary appearance at Daly's, as *The Maid of the Mountains* (1916) seven months later.

Ivan Caryll (1861–1921), born Félix Tilkins in Belgium, was one of the most prolific and popular composers of his day, yet few of his songs are even whistled today, and none of his complete operettas have been recently recorded or performed. He wrote so much that he might easily have been considered a hack, and his adherence to ragtime and other blatantly contemporary music has been criticized by those looking at Caryll as an operetta composer. Yet when Caryll took to writing a comic opera like *The Duchess of Dantzic* (1903) while his fellow composers were wallowing in the Gaiety mire, he was considered old-hat, despite the fact that Caryll was a leading purveyor of the most trivial Gaiety airs.

Caryll began his English career adapting French works for the London stage—the most unfortunate case being his 1899 hack-saw mutilation of Chabrier's *L'Étoile,* based on both the original French and the American editions, and produced at the Savoy by D'Oyly Carte. More respectable and popular was his earlier rendition of Audran's *La Cigale* (1890). The 1893 *Little Christopher Columbus* at the Gaiety was his first big, original success, and *The Shop Girl* the next year launched the new species of British musical comedy on its merry way (Gaiety, 24 November 1894). *The Toreador* (17 June 1901), written with Monckton, was the last show at the old Gaiety. Other than that distinction, it had only Gertie Millar singing "Keep Off the Grass," an ebullient Monckton melody. And so it went, the better-known numbers generally composed by Monckton, or Rubens, or even Talbot, leaving Caryll to fill up the rest of the time with his thoroughly professional, catchy, but not very special compositions. Caryll was, indeed, a house composer *par excellence*.

Outside the Gaiety, he composed one work, above all, that might bear reexamining: *The Duchess of Dantzic* (Lyric, 17 October 1903), a musical version of Sardou's popular *Madame Sans-Gêne* written with Sardou's permission. As one critic mentioned, "Somewhat paradoxically, Mr. George Edwardes has revived at the Lyric Theatre that type of entertainment which his 'musical comedies' helped so largely to suppress, and he has carried out his experiment with customary thoroughness and success." Yet several critics noted that it was almost a drama with music, and the correspondent for *The Illustrated Sporting and Dramatic News* went further: ". . . nothing, either in the acting or in the music . . . [makes] what is sung better than—if as interesting as—what was spoken . . ." A musical version of *Madame Sans-Gêne* had been announced years before for Florence St. John, but this did not materialize. Instead, Evie Greene played the laundress-turned-duchess, a part that had become the property of Réjane and Ellen Terry. Evie Greene was hoarse on opening night, allowing Holbrook Blinn as (a nonsinging) Napoleon to take the audience by storm. Courtice Pounds impressed as Papillon, a singing court milliner, as did Elizabeth Firth and Adrienne Augarde in other roles.

The librettist, Henry Hamilton, had his lyrics attacked, even if the story was strong. "Some were not agreeable or clever," claimed the London *Playgoer,* while the *Daily Graphic* likened them to the "Farnie school of rhymes." The *Daily Graphic* was more laudatory in its comments on Caryll's contribution: "The music often recalls the style of Sullivan, especially in his patter songs and his delightful dance music . . . in the more serious numbers, he is tender without being commonplace." Greatly admired were two duets, in Act I, "Do You Remember?" and in Act II, "Fountain, Fairy Water."

The spectacular Edwardes production, directed by Courtneidge, had sets by Joseph Harker and glamorous costumes and uniforms designed by Percy Anderson. The *Daily Telegraph* described the final act:

> . . . eclipsed by the spectacle of the gold and white throne room, in which the story reaches its end. Here crystal chandeliers and a canopy of purple velvet, studded with golden bees, crown such a display of toilettes as our stage has seldom, if ever, witnessed . . . Mme. Sans-Gêne wears a pale blue *crêpe de chine* Empire dress, with ropes of diamonds hanging down over the front, diamonds across the bodice and over the shoulders, and bordering in a single line the train of blue-shaded brocade.

It was not unusual at this time to devote an entire column of a first-night review to the dresses. Every musical production première was a fashion as well as a theatre event.

The Duchess of Dantzic was imported by Daniel Frohman and presented in New York (Daly's, 16 January 1905) with most of the original London cast. The New York *Dramatic Mirror,* commenting on Evie Greene, liked her "droll" brogue, "half Irish, half Lancashire, in the halls of the Tuileries." A West End revival in 1932 at Daly's paired Dorothy Ward with Frank Cellier. Although not a success, the operetta was admitted by the *Times* to have "a backbone to stand a revival." Whatever the faults of *The Duchess of Dantzic,* its rattling good story gave Caryll the interest and support he got from no other libretto.

The Girl from Kay's (Apollo, 15 November 1902), *The Earl and the Girl* (Adelphi, 10 December 1903), and *The Cherry Girl* (Adelphi, 21 December 1903) were all *hors*-Gaiety hits for Caryll, but they could not stand revival. (How many today remember that Jay's was a famous London store?) Ellaline Terriss may have done wonders in *The Cherry Girl,* but credit was not even given to Caryll when "Goodbye, Little Yellow Bird" was pinched from that musical comedy for the film version of *The Picture of Dorian Gray* (1945). Angela Lansbury sang it, as a cheap music-hall singer of the 1890s.

Eventually exasperated by Lionel Monckton's popularity, Caryll left London for New York, where *The Pink Lady* was the greatest success of his transplanted career. It began its 316-performance run at the New Amsterdam on 13 March 1911. Based on a French play, *Le Satyre,* by Berr and Guillemand, the complicated libretto by G. McLellan revolved around a mysterious man who assaulted ladies with hugs and kisses in the Forest of Compiègne. The lovely Hazel Dawn entranced New Yorkers (and, later, Londoners) as Claudine, the Pink Lady. The best-remembered songs in this frolicsome score were the waltz "My Beautiful Lady," "By the Sasketchewan," and "Donny Didn't, Donny Did," referring to the antique dealer accused of being the satyr. The last act, at the Ball of Nymphs and Satyrs, not only untangled the plot but also had some lively dancing as well. However, *The Pink Lady* did not succeed in London (Globe, 11 April 1912), or in Paris as *La Dame en Rose* (Bouffes-Parisiens, 30 April 1921).

The next Caryll-McLellan hit in New York was *Oh! Oh! Delphine* (Knickerbocker, 30 September 1912), also based on a French farce. This ran less than a year in both New York and London. *The Little Café* (New Amsterdam, 10 November 1913), again with Hazel Dawn, and again based on a French farce (Tristan Bernard's play of the same name), was a bit too similar to *The Pink Lady* to run more than 148 times, and there was no British edition.

The modern revue, ragtime and jazz would seem to have killed off operetta altogether; one notes the shift simply by looking at the list of the productions in 1911 and 1912. The last production of 1911 was the Lyric's revival of *Die Fledermaus* under the title *Nightbirds.* This was not a great hit, whereas *Hullo, Ragtime!,* the last musical show of 1912, was a riotous affair at the Hippodrome.

Even before World War I, revues claimed the attention of the brightest stars and audiences, and even Lionel Monckton found himself composing revue numbers for Gertie Millar, like "Chalk Farm to Camberwell Green." There was little, really, to differentiate revue numbers from musical-comedy songs except that now there was absolutely no need for any plot motivation. The public's fancy for the latest American dance sensation or the big American stars like Ethel Levey was what drew them to the Alhambra, or the Hippodrome, or the London Pavilion. With a few exceptions, such as the success of Victor Jacobi's *The Marriage Market* at Daly's in 1913, continental operettas went out of vogue, and with them the Gaiety type of British musical comedy, which, when produced at all, had to have American dance rhythms to compete with the zippier shows elsewhere.

During World War I, however, tastes were slightly modified. Civvies and soldiers on leave still wanted boisterous music hall and glamorous revue. It was during this period that André Charlot, Charles Cochran, and Albert de Courville raised the revue to new levels of English sophistication, drawing on talented composers and lyricists like Ivor Novello and Arthur Wimperis. And there were great audience-pleasers like *The Bing Boys are Here* (1916), which was simply a vehicle for the music-hall antics of George Robey, Violet Lorraine, and Alfred Lester. But the two musical triumphs of 1914–18 London were two full-fledged romantic operettas: *Chu Chin Chow* (His Majesty's, 31 August 1916) and *The Maid of the Mountains* (Daly's, 10 February 1917), both of which ran for years.

Chu Chin Chow, a "Musical Tale of the East," had a book by Oscar Asche with music by **Frederic Norton** (1875–1940). Norton was the musical director at His Majesty's, and had composed the score for a children's play there in 1908. Oscar Asche had directed and appeared at the Garrick in Edward Knoblock's *Kismet* in 1911, an elaborate Near-Eastern spectacular (later operetta-ized by Robert Wright and George Forrest in America). The Australian Asche, who had appeared in Shakespeare with Tree and Benson, was admired for his portrayal of the poet Hajj. Lily Brayton (Mrs. Asche) played his daughter Marsinah. For rainy Britain it was sunny and colorful claptrap, and some of the ladies' costumes were quite abbreviated. It proved popular, and Asche apparently wanted some kind of follow-up. On tour in Manchester in Shakespeare during the particularly wet 1916 season, Asche and Brayton dreamed up a new pantomime based on *Ali Baba and the Forty Thieves*. After being rejected by several managements, *Chu Chin Chow* wound up at His Majesty's Theatre (31 August 1916) under the aegis of Asche and Brayton themselves.

Chu Chin Chow was nothing more than a cross between a popular pantomime story and an operetta, with the emphasis on the spectacle rather than on the

---

The Maid of the Mountains (Daly's, 1917) was a long-run triumph of World War I London, an escapist farrago that had to be seen (along with *Chu Chin Chow*) by every soldier on leave and those at home as well. José Collins's raven locks and ravishing looks were features of the Fraser-Simson/Tate operetta, which also starred Arthur Wontner.

singing. It cost £5300 to mount. Herbert Beerbohm Tree, who managed His Majesty's, would have approved of the lavish production. In fact, he was in America at the time of the première, and he refused to see *Chu Chin Chow* until late in the run, even though he was earning quite a bit from it. When he did, he called the girls' costumes "more navel than millinery." If he could persuade himself to visit his theatre only once, others could not stay away. It was *de rigueur* for every sailor or tommy on leave to see *Chu Chin Chow* before going overseas. And with their families, which gave the operetta an unprecedented 2,238-performance run, the longest the British stage ever had until *The Mousetrap* exceeded it in 1958.

Frederic Norton's score was hardly distinguished, some of it nothing more than sung neo-Arabesque incidental music, in the style of the then-popular Ketelby, but most of it merely sentimental, un-"Eastern" British parlor balladry. The great hits were "The Robbers' Chorus" and "Anytime's Kissing Time," the latter made touching, originally, by the aging Courtice Pounds singing this unconventional tribute to unyouthful love. As much of Asche's script was strewn with *faux*-Arabian locution, aphorisms, and foodstuffs, the lyrics followed suit, from "Here be oysters stewed in honey" to "When a pullet is plump she is tender," to the even more celebrated "I sit and cobble at slippers and shoon." Though *Chu Chin Chow* had no central finale, and few ensemble numbers—the sprightly "Mahbubah" was an exception—the languorous solos served as a relief from the overwhelming sets of Joseph Harker and glittering costumes of Percy Anderson. Abu Hasan, disguised as the rich Shanghai merchant, Chu Chin Chow, was played by Asche, Lily Brayton again supported him, but this time Violet Essex played the daughter, Marjanah, a close cousin to *Kismet's* Marsinah. *Chu Chin Chow* was supremely silly, hokey escapism, but it was preeminently the right show at the right time.

A German precedent was *Sumurûn,* Reinhardt's notable oriental pantomime, seen in London in 1912. Paris, probably remembering the failure of *Kismet* with Lucien Guitry, never saw *Chu Chin Chow.* The New York version (Manhattan Opera House, 22 October 1917) had a fine cast: Tyrone Power (Senior) in Asche's part, Henry Dixey in Pounds's, with Tessa Kosta and Florence Reed. But, curiously, "the romance, the splendour, the inscrutable mystery of the East," as Asche referred to his play in the lavish American souvenir programme, did not run even a tenth as long in New York as it did in London. The London engagement, when it finally closed, had grossed over £3,000,000. Trying to repeat the success of *Chu Chin Chow,* Asche produced *Cairo,* "a mosaic in music and mime," at His Majesty's. Percy Fletcher composed the music, as Norton had become terrified of income tax. It ran 267 times. When Asche died in 1936, he left £20 in his estate.

The Maid of the Mountains opened a half year after *Chu Chin Chow* at Daly's (10 February 1917). Robert Evett, the turn-of-the-century operetta-tenor-turned-manager who had succeeded the late George Edwardes at Daly's, had been unable to mount any great successes since Edwardes's last production, Jacobi's *The Marriage Market,* which ran more than a year. *The Maid of the Mountains* was seen as the last chance to restore the fortunes of Daly's and the Edwardes name. According to the original Maid herself, José Collins, Frederick Lonsdale sent Evett the script of *Teresa,* a story he had outlined as far back as 1905, in 1917. A decade earlier, Lonsdale and Howard Talbot had some discussion of working together on it, and the manager Frank Curzon expressed some interest in it. But nothing happened. In 1911, Robert Courtneidge followed suit, and again no action. Finally Evett took the plunge and invited Oscar Asche, who had just opened in *Chu Chin Chow,* to direct the operetta. Asche read the script, suggested a number of "drastic alterations," and wanted the title changed to *The Mountain Maid.*

Harold Fraser-Simson (1873–1944), who had written the now-forgotten *Bonita* in 1911, was invited to do the music, and Harry Graham supplied the lyrics. José Collins, who had been brought over from vaudeville stardom in the States only to be given the second female part in *The Happy Day* at a tenth of her American salary, was given the role of Teresa. Opposite her were Thorpe Bates and Arthur Wontner, with Mark Lester and Lauri de Frece as the two comedians. A very cordial Manchester tryout, with one critic prophesying a year's run in the West End, was followed by a fabulous London première (10 February 1917). The *Times* was happy with the score: "Mr. Fraser-Simson's contribution of the evening is no small one. All his music is light and dainty, some of it quite admirable, notably 'Love will find a way' and 'Live for today'; while one of Mr. James W. Tate's interpolated numbers, 'A Bachelor gay,' compelled the producer to break through his stern rule of refusing encores." *The Maid* ran and ran, second only to *Chu Chin Chow* in popularity, for 1,352 performances, and during that time the £80,000 debt of the George Edwardes estate was paid off. Zeppelin raids and blackouts did not keep people from either His Majesty's or Daly's during those difficult times. *The Maid* made a profit of £300,000.

There were several revivals of both *Chu Chin Chow* and *The Maid of the Mountains* in London, most recently a disastrous one of *The Maid* at the Palace in 1968 (which dared to interpolate Rudolf Friml's "Song of the Vagabonds" from *The Vagabond King*). Better business was done in the provinces with this kind of revival. During the Second World War, there was an all-male performance of *The Maid* given by Britons in Palestine. The Australian production, starring Gladys Moncrieff, was a rip-roaring success, but not the American, where Sidonie Espero starred (Casino, 11 September 1918) for only thirty-seven performances. The War nearly over, brigands and Carmenesque leading ladies a-swim in an Edwardian score were hardly the sort of things to interest the Yanks, but this Mediterranean or Balkan sultriness was no doubt attractive to bleak London. Certainly, José Collins—at least in her recordings—possessed a lovely voice, which, when coupled with her dark good looks, must have seemed impressive. Especially when singing "Love Will Find a Way," the waltz song that brazenly took the first part of the refrain of *The Merry Widow* waltz and repeated each note twice. Fraser-Simson wrote several other works in the 1920s, but none was as successful as *The Maid of the Mountains,* which was the perfect example of the Edwardes musical comedy made more romantic and more escapist for wartime audiences, for which credit should be given to Lonsdale and Asche.

The Edwardesian era persisted after Edwardes's death in 1915, a demise hastened by his detention by the Germans—he had had the bad luck to have been at a German spa when war was declared. The Gaiety type of musical comedy would not entirely die, thanks to British composers and lyricists who seemed more partial to the old form than to the newer, brassier, and more tuneful American musicals that hit London in the mid-1920s. The Daly's tradition, fundamentally a European-modeled one, would continue right through the '20s, until Ivor Novello, in the '30s and '40s, managed to lure large audiences to neo-Ruritania with *Glamorous Night* and *King's Rhapsody.* These were direct descendants of the more romantic British operettas of the early years of the century, cleverly streamlined and spectacularized for modern tastes. Drury Lane, from the great success in 1925 of *Rose-Marie,* became the principal operetta theatre, leaving Daly's and the Gaiety to eventual demolition.

FIN DE SIÈCLE

T HE TURN of the century was a paradoxical period for operetta in Paris. Certain theatres disappeared, while others noted for their operettas switched over to non-operetta presentations. The *opéra-bouffe* became an endangered species, while the phenomenon of the *vaudeville-opérette* had escalated, ensuring snappy little comic *couplets,* marches, ballads, and little else. Musical comedy had begun in England, and its somewhat cheapening effects were felt in France, Germany, and Austria, though, to be fair, these countries had always had their farces with songs. By 1901 the number of operettas opening in Paris had dropped drastically, and their level of quality had likewise fallen.

On the other hand, business was not altogether bad. Dance-music variations of the latest operettas proved potent advertising for the new works, and sales of piano arrangements for drawing-room consumption were tremendous. So were postcard sales of the lovely actresses who appeared in operetta. Concurrent with the tremendous growth of music-hall audiences to see what had now become variety or vaudeville, in normal theatres without tables, the operetta saw a similar increase in attendance, with a similar democratization. The upper galleries and pits were more heavily trafficked, and these tastes were generally broader than those of the stalls and circle.

There were a few exceptional operettas by composers who held on to fairly high standards, resisting as much as possible *vaudeville* encroachings. André Messager, probably the most graceful operetta composer of any era, reached his summit in the 1890s and continued right up to the end of the 1920s with his charming compositions. With few exceptions, however, the works of Messager's Parisian contemporaries have been found to be unrevivable, save for sporadic broadcasts on French radio.

A particularly lovely British poster for a particularly lovely French work, Messager's *Les p'tites Michu* (1897), showing the twins Blanche-Marie and Marie-Blanche.

Parisian revues were also very much in demand, and operetta composers found opportunities to contribute songs to them. In Berlin, the revue format was also admired, right up to the Nazi era. As in Paris, several operetta composers, librettists, and stars became famous for their revue work. The days of *opéra-bouffe* and comic opera were over . . . until the Viennese revitalized operetta in 1905.

In **André Messager** (1853–1929) French operetta received its last true titan, a composer forgotten outside France who had his first operettas produced in the early 1880s and his last in the late 1920s, a writing career of nearly half a century which saw complete stylistic changes in operetta, French and otherwise. However, Messager did not necessarily follow these shifts. He brought his operettas closer to *opéra-comique* when many were veering toward music hall at the turn of the century, and he wrote modern "musical comedies" in the 1920s when some of his able contemporaries were harking back to the past with pastiche and even evocations of Messager himself. (Reynaldo Hahn's 1923 *Ciboulette* is a perfect example.) Besides writing three or four outstanding operettas, Messager is remembered today for his conductorial and managerial achievements and his championing of much modern music, particularly for his conducting of the Paris première of Claude Debussy's *Pelléas et Mélisande* in 1902, at the Opéra-Comique.

Messager was born in the central French town of Montluçon in 1853, and his musical inclinations were toward the organ. He studied at the École Niedermeyer, under such masters as Camille Saint-Saëns and Gabriel Fauré (who were to be his lifelong friends). He played the organ in various churches, including Saint-Sulpice, and in 1878 had a symphony performed by the Concerts Colonne. At the same time, he was writing prize-winning cantatas as well as providing little *divertissements,* ballets for the Folies-Bergère with titles such as *Fleur d'Oranger* and *Les Vins de France.* In 1883 he "completed" an operetta started by Firmin Bernicat, *François les Bas-Bleus* (François Bluestockings, Folies-Dramatiques, 8 November 1883), which ran 130 times consecutively. Messager wrote some fifteen of the twenty-five numbers and did the complete orchestration. Bernicat was soon forgotten as Messager began his rise to fame. The year 1885 saw two new operettas. One was *La Fauvette du Temple* (Bouffes-Parisiens, 17 November), a militaristic, patriotic affair with Algerian scenes starring Simon-Max in a strong tenor part and Simon-Girard as the title warbler. Barely a month later, it was outstripped in popularity by *La Béarnaise* (Bouffes-Parisiens, 12 December). This had a libretto by Eugène Leterrier and Albert Vanloo concerning an amorous entanglement of Henri IV, the *roi-galant,* with Jacquet and Jacquette, both sexes portrayed by the ebullient Jeanne Granier. The charming soubrette Mily-Meyer came along for good measure. It had a fetching score with a strong second act that included an ingratiating madrigal, forecasting similarly graceful throwbacks to older musical forms; this would become a Messager trademark. Contemporary critics looked very favorably on the orchestration, which revealed a suppleness and charm entirely lacking in the more obvious and even booming style of the day, and missing in the played-out later compositions of Planquette and Lecocq then being performed. *La Béarnaise* enjoyed a fair run and was seen in London (1886), with Marie Tempest, and in New York (1887, as *Jacquette*).

In 1886, on the recommendation of Saint-Saëns, Messager wrote a ballet for the Opéra, the still-performed *Les Deux Pigeons,* showing orchestral finesse and melodic grace without any vocal supports. Otherwise, the late 1880s saw little success: an *opéra-comique, Le Bourgeois de Calais* (1888), with a boring historical plot, bad lyrics, and a banal score, the musical fairy tale *Isoline* (1888, libretto by Catulle Mendès), and a three-act operetta, *Le Mari de la Reine* (The Queen's Husband, Bouffes-Parisiens, 18 December 1889), which the composer claimed was "the best of my flops." Written merely to be a crowd-pleaser for the Paris Exposition of 1889, the plot concerned the Queen of Kokistan, who had to have a new husband each year.

The 1880s had also seen some song cycles, "sung waltzes," and even a quadrille-fantasy on "favorite themes from Wagner's *Ring"* for four hands, which Messager wrote with Fauré, called *Souvenirs de Bayreuth.* However, the next decade was Messager's finest, and it started resoundingly with the success of *La Basoche* (Opéra-Comique, 30 May 1890). A student is crowned "king of the *Basoche,"* an ancient law guild, and is mistaken for the actual King Louis XII by Princess Mary of England in Albert Carré's somewhat fanciful libretto, woven around the actual poet Clément Marot. The music was warmly praised for restoring good humor and gaiety to the Opéra-Comique, although the score was appreciably heavier than future Messager operettas. It had effective pastiches, lissome orchestration, and fine ensembles in the finales, and it had the added attraction of Lucien Fugère, the old *café-concert* star, who was encored nightly for his singing of *"Elle m'aime! O coeur feminin, curieux problème!"* La Basoche appeared more than two hundred times at the Opéra-Comique.

The London version was the second and last attraction at Richard D'Oyly Carte's Royal English Opera, following the quite successful and unprecedented continuous long-run of Sullivan's grand opera *Ivanhoe* (155 performances). *La Basoche* opened on 3 November 1891 to great acclaim. The *Times* protested that "to enumerate the admirable numbers . . . in the score would be to give a complete catalogue, for there is not a vulgar bar from beginning to end, nor a single section that could be spared." And the *Pall Mall Gazette* liked the "strong story and extremely clever music." But there was little business. *La Basoche* was withdrawn in less than three months and Carte sadly had to sell his ambitious showplace for British opera (which *La Basoche* hardly was) to music-hall interests. The Shaftesbury Avenue edifice still stands in its original state as one of the West End's leading musical theatres, the Palace. *La Basoche* was seen in New York at the Casino in another translation in 1893 and was broadcast by the BBC in the late 1920s.

Madame Chrysanthème, a four-act "lyric comedy" (Théâtre Lyrique, 26 January 1893), was based on the 1887 novel by Pierre Loti which may have furnished at least the germinal idea of both Jones's *The Geisha* and Puccini's *Madama Butterfly*. It had continuous music and is not an operetta; by the time of its New York première in 1920, with the Japanese Tamaki Miura in the title role, the intense popularity of the Puccini favorite made unflattering comparisons with the Messager work inevitable. *Miss Dollar* (Nouveau-Théâtre, 22 December 1893), an operetta about an American heiress long before Leo Fall's *Die Dollarprinzessin,* was more decidedly a hit.

Richard D'Oyly Carte had by no means lost faith in Messager after *La Basoche,* for on 3 July 1894 he presented the Savoy Theatre's first work by a foreign composer, Messager's *Mirette,* with an English book adapted from an apparently unproduced French original by Michel Carré. Messager came to London to prepare and conduct the première. *Mirette* was taken off after a few weeks and put back in October, with lyrics revised by Adrian Ross, but it failed to duplicate even the limited success of the Gilbert and Sullivan work which preceded it—*Utopia, Limited.* The English *Mirette* was by Harry Greenbank and Fred E. Weatherley, with an assist from Hope Temple (who became the composer's second wife), and was a variant of Alfred Bunn's *Bohemian Girl* plot. A band of gypsies finds a baby girl with her dying beggar-mother and raises her as one of their own. But the girl always has the suspicion she is of royal extraction. She has a romantic fling with a marquis's nephew, but in the end returns to her peasant lover. In the final scene, Francal, the gypsy chief, reveals all to Mirette:

FRANCAL: The old parish clerk knows who your mother was, Mirette. She was
                    dressed like a beggar, you know.
MIRETTE: Yes, yes—what was she?
FRANCAL: Well, she *was* a beggar.

In 1896, *La Fiancée en Loterie,* an operetta with Spanish overtones, and *Le Chevalier d'Harmental,* an almost Wagnerian *opéra-comique* adapted from an Alexandre Dumas *père* novel, both failed, and Messager thought he was worked out and washed up. He even considered retirement in England. But he plugged away: a ballet, a pantomime, some songs, and, finally, a sensational hit, *Les p'tites Michu* (Bouffes-Parisiens, 16 November 1897). In the original cast were Alice Bonheur as Marie-Blanche, Odette Dulac as her sister, Blanche-Marie, and Barral as the comic general.

The libretto (Vanloo and Duval) was hardly original; in fact, when *The Little Michus* opened in London one critic called the plot "a feminine version of *The Gondoliers.*" (There was even a game of blindman's buff to make the resemblance more startling.) Two baby girls, one a general's daughter and the other a shopkeeper's, are mixed up in their bath. Years later, and after two and a half complex hours in the theatre, they wind up with the young men they love. With a third act in the by-now-standard operetta locale of Les Halles, the escapades of Marie-Blanche and Blanche-Marie were embellished by a sunny, pulsating, melody-drenched score that earned Messager the operetta mantle worn first by Offenbach and then (primarily) by Lecocq. It was a *partition* that was lilting and elegant, exciting without being at all coarse or overwritten; *"musique de gentilhomme,"* as so many have commented.

Les p'tites Michu is one of those unusual works that begins well enough and gets better and better, with several of the better gems in the third act. Surely outstanding is the Halles ensemble, with its chorus of *marchands* and *marchandes* entering the market bearing flowers, accompanied by one of music's most florid arrangements (in a complimentary sense).

The first act is dominated by the clever, lilting duet of the two Michu: *"Blanche-Marie et Marie-Blanche,"* in which we first see Messager's distinctively personal style. Tripping, gay, never heavy, and perfectly written for the voice. It pulsates with an elegance and grace that other operetta composers have failed to obtain even when using the same rhythmic formula. This Messagerian flow and lyricism over a preponderance of eighth and sixteenth notes is virtually unique. The more *opéra-comique* elements are readily apparent in the trio beginning: *"Michu! Michu! Michu!"* Messager and librettists frequently have each voice begin with a little word or phrase right at the start of an ensemble; the quartet in Act III of *Véronique* begins with four characters singing separately, *"Oh!/Ah!/ Ciel!/Ai-je bien vu?"* Rarely are his ensembles slow or plaintive; many of them are quite rapid. Messager's finales are outstanding, and the second-act finale to *Michu* begins with a brilliant, swelling orchestral introduction, leading to a martial bit, and then to the captivating *"L'une est des Ifs, l'autre est Michu: à vous de deviner laquelle"* (One of the daughters is a des Ifs, the other is a Michu: it's up to you to tell which is which). In Messager's brisk finales, one ingratiating melody quickly follows another, connected by the composer's catchy *enchaînements.* The second act of *Michu* ends with Marie-Blanche's *couplets,* and the chorus merely repeats the refrain. But it is his gracious, well-mannered, craftsman-like approach which makes Messager's style so inimitable. He is thus able to take a sentimental waltz so typical of the turn of the century—which in other hands would be a run-of-the-mill *café-concert* number—and transform it into something much more symphonic. Blanche-Marie's romance in Act III, *"Vois-tu, je m'en veux à moi-même,"* with its refrain *"Ah! soeurette, ma soeurette,"* is a good case in point, a wistful waltz ennobled by the strings singing along with the character.

The London production (Daly's, 29 April 1905), produced by George Edwardes only after the British *Véronique* triumph, was called by the *Telegraph* "a dainty little play, all lilac and prettiness, almost as charming as *Véronique."* Messager himself conducted. "Had not Mr. Messager been severity itself, there might have been a dozen encores," one reporter noted. A New York production followed in 1907, a revival in Paris (in repertory) in 1909, but not much else, save for a charming excerpts-recording which only partly reveals *les délices* of this delicious score.

One reason for this neglect was the even greater success of *Véronique* (Bouffes-

Parisiens, 10 December 1898), which had Messager in better form—certainly as far as hit songs are concerned. This also had a book by Vanloo and Duval which had a slightly less hackneyed and less unbelievable love story but still with the hoary old (flower) market setting for part of the time. If the 1810 setting of *Michu* had appealed to Parisians, the 1840 *Véronique* dresses were even more romantic—perhaps some of the older people in the audience remembered the period. Jean Périer (soon to be the first Pelléas under Messager's direction) was handsome Florestan, and Mariette Sully was the first Hélène de Solanges (Véronique). Two of their duets, popularly known as the "Donkey" and "Swing" songs, assured the international success of the operetta. But there was much more. After an intoxicating overture, *Véronique*, like *Michu*, takes little time to warm up; the opening chorus is diverting and Agathe's air on being a florist is charming, but the entrance of Hélène (Véronique) is Messager at his orchestrally radiant best, using the woodwinds and strings to magical effect. Florestan's entrance song is a holdover from Lecocq or Planquette, but, as such, manly and lilting. The quartet *"Charmant, charmant"* is fairly ambitious for an operetta, and when well sung is one of the reasons why the authors and composer called *Véronique* an *opéra-comique*. The Act I finale is dominated by the gaily rapid and vaguely Offenbachish *"Partons pour Romainville."* Romainville, circa 1840, evidently called forth from Messager (and his librettists) a fair amount of pastiche, including a few rondeaux. The finale for the second act is distinguished by the so-called "Letter Song," a quaint item for Florestan, and the final number for Agathe, plus chorus, heard so delightfully in the overture.

The two big hits, the Donkey and Swing duets, are justifiably celebrated and are much more fluid, youthful, and well-turned-out than the typical, undistinctive love duets of late Victorian or early Edwardian operetta. For sheer high spirits and lyric horseplay (or, should we say, donkey-play), *"De ci, de là, cahincaha"* is the most delightful animal operetta-song since the *"dindons / moutons"* duet in Audran's *Mascotte*. The swing song is a sort of musical evocation of a Fragonard picture: elegant, flowery, romantic, French; in short, the characteristics of Messager's art. Act III has the aforementioned quartet and a charming comic duet for Agathe and Coquenard with a short refrain that again showed the wistful Messager at his most endearing.

The Edwardes London production (Apollo, 18 May 1904) with Lawrence Rea and Ruth Vincent as the lovers and Messager conducting, was attended by the Prince and Princess of Wales and highlighted by Miss Vincent's "dear little" donkey—no doubt suffering first-night jitters—who kept threatening to throw off his rider. After a run of nearly five hundred performances, the British production transferred to New York (Broadway, 30 October 1905), where it did less well. The Theater an der Wien saw it in 1900, as did Berlin, as *Brigitte*, then as now perhaps a sexier name than *Véronique*, but losing the floral connotation

Jean Périer as Florestan and Mariette Sully as Véronique in the first production of Messager's *Véronique* (Bouffes-Parisiens, 1898). Their singing of the Donkey Song, depicted here, made it the operetta's hit tune.

needed in the operetta. The work has been revived several times throughout France; during the German Occupation it was revived at the Mogador (1942) in a production *à grand spectacle* which overpowered its fragility. There was a limited-engagement revival at the Opéra-Comique in 1978–79, revived in 1980–81.

In 1898, Messager assumed the musical direction of the Opéra-Comique (Albert Carré, his *Basoche* librettist, was at the administrative helm) and conducted several new works *(Pelléas et Mélisande)* as well as some notable revivals (Gluck's *Orphée,* Beethoven's *Fidelio,* Mozart's *Così Fan Tutte*), which he preferred to some of the dreary new pieces, like Massenet's *Griséldis.* In 1901, Messager was appointed artistic director of Covent Garden, and arranged the seasons there for seven years.

Messager did not cease composing. *Les Dragons de l'Impératrice* (The Empress's Dragoons, Variétés, 13 February 1905) was again laid in the good old days, this time the heady era of the Second Empire, still a happy memory for much of the audience. The Emperor's élite guard and the Empress's dragoons are rival factions, and in the first act, at St. Cloud, a colonel's wife loses her fan. This sets off complications which take us to the celebrated Bal Mabille in the second act and a salon in the Tuileries in the third (as in *Véronique*). The book, again by Duval and Vanloo, was bright, even though the plot was hardly exciting in itself. But the libretto did furnish Messager with his well-loved opportunity to conjure up another era. Although some considered it Messager's finest score, it appeared only forty times and subsequently dropped into almost total obscurity.

Fortunio (Opéra-Comique, 5 June 1907), a five-act lyric comedy, was based on the Alfred de Musset play *Le Chandelier,* for which Offenbach had written incidental music and his famous *chanson,* later to be used in his one-act operetta, *La Chanson de Fortunio.* This was heavier stuff than usual, as was *Béatrice,* a lyric legend, not presented in Paris until 1917; this was through-composed as well. From 1907 to 1919, Messager was one of the directors of the Paris Opéra, and, aside from *Béatrice* and a little one-act vehicle for the comedian Prince, he composed no stage works until his second British operetta, *Monsieur Beaucaire* (Princes, 19 April 1919). Based on the Booth Tarkington novel, presented by Gilbert Miller and starring the young Maggie Teyte and the American baritone Marion Green, this brought Messager even further back in time, to the eighteenth-century Bath of Beau Nash. The original straight play had been a great success in 1902 in London for Lewis Waller and the story was a conveniently romantic vehicle for Messager's most florid and picturesque score. While it does not reproduce the eighteenth century, it gives a Messagerian view of it, using a turn-of-the-century instrumentation rather than a Mozartian one. The story, used later for American films with Rudolph Valentino, Jack Buchanan, and Bob Hope, was adapted by Frederick Lonsdale, the aspiring playwright who had provided the book to the big wartime hit operetta, *The Maid of the Mountains.* The lyrics were by the veteran Adrian Ross, the perfect man for this throwback to the past. *Monsieur Beaucaire* is the kind of operetta Edward German reveled in *(Merrie England, Tom Jones)* in the first decade of the century—"a romantic opera," as Lonsdale and Messager called it.

"[Messager] does the most delicious things with a single flute, or a pair of clarinets backed by a light pizzicato on the strings, or a simple arpeggio on the harp," noted the London *Times,* which also remarked that the composer had "added the finishing touch of his graceful melodies. It is delightful to stop the play for them . . ." Indeed, one would gladly dispense altogether with the play today, if it will ensure a concert version of this toothsome, bittersweet score.

Adrian Ross might very well have changed his name in 1918 to Rose, as the word pops up a bit too often. The hit "Red Rose" song does not look back to the 1700s; it stops short at 1902 and Edward German's popular "English Rose" from *Merrie England.* Lady Mary's "Philomel" *("Rossignol"* in the French edition) was a glorious tour-de-force for Maggie Teyte. It is hard to fault anything in this soaring number from the pastoral scene in Act II (very much "an existence à la Watteau," as Gilbert's Counsel sings in *Trial by Jury*). The lighter "comic" numbers between Lucy and Molyneux trip brightly along, even if Lucy's "That's a Woman's Way" called for a more humorous setting. However, the "Lightly, Lightly" duet between Beaucaire and Mary harked back winningly to the *Véronique* Messager. Some might accuse *Monsieur Beaucaire* of being saccharine; I would call it genuinely sweet.

Monsieur Beaucaire achieved approximately two thirds of its London run in New York (New Amsterdam, 11 December 1919), a not unrespectable amount of time for an "opera." It was produced in Paris (Marigny, 20 November 1925) in a French adaptation by André Rivoire and Pierre Veber. It had an appealing Lady Mary in Marcelle Denya, and André Baugé sang of the *rose rouge*. In 1954, the Opéra-Comique admitted *Monsieur Beaucaire* to its repertoire, with Jacques Jansen and Denise Duval, but it enjoys today only infrequent revivals. A shame, for it is truly a luscious, rich score, beautiful and, as always, supremely elegant.

Busy with his conducting and administrative duties, Messager had less and less time for operetta, especially as World War I had opened the floodgates for American dances, ragtime, jazz. In 1923, he became president of the French Society of Authors and Composers. He succeeded Fauré as music critic of *Le Figaro*. In 1921 (Mogador, 14 May) he composed an unsuccessful *"comédie musicale," La petite Fonctionnaire,* which had a short run in spite of Edmée Favart's rendering of the lovely *"Je regrette mon Pressigny"* (I miss my Pressigny—a little Loire Valley town where the character grew up). Messager's next attempt in this genre was the delightful *L'Amour masqué* (Masked Love, Édouard VII, 13 February 1923), which had the advantage of a Sacha Guitry libretto and the presence in the cast of the author and his charming wife (second of five), Yvonne Printemps. This was a substantial hit.

Yvonne Printemps (born Wigniolle in 1894) began her career in music hall around 1910; she was noticed by Sacha Guitry in a 1915 revue at the Palais-Royal. She appeared to great acclaim with Guitry from 1917 in his plays, marrying him two years later. Her charm, good looks, the apparently very natural quality of her acting, and the fabled richness of her singing voice earned her fans all over the world. Other French singers, like Edmée Favart and Fanély Revoil, triumphed in both new operettas and revivals of past glories, but they did not achieve the celebrity Printemps had, probably because Yvonne also made films and appeared in many non-musical boulevard hits. Although she recorded some classical operetta songs, Printemps never gave the public the opportunity of seeing her in a revival. Nevertheless, for her creation of leading roles in *L'Amour masqué, Mariette, Conversation Piece,* and *Les Trois Valses,* and for her unique voice, she has joined the immortals in the operetta pantheon, a true descendant of Hortense Schneider.

The seventy-year-old Messager had acceded to the taste for fox-trots and tangos without going overboard. The music has a youthful, fresh quality (perhaps due also to Guitry's witty, sunny lyrics—quite unlike the usual drivel then set

by musical-comedy composers) but retains the old qualities for which Messager was famous, the very qualities which no doubt Guitry sought by asking Messager to compose his new play: elegance, grace, economy of orchestration, and that very personal charm which, it turned out, Mlle. Printemps responded to so memorably. In fact, Messager was not Guitry's first choice; Ivan Caryll was the favorite, but he died before getting around to *L'Amour masqué.*

To cope with the small orchestra for *L'Amour masqué,* which would have to fit into the pit of the Théâtre Édouard VII, Messager studied the instrumentations of the small orchestras playing for silent films. The clever results are invariably charming, and if one misses the dextrous, humming strings of the older works, in truth these would be uncalled for in this "modern" work. Guitry's plot is typically thin, the success of the piece depending on the elegant lines and lyrics and, ultimately, the author and his star present to say them. Guitry did not sing but preferred to speak his lines against the wistful accompaniment, alternating with his singing spouse. (Noël Coward was to do precisely the same thing with Printemps in his *Conversation Piece,* 1934.) Fortunately, their duets were recorded, giving us not only a record of the duo's considerable charm, but also a fairly accurate representation of Messager's orchestration for a small band. After receiving a copy of the score, the ailing composer Gabriel Fauré sent his colleague a letter:

> I'm still forbidden to go to the theatre, alas; I thus can't go to applaud you or divert myself with a play everyone says is very funny and admirably acted. But someone brought me your score. It's always your spirit—that spirit that never grows old— and your charm and your very personal music which always remains exquisite mu-

sic, even in the liveliest buffoonery. That which I am prevented [from hearing] is the amusement of the orchestra, and I can imagine what you must have gotten out of that. I'm content, my good André, and I embrace you with all my heart. Your old friend, Gabriel Fauré.[1]

Guitry was delighted to have obtained Messager's music. He dedicated the script to him, further adding, "This comedy in verse is accompanied on stage by the incomparable and moreover necessary music of André Messager."

The critical reception was virtually unanimous—a triumph, not only for the play but also for Printemps. Pierre Veber stated in *Le Petit Journal:* "Madame Yvonne Printemps is one of our greatest operetta stars, and if I don't say the *only* one, it is because I don't want to depress her comrades." Supporting Sacha and Yvonne in the cast was an extremely proficient bunch of *spécialistes,* including Urban (the original Phi-Phi) as the Baron, and the future stars Marie Dubas, as the second servant, and Henri Garat, as one of the four gentlemen.

With one exception, the songs in *L'Amour masqué* were so ingrained in the plot, and so connected to the dialogue couplets, that they have not lived outside the operetta. That exception is the saucy *"J'ai deux amants"* (I have two lovers), which explains the heroine's joy on her twentieth birthday in keeping two wealthy old boyfriends—she plays one against the other and gets richer and richer. The refrain, echoing sentiments heard in *La Périchole,* runs: "I don't know how we are, but, my God, how dumb a man can be! Well, think of it—two!" Printemps had several other delightful numbers, including *"Vingt ans!"* leading into *"Je m'étais jurée"* (I swore to myself), and the second-act *"Depuis l'histoire de la pomme"* (Since the story of the apple), sung with her two servants. *She* never has a name in the play, being referred to only as *"Elle."*

Quite a bit of amusement and musical charm is derived by having one of her lovers a Burmese nobleman, the Maharajah of Hounk. Accompanied by an interpreter, the Maharajah spouts Guitry's mellifluous "Burmese," and the scene in the middle of Act I, with its *"Ram Padagui, Youm Po, Doborada!"* reminds one of the Turkish ceremony in Molière's *Le Bourgeois Gentilhomme* some 250 years earlier. The *"chant birman"* in Act II, performed "untranslated," is, thanks to Messager, rather beautiful, in spite of lines like *"Lalla vabim ostogénine."*

But, for many, the most entrancing scene of all occurs in the middle of Act II, the duet between *Elle* and *Lui* beginning, *"Viens, s'il est vrai que tu m'attends"* (Come, if it's true you are waiting for me). Sacha's ardent recitations against the music are counterpointed with a delectable waltz for Yvonne.

There were two major revivals, one at the Théâtre des Célestins in Lyon, and another in Paris in 1970, a glamorous production at the Théâtre du Palais-Royal with Jean Marais and Florence Raynal. Marais was dashing as the mature lover

---

[1]Michel Augé-Laribé, *Messager,* p. 201.

Sacha Guitry and Yvonne Printemps in the Guitry-Messager *L'Amour masqué* (Édouard VII, 1923). Paris's most famous acting-couple in the 1920s, until Mme. Printemps discovered Pierre Fresnay.

pretending to be his young son, but Mme. Raynal was vocally unmagical when compared to the mercurial Printemps. The sets, by André Levasseur, evoked the luxury of *les années vingt,* but his costumes had too much of an affinity with the miniskirts then popular, rather than the dazzling frocks that Jeanne Lanvin designed for the original production.

After refusing to set Guitry's *Mozart,* Messager tackled *Passionnément* (Michodière, 15 January 1926), another musical comedy with a text by Maurice Hennequin and Albert Willemetz, the latter a tremendously successful librettist between the wars. He wrote over 2,000 songs, including *"Valentine"* for Maurice Chevalier, and *"Mon Homme"* (My Man) for Mistinguett (and Fanny Brice). Besides being manager of the Bouffes-Parisiens for years, he had at one time been private secretary to Clemenceau. *Passionnément* dealt with a jealous old American millionaire in France who changes personality when intoxicated; his wife, meanwhile, has fallen in love with a young Frenchman.

Enchanting as the score must have seemed then, compared to the existing brash musicals *à l'américaine, Passionnément* is quite assuredly Messager in decline. It was filmed with Fernand Gravet in 1932.

Messager's last operetta, again with Willemetz, was *Coup de roulis* (Marigny, 28 September 1928), written in poor health at the age of seventy-four. The plot was an amorous adventure aboard a warship—à la *H.M.S. Pinafore*—complete with a parliamentary official visiting the ship to inspect it. His daughter inspires tender sentiments from both the captain and a humble sailor, and, as a march tune virtually informs us, "Love levels all ranks." In the last act a disaster in the fog is narrowly averted. The comedian Raimu led a cast of good singers to a considerable success on the first night. It was a lovely way to end a career. Many of the songs were encored, and the critics praised Messager on his delicate, "aristocratic" work. It was revived in 1934 and thereafter several times throughout France. *Coup de roulis* (literally, the lurching movements a ship makes on the high seas) was filmed with Max Dearly in Raimu's role in 1931. André Messager died of a kidney disease in 1929, at the age of eighty-five. There was a posthumous operetta, *Sacha,* produced in Monte Carlo in 1930.

If France has shown a growing interest in Offenbach, with a fairly consistent pattern of reviving his works, Messager has not enjoyed a similar surge of admiration or esteem. Apart from infrequent revivals of *Véronique* or *Monsieur Beaucaire,* the operettas of Messager are unknown quantities on the Paris stage. British amateur operatic societies have staged *Véronique* in the past twenty-five years, but one could confidently guess that Messager's operettas have not enjoyed a single performance in the United States in the same period. Yet there are recordings revealing the treasures in *Véronique, Monsieur Beaucaire,* and *Les p'tites Michu,* plus excerpts from some of the others. Unfortunately, today's theatregoer has probably heard of the ballet *Les Deux Pigeons* rather than *Les p'tites Michu.*

Louis Ganne (1862–1923) had his musical training as a student of César Franck and Massenet at the Paris Conservatoire, specializing, as so many French operetta composers did, in the organ. And like so many operetta composers, he trained for the stage by conducting in the provinces, achieving considerable renown at Monte Carlo with his own concerts. Several of his own marches and dances became great popular successes in and out of the *café-concert,* and he wrote several ballets for the Folies-Bergère and the Casino de Paris. *Rabelais*—not an operetta, as some sources indicate—had Ganne's incidental music at the Odéon in 1892, and the following year, *Les Colles des femmes,* his first operetta (in one act), was seen at the Menus-Plaisirs; the title played with Molière's *L'École des femmes. Les Saltimbanques* (The Tumblers, or The Acrobats, Gaîté, 30 December 1899), his next work, an *opéra-comique* in three acts, was a tremendous success. Its libretto, by Maurice Ordonneau, was a romance of circus life, touching, boisterous, and colorful, cleverly using the circus's spectacular effects to enhance its theatricalism. The Gaîté's cast was headed by Paul Fugère (Paillasse) and Jeanne Saulier (Suzanne).

Ganne's score, although at times tending to a certain *opéra-comique* level, was more in the Planquette-Audran tradition than the Messager, and without the latter's aristocratic touch. But it was essentially a crowd-pleasing work, like its very subject, the circus, and two of the numbers became famous as soon as the first-night audience left their seats. The first occurred at the end of Act I during a very nicely developed finale—the waltz song *"C'est l'Amour,"* introduced by Lise Berty and Lucien Noël. A more voluptuous melody has seldom been written for an operetta, and its sentiments were true enough: "It's love that gives us happiness every day; it's love that gives us liberty!" The second big hit was the big military number in Act II (sung by Émile Perrin) beginning *"Quand la trompette militaire"* and ending with the refrain, *"Va, gentil soldat"* (Go, noble soldier), a surefire patriotic anthem that guaranteed to please as often as it was repeated, and it was repeated often, prominently at the end of Act II, meshed with circus music. The circus music is delightful, and on the stage *Les Saltimbanques* had the novelty necessary to ensure a good run and numerous French revivals—especially outside Paris. A Viennese production appeared at the Carltheater in 1901, as *Circus Malicorne.*

Ganne's next success was *Hans le joueur de flûte* (Théâtre du Casino, Monte Carlo, 14 April 1906), a Frenchified version of "The Pied Piper of Hamelin." With Jean Périer and Mariette Sully as Hans and Lisbeth, the three-act operetta was vigorously applauded. Seen subsequently in Italy, Germany, and America (Manhattan Opera House, 20 September 1910), the work eventually was played in Paris (Apollo, 31 May 1910), where Périer repeated his Mediterranean triumph. One of the finest moments in the operetta was a waltz of the cats, which ended Act I: *"Adieu petits minets, petits minous."* More sentimental than *Les Saltimbanques, Hans* was more of a fairy tale–pantomime operetta; it even sounded like Victor Herbert at times. (It took place in the Flemish village of Milkatz, and opened with a live, musical representation of Rembrandt's *The Night Watch.*)

In 1910, Ganne had another hit in Monte Carlo, *Rhodope,* again with Mariette Sully. It did not reach Paris until after the War (Variétés, 24 December 1918), where it ran over a month. More successful was *La Belle de Paris* (Apollo, 22

October 1921) which used preexistent Ganne melodies and ran almost three months. Both *Les Saltimbanques* and *Hans le joueur de flûte* have been recorded, and it is still possible to see each in the French provinces.

Gaston Serpette (1846–1904) was born in Nantes, the son of a well-to-do industrialist. He gave up his legal studies to study with Ambroise Thomas at the Conservatoire, and at the age of twenty-eight had his first operetta produced at the Bouffes-Parisiens: *La Branche cassée* (The Broken Branch, 23 January 1874), with a strong cast that included Anna Judic, the comedians Berthelier and Brasseur, and Lucien Fugère, making his stage debut. This ran forty nights, and Serpette followed it up with a series of some thirty works written up to 1899, occasionally in collaboration with **Victor Roger** (1853–1903), few of which ran more than a hundred performances and only one of which was revived in this century. Yet his music was attractive, wavering between Offenbachian and Lecocquian styles. The greatest stars appeared in his operettas, and he often had extremely talented librettists. In 1877, at the Bouffes-Parisiens, *La petite Muette* (The Little Mute Girl) ran over fifty performances, with Théo and Madame Peschard and a book by Paul Ferrier. Henri Meilhac was the co-author of the first of two popular Serpette concoctions with diabolic associations, *Madame le Diable* (Théâtre de la Renaissance, 1882). This was a twelve-scene *féerie* with elaborate sets and costumes crammed onto a relatively small stage, plus Jeanne Granier, the great Renaissance star, as Madame the Devil, supported by the ravishing Desclauzas. This confection ran over two hundred performances, though its successor at the Renaissance, *Fanfreluche* (1883) did only a quarter of the Devil's business, even with Jeanne Granier.

Berthelier and Brasseur were in *Le Château de Tire-Larigot* (1884) and also scored in *Adam et Ève* at the same Théâtre des Nouveautés two years later; all Paris had to see Louise Théo as Eve in what then must have been a very daring costume—flesh-colored tights and tunic surrounded by garlands of ivy. Appearing in 1887 was *La Lycéenaire* (The High School Girl) with a libretto by the young Georges Feydeau. Such works as *Cendrillonetti* (1890, with Roger), the *japonaiserie, Mé-na-ka* (1892), and *Cousin-Cousine* (1893) were seen before *Le Carnet du Diable* (The Devil's Notebook), another devilish spectacle, this time at the Variétés, in 1895. This ran for a considerable length of time and was revived as well. That same year saw *La Dot de Brigitte* (Bridget's Dowry) at the Bouffes-Parisiens, again written in collaboration with Victor Roger. Juliette Simon-Girard and Alice Bonheur ably led the cast. In 1921, there was a revival at the Trianon-Lyrique, the last Serpette work heard in Paris, save for radio broadcasts.

Of the approximately thirty works of Roger (another Niedermeyer graduate), only two are remotely remembered: *Joséphine vendue par ses soeurs* (Josephine Sold by Her Sisters, Bouffes-Parisiens, 19 March 1886) and *Les 28 Jours de Clairette,* Folies-Dramatiques, 3 May 1892). *Joséphine* had a *bon-bon* of a libretto by Paul Ferrier and Fabrice Carré that used the familiar Bible story of Joseph, who, for Ferrier and Carré's purposes, was changed into Joséphine. She is the favorite, singing daughter of a Paris concierge and is "sold" into an Egyptian harem rather than an expected theatrical engagement. The literary conceits were somewhat cleverer than the musical ones, although Méhul's then-familiar opera *Joseph* was raked engagingly across the coals. In the original cast were Jeanne Thibault in the title role and Mily-Meyer making another sensational impression as her sister Benjamine. Clairette's twenty-eight days were spent at a Parisian department store and with a detachment of hussars on maneuvers trying to prevent her recently acquired husband from falling into the clutches of his former mistress.

The military aspect of this clever *vaudeville* of H. Raymond and Antony Mars called forth the requisitely martial music then so fashionable on the operetta stage, and Roger was fortunate to have Marguerite Ugalde to sing his *couplets*. *Clairette* was quite often to be seen roaming around the French countryside until World War II.

Claude Terrasse (1867–1913), also organ-trained at the École Niedermeyer, had a career which flourished at the turn of the century. Gounod, it is said, convinced Terrasse to try operetta. He made a name for himself in 1896 when he wrote the incidental music for *Ubu-Roi,* Alfred Jarry's famous and shocking play at the Théâtre de l'Oeuvre. Several early attempts preceded his first operetta success, *La petite femme de Loth* (Mathurins, 1900), which had a particularly fine libretto by Tristan Bernard. But the next work was perhaps his masterpiece: *Les Travaux d'Hercule* (The Labors of Hercules, Bouffes-Parisiens, 7 March 1901), with a very amusing libretto by Robert de Flers and Gaston de Caillavet, those two excellent boulevard-comedy furnishers. Amélie Diéterle became a star overnight as Omphale, the wife of Hercules, who was played by the comedian Abel Tarride.

De Flers and de Caillavet, excellent dramatists though they were, led Terrasse astray, into the terrain of revue and gags. Terrasse's operettas, though well regarded in their day and occasionally revived, are now virtually forgotten. His music seldom imprinted itself on the memory to the extent that his contemporaries' did. Sometimes it bubbles, or even sparkles, but most of it seems flat today. Because of his librettists, their subjects, and the rapidity of his rhythms, Terrasse was ever being called the new Offenbach, though he had neither the melodic gift nor the harmonic talents of *père Jacques.* He (and de Flers and de Caillavet) certainly aped Offenbach in *Le Sire de Vergy* (1903), which burlesqued a medieval story much in the manner of *Barbe-Bleue* or *Geneviève de Brabant;* their next operetta, *Monsieur de la Palisse* (1904), was taken from a celebrated eighteenth-century song. Both were fat hits at the Variétés, with Albert Brasseur and Ève Lavallière leading both casts. In *Le Sire de Vergy,* Mlle. Lavallière stunned all with a *danse du ventre.* Among other Terrasse works one should mention *Le Mariage de Télémaque* (1910), performed at the Opéra-Comique some fifty times, and one of his last works, *Faust en ménage* (Faust at Home, 1924). Terrasse continued writing until his death, but the rage for Viennese operetta put works like *Miss Alice des P.T.T.* (1912) in the shade. *La petite femme de Loth* was revived in Paris no more recently than 1957, with the popular comedienne Jacqueline Maillan and an orchestra consisting of piano and guitar!

Fräulein Loreley

OPERETTE
von Bolten-Bäckers

Musik von
PAUL LINCKE.

Für Piano:			Für Gesang und Piano:		
Klavierauszug ohne Text	M 6.— netto		Klavierauszug mit Text	M 8.— netto	
*Ouverture	2.—		Ja mit ein wenig Weiberlist, Lied	1,50	
Potpourri	2,50		Zahnradbahn-Couplet	1,50	
*Loreley-Walzer	2.—		Ringduett	1,80	
*Vater Rhein, Marsch	1,50		(Dasselbe 1 stimmig) hoch u mittel à	1,80	
*Zahnradbahn-Polka	1,50		Feinsmägdelein, Romanze	1,80	
Quadrille	2.—				
Ringlein am Finger					
Fantasie von O. Lindemann	1,80				

Text der Gesänge — 30 netto.
Die mit ✳ bezeichn. Stücke sind auch für Orchester und MilitärMusik erschien.

Alle Vervielfältigungs-Aufführungs-u Arrengementsrechte vorbehalten

Eigentum für alle Länder

APOLLO-BERLIN VERLAG
LINCKE N. 24. & RÜHLE

für Amerika:
COPYRIGHT.

für Russland:
P. NELDNER, Riga.

Lith Anst v C G Röder Leipzig

Paul Lincke (1866–1946) was the originator of the Berlin school of operetta. Future graduates would include Walter Kollo and Jean Gilbert. Lincke played bassoon in Berlin theatre orchestras, eventually becoming a conductor. He contributed songs and *couplets* for farces, and later songs for the Apollo, a variety theatre in the Friedrichstrasse. His operettas began with one-acters, *Die Spree-amazone* (1896) and *Venus auf Erden* (1897), both at the Apollo, and he conducted two seasons at the Folies-Bergère in Paris. The 1899 summer season at the Apollo opened on 1 May with a one-act "burlesque-fantastical spectacular operetta," *Frau Luna*. (It was later enlarged to two acts.) The libretto by Heinrich Bolten-Bäckers was basically a Berlin variant of *Un Voyage dans la Lune*, the Offenbach operetta which had been seen in Berlin in the 1880s. This time, a party of Berliners reached the moon in a balloon rather than a large bullet. The lunar scenes were suitably idiotic, the characters amusing, and the piece bright. But *Frau Luna's* exceedingly long run was due to Lincke's three big hit songs, still just as catchy and charming as ever: *"Schlösser, die im Monde liegen"* (figuratively, Castles in the Air—the London title of the show), *"Lasst den Kopf nicht hängen"* (Don't be depressed), and a cheery tribute to the invigorating *Berliner Luft* (Berlin air), missed so much on the moon's surface. This would become a great theme song for Berlin.

The *Forward*, reviewing the first night, predicted correctly: "Berlin can pretty safely reckon that 'Frau Luna' will soon issue from every barrel organ and will reach the summit of popular fame." And that it did. *Frau Luna* made its way into all the Central European repertoires, to Paris's Olympia (1904), where the music-hall ambiance effectively approximated the variety-house atmosphere of the Berlin Apollo for *Madame la Lune,* and to London, where, as *Castles in the Air,* the operetta did modest business (Scala, 1911).

The success of *Frau Luna* was derived not only from its hit songs, but also from their music-hall tone, a symptom prevalent throughout European operetta at the turn of the century. Just as the George Edwardes musical comedies had *couplets* and marches that would have been perfectly at home in contemporary London music halls, so did *Frau Luna,* albeit arranged for chorus ensembles, rather than for audience sing-alongs. But, perhaps more significantly, it was an operettic elaboration of a typical Berlin-style farce with songs, reflecting a Berliner atmosphere rather than the usual Viennese transplants, which had been as popular in Berlin as in Vienna up to 1900. Berlin now had its own product, and a somewhat exportable one, too, though never, admittedly, as popular as the Viennese variety.

Frau Luna was filmed in 1941 by the popular comedian Theo Lingen, with Lizzi Waldmüller. The story was altered into a backstage romance, but several

---

Lincke's *Fräulein Loreley* (1901) came between *Frau Luna* and *Lysistrata*. The lovely art nouveau design was used regularly by Apollo-Verlag, Lincke's publishing house.

of the popular songs were performed. (Fritz Lang's 1929 *Frau im Mond* has nothing to do with the operetta.)

Im Reiche des Indra followed (Apollo, 18 December 1899), another one-acter
in three scenes, with a "final apotheosis." This alternated (less successfully) with
Luna until the moon-operetta reached its 350th performance by the summer of
1901. *Lysistrata* (1902) was more successful than other now-forgotten works of
the period, such as *Nakiris Hochzeit* (Nakiri's Wedding) the same year. By the
end of the 1900–10 decade, Lincke was providing operettas for the Apollo (which
had become a major operetta house), the Friedrich-Wilhelmstädtisches Theater,
and material for various revues at other theatres, most notably the Metropol.
And he conducted as well, on tours of his one-acters throughout Germany,
Holland, and Austria. The Cologne production of his 1903 *Am Hochzeitabend*
(On the Wedding Night) starred Fritzi Massary, who would go to the Metropol, Berlin, within a year, singing many Lincke songs to intense acclaim.

Fritzi Massary (born Friederike Massarik in 1882) was Viennese by birth. Her
first notable theatrical engagement was with a Carltheater tour of Russia; she
was later in the Carl-Schultze Theater in Hamburg, where one of her colleagues
in the 1900–1 season was Edmund Loewe, father of the composer Frederick. In
1904, she made a sensational hit singing *"Im Liebesfalle,"* and her popularity
climbed to tremendous heights in Berlin's Metropol-Theater revues in the pre-
World War I period. Her usual partners were two comics, Josef Giampetro and
Guido Tielscher, and their songs were composed by such specialists as Lincke,
Viktor Holländer, and Walter Kollo.

Early in her career, she had appeared as a soubrette in such works as *The
Geisha, Der Vogelhändler,* and *Der Bettelstudent.* During her great wartime operetta reign at the Metropol, she starred in Fall's *Die Kaiserin,* Offenbach's *Grande-
Duchesse,* Kálmán's *Die Csárdásfürstin,* and the immensely popular *Rose von Stambul,*
also by Fall. After the Armistice came Jacobi's *Sybil,* Fall's *Madame Pompadour,*
and works by Oscar Straus, in addition to several revue-operetta revivals in
Berlin. She was unquestionably the most glamorous and talented operetta diva
of her period—an era that ended with her exit from Germany in 1933 on account of her Jewish origins.

Lysistrata, ostensibly suggested by Aristophanes' comedy, contained a trio of
Greek ladies (with ladies' chorus) singing about a *Glühwürmchen* (little glow
worm) to show them the right way through the dark to happiness in love. The
satire was Prussianized, the bit of Aristophanes for the most part watered down
(again by Bolten-Bäckers), but the *Glühwürmchen* flew all over Europe and
America delighting all and making Lincke's tune world-famous. Anna Pavlova
contributed to its success by including a dance version of the trio in her repertoire. In New York, the song was interpolated in *The Girl Behind the Counter*
(1907).

By the end of the first decade of the century, Lincke had left behind him his
greatest successes and best music, like the "Norddeutscher Lloyd Polka" from
Nakiris Hochzeit. With his conducting activities and profitable publishing company, he could easily have retired as a composer in 1910, yet he continued to

write. His last operetta, *Ein Liebestraum,* premièred in 1940 in Hamburg, but he ceased composing, for the most part, after World War I.

One of the few operetta composers who could remain in Germany after 1933, Lincke was given several honors and degrees by the Nazi hierarchy, as well as revivals of his old favorites. While it was true there were few composers left to honor, one suspects there was a certain longing for the old pre-Hitler Berlin that Lincke so cheerfully embodied.

Walter Kollo (Elimar Walter Kollodzieyski, 1878–1940), born in East Prussia (now Poland), gave up his father's merchant trade for the music conservatory. He excelled early in the new century in comic songs, and was a theatre conductor in Königsberg before he reached Berlin and its cabarets. For these, and for several theatres specializing in *Berliner Volkspossen* (popular farces), Kollo contributed many hit songs which had a distinctive Berlin feel to them.

From 1908 to 1918 he composed works for the Berliner Theater, of which *Filmzauber* (Film Magic, 1912) and *Wie einst im Mai* (Like One Time in May, 1913) were typical early examples. The latter is still revived, if infrequently. These were generally paeans to Berlin with typically Berliner characters, their dialect, jokes, and other local color. *Wie einst im Mai* (4 October 1913), which had additional music by Willy Bredschneider, told the story of two Berlin families from 1838 to 1913, a sentimental tribute to the capital by the librettists Rudolf Bernauer and Rudolf Schanzer.

Filmzauber, meanwhile, had been transformed into the typically Edwardesian title, *The Girl on the Film* (Gaiety, 5 April 1913), by James T. Tanner, with lyrics by Adrian Ross. It played an eight-month run with George Grossmith, Jr., Connie Ediss, Gwendolyn Brogden, and Emmy Wehlen (a favorite German star), whereupon it was shipped to New York on the *Mauretania,* opening at the 44th Street Theatre on 29 December. This "musical farce," an exact description, had songs added by Paul Rubens and Albert Sirmay by the time of the New York première. The plot, one of the first in operetta to deal with the movies, concerned a very small town believing a costumed movie crew to be an invading army. During the short London run a clever publicity stunt was perpetrated. A provincial artiste (Prudence O'Shea) was *sent* to the Gaiety as an Easter gift, all wrapped in paper, with label and postage, and delivered to the stage door, where the well-known attendant Jupp signed for the parcel. (The girl later became a well-known literary agent.) The New York production scored less well than the London run, but still managed eight weeks.

Wie einst im Mai was completely overhauled for the New York stage, with a new score by Sigmund Romberg, and an Americanized book by Rida Johnson Young, as *Maytime* (Shubert, 16 August 1917), a tremendously successful Shubert production.

Other works followed at other Berlin theatres: *Der Juxbaron* (The Trick Baron, 1913) was also seen in Vienna, while one of the *Drei alte Schachteln* (Three Old Maids, 1917) was the popular cabaret-operetta star, Claire Waldoff, who had sung Kollo's first hit song a decade earlier. Herman Haller's book for the latter operetta transposed James M. Barrie to Biedermeier Berlin; in 1921, the Messrs. Shubert produced the English version on Broadway, *Phoebe of Quality Street,* which failed.

Music publishing and theatre managing were two new sports for Kollo by the 1920s, a decade which saw Kollo's contributions to the popular Herman Haller revues at the Admiralpalast, such as *An und Aus* (On and Off, 1926) and *Wann und Wo* (When and Where, 1927); the stars included such favorites as Paul Morgan, Trude Hesterberg, La Jana, and lots of Tiller Girls. Meanwhile, there were various operettas, like *Marietta* (1923), and *Drei arme kleine Mädels* (1927), the latter produced in New York as *Three Little Girls* (1930). Various full-length and one-act works continued into the '30s, produced in Vienna as well as in Berlin, and in 1940 Kollo died, leaving behind him not so much cohesive operettas as hit songs that brightened the spirits of the inflationary post-1922 period, still remembered today with affection by older Berliners. Willi Kollo (b. 1904), a successful operetta composer as well, is Walter's son, and René Kollo (b. 1937), Willi's son, is today a popular *Heldentenor,* who often sings operetta on German television.

Jean Gilbert (Max Winterfeld, 1879–1942) is, again, the case of a composer tremendously popular in his day but now chiefly remembered for one work— and, surprisingly, not in his own country. The son of a Hamburg merchant, Gilbert was born in 1879 and, like the Berliners Lincke and Kollo, studied music and became a theatre conductor, first in his native Hamburg and later at Lincke's Apollo-Theater in Berlin. His first operetta, with the spicy title *Das Jungfernstift* (The Apprentice Virgin, 1901), was followed by *Der Prinzregent* and *Jou Jou* (both 1902) at the Carl-Schultze, Hamburg.

In 1907, *Fils à Papa,* a French farce by Antony Mars and Maurice Desvallières, appeared in Berlin with moderate success. Yet the librettist Georg Okonkowski thought its story of a very respectable baron caught at the Moulin Rouge would make a good operetta, and he turned it into *Die keusche Susanne* (26 February 1910, in Magdeburg). In spite of its Parisian setting, the operetta was quite Berlinish, and the 1953 version supervised by the composer's son, Robert, switched the locale to Berlin. Whatever the city, this operetta found particular favor in Latin Europe, particularly France and Spain. It reached Vienna (Carltheater, 18 March 1911), London (as *The Girl in the Taxi,* Lyric, 5 September 1912), and New York (as *Modest Suzanne,* Liberty, 1 January 1912) before it got to Paris (*La Chaste Suzanne,* Apollo, 29 March 1913), and did well in all cities save New York. There have been no less than four film versions: German, English, French, and Argentinian.

The London stage production consolidated the reputation of the French actress Yvonne Arnaud, so beloved for years by British audiences that a theatre was named for her, at Guildford. And the star of the German film was the half-English Lilian Harvey, equally adored in Germany through the 1930s. Essentially a French farce with a central act set in the Moulin Rouge, *Die keusche Susanne* was especially admired for its slow waltz, *"Wenn die Füsschen sich heben und schweben"* (anglicized as "Lilt that's Lazy and Dreamy and Hazy") and the rousing two-step, *"Wenn der Vater mit dem Sohne auf den Bummel geht"* ("When the Old Dog and the Young Dog Go upon the Spree"). Apparently, Spanish-speaking audiences have accepted *La casta Suzanna* as a *zarzuela;* so popular is it in that tongue that the most recent performances of this, or any, Gilbert work in the United States were in Miami in May 1978, for the benefit of that city's large Cuban population.

It would be safe to say that no other Gilbert opus has proved as durable, but there were quite a few others, some of which played outside Berlin and Vienna in their day. *Autoliebchen* (Auto-Darling) and *Püppchen* (Little Doll) both appeared in 1912; 1913 saw *Die Tangoprinzessin,* and *Die Kinokönigin* (Metropol, 8 March), produced in London as *The Cinema Star* (a "farcical musical comedy") with Cicely Courtneidge, Jack Hulbert, and Fay Compton (Shaftesbury, 4 June 1914). In both versions, the big song hit was "In the Night." To counter critics who would accuse him of cheapening operetta and turning it (back, as it were) into farce with songs, Gilbert wrote several works that tried to veer into Lehár territory, attempting more of a romantic style. Many of these works were produced at the Theater des Westens, Berlin: *Die Fahrt ins Glück* (1916), *Der verliebte Herzog* (1917), and, notably, *Die Frau im Hermelin* (The Lady in Ermine, 1919), an elaborately costumed operetta which was the source for Ernst Lubitsch's final film in 1949. It was produced in London in 1921 (Daly's, 21 February) as *The Lady of the Rose,* in an adaptation of Rudolph Schanzer and Ernst Welisch's original by Frederick Lonsdale, with lyrics by Harry Graham. The cast was led by Phyllis Dare, Thorpe Bates, Harry Welchman, and Huntley Wright, and they gave it a run that lasted 514 performances, far longer than the original had lasted in either Berlin or Vienna. Just as successful in London was *Katja the Dancer* (Gaiety, 21 February 1925), an adaptation by the same English team of Jacobson and Oesterreicher's original, *Katja, die Tänzerin* (1923). The British cast was headed this time by Ivy Tresmand, Gregory Stroud, and Gene Gerrard. The fox-trot "Leander" was the big hit, just as "I Love You So" was the outstanding favorite from the previous show. *The Lady in Ermine* was seen, with its original title, in New York (Ambassador, 2 October 1922) with Wilda Bennett and Walter Woolf for a run less than half that of London's; *Katja* (44th Street, 18 October 1926) had only 112 airings, which included Vernon Duke's first interpolations on Broadway.

During 1928 Gilbert was in New York, where *The Red Robe* (Shubert, 25 December 1928) was presented, a musicalization of the 1896 melodrama about the intrigues of Cardinal Richelieu. Walter Woolf was teamed with Helen Gilliland and the operetta ran 127 performances, not nearly as successful as some previous Shubert efforts in this sphere. After work for sound films, Gilbert was forced to flee Berlin in 1933, winding up in Argentina, where he died in 1942.

Grisetten-Lied

Aus der Operette

Die lustige Witwe

Text von
VIKTOR LÉON
UND **LEO STEIN**.

MUSIK
VON
FRANZ LEHÁR.

Aufführungsrecht vorbehalten. Eigenthum des Verlegers für alle Länder
Eingetragen in das Vereins-Archiv Mit Vorbehalt aller Arrangements

Für Gesang und Klavier K 1.8
M 1.5

⟜ WIEN, LUDWIG DOBLINGER ⟞
(Bernhard Herzmansky)
Déposé à Paris   I. Dorotheergasse 10.   London, Ent Sta Hall
Leipzig K. F. Köhler
NEW YORK SHAPIRO, BERNSTEIN & C⁰
COPYRIGHT 1905, BY L. DOBLINGER.
VERLAG U. EIGENTHUM FUR RUSSLAND: P. NELDNER, RIGA.
Musikaliendruckerei v. Jos. Eberle & C⁰ Wien VI

THE MERRY WIDOW
AND HER RIVALS

F RANZ LEHÁR ushered in the silver Viennese operetta with his greatest work, *Die lustige Witwe* (The Merry Widow), in 1905. Though not immediately recognized as such, it was the beginning of a new wave of modern operettas in which the waltz was used for romantic, psychological plot purposes, and danced as much as sung. Some of the old conventions of nineteenth-century operetta remained, but *vaudeville* and revue elements were often kept in check as much as possible.

Lehár's melodic gifts were prodigious, and he had a penchant for sweepingly romantic phrases which at once define his era. By the 1920s, the romance overshadowed any comedy or gaiety in Lehár's operettas, so that any connections with the comic operas of Strauss and Suppé and Millöcker were becoming remote. Similarly, the brilliant comic ensembles that were so much a part of the older operettas were found out of place in relatively intimate love stories. Instead, the chorus was brought in at the finales to comment on some serious love misunderstanding that occurred regularly at the ends of Acts I and II. Comic duets involving the comedian and soubrette were considered sufficient—usually three per operetta. And there were many, many love duets in waltz time. Following the London triumph of *The Merry Widow* in 1907, this Viennese format became world popular. (It is fair to point out that *The Merry Widow* was not yet a completely "silver" creation—it had many delightful choral effusions, elaborate and magnificently glittering finales of the old type, and a plot derived from Henri Meilhac, which made its kinship obvious to such operettas as *Die Fledermaus*.)

The "Song of the Grisettes" from *Die lustige Witwe* (The Merry Widow). Lolo, Dodo, and their sister *cancan* girls were a great enticement for theatregoers to visit the Theater an der Wien during 1906 and in subsequent years. Sales of sheet music from this operetta have remained high to this day; a pity current covers are not as saucy.

In our day, the lasting works of Emmerich Kálmán are the principal rivals of the enduring creations of Lehár. Sadly, few other composers from this period are so consistently revived, even though they created many charming works.

In **Franz Lehár,** born in Hungary 30 April 1870, we meet in all probability the Viennese composer who has made more money from operetta than any other, in death as in life, thanks to copyright laws which were not in existence in earlier days. While by no means the most prolific composer, his few great hits were bigger hits than many other composers' successes, measured in terms of performances around the world, and his *Merry Widow* remains one of the more valuable stage properties in existence. Within two years of its première in 1905 he was a more-than-millionaire (in U.S. dollars) and in subsequent years his wealth would increase many times. He was an impressive melodist, leaving behind him scores of exceptionally popular tunes. These included lovely songs written for Richard Tauber, which one might be tempted to call *Lieder.* Of the thirty or so works he composed, about seven are done with regularity in Europe today, thus ranking him with the most popular of all operetta composers.

After initiating the Silver Age of Viennese Operetta, Lehár opted not for the galoping foolery of Offenbach and his Parisian and Viennese followers but for the heady romanticism of *verismo* composers like Puccini. Had he striven to imitate Johann rather than Richard Strauss, the operetta picture in this century might have been radically different. But Lehár was more interested in lyricism and in beautiful love songs than in brilliance, comedy-through-music, or character delineation. Which is why *The Merry Widow* is so fine a work, by far his greatest. Rather than oozing in total romance, it retained enough of the glitter and silliness of nineteenth-century comic opera to make it a well-balanced work.

Lehár was ultimately responsible more than any other composer for changing the course of Viennese operetta from its original dependence on satire and fantasy to romantic sentimentality. Near the 1930s this silver romance became obsolete, and when Lehár ceased composing, it seemed operetta as a theatrical form ceased as well, save for a few holdout examples. Because of Lehár and his contemporaries, the course of operetta inextricably followed the romantic path. Purveying highly colored sentimentality, usually with late Victorian or Edwardian royalty in the *dramatis personae,* the Lehárian formula of escapism could not compete, essentially, with the more fluent and more realistic sound film or the Broadway musical comedy. If the romantic straight plays of the pre-World War II era became irrevivable after 1945, the faded glamor of Lehár's operettas were redeemable only through their attractive love songs. If the nineteenth-century classics are vintage champagne, Lehár's 1920s operettas are heady perfume, fragrant, even intoxicating.

The son of a military bandmaster, young Lehár was a true army child, roving wherever in the Austro-Hungarian Empire his father's regiment was assigned. He very obviously picked up musical characteristics and folk songs from each of these places: Hungary, Transylvania, Prague, Sarajevo, Vienna. Education was appropriately transitory—from the heights of a Budapest Gymnasium one moment to a rural primary school the next—but he was assimilating at the same time the typical music played by his father's band: Suppé overtures, medleys from Italian operas, Strauss waltzes and polkas. At twelve he was at the Bohemian Conservatory of Music in Prague; Dvořák among others gave him encouragement to compose. At the age of eighteen he was at Barmen-Elberfeld (in the German Rhineland) in the municipal theatre orchestra. This proved boring, and a love affair he was having with a thirty-six-year-old singer was getting difficult, so his father arranged to have him enlisted in the Army in order that the nineteen-year-old Lehár could quit Barmen-Elberfeld without breaking his contract. Rather conveniently, Lehár wound up as an instrumentalist in his father's band; alongside him was the young Leo Fall. At the age of twenty he went to northern Hungary to command his own Infantry Regiment Band, the 25th; he was the youngest bandmaster in the Empire.

Lehár began arranging-composing. Several orchestral arrangements proved attractive to Viennese publishers, but very few songs. Spurred by the great Austrian success of *Cavalleria Rusticana* and *I Pagliacci,* he wrote a one-act opera, *Rodrigo,* which was not produced. In 1896 his grand "Russian" opera, *Kukuschka,* appeared in Leipzig, later for four performances in Königsberg, and a few at Budapest—all well received. Two unpublished and apparently uncompleted operettas, *Fräulein Leutnant* (Miss Lieutenant) and *Arabella, die Kubanerin* (Arabella, the Cuban Girl), also date from this period.

What did bring Lehár a certain fame was a waltz he composed for the Princess Metternich-Sándor's *"Gold-und-Silber"* ball in 1902. He sold it outright to a music publisher for fifty *Gulden*—it would bring in a fortune, but not for Lehár. The budding composer was finally able to quit regimental music for the stage when Wilhelm Karczag, the new director of the Theater an der Wien, appointed Lehár musical director. Around the same time, the librettist Victor Léon, who had collaborated with Johann Strauss II on *Simplizius* and with Richard Heuberger on *Der Opernball,* offered Lehár the book of *Der Rastelbinder* (The Tinker) to set; Léon envisaged a Carltheater production with Louis Treumann. Subsequently, Lehár agreed to compose the music for an operetta for his own Theater an der Wien, *Wiener Frauen* (Viennese Women), for Alexander Girardi.

Wiener Frauen opened at the Theater an der Wien 21 November 1902, and there were raves for Girardi, praise for the new composer, and scorn for the libretto. Everyone admired Girardi's portrayal of Nechledil, and the *Nechledil Marsch,* quite unlike the usual waltz with which Girardi generally stopped the show. In the end the operetta appeared some 69 times—not a bad run by any means—and was accepted by several provincial theatres. It was seen in Berlin as *Der Klavierstimmer* (The Piano Tuner) and had other titles elsewhere. *Der Rastelbinder*'s spectacular première (Carltheater, 20 December 1902) indicated a long run in spite of some unflattering reviews the next day. Treumann played an onion-peddler, Wolf Bär Pfefferkorn. With him was Mizzi Günther playing

Suza; she was originally from Prague, and had been a sensation as O Mimosa San in the very successful Viennese production of Sidney Jones's *The Geisha*.

Der Rastelbinder, set in Slovakia, in Vienna, and in an Austrian Army barracks (allowing for another ebullient march), concerned betrothed youngsters who were mismatched. The variety of the settings allowed Lehár a good opportunity to show off his musical *savoir-faire* in capturing the different areas of the Empire, and in the famous *"Wenn Zwei sich lieben"* (When two are in love) we are introduced to the languorous, sensual Lehár of the future—the distinctive love melodies he did so well. The publisher Josef Weinberger had placed Lehár in another disadvantageous position by buying the rights for *Der Rastelbinder* for a relatively small fee while thousands were made by the new Karczag publishing interests by the *Nechledil Marsch* music sales. In a business sense, Lehár was quite green, but he was not unwise in ingratiating himself from the start of his career with the two big operetta music publishers.

Der Rastelbinder swept across middle Europe and appeared in New York, in German, in February 1909, after *The Merry Widow* had captured the town. It was performed in the Bowery, at the Orpheum Music Hall—nothing more than a small German beer garden with a German band. Henry Savage, whose *Merry Widow* was then on, threatened to stop the production on the grounds that he owned the rights to *all* Lehár works; there was, however, no truth to this contention.

Léon then teamed with his *Wiener Blut* collaborator, Leo Stein, on a new libretto for Lehár, this time a reworking of the Amphitryon legend—entitled *Der Göttergatte* (The Husband God). For its première (Carltheater, 20 January 1904) Louis Treumann and Mizzi Günther were again teamed, but this time in a mythological piece along the lines of Lincke's *Lysistrata* or even an Offenbach *opéra-bouffe*—not ideal ground for Lehár's more emotional talents. There was a lovely waltz, and a few marches, but Lehár did not think comically, as Offenbach had, and the libretto, apparently a clever one, was wasted on him. The press liked his musical farce, *Die Juxheirat* (The Mock Marriage) even less; in spite of the presence of Girardi, it ran for only 39 nights (Theater an der Wien, 22 January 1904). Girardi, dissatisfied with his role as a chauffeur, and with the directors Wallner and Karczag, would leave the theatre for good, after one more appearance in an Edmund Eysler work.

Stein was undaunted. Chancing upon a script of Henri Meilhac's 1861 comedy, *L'Attaché d'Ambassade,* a well-known Burgtheater success, he believed it would make a good operetta libretto. Stein took the play to Victor Léon, who concurred, and they began work on *Die lustige Witwe* (The Merry Widow). Their first choice for composer was Richard Heuberger, with whom Léon had written *Der Opernball.* Unpleased with Heuberger's first-act setting, and wary about giving the libretto to Lehár after the failures of *Der Göttergatte* and *Die Juxheirat,* the librettists and Wallner and Karczag had to be pressured by the Theater an der Wien secretary Steininger into allowing Lehár a trial song.

This, composed in a single day and played over the telephone to Léon, was the *"Dummer, dummer Reitersmann"* (Silly, Silly Cavalier) duet in Act II. Lehár got the job, but when he returned from a working summer at Bad Ischl to play the completed work, Karczag, taken aback by the atypical sensuality of the score, was reputed to have exclaimed, "This isn't music!"

Convinced the new work would not succeed, the management gave it the cheapest possible production, using old sets and tattered costumes. (Part of the décor in Act II may very well have been used in the 1901 productions of the English-oriental operettas *The Geisha* and *San Toy*.) Only the reteamed stars, Louis Treumann (Danilo) and Mizzi Günther (Hanna), and the composer had any faith in the operetta. Karczag at one point offered Lehár five thousand crowns to withdraw the work, but the composer refused.

The first night, 30 December 1905, actually went fairly well: many numbers were encored, and some of the reviews were kind (though one called the operetta "distasteful"). Yet there was very little interest at the box office. Free tickets were distributed in order to reach the fiftieth performance (necessary for reasons of prestige). By that time business had picked up sufficiently to keep the show running until 29 April 1906, when the piece was transferred to the then suburban Raimundtheater—the Theater an der Wien was already booked for various summer guest companies. In the fall, the *Widow* returned to the Theater an der Wien. For the 300th performance, the show was redressed and redecorated; by the end of the 1906–7 season it had been produced in theatres in virtually every city in the German-speaking world.

The greatest foreign triumph was at Daly's Theatre, London (8 June 1907). Produced unenthusiastically by George Edwardes as a stopgap for Leo Fall's then-uncompleted *Die Dollarprinzessin,* the first night made stars of the twenty-one-year-old Lily Elsie and the American comedian Joseph Coyne. Translators Basil Hood (book) and Adrian Ross (lyrics) turned Pontevedo into Marsovia, Hanna Glawari into Sonia, and Baron Mirko Zeta into Popoff, and let George Graves (in the latter part) interpolate much of his own extraneous comic business into the play, including his "Hetty the Hen" monologue. The audience was first subdued but ended cheering, and the press echoed their sentiments the next day. The operetta enjoyed a fantastic run of 778 performances, with some patrons visiting Daly's more than a hundred times—King Edward VII saw it four times—and it created a British vogue for Viennese operetta that continued until the First World War made such entertainment unpatriotic.

The success generated by Colonel Henry Savage's New York production at the New Amsterdam (21 October 1907) with Donald Brian and Ethel Jackson was as much commercial as theatrical: Merry Widow hats, corsets, trains, lunches, cigarettes, cocktails, and so on swept the country. In Paris (Apollo, 28 April 1909), in the memorable adaptation by Robert de Flers and Gaston de Caillavet, the British Constance Drever enchanted all with her English-accented widow. In Buenos Aires, five theatres played the operetta in five different languages on one evening in 1907. Back in Vienna, a frequent galleryite during the long run

K. k. pr. Theater an der Wien.

Direktion: Wilhelm Karczag und Karl Wallner.

Samstag den 30. Dezember 1905.

4. Premieren-Abonnement.

Unter persönlicher Leitung des Komponisten.

Novität!   **Zum 1. Male:**   **Novität!**

Die lustige Witwe.

Operette in 3 Akten (teilweise nach einer fremden Grundidee) von **Viktor Léon** und **Leo Stein.**

Musik von **Franz Lehár.**

Baron Mirko Zeta, pontevedrinischer Gesandter in Paris .	Siegmund Natzler.
Valencienne, seine Frau .	Annie Wünsch.
Graf Danilo Danilowitsch, Gesandtschaftssekretär, Leut. d. Kav. i. R. .	Louis Dreumann.
Hanna Glawari . . .	Mizzi Günther.
Camille Rosillon . . .	Karl Meister.
Vicomte Cascada . . .	Leo v. Keller.
Raoul de Saint-Brioche .	Carlo Böhm.
Bogdanowitsch, pontevedrinischer Konsul . . .	Fritz Albin.
Sylviane, seine Frau .	Bertha Ziegler.
Kromov, pontevedrinischer Gesandtschaftsrat . .	Heinrich Pirk.
Olga, seine Frau . . .	Minna Schütz.
Pritschitsch, pontevedrinischer Oberst in Pension . .	Julius Bramer.
Praskowia, seine Frau .	Lili Wista.
Njegus, Kanzlist bei der pontevedrinischen Gesandtschaft . . .	Oskar Sachs.
Lolo	Mizzi Swoboda.
Dodo	Mizzi Dotzauer.
Jou-Jou	Annie Kienberger.
Frou-Frou	Lina Bauer.
Clo-Clo	Herma Cursa.
Margot	Helene Neumayer.
Ein Diener	Karl Beller.

Pariser und pontevedrinische Gesellschaft, Guslaren, Musikanten, Dienerschaft.

Spielt in Paris heutzutage, und zwar: der 1. Akt im Salon des pontevedrinischen Gesandtschaftspalais, der 2. und 3. Akt im Schlosse der Frau Hanna Glawari.

Die neuen Dekorationen sind aus den Malerateliers Burghart & Frant und Theatermaler Zabransky. — Die neuen Kostüme teils von Maison Hoffmann, teils von Frau Streischofsky und Obergarderobier Staray. Die Tänze hat Herr Professor van Hamme einstudiert.

Die Beleuchtungsgegenstände des 3. Aktes wurden von der Bronzewarenfabrik Erdmann & Kleemann geliefert.

Nach dem 2. Akt ist eine größere Pause.

Operngläser sind bei den Billeteuren und in den Garderoben gegen eine Leihgebühr von 20 Hellern zu haben.

Kassa-Eröffnung ½7 Uhr.   Anfang 7 Uhr.   Ende 10 Uhr.

Sonntag	den 31.	Nachmittags halb 3 Uhr bei ermäß. Preisen (ohne Vormerkgebühr): **Der Zigeunerbaron.** Abends 7 Uhr: **Die lustige Witwe.**
Montag	den 1.	Jänner 1906. Nachmittags halb 3 Uhr bei ermäßigten Preisen (ohne Vormerkgebühr): **Vergeltsgott.** Abends halb 8 Uhr: **Die lustige Witwe.**
Dienstag	den 2.	**Die lustige Witwe.**

☛ Die **Tageskassen:** I. Rothenthurmstraße 16 (Bazar) und VI. Millöckergasse (Theatergebäude) sind täglich von 9 Uhr früh bis 5 Uhr nachmittags geöffnet und werden Karten zu jeder im Repertoire angekündigten Vorstellung abgegeben. ☚

K. k. Hoftheater-Druckerei, IX., Berggasse 7.

at the Theater an der Wien was a young man named Adolf Hitler, who retained a lifelong affection for *The Merry Widow* in spite of the fact that both librettists and the composer's wife were Jewish.

It is difficult to keep track of the amazing statistics of *The Merry Widow*. It has been translated into at least twenty-five languages, has been performed over a quarter of a million times, has been depicted in at least three ballets, has enjoyed a "Holiday on Ice," has been recorded innumerable times, has had enormous sheet-music sales (these alone made Lehár a multimillionaire), and has been filmed many times, from a fourteen-minute Swedish short in 1907 to three Hollywood versions, with Mae Murray and John Gilbert (1925), Jeanette MacDonald and Maurice Chevalier (1934), and Lana Turner and Fernando Lamas (1952), all for MGM. It has been burlesqued, vaudevillized, and broadcast countless times. Among the more celebrated widows: Maria Jeritza, Fritzi Massary (for her 1920s revival in Berlin the locale was switched to South America), Kirsten Flagstad, Kitty Carlisle, and Marta Eggerth. Famous Danilos have included Jan Kiepura, Johannes Heesters, and Cyril Ritchard. *The Merry Widow* was a summer fixture at its birthplace, the Theater an der Wien (even the successful production of *Evita* had to make way for it recently), and it has been done *al fresco* many times, from Budapest to Bregenz.

One reason for the operetta's indestructibility is its ravishing score, which even Viennese operetta connoisseurs will have to admit is as good or better than any other of its day. From its marvelously exciting prelude (any "overture" has been subsequently tacked on, whether by Lehár or someone else) to its finale reprise of the *Weiber* march, there is hardly a tired moment. Besides the fragrant *Vilja,* the Maxim's entrance song for Danilo, and the imperishable waltz (arguably the most famous non-Strauss Viennese waltz), there are several often-overlooked numbers that this writer, for one, cherishes. The "Respectable Wife" duet in Act I, another duet for Camille and Valencienne in the same act, the often-omitted *"Zauber der Häuslichkeit"* (Charm of domesticity), and the absolutely thrilling coda to the Act II finale, *"Das hat Rrrrass'! So trala la la la la!"* Indeed, *The Merry Widow*'s finales—all three of them—are fabulously effective.

But the operetta's endurance is the result of more than just a brilliant score (brilliantly orchestrated, to boot) and a stage-worthy text, which so many operettas of the period lack. There is no better symbol for the *fin-de-siècle,* pre-World Wars era than *The Merry Widow* itself. The Lehár-Léon-Stein creation has come to represent a historical age which has in fact been described as one great operetta itself, with its uniforms, its balls, its political intrigue, and its intoxicating glamor.

During the years that followed *The Merry Widow*'s Viennese première, Lehár supervised various foreign productions and often conducted first nights and anniversary performances. Few operettas had ever been so universally acclaimed.

The programme for the world première of *Die lustige Witwe,* the night before New Year's Eve, 1905. Theater an der Wien.

Robert Bodanzky and Fritz Grünbaum provided Lehár with his next operetta—more a children's pantomime—*Peter und Paul im Schlaraffenland*. (The
Schlaraffia was a club to which Lehár belonged created by artists, musicians,
and writers.) A Christmas-time attraction at the Theater an der Wien in 1906,
it played other German-speaking cities as well. *Mitislaw der Moderne*, a one-act
piece also by Bodanzky and Grünbaum, was produced at the "Hell" *(Hölle)*,
the cabaret-in-the-basement of the Theater an der Wien. It existed mainly to
provide Treumann with the opportunity to burlesque his Danilo. For the full-
length *Der Mann mit drei Frauen* (The Man with Three Wives, Theater an der
Wien, 21 January 1908), the house was sold out weeks in advance, and the
audience seemed to like Lehár's first major work since *The Merry Widow*, but
the critics disliked it for the most part, particularly Julius *(Juxheirat)* Bauer's
libretto. The plot concerned a man who had a wife each in Vienna, London,
and Paris. It was performed in New York with Charlotte Greenwood and Cecil
Lean at Weber and Fields Music Hall in 1912, and appeared as *Les Trois Amou-
reuses* in Paris the same year

On 7 October 1909, at the Johann-Strauss-Theater, *Das Fürstenkind* (The Prince's
Child) arrived to substantially more acclaim. Set by Victor Léon in Greece and
America, it concerned a brigand chieftain and his daughter, Photini, in love
with an American naval officer, Bill Harris. The story enabled Lehár to lay on
the Balkan melodies, plus a couple of attractive waltzes, sung by Treumann and
Günther. After Savage's triumph with *The Merry Widow*, he scheduled but did
not produce it in New York in 1909, as *The King of the Mountains*. *Das Fürstenkind* played provincial theatres within a year of its première and entered the
Theater an der Wien repertoire in 1911, but on reaching Berlin in 1913 it was a
failure, and subsequent performances have been very few.

This was hardly the case with *Der Graf von Luxemburg*, the next Lehár work
and one of his most popular triumphs. A. M. Willner had written *Die Göttin
der Vernunft* (The Goddess of Reason) for Johann Strauss, who only composed
it when he was threatened by a lawsuit to live up to his agreement to set it. It
died in 1897 at the Theater an der Wien. Willner, sensing there was still something to the story, had the libretto legally extricated from Strauss's operetta and
reworked it with Bodanzky. The story told of a marriage arranged between an
impoverished count who needs money and a rich singer who needs a title. During the wedding ceremony, the couple is separated by a screen. In the next act,
of course, they fall in love, and in Act III they realize they are already married
to each other. Hardly a very dramatic plot, to be sure, but the public adored it.

On 12 November 1909, the Theater an der Wien reveled in a brilliant opening-night cast which included Otto Storm as René, Annie von Ligety as Angèle,
Louise Kartousch as Juliette, and, most memorably, Max Pallenberg as Prince
Basil, a minister from what was originally called Luxemburg (sic). It ran for 299
performances in Vienna; by 1911, it had swept through all German theatres,
and in May of that year George Edwardes produced it as a successor to his
Daly's triumphs *The Merry Widow* and *The Dollar Princess* (and also a Daly's
failure, the revival of Straus's *A Waltz Dream*). For the London production,

Basil Hood wisely reduced the book to two acts; the lyrics were by Hood and the reliable Adrian Ross. Leading the cast were the handsome Bertram Wallis (René), the radiant Lily Elsie (Angèle), plus Huntley Wright and W. H. Berry for comedy. King George V and Queen Mary consented to attend the first night, and Lehár himself conducted, adding to the glamor. Lehár politely claimed to a British journalist that the Daly's orchestra was the best he had ever conducted, while he told an American reporter in Vienna in 1909: "Viennese operettas are not written to exploit the chorus. Nor do producers here take liberties with an author's book or a composer's score . . . A New York producer would not think of changing one of the Gilbert and Sullivan pieces, yet they change our operettas."

Edwardes needn't have worried, as he had a six-month advance sale and critics and public adored the new operetta, Lehár coming in for particular praise. "There is many a number in *The Count of Luxembourg* which Sullivan would not have refused to acknowledge," wrote one critic. However magnificent the Terraine sets (and they were), the Comelli dresses, and the Wright-Berry comedics, the waltzes, already familiar to Londoners from dance arrangements, proved the most appealing attraction, sweeping Britain into yet another Lehár frenzy. One was *"Bist du, lachendes Glück"* (Tell Me, Can This Be Love?), and the staircase waltz, *"Mädel klein, Mädel fein"* (Golden Stair We Will Climb), deftly performed by Bertram Wallis and Lily Elsie, was a *coup de théâtre*, helping the work run 345 performances at Daly's. It was no less a sensation in New York, where Klaw and Erlanger produced a new American version, libretto by Glen MacDonough, starring George Leon Moore (René), Anne Swinburne (a celebrity overnight for her Angèle), and Frank Moulan and Fred Walton in the comic parts. "One number after another in the score is of the sort that moves the encore fiend to beat his hands," reported the *Times*.

Paris saw *Le Comte de Luxembourg,* in a beautiful production at the Apollo in March 1912 with Henri Defreyn in the title role, in the *version française* of de Flers and de Caillavet. It ran for 125 performances. This followed an important *"saison viennoise"* at the Vaudeville in 1911 by the Theater an der Wien company, during which *Luxemburg* had been presented in German. And the operetta was supremely successful all over the rest of the world—particularly in Eastern Europe, where it is still played regularly.

Zigeunerliebe (Gypsy Love) followed from the prolific pen of Lehár on 8 January 1910, at the Carltheater. Book and lyrics again were by Willner and Bodanzky; this time they delivered a brooding Romanian-set love story without any of the Parisian gaiety that marked the *Widow* or the *Count*. Again, it was an opportunity for Lehár's Balkan effects (actually rather more Hungarian than Romanian). Especially admired were several dance trios and a czárdás for Zorika, *"Hör' ich Cymbalklänge,"* and best of all a ravishing duet, *"Es liegt in blauen Fernen,"* for the lovers Zorika and Józsi. The Viennese press, to a certain extent, recognized Lehár's aim to be the Puccini of operetta, even if it seemed to prefer the merrier scores of *The Merry Widow* and *The Count of Luxembourg*. The run was not especially long; however, the provinces clamored for the new Lehár work, and *Gypsy Love* still holds the stage, especially in Eastern Europe.

As *Gipsy Love,* the operetta followed the long run of *The Count of Luxembourg* at Daly's on 1 July 1912. "Guv'nor" Edwardes reported in an interview:

> I am just back from Paris, where I have been to confer with Lehár about the play. *Gipsy Love* is undoubtedly his masterpiece. The subject appeals to him, and he pours out his temperament in the music. It is full of luscious melody. It soars into opera, and there is a magical waltz in the second act.
>
> As a rule, you know, Lehár will interpolate nothing. When he has written his score the piece has to be produced as it stands. Not so with *Gipsy Love.* He has written me many new numbers, and the score, I fancy, will take us by storm. The piece will be an entirely new one.

One new number was the stirring drinking song, "Love and Wine."

Edwardes gave *Gipsy Love* a typically sumptuous production, but sensing that this outrightly operatic, romantic operetta was not sufficiently in his musical-comedy style, he had Basil Hood and Adrian Ross devise a part (Lady Babby) for Gertie Millar. She may not have been romantic enough to do justice to Franzi in Straus's *A Waltz Dream;* here she had a new part tailored to her talents. Supporting this queen of the London musical-comedy stage was Budapest's operetta queen Sári Petráss, imported by Edwardes and taught English (at least her part) carefully, with the dashing Michaelis as Józsi, the gypsy vagabond, and the dependable W. H. Berry as Dragotin, Miss Petráss's dad.

Gipsy Love ran a bountiful 299 times at Daly's; not so in New York, where Marguerite Sylva's vocal insufficiencies ruined the first night and doomed the play to failure. *Amour Tzigane* toured France with great éclat in 1911 and reached Paris's Trianon-Lyrique the following year.

Eva (Das Fabriksmädel) (The Factory Girl, Theater an der Wien, 24 November 1911) had a book by Willner and Bodanzky concerning social problems—fellow workers in Paris want to save the factory-girl Eva from her over-interested boss. With Günther, Treumann, Kartousch, and the comic Ernst Tautenhayn in the cast, it pleased the critics, who praised Lehár's orchestrations. The première was also graced by the appearance of a good number of foreign theatre-directors, anxious for what promised to be the next lucrative Lehár triumph. Yet, in spite of a great Viennese success, the operetta failed to be a great hit in New York, with a Glen MacDonough book and Sallie Fisher "miscast" in the

---

Lily Elsie was the undisputed star of Viennese operetta in London, and her loveliness and charm are apparent in the thousands of postcards issued to help popularize these shows during the first years of this century. Her roles included the heroines of four of the greatest and most enduring of the Silver Age operettas: (from top left, counterclockwise) Sonia in Lehár's *The Merry Widow* (1907), Alice in Fall's *The Dollar Princess* (1909), Franzi in Straus's *A Waltz Dream* (1911), and Angèle in Lehár's *The Count of Luxembourg* (1911). All were produced by George Edwardes; all were seen at Daly's, save for the Straus which was first produced at Hicks's. Her romantic co-star was invariably Joseph Coyne (left top and bottom). Two of her supporting comedians are opposite: Huntley Wright (top) and W. H. Berry (bottom).

title role, according to the New York *Times*. The principal waltz, *"Wär' es auch nichts als ein Traum vom Glück,"* was already well known to the fashionable New York audience from cabarets and restaurants, but the orchestrations, "aping the modern French school," were sneered at by critic Charles Darnton, who called *Eva* "a very poor relation of *Louise.*" The *Times* noted a specific instance in the first act when Eva says "yes" to "discords that Schoenberg might have been proud to have written."

Eva's greatest appeal, oddly enough, seems to have been to the Italians and the Spanish. It was first seen in Madrid at the Teatro de la Zarzuela in September 1913, and it has been consistently performed and recorded in Spanish and Italian. Parisians pooh-poohed it (in 1924) in spite of the Parisian setting. Conversely, France has always liked the "Spanish" Lehár, *Frasquita* (1922), more than any other country.

A Spanish subject was proposed by librettists Julius Brammer and Alfred Grünwald in 1913: *Die ideale Gattin* (The Ideal Wife), a new libretto to paste over Lehár's old *Göttergatte* score. There were, however, a few new songs, introduced with verve by the new, young idol at the Theater an der Wien, Hubert Marischka (who eventually would take over its directorship). *Endlich Allein* (Alone at Last) had a triumphant first night at the same theatre (30 January 1914). The New York *Musical Courier*'s Viennese correspondent reported:

> The second act constitutes a precedent in the annals of operetta. There is no spoken dialogue . . . the music, although essentially Lehár, reveals here and there flashes of vivid Italian coloring and more than a suspicion of Wagnerian influence and gesture . . . The leitmotif of the operetta, the slow B major waltz, "The World is Fair" [*Schön ist die Welt*] is possibly a trifle too heavily scored, too scholarly in style to meet the popular taste.

The story concerned an eccentric American, Dolly (Günther), and her ardent lover, an attaché (Marischka), who guides the young beauty to the summit of the Jungfrau. It was an operetta equivalent of the mountain film, a particularly German genre. The public was only somewhat partial to the high-minded piece, which ran some 115 performances. Nevertheless, it was presented spectacularly at the Shubert, New York, on 19 October 1915 (America was not yet, of course, at war) with Marguerite Namara as Dolly and John Charles Thomas as Baron Franz von Hansen, the mountain guide, and with José Collins—just prior to her shattering triumph in London as *The Maid of the Mountains*. The special effects in the second act, starting at the base of the mountain at dawn, going farther up the mountain in wind and snow until the summit was reached, were especially admired.

By this time, British and French stages were closed to Lehár, however innocuous his works seemed. Viennese operetta was no longer officially fashionable in London or Paris. Yet it still raged in Vienna and Berlin, with the composers Kálmán, Fall, and others. Lehár, however, failed to come up with anything quite as popular as such wartime hits as Kálmán's *Die Csárdásfürstin* (1915), Berté's *Das Dreimäderlhaus* (1915), or Fall's *Die Rose von Stambul* (1916). First came *Der*

Sterngucker (The Star Gazer, Theater in der Josefstadt, 14 January 1916, libretto by Fritz Löhner). It did not succeed in Vienna, but it was adapted by Lehár and the Italian operetta manager-author-publisher, Carlo Lombardo, as *La Danza delle Libellule*. This production contained the vastly popular "Gigolette." When *La Danza delle Libellule* was produced in England as *The Three Graces* in 1924 there were boos from the audience due to a lingering feeling against Britain's World War I adversaries. *The Star Gazer* opened in New York (Plymouth, 26 November 1917) just after the United States went to the trenches, and John Charles Thomas was starred again, this time with Carolyn Thomson. The original story concerning the Duc of Nancy was transformed by the respected dramatist Cosmo Hamilton into a story of Bath *à la* Jane Austen. If Lehár was technically an enemy alien, the Shuberts, tactfully, did not advertise this fact.

Wo die Lerche singt (Where the Lark Sings), libretto by Willner and Heinz Reichert, appeared at the Theater an der Wien on 27 March 1918. The folksy Hungarian setting appealed both to the war-weary Lehár, who had done his share entertaining in army hospitals and elsewhere, and to the disillusioned Viennese public, who knew that the upcoming end of the war would be disastrous for them and for their Empire. The original cast included Louise Kartousch and Ernst Tautenhayn. *Wo die Lerche singt* was the last operetta of the old régime, and it was seen a substantial 416 times until its retirement in 1929. A New York production appeared at the Manhattan Opera House in 1920.

In 1920, a few weeks after Lehár's fiftieth birthday, the Theater an der Wien saw *Die blaue Mazur* (28 May), with a Leo Stein–Bela Jenbach libretto set in Poland. A loving couple about to be married, Count Julian Olinski and Blanka von Lossin, had fallen in love during the last dance at a ball—the titular Blue Mazurka. A former mistress turns up and complications ensue, but not enough to disturb a very long run at the Theater an der Wien, with Hubert Marischka, Betty Fischer, Ernst Tautenhayn, and Louise Kartousch in the principal parts. Critics called the score as gracefully charming as any that preceded it, with the added appeal of Polish-accented melodies, but *Die blaue Mazur* has not been revived notably since the 1920s, and out of respect to the memory of librettist Stein (who died in 1921) Lehár did not attempt any revisions. Lehár called it his best score up to then.

London did not see *The Blue Mazurka* until 1927, well after the Viennese craze (Daly's, 19 February). George Metaxa and Gladys Moncrieff starred with Clifford Mollison, in Tautenhayn's part, along with George Graves and Bertram Wallis. With its familiar prewar faces, *The Stage* called it "a typical Daly's production, so typical indeed that, except for the principals, at almost any point one might imagine that it was a revival." It ran only 140 performances, and, unfortunately for Lehár, was only noted for a Herman Darewski interpolation, "The Black Lancers." Nor did the Warsaw setting prove effective in Paris, where it was produced in 1929 with Pépa Bonafé and Victor du Pond.

Following the severe inflation which hit Vienna in 1921, Lehár did his best to entertain the public, though with royalties continuously pouring in from abroad Lehár had no financial worries. In 1921 came *Die Tango-Königin* (Theater an der

Wien, 9 September), a new revision of his *Die ideale Gattin* of 1913; in 1922, a one-act *Frühling*, revised later as *Frühlingsmädel* (three acts). The big success of 1922 was *Frasquita* (Theater an der Wien, 12 May), popular today chiefly for its serenade, *"Hab' ein blaues Himmelbett,"* immortalized by Hubert Marischka, first, and then by Richard Tauber, who created a sensation by singing the encore softly in his first appearance at the Theater an der Wien in a Lehár work. A. M. Willner and Heinz Reichert's book was loosely based on a Pierre Louys novel, *La Femme et le Pantin* (The Woman and the Puppet), which Puccini had at one time considered for an opera and which von Sternberg later turned into the film *The Devil Is a Woman*. Lehár, ever interested in Spanish passion (*Die ideale Gattin*, for one), was obviously influenced here by Spanish dances and *zarzuelas*. He came up with a multicolored score, fandangos and other dances sharing the bill with typical waltzes. The *Serenade* carried the operetta to many European theatres.

Frasquita had the distinction of playing the Opéra-Comique in Paris (5 May 1933) with an enlarged score written and supervised by Lehár. Playing the principal parts were no less than Conchita Supervia and Louis Arnoult; even so, audiences desiring Spanish effects at the Opéra-Comique preferred *Carmen*. In London (Prince's, 23 April 1925), despite a cast including José Collins, Thorpe Bates, and Edmund Gwenn, *Frasquita* ran a meager four weeks. It was not presented in New York until after Lehár's death, in a concert version at Town Hall in 1953 with Ilona Massey. Jarmila Novotna, Hans Heinz Bollman, and Heinz Rühmann appeared in a 1935 film from Germany.

Die gelbe Jacke (The Yellow Jacket, Theater an der Wien, 9 February 1923), in spite of a gorgeous production, was less successful than predicted. In a Chinese setting, librettist Victor Léon told the bittersweet story of an oriental prince in love with a Viennese woman. There was nothing thematically unusual about the work, but in its Berlin revision (1929) as *Das Land des Lächelns* (The Land of Smiles) the work gained immortality, thanks to three new items: (1) a much-improved libretto and score, (2) the magnificent song for Prince Sou-Chong, *"Dein ist mein ganzes Herz"* (Yours Is My Heart Alone), and (3) Richard Tauber to sing it. In 1923, *The Yellow Jacket* held the boards for nearly a hundred performances, not the total failure generally thought. Better on its own terms was the musical farce *Clo-Clo* (Bürgertheater, 8 March 1924), a contemporary story adapted by Bela Jenbach from a 1914 farce. Clo-Clo is a Parisian revue star who runs off to Perpignan, posing as the Mayor's illegitimate daughter. The third act (in jail, as in *Fledermaus*) ends in a joyful champagne party, with Clo-Clo's future secure in her lover's arms. This was a return to the Lehár of old prewar days, gay, lighthearted, uninterested in the tragic, unrequited love stories that distinguished his last works. But, as Bernard Grun aptly noticed, the critics "having faulted [Lehár] for sentimentality and false pathos, now attacked him for frivolity and heartlessness."[1] Louise Kartousch triumphed in the Viennese production. A British company headed by Cicely Debenham opened at the

---

[1] *Gold and Silver*, p. 190.

Shaftesbury in 1925 (9 June), again with Darewski interpolations. The show lasted only 95 performances.

In 1925, Lehár commenced a series of romantic operettas which were, in their unabashed lyricism, the most beautiful the 1920s were to hear, at least in Berlin and Vienna. These were *Paganini* (1925), *Der Zarewitsch* (1927), *Friederike* (1928), and the revised *Gelbe Jacke*, *Das Land des Lächelns* (1929). All four were made world-famous by Richard Tauber, the Austrian tenor, who claimed that he and Lehár were brothers, "without the luxury of a blood relationship."

Tauber was born illegitimately as Richard Denemy in 1891 to a Viennese-Jewish father and a Roman Catholic mother in Linz, Austria. He had a back-stage childhood, his mother being an operetta soubrette in Linz. His father left the household early, but Richard had training at his father's theatre in Wiesbaden. His first noted appearance was as Tamino in a Chemnitz *Die Zauberflöte* in 1913—throughout his career Tauber was one of the greatest of all Mozart tenors. He sang many operatic parts, and memorably recorded selections from these and operetta roles. That same year saw Tauber's debut at the Theater an der Wien in *Frasquita*, his first alliance with Lehár.

Tauber's sensational encore-singing had the Viennese clamoring for more. In 1923, Marischka gave them a revival of Strauss's *Eine Nacht in Venedig*, with numbers like *"Treu sein, das liegt mir nicht"* reassigned by Erich Wolfgang Korngold, the musical arranger, to the Tauber role, the Duke. That same year, Tauber sang at the Salzburg Festival, and agreed to do *Paganini* for Lehár.

The Viennese book publisher Paul Knepler had written what was first called *Der Hexenmeister* (The Wizard), a libretto based on the legends surrounding Paganini's affair with the Duchess of Lucca, Napoléon's sister Anna Elisa. A friend of the librettist, realizing the book deserved a better score than the librettist himself could supply, took it, *incognito*, to Lehár. The composer apparently liked it enough to have composed one half the score before Knepler came to reclaim it. Knepler had only to hear a few bars to leave it in Lehár's hands, and even consented to Lehár's request that the lyrics be polished by Bela Jenbach. Lehár immersed himself in Paganiniana: books, scores, prints, anything to give him inspiration.

Lehár was, however, unwilling to let *Paganini* play the Theater an der Wien alongside Emmerich Kálmán's enormously successful *Gräfin Mariza* and the equally popular *Der Orlow*, by Bruno Granichstädten. The Viennese première therefore took place at the Johann-Strauss-Theater (30 October 1925) but without Richard Tauber, who had a previously contracted Scandinavian concert tour. With Carl Clewing and Emma Kosáry not up to the demands of the roles of Paganini and Anna Elisa, a shabby production and a shortchanged orchestra, *Paganini* failed to please anyone except Tauber, who saw it shortly before the last performance and realized that Lehár was right: he had to save the work by doing it in Berlin.

Vera Schwarz, the opera soprano who had intended to appear with Tauber in Vienna, was finally united with him at the Deutsches Künstlertheater in Berlin

(30 January 1926). The opening night was a triumph, and a sensational surprise. Sophisticated Berliners fell for the powerhouse combine of Tauber and Schwarz singing the luscious melodies of Lehár's gorgeous score, and there were numerous encores for the lovely songs: the spirited entrance of Paganini, *"Schönes Italien,"* in the first act, and the treasure-house of love songs in Act II, *"Gern hab' ich die Frau'n geküsst"* (Girls Were Made to Love and Kiss)—five encores for this *Tauberlied* of the first order—*"Deinen süssen Rosenmund"* (Your sweet rose-lips), *"Niemand liebt dich so wie ich"* (Nobody Could Love You More), and Anna Elisa's *"Liebe, du Himmel auf Erden"* (Love, you heaven on earth), a rapturous tribute to love, not to mention a charming duet for the comedian-soubrette (Pimpinelli-Bella), *"Einmal möcht' ich was närrisches tun"* (For once I'd like to do something crazy), which was so entrancing that Tauber himself recorded it (with his then-wife, Carlotta Vanconti) along with the other hits. *Paganini* remains one of Lehár's finest scores, in spite of what the magazine *Das Theater,* echoing the other reviews, called the "feeble and charmless" book that accompanied it. Moreover, the plump Tauber was by no stretch of the imagination a modern incarnation of the wiry Paganini. No one cared, however, when the operetta tenor of the century (and, perhaps, of all time) sang. As he once stated, "I'm not singing operetta . . . I'm singing Lehár."

Paganini's success in Berlin was contracted to be repeated in some fifty theatres throughout the world within a year of the Berlin first night, though London had to wait until 1937 in order to get Tauber to return there. A new book by Reginald Arkell and A. P. Herbert was commissioned by C. B. Cochran, Evelyn Laye was engaged to co-star, and the Lyceum was engaged. "I felt that in a theatre large enough for plenty of cheap seats—for it is the masses who like singing, and are not so critical about the story—[Tauber] must be a big winner in a show with plenty of good songs," reminisced Cochran.[2] Unfortunately, in spite of generally good notices, the public stayed away. Some, like W. A. Darlington, complained of Tauber's failure to appear a convincing Paganini or even a violinist. "He grasps the whole affair like an Indian club," wrote the *Daily Telegraph* critic. And Tauber and Laye singing fourteen out of the nineteen numbers between them somehow did not prove an inducement. Tauber successfully begged Cochran to let him cover any losses to keep the show open after the producer had cabled the closing notice (from California), but this last-minute effort was in vain. The film fans stayed away from the Lyceum, and the post-Coronation period was not a theatrical highpoint from a business standpoint. Perhaps the public agreed with Cochran himself: "Of its kind, *Paganini* was very good indeed; but I hate the kind."

Paganini was never produced on Broadway; in Paris, it appeared at the Gaîté-Lyrique in 1928 with André Baugé singing the *Tauberlied,* rendered as *"J'ai toujours cru qu'un baiser,"* in the André Rivoire translation. It was filmed silently in 1926, and with sound in 1934, both times as *Gern hab' ich den Frau'n geküsst.*

Lehár's career was entirely revitalized due to Tauber; moreover, it convinced

---

[2]*Cock-a-Doodle-Do,* p. 41.

him that the Berlin public, even though a much less sentimental and much more demanding crowd, was more receptive to this romantic fare than Vienna's. He consequently moved to Berlin, where he had already been delightedly contracted to provide his next opus. This was *Der Zarewitsch,* based on a play of the same name by the Polish Gabryela Zapolska which Lehár had seen in Vienna in 1917. The libretto, which sugared over the realities prevalent in the original play, was by Jenbach and Reichert. According to Bernard Grun, it was first offered to Lehár, who refused it in 1925, then to Mascagni, who took a large advance but did not write anything, and then to Eduard Künneke, whereupon Lehár had second thoughts and got it back for himself.

The story was suggested by the love life of the actual son of Tsar Peter the Great, the young Alexei, who fled Russia with a Finnish girl to live in Italy at the very beginning of the eighteenth century. He was persuaded to return to Russia, where he was put on trial by his father and later died in prison. The sordid ending of this history was expunged. Instead, as in *The Student Prince* (1924), the Crown Prince must return to his country and his duties at the imperial court, leaving his love behind. The time was changed to the end of the nineteenth century to resemble, perhaps, the era of young Nikolai II, whose sad end in 1917 was well known.

Der Zarewitsch (Deutsches Künstlertheater, 21 February 1927) continued in the semihistorical romantic tradition: Lehár was satisfied with *Paganini* and would continue the fashion with *Friederike. Der Zarewitsch* is, however, a singularly run-of-the-mill excuse for Tauberian singing, colored with Slavic spices, generally balalaika accompaniments. Melodically it is not perhaps as rich as *Paganini,* though it does have several effective numbers: Sonja's *"Einer wird kommen"* (Someone will come), the lovers' duet *"Hab' nur dich allein"* (I have only you), the third-act *"Warum hat jeder Frühling, ach, nur einen mai?"* (Why does each spring have only one May?), and the Volga song, with its refrain, *"Hast du dort oben vergessen auf mich?"* (Have you forgotten me?). Save for the balalaikas in the last-named song, any of these could have been placed in any other late Lehár score, but they are nevertheless beautiful and effective here. Tauber was more than satisfied with his role—he claimed it to be his favorite Lehár part—and the Berlin public admired him in it in a luxurious production which was transferred to Vienna the following year. The operetta was produced in Paris as *Rêve d'un Soir* at the Porte St. Martin in January 1935, with Roger Bourdin and Fanély Revoil.

Friederike was considerably more daring—an operetta about the life and love of Johann Wolfgang von Goethe. A British equivalent would have been a romantic operetta about Shakespeare, which probably would have been laughed off the stage in London. The original libretto draft, by Fritz Löhner and Ludwig Herzer, nevertheless appealed to Lehár, who saw the already well-known story of the young poet's romantic entanglements with Friederike Brion, a pastor's daughter in Alsace-Lorraine, as an ideal operetta plot. The rest of Berlin was divided: the left, the intellectuals, and the cabaret crowd saw the operetta-in-the-works as a ridiculous idea; numerous cabaret sketches had caricatures of

Goethe singing and dancing. The middle-of-the-road and lowbrow tastes eagerly welcomed the new Lehár extravaganza. *Friederike* appeared at the Metropol-Theater (4 October 1928) under the management of the brothers Rotter, who were well known principally for studding their plays with big stars and filling cigarette boxes with ticket vouchers, among other publicity ventures. They made the most of the Goethe scandal, while signing up not only Tauber (who had some doubts whether he ought to play the thin poet), but also Käthe Dorsch, the celebrated dramatic actress who began her career in operetta, for the title part.

Friederike is one of the most passionate Lehár works, allowing Tauber a field day. Most of the numbers went to Tauber and/or Dorsch, including *"O wie schön, wie wunderschön"* (O, how lovely, how wondrously lovely) and *"O Mädchen, mein Mädchen, wie lieb' ich dich"* (O maiden . . . how I love you). The critics detested *Friederike,* but the public adored it, and a Viennese production with Tauber and Lea Seidl followed in February 1929. Scores of German theatres produced it, oblivious to any Goethe sensibilities on the public's part. In January 1930, it appeared at the Gaîté-Lyrique, Paris, with René Gerbert and Louise Dhamarys; in September of that year in London (Palace) with Lea Seidl, again, and Joseph Hislop, and in New York (Imperial) in February 1937, with Helen Gleason and Dennis King. None of these foreign productions caused much of a stir. *Friederike* was filmed in 1932, directed by the original stage director Fritz Friedmann-Friedrich, and starring Mady Christians and Hans Heinz Bollmann.

Das Land des Lächelns (Metropol-Theater, 10 October 1929), on the other hand, was a Berlin and an international triumph. In this well-revised *Gelbe Jacke,* the part of Sou-Chong fitted Tauber to a T, especially after a debilitating bout with a severe form of arthritis had partially disfigured his face and left him with a slight limp—the Chinese makeup and long robes hid all this. Léon's original libretto was fixed up by Ludwig Herzer and Fritz Löhner, and in one famous instance new words were fitted to a few bars of incidental music. This was the most celebrated *Tauberlied* of them all, *"Dein ist mein ganzes Herz"* (Yours Is My Heart Alone). Tauber sang it in every possible way during the encores—in German, in French, in English, *sotto voce,* and so forth. The song took him, and the operetta, around the world. (Curiously, *Die gelbe Jacke*'s run of 98 performances at the Theater an der Wien was only seven less than that achieved by the revised "hit" at that theatre.)

The London production (8 May 1931) brought Tauber to Drury Lane. Hopes were high—with Tauber starring—for a sensation. The first night was indeed sensational, but Tauber had to be forced to play the second night, and he missed the third. He thus had an unfortunate reputation confirmed in London: he skipped performances according to his whim. This unreliability killed the London production (71 performances); once, Tauber actually went back to Vienna, at which point the management was reputed to have been training Alfred Piccaver to

---

Richard Tauber in his most celebrated role, Prince Sou-Chong in Lehár's *Das Land des Lächelns* (1929). A scene from the film version made the next year.

take over. As time wore on, Tauber became more trustworthy, appearing often in London on stage and in films. Eventually he became a British subject, when it was impossible to return to occupied Austria.

In Paris, *Le Pays du Sourire* pleased a vast crowd, which came, as in Berlin and London, to hear the tenor (Willy Thunis) sing up to seven encores to *"Je t'ai donné mon coeur."* Like the *Merry Widow* waltz, it became a Lehár signature tune, sung everywhere. But in New York, a disastrously Broadwayized version starring Tauber opened much too late, in 1946. A moderately successful revival in London, by the Sadler's Wells Opera, using a new libretto by Christopher Hassall (Ivor Novello's writer), opened in the 1950s. *Das Land des Lächelns* remains in the repertoires of German theatres to this day. It was filmed in 1930, with Tauber celluloiding his Sou-Chong, and twenty-two years later, with Jan Kiepura in the Tauber role.

For Depression audiences, *The Land of Smiles* contained not only Viennese-Chinese escapism, but a host of luscious melodies, gracefully orchestrated, that demanded robust, operatic singing. *"Immer nur lächeln"* (Patiently Smiling) and *"Von Apfelblüten einen Kranz"* (A Crown of Appleblossoms) are only a few of the more demanding numbers, but a personal choice for the two best would be the two duets *"Bei einem Tee en deux"* (A Tea for Two) and *"Wer hat die Liebe uns ins Herz gesenkt?"* (Love, What Has Given You This Magic Power?).

In the year of Lehár's sixtieth birthday (1930), at Christmas, there were some five hundred different productions of Lehár operettas in Europe, of which two hundred were of *Das Land des Lächelns*. Lehár and Tauber were at their peak financially and artistically (at least in Lehár's own estimation). The Berlin production appeared in Vienna at the Theater an der Wien (26 September 1930) with Tauber in tow, and, after several appearances in New York, Australia, and the film studios, Tauber appeared again at the Berlin Metropol for *Schön ist die Welt* (Fair Is the World), a revision of the *Endlich allein* (3 December 1930). This was an attempt to do for the 1914 work what had been done for the 1923 *Gelbe Jacke*, but the transformation did not fare quite as well. The same mountain story was retained by librettists Löhner and Herzer, with modernized communications, to be sure, and personages of higher rank than previously, plus a modern tango from Rio, but still with the same mountain air. The Rotters did their best with spectacular sets, Tauber, and the Berlin Opera coloratura Gitta Alpar, not forgetting their ruses to keep the show on, but today we only remember, from records, *"Frei und jung dabei"* (Free and young as well) and the title song. Aside from regional performances and a production with Tauber in Vienna (1931), *Schön ist die Welt* has seldom been revived.

Giuditta, the last major Lehár work, was the culmination of Lehár's desire to bring operetta into the opera, literally and figuratively. It was produced at the Vienna State Opera on 20 January 1934. Tauber apparently suggested that it be produced at the Staatsoper; otherwise, it would probably have wound up at the Theater an der Wien, as Lehár had moved back to Vienna in 1933 following the enactment of racial laws that would make life precarious for his Jewish wife. The colorful libretto by Fritz Löhner and Paul Knepler concerned Octavio, an Italian army captain so smitten with Giuditta, a laborer's wife, that he quits the service and ends up as a cabaret pianist. It was set on the Mediterranean coast and in North Africa, and the score was among the lushest Lehár had written. The biggest hit, *"Meine Lippen, sie Küssen so heiss"* (My lips kiss so warmly), introduced by Jarmila Novotna in a luxurious nightclub setting, was supplemented by Tauber's glorious entrance song, *"Freunde, das Leben ist lebenswert!"* and another hit for the tenor, *"Du bist meine Sonne."* The work was entirely out of place in the Staatsoper, and the press was particularly vicious, but it managed 42 well-attended performances. There have been revivals, but none popular enough to spark international acceptance of *Giuditta*.

Lehár's non-stage works, including radio music and the film scores for *Die grosse Attraktion* (1931), *Es war einmal ein Walzer* (1932), and *Grossfürstin Alexandra* (1933), were as unnotable as the various films that were made of his theatrical titles. During the Nazi period, Lehár's works were continually played in the Reich, without mention of the librettists' names, while foreign royalties continued to pour in, until the war. In 1935, bankruptcy forced Hubert Marischka of the Karczag publishing firm to turn over the rights to Lehár's works to the composer himself. The Glocken-Verlag was thus born, still a very prosperous organization. The *Anschluss* of Austria saddened Lehár, and made existence even more dangerous for his wife, but the composer decided in view of their age and ill health to remain in Austria. While many of his theatrical colleagues and friends either emigrated or were sent to their deaths, Lehár remained in Vienna and at his villa in Bad Ischl, even accepting Nazi awards, such as the Ring of Honor from the City of Vienna, or Hitler's Goethe-Medallion. Nevertheless, old friends like Paul Knepler and Richard Tauber visited the old composer after the war, and he died knowing his works still enjoyed their old popularity in the bombed-out Europe of 1947.

Emmerich (Imre) Kálmán was born in the Lake Balaton town of Siófok, Hungary, 24 October 1882. His original intention was to be a virtuoso pianist. This dream unfortunately was shattered when he developed neuritis. He turned to composition and theory, and studied at the Royal Academy of Music in Budapest. Fellow students included Bartók, Kodály, and the operetta composers Szirmai and Jacobi. He dabbled in music criticism and for a time took classes at Budapest University toward a law degree, which he did not receive. His earliest compositions were invariably serious song cycles and patriotic tone poems, but there were also cabaret songs. When Kálmán suggested that he should write the music for a libretto by his friend, the respected Budapest author Karl Bakónyi, Bakónyi consented.

This first operetta, *Tatárjárás,* was produced at the Vígszínház (Comedy Theatre), Budapest, on 22 February 1908. The story of the love of a wealthy widowed baroness and a lieutenant colonel had a marked affinity to the plot of *The Merry Widow*. It was successful enough and sufficiently talked-about to lure managers Karczag and Wallner to Budapest, along with Leo Fall as an adviser. All were entranced, and as *Ein Herbstmanöver* (Autumn Manoeuvres), with a German libretto by Robert Bodanzky, it opened to acclaim at the Theater an der Wien on 22 January 1909 with Grete Holm, Louise Kartousch, Otto Storm, and the newcomer Max Pallenberg, who made a tremendous hit in the third act singing *"Das ist mein Freund—der Löbl."* The composer was twenty-seven and the operetta would achieve 265 performances at the theatre before being taken off. Before settling in Vienna for good, one further work appeared at the Vígszínház: *Obsitos,* which opened in 1910; it played in Vienna the following year with a text by Victor Léon as *Der gute Kamerad* (The Good Comrade) at the Wiener Bürgertheater.

Henry Savage—always on the an der Wien lookout after his *Merry Widow*

triumph—bought the rights for *Ein Herbstmanöver* and presented it at New York's Knickerbocker Theatre on the sweltering evening of 29 July 1909, as *The Gay Hussars,* with a host of bad singers, according to several critics. Florence Reid, however, came off best with an interpolated song, "O, You Bold, Bad Men!" and for comedy one could fall back on W. H. Denny, the English actor who created the part of Don Alhambra del Bolero in Gilbert and Sullivan's *The Gondoliers.* The New York *Dramatic Mirror* did admire the "welcome diversion" of a lack of opening and closing choruses, and liked the "real love story, almost psychological enough to lend a flavor of Pinero . . ." but it still, rather politely, echoed the popular feeling: "I fear the operetta is not congested with hits." Another paper was more blunt, headlining its review "A Savage Massacre."

A totally anglicized version by Henry Hamilton (lyrics by Percy Greenbank) appeared at the Adelphi, London, as *Autumn Manoeuvres* under the aegis of George Edwardes, on 25 May 1912. The Central European setting was expunged, and the comedy, as usual in London, was overblown to fit the talents of Gracie Leigh and Huntley Wright. They and Robert Evett and Phyllis Le Grand as the romantic leads were not enough to save the show. Perhaps the operetta's setting in the neighborhood of "Ambermere Park" and the essentially foreign sounds of Kálmán's score did not mix well.

Kálmán's next work was also very Hungarian in character. *Der Zigeunerprimas* (Johann-Strauss-Theater, Vienna, 11 October 1912) had Alexander Girardi in the title part of a bittersweet story about an aging gypsy violinist of international repute who gives up his Stradivarius to his worthy son by the final curtain. It was well received, and even more so in New York with Mitzi Hajos in the title role of *Sari,* as the Henry Savage production was called (Liberty, 13 January 1914). The New York *Times* commented on "two beautiful stage settings, some excellent music, and an excellent cast, but with a book tremendously dull and uninspiring." "Love Has Wings" was Miss Hajos's song hit, and there were further waltzes of note.

A scant month and a half after the Viennese première of *Der Zigeunerprimas* came *Der kleine König* (Theater an der Wien, 1912). Also in 1912, Kálmán did the score for a short operetta for the London Hippodrome (now the Talk of the Town cabaret), *The Blue House,* and in 1914 a revised, "nationalized" version of *Der gute Kamerad* entitled *"Gold gab ich für Eisen"* (I Gave Gold for Iron) appeared at the Theater an der Wien as a contribution to the war effort. Another wartime work was *Zsuzsi Kisasszony* (Miss Susie), produced at the Vígszínház in Budapest in 1915. Bypassing Vienna, it was transformed by Guy Bolton and P. G. Wodehouse into *Miss Springtime*—A. L. Erlanger wouldn't have anything little at the New Amsterdam, so the *Little* that originally appeared in the title was dropped. With a roster including Sári Petráss in her original part, George Macfarlane, and Jed Prouty, with Joseph Urban sets and Julian Mitchell dances, it ran 230 performances on Broadway and toured even more successfully thereafter across the United States. Rather surprisingly, the propaganda of *"Gold gab ich für Eisen"* was transformed by the "enemy" into Broadway's *Her Soldier Boy* in 1916, with additional music by Sigmund Romberg.

Sweeping all Kálmán's other works aside was the 1915 *Die Csárdásfürstin* (The Csárdás Princess), opening at Vienna's Johann-Strauss-Theater on 17 November. The libretto was by Leo Stein and Bela Jenbach. This was one of the greatest hits of the war years, and it renewed the career of Mizzi Günther as the cabaret star Sylva Varescu, in love with Prince Edwin. The *Neue Wiener Tageblatt* reported the next day that Kálmán "at the same time stands with one foot in the Hungarian soil, and with the other in the dance halls from which the Viennese waltz came." This happy dichotomy enabled the operetta to repeat its triumph all over Central Europe. It played more or less exclusively for over two years (each) in Vienna, Hamburg, and Berlin and has attracted notable stars

---

Emmerich Kálmán placing a wreath at the Lehár family grave, Bad Ischl. Viennese operetta was also virtually dead by this time, as Kálmán must have realized. Frederick Doppelt.

everywhere, most particularly Fritzi Massary, who performed it at the Metro-pol, Berlin, and Hans Albers, who appeared with Rita Georg at the Theater im Admiralspalast in a very elaborate production in 1931. It was revamped for New York audiences as *The Riviera Girl* by Guy Bolton and P. G. Wodehouse, with extra numbers by Jerome Kern (New Amsterdam, 24 September 1917). Wodehouse and Bolton reminisced in 1954:

> The Kálmán score was not only the best that gifted Hungarian ever wrote but about the best anybody ever wrote. After thirty-odd years it is still played constantly on the radio, and last year it was revived, with another libretto, in Paris, and pulled in the cash customers in their thousands. Which seems to place the responsibility for its deplorable failure on Broadway squarely on the shoulders of the boys who wrote the book. They felt, looking back, that where they went wrong was in being too ingenious in devising a plot to replace the original Viennese libretto, which, like all Viennese librettos, was simply terrible.
>
> It was one of those plots where somebody poses as somebody else and it turns out that he really was somebody else, they just think he is pretending to be some-body else. (It would be nice to make it a little clearer, but that is the best we can do.) And the odd thing is that—till the critics got at it with their hatchets—both authors thought highly of it. "Boy," Guy would say to Plum, his eyes sparkling, "you could take that plot down to the bank, and borrow money on it," and Plum, his eyes sparkling, too, would agree that you certainly could.
>
> And then the rude awakening.[3]

The action had been switched from Budapest/Vienna to Monte Carlo. In spite of scenery by Joseph Urban, a cast with Wilda Bennett, Carl Gantwoort, and (Eu)Gene Lockhart, and Julian Mitchell's ensemble staging, *The Riviera Girl* indeed proved a dud, partially due to anti-Viennese feeling in the United States.

Because of the war, London had to wait until 1921. *The Gipsy Princess* ap-peared at the Prince of Wales's Theatre on 20 May with Sári Petráss as Sylva and a supporting cast of Billy Leonard, Mark Lester, and Phyllis Titmuss. The British version had a book by Arthur Miller and lyrics by Arthur Stanley which proved as unmemorable as the U.S. edition's. *A Csárdáskirálynó* had appeared in Budapest at the Királyszínház (King's Theatre) with Emma Kosáry drawing all to see her in November 1916. It remains a repertory staple throughout East-ern Europe, often called *Sylva*. The first Parisian production did not take place until March 1930, at the Trianon-Lyrique, but it was a great sensation, and *Princesse Czardas* is still quite popular in France.

In spite of genial high spirits and a particularly varied score, *Die Csárdásfürstin* until recently failed to attract in Anglo-Saxon areas, though the book is no more contrived or silly than others, and the score is remembered, if in a piecemeal fashion. The waltzes *"Mädchen gibt es wunderfeine"* and *"Tausend kleine Engel singen"* are luxuriant, the songs for Sylva, the *csárdás* and the overflowingly melodious *"O jag dem Glück nicht nach"* in the first act finale, and an excellent Act II finale contribute to a brilliant whole. Even more popular are the comic songs, such as Graf Boni's slow march, *"Ganz ohne Liebe geht die Chose nicht"*

[3]P. G. Wodehouse and Guy Bolton, *Bring on the Girls,* pp. 73–74.

in Act I, which have set Eastern European feet tapping for years. A particularly popular British revival, newly translated by Nigel Douglas, was seen at London's Sadler's Wells Theatre in 1981 and again in 1982.

Die Csárdásfürstin was filmed at least thrice in Germany (and once in Russia), and has also been a television staple in many European countries, including one production in West Germany starring Anna Moffo and René Kollo.

Miss Susie was finally given a Viennese try, as *Die Faschingsfee* (The Carnival Fairy) with Günther again (in a contemporary Munich setting) at the Johann-Strauss-Theater (21 September 1917). It was not successful. However, in Berlin, with Fritzi Massary, it proved popular and its principal slow waltz, *"Lieber Himmelsvater, sei nicht bös' "* was well regarded. Bela Jenbach and Leo Stein provided a more interesting libretto for *Das Hollandweibchen* (The Little Dutch Girl, Johann-Strauss-Theater, 31 January 1920) which ran over 450 performances. Seymour Hicks presented (with J. L. Sachs) the British production, at the Lyric, opening the same year and running 214 performances; the cast included Maggie Teyte and Jack Hulbert, with an English libretto by Hicks and Harry Graham. The title song, a sweeping waltz, is so captivating that modern revivals have been arranged around this one number.

Die Bajadere (Carltheater, 23 December 1921), originally starred Louis Treumann and Christl Mardayn as lovers, with Louise Kartousch and Ernst Tautenhayn in comic parts. *La Bayadère* is the name of an operetta-within-an-operetta playing at the Châtelet, Paris, in the first act. Instead of setting the plot in India—a traditionally fatal milieu for operetta—the librettists Julius Brammer and Alfred Grünwald kept the action in Paris, introducing Prince Radjami, heir to the throne of Lahore, as a visiting potentate. The interior operetta had a Hindu story, with the operetta star Odette Darimonde appearing as the slave girl Leilo Rahi. Needless to say, the Prince falls in love with Odette, finally taking her back to Lahore after mysterious scenes of near-hypnotism and a conventional lovers' quarrel in Act II. The comic subplot between Marietta and Napoléon was particularly built up, and the operetta contained several pleasant songs—exotic "Indian" melodies, Viennese waltzes, and the usual paprika. It could stand a revival if only by virtue of the exotic-1920s situations, like the Indian wedding ceremony, which included the binding of the wrists and lines like "White flower of love, offer me the red of your lips to kiss." Librettists Brammer and Grünwald had already provided big hits for, among others, Leo Fall *(Die Rose von Stambul)* and Oscar Straus *(Der letzte Walzer);* their future triumphs included such Kálmán works as *Gräfin Mariza, Die Zirkusprinzessin,* and *Die Herzogin von Chicago* and other libretti for Straus and Paul Ábrahám.

Erlanger's New York production of *Die Bajadere,* book by William Le Baron, lyrics by B. G. DeSylva, and gorgeous décor by Joseph Urban (Knickerbocker, 2 October 1922) was entitled *The Yankee Princess.* Not to be confused with George M. Cohan's *The Yankee Prince,* the title was no doubt chosen to (possibly) convince the audience that it was a "native" rather than a European musical, and to that end Odette, played by Vivienne Segal, was turned into an American prima donna. Thorpe Bates (in the original cast of *The Maid of the*

Mountains in London) was Radjami. It did not run long, even if the score was praised.

The next work was a true Kálmán *chef-d'oeuvre*, one of the best of all the Hungarian-Austrian conciliations apart from Strauss's *Zigeunerbaron*. *Gräfin Mariza* (Theater an der Wien, 28 February 1924), text by Brammer and Grünwald, stands head high to this day, thanks to its superb score. While retaining the stock format of the earlier Kálmán and other Viennese works of the era—the romantic duets, the subordinate comic numbers, even the order of the songs— the melodic sparkle and instrumental color were remarkably vivid. Produced by and starring the new manager of the Theater an der Wien, Hubert Marischka (as Tassilo), with Betty Fischer (as the Countess), the neophyte variety singer Max Hansen (as Baron Zsupán), and Richard Waldemar and Hans Moser in tow, *Gräfin Mariza* had a sensational première and a basically uninterrupted run of over a year. A total of 396 performances were given until the theatre dropped the work in 1933.

The Shuberts bought the American rights, had Harry B. Smith adapt it, and provided a cast that included Yvonne d'Arle as the Countess Maritza, Walter Woolf as Tassilo, and Odette Myrtil as the gypsy Manja (a relatively unimportant role made significant by Myrtil's accomplished violin-playing). Vivian Hart and Harry K. Morton were the secondary pair, and George Hassell was Prince Populescu. The company included a hundred persons. When Mlle. d'Arle made her entrance in New York (Shubert, 18 September 1926), accompanied by two Russian wolfhounds, a bit of the scenery fell, while Hope Hampton, who had supposedly been considered for the role, sat in her box and no doubt gloated. S. L. "Roxy" Rothafel, the cinema Atlas, had come early: "I like to hear overtures," he claimed. J. Brooks Atkinson reported: "Miss Myrtil is volatile and spirited; and she plays the violin with skill. Her wanton destruction of that instrument . . . may indicate the tremendous overhead expense of all such operettas." Indeed, the Shuberts had ordered a three months' supply of violins before the opening, so confident were they of success. And a success it was, perhaps best characterized by the number Hubert Marischka had thrilled the Viennese with: *"Komm, Zigany,"* here known as "Play Gypsies—Dance Gypsies."

In Paris, the operetta appeared at the Théâtre des Champs-Élysées in May 1931, with Roger Bourdin as Tassilo and Mary Lewis as the Countess. Anton Paulik came from the Theater an der Wien to conduct. London saw it much later, in 1938, with the famed drag artiste Douglas Byng in normal male attire as Zsupán, and John Garrick as Tassilo. Maria Losseff was the British Countess. There have been at least three German film versions: 1925, 1932, and 1958.

Gräfin Mariza shares many musical and structural similarities with *Die Csárdásfürstin*, though its plot is a bit closer to that of *Die lustige Witwe*, with the

Original sheet-music cover for Kálmán's eternally popular *Gräfin Mariza* (Theater an der Wien, 1924).

act-by-act stubborn-lovers-bickering-over-wealth that had become by now a rubber-stamp convention for librettists. The Hungarian elements are as strong as ever, led of course by Tassilo's *"Komm, Zigany"* (added by request of Marischka), and the Viennese waltzes are there, too. *"Einmal möcht' ich wieder tanzen"* is a close cousin to *"Tausend kleine Engel singen."* *Csárdásfürstin's* comedy numbers have a raffishness that those in *Mariza* don't have, but this is more than made up by the long and startlingly romantic Act I finale, so good it rivals the Act II finale of *Die lustige Witwe*. The gypsy sentiment of *"Komm, Zigany"* is brilliantly juxtaposed with the spectacularly rousing invitation by Prince Populescu to go to a local boîte: *"Ja! Heut' um zehn sind wir im Tabarin."*

In Act II, the plot does not so much develop as lie down, but two songs stand out beside *"Einmal möcht' ich wieder tanzen."* The first is the irresistibly "dreamy" *"Ich möchte träumen,"* an airy slow march for the secondary lovers Lisa and Baron Zsupán, late of *Der Zigeunerbaron* and recalled to life by the Countess, looking for a fictitious name for a suitor—who then actually materializes. The other is the yearning *"Sag ja, mein Lieb', sag ja."* The second-act finale and Act III are basically repetitions, a fault of the traditional three-act form.

In 1926 came *Die Zirkusprinzessin* (The Circus Princess, Theater an der Wien, 26 March), almost, but not quite, as popular as the preceding work (344 versus 396 performances *in toto* at the Theater an der Wien). Hubert Marischka, having had such a huge success with *Gräfin Mariza,* again undertook to stage and star in the new Kálmán work, which once more had a Brammer and Grünwald libretto and a cast which included *Mariza* holdovers like Betty Fischer, Richard Waldemar, and the by-now legendary Hans Moser in another of his servant parts. Like *Die Csárdásfürstin* and *Die Bajadere,* it was a mixture of show business and aristocrats. The circus attractions were in some cases real, partially in an attempt to imitate the variety offered by the newly popular revues which were now attracting Vienna as well as Berlin. Marischka got to sing the only song from this operetta that has truly lasted, *"Zwei Märchenaugen."* The circus element was particularly lavish in the Broadway production (Winter Garden, 25 April 1927) which starred Guy Robertson and Desiree Tabor.

In New York in 1927 for *The Circus Princess,* Kálmán wrote some of the score for *Golden Dawn,* to a book by Oscar Hammerstein II and Otto Harbach (Hammerstein, 30 November 1928). There were additional songs by Herbert Stothart and Robert Stolz. Set in German-occupied equatorial Africa, this had a most improbable plot concerning a blonde (Dawn) taken for a native princess by the African villagers (played in blackface by whites). The villain was a Simon Legree-ish overseer, Shep Keyes, who lusted after Dawn. He had the best musical number, "The Whip," sung in New York by Robert Chisolm. How ludicrous

An elaborate costume design shown on the cover of sheet music for Kálmán's *Die Zirkusprinzessin* (Theater an der Wien, 1926). The actual costumes were designed by Gaston Zanel of Paris. By the 1920s, the Viennese expected some of the luxury and spectacle of revue in their operetta productions.

this operetta was can be seen by looking at the 1930 film version, with Noah Beery cracking his whip and with Vivienne Segal screeching the other big song, "My Bwana." Vienna-in-Africa, perhaps, and quite insane.

Die Herzogin von Chicago (The Duchess of Chicago, Theater an der Wien, 5 April 1928), starring Marischka, Rita Georg, and Hans Moser (as the headwaiter, Pelikan), was the next Marischka-Kálmán-Brammer-Grünwald production, with 301 performances, only slightly less moneymaking than its predecessors. The plot dealt basically with the battle between the Charleston and the waltz, then an issue of great urgency in operetta Vienna. Significantly, George Gershwin saw the show on an Austrian visit. Shortly after its première, Kálmán married a young lady he had hired for the chorus, Vera Makinska, who to this day promotes her late husband's *oeuvre* around the world.

Das Veilchen vom Montmartre (The Violet of Montmartre, Johann-Strauss-Theater, 21 March 1930) was the next work, a delicate Parisian romance that remains fairly popular in Eastern Europe (a complete recording—and many performances—are in Russian) but in the West is exclusively remembered for the tango, *"Heut' Nacht hab' ich geträumt von dir."* *Das Veilchen* had its run interrupted at the Johann-Strauss-Theater when that building was converted into a cinema; Hubert Marischka put it on at the Theater an der Wien, in a restaged version later that year. The violet turned up in its native city, Paris, in 1935 (Porte Saint-Martin) with Lotte Schone in the title role, shortly after Kálmán had been awarded the insignia of a *Chevalier* in the *Légion d'Honneur*. One wonders if this was because his latest operetta took place in a garret in Paris occupied by three struggling artists: "Raoul" Delacroix (a painter), Henry Mürger (author of the source of *La Bohème*), and Hervé (the operetta creator). The three were mixed up—most improbably—with a model, Ninon, a street singer, Violetta, and even the Baron Rothschild; the last act concerned itself with Hervé's latest operetta. However flattering Kálmán and his librettists, Brammer and Grünwald, were to French culture, the composer's award was probably given because the French adored *Princesse Czardas* and had revived it constantly. *A Kiss in Spring* (Alhambra, 28 November 1932) was the British title of *Das Veilchen vom Montmartre*.

In 1931 came Kálmán's score for the UFA film *Ronny*, with Käthe von Nagy and Willy Fritsch, and in 1932 *Der Teufelsreiter* rode briefly through Vienna (Theater an der Wien, 10 March 1932), but Kálmán's glory days were over. *Kaiserin Josephine* (Empress Josephine, Zürich, 1936) was his last work before his emigration to America, via Zürich and Paris. Although Kálmán had been decorated by the anti-Semitic, pro-Fascist Nicholas Horthy of Hungary, the dictator nevertheless advised him to leave Europe. And Hitler's representatives failed in their attempt to have Kálmán decreed an honorary Aryan. The large Kálmán *Palais* in Vienna was stripped of its valuables, which were sent to Zürich, and the Kálmán family left Austria.

Lorenz Hart's death, in 1943, stopped the Broadway production of Kálmán's *Miss Underground*, which had a book by Paul and Pauline Gallico. *Marinka* (Winter Garden, 18 July 1945) enjoyed 165 performances in New York. This was a new version of the Mayerling story, which had an upbeat ending, with the royal couple retiring peacefully to Connecticut. Fellow émigré Reinhold Schünzel, the film director, played the Kaiser Franz-Josef. A planned film of *Kaiserin Josephine*, to be directed by Ernst Lubitsch and to star Grace Moore, was thwarted by Miss Moore's death in 1947 in a plane crash in Copenhagen.

There were two more operettas in Europe, *Ronacher* (1950) and *Arizona Lady* (1954), the latter produced posthumously. Kálmán's death in Paris (30 October 1953) was followed by a state funeral in Vienna; he lies near the graves of several other operetta composers in the *Zentralfriedhof*. The composer's son, Charles (1929–   ), is a successful composer in his own right, his most popular work being a musical version of Shaw's *Mrs. Warren's Profession* (1974).

Kálmán appears to have been a quiet, professionally modest, and superstitious man—hardly the type, one would think, to have composed the exuberant *Csárdásfürstin* and *Gräfin Mariza,* his two masterpieces. He was quite as cosmopolitan a composer as Lehár, and in many ways their music was similar. Both were undisputed masters of the Viennese waltz, Kálmán often making it soar as magnificently as Lehár. Kálmán's music was more specifically Hungarian than Lehár's, who, after all, had soaked up the music of other countries in his youthful peregrinations. Kálmán's phrasing was Hungarian; it was not simply a matter of introduced cimbaloms and tambourines. In their searing way, songs like *"Komm, Zigany"* and the entrance song of Sylva Varescu have become virtual Hungarian folk songs as well as the stock international operetta depictions of Hungary itself. Both of Kálmán's masterworks are continually played and recorded. The Hungarians have shown a recent interest in some of the other compositions of its native son, while the British have been busy with Kálmán ever since the unprecedentedly popular revival of *The Gipsy Princess* in London in 1981. With the 1982 Kálmán Centenary behind us, it will be interesting to see what revivals will occur. Probably because of the opportunities for spectacle, *Die Bajadere* would seem the best candidate for reexamination outside of Hungary. It would most likely veer toward pure camp, but if this were resisted, even partially (and a few strong numbers from the other lesser works were interpolated), a colorful piece of 1920s theatre might come vibrantly alive.

THE LAST WALTZ
AT THE GAIETY THEATRE.

SILVER VIENNA

C LOSE on the heels of *The Merry Widow* were numerous Viennese operettas by other composers, mounted by the managers of the Theater an der Wien, the Carltheater, and other theatres, not only for the delectation of the Viennese but also for the scouts of international producers looking for operetta hits of the stature of Lehár's triumph. Almost any halfway decent Viennese work was bought for American, British, or French consumption, in addition to the usual traffic throughout Central and Northern Europe. Not all were presented, but among those that were, there was always the hope that another blockbuster would be found.

Bad Ischl, the spa outside Vienna, was at this time a hotbed of operetta composition, as it had been in the previous century. Composers and librettists would often retreat to hotel rooms and rented villas to turn out their masterpieces and their flops. If the "Tin Pan Alley" of Viennese operetta was not at Ischl, it was possibly at the numerous cafés in Vienna which catered to a theatrical clientèle.

Many composers were once café pianists, including Straus and Benatzky. Although there were doubtless rivalries between operetta creators, there was also a sense of camaraderie, especially among the more successful practitioners who often had their works alternately playing at the same theatres.

Leo Fall and Oscar Straus were consistently popular abroad, often rivaling Lehár and Kálmán, while works by several other composers and their usual librettists attained certain Viennese and Berliner, if not international, popularity. The supply of Viennese works was effectively cut off by World War I, during which time London, for example, was forced to turn to native efforts and ragtime revues for light entertainment. It was during the war that Vienna and Berlin saw some excellent operettas, like *Die Csárdásfürstin* and *Die Rose von Stambul,* shows that failed to repeat their success in the allied capitals after the

---

José Collins as Vera Lisaveta in the London presentation of Oscar Straus's *The Last Waltz* at the Gaiety Theatre in 1922.

war because the vogue for Viennese operetta had been severely dampened. During the 1920s, along with the ultra-romantic Lehár confections, certain operetta composers and authors were forced to kowtow to the post-ragtime forms of American popular music in order to recapture audiences. When the late 1920s operetta, already a watered-down, cheapened commodity, collided with the singing silver screen, operetta's Silver Age was virtually over.

Oscar Straus (1870–1954)—not Strauss—was born into a prosperous Jewish family. His father was a banker, though previous generations had been connected with a feather *(Strauss)* business in Mannheim. He was *not* related to the other operetta titan. Oscar had a luxurious childhood: summers at Bad Ischl, the rest of the year in the Leopoldstadt district, a very comfortable part of Vienna.

At the age of sixteen, he was transfixed by the D'Oyly Carte production of Sullivan's *Mikado* at the Carltheater (1 September 1886). He studied with Max Bruch in Berlin, who thought a classical career was advisable, but Straus instead listened to Johann Strauss II, who urged him to conduct operettas in the provinces. With the great success of *The Geisha* and *Der Opernball* in 1898 in Vienna, Straus was increasingly attracted to the operetta stage, and he and the then-unknown Leo Fall, whose career was to parallel Straus's, became friends in Berlin. While Fall was busy conducting at suburban Berlin theatres, Straus accepted the post of a cabaret pianist at the Secession Theater in the Alexanderplatz. For this *Überbrettl* Straus composed his first song hit, *"Die Musik kommt"* (The music comes), followed over a short period by a great many other *Brettllieder;* these were catchy, often satirical songs.

After several early operas, Straus teamed with the well-known humorist "Rideamus" (Berlin lawyer Fritz Oliven) to write *Die lustigen Nibelungen* (The Merry Nibelungs, 1904), a burlesque of Wagner aimed directly at those "perfect Wagnerites" who showed excessive devotion to the Ring. Produced at the Carltheater that November, the burlesque proved too musically advanced for Viennese ears; Berlin enjoyed it far more. Its revivals have been few; national-socialist pro-Wagnerians caused a disturbance in Graz (Austria) in the early 1900s, and Straus refused to permit a Paris production in 1938. But the book is witty and the music is unusually satiric for 1904. Ignatz Schnitzer (*Zigeunerbaron's* librettist) provided a book for *Zur indischen Witwe,* a flop at the Centraltheater, Berlin, in 1905, while *Hugdietrichs Brautfahrt* (Hugdietrich's Honeymoon) fared no better later that year, in spite of critical raves for the Viennese première at the Carltheater.

With the gradually phenomenal success of *The Merry Widow,* in 1905 at the rival Theater an der Wien, Straus decided to leave his satirical or fantastical libretti and drop the idea of creating an Austrian equivalent of Offenbach's Bouffes-Parisiens at the Carltheater. As soon as he retreated to the comfortable, sentimental Viennese type of operetta, Straus had a world hit.

The librettist Leopold Jacobson was supposedly so taken by the girls' orchestra, "The Prater Swallows," at the Eisvogel Restaurant in the famed Vienna amusement park that he grafted it onto his treatment of *Nux, the Prince Consort,* a tale from Hans Müller's *Adventure Book.* Felix Dörmann furnished the lyrics and *Ein Walzertraum* was produced at the Carltheater on 2 March 1907. The original cast's lovers were Mizzi Zwerenz and Fritz Werner.

One reason it became an intensely popular favorite was because of its sad story, of Lieutenant Niki of the Hussars, already married at the beginning of Act I to Princess Helene of Flaunsenthurn, and his brief fling with Franzi, the orchestra girl from Vienna. The charm of the piece lies in its romantic yearning for old Vienna, a Vienna that was already fading into the romantic mists at the twilight of the Austro-Hungarian Empire. No one song better epitomized this romance than Straus's dreamy waltz *"Leise, ganz leise"* (Gently, so gently), and its impact was of such force that it carried the piece all over the world. It was Straus's finest hour.

Within two years, *A Waltz Dream* was playing at many of the five hundred to six hundred German and Austro-Hungarian city and provincial theatres, its initial Viennese engagement having outrun *The Merry Widow*'s. The New York version (Broadway, 27 January 1908) ran less than six months. Magda Dahl, as Franzi, made little impression, "but it remained for Edward Johnson [later manager of the Metropolitan Opera, New York] in the song of the waltz to first stir the audience to its full fervor of enthusiasm," said one critic. Another, from the *Dramatic Mirror,* remarked that "lavishness rather than taste is displayed in the scenery and costumes," and "the woman's orchestra is rather loud in trumpets and drums." But all the critics admired the girls' fiddling.

For a city that had been one of the first outside the German-speaking world to dote on the silver Viennese operetta, London did not respond to *A Waltz Dream* with much enthusiasm. The first British production (Hicks's, 28 March 1908), produced by George Edwardes, suffered from miscasting: the pert Lancashire-bred musical-comedy star Gertie Millar hardly gave the impression of a sentimental Viennese girl. Weak English lyrics by the usually adept Adrian Ross—"certainly not great, either musically or in a literary sense," said the *Illustrated Sporting and Dramatic News*—and a comparatively sad ending disturbed London audiences. There were first-night compensations: Robert Evett as Niki, George Grossmith, Jr., as Count Lothar (who beefed up his comparatively small part with an interpolated number, "The Gay Lothario," music by Jerome Kern), Straus himself conducting, and Queen Alexandra, the Dowager Empress of Russia, with the Princess Victoria in the Royal Box. But, according to the *Daily Telegraph:*

> . . . the whole cast did not seem to quite catch the right spirit. It was not gay enough, and yet too flippant—that is to say, the whole play loses much of its point unless we realise that to the Viennese the waltz is something of a cult, and more than just a mere adjunct to promiscuous flirtation.

Straus himself, interviewed in London, could not understand the "success" of *Ein Walzertraum* abroad, with its "serious ending—which has never been tried before." In fact, the British public resisted it again, in an improved production (Daly's, 7 January 1911) seeking to capitalize on the huge popularity of Straus's *The Chocolate Soldier*.

In Paris, *Rêve de Valse* (Apollo, 3 March 1910) ran about three months, with Alice Bonheur and Henri Defreyn heading the cast. It has been filmed rather memorably twice, the first time in a silent version (1925) by Ludwig Berger, the second time as *The Smiling Lieutenant* (1931) by Ernst Lubitsch. With attractive casts (Mady Christians, Willy Fritsch; Claudette Colbert, Maurice Chevalier) these were picturesque depictions of a mythical Vienna, in both cases with only the principal tunes played along (and not in any way in their original state). The music did not get in the way of the treacly story.

The score is basically a one-tune affair, and that one tune is of course the "title" song, *"Leise, ganz leise"* which later composers like Sigmund Romberg would use as a model for their sentimental efforts. The rest of the music, whether sprightly *("Piccolo, Piccolo, Tsin Tsin Tsin")* or romantic, while scored with much elegance, has not quite the same wondrous appeal. One exceptional number is the winning "Temperament" trio in Act II.

Der tapfere Soldat (The Gallant Soldier) was another Leopold Jacobson brainchild—a musical version of G. B. Shaw's *Arms and the Man*, which had been a substantial hit in Vienna. Jacobson and Straus, who thought the idea splendid, approached Shaw through his able German translator-agent, Siegfried Trebitsch, but Shaw refused to consider the proposal, arguing that if the operetta were a success his play would be forgotten. Trebitsch, however, did not give up and Shaw ultimately agreed to allow the plot to be used, but no dialogue, providing (a) that all advertising and programmes bear the legend that the play was "an unauthorized parody of Mr. Bernard Shaw's play, *Arms and the Man*" and (b) that he receive no royalties from it. However Shavian the first proviso was, the second proved to be a hugely expensive mistake.

Apparently trying to make up for this tremendous loss of royalties, Shaw asked for an appropriately tremendous sum from Louis B. Mayer when MGM sought to buy the rights of *Arms and the Man* in the 1930s so that they could film *The Chocolate Soldier* with Nelson Eddy and Jeanette MacDonald. Mayer expected them to understand each other and reach a compromise, but Shaw wouldn't budge from his original figure: "No, Mr. Mayer, I fear we two will never understand each other. You're an idealist, you see, whereas I'm only a businessman!" In the end, Molnár's *The Guardsman* was used for the plot of the mediocre 1940 film, without Jeanette.

The Theater an der Wien (14 November 1908) saw the première of the *Praliné-Soldat* operetta, but actual recent Balkan disturbances and some thoughtless miscasting stunted its growth, and with bad notices and resulting poor attendance, the run was short (62 performances) and Vienna forgot about it, save for Max Pallenberg's impersonation of Colonel Popoff. (To this day, it is seldom, if ever, revived in Central Europe.) Manager Fred C. Whitney had bought the American rights before the show's opening and was wary about producing it at all, but *The Chocolate Soldier* (a much catchier and more apropos title) was a great success in its tryout and later on Broadway, where it ran for nine months

(Lyric, 13 September 1909), with Ida Brooks Hunt and J. E. Gardner. There were several touring companies.

Whitney then prepared for the London edition (Lyric, 10 September 1910), with Constance Drever as Nadina and C. H. Workman, the ex-Savoyard, as Bumerli, singing Stanislaus Stange's English version. Character and plot divergences from *Arms and the Man* caused no difficulties here, and Shaw's outbursts in the press against the "chocolate cream soldier" certainly didn't hurt publicity, nor did other helpful but groundless rumors that Shaw actually had a hand in the libretto. B. W. Findon, in the *Play Pictorial,* singled out what had become the operetta's chief drawing card: "Nadina's first song, 'Come, come, my life,' " with its delicious valse refrain, is a vocal gem . . ." A gem indeed, which would be repeated by countless singers for decades to come. "My Hero" remains the chief attraction in this work, like its predecessor having one great waltz surrounded by a number of only slightly less catchy songs and ensembles. One elegant delight is the title duet, with its charming counterpointed refrain.

It was not surprising that most of the London critics remarked how favorably *The Chocolate Soldier* resembled a comic opera rather than a typical musical comedy; one even called it the best since *The Mikado* (1885). This no doubt gratified Straus, who remarked in that London interview of 1908, "I find that the humorous side here is developed so much that the piece becomes almost grotesque. Abroad we insist much more on the sentimental side." Which explains why the too-sentimental *Waltz Dream*—especially its dénouement—displeased Londoners totally. Commenting on the differences in presentation between Vienna and London, Straus went on:

". . . Your choruses too are much bigger, and the ladies, I must admit, are much younger; and also the orchestra—and I must say this—are bigger and better; and, too, you have many more songs than we are content with. Because of this I have had to compose five new numbers for London."

George Grossmith, who had been to Vienna to see *Ein Walzertraum* at the Carltheater, found the production of the "poorest description . . . a 'fit-up,' doing one-night stands in Wales, would have been ashamed of the hideous dresses and tawdry scenery." *Le Soldat de Chocolat* hit the Apollo, Paris, in 1912.

Straus had little luck with *Didi* (1909), which had a plot from Sardou that was all too similar to Lehár's *Der Graf von Luxemburg,* then in the works, but his full-length comic opera *Das Tal der Liebe* (1909) was more of a hit at the Volksoper. *Mein junger Herr* (1910) was not successful in Vienna or in London, where it was seen briefly at the Shaftesbury in 1926 as *My Son John.* There were other minor works, among them a one-act play for puppets with an Arthur

---

OVERLEAF: Oscar Straus's *The Chocolate Soldier* at one time commanded perhaps more popularity in the United Kingdom and the United States than it did as *Der tapfere Soldat* in Austria or Germany. The Act II finale of the first London production (Lyric, 1910), with C. H. Workman as Bumerli.

Schnitzler libretto, *Der tapfere Cassian* (The Brave Cassian), and a ballet, *Die Prinzessin von Tragant*. In 1912, he composed two musicals for the London stage, *The Dancing Viennese* (Coliseum) and *Love and Laughter* (Lyric). The events of 1914 kept Straus in Vienna: his *Rund um die Liebe* (Circle of Love) was based on Goldoni's *Servant of Two Masters; Die schöne Unbekannte* (The Beautiful Unknown), known in America as *Her Lady's Glove,* appeared the following year.

There were other works, but the war seemed to be sapping the lifeblood of some of Vienna's operetta composers and the attitude of its operetta-going public, which greatly preferred the escapist *Dreimäderlhaus* to the more modern, up-to-date Straus works. Straus himself toured for the Red Cross, entertaining wounded soldiers in hospitals.

After the war, Straus settled in Berlin, thenceforward operetta's more luxurious *endroit,* and set a libretto by Brammer and Grünwald eventually called *Der letzte Walzer* (The Last Waltz). In Berlin, the collaborators met Fritzi Massary, who had enjoyed a great triumph during the war as the star of Leo Fall's *Die Rose von Stambul*. Massary was to create six leading roles for Straus, the first and most striking being Vera Lisaveta in *The Last Waltz,* which the authors had to revise extensively for her when she said she would appear in it. *The Last Waltz* appeared at the Berliner Theater (12 February 1920), was a total triumph, and was repeated all over Europe to equal enthusiasm. New York saw it in 1921 (Century, 10 May) presented by the Shuberts, with Eleanor Painter as Vera and Walter Woolf as Lieutenant Jack Merrington, of the U.S. Navy. James Barton was endearing in a comedy role and there were numerous national dances—Russian, Egyptian, Spanish—in the opulent "Vandalian" settings, dreamed up by the Shubert's house designer, Watson Barratt. The Viennese première occurred later (Theater an der Wien, 27 October 1921), with the London edition the following year (Gaiety, 7 December 1922), directed by the eminent comedian Sir Charles Hawtrey. It starred José Collins, now in a continental part, with Bertram Wallis (not singing) and Amy Augarde. The London *Times* called it "a rather heavy light opera," but Alexander Woolcott, on the New York *Times,* had nothing but raves: ". . . no equal in light opera in this city in the last ten years . . . one of the most enjoyable musical shows of recent seasons . . . You suspect 'Charming Ladies' and 'A Baby in Love' of having been baptized in the East River rather than the Blue Danube . . ." No doubt, as they were written by Al Goodman for the New York production. Paris did not see the operetta until 1936, at the Gaîté-Lyrique.

As "heavy" as *The Last Waltz* was, it had an attractively lighter score than either *A Waltz Dream* or *The Chocolate Soldier*. And with its title waltz song, it paved the way for a lighter, better, less pretentious Straus. Among the other waltzes that audiences relished were *"Rosen, die wir nicht erreichten"* (Love the Minstrel, in Reginald Arkell's English) and Vera's final song, *"Flieh hin, du gold'ner Liebestraum"* (Farewell, My Golden Love-dream Bright). The 1920s and '30s were to be Straus's best years, and he had Massary principally to thank.

When *Die Perlen der Cleopatra* (Theater an der Wien, 13 November 1923), the next Massary property, was seen in Vienna, Max Pallenberg and the newcomer

Richard Tauber supported the star. In London, Evelyn Laye was starred in it at Daly's (2 June 1925) in an attempt to have her obtain another smash in a Massary role. But *Cleopatra* was unadmired, lasting only three months in the West End. In 1924, Massary had a less than successful time with *Tanz um die Liebe* (Dance Around Love), but *La Teresina* the next year bolstered her Berlin reputation, and *Die Königin* (The Queen) was an even bigger success in 1926.

In 1928, Straus contributed the music to Sacha Guitry's *Mariette, ou Comment on écrit l'Histoire* (How History is written, Édouard VII, 1 October) a story in which an old woman tells a reporter of her escapades with Emperor Napoléon III years before. Guitry played both Louis Napoléon and the inquisitive journalist, while Yvonne Printemps played the singer, Mariette. Guitry, by 1928, was reputedly jealous of his second wife and reportedly did not relish the idea of leaving his adored Yvonne alone on the stage with another man during the final act. This may have been true, but he also liked the idea of appearing as several characters in the course of one performance. The British critic James Agate mentioned that "Mlle. Printemps a little overstresses the *gaucherie* of Mariette, just as she holds on a little too long to her top notes . . ." but the same writer found Straus's music "charming." The Printemps recording of *"Depuis trois ans passés"* is, at once, a song perfectly tailored for the singer and an indication of the easygoing new, light style of the composer. Like *The Last Waltz* without Massary, *Mariette* succeeded without Printemps elsewhere in Europe: in Vienna and Berlin, Käthe Dorsch very successfully took the part in the expert translation of Alfred Grünwald.

Another product of 1928 was *Hochzeit in Hollywood*, seen in Vienna (Johann-Strauss-Theater, 21 December 1928) and later, fittingly enough, on the Hollywood talking-singing-dancing screen, as *Married in Hollywood*. It starred J. Harold Murray (late of the stage *Rio Rita*) and Norma Terris (late of the stage *Show Boat*). Marcel Silver's Fox film was the first European operetta to be filmed with sound, and it was well received. The New York *Times:* "An especially fine example of vocal recording . . . adroitly interspersed with joviality and extremely clever photographic embellishments. The principal songs are charmingly rendered."

Two Straus works from the 1930s had wide currency: *Eine Frau, die weiss was sie will* (A Woman Who Knows What She Wants, 1932) and *Drei Walzer* (Three Waltzes, 1935). The woman who knew what she wanted was Fritzi Massary, and the Alfred Grünwald libretto was comparatively realistic: a celebrated actress nearing middle age finds she is losing her lover to (of all people) her daughter. The Metropol-Theater première of *Eine Frau . . .* in the autumn of 1932 was one of the last glittering theatrical events Berlin would ever see: the Nazi takeover would deprive Germany of Straus, Massary, Grünwald, and many other operetta specialists. Straus fled to his native Austria, where he was able to stay until the *Anschluss*. *Eine Frau . . .* was produced in London (Gaiety, 27 January 1933), with Alice Delysia, as *Mother of Pearl* in A. P. Herbert's witty version. The big hit song in Berlin (and London) was *Jede Frau hat irgendeine Sehnsucht* (or, Every Woman Thinks She Wants to Wander) with which Massary would enthrall her audiences simply by sitting in a chair. In London, C. B. Cochran's production was played 181 times. Zarah Leander appeared in it in Sweden.

Drei Walzer (Three Waltzes) was written in Vienna and first produced in Zürich (5 October 1935), where it was well received. A few other cities performed it; the Paris production (Bouffes-Parisiens, 22 April 1937) with Yvonne Printemps and Pierre Fresnay, made the operetta world-famous. Not that this was difficult: Paris was at that time hosting a world's fair. The situation exactly paralleled one seventy years before: an operetta by a German-Jewish composer with a magnificent French star was drawing Paris and her international guests like a musical magnet. *La Grande-Duchesse de Gérolstein* was, assuredly, a better work, and its score was wholly original. *Les Trois Valses* was a quasi-pastiche affair, but excellently done. Paul Knepler and Armin Robinson's libretto covered three generations (1865, 1900, 1935) and used for each of its three acts songs by Oscar Straus based on music by, respectively, Johann Strauss I, II, and Oscar Straus. (This was slightly anachronistic, as the first two composers were dead before the times of their acts.) In Act I, Fanny Pichler is a famous ballet-dancer, in Act II, Charlotte Pichler, Fanny's daughter, is a big operetta star, and in Act III, Charlotte's daughter Franzi is a film star. All three, renamed, were played to perfection in Paris by Printemps, and her consorts were romantically incarnated by Fresnay, her husband in real life. He supported her, like her first husband Sacha Guitry, with sonorously intoned dialogue. Each of the three acts had at least one stunning waltz. In Act I, *"Wien ist ein Liebeslied"* (Vienna is a love song, but in French *"C'est la saison d'amour,"* or, It's the season for love); Act II's hit—the biggest in the operetta—was *"Ich liebe das Leben"* (I love life, or, *"Je t'aime,"* I love you, or "Forever," in its British version). And the third act contained *"Man sagt sich beim Abschied adieu"* (One says adieu at parting, or *"C'est le destin, peut-être"*).

There was an attempt to catch the flavor of the past in Straus's use of the Strauss melodies, and there was a finale in the second act that represented the second-act finale of a fictitious operetta in the course of the plot. The French libretto by Léopold Marchand and Albert Willemetz made two very important changes to accommodate the Printemps-Fresnay duo: the male lead was changed from a tenor to a nonsinging role, and the action was switched to Paris, permitting the three acts to coincide with three famous universal expositions (1867, 1900, 1937). Pichler thus became Grandpré, and the family name of the boyfriends became de Chalencay.

Les Trois Valses was an incomparable triumph. *Le tout-Paris* was there for the opening night, and everyone else every night subsequently. Fresnay staged, Marcel Cariven conducted, and the records made of the production were (and remain) best-sellers, spreading the popularity of the operetta all over France. To this day, the French have been the work's staunchest fans. In 1938, the stars took a cue from the show's third act and appeared in a highly successful film version, directed by the exiled Ludwig Berger. Mme. Printemps's Lanvin gowns contributed to the film's gloss.

Three Waltzes was not as popular in English. On Broadway (Majestic, 25

December 1937), an adaptation starring Kitty Carlisle and Michael Bartlett lasted four months, while the London edition (Princes, 1 March 1945), with Evelyn Laye and Esmond Knight, ran only slightly longer. When, in his Straus biography, Bernard Grun stated that Straus's "obituaries are also the obituaries of the Viennese operetta," he was not far from the truth. *Drei Walzer,* in 1935, was the last respectable Austrian work, the last to achieve a worldwide reputation. Yet, it was a part-pastiche creation—the originality of the previous years had perhaps evaporated.

Straus continued writing until his death in 1951, but his last great hit was for the cinema: the waltz theme for the Max Ophuls film *La Ronde* (1950); the follow-up was *"L'Amour m'emporte"* for *Madame de . . .* (1951). Straus's work for films should not be underestimated. During his Hollywood stay in the early '30s, besides the adaptation of his music for *The Smiling Lieutenant,* he wrote several superb numbers for *One Hour with You,* one of the very best of that era's sophisticated operetta films. These included "Day After Day (We Will Always Be Sweethearts)" for Jeanette MacDonald and "Oh, That Mitzi!" for Maurice Chevalier. When Straus was simple, piquant, and (preferably) cheerful, his music was undeniably effective. His waltzes, at their best, had a sentimental Viennese flavor, but often without much *Schwung.* There are exceptions: the title waltz from *Der letzte Walzer* is a melodious, lilting one. And while he occasionally grasped it, he did not always have the bittersweet beauty that Fall, Lehár, or Kálmán so regularly displayed. He was at his best with songs and ensembles that did not strive for too much: the comic numbers from the 1920s and '30s for stage and screen were among his best creations.

Leo Fall (1873–1925) was the son of a military bandmaster, like Franz Lehár, and was born in Moravia (now in Czechoslovakia). His father had written several marches, and an operetta, and Leo's younger brothers Richard and Siegfried were also to become professional musicians. Enrolled at the Vienna Conservatory at the age of fourteen—Edmund Eysler was a classmate—Fall later met Franz Lehár in the violin section of Lehár's father's 50th Infantry Regiment band.

Moving in the early 1890s to Berlin, Fall joined his father's coffeehouse ensemble, later taking up conducting assignments in and around the capital. He contributed numbers to a Viktor Holländer revue at the Metropol-Theater in 1901, *Eine feine Nummer,* and composed songs for cabarets much in the Oscar Straus *Überbrettl* style. An opera, *Irrlicht,* had a Mannheim production (1904) and his first operetta was seen at the Theater an der Wien, *Der Rebell* (29 November 1905). Neither was a success, but the Viennese theatre had faith enough to commission the full-length work that was later to become *Die Dollarprinzessin.* But the Mannheim Hoftheater was the site of Fall's first hit, *Der fidele Bauer* (27 July 1907). Later produced in Vienna after the success of *The Merry Widow* and *The Dollar Princess,* but actually composed before either work, *The Merry Peasant* was at first considered too naïve, its rustic setting and characters too folksy and Eyslerish for the more cosmopolitanized Viennese taste. Nevertheless, it made a substantial impression there, and it was occasionally revived. A

London production appeared at the Strand Theatre with Courtice Pounds and Florence St. John (1909). The songs in this early work show a rhythmic verve and a sensuous sense of melody that only Kálmán and Lehár could match: particularly fetching were the title march and the entrancing waltz *"Jeder trägt sein Pinkerl."* The dialect libretto by Viktor Léon has proved one of the enduring charms of the operetta.

Die Dollarprinzessin (The Dollar Princess)—probably internationally Fall's most successful property—opened at the Theater an der Wien on 2 November 1907 with a stellar cast including Louis Treumann and Mizzi Günther, following their triumph in *The Merry Widow,* and, making a sensational debut, a new soubrette, Louise Kartousch, as Daisy Gray. This was one of the major Viennese works to be set in the New World, with more than a little notice paid to the opulent Anglo/American musical comedy. Its locales were an up-to-date New York City and "Aliceville," Canada; there was an opening chorus of female typists, an *Automobil-Marsch,* a trio, *"Amerika, gib acht!"* and a story that had to do with the taming of the daughter of an American millionaire, John Couder. The A. M. Willner–Fritz Grünbaum libretto, based on a comedy by Gatti-Trotha, was totally up-to-date, and, unlike most of the operettas of its period, more capitalist than royalist, not to mention feminist. Alice, Couder's daughter, proclaims herself a real *"Selfmade-mädel."*

Fall's real gift for conversational duets and ensembles burst forth in *Die Dollarprinzessin.* Stemming naturally from the dialogue, they continued it within the confines of a typically elegant and often quite convoluted series of verses and choruses. The simple romantic duet was too simple for Fall, whose duets were more like the realistic banter of people in love than the usual formalized operetta duets were. Fall's other precious commodity was his melodic genius. In Act II of *The Dollar Princess* comes one of the first great hits: the Hans-Daisy duet beginning *"Paragraph eins,"* and containing the irresistible refrain, *Wir tanzen Ringelreih'n* (We're dancing Ring-a-rosy). Its playful, childish charm and the sophisticated innocence of its haunting melody would influence one American composer prodigiously—Jerome Kern. In fact, Kern supplied two songs for the American première. There were also, obligatorily, several big waltzes, the first tremendous international Fall hits: *"Will sie dann lieben treu und heiss"* and the title quartet, *"Das sind die Dollarprinzessin."*

George Edwardes's London production, planned before *The Merry Widow,* had to wait a very long time before Lehár's triumph began to subside in popularity, so it wasn't until 25 September 1909, at Daly's, that the West End was introduced to Fall's magic. And, as at the Theater an der Wien, the *Merry Widow* stars stepped into their new roles—Lily Elsie, Joseph Coyne (now a millionaire brother rather than father of the heroine), and even W. H. Berry. Robert Michaelis, who had gone into the role of Prince Danilo four months before *The Merry Widow* had its final curtain, played the romantic lead, Freddy Fairfax. Gabrielle Ray was the soubrette, and Gladys Cooper played a Californian. During its tryout in Manchester, "Guv'nor" Edwardes said in an interview to the *Evening Chronicle:*

> It is in presenting a play that the English theatre can outrival the Continent. Take, for instance, *The Merry Widow.* As put before a Viennese audience, the play would not be recognized in England, the presentation in this country was so much superior . . . I saw *The Dollar Princess,* bought it, altered it, and am now producing it."

Some of the changes by Basil Hood (book) and Adrian Ross (lyrics) of Willner and Grünbaum's original included an entirely new third act, set in California, a comedy part for W. H. Berry, and also some song interpolations.

The opening night was naturally a glittering event (after the prior Daly's smash) and the reaction was cheeringly favorable. The *Daily Mail:* "A comedy, it has been set to music which is . . . as in the operettes of Sullivan, Strauss and Offenbach . . . essentially and triumphantly the thing." Coyne as Couder and the lovely Lily Elsie as his sister-heiress, dazzling pastel gowns, ravishing sets by Alfred Terraine and Joseph Harker, and a taut *mise-en-scène* by Edward Royce (a new Edwardes recruit) drove *The Dollar Princess* to a roaring success (428 performances). The Fall score was universally praised, especially for the sheen and expertise of its finales. (Note that the Viennese considered 117 *uncon-secutive* performances of *Die Dollarprinzessin* in six years an overwhelming success.)

Charles Frohman's New York production differed from the London *Dollar Princess,* though it did have a libretto by George Grossmith, Jr. (the Gaiety star) and was directed by J. A. E. Malone—both Edwardes personnel. Opening on Broadway at the Knickerbocker 6 September 1909, it starred, again, a famous ex-Danilo, Donald Brian, paired on this occasion with Valli Valli. It was a strange pair: Valli, an English actress, played the rich American girl while Brian, as American as corned beef and cabbage, played the Englishman. Grossmith's book was hardly admired—one critic claimed that "no one could accuse *The Dollar Princess* of being funny"—and it was odd that Frohman should have picked the English star to concoct a different libretto for American consumption when he might have used the Hood/Ross version.

Grossmith, not satisfied with either Canada or California (too American, no doubt), set his third act at the Franco-British Exhibition in London, not too cleverly basing this on a similar act in *Our Miss Gibbs.* But *The Dollar Princess* succeeded, running over 100 performances in New York and many more on various tours. There were two Jerome Kern interpolations in the Broadway version, and Fall himself obligingly sent four extra songs to Frohman for possible use after he heard of the operetta's Broadway success.

Back in Vienna, *Die geschiedene Frau* (The Divorcée, 23 December 1908) had appeared at the Carltheater with a Viktor Léon libretto and Anny Dirkens, Mizzi Zwerenz, and Hubert Marischka in the cast. It was a huge hit, and its main waltzes swept through European palm-court orchestras, dance halls, restaurants, and streets with a frenzy. *The Divorcée* was a title quite as charmingly scandalous as *The Merry Widow*, and its first act, a great deal of it set to music, takes place in the novel precincts of a Dutch courtroom during a divorce trial. Shades of *Trial by Jury;* perhaps Fall or Léon had seen either of the two versions of Sullivan's great masterpiece in Vienna.

Altered for its George Edwardes London presentation (4 June 1910) and wisely compressed into two acts (sumptuously painted by Alfred Terraine), *Die geschiedene Frau* was changed to *The Girl in the Train*, reflecting the vogue for "girl" in Edwardian titles. It opened with a starry cast at the Vaudeville (Daly's was busy with Fall's previous hit): Robert Evett and Phyllis Dare as the romantic leads, and Rutland Barrington, Fred Emney, Huntley Wright, and Phyllis Monkman in blisteringly funny comic parts. The *Times* stated "the whole thing is a triumph," while the *Daily Chronicle* announced that "Fall's music is delicious."

Again, a modern story with middle-class characters proved refreshingly different, especially in a Dutch setting. The unabashed gaiety of the waltzes and comic numbers, like *"Kind, du kannst tanzen wie meine Frau"* (Now You Are Dancing Just Like My Wife) and *"Man steigt nach"* (In the Park, in London), and the elegant complexity of the finales—especially in the Act I courtroom scene—were heady stuff, even in 1910. Joan Sutherland's comparatively recent recorded medley of tunes from *Die geschiedene Frau*, among them the irresistible *Schlaf-coupé* (Sleeping Car) waltz, ought to have aroused current interest.

Seventy years ago, these operettas had no problem traveling. *A dollárkirálynö* and *Az elvált asszony* were hits in Budapest and all over Central Europe. Paris saw both *Princesses Dollar* (in an adaptation by Willy, Colette's first husband) and *La Divorcée* in 1911. *The Girl on the Train* stopped in New York (Globe, 3 October 1910) and, surprisingly, flopped. The U.S. lyrics by Harry B. Smith did not attract as favorable a response as Adrian Ross's did in the U.K.

On 1 December 1909, Fall's one-act *Singspiel, Brüderlein fein*, was produced in the basement *"Hölle"* (Hell) of the an der Wien. A sentimental tribute to *Kapellmeister* Josef Drechsler (who had tutored Strauss II and had written the song which inspired Fall's title), it was anglicized into *Darby and Joan* for a London production in 1912. A fine waltz, *"Nicht zu schnell und nicht zu langsam"* (Not too fast and not too slow), was the song success. In spite of its miniaturism, this work was eventually staged at the Vienna State Opera, in 1929.

Die schöne Risette (Fair Risette), a romance set in the sixteenth century, opened

---

Hubert Marischka solidified his hold over Viennese operetta by marrying the daughter of his boss, Wilhelm Karczag, who controlled the Theater an der Wien and a lucrative music-publishing firm. At the time of his marriage, Marischka was already one of Vienna's leading tenors. Some of his famous parts were in Fall's *Der liebe Augustin* (Raimundtheater, 1912, upper left with Mizzi Zwerenz), Lehár's *Die ideale Gattin* (Theater an der Wien, 1913, lower left, with Mizzi Günther), Fall's *Die geschiedene Frau* (Carltheater, 1908, lower right, with Zwerenz), and a revival of Jacobi's *Sybil* (Theater an der Wien, 1919, upper right).

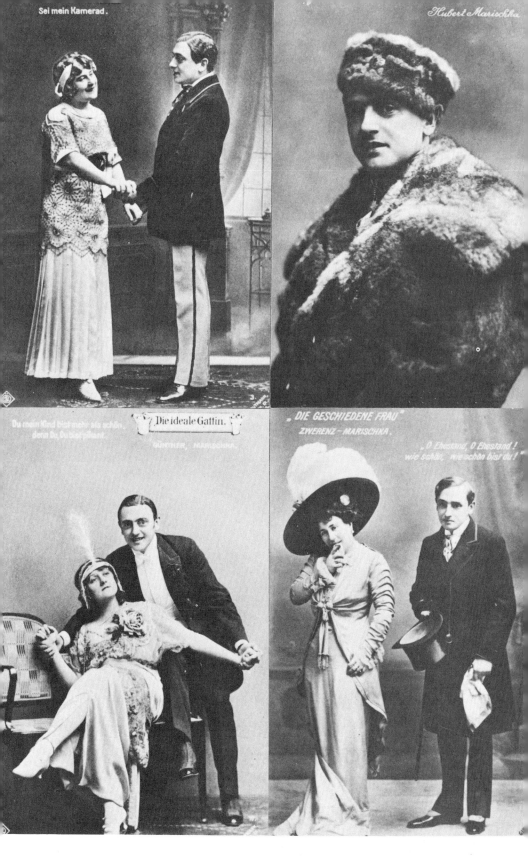

Sei mein Kamerad.

Hubert Marischka

Die ideale Gattin.

Du mein Kind bist mehr als schön, denn Du, Du bist pikant.

GÜNTHER · MARISCHKA

„DIE GESCHIEDENE FRAU"

ZWERENZ — MARISCHKA

„O Ehestand, O Ehestand! wie schön, wie schön bist du!

rousingly at the Theater an der Wien in 1910 (19 November), with many numbers encored and raves from the critics, many of whom liked it more than *The Dollar Princess*. It ran 100 performances in a season. Less popular were its predecessor, *Das Puppenmädel* (The Doll Girl, 1910), and its successor, *Die Sirene* (Johann-Strauss-Theater, 5 January 1911). *The Siren,* with a book by Stein and Willner, had a Napoleonic-Viennese setting. Fouché, the French Minister of Police, hires women to obtain secrets from suspected traitors. Unlike its predecessors, *The Siren* had more dancing than the Viennese usually expected. Charles Frohman's New York production (Knickerbocker, 28 August 1911) starred Donald Brian, Julia Sanderson, and Frank Moulan, the last two having just appeared in the Broadway production of Lionel Monckton's *The Arcadians*. "With Oscar Straus, Fall has almost reinvented the orchestra in operetta. To other and ruder hands he leaves the fat and thumping tunes," noted one critic of *The Siren*. Presumably, these would not have been by Jerome Kern, who also wrote tunes to supplement *Das Puppenmädel*, which, as *The Doll Girl,* had a short run on Broadway in 1913.

At the end of 1911, Fall wrote a short operetta for the London Hippodrome entitled *The Eternal Waltz*, in which a composer, "Feo Lahll," is besought to write a waltz for a musical comedy. This waltz proved to be the only outstanding contribution of both the play-within-the-play and the operetta itself. *The Eternal Waltz* later had the distinction of being presented on the opening bill of the new Palace Theatre, New York, 24 March 1913. For a top price of $1.50 in the evenings, one could see ballet girls from London's Palace Theatre and La Napierkowska in addition to the Fall one-acter.

In 1912 (3 February) the Neues Theater, Berlin, saw a revised version of *Der Rebell,* entitled *Der liebe Augustin,* starring the revue star Fritzi Massary as Princess Helene, niece of the Regent of Thessaly. Rudolf Bernauer and Ernst Welisch revised their old libretto, and Fall's *"Und der Himmel hängt voller Geigen"* (And Heaven is full of violins) and *"Anna was ist denn mit dir?"* (Anna, what is it with you?) intoxicated Berlin. Bernauer and Welisch would be two of the busiest librettists in succeeding seasons. A quintessential Balkan operetta, and a big hit in Berlin, *Der liebe Augustin* was only a fair success in England or in America, as *Princess Caprice* and *Miss Caprice*. In London (Shaftesbury, 11 May 1912), George Graves (Bogumil), Harry Welchman (Augustin), and Clara Evelyn, Cicely Courtneidge, Courtice Pounds, and Fred Leslie led the cast; New York (Casino, 3 September 1913) saw De Wolf Hopper and George MacFarlane (as Bogumil and Augustin). Numbers were added by Jerome Kern.

At first the war seemed to cramp Fall's style (and export possibilities to Britain or France): *Die Studentengräfin* (1913, The Student Countess) and *Der Nachtschnellzug* (1913, The Night Express) were disappointing, even with Massary in

---

Fritzi Massary achieved stardom in revue at Berlin's Metropol, though her major triumphs were in operetta. Fall's *Die Rose von Stambul* (1916) was one of her greatest hits, and the Theater an der Wien's biggest moneymaker since *The Merry Widow*. Fall's score was hardly Turkish, but still a delight with its irresistible Viennese waltzes.

Nr. 159   XIV. Band

Die Rose von Stambul

Operette von Leo Fall

Verlag
Ullstein & Co.
Berlin u. Wien

Musik für Alle

the former and Girardi in the latter. More successful were the Berlin productions of *Frau Ministerpräsident* (1914, set in England, including suffragettes) and *Der künstliche Mensch* (The Artificial Man, 1915) which had a *Frankenstein*-like story of a monster in love with a chemistry professor's daughter, played by Käthe Dorsch. The monster is removed by a jealous lab assistant with a few drops of carbonic acid in champagne—a true marriage of operetta and science fiction!

Even more triumphant was *Die Kaiserin* (1915), the Empress in this case being Austria's Maria-Theresa, as portrayed by Fritzi Massary. According to the Austrian censors, the then-reigning Emperor Franz-Josef's family could not be the subject of an operetta, so the première took place in Berlin's Metropol-Theater. The score was one of Fall's most attractive from beginning to end: two numbers that stood out were the soaring waltz-duet *"Da tanzen Schritt für Schritt,"* (You dance it step by step) and a sentimental tribute to Vienna's Schönbrunn Palace. Massary also appeared in Berlin as Kondja Gül, the Pasha's rebellious daughter, in Fall's 1916 hit, *Die Rose von Stambul,* which had opened in Vienna on 2 December 1916 with Hubert Marischka and Betty Fischer. The Julius Brammer-Alfred Grünwald libretto was set in Turkey and in a Swiss spa, and among its enormous hits were the title song, the irresistible *"Das ist das Glück nach der Mode"* (That is the fashionable way to be happy), and that magnificent floating waltz, seemingly suspended in air on a magic carpet: *"Ein Walzer muss es sein"* (It must be a waltz). The Berlin production was a sensation, and the Viennese production was one of the Theater an der Wien's greatest triumphs, with 480 performances over a relatively short period. It was the Berlin-Vienna equivalent of London's *Chu Chin Chow* but far more jovial. Long after the war, *The Rose of Stamboul* appeared in New York (Century, 7 March 1922), with Tessa Kosta and some substandard Sigmund Romberg interpolations. Die Massary appeared in a silent film of *Die Rose von Stambul* in 1918, and there was a 1953 remake. Fall himself later thought *Die Kaiserin* his greatest work, but *Die Rose von Stambul* is still produced while its predecessor lies dormant. It seemed that little that followed would come up to his older standard, including an opera, *Der goldene Vogel* (The Golden Bird, 1920), which took up four of the last years of his life only to be turned down by the Vienna State Opera. It was produced, without success, in Dresden, with Richard Tauber and Elisabeth Rethberg. In 1921 came *Die spanische Nachtigall* in Berlin, a Massary success, *Die Strassensängerin* (The Street-songstress), not as popular, and *Der heilige Ambrosius,* a failure. A gallbladder condition was beginning to trouble the composer, but in 1922, at the age of forty-nine, he composed what may well be his most enduring masterpiece, *Madame Pompadour,* which many, including this writer, consider his greatest composition.

The Rudolph Schanzer–Ernst Welisch triangle libretto was only loosely suggested by historical fact, and the story of Pompadour, her lover René, and King Louis XV was merely an operetta anecdote. In Berlin (Berliner Theater, 9 September 1922), Massary was partnered with Ralph Arthur Roberts. In Vienna, the Carltheater first night took place on 2 March 1923, with Fritzi Massary in her greatest role, plus Ernst Tautenhayn as Calicot, the dissident poet. The comic duet between Pompadour and Calicot, *"Josef, ach Josef, was bist du so keusch?"* (Joseph, oh Joseph, why are you so shy?), given a shimmy verse, proved the catchiest number, but the score was laden with glorious songs, all Fall at his very best. The entrance waltz of Madame Pompadour, *"Heut' könnt' einer sein Glück bei mir machen"* (Someone will make me happy today), is simply ravishing—not since *"Ein Walzer muss es sein"* had there been so bewitching, so dizzying a waltz. The very next number in Act I, a waltz-duet between *la Pompadour* and René, continued the easygoing, conversational style of duet Fall did so well, this time with a sexy "m-m-m" twist. Their next duet, in Act II, *"Ich bin dein Untertan"* (I am your slave), is a lively martial ditty that calls to mind the love affair in *La Grande-Duchesse de Gérolstein.* And the title slow waltz, *"Madame Pompadour, Kronjuwel der Natur"* (Madame Pompadour, crown-jewel of nature) has a sensuous passion that is effectively put in counterpoint with a soldiers' chorus.

Madame Pompadour, Act II finale: René (Derek Oldham, right) has just been discovered by King Louis XV (Bertram Wallis, center) in the bedroom of his mistress, Pompadour (Evelyn Laye, left, in riding costume). The London production of Fall's great operetta (Daly's, 1923) ran 469 performances, while the New York version flopped.

The analogy with Offenbach was further intensified by a real *Massary-Lied*, *"Dem König geht's in meinem Schachspiel meistens kläglich . . ."* (The King usually does miserably in my chess-game), which reminded one of the *couplets* furnished by Offenbach for Hortense Schneider. Massary was to Fall (and to Oscar Straus, among others) precisely what Schneider was to Offenbach: a rare talent, the greatest operetta diva of the day, one around whom operettas were built. Madame Pompadour was Massary's greatest part. In the 1926–27 season, the operetta was one of several given lavish revue treatment by Erik Charell at Berlin's Grosses Schauspielhaus. Massary again starred, this time opposite her famous husband, Max Pallenberg.

Evelyn Laye, who had just appeared in the London revival of *The Merry Widow* at Daly's (May 1923), was tapped to star in the West End *Pompadour* at the same theatre (20 December 1923). This ran a very substantial 469 times, one of the last big romantic foreign importations of its day, soon to be superseded by the likes of *No! No! Nanette!* (1925). Supporting Mme. Laye were Derek Oldham, the reigning D'Oyly Carte tenor of the 1920s, as René, Elsie Randolph, whose musical-comedy partnership with Jack Buchanan is still remembered, and two old favorites from Edwardian days: Huntley Wright and Bertram Wallis, as Calicot and King Louis XV. Frederick Lonsdale and Harry Graham did the British adaptation, and the lavish sets were the work of Alfred Terraine and Joseph and Phil Harker. The New York production (with a new libretto by Clare Kummer) starring Wilda Bennett opened the new, Byzantine-styled Martin Beck Theatre (11 November 1924), but failed precipitously. In Paris (Marigny, 16 May 1930), it fared better, with Raymonde Vécart of the Opéra as the heroine.

Probably on the strength of the long British run of *Pompadour,* Herbert Wilcox decided to convert the property into a silent film. The British National film was produced by E. A. Dupont, and he collaborated with the versatile Frances Marion on the screenplay. Dorothy Gish was cast in the title role, with Antonio Moreno as René and revue star Nelson Keys as a courtier. Why Dorothy Gish, one might ask? Because Wilcox had previously cast her—against type—as sexy Nell Gwynne in a 1926 film, about which the American critic George Jean Nathan remarked, "It took an Englishman to discover that Dorothy Gish has legs and extremely beautiful breasts."

Leo Fall died in 1925 of cancer. He was at the height of his powers, only fifty-two years old. His death dealt a deadly blow to Viennese operetta itself, for Fall had the gaiety and sparkle of the French in addition to a talent for writing sensational waltzes in true Viennese style. Though many of his later works were frankly written as star vehicles for Massary, they remain as dazzling as ever, waiting for a true star to reinterpret them. (This was proved by a recent

The popular operetta comedian Róbert Ratonyi as King Louis XV in Fall's *Madame Pompadour* in a recent production at the Municipal Operetta, Budapest. MTI Foto.

revival of *Madame Pompadour* at the Vienna Volksoper, which, without a star, was treated as just another ensemble effort. *Madame Pompadour* requires something more.) When *The Dollar Princess* was revived in London in 1925 at Daly's following the solid run of *Pompadour*, with Evelyn Laye and Carl Brisson, it surprised the producers by running only eleven weeks. But *The Dollar Princess* does not require a big star, being more an ensemble piece. Rarely seen today, it would be worth reviving (with a new English libretto). So would, similarly, *Der liebe Augustin, Der fidele Bauer,* and, most of all, *Die geschiedene Frau.* Today, Fall's music would probably sound too delicate to disco ears, and the libretti, uniformly Edwardian, would seem too flimsy and coy to lovers of violence and sex. But, beautifully mounted and crisply directed, they would attract connoisseurs of charm and vivaciousness. Leo Fall was very rarely as maudlin in his love songs as either Kálmán or Lehár—he was too up-tempo for that. Like his disciple, Jerome Kern, Fall's most sentimental songs had a briskness, a joy, a certain lilt, which kept them from becoming too mushy. This was a rare quality in the Silver Age Viennese operetta, so dominated by the heavier Lehár touch.

A song which sums up the Fall spirit might be *"Das ist das Glück nach der Mode"* from *Die Rose von Stambul*. Kálmán could not have written it, nor Lehár. It is too gay, too conversational, perhaps too flippant. Its refrain does not attempt to soar in a Puccini-esque way but the whole is, preeminently, a brilliantly soaring *sung* waltz. One *could* dance to it (one surely did in World War I Berlin), but it is something that is best heard in its theatrical setting. Such charm and lightness of touch were seldom heard in Viennese operetta at this time.

The turn of the century spawned a large number of prolific operetta composers. Among the industrious Viennese, **Edmund Eysler** (1874–1949) had one of the most prodigious outputs of all his contemporaries. In his prime, which spanned roughly 1903–18 with spurts in the 1920s and even later, he wrote well over forty operettas, one or two of which are still performed today. He had a lucky association from the start with Alexander Girardi, writing several operettas for the great star, and these established Eysler's long and prosperous career.

Eysler (Eisler) was born in the suburbs of Vienna, the son of a not-too-successful Jewish businessman. He gave piano lessons for a living while attending the Vienna Conservatory along with Leo Fall, one year his elder. Through a relative, he met the librettist Ignatz Schnitzer, who, after the success of *Der Zigeunerbaron* (1885), had written the libretto of *Der Schelm von Bergen* (The Hangman of Bergen), which Johann Strauss had dropped because of its similarity to *The Mikado*. Schnitzer let Eysler try his hand at the libretto and the finished result pleased publisher Josef Weinberger, who tried in vain to have it produced under the title of *Der Hexenspiegel* (The Magic Mirror). Weinberger later asked Eysler to take the lighter numbers out and to compose a new operetta around them; the new piece was *Bruder Straubinger* (Theater an der Wien, 20 February 1903), with a libretto by Moritz West, of *Der Vogelhändler* fame. Before the première, the theatre director Karczag pleaded with the composer to change his own name to something more exotic: Eisler was for a businessman, not for an artist. "As Eisler you cannot become famous." The composer refused, until Karczag finally convinced him to at least change the i to a y— "they'll think you're from Holland."

With Girardi in the title role, *Bruder Straubinger* was ensured at least some success, but that was not the only explanation for it, as the operetta has been a Viennese favorite without him. The real reason was the waltz song *"Küssen ist keine Sünd"* (Kissing is no sin), with its easygoing refrain. The published song sold more than a hundred thousand copies in a short while.

Eysler's association with Girardi continued with vehicular, vernacular works like *Pufferl* (1905), as well as other operettas for other stars. There were certainly enough compositions to keep a good income coming in, though their librettos were generally poor, no more than transient affairs to keep the local public momentarily amused. Eysler's style was simple, and some were more like typical Viennese farces with songs than true nineteenth-century operettas. There were some thirty or so written until the end of World War I, the best-regarded being *Der lachende Ehemann* (The Laughing Husband, Bürgertheater, 19 March 1913), an operetta that gave the new team of Julius Brammer and Alfred Grünwald an early opportunity to shine. The critic Ludwig Klinenberger remarked on *Der lachende Ehemann:* "Edmund Eysler is one of the best champions of so-called light music, of popular national songs . . . that one can hardly let slip out of one's ears."

A few of Eysler's works crossed European borders, including *The Laughing Husband,* which turned up in London the same year as its Vienna debut. No great hit, it at least provided a hearing for Jerome Kern's delightful song, "You're Here and I'm Here." *The Laughing Husband* was heard at New York's Knickerbocker Theatre in 1914. Before that, Broadwayites had seen *The Love Cure* (1909), a version of *Künstlerblut* (1906), and *The Woman Haters* (1912), based on *Der Frauenfresser* (1911). More successful was the American adaptation of Eysler's musical farce, *Ein Tag im Paradies* (1913), which became *The Blue Paradise* (Casino, 5 August 1915), which ran a full season. Eight of Eysler's songs were retained, supplemented by eight new tunes by Sigmund Romberg. Earlier, the one-act *Vera Violetta* (Carltheater, 30 November 1907), book by Leo Stein, had been seen not only on Broadway (Winter Garden, 1911, with Gaby Deslys and Al Jolson), but also in Paris (Olympia, 1908).

In the 1920s, Eysler found he had difficulty in modifying his essentially prewar style to allow for the jazzy dances that had infiltrated operetta, and his output diminished. In 1927, he had a big success with a throwback to old Vienna, a pre-tango, pre-Charleston Vienna, the Vienna of 1515: *Die gold'ne Meisterin* (The Lady Goldsmith, Theater an der Wien, 13 September 1927). It was based on an 1896 Berlin comedy, which was originally set in Augsburg. A change in the setting permitted the librettists, Brammer and Grünwald, to write lyrics glorifying *alt, alt-Wien:* "*So tanzt man nur in Wien*" (You dance that way only in Vienna), "*In Grinzing is a Gasserl*" (There's a tiny street in Grinzing), and "*So a Wien.*" But the title waltz, "*Du liebe gold'ne Meisterin,*" epitomized Eysler's totally predictable style. Given the song's opening line, you could figure out Eysler's opening notes. Pleasant, but hardly exciting or distinctive.

During the 1938–45 annexation, Eysler was forced into hiding, and his works were unplayed. But after the liberation, he was suddenly, again, a celebrity, and in his last years he was fêted as a grand old representative of the Good Old Days. He died after slipping on a step, going to receive an ovation from an admiring audience.

Leo Ascher (1880–1942), the son of a Viennese umbrella manufacturer, shared his first substantial success with the then-new librettist team of Julius Brammer and Alfred Grünwald. Brammer was a bit-part player at the Theater an der

Wien; Grünwald was an employee of a Viennese theatrical agency; the Bram-mer-Grünwald partnership virtually guaranteed success for the major Viennese and Berliner operetta composers, including Ascher, Fall, Lehár, Kálmán, and Ábrahám. The first collaboration between Ascher and his librettists was *Vindo-bona, du herrlicher stadt* (1910), a *Singspiel* of *alt-Wien*. Their next work was hugely popular, *Hoheit tanzt Walzer* (Her Highness Waltzes, Raimundtheater, 24 February 1912). This took place in and near Vienna early in the 1830s, and its plot was at least suggested by the bittersweet love story of *Ein Walzertraum,* except that here a princess rather than a prince consort was discovered enjoying herself outside the court. The music suitably reflected the play's era with bits of Lanner periodically drifting in. Ascher's other goldmine was for wartime Berlin: *Der Soldat der Marie* (Theater am Schiffbauerdamm, 2 September 1916). This was a typical Berliner *Singspiel* tailored for wartime audiences, but with an uncharac-teristically elegant Viennese refinement in its score. It played all over Germany and Austria.

Oskar Nedbal (1874–1930) was a colleague of Franz Lehár at the Prague Conservatory, under Dvorák, specializing in violin and composition and reach-ing great heights in classical performance. He was a founding member of the Bohemian String Quartet in 1892 and was a conductor of the Prague Philhar-monic from 1896, touring all over Europe with both organizations. From 1906, he was in Vienna with the Tonkünstler Orchestra and the Volksoper (1908–9). After the Great War, he returned to Czechoslovakia and held high positions with several theatres, orchestras, and a radio station.

His serious music, including a sonata for piano and violin, and several piano works, were in their day respectable achievements, and of his early works for the stage, several ballet-pantomimes were considerably admired. His first op-eretta, *Die keusche Barbara* (Chaste Barbara, 1910), was produced in Prague—the music was admired but the libretto was not, and the run was short. The next try, with a libretto by Leo Stein, was *Polenblut* (Polish Blood, Carltheater, 25 October 1913), a Viennese triumph. This had a contemporary Warsaw set-ting, though the plot was suggested by a Pushkin story. Politically and musi-cally, *Polenblut* was an oddity. Its composer was of Czechoslovakian origins, yet the play took place in Russian-occupied Poland. Nedbal was praised for his adherence to his own national music, yet the mazurkas and polonaises he wrote for *Polenblut* were not at all Czechoslovakian. In 1913, Polish nationalist senti-ments were unpopular not only with the Russians, obviously, but with the Austro-Hungarian Government, which had some four million Poles within its own borders.

But the work was a big success, and not merely on account of polkas and other Polish numbers. Two big waltzes were vastly popular as well: *"Mädel, dich hat mir die Glücksfee gebracht"* (Young lady, you brought the Good Fairy to me) and *"Hören Sie, wie es singt und klingt"* (Listen, as it sings and rings).

Nedbal's subsequent works, among them *Die Winzerbraut* (The Vineyard Bride, 1916), *Die schöne Saskia* (1917), and *Eriwan* (1918), never achieved the popularity of the Polish opus. The composer toured again, conducting Czech classics (in

Spain, among other places) until 1930, when the Depression had an adverse effect on the fortunes of the theatre with which he was connected. On Christmas Eve, 1930, right before a performance he was to conduct at the National Theatre in Zagreb, he jumped from a window and ended his life at the age of fifty-six.

Léon Jessel (1871–1942) is remembered today for novelty piano pieces like "The Parade of the Tin Soldiers," and for one operetta, out of sixteen, *Das Schwarzwaldmädel* (The Black Forest Girl, Berlin, Komische Oper, 25 August 1917). This provided Germans and Austrians with some cheer during World War I, and after, thanks to a pleasant score with country touches, beginning with a lively polka right at the start. Highly regarded for its rustic charm, the complicated August Neidhart libretto included accusations of witchcraft in its second act, and a first-act finale that included one of the work's most popular songs, *"Muss denn die Lieb' stets Tragödie sein?"* There have been numerous German films (and television productions) of this property. This *Volksoperette* would probably have attracted German audiences right through the 1930s, but its Jewish composer was not in Nazi favor. In 1936, the authorities attempted to separate him and his wife. In 1941, for sending a letter describing his "difficult circumstances," Jessel was tortured by the Gestapo, which led to his death a few weeks later.

One could not leave the Viennese 1920s without remarking on one of the greatest hits of the Theater an der Wien, Granichstädten's *Der Orlow* (3 April 1925), which received some 428 performances there until its retirement five years later. **Bruno Granichstädten** (1879–1944) had been classically trained, and studied conducting at the Viennese opera. His operetta-idyll from the old, more comfortable days had appeared in 1915, *Auf Befehl der Herzogin!* (The Duchess Commands!); its Maria-Theresa setting enchanted war-weary Vienna. The book for *Der Orlow*, by Ernst Marischka and the composer himself, had an exiled Russian grand duke in New York, in love with a dancer named Nadja. The operetta gave Ernst Marischka's brother Hubert the nightly opportunity to enchant Vienna with a song about a little cigarette, but the real sensation was the appearance of a jazz band. *Der Orlow* was unsuccessfully mounted in London in 1926 as *Hearts and Diamonds,* with Lupino Lane and George Metaxa. Granichstädten and Marischka joined together in 1930 for *Reklame!* (Advertising!), which was also set in New York. The big hit songs included the fox-trot "For You!"

The celebrated violinist **Fritz Kreisler** (1875–1962), whose *Apple Blossoms* had been seen on Broadway in 1919, composed an even more notable operetta in 1932. *Sissy* (Theater an der Wien, 23 December) was a romantic retelling of the courtship of Princess Elisabeth of Bavaria by the young Emperor Franz-Josef. The libretto by the Marischka brothers, Hubert and Ernst, was based on a comedy, and at least some of the score was used before, in *Apple Blossoms.* Starring in the first cast were Paula Wessely and Hans Jaray, the latter later replaced by Paul Henreid, before his Hollywood fame. The success of *Sissy* was long-lasting, with hundreds of performances in Vienna and more throughout Central Europe. In 1936, Josef von Sternberg made a charming American film version, *The King Steps Out,* using some of Kreisler's music—the big hit song was "Stars in My Eyes," agreeably sung by Grace Moore. More lucrative was the series of non-operetta films starring Romy Schneider that treated the same romance, beginning in 1955, and directed by Ernst Marischka.

Robert Stolz (1880–1975) was "the Last of the Waltz Kings." To put it more precisely, Robert Stolz made sure the world knew he was the Last of the Waltz Kings. Whether he was or was not, time will tell. He certainly had proper connections, was associated with the very best composers, and was also requisitely Viennese (even if he was born in Graz). But although he composed a great deal of music for every possible medium, from the operetta stage to films to television to records to ice spectaculars, he will more likely be remembered in operetta chronicles as a champion of composers who preceded him, from Strauss to Straus. As a popular composer he had many song hits, but rarely an operetta (on his own) that today commands more than just a passing glance. He had a very long recording career, and was a world-famous conductor of Viennese light music. In his earlier years, he was fortunate to have been the principal conductor at the Theater an der Wien during the first operettas of the Silver Era, succeeding Artur Bodanzky and beginning with *The Merry Widow.* This must have influenced his composing. He was also one of the first notable composers of German film operettas, beginning with *Zwei Herzen im Dreivierteltakt* (Two Hearts in Waltz Time, 1930).

Stolz's father was conductor of the Stadttheater, Graz, and his great-aunt was the legendary Verdi soprano, Therese Stolz, the first Italian Aïda. He was a piano child-prodigy, and was accordingly sent to Engelbert Humperdinck for training. He started his career as a conductor at the turn of the century at various provincial theatres, while composing his first *Singspiele* and minor operettas; around that time he made his first recordings for the Edison Company. By Christmas, 1905, he was at the conductor's desk at the Theater an der Wien for *The Merry Widow,* and later for *Der Graf von Luxemburg* and several other big successes. His own works, like *Die lustigen Weiber von Wien* (The Merry Wives of Vienna, Wiener Colosseum, 1 January 1909), with a book by the young team of Julius Brammer and Alfred Grünwald, were less enthusiastically received. His 1910 work, *Das Glücksmädel* (Raimundtheater, 28 October), starred Girardi. In 1913, Stolz composed the accompanying music for *Der Millionenonkel,* a film in which Girardi appeared.

Several works appeared during World War I, notably *Der Favorit* (Berlin, Komische Oper, 1916), with its big *Schlager* (hit), *"Du sollst der Kaiser meiner Seele sein"* (You shall be the emperor of my soul). In the 1920s, his fame increased, bolstered by works that enjoyed popularity in some cases outside Germany and Austria. The most successful of these was *Der Tanz ins Glück* (Wiener Colosseum, 18 October 1921), which swept Europe and played London as *Whirled into Happiness* (Lyric, 18 May 1922).

Other substantial hits included *Die Tanzgräfin* (The Dance Countess, 1921), *Mädi* (Berlin, 1923), and *Der Hampelmann* (The Jumping Jack, Vienna, 1923). His hit songs were featured in the repertories of the leading light singers, and

Stolz compositions were heard on the infant radio. The young sound cinema likewise beckoned. Besides *Zwei Herzen im Dreivierteltakt* (1930), with its irresistible waltz, he composed the scores of such films as *Ein Tango für Dich, Das Lied ist aus,* the cinema versions of *Der Hampelmann* and *Die lustigen Weiber von Wien* (all 1930), *Der Prinz von Arkadien, Der Raub von Mona Lisa,* and *Liebeskommando* (all 1931), the big hit from the last-named film being *"Adieu, mein kleiner Gardeoffizier."* In 1930, *Im weissen Rössl* had opened at the Grosse Schauspielhaus, Berlin, with the Stolz songs *"Mein Liebeslied muss ein Walzer sein"* (My love-song must be a waltz) and *"Die ganze Welt ist himmelblau"* (The whole world is a heavenly blue).

The year 1932 was Stolz's most successful as an operetta composer: *Wenn die kleinen Veilchen blühen* (When the Little Violets Bloom) and *Venus in Seide* (Venus in Silk), both of which had foreign productions. The former was first seen in The Hague, the latter premièred in Zürich. *Wild Violets* (Drury Lane, 31 October 1932) achieved a 291-performance run in London. *Venus in Seide* has also been the sole Stolz operetta that the Vienna Volksoper has recently seen fit to revive. He wrote songs for Jan Kiepura films, such as *Mein Herz ruft nach dir* (1933) and *Ich liebe alle Frauen* (1935). *Frühjahrsparade* (Spring Parade, 1934) was a widely acclaimed film score—rewritten for the American remake in 1940 with Deanna Durbin and with the song "Waltzing in the Clouds." *Rise and Shine* (1936), a musical for Drury Lane, with Jack Whiting, was a London failure. By the time of Stolz's voluntary exile from Austria in 1938 (he was a certified Aryan), his career in full-length operettas was dwindling down, but this was at least partially due to the form itself having expired. In 1938, before emigrating to the United States, Stolz added songs to the Paris production of the successful British operetta *Balalaika,* first seen at London's Adelphi in 1936 (22 December). This had a book by Eric Maschwitz and music by George Posford and Bernard Grün. It was filmed in Hollywood (1939) with Ilona Massey and Nelson Eddy. Stolz conducted the Eggerth-Kiepura revival of *The Merry Widow* on Broadway during the war, in addition to several concerts of operetta and waltz music which gained him considerable respect.

Stolz may have thought the responsibility was his to resurrect the medium after the war, but works like *Frühling im Prater* (1949) and *Hochzeit am Bodensee* (1969), the last written for the Bregenz Festival lakeside amphitheatre, were hardly first-class achievements and did not start an operetta renaissance. Stolz did continue recording and conducting until late in life—he signed a long-term recording contract when he was past ninety—as always, serving Viennese music to the world. As a musical evangelist and as a composer of many popular song hits (few of which are regularly heard outside Germany and Austria), his name will be remembered. His style was recognizable in its snazzy, up-to-date use of current dance forms, along with several breezy waltzes for modern consumption which occasionally retained a wistful, sentimental Viennese *Heurigenlied* flavor that touched the hearts of those who were older. And yet, the style was, apparently, not distinctive on the stage, in the way that Lehár's, or Kálmán's, or even Künneke's was.

THÉATRE DES VARIÉTÉS — Chanté par Mlle FAVART et Mr J. PERIER

Nous avons fait un beau voyage

CiBOULETTE

OPERETTE EN 3 ACTES ET 4 TABLEAUX DE MM.
robert de flers et **francis de croisset**
MUSIQUE DE
reynaldo hahn

POUR PIANO ET CHANT
CHAQUE : 3 fr. 50

1. Ce n'était pas la même chose *(Duparquet)*
2. Dans une charrette... *(Ciboulette)*
3. Moi j'm'appelle Ciboulette *(Ciboulette)*
4. Comme frère et sœur *(Ciboulette-Antonin)*
5. C'est sa banlieue... *(Ciboulette)*
6. C'est tout ce qui me reste d'elle *(Duparquet)*
7. Dans le monde quand nous sortons
   (Comtesse de Castiglione)
8. J'sais c'que j'ai *(Antonin)*
9. Amour qui meurs, Amour qui passes *(Ciboulette)*
10. Nous avons fait un beau voyage
    (Ciboulette-Duparquet)
11. Ah ! si vous étiez Nicolas *(Ciboulette-Antonin)*
12. Chanson de route *(Ciboulette)*

POUR PIANO SEUL
CHAQUE : 3 fr. 50

1. Ciboulette - Valse
2. Prélude du 2me acte *(Comme la vie...)*
3. Chanson de route *(Marche-one-step)*
4. Ciboulette *(Fantaisie-Sélection)*

EDITIONS FRANCIS SALABERT
35 B⁴ des CAPUCINES - 107 A⁴ VICTOR·HUGO. 12 B⁴ des ITALIENS

CONTINENTAL VARIETIES

THE 1920s saw a new flowering of operetta in Paris and Berlin. Just before and during World War I there had been several French and German works that on one hand attempted to capture the suavity of the Viennese operettas of the period while on the other managed to retain the boisterousness of the popular topical revues so popular in both capitals. The results were not unlike similar works in London and New York, mixing romantic love songs with satirical or just comical *couplets*. This style persisted throughout the 1920s.

There were also attempts to go back to the formal designs of the nineteenth-century operetta, modifying the structure and using up-to-the-minute, often American, dance rhythms for new effects, or simply streamlining the form without resorting to new music. There were several quite successful operettas of these types: the Brecht/Weill *Die Dreigroschenoper* was the most celebrated.

The French have recently been reappraising some of the big hits of the inter-war years, like *L'Amour masqué, Phi-Phi,* and *Ta Bouche,* with occasionally surprising results. The '20s had an irresistible vitality that wears far better than some of the murkier operettas of the '30s, '40s, and '50s, the *opérettes à grand spectacle* that were seen at the Mogador and other theatres in Paris and in the provinces.

Charles Cuvillier (1877–1955) was a French composer who obtained his biggest success in London and in Germany. A student of Massenet and Fauré, his early waltzes and other dances attracted the management of the very small Théâtre des Capucines, where his first work was presented, *Avant-hier matin* (The Morning of the Day Before Yesterday, 20 October 1905). This unusual "cham-

---

Sheet music from Hahn's *Ciboulette* (Variétés, 1923), the composer's most lasting operetta. The heroine's name means "chives" in English; the part was first played by Edmée Favart.

ber" operetta had only three in its cast: Adam, Eve, and a gardener, in the libretto of Tristan Bernard, one of France's top humorists. Alice Bonheur was Eve. A single piano furnished the accompaniment. It caught the public's fancy, and Cuvillier's stage career was assured. With André Barde as librettist, *Son p'tit frère* (His Little Brother, 1907), a Greek work prefiguring Barde's libretto for *Phi-Phi* (1918), and *Afgar, ou les loisirs andalous* (Afgar, or, Andalusian Leisures, 1909) were substantial hits. In Paris, Marguerite Deval and Henri Defreyn had headed the cast of *Afgar* at the Capucines.

Alice Delysia had created a sensation in 1918 in the English version (by Arthur Wimperis) of the Paris revue *Plus ça change . . .* Called *As You Were,* C. B. Cochran's production featured the new Herman Darewski songs "If You Could Care for Me," "Ninon," and "Helen, Helen, Helen of Troy," which kept both military and civilian quarters cheery. The follow-up was Cuvillier's *Afgar* (London Pavilion, 17 September 1919), already a decade old and showing some signs of age. Fred Thompson and Worton David (book) and Douglas Furber (lyrics) were called in to recondition the Michel Carré–André Barde libretto, and with Delysia in the cast were Harry Welchman as Don Juan, Jr. (a Spanish prisoner at the Moorish court), John Humphries (as Afgar), Lupino Lane, and, making a début for Cochran, Marie Burke. Mona Paiva danced, in what was considered an indecent costume—they were all by Paul Poiret. The song hits of Cochran's extravaganza were the soaring (but fairly boring) "Night Was Made for Love" and "Garden of Make-Believe." It had a run of 300 performances; the run in New York was 171 performances.

But another Cuvillier work had previously conquered London, though it never registered in Paris. It was his most famous operetta, *The Lilac Domino*. The first performances were in Leipzig in February 1911; the score was written to a German libretto by Emmerich von Gatti and Bela Jenbach. *Der lila Domino* played elsewhere in Germany and in Vienna (1912), where it was seen by Andreas Dippel, an American manager, in 1914. The production was shipped by a neutral Dutch ship to New York at the beginning of the war, and along the way it was Americanized by Harry B. (book) and Robert B. (lyrics) Smith. In addition, songs by Benatzky and Lehár were added. The première (44th Street Theater, 28 October 1914) received much favorable notice. The *New York Times* thought the staging was magnificent, and remarked that Eleanor Painter (as Georgine, the daughter of the Vicomte de Brissac) and Wilfrid Douthitt (as Count André de St. Armand) "scored tremendous hits." The *World* called it "the most pleasing comic opera of the season," and the *Globe* noted its "emphatic success." But it lasted only 113 performances, and sought solace on the road—fairly successfully, one might add.

In London, it ran 747 times (Empire, 21 February 1918), one of the great hits of the end of the War-Armistice period. Ironically, a change of locale from Nice at Carnival time to Palm Beach made the operetta more attractive to British tastes. The manager was J. L. Sachs, an illiterate who made a fortune in the theatre and who just happened to love the color lilac. In the London production

Clara Butterworth and Jamieson Dodds were the young lovers. It was a decided novelty for the Empire, a house generally associated with variety and revue, and this operetta attraction had an opening matinée instead of an opening night, thanks to air raids.

The Lilac Domino was last revived in London in 1944, when Pat Taylor was Georgine and Graham Payn appeared in a comedy part. A film was made in 1937 with the locale switched to Budapest, though the story, about a gambling count who falls for a masked noblewoman, was the same. Michael Bartlett and June Knight starred, supported by Athene Seyler, Fred Emney, Morris Harvey, and S. Z. ("Cuddles") Sakall.

In 1913, another Barde-Cuvillier collaboration, *La Reine s'amuse* (a takeoff on the Hugo title *Le Roi s'amuse,* which was the basis of Verdi's *Rigoletto*), was produced in Marseille, and five years later in Paris (Apollo, 1 November 1918), as *La Reine joyeuse.* This and *Phi-Phi* were Paris's great Armistice operettas. Its celebrated waltz was *"Ô! la troublante volupté de la première étreinte"* (Oh, What a Joy Is in the Thrill of the First Embrace). *La Reine joyeuse* was produced in London as *The Naughty Princess* (Adelphi, 7 October 1920), where it ran 268 performances with Yvonne Arnaud, Amy Augarde, Leon Morton, W. H. Berry as the King, and the aging George Grossmith as a young prince, wearing a golden wig and trying to look as youthful as possible.

In spite of alarming reports—circulated for the benefit of the American press—that Cuvillier had been wounded or even killed at Verdun, the composer remained sufficiently vigorous to compose some nine more operettas, none of which attained any lasting popularity in Paris or elsewhere. One, *Florabella,* another product of Cuvillier's German period, had been produced in New York (Casino, 11 September 1916) with Lina Abarbanell as a wife and her (fictitious) twin sister. This lasted 115 performances on Broadway; a 1921 remounting in Lyon did *not* lead to a Paris production. *Annabella* was done in Paris the following year (might it have been a revision of the earlier work?), and in 1924 *Bob et Moi* attempted to be as modern as the Henri Christiné-Maurice Yvain products then in vogue. Cuvillier's charms were more *passé,* however, and he ended his career with what must have been a delightful affair—a Courteline *vaudeville, Le Train de 8^h 47,* with music by Cuvillier (1935).

Marcel Lattès, a composer who moved in high society, wrote several interesting works that entertained—but not the general public. His first full-length work reflected the golden circles in which he moved—*La Jeunesse dorée* (Apollo, 1913)—but despite its stars Henri Defreyn and André Lefaur (later famous as Pagnol's Topaze), and a good première, it was pulled off after two and a half weeks. Lattès then worked on a London show for Charles Cochran in 1919 (Oxford, 22 October), *Maggie.* With Winifred Barnes and George Graves in the cast, there was a dress salon scene which literally reproduced Paul Poiret's studio in Paris. But there were no first-rate tunes to keep *Maggie* running longer than three months. A similar run was registered by the French version at the Gaîté-Lyrique (1921), with principals Yanne Exiane and Henri Defreyn—in Paris,

Maggie became *Nelly*. The principal waltz caught on, but only for a while. *Monsieur L'Amour,* at the Mogador the next year, may not have elicited much interest, but two subsequent works were impressive for both casts and subject matter. *Le Diable à Paris* (Marigny, 1927) had a truly spectacular lineup of actors, with Dranem as Mephisto, Raimu, Aimée Simon-Girard, and Edmée Favart. And Jacqueline Francell, Meg Lemonnier, and the young Jean Gabin were at the Bouffes-Parisiens in 1930 for a rarity indeed: a detective-operetta, *Arsène Lupin, Banquier.* Arletty was in *Xantho chez les courtisanes* (Nouveautés, 1932) and Albert Préjean led the cast of *Pour ton bonheur* (Bouffes-Parisiens, 1935), the last Lattès works.

Émile Lassailly was the *chef d'orchestre* at the Variétés, where his revue *1915* was presented in that year. The cast sparkled: Marguerite Deval, Yvonne Printemps, and Raimu, and one song became very popular with the military, *"On les aura."* Two years later, Lassailly had an operetta performed at the Théâtre Michel, with a libretto by André Barde and Charpentier: *Carminetta* (16 March 1917). The story concerned a Spanish dancer who made a bet that she could steal the hero from the governor's daughter. Heading the Paris cast was Eve Lavallière, who had made a great career *en travesti* at the Variétés at the turn of the century, as Oreste (1899), as Cupidon (1902), as Orlofsky (1904). Eve Lavallière's life was certainly theatrical, but more the stuff of melodrama than operetta. When Eve was fifteen, her father shot her mother and then himself. Her theatre triumphs were such that she was a favorite of King Edward VII, yet shortly after the fifty-odd performances of *Carminetta,* she disappeared. The actress had suddenly left the theatre for good to become a religious zealot, and died after assisting the work of missionaries in Tunisia.

As the title implied, there were echoes of *Carmen* in *Carminetta.* Escamillo was now the portly proprietor of a bar and Carminetta was the daughter of Carmen by Don José. "Musically speaking," claimed one London paper, "she is in fact a very degenerate child." In London, under Charles Cochran's management (Prince of Wales's, 22 August 1917), the title role that might have made a London star of Eve Lavallière was taken by Alice Delysia. Cochran had first seen her in revue in Paris substituting for Irene Castle, the famous ballroom dancer. She appeared in the intimate revues Cochran produced from 1914, where she helped popularize Paul Rubens's recruiting song, "Your King and Country Want You." Throughout the war years, Delysia was to epitomize the glamorous and the saucy, in such successful revues as *Odds and Ends* and *Pell Mell.* Cochran payed Delysia £100 a week to appear in *Carminetta,* her first London operetta, and she dazzled Londoners for 260 performances. The London book for this "operatic cameo" was by Mockton Hoffe, with lyrics by Douglas Furber. Curiously, the most popular songs were interpolated: "Cliquot" and "A Merry Farewell," music by Herman Darewski. The novelty of the operetta was having Delysia, quite alone, closing the show with the latter song, and its "I hate you," "I love you," "I kiss you" sung out to the audience. The song caused a stir and became a signature-tune for the artiste.

Henri Christiné (1867–1941) was the son of a Swiss watchmaker, born in Geneva. There, he became a French teacher, until he married a *café-concert* singer, for whom he wrote songs. These were quite popular and Christiné soon found himself writing them for such popular stars as Dranem, Mayol, and Fragson. Songs like *"Elle est épatante, cette petite femme-là!"* and *"La petite Tokinoise"* are still recalled today. His first operettas were performed in Brussels, *Service d'Amour* (1903) and *Les Vierges du Harem* (1907) among them, but his popular songs enjoyed more popularity.

On 13 November 1918, two days after the ending of the Great War, the Bouffes-Parisiens produced one of its longest-running hits, *Phi-Phi,* with Christiné's score to a libretto by Francis Solar and Albert Willemetz. Originally intended for the tiny Théâtre de l'Abri, there was a risky switch to the Bouffes that was far from financially assured. The decorators and costumiers were offered percentages of the receipts rather than normal payments, an arrangement that later proved very lucrative for them. Tempered undoubtedly by the victorious feeling in the air, the public would probably have reacted enthusiastically to any passably decent operetta, and, in fact, the long and happy fate awarded to *Phi-Phi* was not decided until the spring of 1919, when bookings reached capacity level. *Phi-Phi,* schizophrenically, looked back and looked ahead. The story of Phi-Phi (Phidias, the sculptor) and his domestic life in ancient Greece was typical *opéra-bouffe* material, a risqué plot reveling in puns and anachronisms. Phidias sculpts two model young Greeks; he falls for the woman, his wife for the youth, and they all get entwined with their chief of state, Pericles. (Shakespeare, however, has nothing to do with *Phi-Phi.*) *Phi-Phi* also sought to conclusively explain the disappearance of the arms of the Vénus de Milo and the head from the Victoire de Samothrace: the winsome Aspasie, trying to escape the amorous advances of Phi-Phi, defends herself with an umbrella, which accidentally knocks off those anatomical details.

With the cast in tights and togas (and less), *Phi-Phi* was the perfect sort of silliness to launch the *"années folles,"* the 1920s. And if its book harked back to Plautus and Company, its songs and dances were resolutely up-to-date, in many cases the type of songs heard in the *café-concert* and in revue. This was hardly new to French operetta, which from the start had been based on dance rhythms and popular songs, but the fox-trot, the two-step, and later the Charleston and the shimmy would osmose themselves into the newest Parisian operettas, with *Phi-Phi* as a model. It was the beginning of the *comédie-musicale,* a form of operetta which gained songs based on the latest American dances, but lost the extended finales, the large violin-heavy orchestras, the big choruses, the elaborate scene-changes, and some of the *romance ancienne.* It was snappier, more dance-crazy, more a pretext for popular songs (the very type for which Albert Willemetz had been writing lyrics). In the process it became watered-down *opérette.* But *Phi-Phi* was seen by everyone. By the 1,000th performance, there appeared a celebrated poster showing an insignificant-looking man surrounded by jeering crowds: "The man who did not see *Phi-Phi.*"

The original Phi-Phi was the comic André Urban, who two years before at the Variétés had made his Paris début in the French version of *The Belle of New York*. Aspasie was Alice Cocéa, Madame Phidias was Pierrette Madd (succeeded by Alice Bonheur), and Yvonne Vallée (later Madame Maurice Chevalier) was in the ensemble. In London (Pavilion, 16 August 1922) the principal parts were taken by Clifton Webb (Phi-Phi), June (Aspasia), Vera Freeman (Mme. Phidias), with Evelyn Laye, Stanley Lupino, and old Arthur Roberts. Additional songs were added by Herman Darewski, Nat Ayer, and, surprisingly, Cole Porter ("The Ragtime Pipes of Pan," sung by Clifton Webb). Evelyn Laye made the biggest impression singing, "I'm the Smartest Girl in Greece," and because of this was London's Madame Pompadour (Fall) the next year. The dances were arranged, most engagingly, by the Dolly Sisters. The London book and lyrics were considerably toned down for British tastes by Fred Thompson and Clifford Grey and much of the fun of the French wordplay was lost. An enormously successful Parisian revival began its run in the 1979–80 season.

The next Christiné work was his other big hit, and even more a musical comedy. *Dédé* (Bouffes-Parisiens, 10 November 1921) was written by Willemetz, and starred Urban again, this time as the manager of a Paris shoestore.

One of his salesmen, Robert, was played by Maurice Chevalier, making a formidable first appearance in operetta after having starred at the Casino de Paris with Mistinguett the previous season. With his already familiar lip and his well-established way with a straw hat, Chevalier brought down the house with *"Pour bien réussir dans la chaussure"* (To succeed in shoeselling) and, even more famously, *"Dans la vie faut pas s'en faire"* (roughly, One shouldn't be bothered too much by life). There was a waltz—there was one in *Phi-Phi,* too—but audiences much preferred watching the bright young things dancing away to more modern rhythms. *Dédé* was filmed in 1934 with Albert Préjean and Danièlle Darrieux, and there was a reasonably successful revival in the 1970s with the pop singer Antoine. *Dédé* was unsuccessfully produced in London (Garrick, 17 October 1922) with Joseph Coyne and Gertrude Lawrence. Ronald Jeans's English book failed to capture the English audience.

The Théâtre Daunou picked up the next Christiné operetta, *Madame* (1923). Neither this nor the subsequent Daunou opus, *J'adore ça* (1925), were terribly impressive. *P.L.M.* (Bouffes-Parisiens, 1925) returned to the theme of romance aboard a sleeping car, so delightfully described in Fall's *Die geschiedene Frau* (1908), and *Arthur* (1929) was thought of highly enough to be filmed the following year. Yielding to the fashion for the *opérette à grand spectacle* that hit Paris in the early '30s, Christiné did two for the Châtelet in collaboration with Tiarko Richepin. The first was *Au Temps des Merveilleuses* (1934), with a libretto by Willemetz and Mouëzy-Eon, which starred André Baugé. The second, *Yana,* appeared two years later, with twenty-five elaborate scenes. In these spectaculars, Christiné wrote the more vibrant numbers, leaving the romantic airs to Richepin.

Maurice Yvain (1891–1965) was an even firmer believer in *comédie-musicale.* Born in Paris, he, like Christiné, began his career by writing popular songs for the cabaret and the *caf'-conc'.* His songs were later used in revue, popularized by such stars as Chevalier and Mistinguett. *"Mon Homme"* was probably the most famous, belonging as much to Fanny Brice in America (as "My Man") as to "Mist" in France. The Théâtre Daunou, wanting an operetta to rival the Bouffes-Parisiens's *Phi-Phi,* commissioned Yvain to set the libretto of *Ta Bouche* (Your Mouth, 1 April 1922) by Yves Mirande and Albert Willemetz. The book, which dealt with the adventures of three *nouveau-riche* couples at the seaside, was fiercely up-to-date and delightfully satirical. And Willemetz's lyrics were made virtually unforgettable by having the words appear on a lowered curtain in the theatre. *"De mon temps"* and *"Non, non, jamais les hommes"* were two of the more engaging songs, most of which were in the modern idiom. But a few ensembles of old remained to show that Yvain could actually do them, and his orchestra, though reduced, was not quite the jazzy one Gershwin or Youmans would be using on Broadway. The popular boulevard comedian Victor Boucher—no

Aspasia (June), wife of the sculptor Phidias, gives out invitations to her husband Phi-Phi (Clifton Webb) and Mercury (Stanley Lupino) in the substantially altered British production of Christiné's *Phi-Phi* at the London Pavilion, 1922.

singer—made a spectacular impression in *Ta Bouche,* and was for a long time called Taboucher.

Ta Bouche crossed the ocean in 1923, becoming *One Kiss* (Fulton, 27 November) on Broadway. In Charles Dillingham's production were Ada Lewis, Louise Groody, and Oscar Shaw, and the show ran a quarter season. The British production of *Just a Kiss* (Shaftesbury, 8 September 1926) had extra songs by Vivian Ellis. Included was the title song from Yvain's *Là-Haut* which had recently opened in Paris. A highly successful revival of *Ta Bouche,* mounted in Paris in the 1979–80 season, revealed the work as a sort of *real* French equivalent of Sandy Wilson's *The Boy Friend.*

Bouche à bouche (Apollo) and *Pas sur la bouche!* (Nouveautés) both appeared in 1925. Both had excellent scores, the former perhaps even more carefully regressing to ensembles in the old style, especially the comic petrol trio, with its "Royal Dutch, Royal Dutch . . ." catch-refrain. And there was also a lovely title waltz-duet. *Pas sur la bouche!,* with its bubbly second-act finale *"Sur le quai Malaquais,"* had a long run, and was filmed in 1931. The story actually concerned an American husband who liked to kiss and be kissed, "but not on the mouth"! Such were the dramatic issues of the 1920s.

Yvain was not restricted to titles with the word *bouche,* though very few of his remaining seventeen or so operettas, with three exceptions, were as applauded or remembered as his mouth operettas. *La Dame en décolleté* (1923), *Gosse de Riche* (1924), *Un bon garçon* (1926), *Yes* (1928),[1] *Elle est à vous* (1929), and so on into the '30s, are for the most part forgotten, save for their principal songs. *Un bon garçon* underwent a sex-change operation and appeared on Broadway as *Luckee Girl* (Casino, 15 September 1928), with Irene Dunne in a leading role. Most of Yvain's songs (for which he also, for a change, wrote the words) were replaced by other creations in New York.

Yvain's other exceptional work of the 1920s was *Là-Haut,* an *opérette-bouffe* with book by Yves Mirande and Gustave Quinson, and lyrics by Albert Willemetz (Bouffes-Parisiens, 31 March 1923), which was, again, popularized by the participation therein of Maurice Chevalier and his partner, Yvonne Vallée. The story of a man who dreams he is "up-there" in heaven and who comes to earth to see what his widow is up to, *Là-Haut* combined fantasy and high spirits in a manner that lightly recalled Offenbachian days—though the music was squarely of the '20s. In the role of the guardian angel was Dranem, whose reception by the audience was so enthusiastic that Chevalier jealously quit the cast (along with Vallée). He would never again appear on the operetta stage, though he later recorded both *Dédé* and *Là-Haut,* and we can still enjoy his singing of *Là-Haut*'s big hit fox-trot, *"Le premier, le seul, le vrai paradis, c'est Paris."* Dranem, meanwhile, made a great hit of his laughing song, *"l'Hilarité céleste."*

In 1935, Yvain followed Christiné into the realm of spectacular operetta with *Au Soleil du Mexique* (In the Mexican Sun, Châtelet, 18 December 1935) with a

---

[1]Performed at the tiny Théâtre des Capucines with only two pianos, and considered by historian Florian Bruyas one of Yvain's best works.

book by Willemetz and Mouëzy-Eon that detailed the story of a toreador who at one point found himself in Hawaii (perfect for a volcano!). As in Christiné's case, there was a second composer (Granville) and a cast headed by the elegant André Baugé, this time surrounded by such admirable operetta-specialists as Fanély Revoil, Bach, and Danièlle Brégis. In 1946, after a failed revival of *Ta Bouche* at the Mogador (a theatre much too large for it), Yvain came forth with another spectacular, *Chanson Gitane* (Gypsy Song, Gaîté-Lyrique, 13 December), which is still held dear by many Frenchmen. With André Dassary and Rita Mazzoni heading the cast, and lavish 1820s costumes and scenery, this gypsy extravaganza was popular enough to be revived at the Gaîté-Lyrique in 1950 and again in 1954.

Yvain's wholly successful career spanned the range from popular revue songs to musical comedy to spectacular operetta. He also had time to write film scores, including those for Julien Duvivier's *La belle Équipe* (1936), the Printemps-Fresnay film *Le Duel* (1938), and a vehicle for Tino Rossi, *Lumières de Paris* (1938).

The mantle of *élégance française* was worn, after Lecocq and Messager, by **Reynaldo Hahn** (1875–1947). Born in Venezuela, he was a student of Massenet at the Paris Conservatoire. By the age of thirteen, he was writing songs, like his later *chansons grises,* many of which survived in the repertoire of such concert artists as Maggie Teyte. In 1890, he composed the incidental music for Alphonse Daudet's *L'Obstacle* at the Gymnase, and two years later there followed the first of several ballets, the most famous of which was *Le Dieu bleu,* written for Diaghilev and produced at the Châtelet with Nijinsky and Karsavina in 1912. The Opéra-Comique saw several Hahn works, *La Carmélite* (1902) and *Nausicaa* (1919) being two examples, and he conducted the celebratory Armistice revival of *La Fille de Madame Angot* at that theatre in December 1918.

On 7 April 1923, the Théâtre des Variétés presented a work which brought distinction to that temple of operetta, *Ciboulette*. The libretto, a throwback to those set fifty years before by Lecocq and later by Messager, was by Robert de Flers and Francis de Croisset, and told of a Parisian market girl (*ciboulette* is the French for "chives") destined to meet her lover, Antonin, under some cabbage heads. Rodolphe, Mimi's lover in Mürger's *Scènes de la vie de Bohème* has here grown up into Duparquet, of Les Halles, and there were other colorful Second Empire characters, including the waltz-composer Olivier Métra. A first-rate cast included Edmée Favart and Jean Périer as Ciboulette and Duparquet and Henri Defreyn as Antonin. This only compounded the nostalgia of the evening: Périer had been the first Florestan (in *Véronique*) and Defreyn, the first Paris Danilo (in *The Merry Widow*).

The score to *Ciboulette* restored to operetta the grace and finesse so intimately associated with French music. Instead of the music-hall banalities of the turn of the century, the fox-trots of the late teens, and the jazz of the '20s, Hahn reverted to the romances, scintillating duets, ensembles, and grand finales of the early Messagerian works of the 1890s. Just listening to the overture, audiences knew they would be hearing an unusually well-thought-out work. A work that

went, however, beyond mere pastiche, for Hahn was too accomplished to be a
copyist. There was a modern, breezy feeling in *Ciboulette* that made it fresh
rather than merely antique. Set in 1867, in the Halles beloved of Lecocq, Messager, and their librettists, one might have thought *Ciboulette* was a parody of
their works. But however characteristic the libretto may have been, the music
was imitative of the older masters in the most complimentary sense. *"Nous
avons fait un beau voyage"* (We've had a nice trip) has the running to-and-fro of
a typical Messager duet or ensemble, yet goes further in its contrapuntal exchange. *Ciboulette*'s name song, *" 'Y'a des femmes qui s'appellent Marie"* (There
are girls named Marie), similarly takes off from the usual Lecocquian entrance
couplets by utilizing the chorus from the beginning, rather than waiting for it
merely to echo the refrain. *Ciboulette*'s orchestration sparkles and bubbles with
dozens of sixteenth notes when other composers were infatuated with dotted
syncopations. Yet Hahn could be reflective, touching, and quiet better than anyone else, as in *"Ce n'était pas la même chose"* (It wasn't the same thing) and the
affecting letter song in Act II. Perhaps best of all—how difficult to choose!—
was the finaletto to the second scene of the first act, with its *"Muguet! Muguet!
Joli muguet!"* (Lovely lily-of-the-valley), an ensemble exuding a perfume not
savored in French operetta since Messager's Halles scene in *Les p'tites Michu*
(1897). And there was a great waltz, *"Amour qui meurt, amour qui passe,"* to end
the third act with a grand flourish. Curiously, Hahn's old-fashioned *Ciboulette*
appeared in the same season as Messager's more *moderne L'Amour masqué*, making 1923 a glorious year that French operetta would not again recapture.

Hahn himself would not recapture *Ciboulette*'s glory quite as prodigiously in
subsequent works, though he provided some extremely accomplished scores.
Two were for Sacha Guitry: *Mozart* (1925) and *Ô mon bel inconnu* (1933). The
first (Théâtre Édouard VII, 2 December 1925) was a return to the *travesti* tradition, with Yvonne Printemps in breeches as the young composer in a play with
music lacking the usual operetta ensembles. Bits of real Mozart were incorporated (such as chunks from *Les petits riens*), but Hahn provided his own creations
into which Printemps breathed immortality. (Messager was to have done the
score, but declined to have his music and Mozart's mixed.)

As one critic mentioned, Printemps sang as naturally as she breathed. James
Agate wrote of the London presentation (Gaiety, 21 June 1926):

> It is not exaggerating to say that on Monday evening people were observed to cry,
> and by that I mean shed tears, when Music's heavenly child appeared at the top of
> the stairs and came down them to kneel at Mme. d'Épinay's feet . . . At the moment of her entrance this exquisite artist made conquest of the house, and subsequently held it in thrall until the final curtain . . . Mlle. Printemps uses song and
> speech indifferently, changing almost imperceptibly from one to the other . . . M.
> Guitry plays the Baron with verve and brilliance whenever Mlle. Printemps's occasional absences from the scene call for such display. At other times he stands apart,
> rapt like one who has accomplished a marvel. And we in the audience perfectly
> understand the reason for that rapture.[2]

[2]Agate, James, *Innocent Toys,* pp. 24, 28.

Le Temps d'aimer (1926) was for the Théâtre de la Michodière—an intimate musical comedy that proffered fox-trots and Charlestons, well constructed and orchestrated, said the critics, but not perhaps what Hahn excelled in. Better the period charm of *Brummel* (Folies-Wagram, 20 January 1931), set in Regency England, with such songs as *"Être un dandy, un vrai dandy"* and *"Les dandys de Brummel."* The book was by the revue specialist, Rip (with Robert Dieudonné), and the lovely décors were by Fernand Ochsé. With a cast headed by Marguerite Deval, Louis Arnoult, and the comedian Robert Pizani as Brummel, the operetta might have had a considerable run were it not for the perilous Depression that had hit France.

The second Guitry-Hahn work, *Ô mon bel inconnu* (Bouffes-Parisiens, 5 October, 1933), was the story of a bored middle-aged hatter who poses as a bachelor and corresponds through a box number with his own wife and daughter. This was a modern-dress musical comedy, with the cast headed by Aquistapace (as the hatter), René Koval (in a mute role, apparently cast by Guitry because Koval had once had a liaison with one of Sacha's wives), and Abel Tarride. There were also Mmes. Suzanne Dantès (as the wife), Simone Simon (later of Hollywood fame, as the daughter), and Arletty, as the maid, who opened the proceedings amusingly with a Guitry-Hahn conceit all about breakfast. *Ô mon bel inconnu* was and remains, sadly, exactly what it means, a "beautiful unknown," too refined and slight for a public that was slowly nurturing a taste for thumping spectaculars.

Hahn's last completed operetta was *Malvina* (Gaîté-Lyrique, 23 March 1935), which seemed an attempt to recapture the magic of *Ciboulette*. It was set in 1830, and there was a song about first names in the first act, and a letter song later on, and some of the music had already been used in the '20s, in Hahn's *Revue* of 1926. Hahn became the director of the Paris Opéra in 1945, just two years before his death, at seventy-two. A last work was finished by Henri Büsser, *Le Oui des jeunes filles,* presented posthumously at the Opéra-Comique in 1947. None of Hahn's creations—apart from his salon songs—has been as consistently revived and admired as *Ciboulette,* which entered the repertoire of the Opéra-Comique in 1953 (after several Paris revivals) with Géori Boué and Roger Bourdin, conducted by Albert Wolff. *Ciboulette* had also been filmed in 1933 by Claude Autant-Lara, and in the next year Hahn contributed music to films of both *La Dame aux Camélias* (with Yvonne Printemps) and Daudet's *Sapho.*

Hahn shared with Messager the ability to get the most out of a thinnish melody through entrancing orchestration—one seldom hears a Hahn song hummed in the street. For this, he was probably considered too refined, too much of an academician and not enough of a popular tunesmith. His association with both more ambitious musical forms and composers associated with them might have accounted for a certain *snobisme* in his operettas, but Hahn never looked down on the form.

Modern spectacular operetta in France had its origins at the Théâtre du Châtelet. This theatre had been associated throughout the 1860s with melodrama, such as *Le Courrier de Lyon* (The Lyons Mail) and *Le Juif errant* (The Wandering Jew), until the mid-1870s, when it became principally known for its spectacles. *Around the World in 80 Days* and *Michel Strogoff* were two favorites, each racking up thousands of performances in frequent revivals. There were occasional operettas (Offenbach's *Le Voyage dans la Lune* was one) but it was not until the 1920s that the theatre decided to devote itself consistently to operetta, beginning in 1928 with popular American works that lent themselves to the spectacular Châtelet stage facilities. *Show Boat* and *The New Moon* were the first. Eventually, the works of French composers were produced, such as Christiné's *Au Temps des Merveilleuses* and Yvain's *Au Soleil du Mexique*.

However successful these were, the true passion for *l'opérette à grand spectacle* did not begin until after the Occupation, when Parisians, tired of privations, became enchanted with productions that cunningly mixed the Spanish and other Mediterranean rhythms they had grown to love in 1930s films, syrupy love stories, and the *tableaux* they had always admired at the Folies-Bergère and other music halls. This mixture was, admittedly, not for every taste, but it pleased enough of the *petit-bourgeoisie* to provide the Châtelet and the Mogador and other venues with exceedingly long runs and constant revivals.

The fascination for Mediterranean music, so popular in the 1920s and '30s, made stars of such singers as Luis Mariano, Tino Rossi, and Georges Guétary (who was born Lambros Worlu in Egypt), all of whom appeared in operetta. One of the principal composers in this genre was **Vincent Scotto** (1876–1952) of Neapolitan descent, whose first works appeared in his native Marseille. *Au Pays du Soleil* (1932) was the first significant one, an operetta-revue with a book by Henri Alibert, who wrote most of Scotto's early libretti. His film songs for Joséphine Baker won him more fame. *Trois de la Marine* appeared in 1933, and in 1936 *Un de la Canebière* was mounted at the Variétés, proving once and for all that the new, Mediterranean variety of operetta would attract Paris just as well or better than any more sophisticated or better-composed work. Marseille would soon open the doors to Spain, Mexico, and similar areas.

But the rush did not really begin until after the war, in 1945, when on Christmas Eve *La Belle de Cadix* opened at the Casino-Montparnasse. This was by **Francis Lopez** (1916–   ), born in the Basque country and the composer still associated with this genre perhaps more than any other. *La Belle de Cadix* concerned the movie star Carlos Medina, smitten with Maria-Luisa but admired by an American, Cecilia Hampton, in ten scenes that switched from Cannes to Cadiz. There was a gypsy wedding and even an airport scene, so a comparison to the Ivor Novello spectacles at Drury Lane in the late 1930s would be apropos. What made *La Belle de Cadix* such a triumphal success was the singing and dark looks of Luis Mariano, who had hitherto appeared in opera, variety, and radio without much notice. The operetta ran two years, and Mariano and Lopez were teamed for a total of eight works in Paris and another in Madrid (not to mention several films in the early '50s). *Andalousie* (Gaîté-Lyrique, 1947), *Le Chanteur de Mexico* (Châtelet, 1951), and *La Route fleurie* (A.B.C., 1952) were the other substantial Lopez hits.

The other great theatre for spectacular operetta was the Mogador, long associated with its manager-director Henri Varna. In 1947, Vincent Scotto decided to leave his usual Marseille settings for the apparently more lucrative Spain in *Violettes impériales,* which Varna mounted in costly splendor and for which he also co-authored the book. This took viewers to Seville and Paris, *circa* 1852–54, in some sixteen scenes. The next-to-closing spot was a memorable *tableau-vivant,* an *évocation de Winterhalter,* the famed court painter of the Second Empire, showing the ladies of the ensemble posed in Worth gowns in front of a palace.

This time the plot was somewhat more interesting and less hackneyed than usual (although no less contrived). It told of Eugénie de Montijo, the man she was betrothed to marry, her eventual marriage to Napoléon III, and the sacrifice of Violetta in an attempted assassination of the Empress. *Violettes impériales* similarly brought a male singer to prominence. After a wartime appearance at the Mogador in Straus's *Ein Walzertraum* (Rêve de Valse), Marcel Merkès hit his stride with the Imperial Violets, singing the role of Juan more than two thousand times in a career that is still going strong. With him in the original cast were Lina Walls as Violetta and Raymonde Allain as Eugénie. Curiously, *Violettes impériales* was filmed in 1952 with a new score by Francis Lopez, for Luis Mariano.

Scotto wrote two other operettas of note for the Mogador, *La Danseuse aux Étoiles* (1950) and the posthumous *Les Amants de Venise* (1953). But *Violettes impériales* remains his most famous and most revived work. A version was running in Paris in December 1981.

Francis Lopez is virtually the last popular French operetta composer, his works having earned considerable receipts for many French theatres in Paris and in the provinces. Until the recent conversion of the Châtelet to the Théâtre Musical de Paris (1980), his *oeuvre* could regularly be seen at that theatre. Lopez would then move his operations to the Théâtre de la Renaissance. Three of the biggest Lopez hits were *Méditerranée* (1955), *Le Secret de Marco Polo* (1959), and *Visa pour l'Amour* (1961). Tino Rossi appeared in the first, and Luis Mariano in the last two. The appeal of tango and bolero singers has always been potent in France, as well as abroad, and several of the Scotto and Lopez operettas were sent on tours to the countries surrounding France as well as to Canada. Their scores have nevertheless only the slightest musical interest, admittedly serving as barely melodic accompaniments for the *grand spectacle.* Tunewise, they offer nothing to appeal to Anglo-Saxon ears, which only too happily succumb to the melodies of Ivor Novello, whose effusive scores draped similar spectaculars on the London stage.

Several Frenchmen known in this century for other compositions are the modern equivalents of Delibes, Bizet, and their fellow composers. Although none of these moderns ever came up with as brilliant an operetta as Hahn's *Ciboulette,* it is still useful to record their honorable attempts in this genre. Some critics would categorize Francis Poulenc's *Les Mamelles de Tirésias* (1944) or Ravel's *L'Heure espagnole* (1911) as operetta. I would not. It is not that they are too heavily conceived for their respective libretti, but they are frankly lacking in the lightness of spirit and popular appeal necessary in operetta.

It is encouraging to note that several of *"Les Six,"* and other French composers as well, did not find it beneath their dignity to compose operettas. Erik Satie had his *Coco chéri* produced in Monte-Carlo in 1913, Georges Auric wrote at least two, *Sous le masque* (1923) and *Les Oiseaux* (From *The Birds* of Aristophanes, 1928), while Darius Milhaud did not succeed in 1925 with *Esther de Carpentras*. But Arthur Honegger had a substantial hit at the Bouffes-Parisiens with *Les Aventures du Roi Pausole* (12 December 1930), in spite of a score that had hardly any hit songs. The reason was Albert Willemetz's risqué book and lyrics, and a cast that included (at one time or another) such future film stars as Edwige Feuillère, Simone Simon, Suzy Delair, and Meg Lemonnier. Manuel Rosenthal, who so cleverly arranged Offenbach's music for the ballet *Gaîté Parisienne,* had a success in *La Poule noire* (The Black Hen, 1937), which was put into the repertoire of the Opéra-Comique in 1956.

Very few, if any, of the above were really intended to appeal to a broad cross-section of the French population, whereas two other respected composers at least sought public acceptance.

Louis Beydts (1896–1953) knew and admired Reynaldo Hahn and André Messager, at one time his teacher, and several critics have noted Beydts's elegant touch. *Moineau* (Sparrow, Marigny, 13 March 1931) starred Marcelle Denya and Robert Burnier in a saucy book by Henri Duvernois and Pierre Wolff. There was *hommage* to Messager's *Véronique* in a swing song and in one of the settings (at Romainville), and there was even a song with *"cahin-caha"* to remind one of the Donkey Song. It was easily the most musicianly and classically built operetta of its season (save, perhaps, for Hahn's *Brummel*) and one would like to be able to hear it today. There was also that year at the Madeleine a collaboration with Sacha Guitry, *La S.A.D.M.P.* (an acronym for *Société Anonyme Des Messieurs Prudents*), from which its star, Yvonne Printemps, recorded two charming numbers. The Marigny tried in 1947 to recapture the pleasures of *Moineau* with *À l'aimable Sabine,* but the elegant audiences of prewar days which delighted in the kind of exquisite melody and harmony Beydts supplied were thinning out. A sample of the Beydts style can still be heard in the film music he composed for the 1938 film *La Kermesse héroïque.*

Gabriel Pierné (1863–1937) is today remembered solely for his classical works, though he, in fact, had written operettas as far back as 1893 *(Le Docteur Blanc)* and was well regarded as a conductor—he had studied with Franck and Massenet. *Fragonard* (Porte Saint-Martin, 16 October 1934) was his best operetta, with a cast led by Andre Baugé, as the painter, and Jane Marnac as the dancer La Guimard. It was an eighteenth-century evocation, librettists André Rivoire and Romain Coolus doing for the artist what Lehár and his writers had done for Paganini in their operetta, but it was entirely too delicate, even precious, for the less-refined tastes of 1930s' audiences. Nevertheless, the critics adored it, and in

1946 it entered the repertory of the Opéra-Comique, where Fanély Revoil took the part of La Guimard and charmed all with her ravishing singing.

Eduard Künneke (1885–1953), born in the Rhineland, was a merchant's son. He studied composition in Berlin under Max Bruch, and his first staged work was an opera, *Robins Ende* (1909). This was followed by a spell as composer and musical director for Max Reinhardt at the Deutsches Theater. He conducted the first Berlin performances of *Das Dreimäderlhaus* at the Friedrich-Wilhelm-städisches Theater and provided the house with an original *Singspiel* of his own, *Das Dorf ohne Glocke* (The Village Without a Bell, 1919), set in a German village in Transylvania at the end of the eighteenth century. Two operettas followed. One was *Wenn Liebe erwacht* (Theater am Nollendorfplatz, 3 September 1920), produced as *Love's Awakening* in London (Empire, 1922), without acclaim. Then, in 1921, came *Der Vetter aus Dingsda* (Theater am Nollendorfplatz, 15 April 1921). This played at the Johann-Strauss-Theater, Vienna, all over Germany and Austria, in London, as *The Cousin from Nowhere* (Princes, 24 February 1923), and in New York, set in Civil War Virginia, as *Caroline* (Ambassador, 31 January 1923). It has been filmed twice (1934, 1953).

As in Fall's *Geschiedene Frau,* the action takes place in Holland, and the libretto (by the revue-writers Herman Haller and Rideamus) was the slightest nonsense, a simple romance about a stranger mistaking a country house for a country inn. "I'm Only a Strolling Vagabond" *(Ich bin nur ein armer Wanderge-sell)* was the stranger's anthem, the show's most popular song. There was also the *Strahlender Mond* (Magical Moon) waltz and the enthralling duet, *"Ich trink' auf dein lachendes Augenpaar"* (I drink to your laughing eyes), which was worthy of Lehár. And more: a captivating tango, and a spirited Act II finale-ensemble, *"Der Roderich, der Roderich,"* which mildly burlesqued operatic models. All this could only have seemed even more fresh and charming because the operetta had only two simple sets, contemporary dress, and—more significantly—no chorus. After the more elaborately escapist wartime operettas, *Der Vetter aus Dingsda* must have seemed refreshingly simple. Starring in the original Berlin cast was Ilse Marvenga, who was later the first Kathie in Romberg's *The Student Prince* on Broadway.

Künneke spent the '20s in Berlin and New York (1924–25), where a succession of his operettas appeared, without achieving quite the popularity of *Der Vetter aus Dingsda*. Titles included *Ehe im Krise* (Marriage in Crisis, 1921), *Casino Girls* (1923), and *Die hellblauen Schwestern* (The Light Blue Sisters, 1925).

In New York, Künneke supervised an Offenbach life-and-loves-and-music pastiche, *The Love Song,* and wrote original music for *Mayflowers,* both in 1925 and both for the Shuberts, with whom he was contracted. He also wrote a show for London's Gaiety Theatre, *Riki-Tiki,* which lasted only eighteen performances. *Lady Hamilton* (Breslau, 1926), was set in England, and in its original cast was Anny Ahlers, a soprano rising to the top of operetta stardom. Anglicized completely by Arthur Wimperis and Lauri Wylie, it became, in London,

The Song of the Sea (His Majesty's, 6 September 1928), starring Lilian Davies and Stanley Holloway. A series of tableaux set in 1810 allowed for lovely costumes, seen 156 times. *Die blonde Liselott,* 1927, was revised and revived to better acclaim as plain *Liselott* in 1932. This was set in France in the reign of Louis XIV and was perhaps an attempt to cash in on the newfound success of the Millöcker-Mackeben *Dubarry,* another romance of old France. In the cast was the great German actor Gustaf Gründgens, opposite him an equally fine actress, Käthe Dorsch, and with them the sophisticated Hilde Hildebrand.

Another 1932 work, *Glückliche Reise* (Bon Voyage, Kurfürstendamm-Theater, 23 November) has remained quite popular. This had a contemporary setting (rural Brazil and Berlin) and an unusual combination of tangos and other snappy Latin rhythms (a *paso doble,* a rumba or two), a title march song, and the one soaring duet, *"Liebe kennt keine Grenzen"* (Love knows no borders). *Glückliche Reise* was a happy, elaborate hit, and certainly Künneke's last work of lasting fame. Toothy Lizzi Waldmüller enjoyed great popularity in the leading female part, just prior to her big success in Nazi-era musical films. During the Hitler years, Künneke remained in Berlin to provide such works as *Die lockende Flamme* (1933), *Klein Dorrit* (1933, from Dickens), *Die grosse Sünderin* (The Great Sinner, 1935), and *Traumland* (Dreamland, 1941). All in all, he composed some twenty-five operettas before his death in 1953. One could do worse today than relisten to *Der Vetter aus Dingsda,* preferably with its original orchestrations. Though the plot is numbingly dumb (how could people have sat through it?), a clever producer might do it absolutely straight, for added laughs. And many Lehár-lovers might find a collection of his love duets quite thrilling.

The style of **Kurt Weill** (1900–1950) might have been called eclectic, his works having elements of *Lehrstück* (teaching-piece), *Singspiel,* operetta (in the comic-opera tradition), jazz, blues, and dance-band, dignified by a solid classical background and the influence of modern (1920s) composers. Some are genuine through-composed operas (*Royal Palace,* for example), while others are more *Singspiel*-ish, like *Die Dreigroschenoper*. *Lady in the Dark* is a complete treat: each of the three major "dreams" is like an extended operetta finale, using Ira Gershwin's thoroughly nineteenth-century construction, via Offenbach and Gilbert and Sullivan, with radio-modern crooning juxtaposed with Victorian patter songs. Weill's style was more than eclectic—he wanted to use popular idioms to "write music to express human emotions," as he told a New York *Sun* interviewer in 1940. It was this sense of communication that encouraged his *Gebrauchsmusik,* or music for "practical purposes," as he put it. His direction was clearly toward the opera disguised as "musical drama" of *Street Scene* (1947), but he "never

---

Künneke's *Der Vetter aus Dingsda* reached London's Prince's Theatre in 1923, two years after its Berlin première. This bewitching score—still heard in Germany—must have pleased discriminating theatregoers tired of ragtime and revue. In the final scene, the "Stranger" (Walter Williams, center) reveals himself to the seated heroine, Julia (Helen Gilliland).

acknowledged the difference between 'serious' music and 'light' music. There is only good music and bad music."

Weill had the fortune to have Bertolt Brecht for his librettist for several works; conversely, Brecht was lucky to have had Weill. It was a justly celebrated combination. Weill's search for a more moderate replacement for his hardline-didactic Marxist collaborator resulted in his teaming with several excellent poets: Georg Kaiser, Maxwell Anderson, Ira Gershwin, Langston Hughes, all of whom inspired some brilliant music, but no single work as internationally successful as *The Threepenny Opera*. Much can be said in favor of *Lady in the Dark* and *Street Scene,* but no one seems prepared to mount a full-scale revival of *Lady in the Dark* when the glittering original cast and the production are still lustrous memories in many minds. Yet, as a period piece—in a few years, with a revised book—I have little doubt it will return in glory.

Though Weill probably would not have admitted it, he wrote at least one of the greatest of twentieth-century operettas, and possibly one or two more which are either underrated or not classified operettas by musical-theatre historians. *Die Dreigroschenoper* ranks as perhaps the most original of modern operettas; surprising, as it is concretely moored to one of the *earliest* works, *The Beggar's Opera. Mahagonny* is more ambitious musically, and much more an opera. Modern producers have concentrated on these two works, though recently various European theatres and festivals have mounted more of his pre-1933 German output, while American groups (amateur and professional) have happily rediscovered his Broadway scores.

Die Dreigroschenoper opens with a symphonic overture that was unlike any for an operetta heard up to that time. Its distinctive sound came from Weill's use of what the programme called the Lewis-Ruth Band, under the leadership of Theo Mackeben. This jazzy sound would naturally have shocked normal Berlin operetta audiences, certainly those who were enamored of the Lehár-Tauber collaborations. However, *Jonny spielt auf* (Johnny, Strike Up, 1927, Leipzig), the jazz opera by Ernst Křenek, had already received some notoriety, as had Weill's earlier pieces. Some in the Theater am Schiffbauerdamm audience on the night of 31 August 1928 knew more or less what to expect—Brecht's preaching and Weill's modern sounds—but most did not. They probably did not think they would get a Brecht/Weill piece that was as *entertaining* as *Die Dreigroschenoper*. The celebrated *"Moritat,"* added at the last minute for Kurt Gerron, as the Streetsinger, did not immediately catch on. According to Lotte Lenya, the audience sat quietly through (what was later known as) "Mack the Knife," and the entrance song of Peachum (the part originally intended for Peter Lorre). This was a *Morgenchoral,* the music taken directly from the first number in the Gay-Pepusch *Beggar's Opera*. And they were quiet for the "Instead-Of" duet, and the Wedding Song, until they really sat up and applauded the swaggering *"Kanonen"* Song. From that point on, total glee reigned, as did *The Threepenny Opera*'s assured success in Central Europe, if not for the social reasons Brecht had envisaged. Weill's tinny, bouncy tunes carried Brecht's name further than the dramatist had been able to do himself up to that time. Another in the first-night audience, Robert Lantz, remembered the entire score being enthusiastically received. The cast of the original production was headed by Harald Paulsen as Macheath, Roma Bahn as Polly, and Lotte Lenya as Jenny.

In a score so replete with famous songs—those written for the part of Jenny have become virtual *Lieder*—it is interesting to look at the ensembles, the duets, and those "test" finales. The Cannon Song, in a raucous way, recalls the gaiety of the Symon/Jan first-act duet in *Der Bettelstudent,* though the refrain of the Polish students was totally sweet compared to the savagery of the reminiscence of Macheath's and Tiger Brown's delight in chopping up natives into beefsteak tartar when they were both soldiers.

How charmingly—with his jazz forces—Weill has set Brecht's cynical verses for the two love duets between Macheath and Polly, and how forcefully he has composed his three bitter finales, the first two titled "The Uncertainty of Human Conditions" and "Ballad About the Question: 'What Keeps a Man Alive?' " In the original production, these phrases were projected on a banner, and, according to Brecht's instructions, the singers would seem to cease acting, approach the audience, and sing their parts as in a radio broadcast. These are not typical operetta finales in that they basically contain one song each, and the first finale is a trio, without chorus. Yet, in their melodic variety, counterpoint, and driving fury (especially the very end), they are unequivocally very great operetta finales. The third-act finale contains not only a deliberate parody of operetta, the chorus elaborately announcing the arrival of the King's riding messenger, but also at least a slight reference to Beethoven's *Fidelio,* when Polly and Macheath exclaim, *"Gerettet!"* (Saved!), only to be followed by a sardonic chorale expressing Brecht's profound depression with the human condition. In the dazzling *Eifersucht* (jealousy) duet we note Weill once again borrowing from Gay/Pepusch ("I'm Bubbled, I'm Troubled"). In the end, the audience cared more for Weill's sprightly music than for Brecht's morality. Within a few months numerous theatres in Germany were including *Die Dreigroschenoper* in their repertoires.

The *Threepenny Opera* produced in New York in 1933 (Empire, 13 April) had little appeal in a translation by Gifford Cochran and Jerrold Krimsky, with Robert Chisolm as Macheath and Steffi Duna as Polly. There exists the idea that the production was glossed up for Broadway, but in fact the original designs by Caspar Neher were used, and there was an attempt to be as Brechtian as possible. The New York *Times* found it "worth the seeing," but most of the other critics hated the operetta, which was quite unlike any they had ever seen, and one went so far as to call it "sugar-coated communism." Its twelve performances stood in stark contrast to the more than 2,500 it registered in its celebrated Off-Broadway run at the Theatre de Lys, from 10 March 1954. Lotte Lenya led the cast as Jenny, but her later absence in no way detracted from the excellence of Marc Blitzstein's brilliant adaptation, and the fitting intimacy of the theatre. A later adaptation presented by the New York Shakespeare Festival at the Vivian Beaumont Theatre had a grittier translation by Ralph Manheim and John Gillett but also an affected musical and dramatic production by Richard Foreman that did not really please the public the way the de Lys production had. A brilliant poster was one happy by-product, however. Designed by Paul Davis, it showed Raul Julia as a monocled Macheath.

Productions in Britain and France were never as popular, but a brilliant revival in London in 1972, directed by Tony Richardson with a new translation by the Scottish poet Hugh McDiarmid, was the best this writer ever saw. Two films of *Die Dreigroschenoper* were made in Germany, the celebrated G. W. Pabst version of 1931, with Rudolf Forster and Lotte Lenya, and a forgotten 1963 refilming by Wolfgang Staudte with Curt Jürgens as Macheath and Sammy Davis, Jr., singing "Mack the Knife."

The Theater am Schiffbauerdamm looked to Brecht and Weill for another piece, and *Happy End* was produced there on 2 September 1929. The same directors (Erich Engel and Brecht), designer (Caspar Neher), and jazz band (under Mackeben) were engaged by the show's producer to ensure a success to match that of its predecessor. Though the story did not turn overtly political until Act III, on the first night it provoked a riot. The critics condemned the work as a pale imitation of *Die Dreigroschenoper,* and, after a brief run, the German original lay dormant until 1958, when it was revived in a revised version in Munich. Recorded in Berlin under the CBS auspices that produced successful recordings of *Die Dreigroschenoper* and *Mahagonny* in the 1950s, the work attracted American attention, getting a production at Yale and another in New York, where it ran a few weeks at the end of the 1976–77 season. The Weill-ologist David Drew has correctly pointed out that the songs in *Happy End* are purely decorative; indeed, that is why as a stage work *Happy End* will rarely find producers or audiences. Yet the song hits have an irresistible appeal, especially as sung by Lenya.

Mahagonny, a more ambitious work, started small as *Das kleine Mahagonny,* and there are those who might argue that it ought to have stayed that way. The enlarged version was not performed until after *Happy End,* in Leipzig (9 March 1930, Neues Theater). Like *Happy End,* it betrays Brecht's fascination with America and its gangsters. As sardonic and cynical as ever, *Mahagonny* is not lighthearted, and its music is entirely more operatic than operettic—as proved by excellent productions in East Berlin's Komische Oper (1978) and at the Metropolitan Opera (1979).

It is often forgotten that Kurt Weill's operatic career was well established before he worked with Bertolt Brecht. The expressionist playwright Georg Kaiser provided the libretti for *Der Protagonist,* a one-act piece of 1925 which was extraordinarily well received in 1925, for *Der Zar lässt sich photographieren* (1927, The Czar Has Himself Photographed), a more comic short opera, and for *Der Silbersee* (1933), which was written after the collaboration with Brecht had ceased. Though none of these are operetta, *Der Silbersee* (The Silver Lake) had two pantomimes-within-the-opera, a forerunner of the operettas-within-the-musical of *Lady in the Dark* a decade later. The New York City Opera mounted an impressive reworking of *Silbersee* in 1980. Also stemming from the Brecht-Weill partnership are *Der Jasager,* a *Lehrstück,* several cantatas, and their post-emigration Paris opera-ballet, *The Seven Deadly Sins* (1933)—but these are outside our borders. Also from Paris was Weill's score for the Jacques Deval play *Marie Galante* (1934). In London, *A Kingdom for a Cow* (1935), with libretto by Desmond Carter and Reginald Arkell, was quietly forgotten.

Moving on to New York to provide the incidental music for the Max Reinhardt–Franz Werfel Biblical spectacle, *The Eternal Road* (1935), Weill decided to stay on the Broadway scene. *Johnny Johnson,* an antiwar tract by Paul Green, produced by the Group Theatre (44th Street, 17 November 1936), was a *Singspiel-Songspiel* with just enough of the German Weillisms to remind those in this country who knew about the composer's work of his former triumphs. But it was not really the stuff of the popular musical theatre.

The next U.S. show made concessions to a more Americanized style on one hand, and, on the other, harked back to comic opera—*Knickerbocker Holiday* (Ethel Barrymore, 19 October 1938), one of Weill's most attractive works. At the time, the score was chiefly admired for one number, the celebrated "September Song," which quickly became a radio favorite. In the play, the aging Pieter Stuyvesant (Walter Huston) reflected on his fading chances as an amorous swain. The part was originally conceived for the D'Oyly Carte star Martyn Green, and the rest of Stuyvesant's material has a definite Gilbert and Sullivan spirit. The chorus constantly responds to transpiring events, supporting Stuyvesant in two effective ensembles, "The Scars," and "All Hail the Political Honeymoon," with a forceful, mock-fascist close to Act I using the latter song. The seventeenth-century setting and costumes gave the undertaking an unusually pleasant and very operetta-like atmosphere, though Maxwell Anderson's libretto was purposefully anti-totalitarian and unfortunately up-to-date. Also contemporary were such songs as "It Never Was You" and "How Can You Tell an American?" though both were housed in European song verse-refrain packagings that echoed back to the past. *Knickerbocker Holiday* ran 168 performances, and was revived in California in the 1970s, with Burt Lancaster, but without enough acclaim to bring it back to New York.

Lady in the Dark (Alvin, 23 January 1941) still seems a tour de force; that it is unplayable today is the fault of Moss Hart's overbearing book. As late as 1941, psychoanalysis still may have seemed mysterious, and while it has lost much of its thrill as a theatrical theme today, it remains a convenient way of introducing dreams or similar psychological scenes into a musical comedy. But whereas *Peggy-Ann* (1926), the Rodgers and Hart work, the Lerner-Lane *On a Clear Day You Can See Forever* (1965), and even *Oklahoma!* (1943) had extensive sequences of this type, none was as musically developed or as startling as Weill's and Ira Gershwin's for *Lady in the Dark*. The spartan Liza Elliott edits a glossy fashion magazine; two of her four troubled dreams are the glamorous "theme" issues come to life—the circus and the wedding; the other two are a generalized glamor dream and the final childhood dream, in which her problems are finally ironed out by a glimpse into her traumatic past.

The glamor and circus dreams are easily the best, with Ira Gershwin's words causing as much excitement as Weill's music. From sophisticated, pattery, name-dropping ("Huxley Wants to Dedicate His Book to You"), to sheer wordplay, the exuberance of Gershwin's verses, set in what are basically extended Offenbach-Sullivan finales, are refreshingly comic and elegant. Their apotheosis is reached in that combination of name-dropping and wordplay that is "Tschaikowsky," originally sung by Danny Kaye as the Ringmaster in the circus dream.

Weill's music ranges from contemporary pop croon-tunes ("This Is New") to an effective use of a Latin dance to underscore the heroine's dream-state unease. The rumba that ends the glamor dream ("Girl of the Moment") uncannily recalls another Latin coda to an operetta act, the dance at the end of the first act of Offenbach's *Barbe-Bleue*.

The brilliant New York production, with sets by Harry Horner (utilizing four concentric revolving stages), costumes by Irene Sharaff, dances by Albertina Rasch, and direction by Hassard Short—all of whom save Horner had worked with Hart on *The Great Waltz*—guaranteed a tour de force for the Liza Elliott of the radiant Gertrude Lawrence.

An extremely watered-down, though lavish, color film of *Lady in the Dark* was made in 1944, with Ginger Rogers giving an effective performance as the heroine. Unfortunately, the book was overstressed and the dreams hacked into little bits. Had Vincente Minnelli made the film for MGM (rather than Mitchell Leisen for Paramount) the results would probably have been very different. A concert version of the work was performed in New York's Philharmonic Hall in the early 1970s, with Angela Lansbury as Liza Elliott, but the operetta would need a spectacular production in order to achieve a match for its original 467–performance run.

One Touch of Venus (Imperial, 7 October 1943) ran a hundred performances more, but was much less of an operetta, offering Weill fewer chances to write extended scenes and finales. However, Ogden Nash fashioned some clever lyrics, and the classical tinge (a statue of Venus coming to life) combined with experienced operetta voices, Mary Martin, John Boles, and Kenny Baker, kept this from becoming a pure musical comedy.

The Firebrand of Florence (Alvin, 22 March 1945), Weill's final collaboration with Ira Gershwin, was unquestionably a full-fledged operetta, and one this writer would dearly love to see today. It was based on a Broadway play of the 1920s about Benvenuto Cellini that had originally starred Joseph Schildkraut. The musical version had Earl Wrightson, with Melville Cooper and Lotte Lenya in support. Weill's apparently ambitious score was—according to the critics—sabotaged by his wife (Lenya), miscast, and by the poor libretto. A very lavish investment was not recouped by a run of only 43 performances.

Street Scene (9 January 1947) was a "Broadway opera." Even without music, Elmer Rice's *Street Scene* (1929) was called a "tone poem." This must have attracted Weill, looking since his arrival in America for an emotional, real-life story to appeal to average Americans; that is, those who visited Broadway, rather than the Met. A year before *Lady in the Dark* (1941), in an interview with the New York *Sun,* Weill repudiated the U.S. operatic establishment and its museum-like entombment of old works, claiming that opera would develop within the Broadway theatre. Weill had seen *Porgy and Bess* catch on (1942 revival) with Broadway audiences, followed by "serious" musicals like *Carmen Jones* and *Carousel.* Shortly after the first night he came out and called *Street Scene* "a real Broadway opera."

But the critics, reviewing the première and subsequent revivals, have not been in any agreement about what to call *Street Scene.* Whatever *Street Scene* was, it is now treated as an opera, the New York City Opera being its greatest champion. Technically, we might call it an *opéra-comique,* by virtue of its spoken dialogue, or even a *Singspiel,* but Weill's own term "Broadway opera" is a better definition.

The music is a curious amalgam of Broadway tunes (*à la* Richard Rodgers), 1940s Hollywood mood music, virtuoso operatic flights (including several thick, brilliant ensembles), blues and jitterbuggy dances, and reflections of the Weimar Weill (but not too many). At first, it might seem rather much, but the ethnic character and low-end milieu of Rice's melodrama call for this treatment, and the lyrics, by Rice and Langston Hughes, seldom betray and generally enhance the realism of the dialogue. Appearing in the Golden Age of Broadway musicals (just before *Finian's Rainbow* and *Brigadoon*), it still managed to survive for four months in 1947, and, with its subsequent revivals, it is among the most popular of modern American operas.

Love Life (46th Street, 7 October 1948), written with Alan Jay Lerner, was a fantastical cavalcade of a marriage through 150 years of American history. Pretentiousness, the force that killed Rodgers and Hammerstein's *Allegro* the previous season, also helped defeat *Love Life*. The next season's *Lost in the Stars* (Music Box, 30 October 1949) was Weill's last attempt to keep the Broadway opera rolling along, albeit without quite the same amount or magnificence of music *Street Scene* enjoyed.

Internationally, **Ralph Benatzky** (1884–1957) today stands principally for one thing: *Im weissen Rössl* (White Horse Inn, 1930, for which, incidentally, he did not compose *all* the songs). Although absolutely an operetta now, and so dignified by an elaborate production at the Vienna Volksoper in 1976, *Im weissen Rössl* was actually one of a series of spectacular "revue-operettas" Benatzky wrote for producer-director Erik Charell at the Grosses Schauspielhaus, Berlin, in the late 1920s. But before that, he had written several regulation revues and operettas, now forgotten, and afterward wrote a number of musical comedies and film scores that are still remembered—he moved very much with the times.

Benatzky was born in Moravia (now Czechoslovakia) in 1884, conducted at a theatre in Munich in 1910, and that year saw his first one-acter appear. He wrote many songs and short works for cabarets in Vienna. By World War I he had several full-length works produced, none of them very notable. In Berlin in the '20s, Benatzky contributed to virtually all the Charell Grosses Schauspielhaus revues, culminating in three big revue-operettas: *Casanova* (1928), *Die drei Musketiere* (1929), and *Im weissen Rössl* (1930). *Casanova* was adapted, with considerable tact and finesse, from Johann Strauss II melodies by Benatzky and his librettists, but the evening was, of course, an excuse for brilliant scenes, following the amorous exploits of the leading character all over eighteenth-century Europe: Vienna, Spain, Germany, and naturally Venice. And this meant appropriately "national" tunes, cunningly arranged by Benatzky from lesser-known Strauss material, with several ballet scenes.

The star-studded original cast of *Casanova* in Berlin included Michael Bohnen, the well-known opera bass-baritone, in the title role, Anni Frind, Anny Ahlers, Paul Morgan, Emmy Sturm, and Siegfried "Sig" Arno. In London, Oswald Stoll mounted *Casanova* as the successor to the British production of *White Horse Inn* at the same Coliseum (24 May 1932), with two shows daily, and a cast that featured Arthur Fear (Casanova), Dorothy Dickson, and Marie Löhr as the Empress Maria Theresa. It played 432 performances.

The most famous number was the nuns' chorus, with soprano and organ, near the middle of the operetta *("O Madonna, auf uns sieh")*. Charell directed the London as well as the Berlin production, and Professor Ernst Stern designed both, complete with multiple revolving stages and huge drops.

Die drei Musketiere, book and lyrics by Schanzer and Welisch, was called "a play from the romantic era with music from yesterday and today" (a tango, for example) with the interpolations arranged by Benatzky. This was possibly influenced by Rudolf Friml's operetta of the same name (13 March 1928) but not necessarily—the Dumas *père* original was, after all, an international favorite. The musketeers played in Vienna and elsewhere in Germany.

Meine Schwester und Ich (My Sister and I, 29 March 1930) was a reaction to the overblown spectacles at the Grosses Schauspielhaus, a Parisian-inspired *comédie-musicale* inspired as much by the Christiné and Messager miniatures as by the original source, a play by Berr and Verneuil. Benatzky's own libretto told of a nobly born girl masquerading as her "twin sister," who was *"nur eine Verkäuferin in einem Schuhgeschäft"* (only a shop girl in a shoe store), as the famous song went. In this sense, it bore an unmistakable resemblance to the Christiné-Willemetz *Dédé*, in which Maurice Chevalier had triumphed as an amorous shoe salesman in 1921. *Meine Schwester und Ich*, in its simple, *intime* way, has survived well, the prime German-language musical comedy of the 1919–33 period still played today. Later, there were others like it by Benatzky— including *Zirkus Aimée* (1932) and *Bezauberndes Fräulein* (1933).

My Sister and I traveled to the United States. When the Shuberts decided to mount it in New York, they wanted its well-thought-of star. J. J. Shubert signed up Walter Slezak in Berlin, not knowing that he was substituting for the vacationing Oscar Karlweis. When Lee Shubert met the "star" in New York, he was taken aback by the fine figure of young Slezak, as he had expected a short and slight actor. When questioned by the producer, Slezak cleverly responded: "Oh, you must have seen my understudy."

George Grossmith and Bettina Hall rounded out the production, which was seen 167 times at the Shubert, from 30 December 1930.

In 1930, Erik Charell took what would turn out to be a very profitable holiday around the time of the première of *Meine Schwester und Ich,* meeting with Emil Jannings and his wife on the Wolfgangsee in the Austrian Tyrol. There Jannings remembered an old farce in which he had once appeared which was set in the famous inn in which they were all sitting, *Zum weissen Rössl* (At the White Horse). The farce, by Kadelburg and Blumenthal, was first presented in Berlin in 1897. Charell immediately saw in his head the entire Wolfgangsee recreated on the stage of the Grosses Schauspielhaus. And not only on the stage, but in the audience, in the lobby—everywhere. The old plot concerning the mistress of the inn and her head waiter was merely a peg on which to hang, build, float, revolve, and steam in sets, mountains, boats, trains, and the Emperor Franz-Josef. A huge cast of singers, actors, dancers, and children helped reduce, however slightly, the chronic 1930 unemployment.

As there was only a half year to devise and put the show on, Charell worked with Hans Müller on the book, and commissioned several composers to help out with the score. Thus, Benatzky did most of the "incidental" music, plus the ebullient title song and a few others, Robert Stolz contributed the ever-popular *"Die ganze Welt ist himmelblau"* (Your Eyes Have Brought a Deeper Blue) and *"Mein Liebeslied muss ein Walzer sein"* (My Love Song Is a Waltz Refrain), Bruno Granichstädten had a number, and Robert Gilbert (who wrote the lyrics) also composed *"Was kann der Sigismund dafür,"* the snappy comic's song. And even Eduard Künneke helped out with the choruses. The result, with a cast including Trude Lieske, Camilla Spira, Otto Wallburg (as a gruff Berlin businessman), Paul Hörbiger (as the Kaiser Franz Josef), Max Hansen (as the pivotal head waiter), and Sig Arno as the buffo *Sig*-ismund, opened at the Grosses Schauspielhaus 8 November 1930 and became an immediate sensation, overshadowing any motion picture, however spectacular, for over a year. If the cinema had finally met a serious theatrical threat, film producer Erich Pommer responded instantaneously by offering Charell complete charge of a film spectacle, the result being the immortal *Der Kongress tanzt* in 1931.

Some two million Berliners enjoyed *Im weissen Rössl,* as did numerous foreign managers. The Viennese production was first seen at the Wiener Stadttheater (25 September 1931) and then at the Theater an der Wien. The essentially Austrian story touched the hearts of even the most sophisticated Viennese, and the production ran twice as long as the Berlin version. The London version saved Oswald Stoll's Coliseum from a demoralizing music-hall death (8 April 1931). Harry Graham did the English words, though London audiences would doubtless have enjoyed the play in Swahili. Charell staged, and Ernst Stern's original designs were reproduced. Several critics were astute enough to realize that they were, fundamentally, being given a musical-comedy variation of Max Reinhardt's *The Miracle.* The entire theatre was turned into the Tyrol; there were one hundred and sixty actors, not counting three orchestras, extra native yodelers and dancers, horses, dogs, goats, a real rainstorm, *et cetera.* The bill for this was between forty and fifty thousand pounds (a great sum then), but Stoll won his gamble within twenty-four hours after the opening and the reviews: the theatre-ticket agencies booked £60,000 worth of seats. It was one of the most staggering things to hit London. "You have not time to breathe in watching this wonderful spectacle . . ." gasped the *News Chronicle.* In all, patrons visited the Coliseum twice daily for a total of 651 performances.

The original cast contained Amy Augarde, Lea Seidl, Bruce Carfax, George Gee, Frederich Leisteg as the Emperor, and Clifford Mollison as the head waiter, Leopold. If the British had shown an uneasiness for overtly Austrian (as opposed to Ruritanian) subjects after the Great War, *White Horse Inn* declared a total armistice. In Paris, as well: the Brothers Isola presented *L'Auberge du Cheval Blanc* (Mogador, 1 October 1932), the hugest hit for that theatre since *Rose-Marie.* Gabrielle Ristori and Milton led the cast, with Robert Allard as Célestin (read Sigismund). This, too, ran two years.

In New York, the Center Theatre production, headed by William Gaxton and Kitty Carlisle, had new book (David Freedman) and lyrics (Irving Caesar), and the regulation Charell-Stern direction-décor, enlarged by about a third for the huge stage. Again, twice-daily performances were given for more than a year from 1 October 1936. *Im weissen Rössl* was one of the greatest hits of its day, a *revue-opérette,* to be sure, but an operetta all the same. Because of the haste in preparation, and because of the numerous scene changes, there are all too many reprises, the concerted numbers are few, and the tunes hardly evoke the turn-of-the-century period, being for the most part pure contemporary *Berliner Schlager,* however attractive. Yet even when the spectacle is minimal, as in

touring companies, or in current productions at smaller German provincial theatres, or in amateur performances on tiny budgets, the appeal of *White Horse
Inn* has proved very durable.

There have been numerous major revivals, particularly in Paris, where the
Châtelet has mounted it with assiduous regularity, and, significantly, in Vienna,
where the Volksoper has admitted it to its repertoire of standards. The French,
at one time, had a complete two-record version in French, which very few
other German-Austrian works had been awarded. What so pleased Depression
audiences was undoubtedly echoed in Brooks Atkinson's original notice in the
New York *Times:* ". . . this holiday set to music . . ." For Charell's own
holiday had become a colossal vacation for many who could not have afforded
actually to go to Austria; people from Europe, Australia, Israel, and South America
had an afternoon or evening in the Tyrol that seemed like a week and which
cost only a few pennies.

By the time *Im weissen Rössl* was ready for a filmization, the Nazis had banished Charell, Arno, Stern, and much of the creative staff from Germany. Three
films suggested by the piece were later made, but it was perhaps considered ill
advised to film what was so essentially a stage spectacular. Benatzky had left
Germany in 1933.

In 1936, Benatzky wrote another musical, for the Swedish actress Zarah

Leander. This was *Axel an der Himmelstür* (Theater an der Wien, 1 September 1936) and it made Leander a potent star for German-speaking audiences, leading to a film career. Benatzky provided the songs for Leander's first UFA film, *Zu neuen Ufern* (To New Shores, 1937), like most of her films a melodrama with several songs. *"Ich steh' im Regen"* (I stand in the rain), one of the Benatzky songs from *Zu neuen Ufern,* became a Leander standard. As some of his songs were used in UFA films in the late '30s, one wonders if there were "racial" reasons for this departure from Vienna, but he nevertheless spent some of the war years in Hollywood. In all, Benatzky wrote over a hundred stage works, composed music for scores of films, and had some five thousand songs published—for which he often wrote the lyrics. He is buried in Austria, fittingly enough in St. Wolfgang am Wolfgangsee, the site of the White Horse Inn he made famous.

The operetta composers who remained in Berlin and Vienna during the Nazi years had the unenviable task of writing light music during the darkest era of European history. Their profits were increased by the lack of competition from Jewish composers who had dominated the scene up to 1933. Of the old school of Silver Age masters, only Lehár, Künneke, and Lincke were permitted or encouraged to stay and compose, and of these, only Künneke could be said to have been truly active after Hitler's rise to power. Lehár, an Austrian, virtually stopped composing after 1934, and Lincke belonged to another era that had long since passed. The names of the primarily Jewish librettists were simply omitted from programmes of the 1933–45 period, during which time several died in concentration camps.

The sprightly late-Weimar German musical films of 1930–33 set the tone for a much less musically complicated type of stage dance-operetta that retained its popularity in Berlin even after its main practitioner, Paul Ábrahám, was forced to leave. To help fill the gap, film composers were corraled onto the operetta stage.

One of the leading operetta composers of the period was **Nico Dostal** (1895–1981), born near Vienna. He went from law studies to church music to the First World War, and was afterward a theatre conductor. His own operettas were not at first remarkable, but he was a leading orchestrator; one example was Stolz's *Zwei Herzen im Dreivierteltakt* in 1933. In 1932, he had a hit film score, for *Kaiserwalzer.* The following year saw his first stage hit, *Clivia* (Theater am Nollendorfplatz, 23 December), the story of an American financier and a film star visiting the South American Republic of "Boliguay." The dancing scenes were reported to have made it popular (more than 250 performances),

---

The 1976 Vienna Volksoper production of *Im weissen Rössl*. Though never produced now on the vast scale of the original 1930 Berlin spectacular—it would cost too many millions today—*White Horse Inn* remains extremely popular in Germanic lands because of its sentimental depiction of the good old days under Kaiser Franz-Josef before World War I. Volksoper/Elisabeth Hausmann.

which is easy to believe, as the songs are nearly all unremittingly awful. Among the works that followed were *Monika* (1934) and *Die ungarische Hochzeit* (The Hungarian Wedding, Stuttgart, 4 February 1939). The latter, Dostal's most enduring work, is still revived in Germany and Austria. A lavish production at the Vienna Volksoper in 1980 failed to reveal any qualities to justify its revival. (According to the Volksoper management, the motivation was to honor the last living Austrian operetta composer.) Only Dostal's comedy numbers have any life, in a rather blunt, thigh-slapping way, and his attempt to be a replacement Kálmán was confounded by his distinctly lesser talent.

Fred Raymond (1900–1954) was also Viennese-born (real name Friedrich Vesely) and began his career in the city's cabarets. A huge song hit, *"Ich hab' mein Herz in Heidelberg verloren"* (I lost my heart in Heidelberg) became a hit operetta in 1927 in Vienna, though it had nothing to do with Romberg's *The Student Prince.* From 1934, Raymond was the house composer of Berlin's Metropol-Theater, writing a new operetta each season. His biggest hit came in 1937, with *Maske in Blau* (27 September). This lavish revue-operetta in eight scenes took place, like *Clivia,* in a thoroughly operetta Latin America, supposedly Argentina this time. The general Nazi-era passion for South American songs and dances may have had a subversive bent, as the government was trying to infiltrate the continent. *Maske in Blau* also had scenes set on the Italian Riviera; Mussolini was visiting Hitler at that very moment. Featured in the production was the Chilean Rosita Serrano, who became a big recording, radio, and film star. Many of the operetta's songs became instant (and still-remembered) hits, like *"Die Juliska aus Budapest"* (Little Julie from Budapest). *Saison in Salzburg* (Kiel, 1938) is the only other Raymond still produced today.

Heinz Hentschke was the crafty librettist-director of the Metropol operettas, under the strict supervision of the Goebbels cultural office. In 1942 came his text for the hit *Hochzeitnacht im Paradies* (Wedding Night in Paradise), with music by the popular film composer Friedrich Schröder (1910–1972). German film operettas and musicals, nearly all modified revues or simply romances with a few songs, were great competition for any staged operettas, and their songs have frankly outlasted any '30s stage numbers, thanks to big film stars like Zarah Leander or Johannes Heesters.

Curiously, the stage operetta hits of this period were not filmed until after the war, in the early 1950s. For whatever unsavory reasons, a few of these tainted works remain in provincial repertoires, though it seems unlikely that they will outlive the dying generation that saw them originally and remembers them today.

Lehár and Kálmán are the two major Hungarian-born composers whose success was made in Vienna. There are at least three other outstanding Magyar operetta composers who, notwithstanding considerable success in Vienna and in other cities, are mostly remembered and performed today in Budapest. One is **Jenö Huszka** (1875–1960), whose *Bob herceg* (Prince Bob, 1902) and *Lili bárónö* (Baroness Lily, 1919) are still performed in Hungary. Huszka wrote some twelve other operettas, the last of which, *Szabadság, Szerelem* (Freedom, Love, 1955), would seem from its title to have conformed to the modern Hungarian political strictures for operetta. *Bob* and *Lili* have a certain grace about them, with appealing choruses and well-constructed finales looking back to the previous century, but they lack the fiery Hungarian csárdás strains which foreigners, if not the Budapestians themselves, admire in Hungarian operettas.

Victor Jacobi (1883–1921) was more exportable. In fact, he exported himself to New York from London in 1915 on the *Lusitania* (London then was not fond of enemy aliens), where he wrote several works for Broadway. He died in 1921 at the comparatively young age of thirty-seven, in New York, leaving behind him about a dozen works, of which two are still performed. The first was *Leányvásár* (Girls' Fair, Király [King's] Theatre, 14 November 1911), which had in its cast the two best-remembered Hungarian female operetta stars of all time: Sári Petráss and Sári Fedák, along with the illustrious comic Árpád Latabár and the handsome leading man Ernö Király. The score remains immediately delightful—a profusion of charming waltzes and irresistible up-tempo comic duets and *couplets* with chorus—placed in an exotic American setting, with cowboys and sailors. The libretto, by Miklós Bródy and Ferenc Martos, had its melodramatic overtones: through an auction of eligible young ladies, a man vengefully marries the daughter of the man who ruined his father years before. The score, however, is anything but melodramatic, being melodically exuberant throughout.

Leányvásár was immediately picked up by the Carltheater, Vienna, and Edwardes-ized for Daly's Theatre, London, where it followed (with basically the same cast) Lehár's *Gipsy Love* and a revival of Oscar Straus's *Waltz Dream,* on 17 May 1913. The English title of the Gladys Unger book was *The Marriage Market,* and with a cast including Petráss in her original part, Gertie Millar, W. H. Berry, Robert Michaelis, plus G. P. Huntley, Tom Walls, Hugh Wakefield, and Ronald Frankau (then called Frank Ronalds), the play ran an admirable 423 times. Sári Petráss, who stayed in Britain and married an Englishman, was an expert horsewoman, a talent she put to some use when making her entrance in *The Marriage Market* on a donkey named Jenny. Athletic prowess did not save her life, however, when in 1930, at the age of forty, a car in which she was traveling plunged into a river in Belgium.

In New York, the Charles Frohman production of *The Marriage Market* was headed by Donald Brian and Venita Fitzhugh. Audiences enjoyed seeing their Danilo as "Slippery Jack" Fleetwood, the cowboy, and also relished the lariats, shoot-outs, and the yip-yip cowboy number, "The Mendocino Stroll," as well as a second act on board a ship anchored off San Francisco. The Wild West plus naval maneuvers proved a potent draw.

An even more shimmering score came in 1914, for *Szibill* (Sybil), still very popular in Budapest (Király, 27 February 1914). The libretto, again by Bródy and Martos, was a complicated affair about a French singer on tour in (pre-1917) Russia who falls in love with a Captain of the Imperial Guard and who later poses as a visiting Grand Duchess to prevent her Captain from being arrested for non-possession of papers. While Sybil masquerades as his wife, the *real* Grand Duke makes love to *her,* and their duet is one of the loveliest slow waltzes of the Hungarian repertoire, *"Illúzió a szerelem"* (Love May Be a Mystery), depending importantly on a vast pause before *"szerelem."* George Edwardes optioned *Sybil* for London after the long run of *The Marriage Market,* but he was forced to abandon the idea of producing the work of an enemy alien when the war broke out. Jacobi, himself in London, was forced to leave Britain, and came to neutral New York at the beginning of 1915. The Broadway production of *Sybil,* with a few new numbers by the composer, opened a year later with Donald Brian, Julia Sanderson, and Joseph Cawthorn as the comic lead (now the "Dutch" character "Otto Spreckles" rather than "Poire")—all three were fresh from Jerome Kern's *The Girl from Utah.* The first night was attended by such musical notables as John McCormack, Fritz Kreisler, Efrem Zimbalist, and Alma Gluck; curiously, the New York *Times* found the score "no matter for enthusiasm." The British production (1921—it had to wait till after both the Great War and the great Daly's run of *The Maid of the Mountains)* was more spectacularly produced, better sung, and much better-received. With José Collins, Harry Welchman, and Huntley Wright in the roles originated by Sári Fedák, Ernö Király and Márton Rátkay, it ran 346 performances.

Jacobi remained in the United States to write a few more scores, generally forgotten today except by a few old-timers. One was *Rambler Rose* (1917), which was only distinguished by an Irving Berlin interpolation, "Poor Little Rich Girl's Dog." It was based on a French play that had once served as a Billie Burke vehicle, as well as on an operetta Jacobi had written a decade earlier in Budapest, *Tüskerozsa. Apple Blossoms* (1919) had a score written with Fritz Kreisler; it included "On the Banks of the Bronx," which was given to John Charles Thomas to sing and to that young dancing couple, Fred and Adele Astaire, to dance. *Variety,* however, complained that there was "no big smash in the numbers." Charles Dillingham, who had produced Jacobi's New York shows, continued giving him chances: *The Half Moon* (1920) and *The Love Letter* (1921), the last again with the Astaires. *The Love Letter* predated *Carousel* in one significant aspect: it was based on a Molnár play, namely *The Wolf* (*A farkas,* 1911). John Charles Thomas appeared as a soldier, a statesman, an artist, and a servant in this "musical play." *The Love Letter* was Jacobi's last work.

The case of **Albert Szirmai** (later Sirmay, 1880–1967) is quite mysterious. One wonders to what extent Sirmay influenced the Broadway scores of Richard Rodgers and Cole Porter, in particular, among composers whose work was published by Harms and Chappell's, where Sirmay worked as editor for many years. Charles Schwartz, in his biography of Cole Porter, claimed that Porter had Sirmay speak for him at rehearsals: "It would be Sirmay's duty to suggest changes in tempo, phrasing, orchestration, and so on during rehearsals."

José Collins as the star on tour in Russia in Jacobi's *Sybil,* produced in London at Daly's, 1921. This intoxicating Hungarian score can still be heard in Budapest; Fritzi Massary sang it in a Viennese revival in 1919.

Sirmay's first operetta, *A sárga domino* (The Yellow Domino), appeared in 1907, *Táncos husárok* (The Dancing Hussars) in 1909 (and in Vienna the same year, as *Tanzhusaren*), and others followed, until *Mágnás Miska* (Mike the Magnate, Király, 12 February 1916), which has proved to be Sirmay's main surviving work. A simple tale of a country stableboy who somehow becomes an awkward swell, the story serves as a framework for the typical Hungarian goulash of rustic comedy, sensual love music (though not necessarily waltzed), and sprightly native-accented dance numbers. *"Hoppsza, Sári,"* sings and swings Miska with his girlfriend, Marcsa, a laundress, and the Budapest audience feels almost compelled to join in the action. The original parts were taken by Márton Rátkay and Sári Fedák. Melodically, even harmonically, Sirmay was often more interesting than Jacobi, even if he lapsed into banal refrains; his verses have considerable flair. If Jacobi looked back to the turn of the century, Sirmay often looked ahead, though generally without having to deploy Charlestons and shimmys in rural Hungarian settings.

Sirmay came to New York in the 1920s and stayed there. He contributed to Ziegfeld's *Follies* of 1924, sent back to Budapest scores written to Hungarian libretti, and had one, at least, reworked for American and British audiences. This was the '20s work *Princess Charming* (Palace, 21 October 1926), based on *Alexandra* (1925), a Budapest hit also produced in Vienna. Following the Palace's fabulously successful *No! No! Nanette!* (1925), it ran in London for nearly a year, with Alice Delysia and W. H. Berry starred. In New York (Imperial, 1930), in spite of Evelyn Herbert, Robert Halliday, Jeanne Aubert, Victor Moore, and George Grossmith repeating himself in his London role, the operetta lasted a mere 56 performances. Ruritania had lost its appeal to post–Wall Street–crash Broadway, but not, apparently, to the British film studios. Gainsborough released a film version in 1934 which eradicated the entire score but still allows us the opportunity to see Grossmith in his part, with Yvonne Arnaud, the music-hall's "cheeky chappie" Max Miller in the Berry/Moore role, and Evelyn Laye, radiant, singing Ray Noble's "So Near and Yet So Far."

Lady Mary (Daly's, 23 February 1928) was a new musical play by Frederick Lonsdale (and J. Hastings Turner) set in London and a romantic cattle station in Australia. Herbert Mundin and Paul Cavanagh, both later familiar Hollywood faces, made respectively comic and romantic impressions, but the story "it is true, is pathetically slight—so slight, indeed, that it has to be wound up with a most unexpected and inconclusive jerk . . ." wrote the *Times* critic. *Lady Mary* played 181 performances. Successes thereafter were confined to Budapest: *Eva grófnö* (1928), *A ballerina* (1931), *A kalóz* (The Pirate, 1933), while in 1930 Sirmay collaborated with Oscar Levant on *Ripples!* (New Amsterdam, 1930), with the veteran Fred Stone, but this ran only a bit more than a month.

Paul Ábrahám (1892–1960), of Hungarian origin, enjoyed an inflated reputation exceeding his talent, as far as great operettas were concerned. Yet his film scores, written at the beginning of the sound era, were somehow just right for that unpretentious medium and time. One might be tempted to throw a great deal of the blame on the insipidity of his libretti, but, in fact, they were not much worse than those written for Kálmán and Lehár, and, in some cases, were written by the same authors. Ábrahám was born in 1892 in Apatin, Hungary (now Yugoslavia), going to Budapest to study, becoming a professor of liturgical music and theory, writing serious works. But in 1927 he became conductor

---

By the late 1920s, the disintegration of Viennese operetta into musical comedy and revue was steadily progressing. Foreign musicals enjoyed a vogue, as this Vienna kiosk (April 1928) shows: Youmans' *No! No! Nanette!*—billed as an operetta—had already passed its 600th performance. Also playing at the same time were Kálmán's *Die Herzogin von Chicago*, Stolz's *Eine einzige Nacht*, and the more traditional *Der Zigeunerbaron*.

of the Municipal Operetta in Budapest, where he contributed to *Zenebona*, an operetta which premièred in the next year. In 1930, after two other forgotten works, *Viktoria* became a huge popular attraction, likewise as *Viktoria und ihr Husar* (Theater an der Wien, 23 December 1930) in Vienna, and even more forcefully in Berlin. It was about a Hungarian countess and her hussar captain, who, having been presumed killed in World War I, winds up at the American legation in Tokyo. Viktoria had in the meantime married an American. When all three parties meet in St. Petersburg, the American, realizing his wife's undying affection for her Hungarian, allows Viktoria her freedom. There was a prologue in Siberia, plus three acts in Toyko, St. Petersburg, and a Hungarian town.

Spectacular and adventuresome, with the fatal romance of the recent war in Alfred Grünwald and Fritz Löhner-Beda's book, *Viktoria* had a sort of pre-*South Pacific* effect on its audiences, which ate everything up. The score right away typified what Ábrahám would provide: a bit of foreign color, a profusion of catchy 1920s dance tunes not necessarily reflecting the time or the place of the action, and languorous "pop" love songs—generally with a "sophisticated" foreign phrase as the title. *"Pardon, Madame (Ich bin verliebt)"* is one. More significantly, the orchestra pulsated with trombones and saxophones, previously rare in operetta pits.

Yet even if the score was immediately attractive and more up-to-date than most, the audience chose *one* number as its undisputed favorite: *"Mausi, süss warst du heute Nacht"* (Mousie, you were sweet last night), sung and recorded by the Budapestians Oskar Dénes and Rosy Barsony. More or less on the strength of this fox-trot, the show journeyed to London (Palace, 17 December 1931) with Dénes in tow. It was filmed twice (1931, 1954), the first time by Richard Oswald. *Viktoria* was followed by two operettas written for Berlin which remain fairly popular: *Die Blume von Hawaii* (The Flower of Hawaii, 1931) and *Ball im Savoy* (Ball at the Savoy, 1932). Both had texts by Alfred Grünwald and Bela Löhner-Beda, fresh from respective triumphs with Kálmán and Lehár, and all three can still be heard at various German theatres, where "My golden baby" and *"Toujours l'amour"* continue (somehow) to enchant. The Hungarian "nightingale," Gitta Alpar, made a great reputation with the latter song in Berlin, leading to several choice parts in sound films. Though not especially beautiful, she had an ingenuous, pleasant charm, and a clear voice. *Ball at the Savoy* (Drury Lane, 8 September 1933) was another excuse to give Oskar Dénes and Rosy Barsony exposure to London audiences; this time they sang "Oh, Why, Oh, Why, Oh, Why?", a "laughing song" similar to *"Mausi."* *Ball at the Savoy* was not produced in New York, in spite of its Oscar Hammerstein II book and lyrics. It was filmed in 1955, in Germany, as was *Die Blume von Hawaii*, twice (1933, 1953), the first time by Richard Oswald, with Marta Eggerth and Iwan Petrowitsch.

The early '30s vogue for screen operetta caused Ábrahám to be contracted for original scores, and the best of these was for Wilhelm Thiele's 1931 *Die Privat-*

sekretärin, with its irresistible *"Ich bin ja heut' so glücklich"* (Today I Am So Happy) as sung by Renate Müller.

Ball im Savoy ran at the Grosses Schauspielhaus, Berlin, right through the beginning of 1933; it took the new régime a little time to drive Ábrahám, his librettists, and Gitta Alpar off the stage—their Jewish blood was "unwanted." Ábrahám was forced first to Vienna, next to Budapest, then to Paris, and finally New York (via Cuba), always running ahead of the Nazis. His Viennese works, at the Theater an der Wien, included *Märchen im Grand-Hotel* (Tales from the Grand Hotel, 1934) and *Roxy und ihr Wunderteam* (1937), but these are as little known today as his subsequent Budapest creations.

His final years were unproductive. In 1946 he was admitted to a New York mental home, having suffered memory lapses, which "did not affect his musical ability," according to the press. In the 1950s, the West German Government was prevailed upon to invite him back by the Paul Ábrahám Society, which raised the money to transport him. The German Consulate issued an invitation "to come back to the country where he wrote his well-loved operettas and musicals and spend his remaining days in one of our institutions." Well-loved, yes, but not in the 1933–45 period. He died in Hamburg after an operation, a grim conclusion to what might have been an even greater career.

KISS ME

CHARLES B. COCHRAN

presents

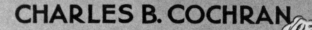

BITTER SWEET

by
NOËL COWARD

An Operette in Three Acts

CHAPPELL & CO. LTD.
50, NEW BOND ST, LONDON, W.1.
NEW YORK & SYDNEY

PRINTED IN ENGLAND

THE WEST END

B RITISH operetta had a difficult time after World War I recapturing the glorious years of Gilbert and Sullivan and the Edwardes era, when English shows were in demand internationally. With the exception of Sullivan, however, Britain was not able to come up with a truly outstanding operetta composer, although her librettists often shone. In the 1920s, American composers in England wrote scores for some British shows, while Broadway musicals and operettas enjoyed an enviable vogue. Several British composers attempted to write works that would withstand the American flood, but few succeeded, except in the realm of intimate revue, in which the London stage excelled.

Out of the small-scale revue came three composers for operetta, Noël Coward, Ivor Novello, and Vivian Ellis. Although none of their operettas has been successfully revived in recent years (as opposed to so many American works), their music (and lyrics) live on, through recordings.

The legitimate successor to Sullivan and Monckton in Britain was **Noël Coward** (1899–1973), unlikely as it may have seemed in 1929, when *Bitter-Sweet* had its première (Her Majesty's, 12 July). Known through the '20s principally for his smart revues and even smarter straight plays (like *The Vortex,* 1924), the proto-Strauss (more like Straus) Vienna of *Bitter-Sweet,* admittedly influenced by gramophone records of *Die Fledermaus,* no doubt surprised London audiences expecting something very different.

The role of Sari Linden was envisioned originally for Gertrude Lawrence, but her limited vocal range had Coward, reluctantly, looking for someone else. The second choice was Evelyn Laye. Unfortunately, Miss Laye was bitter over the

---

Sheet music from Coward's *Bitter-Sweet* (His Majesty's, 1929) with an attractive drawing by Coward's favorite designer, G. E. Calthrop.

fact that her former husband, Sonnie Hale, had met and romanced Jessie Matthews during Coward's revue *This Year of Grace* (1928, where they had sung
"A Room with a View," among other songs). Miss Laye turned down the part.
She was later to head the New York company (Ziegfeld, 5 November 1929)
after her *succès d'estime* in the Drury Lane company of *The New Moon*, and
subsequently went into the London production, which ran well over 700 performances at His Majesty's, the Palace, and the Lyceum theatres. The original
Sari/Sarah was Peggy Wood (New York's *Maytime* star in 1917); her Viennese
lover was George Metaxa, a Romanian who had been in several London shows.
He was appearing in Cochran's *Wake Up and Dream,* the 1929 Cole Porter revue
at the Pavilion, just a few weeks before being snatched away for the *Bitter-Sweet*
role. Also in the first cast were Ivy St. Helier, Robert Newton, Alan Napier,
and (in the trvout at Manchester) "Hugh" Cuenod.

The story of a proper upper-class English maiden (c. 1875) who escapes an
arranged marriage and runs off with her music teacher to Vienna, then loses her
husband in a duel with a thwarted Captain at the café in which the married
couple work, was thin stuff. Coward wisely placed the entire thing within a
flashback framework, allowing for the heroine's rapid change (effected by an
onstage dressing corner) from Lady Shayne to the fifty-four-years-younger Sarah
Millick while singing the song "The Call of Life." And, at the end of the operetta, back to the 1929 beginning again. The play cleverly begins with a contemporary jazz dance, rather than a Viennese waltz.

Coward's proverbial ease of composition was naturally backed up by weeks
and weeks of intense, disciplined work, often during which (from 8 A.M. to 1
P.M. every day) nothing much would appear on paper. "The score had been
causing me trouble, until one day. When I was in a taxi on my way back to the
apartment after a matinée, the "I'll See You Again" waltz dropped into my
mind, whole and complete, during a twenty minutes' traffic block."[1]

The "word" on *Bitter-Sweet* was unpromising, and, in spite of a good reception at the Palace, Manchester, tryout, the première at His Majesty's was, as
Coward put it, "definitely an anti-climax . . . the audience was tremendously
fashionable, and . . . almost as responsive as so many cornflour blancmanges."
The notices were "remarkable for their tone of rather grudging patronage."
Indeed, the press and public were hardly sure how to react to this atypically
uncynical and unwitty Coward *operette*. James Agate used the event to comment
on the state of the art:

> The programme bears the notification, "The Entire Production by Noël Coward,"
> and perhaps a good way of attacking, in the friendly sense, the stupendous opus
> which is this "operette" would be to consider how much Mr. Coward has really
> put into it. I suggest that to arrive at this estimate we must subtract from "the entire
> production" the delightful scenes and dresses designed by Professor Ernst Stern, the
> dance arranged by Miss Tilly Losch, and, of course, the brilliant orchestration of
> the play's tunes by Mr. Orellana. This leaves the plot, the dialogue, the lyrics, the
> melodies as originally executed on a baby grand, the stagecraft, the evening's spar-

[1]Noël Coward, *Present Indicative,* p. 348.

kle, irresponsibility, wit, and fun, the power to conceive its visual delight, and the general notion of what makes a thoroughly good light entertainment.

. . . Consider what Mr. Coward's achievement means. Mozart had need of Beaumarchais, Richard Strauss of Hoffmansthal, Johann Strauss of lots of people, and ditto Oscar Straus, Offenbach, Lecocq, Planquette, Hervé, Audran, Messager— all the Frenchmen had their librettists, and it might be conveniently remembered here that in the days when Meilhac and Halévy were writing for the French vaudeville and comic opera stage, the librettist was a more important person than the provider of the music. Gilbert and Sullivan were the perfect marriage, after which comic opera rapidly degenerated into musical comedy and the licentious state whereby the composer took at least sixteen lyric-writers to his bosom.[2]

That *Bitter-Sweet* became a resounding hit (less resonant in its Ziegfeld New York production) is well known, but, curiously, it has been revived only twice professionally in London and never in New York since 1931. Amateur societies have been very fond of it and there were several recordings in the 1950s and '60s, although no one has seen fit to record all the numbers. This situation changed in 1988 with the popular success of a revival presented by the New Sadler's Wells Opera, which was recorded.

Coward left the actual mechanics of the score to his musical "secretary" and friend, Elsie April, and to his able orchestrator, De Orellana. Nevertheless, he came up with a surprisingly good batch of tunes and some effective ensemble notions. Rarely was an entire chorus involved—Coward preferred quartets or sextets, in situations that were more believable than full operetta finales. When a boy, Coward and his mother probably saw every Edwardian operetta on successive Saturday matinées, and they left as distinct a mark as did the Gilbert and Sullivan songs everyone in his family sang on any given occasion. Thus, lyrically, Coward was a true successor to Gilbert, while his musical background was Monckton, Caryll, and the Viennese composers in vogue after 1907. There is also a trace of Edward German in Coward's continuous use of "comic" ensembles, occasionally used in Coward's case to change scenery behind. In *Bitter-Sweet,* the effect was a fresh one, but by the time of *Operette* (1938) the convention was going stale. The Aesthetic quartet "Green Carnations" was certainly far above the average twentieth-century level for musical lyrics. For a true man-of-the-theatre and jack-of-all-trades, Coward had difficulty, at times, with the lyrics of his loveliest melodies, and, conversely, the melodies for his wittiest lyrics. *Bitter-Sweet,* fortunately, has a lot of wonderful exceptions: "If Love Were All," easily the most moving song Coward wrote, and superbly café-chanted by Ivy St. Hélier as an avowed cross between Loie Fuller and Yvette Guilbert, "Ladies of the Town," clever *and* tuneful, and the immortal signature tune, "I'll See You Again." *Bitter-Sweet* has other attractions: "Zigeuner," a bewitching song, "Tokay," a rousing drinking song, and the charm-duet, "Dear Little Café," plus a true finale to Act I, built around a blindman's-buff game, as in the ensemble in *The Gondoliers.*

There were several other waltzes: "Kiss Me," "Tell Me What Is Love," and

[2]*Immoment Toys,* pp. 69–70.

numerous character choruses for the waiters, the officers, and for the partygoers who open Act III with a variation on the music-hall standby, "Tarara-Boom-De-Ay." Both films of *Bitter-Sweet* (1933, 1940) omit great sections of the singing, and since there are few stage revivals, it is forgotten how rich Coward's work is, and how overdue it is for a faithful stage revival. *Bitter-Sweet* was produced in Paris in 1930 (Apollo, 2 April) as *Au Temps des Valses,* but did not prove a moneymaker.

Conversation Piece (His Majesty's, 16 February 1934) was conceived for Yvonne Printemps. C. B. Cochran prevailed upon Coward to write a play that would allow Mme. Printemps to fall back on her native French when her (nonexistent) English might fail her. Coward came up with a story of a *"ci-devant* French aristocrat," the Duc de Chaucigny-Varennes, trying to pass off a café-girl in Regency Brighton as an orphan of a guillotined marquis, in order to make a rich marriage and receive a commission. The story was not a bad one, containing such complications as a pack of courtesans and a scheming old flame of the Duc's. As a vehicle for Printemps and as a pageant of old Brighton, it succeeded beautifully. Gladys Calthrop's designs again contributed to the show's physical loveliness.

Not as musically varied as *Bitter-Sweet, Conversation Piece* nevertheless had most attractive music. "I'll Follow My Secret Heart," a gorgeous waltz, is set in the context of an extended conversation with Melanie and the Duc (played, reluctantly, by Coward after the original actor bowed out during the rehearsals). This was similar to the conversation pieces between Printemps and her nonsinging former husband Sacha Guitry in *Mozart* and *L'Amour masqué.* Other attractive waltz songs were "Nevermore" and *"Danser, danser, la vie est gaie,"* and Melanie's passionate declaration of love to the Duc de Tramont, *"C'est assez de mensonge . . . Plus de coeur discret."* The two main comic ensembles were "Regency Rakes," sung by a quartet that included the young George Sanders, and a duet, "There's Always Something Fishy About the French," sung first by Heather Thatcher and Moya Nugent. Each bristled with internal and external rhymes of incredible brilliance, and the orchestrations by Charles Prentice were as warm and sunny as Brighton can be.

In 1936 at the Phoenix (9 January), Coward's ambitious series of ten one-act plays, *Tonight at 8:30,* started with *Family Album,* "a Victorian comedy with music." This delightful 1860 pastiche was abridged for a two-sided 78-rpm record, making it sound rather like an operetta. Coward called his play "a sly satire on Victorian hypocrisy, adorned with an unobtrusive but agreeable musical score." With its fragrant music-box waltz, "Hearts and Flowers," its bouncy toast sequence, "Harriet Married a Soldier," and another music-box "hymn," "Let the Angels Guide You," *Family Album* was a tasteful throwback, in its way, to the old German Reed entertainments and to the one-act operetta form in the general, Offenbach style. Though there were delightful songs in *Red Peppers, We*

A flyer announcing the (limited) Broadway engagement of Yvonne Printemps in Noël Coward's *Conversation Piece* (1934).

"*The Town's Prettiest Pet*"

Engagement
Positively
Limited To
12 Weeks

Seats on Sale
at Box Office
Four Weeks
in Advance

ARCH SELWYN and HAROLD B. FRANKLIN
present

YVONNE PRINTEMPS

in NOEL COWARD'S musical romance

"*CONVERSATION PIECE*"

CHARLES B. COCHRAN'S London Success

WITH

PIERRE
FRESNAY

IRENE
BROWNE

ATHOLE
STEWART

Cast of 60 — Orchestra of 30

✛

44th ST. THEATRE (WEST OF BROADWAY)

Matinees THURSDAY and SATURDAY

Were Dancing, and, most particularly, *Shadow Play*, none of these involved an ensemble in the way *Family Album* did, and, sadly, Coward's noble experiment with short musical works did not goad other composers and lyricists into reviving the short operetta format.

One noted a certain banality of Coward's love lyrics by the time of the next operetta, *Operette* (His Majesty's, 16 March 1938), which starred Fritzi Massary. The charm of *Operette*, if any, lies in its Gaiety parody, *The Model Maid*, supposedly produced by "Charles Hobson" (a reference to producer Charles B. Cochran), with lyrics by "Hereford Blake" (Blake was Cochran's dachshund), according to a mock programme for the "Jubilee Theatre" inserted in the actual His Majesty's programme. Let Coward describe his virtues and faults in *Operette*:

> *Operette*, from my point of view, is the least successful musical play I have ever done. The reason for this is that it is over-written and under-composed. The story of an imaginary "Gaiety Girl" of the early nineteen-hundreds who achieves overnight stardom and then has to sacrifice her love-life to her career, while not fiercely original, is an agreeable enough background for gay music and lyrics and beguiling "period" costumes. Unfortunately, however, the plot, which should have been the background, became the foreground, and the music, which should have dominated the action, established the atmosphere, and whirled the play into a lilting success, was meagre and only at moments adequate.
>   . . . The four principal players were Peggy Wood, Fritzi Massary, Irene Vanbrugh and Griffith Jones. Fritzi Massary, one of the greatest stars of middle Europe, emerged from her retirement and studied English for months in order to play Liesl Haren. Her performance was exquisite and her behaviour magnificent. She knew as well as I knew, during the try-out in Manchester, that neither her part nor the songs she had to sing were worthy of her, but never, at the time or since, has she ever uttered a word of reproach . . . Another aspect of *Operette* was the triumphant confusion it established in the minds of the audience. This was cunningly achieved by the switching of the action back and forth between the stage play and the real play. I remember peering from my box in the Opera House, Manchester, and watching bewildered playgoers rustling their programmes and furtively striking matches in a frantic effort to discover where they were and what was going on. By that time, however, it was too late to do anything about it, beyond cutting and simplifying whenever possible.[3]

By this time, Coward had a serious rival in his romantic efforts with the Drury Lane successes of Ivor Novello. Coward later stated that Novello was the "one outstanding exception" to the dearth of "English composers of light music capable of creating an integrated score."

Involved as he was with wartime films (*In Which We Serve, Brief Encounter*) and propaganda work, Coward's answer to Ivor Novello had to wait until 1946, with the production of *Pacific 1860* at Drury Lane (19 December), home of Novello's prewar triumphs. It was a particularly severe winter, with terrible fuel shortages, which meant that tickets were sold by candlelight and that the theatre was ice-cold. Another grave problem was that *Pacific 1860* was not a

[3]*Play Parade*, Vol. II, Introduction.

Drury Lane show—it was designed for a smaller house. Apart from a boat moving in the water and the lovely Calthrop designs, there was virtually no spectacle. Mary Martin (before her U.S. triumphs in *Annie Get Your Gun* on tour and in *South Pacific*) headed the cast, and opposite her was Coward's long-time friend, Graham Payn. Coward considered *Pacific 1860*, musically, his best work, and it is an undeniably lovely score, though without the smash-hit songs to keep its name alive. It has never been revived. After 129 performances it disappeared. Fortunately, the score was recorded by the original cast. "The Press blasted the book, hardly mentioned the music or lyrics, and that was that," grumbled Coward.

Pacific 1860 did have an old-fashioned libretto, one that would hardly grip a present-day audience but, on the other hand, one that might have been expected to entertain a cold, war-weary 1946 one. Set in the fictitious island of Samolo, the story concerned an opera diva and her affection for the son of a sterling Victorian plantation family named Stirling. (Could Miss Martin have known she would be back at the Lane a few seasons later, again, triumphantly, playing a woman in love with a Pacific planter?) It was an extended version of the Victorian skits in *Bitter-Sweet* and *Family Album,* allowing for further 1860 pastiche, such as the second-act "Invitation to the Waltz," another ebullient Coward valse scene, and the startlingly Novelloesque ladies ensemble, "This Is a Night for Lovers," which might be taken for an outright burlesque of "The Wings of Sleep" or "We'll Gather Lilacs" were it not for its sincerity and beauty.

Otherwise, there were typical signature-Coward romantic waltzes: the first-act duet "Bright Was the Day" and the second-act "This Is a Changing World." Comic ensembles suffered from overpopulation; the lyrics were superb, but the Cowardian patter sounds much better when Coward alone sings "His Excellency Regrets" or "Uncle Harry," the latter introduced after the first night. But there were several remarkably fine musical scenes: one beginning with Kerry's (Graham Payn's) letter to the diva, "Dear Madam Salvador," leading into the well-mannered "My Horse Has Cast a Shoe" duet, with its nimbly scored passages, the native chorus, "Fumfumbolo," which has a seemingly authentic (though perhaps African) feeling, plus some—rare—counterpoint, and "I Saw No Shadow on the Sea," which was an easygoing 1940s-style crooner's song plunked down brightly in the middle of the Victorian tropics. Coward proved he could write a contemporary song with charm and loveliness in his previous revue, *Sigh No More* (1945), which included "Matelot," "That Is the End of the News," and the deft title song. For *Pacific 1860,* the programme listed a "musical assistant to Noël Coward," Robb Stewart, as well as the orchestrators, Ronald Binge and Mantovani. The show might have been more amusing had "Alice Is at It Again" not been cut as Miss Martin's second-act entrance song. Coward later recorded it.

If *Pacific 1860* had not appeared at Drury Lane in 1946, there would have been almost no chance for it the following year, after the wild success of *Oklahoma!,* which presumably showed the British that dancing—on a much larger scale than had previously been attempted—must be part of a musical. In 1948, Coward did not act upon Maggie Teyte's suggestion that he turn his 1927 play, *The Marquise,* into an operetta for her. Coward's *Ace of Clubs* (1950) was at least an attempt to grow with the times, an enlarged nightclub show with gangster touches. Very few of the numbers were more than cabaret turns. There were only two big dances, a few attractive "modern" songs, like "I Like America" and "Sail Away," both used later in actual nightclubs and in a future show, and some which reeked of the Edwardian pub or music hall, like "Chase Me, Charlie," or "In a Boat on a Lake with My Darling." To intensify this out-of-place turn-of-the-century feeling, the nightclub owner (Sylvia Cecil) was given a typical Coward operetta waltz, "Nothing Can Last for Ever."

After the premières of the comedies *Relative Values* (1951) and *Quadrille* (1952) and finally the period operetta *After the Ball* (Globe, 10 June 1954), Coward must have been thought of as the Cecil Beaton of dramatists and composers, a purveyor of period charm. In *After the Ball,* his retreat to the previous century— the 1890s of Oscar Wilde's *Lady Windermere's Fan*—was merely a step backward, stylistically, to the 1930s and '40s of *Operette* and *Pacific 1860,* both failures. It showed that Coward still cherished the romantic operetta as his favorite musical form, though this time it could be bolstered with lashings of Wildean and Cowardian wit. Nevertheless, the soap-operatics of the plot could not be overcome, and these weighed down on the graceful songs, sets, and costumes (by Doris Zinkeisen), restricting the run to six months. Individually, quite a few of the songs were delightful: "Mr. Hopper's Chanty" and the wistful "Faraway Land," both sung by Graham Payn, "London at Night," a very catchy, comic male sextet in the vein of "Regency Rakes," and "May I Have the Pleasure of This Dance?", an elegant and effective mini-musical comedy of manners. Otherwise, there were the by-now thoroughly clichéd valse songs, "Sweet Day," and "Light Is the Heart," melodically vapid and interchangeable with those in *Operette* or *Pacific 1860,* with lyrics that had as much to do with those stories as with Wilde's. Norman Hackforth was in Jamaica to take down Coward's compositions in January 1954. During the tryout the orchestrations by J. Marr Mackie were redone by Philip Green, but the finished instrumentation lacked the polish usually associated with the Coward shows. The cast included Mary Ellis, Peter Graves, Vanessa Lee, Graham Payn, and Irene Browne—scoring a great hit as the Duchess of Berwick, singing "Something on a Tray."

The late Noël Coward musical plays were not up to the master's previous high standards, nor were the last Coward straight plays. *Sail Away* (Broadhurst, 3 October 1961) was an attempt at American musical comedy, and a frankly uninteresting one at that. Conceived with Rosalind Russell in mind, this cruise-ship saga wound up with Elaine Stritch as its star. Coward's first musical production to originate in America, it stylistically attempted in a rather dull way to be as breezily Broadwayish as possible, though there were the usual quotient of English music-hall melodies fitted out with complicated lyrics, an extension of the male and female quartets from the former operettas. The music-hall element provided the only real interest in the next Broadway show, *The Girl Who Came to Supper* (Broadway, 8 December 1963), which gave Tessie O'Shea a sequence of mock turn-of-the-century variety or pub songs that stopped the show but also caused one to suspect that Coward was now good merely for pastiche. Terence Rattigan's play *The Sleeping Prince* was the basis for *The Girl Who Came to Supper,* and every attempt was made to have the show prove another *My Fair Lady,* even a bid to get Rex Harrison to do the part finally played by Jose Ferrer. But Edwardian sets and costumes and even another period musical-comedy show-within-a-show ("The Coconut Girl") failed to capture the wonderful mixture of old and new that Lerner and Loewe had so successfully purveyed in *My Fair Lady.* As Coward only provided music and lyrics, he was not entirely to blame. The Philip J. Lang orchestrations were what made Coward's tunes listenable, but the lyrics were still up to their old tricks, especially in "Long Live the King—If He Can," a song about assassinations that had to be cut out-of-town because of the 1963 Presidential tragedy. Where some of his music was less than effective, the comic lyrics would come to the rescue, just as in Gilbert and Sullivan.

Technically, one cannot compare Coward with Sullivan, though both were champions of British light music and also crowd-pleasers. But Coward was incontestably Gilbert's successor as an English lyricist, and even a quick perusal of his *Collected Lyrics*—virtually impossible because of their deliciousness—will bear this out.

Nevertheless, his romantic or sentimental songs are perpetually endearing, harking back to the sweet simplicity of English-Irish folk songs or, occasionally, to Viennese waltzes. In the first category are such items as "Faraway Land," from *After the Ball,* or the patriotic "London Pride," sung during World War II (and actually modeled on a folk tune), while his romantic, sweeping waltzes might have come from the pen of Leo Fall or Oscar Straus: "I'll See You Again," or "I'll Follow My Secret Heart."

Ivor Novello (1893–1951) represents British operetta of the most spectacularly romantic type, proving that the masses of 1930s British audiences, many outside of London, had musical tastes that had not progressed since Edwardian days. However popular *No! No! Nanette!* and the fast, dancing musicals had been in the 1920s, the average family in any local High Street would have felt a positive nostalgic twinge for the era bordered by Gilbert and Sullivan and the Gaiety/Daly's shows on one side and *Chu Chin Chow* and "Keep the Home Fires Burning" on the other. Novello, who himself provided that popular song, responded to this twinge with a series of sensuous and fiendishly memorable songs (going right up the scale), fitted into a succession of incurably romantic shows written from 1935.

Like his friend Noël Coward, Novello had extra-operetta talents. He wrote several creditable straight comedies and dramas (none of which might survive revival today), and contributed charming music and lyrics to numerous musicals and revues from 1916. Many of these songs lack the pretentiousness of some later songs. "And Her Mother Came Too," sung originally by Jack Buchanan in the revue *A to Z* (1921), is a good example, and two lovely romantic

songs "I Want the Sun and Moon" and "Every Bit of Loving" were for the same year's *A Southern Maid*. The national "Our England," used in the first-act finale of another José Collins vehicle, *Our Nell* (1924), was another Novello interpolation in a Fraser-Simson score. Referring to his material for *Arlette* (1917), the *Times* commented on his "light and pretty numbers, without much character, but with plenty of agreeable melody." This criticism would be leveled at virtually anything he wrote until his death in 1951. He did not, contrary to popular belief, eschew modern themes or stories. His first complete score was for *The Golden Moth* (1921), a modernization of the *Robert Macaire* plot that had been used in Jakobowski's *Erminie,* with lyrics by P. G. Wodehouse, and only two of his later spectaculars were specifically "Ruritanian."

Ivor Novello was arguably the handsomest leading man Britain had in the silent cinema, even if he was not a very effective sound actor. He managed to appear in some of the better English silents: *The Bohemian Girl* (1922), the filmed version of Coward's *The Vortex* (1928), and the Hitchcock film *The Lodger* (1926), as well as in D. W. Griffith's *The White Rose* (1922). On stage, however, he was a deft comic actor (though perhaps a bit too forced for present tastes) as well as an excellent romantic one.

Throughout the early 1930s, Drury Lane had endured a succession of flops. The management dearly wanted a succession of hits like *Rose-Marie* and the Hammerstein-Romberg collaborations that followed, but these were not forthcoming, at least from Broadway. Neither Oscar Hammerstein, Jerome Kern, nor Paul Ábrahám could revive its fortunes with shows like *Ball at the Savoy* or *Three Sisters*. Only one show had brought distinction to the Lane, and that was Noël Coward's *Cavalcade* (1931), which realized the full physical potential of England's most lavishly equipped theatre. No doubt inspired by *Cavalcade,* and probably more so by the Coliseum spectaculars *White Horse Inn* and *Casanova,* Novello sketched out during a lunch with H. M. Tennent a wildly spectacular story with a gypsy wedding, a shipwreck, and other sensational scenes that eventually became *Glamorous Night* (2 May 1935). To his surprise, Drury Lane accepted the play—and Novello's score. For this production, Leontine Sagan, who had recently directed Novello's last (straight) play, staged, Christopher Hassall supplied the lyrics, and Mary Ellis, fresh from her triumph at His Majesty's in *Music in the Air,* starred with Novello. *Glamorous Night,* "a musical play," had an Edwardian Ruritanian plot plus the added attractions of a Fascist revolution, television, the shipwreck (shades of the S.S. *Morro Castle*), the gypsy wedding, an operetta-within-the-play; in short, any number of excuses for spectacular scenes and incidental numbers (including two for a black stowaway). The principal love songs were introduced in the operetta, or, in what was to be a typical Novello convention, in *rehearsals* or music lessons for this or that operetta. By placing operettas within his stories Novello could have his *Schmalz*-covered cake and eat it too; the public, similarly, didn't mind being conned so long as the songs were passionate. And, in *Glamorous Night,* they were: "Fold Your Wings of Love Around Me," "Shine Through My Dreams," and the title song being the major examples. Luxuriantly orchestrated by the Drury Lane conductor, Charles Prentice, they showed Novello at his lushest and most typical. Novello himself did not sing; he left this task to better voices. Only in the rarest instances was the singing integrated within the plot in the normal operetta/musical-comedy sense. There were ballet scenes, "skating" and "singing" waltzes, a "rumba," and two blues-y numbers for Broadway songstress Elisabeth Welch. The skating waltz, incidentally, was a revision of a number for an unproduced operetta of 1913, *The Fickle Jade*.

It was a happy marriage between the old Drury Lane melodrama and "modern" operetta, clearly as much of an answer to the cinema as the Coliseum and Alhambra spectaculars, but with the added attraction of modern rather than antique characters. Not that this prevented glittery costumes and flashy uniforms, plus purposely overbearing décor designed by the usually ingenious Oliver Messel—the kingdom of Krasnia was given every pictorial consideration. In its

---

The "gypsy wedding" between Ivor Novello and Mary Ellis in the 1935 Drury Lane production of Novello's *Glamorous Night*. The author-composer's wedding of melodrama and romantic operetta proved an unexpected success; there were several similar follow-ups at the Lane.

way, it was the British version of the Parisian *opérette à grand spectacle*. The critics were impressed, so was the public, and *Glamorous Night* might have ran and ran were it not for the fact that the theatre had arranged for a pantomime that Christmas. *Glamorous Night* was filmed in 1937, the first of three British films based on Novello musicals.

After a slight snag, Novello came back with another Drury Lane show, *Careless Rapture* (11 September 1936). Marlene Dietrich attended the glamorous première, which starred Novello, Dorothy Dickson, and Zena Dare. It began in a West End beauty parlor and ended with a "wedding in white" in China, by way of a fictitious musical, *The Rose Girl,* bank-holiday Hampstead Heath, an earthquake in Fu-Chin, a dream ballet at the Temple of Nichaow, and an escape from a subterranean cavern. There was an ever-so-slight reference to the Drury Lane production of *The Land of Smiles* with Novello as Prince Meilung (actually his character, Michael, in disguise) and there was an oriental specialty-dance (à la "The Continental") called "The Manchuko," danced by the American Walter Crisham. The loveliest song was introduced in the most improbable manner: two soloists from the Fu-Chin Amateur (Operatic) Society, who happen to be putting on *The Rose Girl,* sing "Love Made the Song" for an audience including Prince Meilung. The other numbers of note included "Music in May," part of the score to *The Rose Girl,* and an "operatic" burlesque, the Studio Duet. This proved that Novello did not really have the talent (or at least the inkling) to do extended operetta ensembles well. It was actually sung by Novello (who had taken a few voice lessons) but was dropped from the show after the first performances. Novello's Lehár "tribute" was not only in the choice of his setting; his music was becoming increasingly lush and almost as carelessly rapturous as his mentor's scores.

Careless Rapture was succeeded by *Crest of the Wave* (Drury Lane, 1 September 1937), which again had Novello in two roles and allowed Dorothy Dickson (always first a dancer) and Walter Crisham to do a mazurka, in the production of a fictitious British musical film entitled *Fair Maid of France,* and a tango in Rio de Janeiro. The plot was more unbelievable than the two preceding it, the score was thinner, and, in spite of a colossal train wreck in Act II, audiences may have felt that the formula was wearing thin. Indeed, a regular stock company of actors had been developed (Minnie Rayner, Dorothy Dickson, Walter Crisham) and the songs were dispiritingly similar to one another, if still quite tuneful.

After a short spell as/in Shakespeare's *Henry V,* Novello was given a further chance at Drury Lane. *The Dancing Years* (23 March 1939), an operetta inspired by a viewing of the 1938 film of *The Great Waltz,* was originally thought out shortly after the *Anschluss* of that year. The original intention was to set the play within the framework of invaded Vienna, the old hero-composer having been condemned to death for his help in aiding Jews to escape from Austria. The romance which followed this opening prologue was to have been a flashback. In the final version, watered down by the timid Drury Lane management, the prologue appeared at the end of the play, and overt references to Hitler were cut out. It is, still, Novello's most serious play, and one of the least spectacular (a reason for its enduring popularity with amateur societies).

Mary Ellis was another prima donna, Novello was Rudi Kleber, the composer, Leontine Sagan again produced, and Charles Prentice was joined by Harry Acres, Novello's new conductor, for the orchestrations. As *The Dancing Years* was less spectacular, so was it more plausible, combining the well-remembered romanticism of *Autumn Crocus* (*Lederhosen* and all), a realistic romance ending in premarital pregnancy, and the Nazi invasion of Austria. Scenes of "A Masque of Vienna" ending Rudi's first operetta, *Lorelei*, at the Theater an der Wien, backed up with several composition and rehearsal scenes, provided a canvas for a suitably Viennese-escapist score containing several prospective favorites: "Waltz of My Heart," "My Life Belongs to You," "My Dearest Dear," and "The Wings of Sleep," a lovely duet for contralto and soprano which had a notable successor in Novello's next show. "I Can Give You the Starlight" was an actual love song, from the heart, and not supposedly from an interior operetta, and "My Dearest Dear" was used, emotionally, for non-stage scenes.

Genuine romantic sentiment, rather than spectacle, would have ensured a long run at Drury Lane in the dark post-Munich days, but in September 1939 the outbreak of war caused the closing of all theatres. Drury Lane became ENSA (the British USO) headquarters. *The Dancing Years* was able to tour with great success, when provincial theatres reopened some weeks later, and in 1942 the show reopened at the smaller Adelphi, where it ran and ran—World War II's answer to *Chu Chin Chow* and *The Maid of the Mountains*. The combined Drury Lane/Adelphi run was 1,156 performances—Novello's greatest achievement and still the only work to have been revived in the West End (1968). *The Dancing Years* was filmed in 1950, in Technicolor, with Dennis Price compared unfavorably to Novello. In 1954, it had the distinction of appearing as an ice spectacular.

Arc de Triomphe (Phoenix, 9 November 1943) was on a smaller scale, and without Novello, though with Mary Ellis as a character patterned after Mary Garden; it involved French patriotism during World War I. This time the show-within-the-show was an opera, about Joan of Arc. Elisabeth Welch made a welcome reappearance—singing the wistful "Dark Music"—as a nightclub singer. It was the best song in this weak effort, though "You're Easy to Live With" had a charming bounce.

Perchance to Dream is Novello's most beautiful score, and perhaps his most romantic plot (Hippodrome, 21 April 1945). Surprisingly, he did all the lyrics himself. The story of an English house had been used in *Crest of the Wave;* here, it was a *Wie einst im Mai/Maytime* sort of epochal plot taking place in the same great hall in 1818, 1843, and 1945, the characters descendants of ancestors in previous scenes. Novello was a dashing Regency-era highwayman, Sir Graham Rodney, a Victorian balladeer and choirmaster, Valentire Fayre, and a modern chap, Bay. In the cast with Novello were Olive Gilbert (by this time in all his shows), Roma Beaumont, a young singer who had made an impressive debut in *The Dancing Years,* and Margaret Rutherford, as Lady Charlotte Fayre. Presented as a "victory presentation," this "musical romance" helped dispel the difficult post-VE days in Britain, achieving a run of 1,022 performances at a very large theatre. Although there were typical scenes with Novello *au piano*, there were no internal theatrical performances, save for a Victorian "singing ballet" entitled "The Triumphs of Spring." Aside from this there was little spectacle other than the changing costumes, and no violent scenes of spectacular destruction. The music avoided any modern dance rhythms, sticking to "antique" effects. At least one passionate song sprang from the action, rather than from an interior operetta: "Love Is My Reason for Living," though the rollicking "Highwayman Love" was rather obviously "planted" as a request number. But having Novello play a competent pianist in both acts allowed him to accompany both the Act I pastiche quintette (reminiscent of Edward German) and the show's most endearing and enduring song, the duet in Act II, "We'll Gather Lilacs." This lovely song, also released with a more modern verse for recording purposes, was intended to be a typical Victorian sentimental ballad, sung by soprano and contralto against a sugary accompaniment. But the refrain struck many British hearts in wartime the way the same composer's "Keep the Home Fires Burning" did in the Great War, and sheet-music and record sales were large. The song's effectiveness is best realized, however, in hearing it sung by two females, as originally written.

Perhaps the most enjoyable sequence in *Perchance to Dream* was the Victorian wedding. Following a happy wedding chorus ("Ring out sweet bells"), a lively bridesmaids' dance, a quaintly lugubrious contralto wedding prayer, the bride launches into a sparkling *valse brillante,* "My heart's afire and filled with desire," one of Novello's most ebullient creations. All in all, *Perchance to Dream* had the dreamiest assortment of sweetmeats of any Novello score, and was one of the last British shows to be popular before the American onslaught of 1947.

King's Rhapsody (Palace, 15 September 1949), produced when the composer-star was fifty-six, was a farewell to Ruritania that lasted 841 performances, beyond Novello's death. One of its virtues was to have in the same show both Zena and Phyllis Dare, two of Novello's Edwardian favorites, though he rather undiplomatically had Phyllis play his mistress and Zena his mother. (Zena Dare's last great part was as Mrs. Higgins in the Drury Lane production of *My Fair Lady* in 1958.) The *Sunday Times* echoed the public's general reaction:

> A romantic confection which employs every imaginable stand-by of the light musical stage and which ends with Mr. Ivor Novello kneeling alone upon the altar steps might be supposed to embody the ultimate in saccharine banality. Perhaps it does, but the result is an uncommonly pleasant evening in the theatre.

Originally entitled *The Legend of the Snow Princess, King's Rhapsody* reunited several of Novello's friends: Olive Gilbert, Robert Andrews, Vanessa Lee, and the Dares, plus orchestrator Harry Acres and lyricist Christopher Hassall. Murania and Norseland were the kingdoms, and the story involved an exiled king living with an actress forced by the Queen Mother to accept the crown and to beget an heir. It was an elaborate production, with ten different scenes taking place in such *endroits* as the Summer Palace at Kalacz and the Cathedral of Bledz. As described in the Samuel French play catalogue, the chorus is kept busy:

> There are birthdays to celebrate, a King to greet, a betrothal to honour, a bride to serenade, royal amateur theatricals to rehearse and perform, a revolution to incite and a coronation to attend . . .

The popular songs, some given sneak previews during a provincial tour of *Perchance to Dream,* were "Some Day My Heart Will Awake," "And Then a Violin Began to Play," and "Fly Home, Little Heart." Phyllis Dare had a humorous round, "The Mayor of Perpignan" (originally cut from *Arc de Triomphe*), and some songs found at a piano, dedicated to the actress, but sung by the Queen, including "The Gates of Paradise," a rapturous throwback to the Drury Lane Novello. The "Muranian Rhapsody" was a national ballet with choral embellishments, peopled with a Tartar chief, a Georgian girl, and an Albanian bridal couple. There was even a coronation chorus at the end, in Greek.

King's Rhapsody was filmed by Herbert Wilcox and released in 1955. The principals were Errol Flynn, Anna Neagle, and Flynn's wife, Patrice Wymore. An Anglo-Yugoslav co-production, *King's Rhapsody* was "a headache from the beginning," according to Anna Neagle.

No one complained about the lavish hokum Novello spun for the stage. Though it may not have appealed to more sophisticated tastes, it was, of its kind, exceedingly well done, and unique in its marriage of romantic operetta music with Drury Lane melodrama. Serious music critics did not deign to discuss Novello, and today his music would hardly appeal to the generations born since the composer's death. Novello would surely have been the last person to consider himself a serious composer, in the sense that Arthur Sullivan did, and the names of his orchestrators (Charles Prentice and Harry Acres), who filled Drury Lane, the Adelphi, the Palace, and the departed Hippodrome with the swelling "Novello sound," were always listed prominently in the programmes.

But as a romantic melodist, he had few equals in British music. With the melodies composed first, and the lyrics added later, Novello indulged in soaring, rapturous flights that were easily remembered. Nevertheless, his songs were definitely attractive and resplendently romantic. His sense of theatre was always sure, and he obviously knew how to keep audiences on cloud nine of escapist delirium. If a character did not sing a romantic song in a romantic situation, he or she sang it in the rehearsal or the performance of a new operetta in the course of the plot. Obviously, Novello the actor wouldn't have wanted a tenor to upstage him with a *genuine* love duet with his leading soprano, so he distanced these songs by a play-within-a-play format. It might also have stemmed from a certain British reserve in depicting romantic scenes with the voluptuousness of the Viennese or the Italians. Instead of singing, Novello would play his own songs on the piano while his leading ladies would sing them. The *Times* commented on this practice in its review of *Perchance to Dream* (1945): ". . . all the songs gain much from the rapture with which Mr. Novello listens to them."

Vivian Ellis (1904–   ) confessed admiring André Messager, Reynaldo Hahn, Paul Rubens, and Jerome Kern, who all had, as he stated, "the secret, the talisman, the open sesame—Melody," though throughout his career he was sometimes considered a composer in the shadow of Noël Coward. This was true, not only in his revue and musical-comedy songs, which had the nostalgic tinge of Edwardian melody Coward favored, syncopated into a quasi-Broadwayish 1920s idiom, but also in his delight in providing pastichey scores for period operettas. Many of his tunes had the wistfulness that Richard Rodgers often achieved: "I Will" and "Kiss Me Dear," both from the 1934 revue *Streamline,* both with the touching quality Rodgers had in the 1920s. But very few of his songs crossed the Atlantic to become popular American favorites, nor did any of his shows, unlike Coward's. He did not write the lyrics to his songs, as did Coward, though for a long period he had the services of one of Britain's cleverest, wittiest wordsmiths, Alan P. Herbert. Herbert was perhaps *too* clever; in spite of their application in the shows, few of his lyrics were memorable out-of-context, as Coward's were. They were so topical to either the book or current events that they resembled *Punch* poems—which some of them indeed were. And they were often so pithy that singing, or understanding them, became troublesome.

Ellis's outright revues and musicals, such as *Mr. Cinders* (1929) and the Cochran production of *Streamline* (1934), need not concern us, though the latter contained a piece of pastiche called "Perseverance" by "Turbot and Vulligan," which had the benefit of A. P. Herbert's right-on-target libretto. Ellis's music sounded more like Edward German or other Edwardians at times, and if the Sullivan cadences were sometimes achieved, "Perseverance" proved once again how difficult it was for any British composer to even *imitate* the Sullivan sparkle. The press liked it, but it was "received in almost complete silence," according to its composer.

In the same revue was "The First Waltz," a Rex Whistler–designed piece of Victoriana, used again in Ellis's great postwar success, *Bless the Bride* (Adelphi, 26 April 1947). A prior effort with A. P. Herbert, *Big Ben* (Adelphi, 17 July 1946), had a fairly patriotic theme, ending with the entire company with their backs to the audience listening to the famous clock chime midnight. But it was basically postwar British satire, with a Herbert libretto that recalled *Of Thee I Sing,* complete with a beauty pageant in Act I. *Big Ben* enjoyed the rewarding prestige of a first night attended by the present Queen (then Princess) Elizabeth, Field-Marshal Viscount Montgomery, the Prime Minister, and half the Cabinet. Unfortunately, the presence of the clock tower reminded the press of *Iolanthe,* to which the Ellis-Herbert work was unfavorably compared, and the public was not too keen on seeing a "light opera," as the piece was accurately, but fatally, billed. After a short run it was withdrawn.

Bless the Bride, more wisely billed "a musical show," opened a few days before the fabulous première of *Oklahoma!* at Drury Lane, and was naturally overshadowed by it, but after several weeks it played to capacity and had a very happy run of 886 performances (Cochran's longest). *Big Ben* had been modern, *Bless the Bride* (originally called *Little Lucy*) was Victorian, and apparently better-so than Coward's *Pacific 1860*, which had tried the same period and failed. A lot in it was pleasantly pastichey, like "The First Waltz," but the big songs were resolutely of the mid-twentieth century, such as *"Ma belle Marguerite"* and "This Is My Lovely Day." The story was slightly reminiscent of *Bitter-Sweet*, about an English girl who elopes with a handsome foreigner, though the details were more cheerful. The Egyptian-born Georges Guétary, who had been popular in France with Latin tangos, was hired to play the lover, opposite Lisabeth Webb as Lucy Veracity Willow. Tanya Moisewitsch's charming period designs (including a lovely programme cover) helped immensely—particularly the scenes at *la plage*, Eauville (a suggestion of Cochran's).

Tough at the Top, again with A. P. Herbert, and about a boxer, was not a success in 1949, though Ellis's musicalization of the old J. B. Fagan comedy about Pepys, *And So to Bed*, had a nice run in 1951–52. With Leslie Henson, Betty Paul, and young Keith Michell in the cast, this semi-pastiche period musical play—by no means an operetta—had two delightfully *olde* numbers, a madrigal, "Gaze Not on Swans," and "Love Me Little, Love Me Long." In 1955 (Winter Garden, 31 August) came the last A. P. Herbert–Ellis collaboration, *The Water Gipsies*, based on Herbert's 1930 novel of the same name. With a cast that sported Dora Bryan, Doris Hare, and Jerry Verno, the story was modern, but the best songs in this "play with music," had a decidedly old-fashioned lilt, and the spirit of the English countryside, particularly "Clip-Clop," the song about the river barge-horse, and "Little Boat," originally written by Ellis for the 1932 film of *The Water Gipsies*. This saga of the Thames managed to play 239 performances.

Besides providing English versions of *La Belle Hélène, La Vie Parisienne*, and *Die Fledermaus*, Alan P. Herbert will be remembered in operetta annals for his books for two 1930s works that are entirely forgotten: *Tantivy Towers* (Lyric, Hammersmith, 16 January 1931, transferred to the New Theatre) with music by Thomas F. Dunhill, and *Derby Day* (Lyric, Hammersmith, 24 February 1932) with a score by Alfred Reynolds. These did not pull the crowds out to Hammersmith for years, as *The Beggar's Opera* had done in the previous decade, but the public and critics *might* have imagined that Herbert and Dunhill or Herbert and Reynolds would possibly have developed into the new Gilbert and Sullivan. Again, Herbert's overwriting may have kept them too "special" for mass appeal—*Tantivy Towers* had no prose dialogue—though their typically English, modern themes were refreshing in an era of escapism to the spectacular past. Both had to do with "hosses." *Tantivy Towers* had the equine set visiting bohemian Chelsea and returning to the titular towers for a hunt ball. *Derby Day* was about just that—the derby. In the former, an unaccompanied quartet in Act I caused comment, while Rose's songs in *Derby Day*—"I'm Going to Be Rich!" and "Oh, Pretty, Pretty Horse"—attested to Reynolds's talent (especially on the recordings that survive from the operetta, sung by Gwen Catley).

AMERICAN OPERETTA

T HE CREATION of American operetta, like the Austrian and British varieties, was provoked by the overwhelming reception given to foreign works. In the eighteenth century, British ballad operas were popular in the colonies and led to American imitations, along with Shakespeare, farces, and other English fare. By the middle of the nineteenth century, New York was the principal theatrical city, with its cosmopolitan audience supporting Italian opera, serious drama, and, from 1841, the native minstrel show, along with lower-class diversions centered around the Bowery. Extravaganzas of the British type and burlesques, travesties, and pantomimes flourished. The music hall—usually a disreputable saloon with "waiter-girls" dispensing more than drink—was given a certain respectability by the impresario Tony Pastor, who opened his Music Hall in 1864.

Americans were—and have always been—attracted to anything new (which explains the frequent U.S. resistance to operetta revivals). Along with this quest for novelty, spectacle was always desirable. Thus, the extravaganzas and pantomimes of the 1840s and '50s generally featured extraneous diversions, like elaborate dancing or scenic effects, that often had little to do with the main plot. These erratic combinations reached a famous zenith in 1866, with the production of *The Black Crook* (Niblo's Garden, 12 September 1866), often regarded the "first" American musical comedy. This five-and-a-half-hour spectacular was the amalgam of two separate attractions. One was a Parisian ballet company, performing the 1845 *féerie, La Biche aux bois,* contracted to play a New York theatre that had burned down; the other was a derivative melodrama by Charles M. Barras called *The Black Crook,* at least suggested by the plot of Weber's

---

A poster for De Koven's *The Highwayman* (Broadway, 1897), his best-known work after *Robin Hood*. Operetta has always been partial to highway robbers and masked men, from *The Beggar's Opera* (1728) to *The Desert Song* (1926) to *Perchance to Dream* (1945). Library of Congress.

357

romantic opera *Der Freischütz*. The importers of the ballet easily convinced William Wheatley, Niblo's manager, that the addition of their ballet to the melodrama (which admittedly needed some padding) would improve the success of *The Black Crook*.

At the then unheard-of cost of perhaps $35,000, Wheatley had the Niblo's Garden stage totally redone and filled it with all-new sets and costumes imported from London. However spectacular the costumes may have been, the greatest effect was made by the least clothes—four girls in pink tights, then, for all practical purposes, considered nude. This elicited damnings from pulpit and press, and insured a healthy run.

Though not an operetta by any means, *The Black Crook* was a significant milestone in American musical theatre history as an early example of showmanship and publicity, and an early confirmation that Americans would crave spectacle, dancing, and attractive girls in their musical entertainments.

American audiences, which relied on Britain for a great deal of their theatrical properties and actors, gave a rousing welcome to Lydia Thompson and her British blondes in 1868. By performing rather undistinguished English burlesques in which these ladies invariably appeared as males, scanty attire and transvestism reigned in American theatres, and when Parisian and Viennese operettas were first performed in America, this fashion was perpetuated.

By the late 1860s, Offenbach's *opéras-bouffes* had created a sensation with the intelligent, cultivated sectors of the American theatre audience. Whether in French (to be understood only by the educated) or in the punning English versions of H. B. Farnie and his school, the *opéra-bouffe* was the first acquaintance Americans had with European operetta.

Just as the rage for Offenbach in London dated from the first production of *La Grande-Duchesse* at Covent Garden in 1867, its triumph at New York's Théâtre Français made Offenbach and Lucille the toasts of the town. The following summer, *Barbe-Bleue* was presented at Niblo's Gardens, and in 1870 both Tostée and her rival Marie Aimée were featured in a seven-and-a-half-month season of *opéra-bouffe* at the Grand Opera House (originally known as Pike's Opera House) then at Eighth Avenue and Twenty-third Street. It was one of the grandest and most luxurious theatres of its day. Both Aimée and Tostée were also responsible for bringing Offenbach to Americans living outside of New York City.

By 1870, Maurice Grau was the leading importer of French *opéra-bouffe,* and after that year it was Lecocq who, as in Paris, provided the biggest successes. Long runs were not generally the norm for *opéra-bouffe* in French: a French star would generally come to New York to play five or six of her best parts in a season of several weeks. When Lecocq's *La Fille de Madame Angot* was first seen in New York with Aimée (Broadway, 25 August 1873), the score was seized by Lydia Thompson and used in *Mephisto and the Four Sensations,* a burlesque that had the devil luring a quartet of French characters (including la belle Hélène and Geneviève de Brabant) down to hell. This was followed (at the Olympic Theatre) by the first English presentation of Lecocq's masterwork.

In that same season came an American answer to *opéra-bouffe, Evangeline* (Niblo's, 27 July 1874), which was more accurately a burlesque of Henry Wadsworth Longfellow's epic. Written by J. Cheever Goodwin and composed by Edward Rice, *Evangeline* had its lovers both played by women, and its locales considerably expanded from the poem's. The work's chief merit was its original score, rather than the usual hodgepodge borrowings that were such a natural facet of burlesque. Elaborated Irish-American sketches (by Harrigan and Hart), spectacular extravaganzas like the Kiralfy Brothers' *Around the World in Eighty Days* (1875), and mindless burlesques competed with seasons of French *opéra-bouffe* in the 1875–79 period. The same years saw the first American productions of the new Viennese operettas, including Johann Strauss's *Indigo* (in its French version) and Suppé's *Fatinitza*.

The mania for Gilbert and Sullivan's *H.M.S. Pinafore* in 1879, and for *The Mikado* six years later, produced a wave of native parodies, in addition to the many performances of these works unauthorized by the D'Oyly Carte organization. It also led to managers and impresarios seeking out further British works as well as commissioning new American operettas. Both, ideally, were to be as much like Gilbert and Sullivan as possible. The most obvious manifestation of a new British operetta in America was Gilbert and Sullivan's own *The Pirates of Penzance* (Fifth Avenue, 31 December 1879), which had its "official" première in New York after the "secret" British copyright performance in Devonshire. The "comic military opera" *The First Life Guards at Brighton,* set in England, was an early example of post–Gilbert and Sullivan Anglophilia in January, 1880. Genée's *Der Seekadett,* probably because of its naval setting, was staged the same month. Two short British operettas were staged in 1880 at New York's Bijou, managed by John A. McCaull, who became one of the leading operetta impresarios of the 1880s. These were Gilbert and Frederick Clay's *Ages Ago,* first produced at the German Reeds', and *Charity Begins at Home,* by Gilbert and Sullivan conductor Alfred Cellier and B. C. Stephenson (librettist for Sullivan's *The Zoo*).

Richard D'Oyly Carte was himself responsible for presenting British works in New York that he did not produce in London. *Billee Taylor,* the Edward Solomon nautical comic opera, was first presented in New York in 1881; Lillian Russell (later Mrs. Solomon) was to appear in a later revival. She was also seen in an unauthorized *Patience* the following season, by which time her rise to stardom had begun. Lillian Russell was incontestably the greatest American operetta diva of the nineteenth century, a U.S. equivalent of Hortense Schneider, or Florence St. John, or Marie Geistinger. She was musically well trained (under Leopold Damrosch) and, like Schneider, had her beginnings in music hall—at Tony Pastor's. She appeared in Audran's *Le grand Mogol* in the autumn of 1881 for John McCaull, and also was seen the next season as Aline in Gilbert and Sullivan's *The Sorcerer* (into which she interpolated outside songs).

London successes, whether of British or foreign extraction, continued to hold the boards, and various "English" opera companies toured the United States profitably with operettas performed in English translations. Lecocq, Audran, Planquette, Millöcker, Strauss II, and Suppé works were heard in English, along with English operettas by Solomon, Clay, and, of course, Sullivan. The new Casino, featuring mostly Viennese operettas in English, McCaull's Bijou, Daly's, and the Fifth Avenue were the principal New York operetta houses.

The Bijou had a monumental hit with a burlesque, *Adonis* (4 September 1884), again composed by Edward Rice, who had written *Evangeline* ten years earlier. It was a variation on the Pygmalion and Galatea theme kept alive week after week with topical barbs. Owing to the presence of handsome Henry E. Dixey in the title role, *Adonis* ran longer than any Broadway offering (and certainly any foreign operetta) ever had, just over 600 performances. Even the spectacular success of the D'Oyly Carte *Mikado* in 1885 (Fifth Avenue, 19 August) only lasted 250 performances. In fact, *The Mikado* would prove very influential to American operetta, resulting in a number of far-lesser works set in "oriental" locales.

Another long run was registered by a British work, *Erminie* (Casino, 10 May 1886), which had run just over three months at the Comedy Theatre, London, the previous year. The music was by Edward Jakobowski; the plot was based on a French play, *L'Auberge des Adrets,* a melodrama so ridiculous it was famously burlesqued on its first night by its star, Frédéric Lemaître, and turned into a broad comedy.

Francis Wilson, a spry comedian, made the role of Cadeaux (or "Caddy") his own, while W. S. Daboll was Ravennes ("Ravvy") and Pauline Hall, Erminie. The New York *Times* commented on Wilson's performance: "a very comical sketch of a petty thief masquerading in polite society and bringing his slang and jail manners into the salons of the aristocracy, to the intense amusement of the looker-on." The paper had little that was favorable to say about the score: "If the composer . . . is possessed of any originality or felicity in invention, he has carefully concealed it, and his music, although bright, fluent, and pleasantly rhythmical, cannot be compared with the second-rate efforts even of Strauss and Millöcker." On the other hand, the *Times* did admire "an exceptionally good libretto."

Erminie played well over 1,250 performances at the Casino (not consecutively) and made fortunes for several people. Many of its numbers were popular, including a duet for the two robbers, "We're a Philanthropic Couple," and a song for the soubrette (Marie Jansen), "Sundays After Three, My Sweetheart Comes to Me." The biggest song hit was Erminie's "Lullaby," "Dear Mother in Dreams I See Her." After 500 performances, Francis Wilson wanted out of the production. Like most actors then, he was not used to long runs of this type. Wilson, however, played "Caddy" the rest of his career—it became a signature part.

In the midst of French, Austrian, and British imports, *The Begum,* presented by McCaull at the Fifth Avenue Theatre in 1887 (21 November), was an important American first. It served as the debut of the composer **Reginald De Koven** (1859–1920) and the librettist Harry B. Smith. De Koven, Oxford-educated and musically trained by Delibes, among others, would become best known by his second score, *Robin Hood* (1891), while Smith was one of the most prolific author of operetta books and lyrics that ever lived. In *The Begum*'s cast were Mathilde Cottrelly as the Begum and (William) De Wolf Hopper as her husband, Howja-Dhu. The "Hindoo comic opera" capitalized on the fascination for things oriental that *The Mikado* had started two years before, though the Indian coloring was clumsily smeared over plot, characterizations, and lyrics without much of Gilbert's ingenuity or finesse.

Robin Hood (Standard, 28 September 1891) was a national triumph, though it never enjoyed any particularly lengthy New York stay. Produced first in Chicago by the Boston Ideal Opera Company, without any faith or much expenditure, the new De Koven–Smith surprised the company with its drawing power. *Robin Hood*'s first cast included Tom Karl (Robin), Henry Clay Barnabee (Sheriff of Nottingham), Caroline Hamilton (Maid Marian), and Jessie Bartlett Davis (Allan-a-Dale). To the breeches part of Allan-a-Dale went the operetta's principal song hit, "Oh, Promise Me," the success of which was so great that it ensured frequent revivals of *Robin Hood* for years to come. The rest of the score was more ambitious than this simple song, full of elaborate ensembles, including a hunting chorus, Morris dancing, an armorer's chorus, duets, trios, quartets, and a sextet. Its olde English atmosphere might have given some inspiration to Edward German some years later—especially the quaint phraseology of Smith's lyrics. It was seen on Broadway for the last time in 1944; Bandwagon, an enterprising group devoted to old American works, produced an Off-Off-Broadway remounting in 1982.

The Fencing Master (Casino, 14 November 1892), the next De Koven–Smith work, was the first American work to play the Casino, even though its setting, early 1400s Milan and Venice, was hardly native. The leading role, that of the fencing master's daughter, Francesca, was taken by Marie Tempest (who—as usual—spent most of her time masquerading as a boy). The music was this time Italianate rather than "medieval English," with the structure of music and book based on European models. Mediterranean forms were used, such as the barcarole, habanera, tarantella, as well as *two* quintets and an elaborate second-act finale that depicted the traditional Venetian "marriage" ceremony with the Adriatic.

The Knickerbockers and *The Algerian* (both 1893) were less popular, but *Rob Roy* achieved a 235-performance run on Broadway (Herald Square, 29 October 1894). *Rob Roy* concerned itself with the young Pretender, Bonnie Prince Charlie, and the Highland chief, Rob Roy, the latter secretly married to Janet, daughter of the Mayor of Perth. The show was stopped on the first night by Janet's "There Was a Merry Miller of the Lowland," but the critics most admired De Koven's formal overture, as well as several songs written in an imitation Scottish folk style. *The Tzigane* (1895), the same season, had Lillian Russell and Jefferson de Angelis; this lasted a bit more than a month, as did *The Mandarin* (1896), a bit of *chinoiserie* attacked for its derivativeness.

The Smith–De Koven partnership tried again with *The Highwayman* (Broadway, 13 December 1897), returning to the British Isles of their earlier hits and another eighteenth-century story. This time they succeeded, as the show ran six

THE MARCH WE SHALL ALL HAVE TO WHISTLE

months with Joseph O'Hara, Hilda Clark, and Jerome Sykes starring. The leading musical gem was the love duet, "Do You Remember?" *The Highwayman* was revived in 1917 with John Charles Thomas as the "desperate young Irish blade," but never again. Nor were any of the subsequent, middling, De Koven creations: *The Three Dragoons* (1899), *Foxy Quiller* (a sequel to *The Highwayman,* 1900), and *The Little Duchess* (1901, with Anna Held).

Maid Marian was the last glowing ember in De Koven's career (Garden, 27 January 1902), again a sequel to *Robin Hood.* The Bostonians commissioned it, and put Henry Clay Barnabee and W. M. MacDonald in the cast again as the Sheriff of Nottingham and Little John. The locales of the operetta this time alternated between Sherwood Forest and Palestine, with Robin Hood participating in the Crusades on behalf of Richard the Lion-Hearted. Most admired, musically, were the concert overture, another song for Allan-a-Dale in Act II ("Tell Me Again, Sweetheart"), and the mostly choral third act, set in England during the Yuletide season. George P. Upton, in his *Standard Light Operas* (1902), claimed that "the music gains in dramatic power and seriousness of purpose, and at the time is full of life and vivacity."

The Jersey Lily (1903) lasted but three weeks; *The Red Feather* (Lyric, 9 November 1903) had a book by Charles Klein (a Sousa collaborator) and a spectacular production by Florenz Ziegfeld. This time the *heroine,* the Countess Von Draga, was a bandit in disguise, the Red Feather. *Happyland* (Lyric, 2 October 1905) had a much happier run, while works like *The Student King* (1906), *The Girls of Holland* (1907), *The Golden Butterfly* (1908), *The Beauty Spot* (1909), *The*

Wedding Trip (1911), or *Her Little Highness* (1913) were substantially weaker efforts.

De Koven will be remembered as *Robin Hood*'s composer, though as "Oh, Promise Me" is seldom sung at American weddings anymore, the composer and his leading operetta are in danger of sinking further into obscurity. However, Julie Andrews surprised film audiences by singing the song during a funeral scene in the 1980 Blake Edwards film, *S.O.B.* De Koven's works come from the palmy days of American composers and librettists writing about romantic old Europe, rather than seeking native inspiration. Not having heard *Robin Hood, Rob Roy,* or *Maid Marian* with their full orchestrations, which might reveal what many contemporary critics admired, it is difficult to comment on De Koven's talents.

John Philip Sousa (1854–1932) was the March King, as inextricably allied to his favorite form as Strauss II was to the waltz. It was not, perhaps, Sousa's original intention to be remembered solely for his marches, but he had a band background, and his music seems best suited for martial ensembles, heavy on the brass and percussion.

Sousa is a Portuguese name; his mother was Bavarian. He was appropriately enough born in Washington, D.C., and his patriotic feelings lasted a lifetime. He ran away from his home at the age of thirteen to join a circus band, where he must have learned exactly how to please a crowd. But he came back to his parents, and his father had John Philip apprenticed to the United States Marine Band. After seven years with this even more decisively influential organization, Sousa spent a similar length of time playing in theatre orchestras, notably in Philadelphia. He was in the "Offenbach Garden" orchestra in 1876 in Philadelphia, and also played Sullivan, Strauss II, and other popular operetta scores during this period. He began his own stage attempts during the 1878–79 season. *Katherine* was unproduced, but *Our Flirtation* (1880) was seen in Philadelphia, as was his variant of the Sullivan–Burnand *The Contrabandista* (1867), entitled *The Smugglers,* given a few performances in the beginning of 1882 with a largely nonprofessional cast. The libretto was by Wilson J. Vance, who smuggled his ideas from Burnand. The one-act *Queen of Hearts* (1886) was no more successful, but by this time Sousa had been the leader of the Marine Band for some six years, and his career seemed set in the bandstand, rather than in the theatre. In 1884, *Desiree* was presented by the McCaull Opera Company; the book was partly the work of *Box and Cox*'s author, John Maddison Morton. Some sources credit Sousa with the orchestration for *The Merry Monarch* (1890), the J. Cheever Goodwin–Woolson Morse rehash of Chabrier's *L'Étoile* (1877), as well as for

---

Cartoon of the London presentation of Sousa's *El Capitán* (1896), which ran longer than the first Broadway edition. De Wolf Hopper (in helmet) towers over the rest of the cast. *El Capitán* is still revived, and the famous title march remains its best feature (and advertisement).

the Americanization of Lecocq's *Le Grand Casimir,* called *The Lion Tamer* (1891). During the period of his tenure with the Marine Band, Sousa was achieving considerably more fame for his marches, including, most famously, *The Gladiator* (1886), *Semper Fidelis* (1888), *The Washington Post* (1889), and *The Stars and Stripes Forever* (1896).

In 1896, Sousa tried once more for a stage hit and got it, on Broadway, with *El Capitán* (Broadway, 20 April 1896). Charles Klein provided the silly libretto that had elements of *La Périchole, The Mikado,* and other works, as did the lyrics, by Thomas Frost and the composer, and, predictably, Sousa's score. But audiences were enthusiastic over De Wolf Hopper in the title role (actually the Viceroy of Peru disguised as the rebel bandit, El Capitán). Hopper, who also produced *El Capitán,* had a hit vehicle on his hands, with which he delighted thousands of patrons in the United States and London (Lyric, 10 July 1899, 140 performances). His appearance in the Sousa work followed a long career with the McCaull Opera Company, playing parts in *Der Bettelstudent, Die Fledermaus, Joséphine vendue par ses soeurs, Fatinitza,* and many other works, as well as in the native operettas *Wang* (1891) and *Dr. Syntax,* a musical version of Tom Robertson's *School* (1895).

Hopper's appearance as the conquistador-bandit, in ridiculous ill-fitting armor and a plumed helmet, was calculated to provoke mirth, as was his voice,

> . . . modelled after the involuntary bass and treble of the schoolboy whose throat mechanism is in that settled condition known as "changing," [which] startles one into amazed laughter because of its ludicrous contrast with his six feet and several inches of height. His abnormally long legs and his loose-jointed awkwardness also strike the person . . . as vastly amusing.[1]

El Capitán remains the only Sousa work to be regularly revived, generally in a revised version. The most recent productions were at the Goodspeed Opera House in 1973 (with John Cullum), the Minnesota Opera, the Texas Opera Theater, and by the Eastern Opera Theatre in New York. The operetta's most famous song is, of course, its rousing title march, which is first heard as the refrain of the entrance song of the disguised Viceroy, "You see in me, my friends." The rest of the score has a number of worthwhile melodies, but none approaches the march in appeal, and many are embarrassingly derivative. "The Typical Tune of Zanzibar" reminds one of "Titwillow," and a love ballad or two are common and trite. Echoes of Sullivan, Suppé, and Offenbach were unavoidable, given Sousa's career, but all too seldom in *El Capitán* is there a great ensemble or even a glittering *couplet.* The marches—and there are more than one—dominate.

The following year saw the production of *The Bride Elect,* with a libretto by the composer, which toured the country for five months before its New York debut (Knickerbocker, 11 April 1898). This starred Christie MacDonald and

[1]Lewis C. Strang, *Celebrated Comedians of Light Opera and Musical Comedy in America,* pp. 64–65.

Hilda Clark. The principal march was thought by the composer his finest, but some critics did not care for the preponderance of march time:

> Sousa is the most eminent composer for the bass drum and cymbals that we have . . . and the American public thinks that it is great stuff. So it is, the finest music for a military parade that ever came out of a brass band . . . His strong point is marches, and he knows it . . . The score [to *The Bride Elect*] was undoubtedly catchy, and the tunes pleased for the moment. As for the book, which was also by Sousa, it was nothing to boast of. It served admirably as a ringer-in for the marches.[2]

The Spanish-American War called upon Sousa's patriotic talents, and his band's lengthy recording career began around that time. In 1898, after a nervous breakdown caused by hectic activities during the war, Sousa, with Klein and Hopper, sought to duplicate the success of *El Capitán* with *The Charlatan* (Knickerbocker, 5 September 1898), which did better on the road than in New York. Sousa again played it safe by designing the work expressly for De Wolf Hopper and his company, which was able to profitably tour the operetta outside of New York prior to its Broadway debut. The plot, again the work of Charles Klein, was set in Russia.

Chris and the Wonderful Lamp (Victoria, 1900) opened on the first day of the new century, a Sousan precursor to the successful fairy-tale operetta-spectacles that Victor Herbert and Glen MacDonough would do several years later; MacDonough was Sousa's librettist. Harry B. Smith, another frequent Herbert and De Koven librettist, provided the book and lyrics for *The Free Lance* (New Amsterdam, 16 April 1906), which was too steeped in the 1870–80s comic tradition to have caught on in the new century. Echoes of *Patience, La Périchole,* and *Der lustige Krieg,* not to mention *The Bride Elect* and even *El Capitán,* were present in the score and in Smith's libretto. Nevertheless, critics (no doubt decrying the watering-down of the operetta form) thought it Sousa's best, or nearbest, work. A recent production by the Opera Company of Philadelphia (1979) revealed few musical or dramatic riches one might have been missing all these years, but it was all pleasant enough. Again, the marches predominated. The original production lasted about a month, with the comedian Joseph Cawthorn in a leading role. Sousa's last Broadway production lasted less than half the time: *The American Maid* (Broadway, 3 March 1913).

With isolated exceptions, the turn of the century was a great age for operetta in terms of productivity only. Hundreds of operettas were written and produced in the 1890–1905 span in Europe and in America. The distinctions between operetta, musical comedy, and revue were in many cases still muddy; many of the works presented in this period combined elements of each. Gilbert and Sullivan's patter songs were somehow thought to be licenses for the inclusion of any topical song in the context of a comic opera, while the lavish trappings of extravaganza, which were later concretely exploited in revue, were still expected in operetta. In all operetta cities, the *vaudeville* element had already

---

[2]Lewis C. Strang, *Prima Donnas and Soubrettes of Light Opera and Musical Comedy in America,* pp. 256–57.

overtaken either the romantic or the socially-politically satirical plots, returning to the farcical elements that Gilbert and Sullivan had (at least) tried to refine. In America, low comedians, like James T. Powers or Jefferson De Angelis, who had training in the well-written Gilbert and Sullivan roles, began to have less rigidly constructed vehicles written for them, to capitalize on their broad styles. The leading sopranos and mezzo-sopranos, who had had *opéra-bouffe* companies built around them in the 1870s and '80s, began to lose their prominence, though Lillian Russell still had drawing power. This explains the popularity of comic operas like *Wang* (1891) and even some of Sousa's works, which were—effectively—tailored specifically for De Wolf Hopper in the '90s.

Significantly, the resurgence of modern-dress *vaudeville* in England and America gave rise, by the mid-'90s, to what became the modern musical comedy, as opposed to the future "musical play," often a euphemism for the romantic operetta. As usual, London was first, with the Gaiety musical comedies of George Edwardes and his fellow managers produced along with more florid operettas at Daly's and other theatres. In New York, British musical comedies like *A Gaiety Girl* and *An Artist's Model* were eagerly devoured, while only a few American shows were reciprocally appreciated in the West End, *The Belle of New York* being the principal example.

When **Victor Herbert** (1859–1924) began his ascent to fame, his main occupation—and that of his librettists—was to provide operettas that were *not* simply vehicles for popular comedians like De Wolf Hopper and Jefferson De Angelis (although Herbert did do a few tailor-made works in his career). Herbert's musical ambitions were to create cohesive scores to support libretti that were romantic as much as or more than comic. What, exactly, one might ask, were Herbert's models? Given Herbert's German training, it is probable he was acquainted with the works of Lortzing, Flotow, and presumably the major Viennese operetta composers, like Suppé and Strauss II. Having played in the Stuttgart and Metropolitan Opera orchestras, he obviously knew his grand opera. His scores betray a knowledge of French operetta, and he may also have had acquaintance with the scores of Auber and Adam. He adored Schubert.

Herbert was born in Dublin in 1859 and, in spite of half-German parentage and German upbringing and training, the folk tradition of Ireland had an irresistible effect on his music. In the ballads and romantic numbers for which Herbert remains famous, this Irishness gave his music an unmistakable wistfulness and charm—whether the setting of the operetta was in Hungary, New Orleans, or Toyland. When the locale *was* Ireland, as in *Eileen* (1917), this pe-

---

Lillian Russell in Jakobowski's *The Queen of Brilliants* (1894), which failed to capture the public that the composer's *Erminie* had conquered. Miss Russell reigned as America's operetta queen as well as its standard for feminine beauty. She was, however, allowed to get away with interpolations in the finer scores she performed. This would have infuriated Gilbert and Sullivan, in whose *The Sorcerer* and *Patience* she appeared, among other works.

culiarity was indeed welcome. Nothing was intrinsically wrong with an Irish style, but Herbert was also guilty—with his librettists—of lapsing into the childish triteness and quaintness so unfortunately popular at the turn of the century. The banality came directly from Sousa and his school, the type of songs written for the 1890s extravaganzas for which the public clamored, like *Wang* or *El Capitán*. *Couplets* had become more infantile than usual, and so had any attempts at ensemble elegance. But Herbert's orchestrations for these effusions were brilliantly effective; and his ensemble writing was certainly more polished than that of most of his contemporaries.

Herbert was trained at the Stuttgart Conservatory as a cellist (like Offenbach) and was a cellist for the Stuttgart Opera. When his fiancée, a soprano with the Opera, was engaged for the Metropolitan Opera in New York, Herbert was also contracted as a cellist for the orchestra. While in New York he also became a military bandmaster; the combination of opera and the regimental band was a promising one for an operetta composer.

In 1894, his first stage work was presented in New York by the Bostonians, the prominent operetta company. *Prince Ananias* (Broadway, 20 November 1894) had a libretto by Francis Neilson set in France in the 1500s, perhaps influenced by Messager's *La Basoche,* seen a few years before at the Casino. The libretto—concerning a group of strolling players presented before the French court—was condemned, though not Herbert's score. The Bostonians took *Prince Ananias* on the road for a few months after the Broadway run of 55 performances, but it never achieved the popularity of its principal repertory favorite, De Koven's *Robin Hood.*

Harry B. Smith furnished the book for *The Wizard of the Nile* (Casino, 4 November 1895), Herbert's second work, and one which ran nearly twice as long as *Prince Ananias.* Frank Daniels, who had begun his stage career in *Les Cloches de Corneville* with the Boston Opera Company in 1879, was the popular comedian who starred as a traveling fakir, Kibosh, in the Egypt of Cleopatra (played by Dorothy Morton in a blond wig). When Smith first heard the composer play a portion of the score, he remembered that "it was rather obscured by Herbert's piano playing." Herbert finished the score in great haste, as usual composing away from the piano and orchestrating it entirely himself. Daniels' popular catchphrase was "Am I a wiz!", and his antics were indeed more catchy than the score, remembered only for the waltz, "Star Light, Star Bright." *Der Zauberer von Nil* was produced at the Carltheater in Vienna in 1896 (26 September) and also in New York in its German translation.

The Bostonians returned to Herbert and Smith for *The Serenade* (Knickerbocker, 16 March 1897) after *The Gold Bug* (1896) failed at the Casino (it had nothing to do with Edgar Allan Poe). The Bostonians—Jessie Bartlett Davis and Henry Clay Barnabee among them—were joined by the Nashville-born Alice Nielsen, who had sung Yum-Yum and La Périchole at the start of her career in California. Her brilliant voice and high spirits brought her to the attention of a San Francisco opera company, and later to the Bostonians, where she sang small parts in *Prince Ananias* and *Robin Hood*. Her Yvonne in *The Serenade* was so successful in stopping the show that she launched her own operetta company after appearing in the Herbert work. The show's most popular musical item was the title serenade, though some critics thought the entire score was excellent. Smith's libretto—loosely suggested by Richard Genée's *Nanon*, transplanted to Spain—also had elements of Sullivan's *The Chieftain* in its plot.

The Idol's Eye was another Eastern vehicle for Frank Daniels (Broadway, 25 October 1897) and ran a mere two months, distinguished merely by a comic number about a tattooed man. *Plays and Players* criticized the score: "The music of this opera is what we have learned to expect from Victor Herbert—upon one hand, not trashy; upon the other, not strikingly original."

In 1898, Herbert conducted the Pittsburgh Symphony Orchestra, alternating symphonies with miscellaneous pieces by such operetta composers as Saint-Saëns, Delibes, Chabrier, and Bizet. Meanwhile, his operettas continued. *The Fortune Teller* (Wallack's 26 September 1898) had in its première cast Eugene Cowles, Joseph Cawthorn, Marguerite Sylva, and Alice Nielsen, for whose company Herbert had composed the work. Harry B. Smith's libretto detailed the story of a gypsy fortune-teller and Irma, an heiress from Budapest studying for the ballet who looks just like her—both played by Miss Nielsen. Picturesquely set in the Hungarian countryside, some of the melodies had charming gypsy-Hungarian colorations. "Romany Life" ("In the Forest, Wild and Free") and the hussar chorus were undeniably rousing. The "Gypsy Love Song" ("Slumber On, My Little Gypsy Sweetheart") was more Irish than Magyar, but Eugene Cowles made a tremendous hit of it. There were a number of lesser items: "Always Do as People Say You Should" was the most memorable.

Alice Nielsen in one of Victor Herbert's early successes, *The Fortune Teller* (Wallack's, 1898).

The Fortune Teller lasted five weeks in New York, but toured extensively, and has been revived, the last time Off-Broadway by the Light Opera of Manhattan in 1980. A thoroughly revamped version by Arthur Kay and Robert Wright and George Forrest, *Gypsy Lady,* was seen for ten weeks in New York in 1946; it was retitled *Romany Love* for London in 1947. The setting was changed to France and there were a number of other Herbert songs interpolated. This was one of the few times Herbert was heard in England since Alice Nielsen brought *The Fortune Teller* to London in 1899 (Shaftesbury, 9 April).

The 1899–1900 season saw four Victor Herbert works. The first was a failure, a musicalization of Edmund Rostand's *Cyrano de Bergerac* (Knickerbocker, 18 September 1899), barely two years after the play's Paris première. The idea was that of Francis Wilson, who starred as Cyrano; the blend of burlesque and romance did not work. Another vehicle for Frank Daniels, *The Ameer* (Wallack's, 4 December 1899), was a popular, though not critical, success. Daniels was set loose this time in Afghanistan. *The Singing Girl* (Casino, 23 October 1899) was similarly written as a star vehicle, for Alice Nielsen; Stanislaus Stange's silly book took place in Linz (Austria). "The libretto [of *The Ameer*], which is credited to Kirke La Shelle and Frederick Ranken," wrote one critic, "is a trivial and infantile affair, without wit or point or grace of anything else that is of the slightest moment." Nor was Harry B. Smith one to contribute much of literary worth: his book for *The Viceroy* (Knickerbocker, 30 April 1900) inspired little of value from Herbert.

It was not until 1903 that Herbert, busy with the Pittsburgh Symphony, returned to Broadway, and with one of his most famous works, *Babes in Toyland* (Majestic, 13 October 1903). Attempting to repeat the success of the previous season's *The Wizard of Oz,* this extravaganza introduced nursery-rhyme characters in a children's adventure libretto concocted by Glen MacDonough. Commencing a country-wide tour in Chicago that lasted—with other companies—for years, *Babes in Toyland* depended on spectacular effects, to be sure, but was aided by a catchy and often lovely Herbert score. Best were the lullaby-like "Toyland," and the marvelous, grand "March of the Toys." The operetta has not seen any recent major revivals on Broadway (there was a Shubert production in 1929–30), but the Light Opera of Manhattan mounted a small-scale production, to considerable approbation, in 1978.

Two musical films were made of the property: in 1934, with Laurel and Hardy, and in 1961, a Disney production. A large arena attraction entitled *The Babes in Toyland* toured in the 1979–80 season with a modernized book and score.

Babette (Broadway, 16 November 1903) made little impression on the public, but Herbert's new Viennese prima donna did. Fritzi Scheff, with Metropolitan Opera appearances behind her (among them, Papagena in *Die Zauberflöte*), was the critics' pet, and her solid vocal talents allowed Herbert an increased range of composition. During the calls following the second act of *Babette,* Scheff planted a "little" kiss on Herbert's cheek, which caused a slight scandal at the time, and may have influenced the composer's biggest hit song for the singer, "Kiss Me Again," two seasons later.

It Happened in Nordland (Lew Fields, 5 December 1904) and *Miss Dolly Dollars* (Knickerbocker, 4 September 1905) proved acceptable vehicles for Marie Cahill and Lulu Glaser, respectively. The former star made *Nordland* the greater success of the two, and "Absinthe Frappé" remains the show's best-remembered song. *Wonderland* (24 October 1905) was an attempt to duplicate *Babes in Toyland,* again with a Glen MacDonough book. Curiously, the Lewis Carroll characters that the piece had on its tryout were eliminated by the time of the Broadway première—even though the sheet music and posters depicted them.

Mlle. Modiste (Knickerbocker, 25 December 1905) was indeed a Herbert Christmas present, possibly his best work. In its Parisian hat shop setting, Henry Blossom's book conjured up both Messager and Monckton, and Herbert's score owed something to both styles, without managing to be as truly brilliant as the former or as genuinely piquant as the latter. This time the tryout went very well, with President and Mrs. Theodore Roosevelt enjoying Herbert and Scheff in Washington. It was adoringly received on Broadway and later on the road, and it had the fortune to produce at least four Herbert standards: "Kiss Me Again," "The Mascot of the Troop," "The Time and the Place and the Girl," and "I Want What I Want When I Want It." The modest but tasteful revival by the Light Opera of Manhattan in 1977 reaffirmed the work's sprightly good spirits and inoffensive ensembles, married to a clichéd but not boring book. As *Kiss Me Again,* the operetta was entertainingly filmed by First National in Technicolor at the beginning of the sound period, but sadly without most of its score.

The Red Mill, which usurped *Mlle. Modiste* at the Knickerbocker the following season (24 September 1906), was perhaps an even better work. Charles Dillingham produced it for the comedy team of Montgomery and Stone, who played two Americans in Holland. Again, a succession of sterling songs ensured a long run: "The Streets of New York," "Moonbeams," "Every Day Is Ladies' Day with Me," and "The Isle of Our Dreams." Better yet, the Dutch setting and costumes were invitations to the Knickerbocker, as was the large illuminated windmill in front of the theatre set up for producer Dillingham.

A double bill for the Weber and Fields' Music Hall, *Dream City* and *The Magic Knight* (25 December 1906), concerned an imagined housing scheme in Long Island, complete with opera house, at which *The Magic Knight* is performed. The latter work, an outright burlesque of Wagner's *Lohengrin,* was particularly well liked by the more astute critics. *The Tattooed Man* (Criterion, 18 February 1907) was another tailor-made piece for Frank Daniels, this time set in Persia.

The prolific pen of Victor Herbert kept on composing, undaunted by dreadful libretti that seem to have prevented continued popularity. *Algeria* (1908) ran six months; *Little Nemo* (1908), based, again, on children's reading matter—this time the comic strip—ran a bit over three months, helped by its spectacle; *The Prima Donna* (1908) had Fritzi Scheff for 72 performances in a spin-off of *Mlle. Modiste.* And *Old Dutch* (1909) was notable merely for having given the very young Helen Hayes her first Broadway role.

But with *Naughty Marietta* (New York Theatre, 7 November 1910), Herbert reached what many considered his apex. Having failed in his attempt to rival New York's Metropolitan Opera, producer Oscar Hammerstein (I) had Herbert and Rida Johnson Young write their "creole comic opera" for two of the singers of his Manhattan Opera House: Emma Trentini and Orville Harrold. *Musical America* remarked on the première:

> . . . The entire orchestral part is replete with felicitous touches better than anything of their kind their writer has yet done. Mr. Herbert himself wielded the baton on the first night with the result that everything went for its full value. At the close of the first act the enthusiasm was positively riotous and the principals were showered with flowers. Victor Herbert received a stormy welcome when dragged on the stage by Miss Trentini, but the audience would not calm down until Mr. Hammerstein had risen in his box to bow four or five times . . .

Naughty Marietta was assuredly a triumph for American operetta, and refreshing in its use of an American setting, eighteenth-century New Orleans. The story, about a noble young lady escaping her betrothed back in Europe, could just as easily have taken place there, but the native color of Louisiana made the piece that much more novel. Seen today (for example, the lavish revival by the New York City Opera in 1978), the book—no matter how thoroughly revised—remains a silly framework for the treasury of stirringly effective songs which continue to weave their spell on the public: "Tramp! Tramp! Tramp!", " 'Neath the Southern Moon," the "Italian Street Song," "I'm Falling in Love with Someone," and "Ah, Sweet Mystery of Life." Five numbers like this in one work are certainly enough to keep it on the boards. Musical adapter Herbert Stothart and the scriptwriters kept these in the famous 1935 MGM film, directed by W. S. Van Dyke, the first to team Jeanette MacDonald and Nelson Eddy. It was acclaimed for its charming cast (Frank Morgan, Elsa Lanchester were in it also), its glossiness, its verve, and, primarily, for the five hit songs retained. The rest had been exorcised.

If *Marietta* was the high point of Herbert's career, the rest was not entirely a downhill slide. *The Duchess* (1911), for Fritzi Scheff, failed to please (and resulted in a tiff that ended the partnership of composer and star), but *The Enchantress* did quite well (New York, 19 October 1911). This was a Ruritanian affair by Fred de Gresac (the wife of opera baritone Victor Maurel) that featured the glamorous Kitty Gordon as a prima donna. The most enduring number was the star's entrance song, "The Land of My Own Romance." The next operetta, *The Lady of the Slipper* (Globe, 28 October 1912), was a variation of the Cinderella story, produced lavishly by Charles Dillingham with a stellar cast led by Elsie Janis and Montgomery and Stone. This ran some 232 performances.

But *Sweethearts* (New Amsterdam, 8 September 1913, 136 performances) was vintage Herbert, with songs that are still immensely attractive. This time, the singers (Christie MacDonald and Thomas Conkey) were more attuned to the operatic operettics of the title waltz, "Every Lover Must Meet His Fate," and the moving "Angelus." The lighter numbers were top drawer as well, especially "Jeannette and Her Wooden Shoes," which did not have a very "Flemish" feeling but which best approximated the catchy, but not cheap, wistfulness of Herbert's British contemporary, Lionel Monckton. The story, based on a fifteenth-century tale about a princess brought up by a Belgian laundress, was impossibly full of mistaken identities, but the Fred de Gresac and Harry B. Smith plot and Robert B. Smith's lyrics were more or less unaltered (save for the dialogue) in the 1947 revival on Broadway. This saw Bobby Clark in what was once a very small part. Songs from *The Enchantress* and *Angel Face* (1919) were added to the score.

The Madcap Duchess (Globe, 11 November 1913), despite a big new star (Ann Swinburne, lately of the New York production of *The Count of Luxemburg*) and period sets and costumes (eighteenth-century France), and a very conscientious, pastichey score, did not attract, probably because no hit tunes were there. *The Debutante* (Knickerbocker, 7 December 1914) was similarly unmemorable. Hazel Dawn, the original Pink Lady, headed the cast. Critics enjoyed Herbert scholar Frederick S. Roffman's revival in 1980, as produced by New York's Bel Canto Opera. Compared with contemporary musicals, even minor Herbert sounded quite special.

The Princess Pat (Cort, 29 September 1915) was set in modern Long Island and was termed a comic opera—a markedly more ambitious score than some of Herbert's prior efforts. It was very different from the following season's *The Century Girl* (Century, 6 November 1916), a lavish revue with other numbers written by Irving Berlin, with Hazel Dawn and the popular comedian Leon Errol.

Eileen (Shubert, 19 March 1917) was Herbert at perhaps his most rhapsodic. The patriotic subject matter appealed to the pro-Irish composer, and he poured out at least two of his most gorgeous creations, the title song and "Thine Alone." The rest of the operetta's score reflected the Irish setting—finally an excuse for the essential Irishness of Herbert's melodies—and was admired by the critics, some of whom claimed it surpassed his more popular earlier works, like *Naughty Marietta*. *Eileen* ran only 64 performances at a time when the public's mind was on the effects of the European war in the North Atlantic and not on the Irish Rebellion of 1798, as filtered through Henry Blossom's romantic libretto. Herbert always thought highly of *Eileen* (perhaps for patriotic as much as musical reasons) and it is certainly high on the list of Herberts awaiting rediscovery.

Her Regiment (Broadhurst, 12 November 1917) did not effectively interest a nation at war, but the post-Armistice *The Velvet Lady* (New Amsterdam, 3 February 1919) had a 177-performance run. No subsequent Herbert work ran as long. *Angel Face* (1919), *My Golden Girl* (1920), *The Girl in the Spotlight* (1920), *Orange Blossoms* (1922), and the posthumous *The Dream Girl* (1924) followed, along with contributions to various revues and even the dance music for Kern's *Sally* (1920). Most of these did not do well financially. At the time of the settling of Herbert's estate, his publishers branded these operettas as failures: *Sweethearts, The Madcap Duchess, The Debutante, Angel Face,* and *Orange Blossoms*.

Revenues to the Herbert estate undoubtedly blossomed as radio developed in the mid-'20s and after the surprisingly successful Shubert revival of *Sweethearts* in 1929, which led to further remountings: *Mlle. Modiste* (with Fritzi Scheff), *Naughty Marietta* (with Ilse Marvenga), *The Fortune Teller, Babes in Toyland,* and even *The Serenade.*

The 1934 film of *Babes in Toyland* and the 1935 film of *Naughty Marietta* re-awakened interest in Victor Herbert, with the result that MGM filmed *Sweethearts* in 1938. The story was thrown out altogether in this lovely Technicolor mounting starring MacDonald-Eddy, and so was most of the score. Barely five numbers remained.

After the 1940s revivals of *The Red Mill* and *Sweethearts,* Herbert's popularity declined, though *The Red Mill, Sweethearts, Naughty Marietta,* and *Babes in Toyland* continued to be revived in summer stock. In the late 1970s, Beverly Sills recorded a best-selling disc of Herbert songs with conductor André Kostelanetz that broke the silence. From that time on, frequent performances in New York by small amateur and professional groups (many restored and conducted by Frederick S. Roffman) and excellent reissues of old recordings, as well as some new ones, have prompted organizations like the New York City Opera to look at the popular works once more. These certainly deserve reexamination, as well as revised libretti.

Gustav Luders (1865–1913), **Ludwig Englander** (1859–1914), and **Gustave Kerker** (1857–1923) were all German or Austrian-born conductors turned operetta composers. Luders was formally trained in Germany, coming to the United States in his twenties. One of his earliest efforts, *The Burgomeister* (Manhattan, 31 December 1900), had a Frank Pixley libretto concerning Peter Stuyvesant falling asleep and reawakening in 1900. Henry E. Dixey was Stuyvesant (long before Walter Huston's memorable portrayal in the Anderson-Weill *Knicker-bocker Holiday* thirty-eight years later). A previously written Pixley-Luders effort was a greater success, *King Dodo* (Daly's, 12 May 1902), which had pleased Chicagoans for months before the Broadway opening. This reversed the plot of *The Burgomeister,* by having time set back thirty years. Raymond Hitchcock, the original American Charley in *Charley's Aunt,* made a great impression as a musical-comedy comedian, especially with his topical *couplets,* "They Give Me a Medal for That."

The next Pixley-Luders effort was their best: *The Prince of Pilsen* (Broadway, 17 March 1903). This had a much less absurd, extravaganza-ish plot than its predecessors, and was about mistaken identities, involving Americans and Europeans on holiday in Nice. The attractive numbers included the Heidelberg students' choruses (the same season that the play *Old Heidelberg* was first seen in New York), a sextette (à la *Florodora*) entitled "Song of the Cities," and the love duet "The Message of the Violet." The Prince was Arthur Donaldson, the daughter was Lillian Coleman, and her father, John W. Ransome. *The Prince of Pilsen* did excellent out-of-town business for years.

Nothing Luders composed subsequently has approximated the fame or fortunes of *The Prince of Pilsen*. *The Sho-Gun* (1904) was set in Korea, probably to avoid comparisons with *The Mikado*, which were nevertheless unflatteringly made. *Woodland* (1904) had a cast of birds.

Ludwig Englander was Viennese, arriving in New York in 1882. He was conductor at the Thalia, a leading German-language theatre, and in 1883 had his own operetta, *Der Prinz Gemahl* (The Prince Consort), done there, securing an ultimately unsuccessful transfer to Broadway. He did achieve real success by writing a series of comic-opera vehicles for stars like Jefferson De Angelis and Francis Wilson, as well as lightweight revue-ish pieces, and also by replacing Karl Ziehrer's score with his own in the 1901 *The Strollers (Die Landstreicher)*. Englander collaborated with Harry B. Smith on a musical version of the popular novel *When Knighthood Was in Flower*, entitled *A Madcap Princess* (Knickerbocker, 5 September 1904). Lulu Glaser was Mary Tudor, in love with Charles Brandon, portrayed by Britain's heartthrob, Bertram Wallis. Another literary adaptation, *The Two Roses* (Broadway, 21 November 1904), was based on Oliver Goldsmith's *She Stoops to Conquer*. The argument was resettled in Europe by librettist Stanislaus Stange to accommodate Fritzi Scheff.

Gustave Kerker, who contributed numbers to *The Two Roses*, came to the United States in 1867, when he was ten and already adept at the cello. He became the principal conductor at the Bijou and the Casino, New York, leading a succession of notable European (and later American) operettas.

After weak efforts in the mid-'90s (*Prince Kam, Kismet, The Lady Slavey*—with Marie Dressler as a music-hall singer), Kerker had a sizable hit in the revue-ish *The Whirl of the Town* (1897). The same year's *The Belle of New York* (Casino, 28 September 1897) ran only 56 performances—in New York. Transported to London (Shaftesbury, 12 April 1898) with its original star, it was the first Broadway musical to electrify the West End. The story of a Salvation Army girl enthralled the Londoners for 674 performances. Charles Morton's story was not far removed from the typical Gaiety musical comedy, though the first-act finale took place in New York's Chinatown. Edna May triumphed in the title part; her rendition of "The Purity Brigade" was considered the last word in fast, American vitality. The title song was probably the most catchy number, as sung by the character of Blinky Bill, played in New York by William Cameron and in London by Frank Lawton. In its initial run in London, the show earned a profit of £100,000, and a further £87,000 from the provincial rights. In Paris, the Moulin Rouge presented *La Belle de New York* in 1903, and that same year a young singer named Yvonne Printemps took Edna May's part in Brussels in an auspicious debut. Vienna saw *Die Schöne von New York* in 1900, while a company performed the work in English at the Carltheater the following year.

Both *The Telephone Girl* (1897) and *The Girl from Up There* (1901) tried to duplicate the style that made *The Belle of New York*, but these and subsequent Kerker scores never approached that level, and were received by some critics with—probably deserved—derision.

ALFRED BUTT in conjunction with LEE EPHRAIM presents
The THEATRE ROYAL, DRURY LANE Production

The DESERT SONG

BOOK & LYRICS BY
OTTO HARBACH
OSCAR HAMMERSTEIN 2ND
& **FRANK MANDEL**
MUSIC BY
SIGMUND ROMBERG

VOCAL SCORE (Complete) 8/- NET

SEPARATE NUMBERS

The Desert Song	2/- NET
Romance	2/- "
The Riff Song	2/- "
"It"	2/- "
One Alone	2/- "
One Flower grows alone in Your Garden	2/- "
Piano Selection	2/6 NET
Desert Song Valse	2/- "

BROADWAY

THE GENUS *Broadway operetta,* as distinct from the nineteenth-century comic opera, had two major influences: Victor Herbert and the Viennese operettas of the Silver Era. Sigmund Romberg and Rudolf Friml were the leading composers of the late teens and 1920s, and both had middle-European backgrounds. Though much of their work in the teens was frankly, requisitely imitative of Herbert, their operettas of the '20s were as spectacularly romantic as the gushing costume operettas of Lehár, if not more so. The uniformed male choruses that Herbert had held over from the older comic operas were retained by Friml and Romberg, and given similarly stirring marches. Perhaps influenced by the close-up intimacy and spectacular passion of the hugely popular silent screen, operettas were forced to be increasingly romantic and full-blooded, rather than satiric or comic.

What is astounding about the '20s is that while these hot-blooded romantic operettas were being created and consumed, the same years saw the birth of the fast, dancing, jazz musical comedies of Gershwin, Youmans, and other composers, as well as excellent revues, both spectacular and intimate, and also attempts to modernize operetta into something almost as zippy as musical comedy. It was truly the Golden Age of the American musical theatre, and one that did not really end in 1929. The potent romantic and sentimental elements that had made *The Student Prince* and *Show Boat* such superb operettas were simply streamlined in the 1940s and transformed into the "musical play," a euphemism for romantic operetta. The main differences between the 1920s and the 1940s operetta involved the replacement of passion with compassion and psychology, cleverer segues into songs that had to do more sophisticatedly with character and plot than before, an attempt to use the comedian and soubrette more effectively in the story, and, most importantly, the use of ballet for story or mood

---

Romberg's *The Desert Song* (Casino, 1926) was one of the 1920s greatest operettas, and one still revived frequently today. The lure of romance on burning desert sands is depicted on sheet music from the London production at Drury Lane in 1927, one of a golden string of hits at that theatre for librettist Oscar Hammerstein II.

purposes, sometimes replacing the central finales altogether. Some acclaimed modern musical plays are very apparently and decisively operettas, though critics do not care to admit that they are. Recently revived on Broadway, shows like *Oklahoma!*, *Brigadoon*, *The King and I*, *West Side Story*, *My Fair Lady*, and *Camelot* are all to varying degrees romantic operettas, and there are those who would consider *The Most Happy Fella* and *Porgy and Bess* operettas as well, if not American operas. There are several other classic "musical plays" that are so much operettas that there seems to be a slight hesitation in reviving them, in spite of their magnificent scores: *Carousel* and *South Pacific* are two examples. The latter was however recalled to life in 1987, with a recording, a New York City Opera mounting, a popular revival at London's Prince of Wales Theatre, and a touring edition with Robert Goulet.

(Charles) Rudolf Friml (1879–1972) was born in Prague and was a star music pupil at its Conservatory, which he entered at the age of fifteen. In Friml's last year there, Antonin Dvořák was one of his teachers. His talents as a pianist were for many years employed by Jan Kubelik, the violinist, with whom he first visited the United States in 1901. During these years, many of Friml's piano compositions were published. By 1904, he arranged his own tour of the United States, including in his repertoire his own Piano Concerto in B. In 1906 he settled in New York.

His piano works apparently attracted the attention of music publishers Max Dreyfus and Rudolph Schirmer, who reportedly suggested Friml as a replacement for Victor Herbert as the composer for Arthur Hammerstein's production of *The Firefly* (Lyric, 2 December 1912). Emma Trentini and Herbert had quarreled after *Naughty Marietta*, and Hammerstein quickly had to find a new composer for the Otto Hauerbach (Harbach) libretto. Miss Trentini played an Italian street singer (of course!) who travels to Bermuda as a cabin boy and ends up a famous opera star. The "cabin boy," Tony, got to sing *"Giannina Mia"* and his alter ego, Nina, thrilled audiences with the title song, "(Love Is Like a) Firefly." Another song hit was "Sympathy." The Broadway run was 120 performances, and there were reprises in later seasons. The 1937 MGM film jettisoned the Hauerbach plot and substituted one by Frances Goodrich and Albert Hackett, with Ogden Nash that concerned a female spy in Spain during the Napoleonic era. Jeanette MacDonald sparkled in Oliver Marsh's camera setups. The big song hit from the film was "The Donkey Serenade," an adaptation of a 1920 piano piece. Sung by Allan Jones, it became his trademark.

High Jinks (Lyric, 10 December 1913) was a lighter story, concerning a perfume which made its wearers giddy. "Something Seems a Tingle-ing-eling" was the best song (later sung by Cyril Ritchard in his last Broadway appearance in a revue). This ran longer than *The Firefly* and was reproduced in London (Adelphi, 24 August 1916) with an interpolation by Jerome Kern, the wonderful "It Isn't My Fault," sung by W. H. Berry and Marie Blanche. The London run nearly doubled Broadway's. *Katinka* was a return to the more romantic style of

The Firefly and was popular both in New York (44th Street, 23 December 1915), with Franklin Arcade and Adele Rowland, and in London (Shaftesbury, 30 August 1923), with Joseph Coyne and Binnie Hale. Hauerbach's libretto switched from Russia to Austria (France, in the British production), and Friml's score had a number of delectable melodies: the sumptous "Allah's Holiday" showed the path that led to *Rose-Marie*'s "Indian Love Call." *You're in Love* (1917), *Sometime* (1918), *Glorianna*—no relation to Britten's opera—(1918), *Tumble In* (1918), *The Little Whopper* (1914), and *June Love* (1921) were not musically in the same category as *The Firefly* or *Katinka*, but *Sometime* had a startling cast that contained Ed Wynn, Francine Larrimore, and Mae West as a vamp. *The Blue Kitten* (Selwyn, 13 January 1922) further confirmed the musical-comedy bent Friml seemed to be pursuing: he even contributed to the Ziegfeld *Follies* that season.

Cinders (1923) was unnotable, and it would have seemed that Friml's career was at a standstill. Until the second of September 1924, when the Imperial Theatre presented *Rose-Marie* to an enraptured audience. Arthur Hammerstein had wanted an ice spectacular, but this became unfeasible. Retaining a Canadian setting, however, the producer had Hauerbach (now Harbach) and Oscar Hammerstein II map out the fundamentally serious love story of the Rockies concerning a singer and her lover, implicated in the murder of an Indian, Black Eagle. This added a bit of excitement to what was otherwise a fairly common Leháresque plot of impossible love in some strange place—*Endlich Allein* had a mountain plot as well. But *Rose-Marie* rather cleverly managed to merge the vivacious rhythms of contemporary Broadway with the dreamy Lehár; even the most romantic songs had a dash and verve that had hitherto been lacking.

The original Imperial Theatre programme declined to list the songs, rather pretentiously stating: "The musical numbers of this play are such an integral part of the action that we do not think we should list them as separate episodes." (In London, however, the songs *were* listed separately.) Certainly, there was a cinematic flavor to the proceedings, with constant use of *mélodrame,* perhaps in an attempt to give spectacular scope to the operetta to compete with the motion picture, which by this time had reached new plateaus of elaborateness in films like *The Thief of Bagdad*. *Rose-Marie* also had general and specific screen antecedents. Between 1921 and 1923 there were no less than forty feature films with Canadian Northwest Mounted Police plots, and one of them, *Tiger Rose* (1923, based on a 1917 stage melodrama), had a plot vaguely similar to the following season's *Rose-Marie*.

The operetta had two male singing leads: Jim Kenyon, with whom Rose-Marie is in love, and Sergeant Malone of the RCMP. Plus the buffo part (instrumental in unraveling the murder) of Hard-Boiled Herman. In New York, the classically trained English actor, Dennis King, originated the part of Jim, with Arthur Deagon as Malone and William Kent as Herman. In London, Derek Oldham, of D'Oyly Carte fame, was Jim, John Dunsmure was Malone, and Billy Merson (later Nelson Keys) was Herman. On the distaff side, the

Metropolitan Opera soprano Mary Ellis was the world's first Rose-Marie, while Edith Day, the American singer who had conquered London in Tierney's *Irene*, played the part at Drury Lane (20 March 1925).

Rose-Marie was not the first operetta to involve a murder. Offenbach's first full-length operetta, *Orphée aux Enfers* (1858), had Eurydice killed in the first act by Pluton. But *Rose-Marie*, building on the turn-of-the-century libretti furnished for Victor Herbert, provided the "serious" romantic mold set in some exotic locale that would become stylish in the 1920s. The plots might deal with a doomed love *(The Student Prince)*, or political upheaval *(The Vagabond King, The New Moon)*, or even racial strain *(Show Boat, Golden Dawn)*, but there was definitely a new effort to avoid the trivialities of musical comedy and the purely romantic escapades of royalty and disguised-royalty that still dominated the Central European operetta in the '20s.

This is not to say that operetta libretti suddenly became serious. Most of them were still the familiar drivel, and the quality of the lyrics on the whole showed no improvement. But there was definitely a vibrancy and a stoutheartedness about these shows that proved immensely popular, as did the exoticism and glamor found necessary to rival the spectacle offered to the public so inexpensively any week on celluloid.

And it was in its spectacle that *Rose-Marie* proved so influential. One great attraction of the first productions was the "Totem Tom-Tom" number near the end of Act I. The words were arrant nonsense, with silly rhymes that harked back to the *Geisha* era, and the song—like so many memorable production numbers—advanced the plot not one whit. But when one hundred dancers appeared in formation dressed as totem poles (the young Anna Neagle was one at Drury Lane), the effect was quite spectacular. And it was truly an operetta *à grand spectacle,* with ten elaborate scenes to suit Parisian tastes. The Paris production (Mogador, 9 April 1927) was, incredibly, the longest-running of all (1,250 performances), with more revivals in that city than anywhere else. The French version was led by Robert Burnier (Jim), Felix Oudart (Malone), and Cloe Vidiane (Rose-Marie). Drury Lane saw 851 performances, and without a ticket-broker deal prior to the première, as the agencies were unconvinced the show would be a hit. The Imperial run was the least impressive—only 557 showings—but it made more money than any Broadway musical play until *Oklahoma!* in 1943, and it made Oscar Hammerstein II a millionaire in seven months. Moreover, *Rose-Marie* appeared all over the world to great acclaim, and it is still a staple of repertoires in Eastern Europe, particularly in the Soviet Union, where it is often used for mildly anti-American jokes, as in a recent production at Leningrad's Musical Comedy Theatre.

Rose-Marie was King George V's favorite show—he saw it no less than three

---

Jeanette MacDonald and Nelson Eddy in the famous MGM film version of Friml-Stothart's *Rose Marie* (1936). Even today, "MacDonald and Eddy" mean operetta to many Americans. MGM.

times during its original Drury Lane run, and again on revival. It was so popular that it was decided not to hold up the first film version in order to wait for the perfection of sound recording. MGM released *Rose-Marie* in 1928, with Joan Crawford in the title role, and with a somewhat altered plot, but with a musical score based on Friml and Stothart, though without actual singing. Herbert Stothart let himself go on the MGM remake in 1936; he also let most of Friml's score go as well, to be replaced by items ranging from the "St. Louis Blues" to scenes from Gounod's *Roméo et Juliette* and Puccini's *Tosca*. Nevertheless, W. S. Van Dyke's *Rose-Marie* remains, to many, the most characteristic of the Jeanette MacDonald–Nelson Eddy epics. The mountain scenes, filmed at Lake Tahoe, gave a breadth to "Totem Tom-Tom" and the "Indian Love Call" that was obviously impossible to achieve on the stage. Unfortunately, songs like "Door of My Dreams," "Pretty Things," and "Minuet of the Minute," all of which would have been perfect material for Miss MacDonald, were not used. A sensible plot emendation had the Mountie sergeant becoming Rose-Marie's swain, making the story less complicated. Mervyn LeRoy's 1954 version had several things going for it: CinemaScope, Eastman Color, Bert Lahr (as the "Mountie

Who Never Got His Man"), and Howard Keel, reverting to the original conception of the Mountie sergeant who doesn't get his girl.

It would have been nice to report that the next Friml hit was also a resounding success in Paris, but *The Vagabond King,* based on the romanticized exploits of François Villon, was never seen there. Nevertheless, it proved dramatically popular in the English-speaking world. Based on Justin Huntly McCarthy's *If I Were King,* which had been a vehicle for E. H. Sothern from 1901 in the United States, and for Sir George Alexander from the next year in the United Kingdom, the story took considerable liberties with history, and the characters were musical-comedy-ized to an extent. But the plot was sufficiently romantic and robust to attract Friml and W. H. Post and Brian Hooker (the librettists). Structurally, it was similar to *Rose-Marie* in its use of a wanton rival for the attention of the hero. In the former, the Indian girl Wanda; in *The Vagabond King,* the prostitute Huguette.

Producer Russell Janney's "New Spectacular Musical Play" at the Casino (21 September 1925) was carefully tailored for Dennis King, whose Shakespearean training and thrilling singing voice could finally be used at the same time. Opposite King was Carolyn Thomson as Katherine de Vaucelles, Jane Carroll as Huguette. Max Figman played King Louis XI and also staged the operetta for its producer. The Casino registered 511 performances. In London, the tally at the Winter Garden (19 April 1927) reached 480. Leading the London cast were Derek Oldham and Winnie Melville (who were actually husband and wife) as the lovers, while Norah Blaney and H. A. Saintsbury were streetwalker and monarch, respectively. The operetta was filmed in 1930 with King repeating his stage role and Jeanette MacDonald as Katherine, directed by Ludwig Berger. There was a dull remake in 1956.

The Vagabond King is arguably Friml's best score. In order of their appearance, the better songs are: "Love for Sale," the drinking song, "A Flagon of Wine," the "Song of the Vagabonds," "Some Day," "Only a Rose," "Tomorrow," the "Huguette Waltz," and "Love Me To-night." The comic numbers were only marginally less successful, the second-act trio "Lullaby! Plim-Plum" being quite likable, and there are any number of other captivating marches and flourishes. The reprises—and there were many—were not discomfiting: one could listen to "Only a Rose" and "And to *Hell* with Burgundy!" over and over. Today, the medievalistic dialogue and idiotic jokes would seem contrived, but the force and amorousness of the songs are not dated. Major revivals of *The Vagabond King* have been attempted outside of New York, but a truly thrilling leading man would be required to sell the show on Broadway, along with extensive dialogue revisions.

Both *The Wild Rose* (1926) and *The White Eagle* (1927) were failures. The first concerned Americans in Monte Carlo, the second was set in Indian territory, a musical version of *The Squaw Man,* the 1905 play that had been the basis of a famous 1913 Cecil B. De Mille film. Too much Americana probably convinced Friml that a return to European romance was in order, and to Alexandre Dumas *père,* at that. *The Three Musketeers* (Lyric, 13 March 1928) was a Ziegfeld production, with book by William Anthony McGuire, sets by Joseph Urban, glorious costumes by Jack Harkrider, a leading Ziegfeld costumier, and lyrics by P. G. Wodehouse and Clifford Grey. McGuire had difficulty supplying the script in time, and so insisted on having the entire company see the 1921 Fred Niblo/Douglas Fairbanks film of *The Three Musketeers* prior to the last rehearsals so he could finish his work. McGuire also had to stage the production, and rehearsals were far from amicable due to the intense rivalry of Dennis King (as D'Artagnan) and Vivienne Segal (as Constance). Reginald Owen was Richelieu. The musketeers were Douglass Dumbrille (Athos), Detmar Poppen (Porthos), and Joseph Macaulay (Aramis).

Surprisingly, Friml's melodious score and the time-proved plot did not add up to a very long run: only 318 performances in New York and 240 in London (Drury Lane, 28 March 1930), where Dennis King repeated his part opposite Adrienne Brune (Constance), Webster Booth (Buckingham), Lilian Davies (Queen Anne), and Arthur Wontner—a well-known Sherlock Holmes impersonator (Richelieu). Raymond Newell, as Aramis, stopped the show cold with his rendition of *"Ma Belle,"* just as Joseph Macaulay had done on Broadway. But King stole all hearts. "From the moment when D'Artagnan arrived at the Inn of the Jolly Miller on a white horse painted to represent emaciation, and the young Gascon clad in rags leapt from the steed, Dennis King was the favorite with the audience," reported the critic of the *Daily News.*

The score to *The Three Musketeers* nearly rivaled that for *The Vagabond King,* even if some of the songs were very patently suggested by those from the earlier show: "One Kiss" was alarmingly similar to "Love Me To-night," for one example. But the swaggering anthems and marches were so excellent that they swept almost all else aside and easily conquered audiences: "Gascony," "My Sword and I," "March of the Musketeers" being the principal examples. Dennis King's swashbuckling was admired in both song and action. During the London run a bit of D'Artagnan's épée broke during a particularly active fight and sailed out into the audience, landing on a lady's lap. She took her souvenir home, and before the nervous management thought they would receive a lawsuit, the lady had written a kind letter inquiring whether she could keep her memento.

Luana (Hammerstein, 17 September 1930) was originally intended as a film musical of the Richard Walton Tully play *The Bird of Paradise* (which was eventually filmed as a straight romance in 1932 with Dolores del Rio and Joel McCrea, and remade in 1951). With the famous theme-song for Ramona in the Del Rio film proving such a potent advertisement, one can almost hear Hollywood asking Friml for "Luana." But the property was instead retailored for the musical stage, with Ruth Altman as the South Sea Luana, and Joseph Macaulay, the previous year's stalwart Aramis, as her American lover. The material was obviously better suited to screen. Macaulay was a Friml protégé, used in Friml's first Hollywood score, *The Lottery Bride,* released the same year as the Kálmán-Stothart-Hammerstein II *Golden Dawn* (1930), but set in Norway rather than Africa. Typical of this era in its ridiculousness was the big song from *The Lottery Bride,* "Your Eyes Are Like the Northern Lights," sung by John Garrick.

Much more acceptable was the rousing "I'll Follow the Trail," sung by Macaulay.

Friml wrote the scores for two other film musicals, *Music for Madame* (1937) and *Northwest Outpost* (1947), but neither contained anything worthwhile, musically or otherwise. Nor did *Music Hath Charms* (1934), Friml's last Broadway effort.

Sigmund Romberg (1887–1951) was born in the Hungarian provinces, and trained for careers in both music and engineering. He worked at the Theater an der Wien during his studies in Vienna. Later he came to New York, where he was a pianist and restaurant orchestra-leader. He contributed songs to a revue, *The Whirl of the World* (Winter Garden, 10 January 1914) and followed this with the basic scores of *The Midnight Girl* (1914), *The Passing Show of 1914* (and later, 1916, 1917, 1918, 1923, 1924) and other revues, including *Dancing Around* (1914) and *Maid in America* (1915), before he added songs to Eysler's *The Blue Paradise* at the Casino in 1915. From this came his first standard, "Auf Wiedersehen," sung by Vivienne Segal, making her Broadway debut, and Cecil Lean.

In 1917 came *Maytime*, Rida Johnson Young's Americanization of Kollo's, Bernauer's, and Schanzer's *Wie einst im Mai* (1913), with a new Romberg score (Shubert, 16 August 1917). The locale was switched from Berlin to New York, and the story was centered on the fortunes of a house in Washington Square during the course of sixty years. With the show's nationality changed, there was no need to mention its German origins. Peggy Wood played a colonel's daughter and later *her* granddaughter, and Charles Purcell an apprentice and then *his* grandson. It was a charming, extremely sentimental show, so popular with wartime audiences that the Shuberts opened a second company at a theatre across the street. The song that tied the eras together, and which became a great success, was "Will You Remember?", later re-immortalized in the filmed *Maytime* (1937) by Jeanette MacDonald and Nelson Eddy.

Romberg continued contributing to slews of revues and musicals at the Winter Garden, including *Sinbad* (1918), with Al Jolson, and created a new operetta that was a bit too much like *Maytime—The Magic Melody* (1919)—until he came up in 1921 with another Americanized European piece, *Blossom Time* (Ambassador, 29 September 1921). This was a revamped *Das Dreimäderlhaus* (1916) with a new book and characters and a basically new score by Romberg, but still adapted from Schubert themes. Berté's *Dreimäderlhaus* had opened during the war, accounting for its delay before U.S. audiences, and as Romberg had produced a winner with *Wie einst im Mai,* the Shuberts were only too eager to entrust the Viennese piece to him. In New York, 536 performances were achieved (there was a slight interval in that period), and there were thousands more on tour, with several Shubert companies of decreasing sparkle traveling about. In spite of *Blossom Time*'s success, British audiences saw its own *Lilac Time* in 1922, which hewed closer to Berté, though when another Schubert story was filmed in England with Richard Tauber in 1932, as *Blossom Time,* some of the songs were from *Lilac Time*. Both *Maytime* and *Blossom Time* were seen again in stage revivals and were great favorites with stock and amateur companies.

The success of both *Maytime* and *Blossom Time* convinced the Shuberts that Romberg's heart lay in the bittersweet operettas he was adapting from European models, rather than in the Winter Garden revues and Jolson vehicles which had their biggest song hits by others. This accounted for *The Rose of Stamboul*, Broadwayized with Tessa Kosta in the role written for Massary, which had some dismal Romberg interpolations (Century, 7 March 1922), and *Springtime of Youth*, adapted from Kollo's *Wenn zwei Hochzeit machen* (When Two Get Married, 1915), very much like *Maytime* and reset this time in Portsmouth, New Hampshire, in the 1812 era, which prefigured *Carousel* in having Central Europe New Englandized (Broadhurst, 26 October 1922). The reviews were excellent but the public resisted the Kollo-Romberg mix, as they had the Fall-Romberg mélange. Finally, in 1924, following the triumph of Friml's *Rose-Marie* at the Imperial (for the Hammersteins), the Shuberts' production of Romberg's first great original operetta, *The Student Prince*, came to Broadway.

The annals of *The Student Prince* begin in 1899 with a romantic German novella by Wilhelm Meyer-Förster, ostensibly modeled on a prince from Karlsruhe who had an affair with a commoner while attending the University of Heidelberg. In its dramatization, *Alt-Heidelberg* was a success all over Germany and Austria, and following the successful London run of *If I Were King*, Sir George Alexander produced and appeared in the first English version, *Old Heidelberg*, at the St. James's Theatre in 1903. Though Alexander was well over forty at the time, he made a favorably romantic impression, as did the equally aged Richard Mansfield, who appeared as the nineteen-year-old Prince Karl Heinrich when the show opened the same year at the Lyric Theatre in New York.

In their musicalization of *Old Heidelberg*, Romberg and his librettist Dorothy Donnelly retained at least one of the familiar student songs which had been used in the Mansfield version, *"Gaudeamus igitur."* The tryout tour began in the autumn of 1924, under the title *In Heidelberg*. This became *The Student Prince in Heidelberg*. The producers were unhappy with the sad ending and with the near-operatic "Serenade," but Romberg resisted any change. The Shuberts barred him from the theatre, the composer sought his lawyers, and matters were eventually straightened out proving Romberg right.

The "Stupendous Musical Production," staged by J. C. Huffman, and starring Ilse Marvenga and Howard Marsh, arrived at Jolson's 59th Street Theatre on December 2, 1924. The "Chorus of 100" indeed included some forty males, who gave a huge sound to the marching and drinking choruses (the latter especially popular during Prohibition)—a sound we no longer hear on Broadway, thanks to the great costs of mounting musicals today. Orchestrations were by Emil Gerstenberger. It was a huge popular success from the start, enjoying a fabulous run of 608 performances—Romberg's longest—and quite unusual in those years. And, of course, the Shuberts sent out nine extremely profitable touring companies, which played all over the country for years and years.

The London production (February 3, 1926), built up with a great deal of advance publicity from America, and rather tactlessly omitting any English leads, was not well received at His Majesty's Theatre. The critic James Agate admired the well-drilled chorus, the costumes—some designed by Erté—including a "magnificent affair in ermine and blue velvet in which the Prince made the railway journey from Karlsberg to Heidelberg" and "a parquet flooring at a hundred pounds a foot laid down by Messrs. Shubert's own men . . ." The main reason given for the lack of success was the lack of British sympathy for a German story so soon after the Great War, but I suspect that Allan Prior, to judge from some of the notices, was not up to snuff. Though he may have appeared briefly as a replacement prince on Broadway, Agate described his Karl as a "chubby, confident personage in whom there was no possible wistfulness, melancholy, or any kind of nostalgia." Fortunately, the superb Harry Welchman was secured to head an all-English touring company, which did better in the provinces than the troupe in the West End, which was seen for only 96 performances. Two notable revivals were at the Cambridge Theatre, London, in 1968, and at the New York State Theater, sung by the New York City Opera, in 1980.

In September 1927, Metro-Goldwyn-Mayer released Ernst Lubitsch's silent operetta film, with Ramon Novarro and Norma Shearer as the lovers, and a musical score by David Mendoza and William Axt. That same year, instead of translating *The Student Prince* into German, the Viennese saw *Ich hab' mein Herz in Heidelberg verloren* (I Lost My Heart in Heidelberg), a totally new *Singspiel* by Fred Raymond with nothing to do with the Romberg operetta.

As the Lubitsch film had no singing, Americans had to wait until 1954 for a sound version, this time with Mario Lanza's voice and Edmund Purdom's looks—neither had both. Ann Blyth and some lovely color photography furnished support, and three songs by Nicholas Brodzsky were added, for whatever reason. Things came to a full circle in 1974, when *The Student Prince* was finally performed in Heidelberg by the Heidelberger Schloss-Spiel company in the courtyard of the castle.

The Student Prince remains the most adored of the Romberg creations, probably because the score has more familiar hits than the others: the Drinking Song ("Come, Boys"), *"Gaudeamus igitur,"* "Deep in My Heart, Dear," and "Overhead the Moon Is Beaming" (the Serenade). And others are quite lovely: "Golden Days," and "Just We Two," among them. Possibly because the story was a sad one, of young lovers, and because the Prince does nothing to conceal his identity, it seemed less preposterous than the usual Ruritanian romances that figured with numbing regularity in prior operettas. For its songs, but more specifically for purely sentimental story reasons, *The Student Prince* has remained a favorite.

Princess Flavia (Century, 2 November 1925) was an operetta version of *The Prisoner of Zenda,* the piece that introduced Ruritania to the world. In spite of a lavish production, with a cast headed by Britain's gallant Harry Welchman, and Evelyn Herbert, and another large male chorus, *Flavia* expired on Broadway after 152 performances. It was too frankly imitative, musically, of *The Student Prince,* though a much more opulent show, physically. Part of the problem was that *Princess Flavia* was composed at the same time as *The Desert Song,* which I consider the best and, certainly, lushest of Sigmund Romberg's romantic operettas. In 1965, Vernon Duke composed an operetta-ish version of the Anthony Hope property entitled *Zenda,* which appeared in California with Anne Rogers, as Princess Flavia, and Alfred Drake.

The Desert Song was, unlike *The Student Prince* and *The New Moon,* a contemporary "musical play," set in modern French North Africa. In this sense it was unusual for a 1920s operetta, but there was no stinting on either exoticism or spectacle. Arabian Nights and similar Near Eastern stories and locales had frequently been used for earlier operettas. Sullivan's *The Rose of Persia* (1899), Herbert's *The Rose of Algeria* (1909), and Fall's *The Rose of Stamboul* (1916) were three that were heavily scented with the attar of Arab roses. *The Desert Song,* however romantic it may seem today, was as up-to-date as the latest headlines.

The exploits of Lawrence of Arabia, aiding native guerrillas in their struggle against the colonial government, had been published, as were accounts of Riffian uprisings against the French rule of Morocco in 1925–26. In 1925, Percival Christopher Wren's novel *Beau Geste* appeared, sparking interest yet again in the French Foreign Legion, culminating in 1926 with the spectacular film of the same name with Ronald Colman, William Powell, and Victor McLaglen. In early 1926, the exceedingly popular Rudolph Valentino scored a tremendous success as *The Son of the Sheik,* a film made to capitalize on the previous hit, *The Sheik* (1922), both based on novels by E. M. Hull. The public's fancy for "The Sheik of Araby" and such trappings had reached a high point by August 1926, when Valentino's death plunged a considerable segment of the population into deep mourning. In his first-night review of *The Desert Song,* the New York *Telegraph* critic Burton Davis imagined the librettists having had a "romantic nightmare" combining all these elements: ". . . Waking, they had only to write it down, add comedy, garnish with Sigmund Romberg's music, and serve."

Which is probably just what Oscar Hammerstein II, Otto Harbach, and co-producer Frank Mandel did when they drafted *Lady Fair,* as the show was first called when it opened in Wilmington, Delaware, on 21 October 1926. By the beginning of November, in Boston, *Lady Fair* was getting good notices, though along the road to Broadway it was necessary to expunge songs like "Ali-Up" and "Women, Women, Women!" The original cast, marshaled by Arthur Hurley (direction) and Bobby Connolly (musical numbers), starred Robert Halliday and Vivienne Segal, with Eddie Buzzell and Nellie Breen as the comedian/soubrette duo. The retitled show opened in New York on 30 November 1926, at the Casino Theatre. The New York *Times* noted that *The Desert Song* "seemed to have been especially devised for the fancy Moorish interior of the theatre." (The first New York revival, coincidentally, played twenty years later at the equally Moorish City Center.)

The reviews in 1926 were kind, but little more—it is comforting to know that even then the critics thought the libretto quite ridiculous. Said Richard Watts: "With so many pleasant people in the cast and so much music, color, and romance, I am perhaps ungrateful in regretting that, with the exception of one song called 'It,' the lyrics gave indication that W. S. Gilbert lived and died in vain." Few took the ludicrous twists of the plot seriously. Romberg's sensuous melodies (ably orchestrated by Emil Gerstenberger) were what counted, along with the Moroccan ambiance.

Within a month after the première, business had increased to the point that producers Schwab and Mandel knew that they had a big hit on their hands, a hit that would run 471 performances. A London presentation was arranged to follow the phenomenally successful *Rose-Marie* at Drury Lane. Edith Day, the American actress who had so favorably impressed Britons as Rose-Marie was co-starred with Harry Welchman. With a large company of over a hundred, it could hardly miss, and people queued for the gallery in a cold rain from early morning on the day before the first night (7 April 1927). It was enthusiastically received by the audience–the London *Times* thought "the massed dancing the chief pleasure of the evening." It ran longer than both *Show Boat* and *The New Moon,* which followed it at the Lane. As in London, in Paris (1930), *Rose-Marie* gave way to *Le Chant du Désert,* at the Mogador. "One Alone" was rendered as *"Je ne veux que son amour."*

There have been three Warner Brothers filmizations. The first, released in April 1929, was the first Broadway operetta to receive the Vitaphone treatment. It starred John Boles and Carlotta King, with Myrna Loy as Azuri. This managed to retain a good percentage of its score, and was partially filmed in the Great American Desert. In 1943, Dennis Morgan played a 1939 American pianist, Paul Hudson, while the Riffs were being used as slave labor to build a railroad to Dakar financed by the Nazis. This action-packed updating was followed a decade later by a more traditional but equally Technicolored version starring Gordon MacRae.

The Desert Song continued to be heard on stages everywhere. In London, a company headed by the provincial idol John Hanson opened at the Palace Theatre in 1967. Sophisticated West Enders who might have laughed at the very thought of the whole enterprise found themselves adoring the show, among them Queen Elizabeth II, the Queen Mother, and Princess Margaret. The Shah of Iran took a party to the Kennedy Center in Washington to see the pre-Broadway 1973 revival.

The Desert Song possesses the most glorious succession of romantic melodies of any '20s operetta, well orchestrated by Gerstenberger to capitalize on as much French North African exoticism as possible. From the opening chorus and the rousing Riff Song—by now the stirring male chorus was *de rigueur* in these works—through such high spots as the French Military Marching Song (a delightful double chorus), "Romance," "I Want a Kiss," "Then You Will Know I Love You," the enthralling title song, the spectacular sequence entitled "Eastern and Western Love," with its "One Alone," finally to the near-operatic Saber Song, the score very rarely dives down to the banality Romberg had so long wallowed in. *The Desert Song* had also the most romantically titillating story: millions of women dreamed of being in the arms of the masked Red Shadow, while men imagined how easily they could conquer.

The year 1927 saw four Romberg shows. *Cherry Blossoms* (44th Street, 28 March 1927), a musical version of a 1917 play with a Japanese-American theme somewhat resembling *Madama Butterfly,* was a failure, but *My Maryland* (Jolson, 12 September 1927) ran almost a season. This was Dorothy Donnelly's version of the Barbara Frietchie story, with a Civil War setting, distinguished principally by "Your Land and My Land," which ended with a snatch of "The Battle Hymn of the Republic." *My Princess* (Shubert, 6 October 1927) and *The Love Call* (Majestic, 24 October 1927) were less well received.

Rosalie (New Amsterdam, 10 January 1928), lavishly produced by Florenz Ziegfeld with a score by Romberg and George Gershwin, was written for Marilyn Miller. Yet none of the Romberg songs proved as popular as Gershwin's "Oh, Gee! Oh, Joy!" or the title song Cole Porter wrote for the 1936 film. Much more to the public's (and Romberg's) liking was *The New Moon,* which was "A Musical Romance of the Spanish Main." It was ostensibly "founded on the life of Robert Misson, a French aristocrat whose autobiography was written in the late eighteenth century," as the program stated. The original libretto, by Oscar Hammerstein II and the writers-producers Laurence Schwab and Frank Mandel, was set in New Orleans, conjuring up the pirates, casquette girls, and French government of New Orleans in Victor Herbert's *Naughty Marietta* (1910). (In the 1936 film of the Herbert favorite, the MGM scenarists appropriated some *New Moon* ideas, in return.)

After an interrupted tryout, *The New Moon* opened in New York (Imperial, 19 September 1928) and remained there for 509 performances. The original cast included Evelyn Herbert (who had just appeared as Barbara Frietchie in *My Maryland*) as Marianne, while the dashing Robert was portrayed by Robert Halliday (the original Red Shadow in *The Desert Song*). Gus Shy was "gorgeous" Alexander, the comedy "relief," and appearing as the New Orleans shipowner M. Beaunoir was Pacie Ripple, who had appeared in 1906–7 in the first repertory season of the D'Oyly Carte Opera Company at the Savoy, London. The direction (probably by Hammerstein) went uncredited, but the musical numbers were staged by Bobby Connolly. The glittering orchestrations were the joint work of Romberg's usual man, Emil Gerstenberger, and the conductor Al(fred) Goodman. Seven colorful sets were designed by Donald Oenslager, with sumptuous dresses by Charles Le Maire.

The critic Percy Hammond called the new operetta "a distinguished song-service performed by many soulful musicians dressed splendidly in the pompous clothing of romantic opera . . . No doubt it would have been an error if the librettists . . . had demeaned their stately oratorio with the jest and banter of Broadway's laughing gases." But no one condemned the barrage of melody: "Marianne," "Softly, as in a Morning Sunrise," "One Kiss," "Stouthearted

Men," and "Lover, Come Back to Me," just to name the five obvious standards. Ring Lardner *did* wonder about the morning sunrise, "as distinguished from the late afternoon or evening sunrise . . ."

Arrangements were made for *The New Moon* to follow *Show Boat* at London's Drury Lane, making Hammerstein easily the Theatre Royal's favorite librettist—four operettas in a row in the 1920s. (He later equaled this record with *Oklahoma!, Carousel, South Pacific,* and *The King and I,* again at the same theatre.) Evelyn Laye was the female star, while Howett Worster, the Drury Lane Gaylord Ravenal, was Robert. It opened 4 April 1929, but ran only 148 performances. A spectacular Paris production appeared at the Châtelet as *Robert le Pirate* in 1930.

The movie rights were sold to Metro-Goldwyn-Mayer for what was reputedly a very high price and in December 1930 the first version appeared. Lawrence Tibbett was Lieutenant Michael Petroff, and Grace Moore Princess Tanya Strogoff; yes, the locale and time were changed, to twentieth-century Russia. The second film (1940) was reset in old New Orleans, and starred that ideal romantic couple, MacDonald-Eddy.

The musical screen, ironically, helped kill the spectacular romantic Broadway operetta, of which *The New Moon* was a late example, as films could do everything so much more spectacularly. The success of the screen *Desert Song* had, in fact, prompted Warner Brothers to offer Romberg and Hammerstein a contract to provide original screen operettas—*Viennese Nights* (1930) being the first of these.

It was a downhill path for Romberg after *The New Moon,* a combination of watered-down scores lacking the vibrancy of the '20s creations and the public's waning interest in romantic operetta. After his 1929 film work, Romberg returned to the Shuberts for *Nina Rosa* (Majestic, 20 September 1930), book by Otto Harbach and lyrics by Irving Caesar, which was far more popular in Paris (Châtelet, 14 January 1932) than on Broadway. Perhaps its setting reminded Parisians of *La Périchole:* it was one of those rare operettas set in Peru. Even more exotic was *East Wind* (Manhattan, 27 October 1931), set in Saigon—it did not last a month, even with a Hammerstein libretto. *Melody,* the last show to play the Casino (1933), another collaboration with Hammerstein, *May Wine* (1935), another with Harbach, *Forbidden Melody* (1936), and one more work with Hammerstein, *Sunny River* (1941) were, with one exception, failures of varying degrees. *May Wine* was the 213-performance exception, based on a story co-authored by Erich von Stroheim, "The Happy Alienist." The cast included Walter Woolf King, Walter Slezak, and Leo G. Carroll. *May Wine* dispensed with a chorus (was this really a good idea where Romberg was concerned?) and dealt with, peripherally, at least, a Viennese psychoanalyst.

Up in Central Park (Century, 27 January 1945), produced near the war's end and very typical in its evocation of old-time Americana, was a comeback of sorts for Romberg. The score was pleasant ("Close as Pages in a Book," "The Fireman's Bride") and low-keyed, with the right amount of music-hall boisterousness to suit the story of Boss Tweed and his nasty associates. Splendidly produced by Mike Todd, it included a skating ballet, a Currier & Ives print come to life that harked back in a way to the *tableaux vivants* of Romberg's Winter Garden revue days. It was picturesque escapism, lighter than *Bloomer Girl* and *Carousel,* both of which opened that season, the latter being the natural 1940s extension of Romberg's 1920s romantic operettas.

Encouraged by the 502-performance run of *Up in Central Park,* Romberg wrote two more Broadway shows. *My Romance* (Shubert, 19 October 1948) was the last he saw in his lifetime. It only ran three months. *The Girl in Pink Tights,* produced posthumously (Mark Hellinger, 5 March 1954), was a musical comedy about the *first* American musical comedy, *The Black Crook* (1866), but, as the title suggested, attention was focused on the dancing (by Zizi Jeanmaire) rather than on Romberg's melodies.

Harry Tierney (1894–1965) functioned primarily as a house composer for producer Florenz Ziegfeld, contributing songs for several musicals and revues in the late teens and early '20s, including many editions of the *Follies.* In 1919 came *Irene* (Vanderbilt, 18 November), which catapulted Edith Day to instant stardom as the Irish-Cinderella heroine, Irene O'Dare. In its New York–set, modern, easygoing way, *Irene* was a musical comedy that owed something to the Kern-Bolton-Wodehouse Princess Theatre shows. A rejection of European operetta, musically? Perhaps, but not James Montgomery's book, which, with a few changes of nationality, might have done service in London or Vienna. The two songs (with lyrics by Tierney's partner Joseph McCarthy) that charmed New York and London (Empire, 7 April 1920) during the long runs in those cities were the title song and "Alice Blue Gown," both contributing to the success of successful revivals in both cities in the 1970s.

Rio Rita (Ziegfeld, 2 February 1927) was a regulation '20s Broadway operetta, and one of the best examples of the genre. Its models were clearly Friml's *Rose-Marie* and Romberg's *The Desert Song,* and one can almost imagine Ziegfeld commissioning songwriters Tierney and McCarthy and librettists Guy Bolton and Fred Thompson to provide the producer with something similar to these successful shows. Set "along the River Rio Grande," *Rio Rita* had a disguised bandit (the Kinkajou), an eponymous local heroine, and a robust male chorus of law enforcers. The Texas Ranger Jim (J. Harold Murray) was in love with Rita (Ethelind Terry), and lending comic support—for the first time together on the Broadway stage—were Bert Wheeler and Robert Woolsey. The songs were smashing: the lovely title song, especially when sung against the "River Song," "If You're in Love, You'll Waltz," the "Kinkajou" chorus (rather like "Totem Tom-Tom"), the Rangers' chorus ("You'd Better Look Out for the Lone Star Rangers Texas Way!"), "Following the Sun Around," and even a vibrant comic number, "Out on the Loose." Plus numerous Mexican dances, performed by the Albertina Rasch dancers in magnificent Jack Harkrider costumes in front of luscious Joseph Urban sets. From the film version (1929) came the enchanting waltz, "You're Always in My Arms (But Only in My Dreams)," which was added to the London production (Prince Edward, 3 April 1930).

The New York *Times* critic Brooks Atkinson wrote: "In decorative show-manship, Mr. Ziegfeld is the master of style . . . for sheer extravagance of beauty, animated and rhythmic, *Rio Rita* has no rival among contemporaries . . . In the most lustrous costumes—silver sombreros, blood-red shirts, fluffy ballet stuffs, embroidered velvet waistcoats—[the dancers] whirled in squads, one on the heels of another, until the stage was as furious with design as the wall dec-orations." The wall decorations of the brand-new egg-shaped Ziegfeld Theatre were Urban's elaborate murals around the proscenium and throughout the au-ditorium, a riot of flora and fauna on a gold background. Ziegfeld's canny ge-nius for the spectacular and his insistence on movement and fluidity were finally applied to Broadway operetta. In operetta terms, the success of *Rio Rita* (it ran in all 494 performances) was a dress rehearsal for the great *Show Boat* eleven months later.

Jerome Kern (1885–1945) had the double distinction of having written America's greatest operetta, *Show Boat* (1927), as well as having helped to ini-tiate the modern intimate musical comedy, as opposed to the modern "musical play." His early career was devoted to interpolating sprightly numbers into foreign works that needed padding either at the beginning of the evening (fash-ionable audiences arrived late) or during the long, sometimes turgid hours that followed. These songs were used on Broadway and in London, where Kern stayed for a number of months (taking a British wife). Many of these shows were hit Edwardesian musical comedies, at the turn of the century quite popular in America; others were Viennese operettas.

For the record, Kern had songs interpolated in New York or London pro-ductions of—among others—the following British musical comedies: *The Catch of the Season*, *The Earl and the Girl*, *The Beauty of Bath*, *The Spring Chicken*, *The Little Cherub*, *Lady Madcap*, *The White Chrysanthemum*, *The Dairymaids*, *The Girls of Gottenberg*, *Kitty Grey*, *The King of Cadonia*, and *Our Miss Gibbs*, and, follow-ing the huge success of *The Merry Widow*, in these German-Austrian operettas: *A Waltz Dream*, *The Dollar Princess*, *The Gay Hussars*, *The Siren*, *The Kiss Waltz*, *The Opera Ball*, *Das Mädel von Montmartre*, *The Polish Wedding*, *The Doll Girl* (Fall), *Der liebe Augustin*, *The Marriage Market*, and *The Laughing Husband* (Eysler).

Some of the interpolations became substantial moneymakers, most notably "They Didn't Believe Me," first sung in Rubens's *The Girl from Utah* (Knick-erbocker, 24 August 1914), which became just as sensationally popular in En-gland as it was in America after being put into the Gaiety production, *Tonight's the Night* (28 April 1915).

In 1915, Kern composed the first of several musical comedies for the intimate Princess Theatre, *Nobody's Home* (20 April). There were several other Princess shows, some with books by Britons Guy Bolton and P. G. Wodehouse, includ-ing the recently revived *Very Good Eddie* (1915), *Oh, Boy!* (1917), *Leave It to Jane* (1917), and *Oh, Lady! Lady!!* (1918). The Princess Theatre musical come-dies looked ahead by reinstituting—at least partially—songs that had something to do with, or even stemmed naturally from, the plot. In a construction sense, the musico-dramatic continuity and fluidity of the *offenbachiade* or the Savoy operetta again served as models. Musically, however, Kern was not dedicated to presenting a nineteenth-century style, choosing rather to build his scores around the very types of light, two-steppy, ragtime, or whimsical numbers he had interpolated in other composers' scores. The spell of watered-down European comic opera had been broken by an American composer, but a composer who had had his training (and it showed) in Edwardesian musical comedy.

Kern's Princess Theatre shows were the lightest scores he wrote, and perhaps the freshest, though the general public still prefers his later, much more romantic works for stage and screen. Recent Broadway and Off- and Off-Off-Broadway revivals of *Very Good Eddie, Leave It to Jane, Oh, Lady! Lady!!,* and *Oh, Boy!* have proved that these works are capable of being seen again, though with apologies, and a certain tinkering to make them more palatable to modern audiences. They are defiantly musical comedies, yet the best songs in each are often the most wistful: *Very Good Eddie*'s "Babes in the Wood" and *Oh, Boy!*'s "Till the Clouds Roll By," for example. Although Kern's style at this time was much less florid than the Viennese composers to whose works he added interpolations, there is one composer whose charms very obviously rubbed off on Kern: Leo Fall.

Few other composers were capable of writing such similarly wistful, heartfelt melodies as Fall and Kern. "Babes in the Wood," for example, is directly modeled on *"Wir tanzen Ringelreih'n,"* the "Hänsel und Gretel" duet in the second act of *The Dollar Princess,* to which, as we have mentioned, Kern added songs. Fall's music required weightier singing, and Kern seldom wrote as thrilling a waltz as *"Ein Walzer muss es sein"* (from *Die Rose von Stambul*) or Madame Pompadour's entrance from the operetta of that name. But both composers knew, particularly in the bridge or release sections of their songs, how to bring you very close to tears while you were smiling. With many composers, this can be forced and oversentimental. Fall and Kern managed it gracefully.

Kern had numerous song hits in his two most famous shows of the early 1920s, *Sally* (New Amsterdam, 21 December 1920) and *Sunny* (New Amsterdam, 22 September 1925), the first being Ziegfeld's answer to the Tierney-McCarthy *Irene* (1919), the second, Dillingham's revue disguised as a book musical. Both were fashioned for the primarily dancing talents of Marilyn Miller, but also had contributions from formidable stars like Walter Catlett and Leon Errol *(Sally)* and Clifton Webb and Joseph Cawthorn *(Sunny).* Though lavishly produced at large theatres, these two musicals featured Kern scores that carried on the Princess Theatre traditions of lightness and verve, along with the more poignant songs Kern's producers and audiences had by now come to expect. "Look for the Silver Lining" in *Sally* was the most famous of these. These shows had great success in London, too.

Surprisingly, Kern's other musical comedies of the 1920–27 period are totally forgotten. But *Show Boat* is immortal and, in spite of its libretto problems, the greatest of all American operettas. There was little indication in *Good Morning,*

Dearie (1921), *The Cabaret Girl* (London, 1922), *The Beauty Prize* (London, 1923), *The Bunch and Judy,* (1922), *Stepping Stones* (1923), *Sitting Pretty* (1924), *Dear Sir* (1924), *The City Chap* (1925), *Criss Cross* (1926), or *Lucky* (1927), that *Show Boat* was forthcoming from Kern. From Oscar Hammerstein II, yes, as he had already been librettist of many of the best 1920s operettas, including *Rose-Marie* and *The Desert Song.*

What *is Show Boat?* Gerald Bordman, in his definitive study of Kern, quotes an out-of-town critic, Bud Waters, reviewing the original company in its Philadelphia tryout in 1927:

> . . . *Show Boat* is not simply an operetta, although Jerome Kern's distinguished score can easily be ranked with the best of them. No, Mr. Ziegfeld's production, styled in the program "an American musical play," has many of the finer attributes of musical comedy, operetta, even of revue, with a definite suggestion of legitimate drama that is not dragged in by the heels and never falls into the customary mawkish channels that mistake bathos for pathos.[1]

The "legitimate drama" does seem quite mawkish today and the second act is nowhere near as brilliant as the first, in terms of libretto and music, but Waters' definition still holds. Ziegfeld, to be sure, suggested the spectacle and razzmatazz that made *Show Boat* more revue- or musical-comedy-esque; nevertheless, the broadly operettic moments are distinctly Kern's and Hammerstein's.

Show Boat's opening is thoroughgoing operetta. The chorus "Niggers all work on de Mississippi" (later "Colored folk work . . ." and later still "People all work . . .") inaugurates a brilliant opening section with several minutes of singing and only transitional dialogue, ingeniously depicting the arrival of the *Cotton Blossom* at the levee at Natchez, the introduction of the ship's company of players, and a reprise of the invigorating *"Cotton Blossom"* chorus. This is followed by a suave entrance song for the baritone, "Where Is the Mate for Me," and, almost immediately thereafter, a let-us-pretend love duet, "Only Make Believe" (like the let-us-pretend duet in Millöcker's *Der Bettelstudent* a half century before). The principal characters have been introduced, the love story is on its way, and nothing has seemed unrealistic or arbitrary, save possibly for the instant attraction of Gaylord and Magnolia, which was staged to resemble the balcony scene of *Romeo and Juliet.* This is the novel integration of song and plot with which some historians credit *Show Boat,* fifteen years before *Oklahoma!*

These historians obviously do not know their operetta. This "integration" was part of operetta since Offenbach, and any observer has merely to look at French, Viennese, or Gilbert and Sullivan operettas to find models for much of *Show Boat.* What was special about *Show Boat* was that it was an *American* romantic operetta; *Rose-Marie* (also by Hammerstein) was its obvious antecedent. But *Show Boat* had a social consciousness. The lyrics of "Ol' Man River" are read as a sort of slave's litany, and there is a dramatic scene involving miscegenation. While not denying *Show Boat*'s seriousness of purpose in 1927, the main plot concerns a love affair between a riverboat gambler and the captain's daugh-

[1]*Jerome Kern: His Life and Music,* p. 286.

ter, and its bittersweet aftermath. At the end of the story (1927), the principals are rediscovered at Natchez with no substantial improvement in the racial picture. Former stevedores and servants have not become bankers and society ladies; indeed, this is never brought up. "Ol' Man River" just keeps rolling along as Gay and Magnolia are reunited and "niggers all work on de Mississippi," as before.

"Ol' Man River," "C'mon Folks" (now "Queenie's Ballyhoo"), and "Can't Help Lovin' Dat Man" are undoubtedly influenced by black music—spirituals, jazz, and blues—and there is a Southern coloration in Robert Russell Bennett's orchestrations, which use banjos prominently. These are mixed, quite effectively, with operetta sections (that could well take place anywhere) and the juxtaposition of operetta and black music must have seemed novel in 1927.

Ziegfeld cast Helen Morgan to play the bitterest-sweetest part in the story, the mulatto, Julie. She sings two songs, perhaps the least operetta-ish of the score's numbers: "Can't Help Lovin' Dat Man" and "Bill." The first is performed as a slow blues number, though the second time it is done it becomes a rousing Charleston. The contrast is spectacular, and it does not fail to stop the show. "Bill," words by P. G. Wodehouse, was originally dropped from *Oh, Lady! Lady!!* In *Show Boat* it becomes a torch song. The songs for the soubrette and comedian (Ellie and Frank) are excellent, lively, to the point, and charming in their use of the chorus.

Then there are the three rapturous love duets between Magnolia and Gaylord Ravenal, "Only Make Believe," "You Are Love," and "Why Do I Love You?", which have seldom, if ever, been equaled in American operetta. All are long, attractively convoluted, passionate and beautiful in an extended, lush, heretofore unheard Kern manner. The spectacular settings against which these numbers are sung add an all-American romantic glow—the upper deck of the showboat and the Chicago World's Fair grounds.

Spectacle in the grand Ziegfeld manner was certainly provided: an integrated company of over one hundred, including the Jubilee Singers (a black choir) and the Dahomey Dancers, and sumptuous settings and costumes by Ziegfeld's most opulent designers, Joseph Urban and John Harkrider.

The original production at the Ziegfeld was a triumph (27 December 1927, 572 performances), with Helen Morgan, Norma Terris (Magnolia), Howard Marsh (Gaylord), Charles Winninger (Captain Andy), Edna May Oliver (Parthy Ann Hawks), Jules Bledsoe (Joe), Sammy White (Frank), Eva Puck (Ellie), and Aunt Jemima (Queenie). Ziegfeld had announced Paul Robeson for Joe, to introduce "Ol' Man River," but he was only able to appear in the London production (Drury Lane, 3 May 1928), along with an equally winning cast that included Cedric Hardwicke (Captain Andy), Marie Burke (Julie), Edith Day (Magnolia), and Howett Worster (Gaylord). The London production was seen 350 times, and there have been major revivals in both cities, the most successful in New York in 1946 and in London in 1971. Both used new orchestrations, and there were several changes in the script and score. By far the most apropos revivals were staged at the Jones Beach Marine Theater, Long Island (1956,

1957), with a real showboat floating into view, later revealing a theatre within its bulk. The Chicago World's Fair scenes were massive, and a revival of this production in the 1970s could not duplicate the lavishness of the production twenty years before because of the economic situation.

There were three *Show Boat* films, all meticulously documented in Miles Kreuger's elaborate study of the show.[2] The first film was planned by Universal at the same time Ziegfeld was preparing the stage version, and it was put into production as a silent film. By the time of the film's release in 1929, the rage for talking-singing pictures was so strong that a sound prologue had to be tacked on the film, featuring several members of the original cast performing their songs. Otherwise, Laura La Plante and Joseph Schildkraut carried on the romance in the silent body of the film.

[2]Miles Kreuger, *Show Boat: the Story of a Classic American Musical*.

Universal's 1936 remake, directed by James Whale, with Irene Dunne (Magnolia), Allan Jones (Gaylord), Helen Morgan (Julie), Paul Robeson (Joe), Charles Winninger (Captain Andy), and Hattie McDaniel (Queenie), was easily the best version, though quite a bit of the music was expunged. It was extremely well cast, and the period flavor of the operetta was particularly well served. The 1953 MGM version, while admittedly colorful and lavish, was only partially successful because of the misguided participation of Ava Gardner as Julie, a role intended for Judy Garland. Some of the other cast members weren't bad: Howard Keel (Gaylord) and Kathryn Grayson (Magnolia), in particular, but the dark Mississippi Victorian Gothic, so beautifully captured by James Whale, was missing in George Sidney's later direction.

In London for the Drury Lane *Show Boat,* Kern provided a fairly undistinguished score for the opening show at the new Piccadilly Theatre, *Blue Eyes* (27 April 1928), starring Evelyn Laye. The story was about a real actress who assists the thwarted plans of Bonnie Prince Charlie in eighteenth-century Scotland. Aside from a medley of Scottish airs in the first act, there was little attempt to pastiche the style, and only "Do I Do Wrong, Dear?" from the finale, has endured—as "You're Devastating" from the later *Roberta.* A more conscientious attempt at period pastiche was the next Kern-Hammerstein show, *Sweet Adeline* (Hammerstein's, 3 September 1929). Helen Morgan led the cast in this view of Broadway and Hoboken in the 1890s, which was praised by the critics but dealt a blow by the stock market crash. Hammerstein's libretto had none of the spine Edna Ferber's material gave him in *Show Boat,* and Kern's score was correspondingly less passionate, and less an operetta score. The numbers were basically songs performed in shows-within-the-show (one, a period operetta, *Oriental Moon*). The biggest hit song was "Why Was I Born?", perfect material for Helen Morgan, but for few other performers.

The Cat and the Fiddle (Globe, 15 October 1931), written with Otto Harbach, was a Brussels-set musical play that dealt with classical versus popular music, embodied by two composers who fall in love, played by Bettina Hall and George Metaxa. As with *Rose-Marie,* the songs were so inherently part of the "musical fabric" that they were not listed by title out of town. The musicians were listed by name as "soloists," and there was a conscious attempt to have music woven in and out of the play as underscoring, an elaboration of the *mélodrame.* This in itself was not necessarily operetta-ish (rather more cinematic), and the play's modern setting, unlike the historical periods of Kern's past two works, would not have been expected to call forth any soaring lyricism from the composer. But Kern let himself go with some of the loveliest songs he had yet written, including "The Night Was Made for Love," "The Love Parade," "Try to Forget," and the sprightlier "She Didn't Say Yes." It is now impossible to hear Robert Russell Bennett's original orchestrations, but a good indication of the

---

The first Jones Beach Marine Theatre production of Kern's *Show Boat* (1956). Possibly the most spectacular and memorably realistic production of this great American operetta, although the show boat itself was not exactly accurate.

score's beauty can be heard in the excellent film version (1934), directed by William K. Howard and well sung by Jeanette MacDonald and Ramon Navarro. The original Broadway run was 395 performances; more were registered at the Palace, London, in 1932. with Peggy Wood (4 March).

Music in the Air (Alvin, 8 November 1932) had an even more pretentious programme than *The Cat and the Fiddle*'s. The chorus was identified as members of various Edendorf (Bavaria) societies—the choral society, the walking society, and the girls' club. The scenes were listed not only by locale but also with special titles: "Leit Motif," "Etudes," "Pastoral," and so forth. *Music in the Air* in some cases used choral singing where orchestral and piano music were used in *The Cat and the Fiddle,* so that the relatively few songs are repeated in various combinations throughout the show. There were two substantial hit songs, "I've Told Every Little Star" and "I Hear Music . . . The Song is You," but other numbers were just as fine, even if Oscar Hammerstein's libretto was severely clichéd, set in modern Germany just before the Nazi takeover a few months later, which few could forecast in the middle of 1932.

Walter Slezak, after the *succès d'estime* of Benatzky's *Meet My Sister,* had a good part in *Music in the Air,* introducing the immortal "I've Told Every Little Star." Natalie Hall continued her operetta career as an operetta singer, Frieda, this time courted by another Latin lover, Tulio Carminati. The operetta-within-an operetta format must have attracted Ivor Novello, who undoubtedly saw his future co-star Mary Ellis in the London production of *Music in the Air* (His Majesty's, 19 May 1933) which had a 275-performance run, less than Broadway's total of 342.

Roberta (New Amsterdam, 18 November 1933), like *Music in the Air,* took place in modern Europe (Paris). Otto Harbach's weak book harked back to the Edwardian era, with a princess disguised as a shop assistant. Again, a great romantic song hit helped propel the latest Kern show to success: "Smoke Gets in Your Eyes." There was less of an attempt on Kern's part to fill *Roberta* with continuous music, and there was far less chorus work than in its heavily choraled predecessor. *Roberta*'s fame nowadays rests somewhat on its original cast, which included the old musical-comedy star Fay Templeton (out of retirement) and Bob Hope, for the first time in a substantial part on Broadway. Several other songs have achieved classic status, including "Yesterdays" and "You're Devastating," the latter originally in *Blue Eyes.* There were 295 performances on Broadway. The painfully dull 1935 film confirmed the show's serious failings; even the dancing of Fred Astaire and Ginger Rogers failed to enliven the film more than momentarily. "I Won't Dance," their big number in the film, was part of the score of *Three Sisters,* a British Kern-Hammerstein failure at Drury Lane in April 1934.

Kern next went to Hollywood, where he wrote several excellent film scores: *I Dream Too Much* (1935, with Lily Pons), *Swing Time* (1936), and the marvelously operetta-ish *High, Wide and Handsome* (1937), written with Oscar Hammerstein II and directed by Rouben Mamoulian, which included the lovely songs "Can I Forget You?" and "The Folks Who Live On the Hill." The Broadway

production of *Very Warm for May* (Alvin, 17 November 1939) is remembered
solely for "All the Things You Are," although several other songs in this back-
stage story—not unlike *The Cat and the Fiddle* or *Music in the Air*—are quite
attractive. There were, however, only 59 performances.

Back in California, Kern's further films included *You Were Never Lovelier* (1942),
Can't Help Singing (1944), *Cover Girl* (1945), and *Centennial Summer* (1946), each
containing a wonderful song or two. Kern died before the acclaimed revival of
Show Boat in 1946, and before he had a chance to compose the score of the
musical comedy *Annie Get Your Gun*. After his death, the job of writing the
music for the new show was given to Irving Berlin.

Richard Rodgers (1902–1979) first sprang into prominence with his great
lyricist **Lorenz Hart** (1895–1943) in revue, with *The Garrick Gaieties* in May
1925. Rodgers had already composed scores for amateur musicals, while Hart
(distantly related to the poet Heinrich Heine) had been doing translations of
Viennese and Berliner operettas for the Shuberts. By the following fall (Knickerbocker, 18 September 1925) the team's first musical play, *Dearest Enemy,* was
appearing in New York. Based on a true incident that occurred during the
American Revolution, the plot had Mrs. Mary Lindley Murray (of New York's
Murray Hill) detaining General Howe and other British officers at her home
during which time an American army contingent was allowed to escape. Hart's
lyrics had a wit and sheen quite unusual for their era, and Rodgers's score occasionally went into operetta territory. The use of the chorus and the colonial
British setting brought W. S. Gilbert to mind to several reviewers; a not unexpected inference, as Hart idolized Gilbert. But there was more to produce the
correspondence than Hart's contributions alone. Just as Sullivan's sweet, tuneful
music sweetened and made irresistibly tuneful Gilbert's irony, Rodgers's music
did much the same thing for Hart's words. While *Dearest Enemy* provided at
least one enduring standard, "Here in My Arms," little else has achieved classic
Rodgers and Hart status, and there has been only one major revival since 1925,
at the Goodspeed Opera House, Connecticut, during the Bicentennial year of
1976.

The operetta elements that had provided some of the pleasures of *Dearest
Enemy* were pilloried in the "Rose of Arizona" sketch in the 1926 *Garrick Gaieties*. Indeed, Rodgers and Hart forsook operetta the rest of the 1920s, offering
more zippy musical comedies like *The Girl Friend, Peggy-Ann* (both 1926), *A
Connecticut Yankee* (1927), and *Present Arms* (1928). *A Connecticut Yankee* might
easily have been turned into a modern comic opera, especially with its elaborate
Act I finale, but it was more regulation musical comedy, and with a great score.

Chee-Chee (1928) was almost an operetta, and it didn't last a month. The
unpalatable subject of castration provided the plot momentum, but unlike the
grisly genius of Gilbert's *The Mikado*, Herbert Fields's book was unfunny. There
was a yeoman attempt to provide variety and integration with the songs (some
of which were mere snippets), but none appealed to an audience that found the
whole idea fundamentally unentertaining. Rodgers and Hart were nevertheless

to remain fond of setting whole scenes in music and verse and of using extended recitative or rhyming dialogue, and they were curiously allowed to get away with this anachronistic behavior in Hollywood during the next decade.

Both *Spring Is Here* and *Heads Up*, 1929 Rodgers and Hart musical comedies, were transferred to celluloid the following year, and a version of *A Connecticut Yankee* was released in 1931. *The Hot Heiress* (1930) was an unremarkable original screen musical, but their next work was very possibly the greatest U.S. film operetta, *Love Me Tonight* (1932). Starring Maurice Chevalier, Jeanette MacDonald, Charlie Ruggles, Charles Butterworth, and Myrna Loy and peerlessly directed by Rouben Mamoulian, it out-Lubitsched Lubitsch in its definitive rendition of the intimate European-style operetta made in Hollywood. Here, Rodgers and Hart could blend singing, music, and dialogue perfectly, and, under Mamoulian's expertise, the innate theatricality of operetta was captured on screen in a completely cinematic and charming way.

There were certain slight changes in style and operetta sources. During the '20s, Hart was evidently smitten primarily by Gilbert and Sullivan. By 1932, one could easily tell Rodgers and Hart had been watching the parade of German musical films, as well as the Lubitsch screen operettas, very closely. While *Love Me Tonight* in certain places parodies these, the parody is affectionate, and the satire and pure verbal byplay on Hart's part had softened. National film audiences were not sophisticated Broadway audiences. Not that Hart's verbal dexterity and satire had disappeared—they turn up rather prominently in the next two Rodgers and Hart film musicals, *The Phantom President* (1932) and *Hallelujah, I'm a Bum* (1933), both with extended social-political sung scenes. George M. Cohan starred in the first, Al Jolson in the second, both formidable stars demanding special handling.

When asked by MGM to do the musical adaptation for the Lubitsch version of *The Merry Widow* (1934), Rodgers bowed out, unwilling to tamper with Lehár. Hart did some of the new lyrics, with Gus Kahn, a throwback to Hart's Broadway apprenticeship.

Back on Broadway in 1935, Rodgers and Hart provided a run of memorable musical comedies with interesting new slants: *Jumbo* (1935—a circus spectacle), *On Your Toes* (1936—with its George Balanchine ballets), *Babes in Arms* (1937—a story of youngsters putting on their own show), and then, *I'd Rather Be Right* (1937), which marked a return to Gilbert and Sullivan, or, more precisely, Gilbert and Sullivan as seen through George and Ira Gershwin in *Of Thee I Sing* (1931). Hart's lyrics were undeniably clever, but they and the Kaufman–Moss Hart book were too mired in topicality to have ever lasted. And Rodgers's score was in no way a match for Gershwin's, unfortunately. George M. Cohan made a fabulous impression as FDR, triumphing in spite of his dislike for Roosevelt and Rodgers and Hart.

I Married an Angel (1938), based on a Hungarian play, had been written during the Rodgers and Hart stay in Hollywood, which probably accounts for its extended rhymed dialogue/recitative sections, so closely resembling those in *Love*

Me Tonight. The fantasy of the story was uniquely suited to the screen: an angel (Vera Zorina) journeys down from heaven to be married to a Budapest banker (Dennis King). However, when later filmed with Jeanette MacDonald and Nelson Eddy—their last movie together (1942)—the fun had turned to stone and the score had been reduced. *The Boys from Syracuse* (1938) had a lovely score, but the best songs were resolutely of the 1930s. The temptation to allow a classical setting (ancient Ephesus) and a classical source (Shakespeare) to dictate a comic-opera treatment was basically resisted, but there were several pure operetta sections, including the opening. *Pal Joey* (1940) had an even greater score, but was the type of realistic show that would kill off operetta. *By Jupiter* (1941), the last Rodgers and Hart show, was again a return to classical times, and, like *The Boys from Syracuse,* was popular for its musical comedy elements.

At the time of *By Jupiter,* the Theatre Guild, by then going broke, announced a musical version of their earlier western play, Lynn Riggs's *Green Grow the Lilacs*. The score was to be written by Rodgers and Hart. Hart was not interested, because of the subject matter, and also because of his mental and physical condition, then deteriorating rapidly. Rodgers discussed switching partners with Ira Gershwin and Oscar Hammerstein, who, throughout the late '30s, had not had a substantial hit in the theatre. Gershwin declined, but Hammerstein was more than willing, and Lorenz Hart generously approved of the merger. The two lyricists were not entirely disparate.

Oscar Hammerstein (1895–1960) was basically a romantic-operetta librettist. Hart, who did not write dialogue, was a lyricist usually more concerned with wit than romance, though he—like Cole Porter—wrote some of the most lyrical love songs of the American stage. Oscar Hammerstein was interested in a cohesive, integrated structure, with song flowing out of dialogue, often using standard operetta *recitative*. Hart had shown his skill in the *parlando* couplets heard in some of his 1920s shows and, more potently and memorably, in his Hollywood films, especially *Love Me Tonight*. The "honesty" and "maturity" of the American musical had been achieved before Rodgers and Hammerstein, not only in *Show Boat,* but also in Rodgers and Hart's *Pal Joey*.

But *Oklahoma!* (St. James, 31 March 1943) was a tremendous and fairly unexpected triumph, and a "musical play," that euphemism for a romantic operetta. What made it seem less operetta-ish was its emphatic Americana, especially the dialect dialogue and the setting in the Oklahoma Territory. The show fit right in with the wartime escape to the past, a perfect evocation of simpler times without any European or Asian menace. The plot had the added interest of a psychopathic villain, reflecting the fashionable interest in psychology and psychiatry that had shown up earlier in the Weill-Hart-Gershwin *Lady in the Dark*. And there was a great deal of dancing—though *On Your Toes* had quite a bit as well. Agnes de Mille, not at that time the celebrity she was later to become, was responsible for the dream ballet that closed Act I and set a style that persisted for seasons. Interestingly, the dream ballet replaced what would ordinarily have been the first-act finale, considered too artificial for the 1940s. De Mille also staged the other effective dances that were more "integrated" in the plot, including the lively social dancing at the opening of Act II.

Rouben Mamoulian, who directed *Love Me Tonight* and the stage *Porgy and Bess,* knew very well how to unite song and dialogue into a seamless flow, and he was perhaps as much responsible for the integration of *Oklahoma!* as anyone else. The production was also lucky in having the fetching sets of Lemuel Ayers, with their very stylized backdrops reminiscent of children's illustrations. The sunny, unsardonic, seeming unsophistication of *Oklahoma!* was the right restorative tonic for a country at war. With its strong accent on dance, *Oklahoma!* was considerably more stylized than *Show Boat,* and the novelty of de Mille's and Mamoulian's achievement with the fluid Hammerstein libretto caused audiences (and subsequent historians) to think that a new, American art form was born. Time has shown Hammerstein's libretto to be almost as dated as those he wrote for *The Desert Song* or *The New Moon,* if perhaps less cliché-ridden, and certainly more interesting. *Oklahoma!* was an undeniably effective American operetta, though Rodgers's score was not as entirely country-western as it might have been.

The composer's propensity for soaring waltzes reflected his early childhood memories listening to piano renditions of the big European operetta hits of the day, particularly those by Oscar Straus, which he then memorized. "Oh, What a Beautiful Mornin' " is the most celebrated of *Oklahoma!*'s waltzes, but the complete version of another, "Out of My Dreams," with its chorus sections, reminds one of similar scenes in many previous Hammerstein creations, including those in *Rose-Marie* and *The New Moon.* The great experiment of beginning *Oklahoma!* without a chorus had already had a memorable precedent in the opening of Gilbert and Sullivan's *The Yeomen of the Guard* (1888). The conventional operetta supporting-couple, the soubrette and the comedian, were quite apparent in *Oklahoma!* The original cast included Alfred Drake, Joan Roberts, and Celeste Holm.

In short, *Oklahoma!* was a streamlined version of the 1920s romantic operetta, eliminating superfluous spectacle and novelty numbers, adding psychology to a routinely melodramatic plot. Lorenz Hart, genuinely pleased for his ex-partner, was reported to have gushed to Rodgers at the opening-night party that "the thing will run longer than *Blossom Time.*" Hart knew his operettas.

Oklahoma! enjoyed an emotional and triumphant première in London (Drury Lane 29 April 1947, 1,543 performances), where it blew in like a sunny prairie wind into a city that was still suffering the postwar blues. Rodgers and Hammerstein's occupation of Drury Lane lasted almost twice as long as World War II, through *The King and I.* The original Broadway productions of the Rodgers and Hammerstein works had conspicuously long runs; Continental theatres are not geared to such runs, but *Oklahoma!* and some of its successors have had popular engagements in Europe. (Parisians, once again, have persistently resisted modern American operettas.) The film versions of the Rodgers and Hammerstein *oeuvre* have been seen all over the world, and quite recently revivals of *Oklahoma!* have been winning new fans in New York, London, West Berlin, and Australia.

Oklahoma! was, financially, the greatest triumph Broadway had seen in years, making its creators, producers, and backers millions and millions of dollars. The Theatre Guild was anxious to continue its association with the new team, and the next project announced was a musicalization of another Guild property, Ferenc Molnár's *Liliom*. *Carousel* (Majestic, 19 April 1945) accentuated the psychological-supernatural dream elements of *Oklahoma!* (with Mamoulian and de Mille) in the context of an even more melodramatic story. Vocally, *Carousel* was far more demanding, and with its increased choral work, its heaviness of texture, and less comedy, it was even more a romantic operetta than its predecessor. Unfortunately, the freshness of *Oklahoma!* was absent, and an earnest, religious, pretentiousness replaced Molnár's affecting whimsy. Rodgers's score did not avoid maudlinity, and Hammerstein's preaching, first encountered in Aunt Eller's dialogue in Act II giving advice to *Oklahoma!*'s depressed heroine, burst into hymn-singing in *Carousel*. In the true Gilbert and Sullivan style, the contralto became a stock figure for Rodgers and Hammerstein, though she was never as fascinating a character as Lady Jane or Katisha. Aunt Eller's descendants were Nettie (in *Carousel*), Bloody Mary (as bizarre as they could make her, in *South Pacific*), Lady Thiang (Madame Conscience in *The King and I*), and the Mother Abbess in *The Sound of Music*. Many of these characters had a hymn to sing: "You'll Never Walk Alone," "Something Wonderful," "Climb Ev'ry Mountain." Rare, indeed, in operetta, to send the audience out on a ray of hope rather than one of jollity.

In *Carousel*, Hammerstein de-Budapestized the setting, putting it in late nineteenth-century New England to keep it escapist, and to allow for more luscious Rodgers waltzes. A suite of these, originally planned for Paul Whiteman, replaces the overture. After the simplicity of *Oklahoma!*, the choral platitudes of *Carousel* seem a bit forced, with perhaps too many production numbers having little to do with the plot, reinforcing *Carousel*'s throwback to older operettas. But these choruses, like "June Is Bustin' Out All Over" (a rustic paean to rising sap) and "Blow High, Blow Low" (the sea chantey), had dances by de Mille, a huge celebrity after her *Oklahoma!* ballets, which the producers thought the audience wanted to see recreated.

Carousel nevertheless had an extremely effective first part, in which Mamoulian's seamless direction and the almost continuous music fused to create one of the most picturesquely romantic of American operetta openings. If the essentially middle-European whimsy of Molnár's original was not recreated in the heavenly scenes in Act II, Rodgers's score and Hammerstein's charm enabled at least the first earthbound scenes to take on a rare, poetic sheen that was, again, very effectively escapist in wartime. The pantomimed Carousel Waltz, "You're a Queer One, Julie Jordan," "When I Marry Mister Snow," and the long love

duet culminating in "If I Loved You" were together perhaps the finest sustained portion of any Rodgers and Hammerstein show. Leading the Broadway company were John Raitt and Jan Clayton.

Oscar Hammerstein II greatly admired his next musical, *Allegro* (1947), which was no doubt thought ahead of its time. There was even more choral work here, with the musical-comedy equivalent of a Greek chorus. Unfortunately, the librettist's preachy moralizing would probably not be welcomed on Broadway today, although Rodgers's score has many fine moments.

The dramatic appeal of *South Pacific* (Majestic, 7 April 1949), drenched with an irresistible, gorgeous Rodgers score, is the same as that of a 1920s Romberg-Hammerstein operetta: a love story between two big-voiced opposites caught in an exotic setting, with songs describing the locale *("Bali Ha'i")*, a rousing male chorus (this time more or less half-naked—probably as much a jolt as the nudes in *Hair* twenty years later), and either a romantic conflict (the racial business with Émile de Becque's former marriage) or another kind, in this case, the Pacific War, which naturally had a very immediate connotation for the original audience. *South Pacific,* rather brilliantly, managed to bring in these two conflicts at once, reinforcing them with an equally dramatic subplot with further racial problems. The preaching morality (which had so disfigured *Allegro*) and the seriousness of tone of *South Pacific* now seem faintly ludicrous, but in 1949 they were considered mature. Because of its unabashedly romantic score and dated histrionics, *South Pacific* is now very much an operetta, as distanced by time. In its original production, which has never been satisfactorily recaptured, Ezio Pinza played the French planter opposite Mary Martin's American nurse, in a production by Joshua Logan (direction) and Jo Mielziner (settings) that was a model of fluid modernity.

The King and I (St. James, 29 March 1951), similarly, is a pure operetta, and the moral issue here—slavery—is perhaps better dealt with. The romantic plot is an American answer to *Das Land des Lächelns:* Western girl meets Eastern potentate, and to what extent will the twain meet? Musically, however, it is not quite as lavish as the Lehár work, and the love songs are given to the soubrette/second-male-lead, this time a tragic couple. These songs are particularly lovely ("We Kiss in a Shadow" and "I Have Dreamed"), plus the dramatic first song of Tuptim ("My Lord and Master"), which soars away all too soon. The rest of the rich score, with some exceptions, attempts to be "oriental" in much the same way as Lehár's. As Rodgers pointed out, Western ears wouldn't be able to stand authentic Thai sounds for very long. Whether the King's songs were written specifically for Yul Brynner's savage, tartar voice or not I cannot say, but his harsh intonation suits them perfectly. Anna's (Gertrude Lawrence's) whistling song and "Getting to Know You," though they have an easy charm, are not as appealing as her waltz song, "Hello, Young Lovers," which, again, is a dramatic plus.

Both the modern-dress musical comedies *Me and Juliet* (1953) and *Pipe Dream* (1955) were unpopular with the Rodgers and Hammerstein public, which simply preferred costumed romance or at least some sort of exoticism. The television version of *Cinderella* (broadcast 31 March 1957 by CBS) was a somewhat happier event for Rodgers, if not for Hammerstein, and its European fairy-tale setting brought out echoes of the Rodgers (and Hart) of the *Love Me Tonight* era. It was ideal operetta material, but the singing chorus was sadly underemployed—again, the dancing in the ball scenes took its place. There were, however, two attractive romantic duets, "Do I Love You Because You're Beautiful?" and "Ten Minutes Ago." And best of all were the extended scene, "A Lovely Night," which finally allowed more than two people to sing at once,

---

Rodgers and Hammerstein's *Carousel* at the Vienna Volksoper (1972). Not a big success, as the Viennese and other Europeans still prefer their indigenous works, with rare exceptions like *My Fair Lady* and *Kiss Me, Kate*. Volksoper/Elisabeth Hausmann.

complete with recitative, and the comic "Stepsisters' Lament," which was Hammerstein at his most amusing. The early nineteenth century was elegantly depicted in the William and Jean Eckart period dresses and settings, and the title role was a natural for Julie Andrews, who had shown all she could transform herself in *My Fair Lady* a year previously. The other roles were similarly well cast, especially the two ugly sisters of Alice Ghostley and Kaye Ballard. (An even more glittery cast—Cyril Ritchard, Dennis King, and Basil Rathbone—appeared 21 February 1958 on the same network in another musical fairy tale, Cole Porter's *Aladdin*. One should also note here, while on the subject of television, that American broadcasting during the 1950s was far more willing to present older operettas, whether complete or excerpted, than it has been recently.)

Flower Drum Song (1958) was an attempt to be as modern American as, let us say, *Me and Juliet,* while at the same time offering the oriental elements that made both *South Pacific* and *The King and I* so popular. Unfortunately, it would be impossible to revive the book today, as its racial stereotyping or patronizing would be considered quite offensive, and Rodgers's score is only fitfully interesting.

The final work of the partnership, however, is not only its most popular product, but also one of the most popular operettas of the century. And operetta *The Sound of Music* (Lunt-Fontanne, 16 November 1959) certifiably is, as some of the critics pointed out in their original reviews, including both Brooks Atkinson of the New York *Times* and London's Kenneth Tynan. The true story of a postulant-governess who charms a stern Austrian baron and his children, the story had obvious parallels to that of *The King and I,* except that its ending, involving an escape from the Nazis, was more exultantly exciting. The Austrian locale might have inspired Rodgers to Lehárian heights, but because the two principals (Mary Martin and Theodore Bikel) then had unoperatic voices, the rapturous moments were minimal. Most of the soaring music was written for the nunnery, examples being the "Preludium" that opened the show and the hymn for the Mother Abbess, "Climb Ev'ry Mountain." But Miss Martin's songs, especially those sung with the von Trapp children, gained worldwide currency. "Do-Re-Mi" was an exceptionally catchy (and unbelievably speedy) singing lesson. And "The Lonely Goatherd" used the *tyrolienne* effects which so delighted audiences at the time of Offenbach. Other musical highlights included Rodgers's stabs at purely Austrian melodies, the *Ländler* near the end of Act I (the operetta's big dancing scene, and *not* a dream ballet), and the effectively wistful "folk song," *"Edelweiss."* But even more operetta-like were the little ensembles that served as the relatively few comic or ironic spots in the story: "(How Do You Solve a Problem Like) Maria," "How Can Love Survive?", and "No Way to Stop It." The last two were apparently found so stagy that they were omitted from the fabulously successful Robert Wise film version released in 1965. If the plot was sentimental in a way that was considered quite operetta-like, it was, after all, based on a true story, something one cannot claim for most operetta stories, and a fact that served as a positive publicity factor for *The Sound of Music*. If the combine of nuns and motherless children was found too cloying for some, the real intrusion of the Nazi menace engineered by librettists Howard Lindsay and Russell Crouse shrewdly managed to offset the treacle for most viewers.

The Sound of Music ran very successfully on Broadway (1,443 performances) and even more triumphantly in London (2,385 performances), where it began its run 18 May 1961 at the Palace Theatre. A decade before, Ivor Novello's *King's Rhapsody* had been what might have been thought the last big operetta to play the Palace. Subsequent revivals in English-speaking countries have been either overshadowed or provoked by the success of the film version, which solidified universal admiration for the talents of Julie Andrews. One particularly extravagant reprise was at the Jones Beach Marine Theatre in 1967; another was seen in 1981–82 at London's Apollo Victoria. Although the film has met with success in Europe, the original stage version has been produced there only rarely, and not in Austria, a country that would ordinarily admire this kind of show but one that probably would not like to be reminded of its embrace of Naziism in 1938.

The death of Richard Rodgers in 1979 did not prompt any retrospective look at his career, as his music is still very much alive today. Admittedly, his *oeuvre* was remarkably rich, and, like Jerome Kern, he managed to present operetta to the public in what was thought to be a new and modern way. He was also Kern's successor as a melodist, likewise achieving many of his effects with the help of able orchestrators like Robert Russell Bennett. Furthermore, Oscar Hammerstein, the principal librettist for both, kept the two composers firmly in operetta terrain. The lovely catalogue of songs Rodgers left his public is of course partially the work of Lorenz Hart, but the libretti for the Rodgers and Hart shows have not been found as enduring as the much more romantic concoctions created by Hammerstein, again proving the lasting appeal of the romantic operetta.

The collaboration of **Alan Jay Lerner** (1918–1986) and **Frederick Loewe** (1904–1988) has provided the Broadway stage with three of the greatest operettas of the postwar era, though none of them was so termed. Lerner was born in New York, and spent some of his school days in England. He began his show-business career in radio. Loewe, the son of a notable Berlin Danilo in *Die lustige Witwe,* had a classical background, including studies with Ferruccio Busoni and Eugène d'Albert. He held a variety of not-too-auspicious jobs when he first came to America. After an early song effort, "A Waltz Was Born in Vienna," was included in a 1936 revue, he was entrusted with the full score for the unsuccessful *Great Lady* two years later.

The first joint effort of Lerner and Loewe was the musical-comedy *What's Up?* (1943), a failure, but their next show, *The Day Before Spring* (National, 22 November 1945), was somewhat better received. Both were bright, supposedly intelligent and cheery musical comedies, perhaps too clever for wartime audiences. *Brigadoon* (Ziegfeld, 13 March 1947) was a "musical play," and though it subscribed to a number of '40s conventions, particularly in its use of dance-drama (by Agnes de Mille), it was the most romantically escapist operetta of the decade, and a hopeful sign that operetta had indeed been reborn in the United States after the Nazis had killed it in Europe. *Brigadoon's* libretto was sufficiently original, and its score so entrancingly lovely, that it delighted 1947 audiences and still holds the stage. The story is about the love of a weary modern American for a Scottish lassie who turns out to be living in the mid-eighteenth century, along with the rest of Brigadoon's inhabitants. Through the power of love, the hero indeed retreats into the past at the end of the play. The plot was reputed to have been suggested by a German folktale, but a more obvious suggestion might have been John Balderston's *Berkeley Square* (1926), a play that played with the eighteenth and twentieth centuries, or Robert Nathan's popular novel, *Portrait of Jennie* (1940), or, even more apparently, the book and film of *Lost Horizon,* by James Hilton (1933 and '37, respectively).

The most ostensibly Scottish elements of the original production were the tartan costumes by David ffolkes and the gloomily evocative and rather ballet-like settings of Oliver Smith, along with more obvious effects like burred accents and bagpipes. The music was only occasionally Scottish-sounding, and Loewe admitted that his main stylistic influence was Brahms. The composer's vocal arrangements and the Ted Royal orchestrations accentuated the bagpiping sound, but there was no gainsaying the charming, folkish "Come to Me, Bend to Me" and "I'll Go Home with Bonnie Jean," which sounded quite Anglo-(Scots)-Irish. The two most popular songs from the show were not at all Scottish in flavor, but had a wistfulness and charm that recalled another great Anglophile, Jerome Kern. These were "The Heather on the Hill" and "Almost Like Being in Love," both love duets. Lerner's lyrics echoed Harry Lauder's "Roamin' in the Gloamin' " in the first quatrain of "The Heather on the Hill," but no one minded. (It was simply, beautifully, a charming duet in the play, but it was turned into something much more balletic with Gene Kelly and Cyd Charisse in the strange 1954 MGM movie.) By the time the lovers have finished their walk "up the brae," they know what it is like to be "Almost Like Being in Love," and their joy is contagious.

The rest of the score is remarkably effective, with hardly a weak number in it, and with the richness of invention and prodigality of music that made the 1940s and '50s so memorable. It is very much an operetta score. After a mystical prologue involving a short, expository dialogue scene surrounded by two ghostly choruses, *Brigadoon* launches into a typical village-green opening chorus, followed by the typical entrance songs of the heroine, Fiona, and an expectant bridegroom, Charlie Dalrymple, supported by the female and male choruses, respectively. Meg, the comic soubrette, has two comic *couplets*. Where *Brigadoon* differed from the normal operetta was in its use of dance, no better illustrated than by the incorporation of two characters, Jean and Harry, whose dancing provided the electrifying drama on which the first act ended and the second began. Agnes de Mille had done the same thing at the end of Act I of *Oklahoma!,* though in a dream ballet; in *Brigadoon,* the Act I finale was dominated not by a dream but by a real sword dance, after which Harry dances maniacally with the girl he could not marry, and runs away from Brigadoon—a deed that will cause it to vanish forever. The use of dance as a dramatic device was nothing new in operetta—a waltz had been sensuously used as an act ending by Lehár in *The Merry Widow*.

The second act of *Brigadoon* became rather churchy, with hymn-like (but lovely) songs like "There But for You Go I" and "From This Day On," and there was a New York bar scene with Brigadoon recollections seen and heard behind a scrim, somewhat like the *Student Prince* reminiscence scene twenty-two years earlier. But the impending mystery and romance of the end, with the ghostly "Brigadoon" chorus heard through the mist and the reunion of the lovers on the footbridge border of the spectral town, were wondrous enough to wait for. The London production of *Brigadoon* (His Majesty's, 14 April 1949) ran 685 performances; several of the Scottish surnames were changed in the *dramatis personae,* for whatever reason.

Paint Your Wagon (Shubert, 12 November 1951), a gold-rush musical comedy, had a number of attractive songs ("They Call the Wind Maria," "I Talk to the Trees") but the story was insufficiently exciting or romantic to make it a financial hit. Excitement, romance, glamor, and a return to operetta were features of the next and greatest Lerner and Loewe show, *My Fair Lady* (Mark Hellinger, 15 March 1956). The rights to George Bernard Shaw's popular *Pygmalion* (1913) were in the hands of Gabriel Pascal, who produced the brilliant 1938 film version with Leslie Howard and Wendy Hiller. Rodgers and Hammerstein, among others, were approached by Pascal himself to do a musical version, but after their attempts failed, Lerner and Loewe began their own treatment. The rights were ultimately granted to Lerner and Loewe only after they had done a considerable amount of writing. *Pygmalion* had already been "opened up" in a 1935 German film, starring Gustaf Gründgens as Higgins, and ideas from both film versions may have influenced Lerner's libretto. The racecourse scene was in the German film; the Embassy Ball was in the British.

Critics have praised Lerner for retaining so much of the original Shaw dialogue, and Shaw's original tone was admirably caught in Lerner's exceptionally crystalline lyrics, in every case either revealing a personality or exploiting a situation by making it sing. And there is a marvelous pun in the title—intentional or not: "My Fair" is how Eliza would say "Mayfair." Loewe's score, again brilliantly orchestrated by Robert Russell Bennett and Philip J. Lang, harked back not only to the Edwardian era but also to the early '30s screen operettas, particularly the charming confections of Mamoulian and Lubitsch.

There is comparatively little use of the chorus in *My Fair Lady,* compared with *Brigadoon* or *Paint Your Wagon.* It is *there,* parading around the opening scene in front of Covent Garden in its glamorous Beaton creations, but it doesn't sing an opening chorus, nor does it support Professor Higgins in his first patter song, "Why Can't the English?" A few Garden types hum along with Eliza's "Wouldn't It Be Loverly?" and assist Doolittle's "With a Little Bit of Luck."

From then on, the entire chorus is heard only twice: in the brilliant "Ascot Gavotte," and in the one real production number in Act II, "Get Me to the Church on Time." Professor Higgins's house staff makes fleeting appearances in "I Could Have Danced All Night" and "You Did It," and before that glorious trio, "The Rain in Spain," probably the greatest "Spanish" number in operetta since the first-act finale of *Barbe-Bleue* or the cachucha in *The Gondoliers.* Here, a small contingent of the chorus continuously remarks on the non-progress of Eliza's speech lessons, until, early in the morning when all are bone-tired, she magically pronounces the cabalistic sentence without any cockneyisms. Slowly, the Professor and his friend the Colonel ask her to repeat the sentence, which she does, this time to a slow tango rhythm. This gets faster, and the joy of the three is celebrated "with a little dance," as the record notes modestly remark.

Virtually two thirds of the musical numbers in *My Fair Lady* are small-scale, mostly solos. "You Did It," in Act II, is a true operetta scene in which events are relayed musically, and cleverly, with a number of melodies. As in *Brigadoon,* the first-act finale is basically a dance-with-dialogue affair, and in the same act's famous Ascot scene, Lerner and Loewe managed to embody upper-class British snobbery very effectively. Cecil Beaton's black-and-white-and-gray costumes and Oliver Smith's awnings produced a stage picture that transfixed audiences.

"Those verbal class distinctions" that Professor Higgins mentions in his opening song account for the brilliant idea of giving Alfred Doolittle two songs with the flavor of the Edwardian music hall, "With a Little Bit of Luck" and "Get Me to the Church on Time," both supported with sing-along choruses. Higgins has a succession of patter songs that smack of the upper-class statements of Gilbert's dignified (and often manic) comedy-baritones. Eliza begins with the "simple" "Wouldn't It Be Loverly?" and the angry "Just You Wait, 'Enry 'Iggins," ultimately arriving at the cool British dignity of "Without You." The most challenging song she has to sing is "I Could Have Danced All Night," which has a slightly Latin beat behind it, reflecting popular music of the '50s. Rarely had music been so memorably tailored to fit the characters of an operetta.

And an operetta it is, as the New York *Times* reviewer Clive Barnes called it on its revival in 1976. The *Post*'s Martin Gottfried, reviewing the same production, called it "among the very best of the Broadway book musicals," adding, "We have since seen more integrally conceived musicals, ones more likely to remain theater artworks." I sincerely doubt it. *My Fair Lady*'s international popularity has made it probably the most successful operetta since *The Merry Widow*, a work Lerner once admitted he could listen to every day and a work that made Loewe's father famous. Major productions have appeared in capitals the world over (with the notable exception of Paris) to unanimous acclaim. Recently, there have been major, elaborate revivals at London's Adelphi, a company touring the United States (with Rex Harrison), and a production at the Vienna Volksoper (as much of a hit as any native operetta in recent years). The Warner Brothers film version of 1964 was popular, though the film had the unenviable task of having to be faithful to a *mise-en-scène* (the Moss Hart staging, the Smith-Beaton décor and costumes) as familiar to the world as the libretto and music themselves. As such, it could not stray too much from the stage version, for fear of audience rejection. This accounts for a certain stodginess, but as a filmed version of a famous production it is quite admirable, with basically new Art Nouveau sets by Beaton that had to be more realistic than the stylization possible on Broadway. Rex Harrison close up was similarly less theatrical than on the stage, but Audrey Hepburn gave a nice film performance as Eliza, buttressed by Stanley Holloway from Broadway.

The role of Mrs. Higgins seems to have attracted the most interesting players: Cathleen Nesbitt, who at the age of ninety-one repeated her original Broadway role, Dame Anna Neagle, in the London revival, and, in the first London production, Zena Dare, a fabulous echo of the Edwardesian period that lent further glamor to the Drury Lane run that began 30 April 1958.

Loewe's *My Fair Lady* at the Vienna Volksoper (1979): Dagmar Koller as Eliza and Franz Waechter as Freddy in the Ascot scene. This spectacular production could not fail to be a great hit with the Viennese because of its basic operetta structure and its Edwardian trappings. Designed by Rolf Langenfass. Volksoper/Elisabeth Hausmann.

Germany, Austria, and Switzerland have had the advantage of hearing *My Fair Lady* in German, a language that often accentuates the operettics of the score and which has a sentimental right to the show: the world première of *Pygmalion* took place at the Vienna Burgtheater on 16 October 1913. The able translation of the Lerner libretto was done by the master of these transformations, Robert (son of Jean) Gilbert.

After the international furor caused by *My Fair Lady*, Lerner and Loewe were put in the position of Gilbert and Sullivan after *The Mikado*. How could they top it? They went to Hollywood—and Paris—and transformed Colette's *Gigi* into a musical film, using many of the stylistic tricks they had used in *My Fair Lady*. Cecil Beaton was in charge of costuming *and* décor, to ensure elegance and *ton,* and the stylist Vincente Minnelli was on hand to make sure the film was elegant and mobile. *Gigi* did for *fin-de-siècle* Paris what *My Fair Lady* did for 1912 London. It recreated a period without necessarily resorting to the music of that era. The stories were fairly similar. The character of Gaston (Louis Jourdan) was another professedly unromantic, pattering hero in the mold of Henry Higgins, and in Gigi (Leslie Caron) was another heroine changing with the aid of tutorials from a schoolgirl into a beautiful woman—ostensibly a courtesan.

In its absence of chorus and in its witty numbers—patterned after the intimacy of *My Fair Lady*—*Gigi* reflected the sophisticated operetta films of the early '30s. This was further reinforced by the casting of the early '30s' greatest star, Maurice Chevalier, as the hero's uncle. "Thank Heaven for Little Girls" and "I'm Glad I'm Not Young Any More," both sung directly to the audience, reminded one of his Oscar Straus numbers in *One Hour With You*. *Gigi* had a charming sung waltz, "She Is Not Thinking of Me," which was one of several delightfully introspective numbers that also included the title song, a long, rambling (all over Paris) song of realized love related to "I've Grown Accustomed to Her Face."

It was an error of judgment to put *Gigi* on the stage (Uris, 13 November 1973), but this did enable Lerner and Loewe to add at least one good new number, "The Contract," a true operetta-ensemble scene. Alfred Drake had the necessary panache to do justice to the Chevalier songs, and Daniel Massey was a reliable Gaston, but the intimacy-*cum*-spectacle of the film was not conveyed on the stage. By a strange coincidence (that no one seems to have noticed) the Oliver Smith set for Maxim's turned up in the 1978 film, "10," as a background for Julie Andrews during her rehearsal rendition of "I Give My Heart" *("Ich schenk' mein Herz")* from the Millöcker-Mackeben *Die Dubarry*.

Camelot (Majestic, 3 December 1960) had the challenging task of following *My Fair Lady* (whose run had not yet by any means ended) on Broadway and in the West End. With many of the same names involved, including Julie Andrews, Robert Coote, Moss Hart (the director), Oliver Smith (the designer), Franz Allers (the conductor), Robert Russell Bennett and Philip J. Lang (the orchestrators), as well as a British story set in the past, *Camelot* was found, again, an attempt to recreate the successful elements that had made its predecessor a triumph. If anything, *Camelot* was even more a standard old-fashioned operetta than *My Fair Lady,* depending far more on romance and spectacle. Otherwise, the dichotomy between the intimate domestic scenes and the hollow pageantry was made more jarring because of a libretto that failed to really ignite. The scenes between King Arthur (Richard Burton) and Queen Guenevere (Julie Andrews) and the love scenes between the Queen and Lancelot (Robert Goulet) were for the most part wearisome. A true operetta would have let go with some love duets—even *Brigadoon* had several—but for some reason the most romantic songs were sung as solos by Mr. Goulet ("If Ever I Would Leave You") or Miss Andrews ("I Loved You Once in Silence").

Otherwise, everything was quite splendid, the music and lyrics preeminently. A dazzling succession of patterish entrance songs, wistful, charming duets for the King and Queen, stirring choruses, quasi-Korngold "medieval" music (as for an MGM film), and a wonderful quartet for Guenevere and three knights, "Then You May Take Me to the Fair," which once again proved how effective Lerner and Loewe were with operetta ensembles. (Sadly, this outstanding number was eventually cut from the original production and several subsequent revivals.) As usual, songs that in the '20s would have been backed by a chorus ("Where Are the Simple Joys of Maidenhood?", *"C'est Moi"*) were not.

Camelot was not unlike *The Vagabond King* in its tale of kings and fair ladies, but the derring-do of François Villon would not have been enough for the more psychologically minded '60s. Part of *Camelot*'s problem was its source, T. H. White's *The Once and Future King,* a long novel that covered a lot of territory. (Disney turned the early part, *The Sword and the Stone,* into one of his least effective cartoon features.) In any event, the score is radiant, romantic, and enchanting, and gave Richard Burton the (musical) part of his lifetime. He did not appear in the Drury Lane production (19 August 1964), which succeeded with Laurence Harvey in spite of reviews that were even less kind than those received on Broadway. But in 1979 Mr. Burton began a U.S. tour that grossed amazing sums (more than $400,000 a week) in several cities played. This, in spite of a disagreeable physical production and a less than adequate supporting cast that were not a patch on the originals, save for the splendid King Pellinore of Paxton Whitehead.

The film of *Camelot* (1967), though largely underrated, is perhaps the most self-indulgent Hollywood transformation of Lerner and Loewe. Joshua Logan's direction and the sets and costumes of John Truscott had little to do with the stage originals, but they created a milieu that was at once regal and even believable. Richard Harris and Vanessa Redgrave made a fetching King and Queen, and Franco Nero, though he could not sing, brought a sexuality to his Lancelot that made his rather sensual love scenes with Guenevere quite believable, thus making the plot bearable (as it seldom was on the stage). Though many scenes in *Camelot* threaten to turn into a British pantomime, especially those involving the fantasy of the sorcerer Merlin, the score and the basic appeal of the Arthurian legends will ensure the survival of the work.

On a Clear Day You Can See Forever (Mark Hellinger, 17 October 1965), with a score by Burton Lane, combined the elements of time-travel and Anglophilia so beloved by Lerner in a romantic musical comedy. The original book caused problems, however, in spite of effective dialogue and amusing lyrics. Several scenes laid in the eighteenth century evoked an older operetta style while the modern moments obviously tried to be modern; somehow the shifts were not as adroitly handled as in *Brigadoon,* or as in *Berkeley Square,* for that matter. But Lane's score was quite lovely, especially at its most romantic: "Tosy and Cosh," "She Wasn't You," "Melinda," and the endearing title song. *1600 Pennsylvania Avenue,* which promisingly paired Alan Jay Lerner and Leonard Bernstein, lasted only a week on Broadway (Mark Hellinger, 4 May 1976). This was more of an operetta, with a more ambitious score than was the usual Broadway wont. It was also a pageant, and an unwieldy one, celebrating the occupants of the White House as seen by their black servants, and the lack of a central plot killed the show. Patricia Routledge will be remembered by those who saw her for a show-stopping aria in which she portrayed *both* Mrs. Ulysses S. Grant and Mrs. Rutherford B. Hayes.

There were several major American theatre composers who are today remembered primarily for their musical comedies (or musical-comedy songs), although their infrequent forays into operetta were quite memorable. In many cases, a long period of success with strict musical comedy and revue led to a desire for something grander, though still generally comic. Operetta was found to be more or less the ideal form for their expression, though there were naturally concessions for the modern tastes of Broadway audiences supposedly weaned of both turn-of-the-century comic opera and the more romantic operettas of the 1920s.

There was also the tenor of the times. The stock market crash and the Great Depression would have been thought to have instigated a series of purely escapist-romantic operettas to turn the public's attention away from its problems. Instead, the revue triumphed, not only on Broadway *(The Band Wagon, As Thousands Cheer)* but also in the Hollywood backstage musicals of the early '30s. Those romantic operettas that were produced on Broadway in the 1930s were generally failures. There was nothing, for example, to effectively follow the lead taken by *Show Boat* (1927) in providing a historical, thoroughly romantic operetta until the 1940s. (With a few exceptions, this was also the case in Europe, where revue-type material was popular.)

Instead, the satire found acceptable in revue was sometimes parlayed into a book musical. The Gershwins' *Of Thee I Sing* is one of the most satirical shows of the 1930s, but it is more remarkable for its having satisfied the craving of its creators to revive the style of Gilbert and Sullivan on the modern American stage.

The career of **George Gershwin** (1898–1937) in musical comedy and serious orchestral music is very well documented. By 1924, the year of *Lady Be Good!* and *Rhapsody in Blue,* his talent in both terrains was evident. The musical comedies he wrote with his brother, Ira (1896–   ), would come to be regarded as among the better creations of their kind, though no revivals have ever really recaptured what must have been the aura surrounding the original stars, principally, the Astaires and Gertrude Lawrence. Nevertheless, many songs from *Lady, Be Good!, Tip-Toes* (1925), *Oh, Kay!* (1926), *Funny Face* (1927), and *Treasure Girl* (1928) remain unquenchably brilliant.

Early indications of a more florid operetta style, as opposed to the more recognizable upbeat musical-comedy one, had appeared in works like London's *Primrose* (Winter Garden, 11 September 1924), especially in songs like "This Is the Life for a Man." The influence of Gershwin's idol, Jerome Kern, was very apparent in another, "Some Far Away Someone." The Gershwins' awesome musical-comedy songs overshadow the less-well-known numbers composed for *Song of the Flame* (44th Street, 14 December 1925) or *Rosalie* (New Amsterdam, 10 January 1928), the former a typical '20s operetta co-composed with Herbert Stothart, the latter an extravaganza with more romantic music composed with Sigmund Romberg. *Song of the Flame* was called a "romantic opera," and its Russia-and-Paris-set libretto by Harbach and Hammerstein II was purely operettic, concerning the 1917 Revolution. Tessa Kosta and Guy Robertson were the stars, and there was an unusually loud orchestra and a large chorus to help put over the rich score. Only the title song is even vaguely remembered, probably because it was the centerpiece of the film version, released in 1930. For *Rosalie,* Gershwin contributed "How Long Has This Been Going On?"

Strike Up the Band, which closed out of town in 1927, was in an altogether new direction, a satirical operetta in an obviously Gilbert and Sullivan style that attacked war and peace-making efforts, big business and politics. The book was originally George S. Kaufman's; Morrie Ryskind revised it for the version that reached the Times Square Theatre on 14 January 1930. It was a more ambitious score for both Gershwins, requiring patter songs and ensembles hitherto unknown in their shows, and its 191-performance run (greatly helped by hit songs like the title march and "I've Got a Crush on You") persuaded the creators that another show in this style would be perhaps even more effective, both aesthetically and financially.

Of Thee I Sing, produced two years later (Music Box, 26 December 1931), was *so* much more effective that it became the first musical show to win the Pulitzer Prize, although the citation was for the libretto alone. It was more effective than its predecessor, probably because it dealt primarily and more humorously with American politics, and ultimately because its score was better. The Kaufman-Ryskind book at times allowed the Gershwin-Gershwin score to flagrantly adopt the mannerisms of Gilbert and Sullivan, so that sections came out sounding quite like the first-act finale of *Iolanthe* or much of *Trial by Jury.* Diana Devereaux, the "jilted" winner of the beauty contest, functions as a modern Broadway equivalent of the Katisha-type spinsters in Gilbert and Sullivan.

The amiable surreality, topsy-turvy satire, and progression of the story through song were thoroughly Gilbertian, and these qualities had a fair amount of influence on Hollywood musicals, perhaps more than on those on Broadway, especially on the singing parts of the Marx Brothers movies and recitative-laden films like Rodgers and Hart's *Love Me Tonight* (1932) and *Hallelujah, I'm a Bum* (1933). *Let 'Em Eat Cake* (Imperial, 21 October 1933) was a sequel to *Of Thee I Sing*, by the same creators, and with the same stars (William Gaxton, Victor Moore, Lois Moran) as its predecessor. Unfortunately, the Kaufman-Ryskind-Ira Gershwin libretto swung back to topics that were too unfunny to be satirized. In *Strike Up the Band*, war had been bandied about; here, fascist dictatorships and revolution were among the more dangerous plot developments. There was a fair amount of fun, and the song "Mine," but the show lasted only 90 performances as opposed to *Of Thee I Sing*'s 441. The satirical operetta had a short life-span on Broadway, though George S. Kaufman, in particular, would never tire of it. His tiresome reworking of W. S. Gilbert's libretto for *Hollywood Pinafore* (Alvin, 31 May 1945) was a summer-camp style burlesque that did not enhance or even parody a masterpiece that certainly did not need any modernization. There were the expectedly clever *couplets* and gags, but no one preferred it to the real *Pinafore*. (*Memphis Bound*, another remade *Pinafore* earlier that season, was seen for only a few more days—36 performances in all—thanks to Bill Robinson and a black cast attempting to cash in on the prior success of *The Hot Mikado*.)

Kaufman, however, directed the brilliant *Guys and Dolls* (1950), the **Frank Loesser** (1910–1969) musical comedy that is simply too brash, brisk, and Broadway to be called an operetta. Had the opening number ("A Fugue for Tinhorns") set the tone for all the others, a true comic opera might have been achieved. As it stands, it is one of those rare pieces that created an environment through plot, dialogue, lyrics, music, décor, costuming, casting, and staging that was as distinctively controlled as anything that had been seen on the Broadway stage. Numbers like "Adelaide's Lament" and "Marry the Man Today" also had unusual constructions that recalled the clever solos and duets from nineteenth-century French operetta, however unconsciously. Loesser's *How to Succeed in Business Without Really Trying* (1961) was a brash, musical-comedy big-business satire that, in its modern way, effectively approximated the Offenbach *opéra-bouffe* style with its hilarious numbers and generous use of the chorus. *The Most Happy Fella* (1957) openly attempted to become the sort of Broadway opera Weill's *Street Scene* was, and succeeded handsomely. In both cases, serious *intent*, both music- and plot-wise, was enough to prevent their being outright operettas. Revivals and telecasts of both works in recent years have proved there is a large audience for this genre, a prime example of which is Gershwin's most celebrated achievement, *Porgy and Bess* (1935). This was "an American folk opera," and the original operatic version is the one heard and admired today, not the (admittedly popular) Broadway-ized revival edition of 1942, which substituted dialogue for the recitative sections and cut some of the music. One question: Did a trip to Europe in 1928, during which the Gershwins saw Coward's *This Year of Grace* in London and Kálmán's *Die Herzogin von Chicago* in Vienna, have any influence on the future Gershwin works?

Like Gershwin, **Cole Porter** (1891–1964) had classical training, and both began their careers quite similarly with revues and musical comedies in New York and London. Of course, Porter wrote his own, brilliant lyrics, ranking with the best of Noël Coward, Lorenz Hart, and Ira Gershwin. His great successes of the 1920s, '30s, and '40s, including *Fifty Million Frenchmen* (1929), *Anything Goes* (1934), *Red, Hot and Blue!* (1936), *Du Barry Was a Lady* (1939), *Panama Hattie* (1940), and *Let's Face It* (1941), were the brightest of Broadway musical comedies. Most of them starred the irrepressible Ethel Merman, who got to introduce many of the Porter standards still cherished today.

In 1948, after two less-than-wildly-successful shows, a revue (*Seven Lively Arts*, 1944) and an extravaganza (*Around the World in 80 Days*, 1946), *Kiss Me, Kate* opened at the New Century Theatre on 30 December 1948, and ran 1,077 performances, Porter's greatest hit and his greatest . . . operetta? Not really, as the plot and most of the numbers are pure musical comedy. There are no real extended ensemble sections, as there are in *Of Thee I Sing*, although the second-act finale *might* have been so easily turned into one. Nevertheless, the basically European style of so many of the songs, their ABAB format, their very convoluted lyrics, the giddy accompaniments, and the operetta voices required to sing them have made *Kiss Me, Kate* one of the most popular of shows in the operetta theatres of Eastern Europe. (A revival was staged at the Vienna Volksoper in 1981.)

Shakespeare was the cause for this elevation of Porter's usual style, and he even used the Bard's lines in his songs, like "I've Come to Wive it Wealthily in Padua" and "I Am Ashamed That Women Are So Simple."

The *Candide* of **Leonard Bernstein** (1918–   ) is one of the most successful modern American operettas. In any event, it was the only one to be billed as a "comic operetta," a fairly daring and possibly pretentious move in 1956 (Martin Beck, 1 December). Pretentious, one must qualify, in the best sense of the word. Leonard Bernstein and his librettists, Lillian Hellman (book) and Richard Wilbur (most of the lyrics), probably did not know that theirs was not the first musical version of Voltaire's 1759 satire. At least two *vaudevilles* had been seen in nineteenth-century Paris alone: *Candide, ou Tout est pour le mieux* (Everything Is for the Best) at the Variétés in 1848, and an earlier *Candide et Cunégonde* at the Panthéon theatre in 1837. Hellman's book was thought to have been the chief fault of the original production (73 performances), which was otherwise stuffed with wonders: a cast that could sing (Robert Rounseville, Barbara Cook, Irra Petina, William Olvis, William Chapman), an elaborate and colorful production designed by Oliver Smith (sets) and Irene Sharaff (costumes), staging by Tyrone Guthrie, Bernstein's marvelous score, and Wilbur's often brilliant lyrics, with others, equally interesting, by John Latouche and

Dorothy Parker. In addition, the rasping Max Adrian was the first Dr. Pangloss.

The original production was criticized for its heavy, sluggish ways, as though Voltaire's story was simply too unwieldy for a Broadway musical—or operetta. Perhaps only an extremely innovative film could attempt to depict not only the irony of Voltaire's narrative but also the actual disasters so crucial to the optimistic plot. In realizing its limitations in stage trickery and spectacle, the musical *Candide* delightfully overemphasized its score, the result being Bernstein's greatest and most accomplished work for the stage.

It is unabashedly an operetta score, and Bernstein must have been delighted to have been able to trot out the ruffles and flourishes that lavish, international, eighteenth-century settings allowed, rather than the modern Manhattan that had produced the musical comedies *On the Town* (1944) and *Wonderful Town* (1953). (Interestingly, co-librettist Adolph Green has pointed out that *On the Town* was a conscious attempt to modernize and Americanize nineteenth-century comic opera.) There are patter songs with chorus, love duets that did not have to be written with the radio or jukebox in mind, elaborate ensembles the likes of which were rarely heard on Broadway, and, to top it all off, an overture of such brilliance that it has become a concert-hall favorite. The humor of Voltaire was ably caught in lyrics like "You Were Dead, You Know," and "What's the Use?" There were, miraculously, many other instances of ironic or humorous words mated to sweet music, a prime operetta virtue, as in the first Candide-Cunegonde duet, "Oh, Happy We." What sweet, lovely music this is, approximating an eighteenth-century tune of almost Mozartian grace. More miraculously, Bernstein obviously demanded not only formal opening choruses ("The Best of All Possible Worlds") but also formal finales as well (the quartet finale of Act I and the monumental chorale, "Make Our Garden Grow"). There were at least four quartets, four trios, a mazurka, a gavotte, and the operetta's most famous number, "Glitter and Be Gay," a clever (but affectionate) parody of Marguerite's jewel song in Gounod's *Faust,* the type of operatic burlesque Offenbach and Hervé would have adored. A great help to Bernstein was his orchestrator, Hershy Kay.

The original Broadway failure, and one in London as well (Saville, 30 April 1959), did not stop the original-cast record from prompting further theatrical and concert versions. Nearly two decades later, a Broadway revival based on a production by Harold Prince for the Chelsea Theatre of Brooklyn opened at the Broadway Theatre (8 March 1974). This had a new book by Hugh Wheeler that helped melt some of the stodginess of Hellman's version. On an orchestra level with its seats torn out, on a tatty, ragged skeletal set by Eugene and Franne Lee, Prince led an enthusiastic but far too young cast through a circus version of the story, straying alarmingly far from Bernstein's very elegantly ironic musical conception. Furthermore, the reduced orchestra could not compete with the sound of the forces heard on the first-cast album. Somewhere in between the vibrancy and pacing of the revival and the experienced vocalism and elegance of the original is the ideal production of *Candide*. This was realized to some degree by the New York City Opera 1982 revival.

Like Porter's *Kiss Me, Kate*, Bernstein's *West Side Story* (Winter Garden, 26 September 1957) is today in the repertoires of several Central European operetta theatres. *West Side Story*, the dramatic resetting of *Romeo and Juliet* in New York's West Side in the 1950s, would seem to be another of the more successful "Broadway operas," this time infused with the electrifying dances of Jerome Robbins. What would have been chorus numbers are in this work invariably danced. As with *Candide*'s music, Bernstein's score is on a much higher level than that generally expected from a Broadway musical, and the romantic exuberance of "Tonight," "Maria," and "One Hand, One Heart" recalls similar love songs in the operettas of the 1920s. And, like the '20s operetta, *West Side Story* has similarly dated—in a not unpleasant way. Bernstein's subsequent works for the stage have not been well regarded; however, one is left with the impression that, if he wanted, the composer could write another successful operetta. Though sections of *1600 Pennsylvania Avenue*, written with Alan Jay Lerner, harked back to *Candide* or other operettas, the unevenness of the whole defeated its creators and its audiences. But with an operetta as mercurial as *Candide*, Bernstein's place in the honor list is assured.

The impressive narrative techniques of Rodgers and Hammerstein, carefully honed by forty years of combined experience before the two titans embarked on *Oklahoma!*, were extremely influential on contemporary and future musical comedies and "musicals" by other composers. The late 1940s and '50s proved to be very definitely a Golden Age of the Broadway musical. Most of the productions of this era were essentially lighthearted musical comedies, like Irving Berlin's triumphant *Annie Get Your Gun* (1946), or the enchanting combination of satire and fantasy, *Finian's Rainbow* (1947, music by Burton Lane and lyrics by E. Y. Harburg). In the 1950s, two outstanding examples of a breezier, more modern style were *The Pajama Game* (1954, by Richard Adler and Jerry Ross) and *Bells are Ringing* (1956, music by Jule Styne, lyrics by Betty Comden and Adolph Green). All four shows were secure in their narrative techniques, each had a marvelous, rich score (with extractable hit tunes), each used the chorus in important ways, and at least two were vaguely satirical. Though their scores were not as developed as those of the nineteenth century, they were nevertheless among the rightful descendants of operetta at the mid-twentieth-century point, for they were comic, romantic, unpretentious, and bubbling with vitality.

Annie Get Your Gun might be seen as a costumed romance enlivened by spectacular scenes and comic *couplets*. *Finian's Rainbow* was perhaps closest to Gilbert and Sullivan, with its supernatural visitation and its pointedly satiric social comments. *The Pajama Game* had the flow of a Rodgers and Hammerstein romance, but with more developed comic characters and situations; *Bells are Ringing*, almost a revue in disguise, had even more buffoonery and a silliness that recalled the heyday of *opéra-bouffe*. In the 1960s, the jovially unpretentious musical comedy reached an apex with *Hello, Dolly!* (1964, by Jerry Herman), which curiously enough was descended from Johann Nestroy's *Einen Jux will er sich machen* (1842), a *Posse mit Gesang* of the type that would influence the infant Viennese operetta.

Even more structurally similar to comic or romantic operettas were such delightful confections as *Brigadoon, Kismet, The Golden Apple* (1954), *My Fair Lady,* and *Candide.* Other musicals with extremely romantic, often serious, and usually operetta (or *opéra-comique*) tendencies occasionally broke through the public's general taste for light musical comedies: *Fanny* (1954), *The Most Happy Fella, West Side Story, The Sound of Music,* and *Man of La Mancha* (1965). *Juno* (1959), a failure, had an entrancing score by Marc Blitzstein. Three-dimensional musical love stories and dramatic, even depressing situations were becoming acceptable to modern audiences. *West Side Story* and Jule Styne's *Gypsy* (1959) had one thing in common besides their quite realistic depictions of comparatively sordid subjects: their lyricist, Stephen Sondheim (1930–   ). Apart from *A Funny Thing Happened on the Way to the Forum* (1962), a lighthearted, clever Broadway retelling of Plautus, Sondheim did not resurface in a major way until 1970, alongside the champion of the concept musical, Harold Prince.

This type of musical changed what had hitherto been straightforward musical libretti to a new, fragmented method of storytelling, in which the plot and dialogue became subject to the whims of the musical and mechanical elements that sought to establish the mood of the piece. These shows developed from *Fiddler on the Roof* (1964), *Cabaret* (1966), *Company* (1970), *Follies* (1971), *A Little Night Music* (1973), *Pacific Overtures* (1975), *Evita* (1978), and *Sweeney Todd* (1979), to two recent misfires, *Merrily We Roll Along* (1981) and *A Doll's Life* (1982).

Six of these ten shows produced and/or directed by Harold Prince had scores by Sondheim, and although all had comic elements, they were essentially serious creations. Sondheim's lyrics and music reached new levels of complexity and sophistication, and earned him many critical accolades and fans, but not perhaps the universal popularity enjoyed by other musical comedy (or operetta) creators of the past. Many feel that his classically schooled music—brilliantly orchestrated by Jonathan Tunick—is too rarefied to be generally admired. As produced by Prince, the Sondheim shows were inclined to be icily spectacular, with an emotional distance that put off some spectators.

A Little Night Music was seen by critics and the public as an attempt to create a modern equivalent of a Viennese operetta, though its period trappings did not mask the unlikelihood that any Viennese composer would have written every song in a variant of three-quarter time, as Sondheim proudly did. The musical (Shubert, 25 February 1974) had a definite bittersweet quality Oscar Straus might have admired, but the disillusioned unsentimentality of its lyrics and its Hugh Wheeler book (based on the Ingmar Bergman film *Smiles of a Summer Night*) and its lack of true gaiety made it an unexpectedly somber show. Although the Broadway version ran 600 performances, it was not an international favorite. An attempt to present the work to the Viennese at that hallowed temple of operetta, the Theater an der Wien (14 February 1975), was not rapturously received. After 65 performances it was not brought back, as were other Broadway shows that played there. An aging Zarah Leander appeared in the role created by Hermione Gingold on Broadway.

Succeeding Harold Prince shows delved into the historical or literary past, with correspondingly weighty scores. *On the Twentieth Century* (St. James, 19 February 1978) was a highly unusual and entertaining effort by Betty Comden and Adolph Green (libretto) and Cy Coleman (music) to recreate a nineteenth-century comic opera in an art déco atmosphere. But the unpretentiousness necessary to operetta was absent in *Pacific Overtures, Evita,* or *Sweeney Todd,* the latter a reasonably good stab at turning a gruesome melodrama into something that veered toward opera. *Evita* was a rock opera, an oratorio-like form that eliminated dialogue entirely (and which was in some cases born in the recording studio). This has developed more recently into the spectacular and spectacularly successful *Cats* (1981), music by Britain's Andrew Lloyd Webber, who also composed *Evita.* These have been staged as concept musicals with an emphasis on the physical production, but *Cats* at least has a good amount of humor, despite its pretensions—a ray of hope for the future. What had started innocently enough as a framing device by Prince and his creators in *Fiddler on the Roof* and *Cabaret* has by now so utterly taken over musicals that straightforward libretti are regarded as old-fashioned. The *conférencier* in *Cabaret* (brilliantly played by Joel Grey) has led to a host of succeeding narrators and Greek choruses to help relate stories.

Because today's musicals often have more extended musical sections than 1950s shows, and heavier singing requirements, they are often mistaken for operettas. But they are not, for their pretensions are usually higher. When elected Chairman of the Board of the National Opera Institute in 1982, Harold Prince made the statement that "opera and musical theatre are exactly the same thing." This is no doubt an indication of the direction Prince is headed these days—directly to the opera house. His lighter comic and romantic productions of the past—*The Pajama Game, A Funny Thing Happened on the Way to the Forum,* or the adorable *She Loves Me* (1963)—apparently have little appeal for him today. They might seem too antique to today's television audiences, weaned on ponderous, "meaningful" dramas, sexy, violent crime action, and—most fatally—plotless rock concerts and variety shows. Perhaps because of the volatile times in which we live, the fanciful escapism in which operetta specialized has been seen as archaic. Fortunately, operettas are still being revived (if not written) to please audiences that still crave frivolity and romance, elegance and wit, and music that reflects these qualities without having to resort to deafening rock or disco.

A Monsieur Philippe DUCAZCAL

LA GRAN VIA
(LA GRANDE VOIE)

OPERETTE ESPAGNOLE EN 1 ACTE
de MM Maurice ORDONNEAU & J.B. ENSEÑAT
D'APRÈS LA ZARZUELA
de MM F. PEREZ et GONZALEZ

MUSIQUE de
MM. CHUECA & VALVERDE
SOCIEDAD ANÓNIMA CASA DOTESIO
Carrera de St Jeronimo, 34 y Preciados, 5 - MADRID

AGENCE POUR LA VENTE EN FRANCE ET À L'ETRANGER Lr E. DOTESIO et Cie
47, Rue Vivienne, 47. PARIS
Propriété exclusive pour tous pays
y compris la Suéde et la Norwège Deposé selon les traités internationaux

PASTICCIO AND ZARZUELA, ITALY AND RUSSIA

P ASTICCIO is an Italian word for pie or pudding; it can also mean a jumble or a mess. Operettas employing preexisting music were not uncommon (e.g., *The Beggar's Opera*), but the fashion for the operetta-*pasticcio* based on one composer did not really take hold until this century.

Wiener Blut (Carltheater, 26 October 1899), concocted from Strauss compositions by Adolf Müller, Jr., to a text by Viktor Léon and Leo Stein, was ordered by the Carltheater's manager Franz Jauner. Léon was Jauner's head director at the Carltheater; with Stein he wrote a rather ordinary, sentimental romance of mistaken identities, set at the time of the Congress of Vienna (1814–15). Strauss wanted to arrange the melodies from his old compositions (and presumably orchestrate them) but was too infirm. It was suggested that Müller, the house composer and conductor at the Theater an der Wien, do the task. Strauss was agreeable, but a few months before the première, Strauss was dead. The waltz-king and his century had gone.

In fact, *Wiener Blut* has not too much to do with the Congress of Vienna or its principals; the story might well have taken place at any other time. (Erik Charell's 1931 film, *Der Kongress tanzt,* was the definitive operetta depiction of this period.) There is a certain Viennese flavor to the character names, the dialogue, and, of course, the prior association of so much of Strauss's music to Vienna itself. The première was an almost complete fiasco and *Wiener Blut* barely managed to stay on the boards a month, after which it was hastily transferred to the Raimundtheater. In 1905, a revival with a rearranged book at the Theater an der Wien was unaccountably a huge success, and the *pasticcio* appeared at the Volksoper in 1928, where it has reappeared ever since.

A French music-cover showing characters from *La Gran Vía* (1886), one of the few Spanish *zarzuelas* to appear on non-Spanish stages.

423

As a medium for hearing attractive Strauss II music *sung, Wiener Blut* will have its adherents, though the word setting is quite often atrociously handled. The story and characters, now considered an accurate depiction of old Vienna, are singularly uninteresting, though there are those who think Franzi, a ballerina, and Pepi, a dress-fitter, are the embodiments of the Viennese spitfire. *Wiener Blut* tries rather desperately, in its mixture of high and low classes and its amorous intrigues, to be to Vienna what *La Vie Parisienne* is to Paris, but this honor falls unmistakably to *Die Fledermaus,* the very essence of *Alt-Wien.* With the exception of perhaps one or two effective numbers, most especially the title waltz, *Wiener Blut* fails to enshrine the Strauss melodies in a theatrical setting. One wishes a good orchestra would perform them and throw out the lyrics.

The successful revival of *Wiener Blut* at the Theater an der Wien did not immediately start a vogue for *pasticcio* operettas, new works based on used melodies, but once the fashion started, it did not let up. In 1903, there had been *Frühlingsluft* (Spring Air) based on the tunes of Josef Strauss. In 1911 came *Alt-Wien,* a *Singspiel* using Josef Lanner's music. The year 1913 saw *Die tolle Therese* (Crazy Therese), with Johann Strauss I music and a story about the legendary actress Therese Krones, and the following year there was a Waldteufel *pasticcio, Teresita.*

The greatest hit of the World War I years in Vienna was an utterly pseudo-biographical pastiche operetta of Franz Schubert picturesquely entitled *Das Dreimäderlhaus* (The House of the Three Girls, Raimundtheater, 15 January 1916). Billed as a *Singspiel,* the score was cleverly arranged by Heinrich Berté from Schubert compositions to accompany a fanciful libretto by A. M. Willner and Heinz Reichert. In their story, the shy composer is smitten with Hannerl Tschöll (sister to Hederl and Haiderl), only to lose her to his poet friend, the Baron Schober. The story was adapted from *Schwammerl* (Little Toadstool), a novel by Rudolf Hans Bartsch.

Heinrich Berté (1858–1924) had written a depressing series of middling operettas in the first years of the twentieth century before he was first asked to write *Dreimäderlhaus.* The original concept was to have Berté do a completely new score around one authentic Schubert interpolation, the "Impatient" Song. This idea was jettisoned when it was discovered that the one Schubert song was infinitely more effective than all of Berté's score. The composer's brother then suggested that Schubert "supply" the entire score, and it was Berté's task to find the appropriate melodies. The Schubert *oeuvre* was examined, suitable songs and orchestral pieces were picked out, the tunes were then extracted, and these were effectively orchestrated—but not by Berté.

Das Dreimäderlhaus was the most popular Viennese operetta during World War I, playing the Raimundtheater continuously for several seasons. This *Schubertiade* has had several English-language versions, one being the London production of *Lilac Time* (Lyric, 1922). Courtice Pounds entreats Clara Butterworth, but to no avail; in the end he is left with only "my music and my dreams." Courtice Pounds was the original Marco in *The Gondoliers* in 1889.

The music was charming enough; what really sold the operetta was its combination of score and setting. Old Biedermeier Vienna was lovingly recreated on the Raimundtheater stage. Not only would one be able to hear Schubert, one could *see* him, the shy lover too timid to propose, in a quaint old Viennese courtyard, a dainty salon, or a Hietzing square in 1826, two years before the composer's death. This failure-proof combination hit a sensitive spot in the heart of every sentimental Viennese, especially in the difficult war years, and propelled the work to a sensational, seemingly endless run. In the original cast were Fritz Schrödter as Schubert and Anny Rainer as Hannerl. Serious music critics may have objected, but the public would not stay away, and "*Schu*-berté" was no doubt quite pleased.

The operetta was eventually translated into some twenty-odd languages and is probably the most popular *pasticcio* of them all. In Paris, *Chanson d'Amour* (Song of Love) opened to cheers with Henri Fabert (*de l'Opéra*) as Schubert; the three girls called Annette, Jeannette, and Nanette (Marigny, 7 May 1921). In London, a new version with new adaptations by G. H. Clutsam opened as *Lilac Time* (Lyric, 22 December 1922), with a libretto by Adrian Ross, and Courtice Pounds as Schubert, plus Tili, Lili, and Wili. This had a shaky start, but a happy end, achieving 626 performances. *Blossom Time,* the New York version (Ambassador, 29 September 1921), ran almost as long, and was revived and toured endlessly by the Shuberts. *Blossom Time* differed most radically from the Viennese original, with a recomposed score by Sigmund Romberg and a new libretto by Dorothy Donnelly. Bertram Peacock was Schubert, and the three sisters were now only Mitzi and Vicki. In Budapest, where Berté was born, the sisters were Edi, Hedi, and Medi. There have been three German films on this theme (one silent) and the Viennese original is still constantly revived on the stage. Richard Tauber was closely identified with the role of Schubert, both in Germany and in England.

The *pasticcio* floodgates were now open. Composers right and left—their lives and/or music—were fair game for operetta immortality. One need only skim over them, as most are utterly forgotten. *Fahrende Musikanten* (Traveling Musicians, 1917), based on Schumann, *Der Zigeuner* (The Gypsy, 1918), from Liszt, and *Dichterliebe* (Poet-love, 1920), from Mendelssohn, were all produced in Vienna. Tchaikovsky's music has been used in several cities in works like *Die Siegerin* (1922), *Catherine* (1923), *Nadja* (1925), and *Music in My Heart* (1947), while Offenbach's scores have been pilfered for *Die Heimkehr des Odysseus* (The Return of Odysseus, 1917), *The Love Song* (1925, arranged by Künneke), *König ihres Herzens* (King of Her Heart, 1930), *The Happiest Girl in the World* (1961), and *Christopher Columbus* (1976). Chopin was used no less than four times, in *White Lilacs* (1928), *The Damask Rose* (1930), *Waltz Without End* (1942), and *Polonaise* (1945), while Dvořák's music was used in London's *Summer Song*.

The music of the Strauss family remained the most fertile source of the *pasticcio*-operetta: *Faschingshochzeit* (1921), *Casanova* (1928, arranged by Benatzky), *Walzer aus Wien* (1930, arranged by Korngold), *Freut euch des Lebens* (1932), *Die Tänzerin Fanny Elssler* (1934), and Parisian spectacles like *Vienne Chante et Danse* (Vienna Sings and Dances). In 1945, Robert Stolz dared to write a *new* score for a Broadway production, *Mr. Strauss Goes to Boston*, which rightly failed.

Of all the Johann Strauss *pasticcios*, *Walzer aus Wien*, or, what became of it, has had the most lasting appeal, exceeding even that of *Wiener Blut* in international performance runs and royalty tallies. *Walzer aus Wien* (Waltzes from Vienna) was designed for the Theater an der Wien by Hubert Marischka to cash in on both the nostalgia that was making *Im weissen Rössl* the hit of Berlin, and the well-remembered "biographical" elements that made *Dreimäderlhaus* such a Viennese triumph. The time was again right. Financial instability following the stock market crash and the Depression would turn Viennese audiences to the comforts of the past and particularly their beloved *Schani*. To duplicate the Schubert-*Singspiel* success, the librettists A. M. Willner and Heinz Reichert were rehired, to be assisted by Ernst Marischka. Julius Bittner did the Strauss-picking, with "musical enriching" by Erich Wolfgang Korngold. The piece opened 18 May 1931, but was, rather surprisingly, not one of the Theater an der Wien's triumphs.

Nevertheless, the story of Strauss, father and son, embellished by their music, was apparently attractive to foreign managements, all of whom mounted the show on a far more lavish scale than was the rule in Vienna. In London, *Waltzes from Vienna* (Alhambra, 17 August 1931) ran 607 performances (two performances daily, in an effort to compete with the "talkies"), with a sumptuous production designed by Albert Johnson, staged by Hassard Short, and choreographed by Albertina Rasch. The book was anglicized by Desmond Carter and Caswell Garth, while G. H. Clutsam (who had helped make *Lilac Time* a smash) and Herbert Griffiths did further musical arrangements. An American pair of leads, Robert Halliday (Strauss II) and Evelyn Herbert (Resi) alternated with a British duo, Esmond Knight and Adrienne Brune. Marie Burke was the Countess Olga. In Paris, the Porte St.-Martin saw *Valses de Vienne* in a French version by Mouëzy-Eon, Jean Marietti, and Max Eddy, with further musical arrangements by Eugène Cools. André Baugé was the young Strauss, Lucienne Trajin, Rési, and Fanély Revoil, the Countess.

In New York, the British version of the operetta became *The Great Waltz* (Center, 25 September 1934), and had Guy Robertson, Marion Claire, and Marie Burke in the principal parts, along with Albert Johnson's spectacular effects, including a finale that moved the orchestra from the pit to the back of the stage, transforming Dommayer's Casino Gardens into a ballroom dripping with chandeliers and glistening with uniforms and ball gowns. The *Playbill* bore the seal of the NRA (National Recovery Act) and the show offered jobs to more than two hundred actors, singers, dancers, orchestra players, and technicians. Further revisions on the London version were made by Moss Hart (book) and Frank Tours and Robert Russell Bennett (music). The run of nearly 300 performances was followed by a national tour.

Waltzes from Vienna was filmed in Britain in 1933 by, of all romantic musical experts, Alfred Hitchcock! This was designed to some extent to showcase Jessie Matthews. The stage score could not be used, as the studio could not afford to pay the demanded sum; other Strauss music was—ineffectively—used. The Hollywood film of 1938 was called *The Great Waltz,* though it again had little to do with the stage story or score. Julien Duvivier directed, Dimitri Tiomkin arranged, and Fernand Gravet, Luise Rainer, and Miliza Korjus starred. Revivals of *The Great Waltz* have been frequent, especially in the new version prepared for the Los Angeles Civic Light Opera Company in 1949. A production at London's Drury Lane in 1970 did excellent business.

Participating in the 1949 revisions was the team of **Robert Wright** (1914–   ) and **George Forrest** (1915–   ), whose musical adaptations have produced several immensely popular modern *pasticcios*. Beginning as highschool chums in Florida, they were brought to Hollywood by their early songwriting efforts when each was barely twenty. At MGM, they received credit for "special lyrics" on a number of screen versions of operettas, including *Maytime* (1936), *The Firefly* (1937), *Sweethearts* (1938), *Balalaika* (1939), and *The New Moon* (1940), all for Jeanette MacDonald and/or Nelson Eddy.

For *Maytime,* Wright and Forrest were required to assist Metro's musical arranger Herbert Stothart in reworking public-domain or familiar operatic-symphonic material that would replace the original Romberg score that producer Hunt Stromberg disliked. Thus began the team's experience in reworking the classics. Out of a string of operatic arias they fashioned a comedy number for Eddy called "Virginia Ham and Eggs," from a French folk song they developed his *"Vive l'Opéra,"* and, in their most impressive transformation, Tchaikovsky's

Fifth Symphony was turned into a fictitious grand opera, *Czaritza,* with their original English libretto translated into French.

In the early 1940s, they were approached by Edwin Lester of the Los Angeles and San Francisco Civic Light Opera Associations to devise a *pasticcio* operetta score from the music of Edvard Grieg which would be used to tell the story of Hans Christian Andersen. However, film producer Samuel Goldwyn would not part with the rights to this scenario. (He later filmed the story with Danny Kaye and a score by Frank Loesser.) It was then decided to treat Grieg's love life instead of Andersen's, and the result (book by Milton Lazarus based on an idea by Homer Curran) was *Song of Norway,* which opened on Broadway (Imperial, 21 August 1944) after encouragingly good business on the West Coast. *Song of Norway*'s plot, like those of *Dreimäderlhaus* and *The Great Waltz,* mixed fact and fiction, and, likewise, had a scheming woman to provide romantic conflict. But the libretto was never meant to be the strong point in these super-musical productions. Wolcott Gibbs told his *New Yorker* readers that, in *Song of Norway,* "everything was all right with me as long as nobody talked. Then I tried to think of something else." Lewis Nichols in the Sunday *Times* commiserated with the librettist: "Books for operettas usually consist of a few bare announcements concerning who people are and what they are about to sing . . . and the author is blamed if he adds twelve extra words."

Song of Norway had other things in its favor: lavish settings by Lemuel Ayers, a contingent of the Ballet Russe de Monte Carlo, including Alexandra Danilova and Maria Tallchief dancing to George Balanchine's choreography, and the Metropolitan Opera's Irra Petina leading a cast of singer-actors. The music triumphed. The public supported the show for an 860-performance run—and several respected Broadway composers came to see the show, often. Rodgers and Hammerstein told Wright and Forrest they were so encouraged by the sight of audiences weeping at Helena Bliss singing "I Love You" that they thought they could get away with the sad portions of *Carousel.* Cole Porter adored the show, came constantly to see it, and it is not surprising that his next great hit, *Kiss Me, Kate* (1948), owed something to operetta.

The sources of Grieg's music were carefully noted in the *Playbill.* Some of Grieg's *Lieder* were used, more or less intact, notably *"Ich liebe dich,"* which originally had words by Hans C. Andersen. In other numbers, more than one instrumental piece was used, rearranged and welded together by Messrs. Wright and Forrest. The A Minor Concerto frames the operetta, providing themes for two of the most thrilling songs at the beginning of the show, the "Legend" and "Hill of Dreams." The most famous hit-parade number is "Strange Music," cleverly, if loosely, based on two pieces, "Nocturne" and "Wedding Day at Troldhaugen."

The London version (Palace Theatre, 7 March 1946) ran almost two years, with its choreography by Robert Helpmann, and it remains an amateur favorite in Britain. Easily the most spectacular mounting was Guy Lombardo's and Leonard Ruskin's production at the Jones Beach Marine Theater in 1958 and 1959, which used the watery facility to its best advantage with fishing boats, floating fjords (complete with ice rink), and a Viking ship that had been used in the Kirk Douglas film *The Vikings.*

Hollywood had continually expressed interest in the property (first Universal in the '40s), but Wright and Forrest's script approval was not easily obtainable. Andrew Stone finally made the film in 1970, which turned out to be a travelogue with music (fair enough) unfortunately straddled with ludicrous biographical sections. The New York *Times* (Vincent Canby) noted that "it raises kitsch to the status of a kind of art . . ." while *The New Yorker* (Pauline Kael) claimed that the film was "of an unbelievable badness; it brings back clichés you didn't know you knew." The New York City Opera mounted a well-sung, picturesque revival in 1981 that was criticized for its dated libretto.

After *Song of Norway,* Wright and Forrest went on to provide a string of other adaptations as well as original works: among them, *Gypsy Lady* (1946, from Victor Herbert), *Magdalena* (1948, a new score by Villa-Lobos), *Kismet* (1953, from Borodin), *Kean* (1961—original), and *Anya* (1965, from Rachmaninoff). *Kismet* was the greatest success.

Difficult as it was to obtain Grieg's music during the war in order to adapt it for the stage, getting hold of the scores of Alexander Borodin for *Kismet* was even more of a challenge. The adapters freely admit that they listened to a lot of recordings—everything they could get their hands on. The "musical Arabian Night" was based on the 1911 play by Edward Knoblock that had proved a fabulously exotic vehicle for Oscar Asche in Britain and Otis Skinner in the United States. (Curiously, Lucien Guitry could not make a success of the play in Paris.) The archly Edwardian neo-Near Easternisms of the dialogue were somewhat pruned in the libretto by Luther Davis and Charles Lederer, but the perfumed spectacle of the original was enhanced by an expensive production and the lovely score by Wright and Forrest. (The plot was not dissimilar to that of *The Vagabond King,* or, if you will, *If I Were King,* concerning a poet who becomes Emir for a day and who helps root out evil.) Themes from the Polovtsian Dances from *Prince Igor* became the basis for a magnificent operetta love duet, "Stranger in Paradise," the rousing "He's in Love," and the voluptuous "Not Since Nineveh," while "Baubles, Bangles, and Beads" was adapted from a string quartet.

On Broadway (Ziegfeld, 3 December 1953) and in the West End (Stoll, 20 April 1955), Alfred Drake, Doretta Morrow, and Joan Diener glistened in the original cast. It was a personal triumph for Drake, who had already created Curly in *Oklahoma!* and Fred Graham in *Kiss Me, Kate,* and whose Hajj was thought comparable to those of Oscar Asche and Otis Skinner. *Kismet* was in precisely the same category as Asche's *Chu Chin Chow,* with its heavily scented Arabian Nights mystery and spectacle, but it had the advantage of a far more entrancing (and lasting) score. The London production outran the Broadway, but was still no match for *Chu Chin Chow's* 2,238 performances. Vincente Minnelli directed a filmed *Kismet* (1955), and an all-black version entitled *Timbuktu* was seen on Broadway in 1978.

Of all the foreign varieties of operetta, the *zarzuela* of Spain is surely the most developed without being known outside of Spanish-speaking countries. There have been attempts to translate the more popular works into English and other languages, and companies of *zarzuela* experts have presented this material in places like Vienna and New York (apart from American cities like Miami with large clusters of Spanish-speaking citizens). But the texts apparently will not translate, the music has not enjoyed any widespread foreign popularity, and, more importantly, the style of performance is somewhat alien to non-Hispanic tastes.

The word *zarzuela* refers to the Zarzuela Palace in a section of the Pardo woods near Madrid where bramble bushes *(zarza)* flourished. It was there in the seventeeth century that Philip IV organized royal entertainments. Pedro Calderón de la Barca, one of Spain's Golden Age dramatists, wrote the text for what is considered the first *zarzuela, El Golfo de las Sirenas* (The Gulf of the Sirens) in 1657. This was more or less a Spanish equivalent of a Molière *comédie-ballet*, a play fitted out with songs and dances. As in France, both original and existing music was used in the seventeenth- and eighteenth-century works that followed. When Italian opera began to grow in popularity in mid-eighteenth-century Spain, the old *zarzuela* gave way to the *tonadilla*, a short comic piece in the manner of an Italian *intermezzo;* this also died out in the early nineteenth century.

A precursor of the revitalized *zarzuela* appeared in the 1830s with the Italian-born Basilio Basili (1820–?), who very importantly used native stories, songs, and dances in his works. By 1857, with the opening of the Teatro de la Zarzuela in Madrid, the short *tonadilla* had been superseded by the new full-length *zarzuela*. This was at first modeled on French *opéra-comique*, but, later, on the new Parisian operettas that received productions in Madrid and elsewhere. (Even a British operetta like *H.M.S. Pinafore* was performed in Madrid, in 1885.) The first big success at the Teatro de la Zarzuela was the four-act *Los Magyares* (The Magyars, 12 April) by the composer Joaquín Gaztambide (1882–1870).

The new format was the *género grande,* usually in three or four acts, and—like its French counterpart—not always comic and usually sentimental. But the satiric, short *tonadilla* underwent a welcome transformation into the *género chico,* or short *zarzuela,* and these one-act operettas were invariably more comic, with everyday characters from Madrid, the suburbs, the Spanish provinces, and the colonies. All the Iberian rhythms surfaced: *seguidillas, habaneras, boleros, paso dobles, malagueñas,* and others, to give the new operettas a welcome national distinction. Another composer of Italian descent whose works achieved an early celebrity was **Francisco Asenjo Barbieri** (1823–1894). His great successes were *Jugar con fuego* (Playing with Fire, 1851), *Pan y toros* (Bread and Bulls, 1864), and *El Barberillo de Lavapiés* (The Little Barber of Lavapiés, 1870). The last is, arguably, the greatest of all nineteenth-century *zarzuelas*. A joyous, entirely national score that has no dull moments has been set to a colorful libretto by L. Mariano de Larra. The story is about a political upheaval in the Madrid of 1770, complicated by amorous entanglements. Some of the ensembles have a (not unattractive) *opéra-comique* or *opera buffa* feel to them, but there is nearly always a Spanish accent to the music. Spectacular and memorable chorus scenes are abundant, and there are numerous patter songs. The most memorable moment occurs early in Act I with the entrance song of the dressmaker-*soubrette* Paloma, a number so irresistibly gay and unforgettable that no female Spanish singer can afford to leave it out of her repertoire. Unfortunately, the operetta itself is heard only rarely today, the public generally preferring the more romantic creations of the present century.

The Golden Age of the *zarzuela* really began in the 1880s. In 1886, *La gran vía,* named after the "Broadway" of Madrid, conferred immortality on the composers **Joaquín Valverde** (1846–1910) and **Federico Chueca** (1846–1908). So popular was *The Great Way* that it was produced in several other countries including Austria and England. **Ruperto Chapí** (y Lorento) (1851–1909) wrote over 150 *zarzuelas,* among them *La Tempestad* (The Tempest, 1882), *La Bruja* (The Witch, 1887), *El Rey que rabio* (The Rabid King, 1891), and his enduring masterwork, *La Revoltosa* (The Mischievous Girl, 1897), also about life in working-class Madrid. Another short *zarzuela, La Verbena de la Paloma* (The Festival of the Dove) by **Tomás Bretón** (y Hernández) (1850–1923) gave Madrid's Teatro Apolo a resounding triumph in February 1894. It was technically a *sainete lírico,* related to the French musical *saynète,* or farce. (This was presented at New York's City Center in 1969 in a greatly amplified edition devised by Tito Capobianco and called *Fiesta in Madrid.*) The year 1895 saw another Bretón hit at the Teatro de la Zarzuela, the three-act *La Dolores.* This appeared at the Vienna Festival in 1975—undoubtedly the first Bretón work on an Austrian stage since the production of his opera *Los Amantes de Teruel* at the Oper in 1891.

There were other composers at the turn of the century who enjoyed considerable acclaim, like **Manuel Fernández Caballero** (1835–1906) (*El Duo de la Africana,* 1893), but the true giant was **Amadeo Vives** (1871–1932). Vives was one time professor of composition at the Conservatorio of Madrid, and his scores had an orchestral sheen that few of their contemporaries could match. *Bohemios* (1904) was his most lasting early success, although *Maruxa* (1914) has also endured. Well into the Silver Age of *zarzuela,* Vives produced *Doña Francisquita* (1923), one of the most popular of all *zarzuelas* to this day.

Other famous hits of the 1910s, '20s and '30s (up to the shock of the Civil War) were such works as Vicente Lleo's *La Corte de Faraón* (Pharaoh's Court, 1910), Pablo Luna's *Molinos de Viento* (Windmills, 1910) and his *El Niño judio* (The Jewish Boy, 1918), Siméon (José) Serrano's *La Canción del Olvido* (The Song of Oblivion, 1916), and, more or less finally, Moreno Torroba's *Luisa Fernanda* (1932). There are, of course, many, many more titles.

Like the best operettas, the *zarzuela* has rested on a foundation of national dance music, and the attractiveness of these Spanish rhythms remains undeniable. Europeans and Americans alike have been fascinated by Spanish themes, often filtered through French or even Russian composers (Bizet, Chabrier, Rimsky-Korsakov). Offenbach—his wife was of Spanish extraction—often used Iberian rhythms. The *zarzuela* was an extremely popular form of entertainment because of its sentiment, its fun, and—to an extent unheard of in British or French operetta—its rapport with the audience. One was expected to join in the refrains of the popular songs (a music-hall touch) and to participate with the comedian in verbal exchanges.

As the present century proceeded, Viennese works exercised a fascination for Spanish audiences, particularly the works of Franz Lehár. *Eva* and *Frasquita* could, until recently, be seen in Madrid. Modern musical comedy and revue hit in the 1920s, further weakening the dominance of *zarzuela,* and at this writing *Evita* is a resounding success in Madrid.

Italy played a crucial role in developing what would become, in French hands, operetta—even the word is Italian. *Opera buffa* has many delightful surviving examples still drawing crowds to opera houses the world over. But from the middle of the nineteenth century, when operetta began its rise in France, Verdi's operas were *the* popular entertainment in Italy. Comic relief was provided by Donizetti or Rossini. There were no indigenous new operettas worth mentioning. Verdi's music publisher, Guilio Ricordi, wrote a work or two (under the pseudonym of Jules Burgmein), but there was little else of note, apart from light works by *verismo* composers. Leoncavallo's *La Reginetta delle Rose* (The Little Queen of the Roses, 1912) and *La Candidata* (1915), Mascagni's *Sí* (Yes, 1919), and Giordano's *Giove a Pompei* (Jove at Pompeii, 1921) are forgotten, while Puccini's *La Rondine* (The Swallow, 1917) is still played and recorded. *La Rondine*'s *opéra-comique*-ness prevents it from being a real operetta; Puccini's *Gianni Schicchi* (1918) is hardly one.

These last-named works appeared just after Silver Age Viennese works began playing Italian cities, at the same time that popular native works made their debuts. Noteworthy were Alberto Montanari's *Il Birichino di Parigi* (The Urchin from Paris, 1912), Giuseppe Pietri's *Addio Giovinezza* (1915) and *L'Acqua Cheta* (Still Waters, 1920), Carlo Lombardo's *Madama di Tebe* and *Cin-ci-la,* and Mario Costa's *Scugnizza* (a local term referring to a Neapolitan female urchin). Plot themes tended toward the sentimental and there was too much local color, making these works virtually unexportable. A now-forgotten step in what might have been the right direction was Alfredo Cuscina's *Il Ventaglio* (The Fan, 1927), which had a reputedly fine score and a libretto based on a Carlo Goldoni Venetian comedy.

Even Tsarist Russia was prey to the charms of Offenbach, though before that there had been Russian equivalents of *opéra-comique* and *vaudeville.* Alexander Borodin and César Cui (particularly) wrote several lighter works that are only found today on academy bookshelves. Viennese and British works were instead performed, including Sullivan's *Mikado,* which Constantin Stanislavsky produced very early in his career with a semi-amateur company in Moscow.

The Soviet period's most famous composer was **Isaac Dunayevsky** (1900–

1955), whose work for the stage–and particularly the cinema—has been heard outside the USSR. The themes of the most famous libretti he set continued the *Volksoperette* tradition, but in a purely Soviet way: the joys of collective farming, support for the Red Army, resisting the Germans in World War II. His lasting operetta hit is *The White Acacia* (1955), still performed in Moscow, Leningrad, and the provinces. The films *Jolly Fellows* (1934) and *Volga-Volga* (1938, reputedly Stalin's favorite film), both directed by Grigori Alexandrov, have famous songs by Dunayevsky that are perhaps more in a musical-comedy style.

Another oft-performed operetta composer is **Yuri Miliutin** (1903–1968), whose best-known work is *Young Girls' Alarm* (1945). More recent essays by Dmitri Kabalevsky and Dmitri Shostakovich have not been revived, while so-called "musicals" like the Ukrainian *Fair at Sorochints* (1936, by A. Riabov and having nothing to do with Modest Mussorgsky's charming opera) are still performed and even forced down the throats of Soviet-satellite audiences.

Still, one must give the Soviets considerable credit. Apart from these modern, instructionist works, the musical theatres of Moscow and Leningrad retain an extremely varied repertoire of old and new works which, in some cases, one cannot see elsewhere. During a fortnight spent in Moscow one might catch performances of Suppé's *Donna Juanita*, Offenbach's *La Périchole*, Friml's *Rose-Marie*, Kálmán's *Csárdásfürstin*, and Loewe's *My Fair Lady*, along with *The White Acacia* and a few more current items. The production standards today are quite variable; the Arts Ministry obviously does not give the Moscow Operetta what it gives the Bolshoi! The Soviets have also managed to record things the West seldom has: Kálmán's *Das Veilchen von Montmartre* and Offenbach's *Pomme d'Api*, for example. The conservative Soviet arts policies have at least managed to preserve works that might otherwise be quite neglected.

BIBLIOGRAPHY

Agate, James. *Immoment Toys*. Jonathan Cape, London, 1945.

Allen, Reginald, *The First Night Gilbert and Sullivan*. Heritage Press, New York, 1958.

Arnold, Elliott. *Deep in My Heart*. Duell, Sloan & Pearce, New York, 1949.

Augé-Laribé, Michel. *Messager: Musicien de théâtre*. La Colombe, Paris, 1951.

Baily, Leslie. *Gilbert and Sullivan and Their World*. Thames & Hudson, London, 1973.

———. *The Gilbert and Sullivan Book,* Cassell & Company, London, 1951.

Barrington, Rutland. *Rutland Barrington by Himself,* Grant Richards, London, 1908.

Bekker, Paul. *Jacques Offenbach*. Verlag Von Marquardt & Co., Berlin, 1909.

Bettany, Clemence. *100 Years of D'Oyly Carte Opera Company and Gilbert and Sullivan,* D'Oyly Carte Company Opera Company, London, 1975.

Bolitho, Hector. *Marie Tempest*. J. B. Lippincott Company, Philadelphia, 1937.

Bordman, Gerald. *The American Musical Theatre*. Oxford University Press, New York, 1978.

———. *American Operetta*. Oxford University Press, New York, 1981.

———. *Jerome Kern: His Life and Music*. Oxford University Press, New York, 1980.

Brindejont-Offenbach, Jacques. *"L'Opérette,"* in *Le Théâtre Lyrique et la Symphonie de 1874 à 1925*. Librairie de France, Paris, 1925.

———. *Offenbach, mon grand-père*. Librairie Plon, Paris, 1940.

Brisson, Pierre. *Le Théâtre des Années folles*. Éditions du Milieu, Genève, 1943.

Bruyas, Florian. *Histoire de l'Opérette en France: 1855–1965*. Emmanuel Vitte, Lyon, 1974.

Bruyr, José. *L'Opérette*. Presses Universitaires de France, Paris, 1962.

Castle, Charles. *Noël*. Doubleday & Company, Garden City, New York, 1972.

Cellier, François, and Bridgeman, Cunningham. *Gilbert, Sullivan and D'Oyly Carte*. 2nd ed. Sir Isaac Pitman & Sons, London, 1927.

Claretie, Jules. *Ludovic Halévy*. A. Quantin, Paris, 1883.

Clément, Félix, and Larousse, Pierre. *Dictionnaire des Opéras*. Volumes I and II. Da Capo Press, New York, 1969.

Cochran, Charles B. *Cock-a-doodle-do*. J. M. Dent & Sons, London, 1941.

———. *Showman Looks On*. J. M. Dent & Sons, London, 1945.

Coffin, Hayden. *Hayden Coffin's Book*. Alston Rivers, London, 1930.

Cooper, Martin. *Opéra Comique*. Max Parrish & Co., London, 1949.

Courtneidge, Robert. *I Was an Actor Once*. Hutchinson & Co., London, n.d.

Coward, Noël. *Future Indefinite*. Doubleday & Company, Garden City, New York, 1954.

———. *The Lyrics of Noël Coward*. Doubleday & Company, Garden City, New York, 1967.

———. *Present Indicative*. Doubleday & Company, Garden City, New York, 1937.

Czech, Stan. *Franz Lehár*. Franz Perneder, Vienna, n.d.

Dark, Sidney, and Grey, Rowland. *W. S. Gilbert, His Life and Letters*. Methuen & Co., London, 1923.

Darlington, W. A. *Six Thousand and One Nights*. George G. Harrap & Company, London, 1960.

———. *The World of Gilbert and Sullivan*. The Thomas Y. Crowell Co., New York, 1950.

Decaux, Alain. *Offenbach, Roi du Second Empire*. Librairie Académique Perrin, Paris, 1966.

Decsey, Ernst. *Franz Lehár*. Drei Masken Verlag, Berlin, 1924.

———. *Johann Strauss, ein Wiener Buch*. Deutsche Verlags-Anstalt, Stuttgart, 1922.

De Curzon, Henri. *Léo Delibes: sa vie et ses oeuvres*. G. Legouix, Paris, 1926.

Donaldson, Frances. *Freddy Lonsdale*. William Heinemann, London, 1957.

Dunhill, Thomas F. *Sullivan's Comic Operas: A Critical Appreciation*. Edward Arnold & Co., London, 1928.

Ellis, Vivian. *I'm on a See-Saw*. Michael Joseph, London, 1953.

Engel, Lehman. *The American Musical Theater*. A CBS Legacy Collection Book, New York, 1967.

Ewen, David. *The Book of European Light Opera*. Holt, Rinehart & Winston, New York, 1962.

Fantel, Hans. *The Waltz Kings*. William Morrow & Company, New York, 1972.

Faris, Alexander. *Jacques Offenbach*. Charles Scribner's Sons, New York, 1980.

Ferrier, Henry. *André Messager: mon maître, mon ami*. Amiot-Dumont, Paris, 1948.

Fitzgerald, Percy. *The Savoy Operas*. Chatto & Windus, London, 1894.

Fitz-Gerald, S. J. Adair. *The Story of the Savoy Opera in Gilbert and Sullivan Days*. D. Appleton & Company, New York, 1922.

Forbes-Winslow, D. *Daly's: The Biography of a Theatre*. W. H. Allen & Co., London, 1944.

Fordin, Hugh. *Getting to Know Him: A Biography of Oscar Hammerstein II.* Random House, New York, 1977.

Gammond, Peter. *Offenbach: His Life and Times.* Paganiniana Publications, Neptune City, New Jersey, 1980.

Genest, Émile. *L'Opéra-Comique: connu et inconnu.* Librairie Fischbacher, Paris, 1925.

Goldberg, Isaac, ed. *New and Original Extravaganzas by W. S. Gilbert, Esq.* John W. Luce & Co., Boston, 1931.

Graves, Charles. *The Cochran Story.* W. H. Allen & Co., London, n.d.

Green, Stanley. *Encyclopaedia of the Musical.* Cassell, London, 1977.

————. *Ring Bells! Sing Songs! Broadway Musicals of the 1930's.* Arlington House, New Rochelle, New York, 1971.

————. *The World of Musical Comedy.* Ziff-Davis Publishing Company, New York, 1960.

Grossmith, George (Jr.). G. G. Hutchinson & Co., 1933.

Grun, Bernard. *Gold and Silver: The Life and Times of Franz Lehár.* David McKay Company, New York, 1970.

————. *Prince of Vienna: The Life, the Times and the Melodies of Oscar Straus.* W. H. Allen & Co., London, 1955.

Harding, James. *Folies de Paris: The Rise and Fall of French Operetta.* Chappell & Company/Elm Tree Books, London, 1979.

————. *Sacha Guitry: The Last Boulevardier.* Charles Scribner's Sons, New York, 1968.

Hart, Dorothy. *Thou Swell, Thou Witty: The Life and Lyrics of Lorenz Hart.* Harper & Row, New York, 1976.

Herbert, Sir Alan. *A.P.H., His Life and Times.* William Heinemann, London, 1970.

Herbrich, Othmar. *Robert Stolz.* Wilhelm Heyne Verlag, Munich, 1977.

Hibbert, Christopher. *Gilbert & Sullivan and Their Victorian World.* American Heritage Publishing Co., New York, 1976.

Higham, Charles. *Ziegfeld.* Henry Regnery Company, Chicago, 1972.

Hobson, Sir Harold. *French Theatre Since 1830.* John Calder, London, 1978.

Hollingshead, John. *Gaiety Chronicles.* Archibald Constable & Co., London, 1898.

————. *Good Old Gaiety: An Historiette and a Remembrance.* Gaiety Theatre Co., London, 1903.

Hopper, De Wolf. *Reminiscences of De Wolf Hopper.* Star Books, Garden City Publishing Company, Garden City, New York, 1925.

Hughes, Gervase. *Composers of Operetta.* St. Martin's Press, New York, 1962.

————. *The Music of Arthur Sullivan.* St. Martin's Press, New York, 1960.

Hyman, Alan. *The Gaiety Years.* Cassell & Collier Macmillan, London, 1975.

————. *Sullivan and His Satellites.* Chappell & Company/Elm Tree Books, London, 1978.

Imbert, Charles. *Histoire de la Chanson et de l'Opérette.* Les Éditions Rencontre, Lausanne, 1967.

Jacob, H. E. *Johann Strauss, Father and Son.* Halcyon House, Garden City, New York, 1948 (reprint edition).

Jacobs, Arthur. *Gilbert and Sullivan.* Max Parrish & Co., London, 1951.

Kálmán, Vera. *Grüss' mir die süssen, die reizenden Frauen.* Hestia Verlag, Bayreuth, 1966.

Kaye, Joseph. *Victor Herbert.* G. Howard Watt, New York, 1931.

Khukova, L. L., *V Mire Operetti* (The World of Operetta), Znanie, Moscow, 1976.

Kidson, Frank. *The Beggar's Opera: Its Predecessors and Successors.* The Macmillan Company, New York, 1922.

Kimball, Robert, and Gill, Brendan. *Cole.* Holt, Rinehart & Winston, New York, 1971.

Kimball, Robert, and Simon, Alfred. *The Gershwins.* Atheneum, New York, 1973.

Knowles, Eleanor. *The Films of Jeanette MacDonald and Nelson Eddy.* A. S. Barnes & Company, South Brunswick, N.J., and New York, N.Y., 1975.

Kracauer, Siegfried. *Orpheus in Paris: Offenbach and the Paris of His Time.* Alfred A. Knopf, New York, 1938.

Kreuger, Miles. *Show Boat: The Story of a Classic American Musical.* Oxford University Press, New York, 1977.

———, ed. *The Movie Musical from Vitaphone to 42nd Street,* Dover Publications, New York, 1975.

Láng, Attila E. *Das Theater an der Wien: vom Singspiel zum Musical.* Jugend und Volk, Vienna, Munich, 1977.

Laufe, Abe. *Broadway's Greatest Musicals.* Funk & Wagnalls Company, New York, 1969.

Lawrence, Arthur. *Sir Arthur Sullivan.* J. Bowden, London, 1899.

Lerner, Alan Jay. *The Street Where I Live.* W. W. Norton & Co., New York, 1978.

Lesley, Cole. *Remembered Laughter: The Life of Noël Coward.* Alfred A. Knopf, New York, 1976.

———; Morley, Sheridan; and Payn, Graham. *Noël Coward and His Friends.* William Morrow & Co., New York, 1979.

Lewis, Peter, ed. *John Gay: The Beggar's Opera.* Barnes & Noble, New York, 1973.

Lorcey, Jacques. *Sacha Guitry.* La Table Ronde, Paris, 1971.

Lubbock, Mark. *The Complete Book of Light Opera.* Appleton-Century-Crofts, New York, 1962.

MacKinlay, Sterling. *Light Opera.* Hutchinson & Co., London, 1926.

Macqueen-Pope, W. J. *Carriages at Eleven: The Story of the Edwardian Theatre.* Hutchinson & Co., London, 1947.

———. *The Footlights Flickered.* Herbert Jenkins, London, 1959.

———. *Gaiety: Theatre of Enchantment.* W. H. Allen & Co., London, 1949.

———. *Ivor, The Story of an Achievement: A Biography of Ivor Novello.* Hutchinson & Co., London, 1954.

————. *Nights of Gladness*. Hutchinson & Co., London, 1956.

————. *Pillars of Drury Lane*. Hutchinson & Co., London, 1955.

————. *Theatre Royal Drury Lane*. 2nd ed. W. H. Allen & Co., London, 1951.

Mander, Raymond, and Mitchenson, Joe. *The Lost Theatres of London*. Taplinger Publishing Company, New York, 1968.

————. *A Picture History of Gilbert and Sullivan*. Vista Books, London, 1962.

————. *Revue: A Story in Pictures*. Taplinger Publishing Company, New York, 1971.

————. *The Theatres of London*. Hill & Wang, New York, 1961.

Martinet, André. *Offenbach: sa vie et son oeuvre*. Dentu et Cie, Paris, 1887.

Myers, Rollo. *Emmanuel Chabrier and His Circle*. J. M. Dent & Sons, London, 1969.

Naylor, Stanley. *Gaiety and George Grossmith*. Stanley Paul & Co., London, 1913.

Noble, Peter. *Ivor Novello: Man of the Theatre*. Falcon Press, London, 1951.

Nolan, Frederick. *The Sound of Their Music: The Story of Rodgers & Hammerstein*. Walker & Company, New York, 1978.

Nowak, K. F. *Girardi*. Concordia Deutsche Verlags-Anstalt. H. Ehbock, Berlin, 1908.

Orrey, Leslie. *A Concise History of Opera*. Thames & Hudson, London, 1972.

Oster, Louis. *Les Opérettes du repertoire courant*. Éditions du Conquistador, Paris, 1953.

Pearsall, Ronald. *Edwardian Popular Music*. David & Charles, Newton Abbot, England, 1975.

————. *Popular Music of the Twenties*. David & Charles, Newton Abbot, 1976.

————. *Victorian Popular Music*. David & Charles, Newton Abbot, 1973.

Pearson, Hesketh. *Gilbert, His Life and Strife*. Harper & Brothers, New York, 1957.

PEM. *Und der Himmel hängt voller Geigen*. Lothar Blanvalet Verlag, Berlin, 1955.

Pirchan, Emil. *Marie Geistinger*. Verlag Wilhelm Frick, Vienna, 1947.

Pourvoyeur, Professor Doctor Robert. *Jacques Offenbach*. Eclectica, Brussels, 1977.

Powers, James T. *Twinkle Little Star*. G. P. Putnam's Sons, New York, 1939.

Procházka, Rudolf Freiherr. *Johann Strauss*. Schlesische Verlagsanstalt, Berlin, 1913.

Prosl, Robert Maria. *Edmund Eysler*. Verlag Karl Kühne, Vienna, 1947.

Ratonyi, Róbert. *Az Operett csillagai I*. Szinháztudományi Intézet, Budapest, 1967.

Rees, Terence. *Thespis: A Gilbert & Sullivan Enigma*. Dillons University Bookshop, London, 1964.

Rieger, Erwin. *Offenbach und seine wiener Schule*. Wiener Literarische Unstalt, Vienna, Berlin, 1920.

Rodgers, Richard. *Musical Stages: An Autobiography*. Random House, New York, 1975.

Sanders, Ronald. *The Days Grow Short: The Life and Music of Kurt Weill.* Holt, Rinehart & Winston, New York, 1980.

Schneider, Louis. *Hervé, Charles Lecocq.* Librairie Académique Perrin & Cie., 1924.

———. *Offenbach.* Librairie Académique Perrin & Cie., Paris, 1923.

Schneidereit, Otto. *Berlin, wie es weint und lacht.* VEB Lied der Zeit Musikverlag, Berlin, 1976.

———. *Eduard Künneke, der Komponist aus Dingsda.* Henschelverlag, Berlin, 1978.

———. *Paul Lincke und die Entstehung der Berliner Operette.* Henschelverlag, Berlin, 1974.

———. *Operette A–Z.* Henschelverlag, Berlin, 1971.

———. *Franz von Suppé: Der Wiener aus Dalmatien.* VEB Lied der Zeit Musikverlag, Berlin, 1977.

Schwartz, Charles. *Cole Porter: A Biography.* Dial Press, New York, 1977.

Short, Ernest. *Sixty Years of Theatre* Eyre & Spottiswoode, London, 1951.

Slezak, Walter. *What Time's the Next Swan?* Doubleday & Company, Garden City, New York, 1962.

Smith, Cecil. *Musical Comedy in America.* Theatre Arts Books, New York. 1950.

Smith, Patrick J. *The Tenth Muse: A Historical Study of the Opera Libretto.* Alfred A. Knopf, New York, 1970.

Soldene, Emily. *My Theatrical and Musical Recollections.* Downey & Co., London, 1897.

Stagg, Jerry. *The Brothers Shubert.* Random House, New York, 1968.

Stedman, Jane W., ed. *Gilbert Before Sullivan.* University of Chicago Press, Chicago, 1967.

Strang, Lewis C. *Celebrated Comedians of Light Opera in America.* L. C. Page & Company, Boston, 1901.

———. *Prima Donnas and Soubrettes of Light Opera in America.* L. C. Page & Company, Boston, 1900.

Sullivan, Herbert, and Flower, W. N. *Sir Arthur Sullivan: His Life, Letters and Diaries.* George H. Doran Company, Garden City, New York, 1927.

Tournier, Jacques, ed. *Yvonne Printemps.* La Table Ronde, Paris, 1953.

Walbrook, H. M. *Gilbert and Sullivan Opera.* F. V. White & Co., Ltd., London, 1922.

Wechsberg, Joseph. *The Waltz Emperors.* G. P. Putnam's Sons, New York, 1973.

Williamson, Audrey. *Gilbert and Sullivan Opera: A New Assessment.* The Macmillan Company, New York, 1953.

Wilson, A. E. *Edwardian Theatre.* The Macmillan Company, New York, 1952.

Wilson, Francis. *Francis Wilson's Life of Himself.* Houghton Mifflin Company, Boston, 1924.

Wilson, Sandy. *Ivor.* Michael Joseph, London, 1975.

Witeschnik, Alexander. *Dort wird Champagnisiert oder vom ruinösen Charme der Operette.* Neff Verlag, Vienna, Berlin, 1971.

Wodehouse, P. G., and Bolton, Guy. *Bring on the Girls!* Herbert Jenkins, London, 1954.

Wolff, Stéphane, and Lejeune, André. *Le Théâtre du Châtelet est Centenaire.* Paris, 1962.

Worbs, Hans Christoph. *Lortzing.* Rowohlt Taschenbuch Verlag, Hamburg, 1980.

Würz, Anton. *Reclams Operettenführer.* Philipp Reclam Jun., Stuttgart, 1969.

Wutzky, A. Ch. *Girardi.* Wilhelm Frick Verlag, Vienna, 1943.

Young, Percy M. *Sir Arthur Sullivan.* W. W. Norton & Co., New York, 1971.

Yvain, Maurice. *Ma belle Opérette.* La Table Ronde, Paris, 1962.

Not listed above are the innumerable articles, reviews, clippings, programmes, scores, libretti, records, and personal accounts to which the author has referred. This would also be a good place to give further credit to such eminent historians as Gerald Bordman, Florian Bruyas, Kurt Gänzl, and Otto Schneidereit, whose monumental works are truly outstanding examples of scholarship. And also to the excellent articles appearing in *Tritsch-Tratsch*, the magazine of the Johann Strauss Society of Great Britain, by such scholars as L. A. Hawkey, Andrew Lamb, and others.

Illustrations not otherwise credited are from the Traubner Theatre Collection.

INDEX

OXFORD

Winner of a 1984 ASCAP-Deems Taylor Award

This entertaining, thorough, and richly-illustrated history of operetta documents a delightful form of musical theater which enraptured audiences around the world for over a century. Coming at a time of renewed enthusiasm for operetta, Richard Traubner's timely volume details the creation of the genre's masterworks, from *Orphée aux Enfers* through *Die Fledermaus, H.M.S. Pinafore, The Merry Widow, The Desert Song,* and *White Horse Inn*; covers the careers of the major operetta composers and librettists—such as Offenbach, Lecocq, Gilbert and Sullivan, Lehár, Kálmán, Coward, and Lerner and Loewe—and discusses the minor ones as well in a chronicle of operetta's greatest theaters and most popular stars.

"The first large-scale history of light musical entertainment in the English language, and it's an incredible cornucopia of information, most knowledgeably written by someone who adores the art. . . . Thus far and by far the finest book yet produced on a joyously fascinating subject."
Bill Zakariasen, *The Daily News*

"An indispensable companion for anyone who loves the irresistible tunes, aching nostalgia, and heady effervescence of operetta. Traubner's thorough knowledge of the field—its history, musical cross-currents, and uproarious scandals—should make his fact-filled study the standard operetta reference book for years to come."   Peter G. Davis, *New York Magazine*

"A work that contains not merely the history of the genre but its very essence. It is one of those rare books clearly destined to remain the standard work on its subject for a long time."
Andrew Lamb, *The Musical Times* (London)

"I know of no more readable or . . . more comprehensive treatment of the subject."   *Gramophone*

"A remarkable history of operetta . . . the genre is studied with the same seriousness one exhibits when discussing opera."
Opera International (Paris)

"Told with wit, charm, and a very personal style, and enriched with many illustrations. . . . A standard work of its genre."   *Orpheus* (Berlin)

Richard Traubner is a journalist and lecturer on theater and film. This country's leading operetta historian, he has also translated and directed four Offenbach operettas in U.S. productions.

Cover design by Honi Werner
Cover illustration reprinted by permission of
the Traubner Theatre Collection

Oxford Paperbacks
Oxford University Press
$16.95

90000

9 780195 207781

ISBN 0-19-520778-5